Welfare and Capitalism in Po

This book explains how postwar Japan managed to achieve a highly egalitarian form of capitalism despite meager social spending. Margarita Estévez-Abe develops an institutional, rational-choice model to solve this puzzle. She shows how Japan's electoral system generated incentives that led political actors to protect, if only for their own self-interested reasons, various groups that lost out in market competition. She explains how Japan's postwar welfare state relied on various alternatives to orthodox social spending programs.

The initial postwar success of Japan's political economy has given way to periods of crisis and reform. This book follows this story to the present day. Estévez-Abe shows how the current electoral system renders obsolete the old form of social protection. She argues that Japan's institutions now resemble those of Britain, and she predicts that Japan's welfare system will also come to resemble Britain's system. Japan thus faces a future in which its society is more market oriented and more economically stratified.

Margarita Estévez-Abe is currently associate professor of political economy at Harvard University. She has also taught at the University of Minnesota, served as a research associate at Keio University in Japan, and worked for a senior Japanese policy adviser. She coauthored "Social Protection and the Formation of Skills: A Reinterpretation of the Welfare State," in Peter Hall and David Soskice, eds., *The Varieties of Capitalism* (2001) and "Japan's Shift toward a Westminster System," *Asian Survey* (2006). She is also the author of "Negotiating Welfare Reforms: Actors and Institutions in Japan," in Sven Steinmo and Bo Rothstein, eds., *Institutionalism and Welfare Reforms* (2002) and "State-Society Partnership in Japan: A Case Study of Social Welfare Provision," in Susan Pharr and Frank Schwartz, eds., *The State of Civil Society in Japan* (2003).

Cambridge Studies in Comparative Politics

General Editor
Margaret Levi *University of Washington, Seattle*

Assistant General Editor
Stephen Hanson *University of Washington, Seattle*

Associate Editors
Robert H. Bates *Harvard University*
Torben Iversen *Harvard University*
Stathis Kalyvas *Yale University*
Peter Lange *Duke University*
Helen Milner *Princeton University*
Frances Rosenbluth *Yale University*
Susan Stokes *Yale University*
Sidney Tarrow *Cornell University*
Kathleen Thelen *Northwestern University*
Erik Wibbels *Duke University*

Other Books in the Series

Lisa Baldez, *Why Women Protest: Women's Movements in Chile*
Stefano Bartolini, *The Political Mobilization of the European Left, 1860–1980: The Class Cleavage*
Robert H. Bates, *When Things Fell Apart: State Failure in Late-Century Africa*
Mark Beissinger, *Nationalist Mobilization and the Collapse of the Soviet State*
Nancy Bermeo, ed., *Unemployment in the New Europe*
Carles Boix, *Democracy and Redistribution*
Carles Boix, *Political Parties, Growth, and Equality: Conservative and Social Democratic Economic Strategies in the World Economy*
Catherine Boone, *Merchant Capital and the Roots of State Power in Senegal, 1930–1985*
Catherine Boone, *Political Topographies of the African State: Territorial Authority and Institutional Change*
Michael Bratton and Nicolas van de Walle, *Democratic Experiments in Africa: Regime Transitions in Comparative Perspective*
Michael Bratton, Robert Mattes, and E. Gyimah-Boadi, *Public Opinion, Democracy, and Market Reform in Africa*

Continued after the index

Welfare and Capitalism in Postwar Japan

MARGARITA ESTÉVEZ-ABE

Harvard University

CAMBRIDGE UNIVERSITY PRESS
Cambridge, New York, Melbourne, Madrid, Cape Town, Singapore, São Paulo, Delhi

Cambridge University Press
32 Avenue of the Americas, New York, NY 10013–2473, USA

www.cambridge.org
Information on this title: www.cambridge.org/9780521722216

First published 2008

Printed in the United States of America

A catalog record for this publication is available from the British Library.

Library of Congress Cataloging in Publication Data

Estévez-Abe, Margarita.
Welfare and capitalism in postwar Japan / Margarita Estévez-Abe.
    p.   cm. – (Cambridge studies in comparative politics)
Includes bibliographical references and index.
ISBN 978-0-521-85693-5 (hardback) – ISBN 978-0-521-72221-6 (pbk.)
1. Japan – Economic conditions.   2. Public welfare – Japan – History   3. Welfare state – Japan.
I. Title.
HC462.95.E88   2008
330.952–dc22   2007043012

ISBN 978-0-521-85693-5 hardback
ISBN 978-0-521-72221-6 paperback

For my parents,
Yasuko Abe and Angel Estévez Domínguez

Contents

Tables, Figures, and Appendices

Acknowledgments

An army of people – family, friends, colleagues, and former teachers – helped me at different stages of the long march to finish this book. My first thanks go to Yasunori Sone, my undergraduate adviser at Keio University, who got me interested in the world of ideas and persuaded me to continue my studies in the United States. I am also grateful to Michael Mosher, my first Ivy League–trained teacher, whom I met at Keio University. Michael's letter of recommendation got me into the Harvard PhD program. Hideo Otake at Kyoto University kindly "adopted" me as a student of his and offered invaluable help. At Harvard, I encountered my first female role model, Susan Pharr. She became my dissertation committee chair, later a colleague and a perpetual source of support. Without Susan's help, I probably would have packed up my suitcase and gone back to Tokyo a long time ago. I hope this book repays a small part of my immense debt to her. Special thanks also go to another former adviser and now a colleague, Peter Hall. Peter introduced me to the field of comparative politics of advanced industrial societies, a topic that still fascinates me. I was never satisfied with the way this particular field treated Japan – too often it viewed Japan as an outlier. I believed that Japan's permanent outlier status was a result of the European bias of scholars in the field, and this bias affected how they formulated their theories. Hopefully, my attempt to solve this problem will convince Peter. I am also indebted to Paul Pierson, who was also in my committee. I have benefited greatly from his work.

I owe my knowledge of Japanese politics to a group of Japanese scholars and career bureaucrats. I learned immensely while working under Hiroshi Kato (more popularly known as Katokan in Japan) as a researcher in the latter half of the 1990s. As part of a research group on deregulation in Japan at the time, I benefited greatly from numerous conversations with Haruo Sasaki, Hiroo Ide, and Shintaro Tajiri, in particular. In the latter half of the 1990s, I also participated in a number of study groups led by reformist career civil servants and politicians. Regular discussions in these study groups gave me invaluable insights into the workings of the Japanese government. I particularly want to thank Naoyuki Agawa, Tomoko Fujiwara,

Jun Hajiro, Yoshimasa Hayashi, Sukehiro Hosoda, Taro Kono, Hideaki Shiroyama, Hiroshi Suzuki, Heizo Takenaka, and Jiro Tamura. I have also benefited greatly from conversations and research-related assistance from Kiyoaki Fujiwara, Glen Fukushima, Naokatsu Hikotani, Nobu Hiwatari, Naotaka Kawakami, Yoko Makino, Taku Sugawara, Junko Takashima, Yutaka Tsuchiya, and Taizo Yakushiji. Although I do not have the space to mention each by name, a whole generation of Fellows – Japanese civil servants and businessmen – at the Program on U.S.–Japan Relations at Harvard University generously shared their experience with me and often helped me with interview appointments. My book does not always paint Japanese civil servants in the best light. To protect the honor of my friends in the Japanese civil service, I want to state on the record that they are all truly public spirited and that they care deeply about the future of Japan. Nonetheless, I stand by my argument that the specific features of the Japanese political structure produce some perverse consequences.

My academic friends and colleagues offered valuable advice throughout the whole process. I would like to thank Concha Artola, Mary Dietz, Jorge Dominguez, Peter Gourevitch, Steph Haggard, Yoi Herrera, Torben Iversen, Devesh Kapur, Peter Katzenstein, Dan Kelliher, Isabela Mares, Cathie Jo Martin, Kuniko Yamada McVey, Pratap Mehta, Russ Muirhead, Takehiko Nagakura, Kim Reimann, Rainer Schnell, Theda Skocpol, David Soskice, Kathy Thelen, Ezra Vogel, Steven Vogel, and Deborah Yashar. My special thanks to the following colleagues who kindly read the whole manuscript and helped improve it: John Campbell, Patti Maclachlan, T. J. Pempel, Frances Rosenbluth, and Frank Schwartz.

The real army behind me, as usual, consisted of my very old friends from Japan, former roommates, and family. Heartfelt thanks (*itsumo oen shite kurete arigato*) to Kuniko Doi, Maquie Eklund, Takako Hikotani, Mako Ito, Toshimi Kimura (Doji), Kumiko Miyasaka, Hiroyuki Nagayama, and Rieko Yamada Ivy. (I would also like to thank Laurence Ivy, Rieko's husband, for letting me use his photo for the cover of this book.) These friends were the most devoted cadets who stuck with me though thick and thin. Doji and Mako, in particular, put up with my obsessions with art and politics since our high school days. Takako and Hiroyuki, as fellow political scientists, patiently listened to every permutation of my argument over the years. I would also like to thank my family and former roommates: Maria de los Angeles Estévez Abe, Juan Manuel Angel Estévez Abe, Miguel Angel Estévez Abe, Ann Golesworthy, Katja Krikinkova, and Susan Taylor.

I also would like to thank various organizations and individuals who supported my research and helped in the publication of this book: the Hansa Wissenschafts-kolleg, the Radcliffe Institute of Advanced Study, the Reischauer Institute of Japanese Studies at Harvard University, the Weatherhead Center of International Studies at Harvard University, Japan Society for the Promotion of Science, Keio University, the Social Science Institute at Tokyo University, Yoshinori Furuya, and Lewis Bateman. Yuka Ejima, Yui Hirohashi, and Yu Kanosue provided very able research assistance at different stages of the project. I would also like to thank Margaret Muirhead for her copyediting.

My Spanish grandmother, who passed away more than ten years ago, never understood why I was spending so many years at school. The last time I saw her, apropos of nothing, she asked me about my work for the first (and last) time. As it turned out, she just wanted to know whether I was finishing my school work in time to get married ("time was running out!"). I have taken a long time to complete this book, but my grandmother would be quite pleased to know that my boyfriend whom she met, Glyn, did become my husband soon afterwards and has stayed with me for the whole process. My parents have always admired and thanked Glyn for putting up with their self-obsessed, rebellious daughter. I second it from the deepest of my heart. Without him, I would have not finished this book. This book is dedicated to my parents, Yasuko Abe and Angel Estévez Dominguez.

Introduction

The Puzzle of Japan's Welfare Capitalism

THE REAL VARIETIES OF WELFARE CAPITALISM

Japan's welfare state is puzzling. On most measures, Japan's welfare state is small. Its social spending levels are low; its tax revenue is small; and its benefit levels are meager (Figure 0.1).[1] Japan's social spending programs are among the least redistributive in the advanced industrial world (Table 0.1). At first glance, Japan's small welfare spending appears to confirm the conventional scholarly wisdom that attributes the development of a generous and redistributive welfare state to a strong social democratic party – supported by well-organized and centralized labor unions. Yet despite its meager social spending, Japan has nonetheless managed to achieve a fairly egalitarian income distribution. This situation stands in marked contrast to other countries with similarly small welfare states, including the United Kingdom and the United States, which remain the least egalitarian of the advanced industrial democracies.[2] Japan's "small" welfare state does not, in short, mean that Japan possesses a laissez-faire form of capitalism. On the contrary, the Japanese state interferes frequently and extensively with the market. Just as Sweden uses social policy as a form of industrial policy, Japan uses industrial policy as a form of social policy.[3]

---

[1] Unless otherwise noted, this chapter and Chapter 1 use the year 1990 as the base year of international comparison. I choose this year for two reasons. First, influential comparative studies that established different regime types used the data for the 1980s and the early 1990s, so using the date from the same period is a good strategy to highlight the difference between existing studies and my approach. Second, choosing 1990 as the base year allows me to highlight policy shifts that occurred since then.

[2] I cannot agree more with John Campbell (1992), who emphasizes the heuristic importance of the Japanese case. Japan has so often been treated as an outlier in comparative studies of advanced industrial societies. The literature on neocorporatism best illustrates the enigmatic status of Japan in comparative studies. In particular, see Kenworthy (1995), Korpi (1985), Shalev (1990), Siaroff (1999), and Soskice (1990a, 1990b).

[3] See Pontusson (1991) for a similar point. Pempel (1991) makes a fascinating contrast between Japan and Sweden. For a different Japan-Sweden comparison, see Gould (1993).

TABLE O.I. *Country Ranking on Equality*

Pre-Tax/Transfer	Post-Tax/Transfer
Belgium	Finland
JAPAN	Belgium
Netherlands	Netherlands
Italy	Germany
Canada	Sweden
Finland	**JAPAN**
Germany	Canada
Switzerland	France
United States	Italy
France	United Kingdom
United Kingdom	Ireland
Sweden	Switzerland
Ireland	United States

Source: Provided by Chiaki Moriguchi (The data are based on the mid- and late-1980s.). See Moriguchi and Saez (2006).

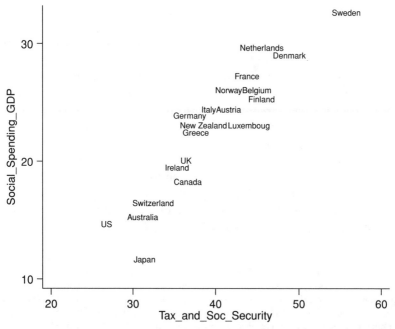

FIGURE O.I. Taxation and Social Spending as Percentage of GDP (1990). *Source:* OECD dataset. (Figures for taxation include revenue from social security contributions.)

This book offers a new way of thinking about welfare states and the politics that produces and sustains such states. Most studies of welfare states focus exclusively on a narrow range of social spending programs and rarely ask how different countries draw upon a combination of nonwelfare policies to protect their citizens' well-being. This book broadens the traditional analysis of the welfare state by introducing the concept of functional equivalent programs.[4] Welfare state studies have long ignored public works, subsidies to rural families, market-restricting regulations, and employment protections as mechanisms to protect the livelihood of citizens. Imagine, for instance, a middle-aged farmer in rural Niigata Prefecture without many nonagricultural job opportunities. The agricultural subsidies that he receives protect not only his job but the livelihood of his family. They are important functional equivalents to full employment policy and to more orthodox income transfers to families.

When viewed in this broader perspective, Japan possesses a much bigger welfare state than comparative welfare state scholars have recognized. Japan, while lagging behind large European welfare states in its public income transfers and social services to working-age citizens, has relied instead on functional equivalent programs, which go uncaptured by statistics on social spending.[5] By extending the analysis to functional equivalent programs, one can identify the specific features of Japan's social protection.

Many of these functional equivalents in Japan either promote work-mediated welfare benefits or protect jobs. The Japanese government has used functional equivalents to deliver protection to very specific groups of beneficiaries – such as industries, occupational groups, and even businesses and citizens in specific geographical areas. Japan's social security programs have, partly as a consequence, developed in a highly fragmented manner. The two largest items – pension and health care – both developed as occupationally based social insurance schemes. In fact, Japan's social spending is heavily concentrated in old-age pension and health care payments.[6] Despite Japan's meager benefits for working-age wage

---

[4] Scholars of American social policy have been much better than scholars of European welfare states in recognizing the importance of functional equivalents. Dobbin (1992), Dobbin and Boychuk (1996), Hacker (2002), Quadagno and Hardy (1996), and Stevens (1990) in particular have looked at employer-provided corporate programs and other market-based welfare products. Howard (1997) focuses on tax expenditures. Salamon (1989) and Kamerman and Kahn (1989) discuss a whole range of policy tools at the disposal of the government to deliver protection. For a rare comparative study that uses a similar concept of functional equivalents, see Bonoli (2003).

[5] In his typically thorough and insightful analysis of Japan's pension policy, Campbell (1992) notes how Japan has resorted to policies that stimulate activity rates of the elderly as a functional equivalent to orthodox programs. Calder's work on the postwar Japanese politics – now a classic – also demonstrates how Japan frequently relied on functional equivalents (Calder 1988). Calder, however, does not use the term functional equivalents nor does he contrast them with social security programs. Generally, scholars working on Japan have long been aware that the absence of social spending does not necessarily mean the absence of welfare provision. Although they rarely use the term functional equivalent, many scholars emphasize the role of companies and families in providing welfare in Japan, whereas others focus on the use of "nonsocial" policies such as industrial and financial policies for welfare purposes. See Dore (1973), Rose and Shiratori (1986), and Nobuhiro Hiwatari (1991) for emphasis on welfare provision by companies and families, and Calder (1988), Hatsuta and Yashiro eds. (1995), Kazuo Shibagaki (1985), and Robert Uriu (1996), among others, for studies that recognize how "nonsocial" policies were used in Japan as tools of social protection. I owe my work to their important insights and try to build upon them.

[6] Lynch (2001) provides an excellent point about how some welfare states are biased in favor of the old rather than the young.

earners, public pensions and health care in Japan are relatively generous even by international standards.

Furthermore, the postwar Japanese state has used "welfare" to squeeze money from society without resorting to taxes.[7] Japanese governments promoted savings-oriented programs of all kinds – both public and private welfare programs – and placed welfare funds under state control. To put it boldly, Japan socialized capital by means of state control over welfare funds. The vast reserves of long-term capital under the state's control, in turn, have provided each Japanese government with a far greater financial capacity than its small tax revenue would otherwise have allowed. Despite its importance, the impact of Japan's welfare system on its distinctive model of capitalism has never been adequately explained.

The concept of functional equivalents is not specific to Japan. More generally, this book challenges the orthodoxy of welfare state studies by arguing that we cannot understand the real scope and full nature of social protection in a country unless we look at the way different policy tools are combined. In this respect, although this book focuses primarily on Japan, it is written for readers more broadly interested in welfare states and the political economy of advanced industrial societies. More than any other advanced industrial society, Japan illuminates the limitations of existing notions of the welfare state. Gøsta Esping-Andersen (1990), in his extremely influential book, *The Three Worlds of Welfare Capitalism*, uses the concept of *decommodification* to capture qualitative differences among welfare states. Decommodification refers to the degree to which the welfare state makes citizens more independent from the wages earned in the market. By exclusively focusing on a few social welfare programs to measure the degree of decommodification, Esping-Andersen entirely overlooks a whole range of functional equivalents that attenuate the effects of market forces. His omissions, which are shared by many others, reflect what I call a *social democratic bias* in traditional welfare state studies. Esping-Andersen and others are mostly interested in identifying those dimensions of the welfare state that promote social rights. Their goal – implicitly or explicitly – is to demonstrate that social democratic countries promote social rights the best. As a result, many dimensions of welfare states that appear unrelated to social rights have been largely ignored. A good example of such neglect is the absence of any interest in the financial dimensions of the welfare state, despite their enormous impact on the nature of a particular market economy. If the task is to understand the real varieties of welfare capitalism, we need to overcome the social democratic bias.

THE STRUCTURAL LOGIC APPROACH

Why did Japan develop generous orthodox programs in some areas but not in others? Why did it so often employ functional equivalents rather than more

---

[7] Calder (1990) and Anderson (1990) also note that the Japanese state has used "welfare" as a reason to promote postal savings and postal insurance to raise capital. As Calder explains, the Japanese government has used welfare funds via the Fiscal Investment and Loan Program (FILP). I demonstrate in this book that the Japanese government's use of welfare funds for policy purposes has been much more extensive than the presence of FILP indicates. Chapter 6 provides the details.

orthodox social spending programs? Comparatively speaking, Japan has developed fairly decent public programs in pension and health care. But when it comes to unemployment benefits and income support to working families – such as family allowance and housing allowance – Japan still lags behind other countries. Where public welfare benefits lag behind, we find functionally equivalent welfare programs. What explains Japan's asymmetrical development of welfare provision? Why has the Japanese state relied so heavily on savings-oriented programs? Once we place Japan in a comparative perspective, it becomes evident that other countries, too, rely on functional equivalents. In fact, there are countries that use sets of functional equivalents similar to those used in Japan. This finding leads us to a broader question in comparative politics. What factors determine why some countries combine certain types of social security programs and their functional equivalents in specific ways?

In answering these questions, this book employs an institutional model of welfare politics to explain why advanced industrial democracies combine specific types of social spending programs and their functional equivalents in different ways. It builds an institutional model of welfare politics on the basis of three features: (i) the government type – for example, majoritarian, coalition, minority; (ii) district magnitude – that is, the number of seats assigned to an electoral district; and (iii) the importance of the personal vote – that is, the personal vote becomes important when voters cast their votes for specific candidates rather than for parties and when candidates need to compete against their fellow party members at the polls. The government type and the importance of the personal vote determine the number of veto players in the government. Specific combinations of district magnitude and the relative importance of the personal vote determine what electoral strategies are most desirable in a given country. Different electoral strategies, in turn, determine what types of social protection possess the most advantageous distributive implications. Because the microlevel logic of welfare politics can be derived from the aforementioned features of the political system, I call my institutional model a "structural logic model."

To put it briefly, the structural logic model claims that the Japanese electoral system (multimember districts and single nontransferable vote) produced strong incentives in favor of highly targeted forms of social protection. Electorally speaking, it made sense for the ruling party in Japan to target social protection at specific constituent groups or areas.[8] Japan thus spent less on comprehensive social welfare programs, because such programs made it difficult to steer distributive benefits to specific areas and groups. Instead, Japan developed social insurance schemes and functional equivalents to social security programs that allowed occupational and geographical targeting. The largesse of functional equivalents in Japan meant that "redistribution" occurred outside the narrowly conceived welfare state. This explains an odd combination: an egalitarian society and meager social spending.

---

[8] Tatebayashi (2004) provides an excellent argument and evidence on the issue of conservative politicians' distributive strategies under the multimember districts combined with single nontransferable vote.

The structural logic model put forth in this book explains three sets of variations: (i) cross-national variations in the pattern of social protection; (ii) cross-policy variations within the same country during the same period; and (iii) historical changes within the same country. In other words, my structural logic offers a new explanation for previously unexplained differences and similarities between Japan and other advanced industrial societies. It also explains policy variations within Japan – both across issue areas and time. The following sections briefly review existing theories that account for each of these three sets of variations. The aim here is to situate my structural logic approach in relevant theoretical debates.

Comparatively speaking, Japan often appears as an outlier. Scholars have had a hard time pinning it down. Japan's public pension and health care schemes resemble those in continental European countries, but Japan also looks very much like the United States in its small social spending.[9] Yet notwithstanding its small social spending, the Japanese government has intervened in the market in multiple ways – much like many continental European governments. To further complicate the picture, Japan's commitment to full employment resembles that of the Scandinavian social democratic welfare states. Existing theories of welfare politics simply cannot explain these similarities and differences.

Partisanship-Based Models of Welfare Politics

The dominant model of welfare politics explains the shape of a welfare state on the basis of the partisan composition of the government. Countries where social democratic parties dominate, so the argument goes, develop generous and universalistic welfare states, which emphasize full employment (Esping-Andersen 1985; Esping-Andersen and Korpi 1985; Hicks 1999; Hicks and Swank 1992; Huber and Stephens 2001; Korpi 1978, 1983; Rothstein 1985; Stephens 1979). Countries with Christian democratic party dominance also develop generous welfare states but they emphasize income transfers to families rather than universalistic coverage (Castles 1978, 1982; Huber and Stephens 2001; Van Kersbergen 1995). At first sight, the partisanship-based models of welfare politics appear to work well when we exclusively look at social spending programs. Small welfare states – Japan being one of them – lack strong social democratic or Christian democratic parties. These explanatory models nonetheless have two weaknesses. The first weakness is that they cannot explain cross-national variations among small welfare states. Partisanship-based models might explain why Japan and the United States differ from Sweden or Germany. But they cannot explain why Japan's social protection

[9] Esping-Andersen (1997) calls Japan a hybrid between a liberal welfare state and a conservative welfare state.

system differs from that of the United States.[10] As existing studies of the Japanese welfare state correctly point out, Japan has managed to introduce many public welfare programs despite its weak labor. Japan has a whole range of social security programs and their functional equivalents that are absent in the United States. The second weakness of partisanship-based models is that they fail to account for similarities that exist between Japan and social democratic or Christian democratic welfare states.[11] Some social democratic welfare states accumulate funds via welfare programs and also spend a lot on public works – much like Japan does. Both Japan and the Scandinavian social democratic countries also emphasize full employment. Japan also shares similarities with continental European Christian democratic countries such as Germany and Italy. They share highly fragmented social insurance schemes and all rely on regulatory interventions in the market – an important functional equivalent to orthodox social security schemes. Clearly, the models that associate partisanship and welfare states cannot explain all these differences and similarities between welfare states. Much of the literature is too Eurocentric. Scholars of Japanese social policy have long noted this failing.[12]

Cross-Class Alliance Model of Welfare Politics

Scholars skeptical of partisanship-based models focus theoretical attention on the preferences of employers and unions concerning social policy outcomes (Mares 1997, 2003; Martin 1995a, 1995b, 2000; Swenson 1991a, 1991b, 1997, 2002). Studies in this camp have greatly improved our understanding of social policy preferences of employers and unions. They have identified a range of factors – insurance against risks, labor cost, control and labor management needs – that affect employers' and unions' calculations over corporate welfare benefits, occupationally fragmented social insurance schemes, and tax-financed universalistic schemes.[13] This approach appears, at least initially, to explain Japan well. Given Japan's highly dualistic labor market, the privileged core workers in large firms preferred company-based benefits over generous universalistic benefits. Indeed,

---

[10] Chapter 1 provides detailed cross-national comparisons.

[11] Japan developed national health care, paid child care benefits, and long-term care insurance as public welfare programs – all of which still remain absent in the United States. Furthermore, a look at functional equivalents also indicates that the Japanese welfare state protects jobs to a much greater degree than the American welfare state does. The Japanese welfare state also interferes into the financial market in ways that the American welfare state does not. This means that not all functional equivalents are market-expanding ones typically emphasized by scholars of American social policy.

[12] Anderson (1990), Calder (1990), Campbell (1979, 1992), Kasza (2006), and Pempel (1982). Some have gone on to write about East Asian models of welfare states; see Goodman, White, and Kwon (1998).

[13] Swenson (2002) has focused more on different types of human management needs as the basis of different employers' social policy preferences. Martin (1995a, 1995b) has focused more on employers' cost calculations. Mares (1997, 2003) advanced the initial insights of Baldwin (1990) that characterized the welfare state as an insurance mechanism against risks. For another application of this idea, see Burgoon (2001). Mares considers both employers' labor management needs and their cost calculations in determining their preference for a specific insurance scheme.

a universalistic policy would have redistributed from better-paid and more secure core workers to their less fortunate peers.[14] Two problems exist, however, when applying this model to Japan. First, this model lacks a general model of political power. It sees welfare politics primarily as a game between unions and employers.[15] Outside a handful of northern European countries, however, welfare politics consists of a much wider cast of actors.[16] When do we know that a cross-class alliance of capital and labor can prevail over opposition by other groups, such as physicians, the insurance industry, or the self-employed (to name but a few possible participants in welfare politics)? Furthermore, in addition to societal actors, state actors also take part in welfare politics (Heclo 1974; Skocpol and Amenta 1986; Weir and Skocpol 1985). Do different types of civil service pursue different social policies to influence final policy outcome? Who prevails when there is a conflict of interest between state and societal actors? Models that emphasize the importance of cross-class alliance tend to ignore these questions.[17] The absence of a general theory of power leads to a second weakness of this approach.

Second, most studies define the range of welfare options for employers and for unions too narrowly. The choices typically considered consist of private corporate welfare, fragmented social insurance schemes, and universalistic public welfare benefits. In the real world, however, unions and employers seek a much wider range of public policies than social insurance and universalistic benefits, including subsidies for private welfare schemes – subsidies that involve government spending or tax expenditures – and a whole range of regulatory interventions.[18] We also observe unions and business demanding market-restricting regulations to protect, respectively, their jobs and profits. These policy options can best be understood, so this book argues, as functional equivalents to orthodox social security programs. The types of protection that unions and employers demand are partly a function of their power. Firms that possess political influence often seek

---

[14] Esping-Andersen (1997) has made this point.

[15] In this sense, it resembles the power resources model it criticizes.

[16] In reality, however, as pointed out by Skocpol (1992), the view that class actors are the most important players in welfare politics must be treated skeptically.

[17] Consider, for instance, whether a similar cross-class alliance in the automobile industry in Germany, Japan, and the United States produces the same amount of political power and policy outcomes in these respective countries. The fact that the U.S. automobile industry pays so much more for the health care costs of their workforce due to the absence of a national health care system in the United States suggests that this cross-class alliance does not possess the same weight in all countries. Katzenstein's work has been an exception (1985). He has not exclusively focused on the two class interests – capital and labor – but has also paid attention to a broader institutional context such as electoral systems that affect the likelihood of these class interests being materialized as public policy. Similarly, Cathie Jo Martin has always been more concerned with the issue of political capacity. Her recent work, in particular, focuses explicitly on the policy capacity of employer organizations (Martin and Swank 2004).

[18] Swenson (2002) offers insights beyond the narrow range of welfare programs. He considers conditions in which employers might prefer cartels. He acknowledges that those employers he calls "segmentalist" might prefer cartel as social protection. He refers to Japan as a possible case of a country with segmentalist employers. Nonetheless, he does not identify when such segmentalist employers succeed or fail in forming cartels.

protective measures targeted at their companies. When lacking sufficient independent power, they might ally themselves with other firms in the same product
market or in the same region to demand industry- or region-specific subsidies.
Risk exposure is certainly an important factor. But political power is more often
the decisive factor.

Institutionalist Models of Welfare Politics

Institutional models of welfare politics provide a theory of power different from
the partisanship-based models of welfare politics. There are different strands of
institutionalist theories. One strand focuses on the historical legacies of earlier
institutional choices such as a choice of a particular type of welfare program or
a state structure (King 1995; King and Rothstein 1993; Orloff 1993; Pierson 1994;
Rothstein 1992; Skocpol and Amenta 1986; Weir 1992; Weir and Skocpol 1985).
Scholars in this group explain cross-national differences in terms of such historical
institutional legacies. The other strand focuses more on the role of institutions in
setting the rules of the political game.[19] Within this second strand, some scholars
focus on the number of veto players, whereas others focus on electoral systems. It
is important to consider theories within the second strand at more length because
the theory I develop in this book belongs to this particular strand of institutionalist theories. The veto player theory attributes the presence of universalistic
programs to the number of veto players in the polity. Most scholars in this group
argue that legislative processes that contain many veto players make policy shifts
difficult (Immergut 1992; Maioni 1998; Moe and Caldwell 1994; Pierson 1995;
Skocpol 1996; Steinmo 1993; Steinmo and Watts 1995; Tsebelis 2002). Veto
players, by definition, are actors (whether political parties or individual politicians) whose consent is necessary to make law. They argue that, for this reason,
when the number of veto players is large, a country is less likely to develop universalistic programs, because it becomes very easy for a minority group to block
what benefits the majority (Immergut 1992; Maioni 1998; Skocpol 1996; Steinmo
1993; Steinmo and Watts 1995).[20]

---

[19] I am exaggerating the contrast here to make distinctions clear. In reality, those historical institutionalist studies that focus on state structures mostly draw attention to the role of federal structures in blocking certain types of social welfare programs. The reasoning behind these arguments
is basically the same with the veto player argument reviewed here as part of the second strand
of institutionalist theories. Orloff (1993), for instance, pays close attention to the role of the
federal structure in explaining welfare state developments in Britain, Canada, and the United
States.

[20] Moe and Caldwell (1994) make a different argument to explain the same policy outcome. Instead
of arguing that universalistic programs are difficult when the number of veto players is large,
they explain why countries with few veto players might be more likely to introduce universalistic
programs. They argue that, because policy reversals are easy in political systems with a small
number of veto players, the current government opts for universalistic programs that benefit the
majority in the hope that popular programs that benefit many are more difficult to roll back in the
future. I would like to thank Terry Moe for bringing this to my attention. Tsebelis (2002) also
agrees with the gist of their argument.

Another group of institutionalists attribute larger welfare states to proportional representation (Birchfield and Crepaz 1998; Boix 2001; Crepaz 1998; Iversen and Soskice 2006; Katzenstein 1985; Lijphart and Crepaz 1991). Most notably, Lijphart and Crepaz (1991) and Iversen and Soskice (2006) develop different causal logics, both of which predict a strong link between proportional representation (PR) and large welfare states. Lijphart and Crepaz (1991) claim that the use of PR gives rise to a more cooperative form of parliamentary politics that they call "consensual democracy." Consensual democracy enables the introduction and expansion of welfare programs by facilitating cooperation among political parties.[21] The use of single-member districts (SMD), in contrast, gives rise to a more confrontational politics – "majoritarian democracy" – leading to a smaller welfare state. Birchfield and Crepaz (1998) and Crepaz (1998) basically take the same view.[22] Iversen and Soskice (2006) claim that PR systems are more likely than SMD systems to give rise to left-of-center governments that spend more on social programs.[23] They make this claim by developing a model focused on the voting behavior of the middle classes. They claim that middle-class voters – the pivotal group of voters in their model – are more likely to support a left-leaning government when a moderate party that represents their position forms a coalition partner (and thus possesses veto power).

An important tension exists between the electorally based account of welfare politics and a subgroup of veto player–based account. Huber, Ragin, and Stephens (1993) and Huber and Stephens (2001) claim that the number of veto players negatively affects the size of the welfare state. On this account, coalition governments should develop smaller welfare states than majoritarian governments because coalition governments have more veto players within the government than majoritarian governments do. Obviously, this argument runs counter to the claims made by Lijphart and Crepaz (1991), Birchfield and Crepaz (1998), Crepaz (1998), and Iversen and Soskice (2006).[24]

---

[21] They focus on differences between consensual and majoritarian democracies. Consensual democracies emerge in countries with PR, and display oversized cabinets, balanced power, executive dominance, and multiparty systems. In contrast, majoritarian democracies use plurality rules – as in single-member district systems – rather than proportional rules, and have minimal winning cabinets and a two-party system. This group associates consensual democracies with politics characterized by cooperation among political parties, whereas they associate majoritarian democracies with a more confrontational style of politics. They suggest that consensual democracies lead to larger welfare states. For a full description and definition, see Lijphart (1984) and Lijphart and Crepaz (1991). Crepaz (1996, 1998) and Steinmo and Tolbert (1998) also develop corollaries of this argument.

[22] Crepaz extends the earlier argument by developing a new concept of collective and competitive veto players (Birchfield and Crepaz 1998; Crepaz 1998). Briefly stated, collective veto players arise in the same institutional arena such as within the parliament, whereas competitive veto players arise in different institutional arenas within the polity. Crepaz argues that the face-to-face transactions among collective veto players make them more cooperative.

[23] Rodden (2005) provides a simpler causal argument with the same implications. Rodden argues that SMD systems generate more representational bias in favor of rural voters, who tend to be more conservative. This is why PR is more likely than SMD to produce left-leaning governments and hence larger welfare states.

[24] Markus Crepaz tackles this tension by distinguishing two kinds of veto players – competitive and cooperative veto players. He considers veto players that arise from the constitutional structure of

Institutionalist theories of welfare politics are difficult to apply to Japan for two reasons. First, standard measures of veto players and the PR/SMD dichotomy fail to locate Japan in a proper comparative context.[25] By any ordinary measure of veto players, Japan comes out as a political system with very few veto players. By this count, Japan should have developed a highly universalistic welfare state. Conventionally considered, Japan's electoral rules – both old and new – defy simple categorization into PR/SMD.[26] As a result, it is not exactly clear how to formulate theories relevant for Japan. The second reason why existing theories fail in the Japanese case is that such theories are themselves poor at explaining qualitative differences across welfare states. Institutionalist theories of welfare politics based on PR/SMD distinctions focus exclusively on social spending levels. This is unfortunate, because electoral studies actually provide a lot more insight into the distributive implications of different types of electoral rules beyond spending levels. This book integrates insights from institutional studies to construct a new theory of welfare politics.

The Structural Logic Approach

Instead of viewing Japan as an outlier that does not fit any institutional category, my structural logic approach takes advantage of the Japanese case to develop an alternative institutional argument of welfare politics in advanced industrial societies. It does so by going beyond the dichotomy of SMD/PR and beyond an exclusive focus on social spending. More specifically, my structural logic approach, while building upon the rich literature on electoral systems, focuses on the distributive implications of district magnitude and the relative importance of the personal vote. Once we use the institutional matrix of district magnitude and the strength of the personal vote, it becomes possible to situate Japan more appropriately (see Chapter 2 for more details). Many experts of electoral systems have been aware of the importance of district size in shaping politicians' behavior: a large district magnitude leads politicians to cultivate organized groups of voters, whereas a single-member district increases the importance of unorganized voters (Cox 1990, 1999; Cox and McCubbins 1986; McGillivray 1997, 2004; Myerson 1993; Powell 1982; Rogowski and Kayser 2002). Others have pointed out the importance of geographical targeting when the district magnitude is small (Baron 1991; Milesi-Ferretti, Perotti, and Rostagno 2002; Weingast, Shepsle, and Johnsen 1981). Likewise, experts of electoral systems point out that the strong

a polity such as federalism and bicameralism to be more "competitive" veto players, whereas he considers partisan veto players that arise in coalition government to be more cooperative (Birchfeld and Crepaz 1998; Crepaz 1998). It is insightful that Tsebelis (2002), who has developed the most detailed theory of veto players, argued that the number of veto players has nothing to do with the size of the welfare state. In his view, the number of veto players only explains the difficulty of changing the status quo. In other words, countries that have large welfare states may find it difficult to shrink their welfare states if there are a lot of veto players. Hicks and Swank (1992) find effects of consensusal/majoritarian distinctions on the welfare state to be indeterminate.

[25] Hicks and Kenworthy (1998) claim that PR/SMD distinction has no predictive value on the level of social spending. See also Boix (2001).

[26] Nor does Japan fit the dichotomy of majoritarian and consensual democracies.

personal vote weakens the party leader and makes money more valuable in politics (Chang and Golden 2007; Cox and Thies 1998; Grossman and Helpman 2005; Johnson 1986; Tsebelis 2002). By extension, this means that in such cases individual politicians rather than the party as a whole is the key player in determining the distributive calculations of the party. In contrast, when the party is strong, the party leader becomes the key person determining the distributive strategy of the party.[27] Existing institutional studies of welfare politics have not registered the importance of these insights.

Briefly stated, my structural logic approach combines these insights to construct expectations for the distributive strategies of politicians in different systems. While leaving the detailed argumentation to Chapter 2, my structural logic approach argues that countries with multimember districts are generally more likely than others to introduce social protection programs that are targeted at specific groups.[28] Many of these programs are likely to be functional equivalents such as protective regulation that pass on the cost of protection to unorganized groups such as consumers. The strength of the personal vote exacerbates this trend. As Chapter 2 shows in greater detail, a theory that combines district magnitude and the personal vote can distinguish: (i) those countries that are likely to introduce universalistic social protection programs in contrast to those that are likely to pursue highly targeted programs; and (ii) those that are likely to seek market-expanding functional equivalents from those more likely to seek market-restricting functional equivalents. This framework explains Japan's similarities to and differences from other countries much better than existing accounts of welfare politics.

Obviously, it matters greatly which parties possess veto power, because their electoral calculations are the ones that matter most in the parliament. For this reason, in addition to district magnitude and the relative importance of the personal vote, it is also important to consider different government types, whether minority government, coalition government, or majority party government (see Weaver and Rockman 1993). The government type not only tells us who possesses veto power in the parliament, but provides vital information as to how capable the government might be in introducing costly policies such as tax increases. Here I build upon the insights of Hallerberg (2002), Bawn and Rosenbluth (2006), and Haggard and McCubbins eds. (2001). The gist of my argument is the following: When there is only one ruling party, it becomes easy for voters to blame the ruling party for an unpopular policy. When the electoral system is SMD based,

---

[27] Weingast, Shepsle, and Johnsen (1981) fail to consider different types of SMD systems – one with weak party and the other with strong party. The precise nature of geographical targeting changes depending on whether the party is strong or not, as illustrated by McGillivray (1997, 2004).

[28] I do not share Persson and Tabellini's view that PR (= large district magnitude) promotes "broad spending" instead of targeted spending (Persson and Tabellini 2000). Many of the existing empirical studies that explore the relationship between the district magnitude (or PR/SMD distinctions) and public policy merely look at which system spends more on public goods overall (Persson and Tabellini 1999, 2000). As a result, they fall short of taking full advantage of the existing insights of electoral studies. I will come back to this issue more fully in Chapter 2.

the high volatility of electoral outcomes makes an electoral backlash against the ruling party much more likely. This means that tax increases are easiest under coalition governments of parties that are elected in multimember districts. Conversely, tax increases are most difficult under majority-party government rule in SMD systems.

Finally, my structural logic also casts light on the preferences and power of bureaucratic actors. Without going into detail, it suffices to mention here that the combination of the three factors – the district magnitude, the relative importance of the personal vote, and the government type – also determines specific constraints that bureaucrats face. To put it crudely, with all things being equal, when the veto players within the ruling party (or parties) are greater in number, the scope of bureaucratic discretion is greater (see Tsebelis 2002).

VARIATIONS WITHIN JAPAN: CROSS-ISSUE AND HISTORICAL VARIATIONS

Scholars of Japanese politics have long puzzled over the persistence of Japan's egalitarianism under conservative governments. There is a consensus that Japan is a very different kind of welfare state from other small welfare states like the United States.[29] Some scholars point to the compromise between capital and organized labor in Japan, whereby large firms and their company unions agreed to share the fruits of productivity increases (Dore 1973; Garon and Mochizuki 1993; Gordon 1985, 1998; Hiwatari 1991; Kume 1998).[30] Others attribute Japan's egalitarianism to (i) the role of electoral competition and (ii) the role of the career social policy bureaucrats (Anderson 1993; Calder 1988; Campbell 1979, 1992; Milly 1999; Pempel 1982).[31] The argument goes like this: When facing electoral threats from the opposition, Japanese conservative politicians embraced egalitarianism

---

[29] There exists, however, an interesting tension within the existing literature. Most American scholars of the Japanese welfare state focus their efforts on demonstrating that Japan developed a welfare state similar to large European welfare states even in the absence of strong organized labor or a social democratic party. Some scholars of the Japanese welfare state nonetheless think Japan indeed has a small welfare state different from large European welfare states. They attribute this difference to Japan's generous corporate welfare, which, in their view, made generous social security programs unnecessary in Japan.

[30] Dore (1973), for instance, argues that Japanese companies were much more *welfarist* than companies elsewhere. He thinks that corporate benefits crowded out public benefits in Japan. Dore's argument is based on his comparison between Japan and the United Kingdom. It is worth pointing out here that large firms in the United States have generally been more welfarist than their Japanese counterparts in terms of their spending on corporate welfare. For other work on Japanese corporate benefits, see Hiwatari (1991), Shinkawa (1993), Shinkawa and Pempel (1996), and Weiss (1993). It is worth noting that while someone like Dore positively evaluates the Japanese model of company-provided welfare, many Japanese social scientists see it as a sign of business dominance in Japan (Shinkawa 1993; Shinkawa and Pempel 1996).

[31] Garon (1987) and Kasza (2002) look at the prewar and the wartime origins of Japan's social security system, respectively. Garon emphasizes the role of social policy bureaucrats, whose goal was to prevent the radicalization of labor movement, whereas Kasza emphasizes the role of World War II.

and welfarism to co-opt voters – including wage earners.[32] The presence of social policy bureaucrats, in turn, ensured that the politicians always had policy ideas at hand to take advantage of these moments of political will for welfare expansions (see Calder 1988; Campbell 1992; and Pempel 1982 in particular).

Existing studies, however, do not explain why the Japanese government's commitment varied so much from one welfare area to another. Nor do they tell us why Japan opted for particular types of social security programs and their functional equivalents – work-based and savings-oriented programs.[33] Electoral competition *per se* does not explain the asymmetrical development of Japan's welfare state. Housing shortages, unemployment, and poverty among households headed by war widows were all extremely pressing issues that were hotly debated at various election times in the early postwar period.[34] Nonetheless, the postwar conservative governments were willing to fund benefits only for certain subgroups of voters. The role of social policy bureaucrats does not explain cross-policy variations either. Most existing studies of welfare politics contrast two kinds of bureaucrats – *redistributors* and *reluctants* (to borrow Pempel's terms). Pempel (1982) sees the Ministry of Finance as the anti-welfare reluctant ministry, and the old Ministry of Health and Welfare as the pro-welfare redistributive ministry.[35] From this perspective, when political windows of opportunity open up due to electoral competition – or what Calder (1988) calls "crisis" – redistributors prevail over reluctants to expand welfare. However, this does not explain why some types of social protection programs were more likely than others. As Calder's *Crisis and Compensation* reveals, Japan's conservative governments introduced many welfare programs and their functional equivalents when they faced electoral competition. Existing studies fail, however, to explain why Japan opted for specific forms of orthodox welfare programs and their functional equivalents rather than others. As a result, they fall short of providing an account of welfare politics that can be generalized.

In sum, this book diverges from existing accounts of welfare politics in three fundamental ways. First, it offers a new account of the highly selective nature

[32] Calder (1988) specifically talks about how electoral threats to the conservatives – he calls them "crises" – prompted redistribution in Japan. Calder, unlike others, discusses a broader range of policy areas beyond social security programs. In this sense, my work is closest to Calder's approach.

[33] Certainly, scholars have been aware of distinctive functionally equivalent programs that Japan possessed. Calder (1990) has paid attention to the use of postal savings as a way of accumulating capital and financing economic development in Japan; Dore (1973) has long noted the prominent role of corporate welfare provision in Japan; Campbell (1992) refers to Japan's policy makers' preference for providing work to old workers rather than paying them pensions. Despite their insights, they do not provide a systematic explanation of why postwar Japan always favored particular types of social protection programs rather than others.

[34] Notwithstanding the image of Japan's *development state*, welfare issues continued to be high priority policy concerns in the decades following the end of the war. See Chapter 4.

[35] Although some ministries were merged and their names changed as of January 2001, throughout the book I use the ministerial name that was used at the time of the legislative developments under discussion. This means that for welfare politics prior to January 2001, I refer to the Ministry of Labor and the Ministry of Health and Welfare rather than the Ministry of Health, Labor, and Welfare, which was created by merging the two ministries in 2001.

of welfare state development under the conservatives in postwar Japan. Under Japan's electoral system based on multimember districts and single nontransferable vote (MMD/SNTV), ruling party politicians favored social protection programs that permitted targeting specific groups and regions to reward their core constituent groups. As a result, while this electoral system remained unchanged, Japan's social protection programs rewarded the same core conservative constituent groups. Furthermore, in its attempt to target distributive benefits to their constituent groups, the ruling party resorted to functional equivalents rather than orthodox social spending programs. Benefits for the core organized constituent groups of the ruling party, once introduced, grew bigger. The cost of these benefits was passed along on to unorganized general tax payers and consumers. The uneven development of Japan's welfare state reflects the persisting distributive bias that emerged under the MMD/SNTV system.

Second, this book also offers a new interpretation of the bureaucrats' preferences and their power. Compared to existing studies, which tend to see Japanese bureaucrats as technocrats focused on carrying out their policy missions, this book highlights the self-interested motivations of bureaucrats in choosing policy options. I explain their selfish motivations as a function of specific personnel management practices in the Japanese bureaucracy. For the reasons identified in Chapter 3, Japanese bureaucrats developed organizational stakes in introducing savings-oriented programs. They were successful in doing so because Japan's legislative process afforded them so much discretion. Whereas most recent studies of Japanese politics see bureaucratic power as greatly constrained by the will of the ruling party leadership, this book offers a more nuanced picture of the relationship between the ruling party and Japan's career bureaucracy.[36] I claim that the importance of the personal vote in Japan increased the scope of bureaucratic discretion by increasing the number of veto players within the ruling conservative party.[37]

Finally, this book differs from existing accounts in providing a more systematic account of historical shifts in the pattern of welfare policy. My structural logic approach offers a new account of historical policy shifts in Japan. It does so by identifying different historical periods on the basis of different combinations of government type, district magnitude, and the importance of the personal vote. Broadly speaking, the structural logic approach distinguishes three periods: (a) the period of conservative dominance; (b) the period of "partial" minority and coalition governments; and (iii) the period of party centralization. The first period sees the development of highly targeted programs – both social security programs and their functional equivalents – to mobilize and organize conservative constituent groups. The second period sees, for the first time, programs for wage earners as the configuration of veto players changed. The third period, a period that continues today, sees Japan develop into a British-style Westminster

---

[36] Ramseyer and Rosenbluth (1993) see bureaucrats solely as the agents of the LDP in their application of the principal agent theory to Japan.

[37] Chapters 2 and 3 provide more detailed arguments on this point.

system. With this change in the structural logic, so this book argues, Japan's social protection system is likely to develop into a British-style welfare state.

CONTRIBUTIONS AND THE ORGANIZATION OF THE BOOK

In addition to a new account of the development and nature of the Japanese welfare system, this book contributes to three more general debates in comparative politics. First, it contributes to the debate on the transformation of Japanese politics since the electoral reform in 1994. Ever since Japan introduced a mixed system of SMD and PR in the Lower House, a major reform of its electoral system, political scientists have wondered aloud about how the new institutions would reshape the Japanese party system and politics (Cox and Schoppa 2002; Krauss and Nyblade 2005; Krauss and Pekkanen 2004; McKean and Scheiner 2000; Mulgan 2002; Otake 2003; Reed 2002; Reed ed. 2003; Reed and Thies 2001). This book takes a bold position on this debate. It claims that the new political reforms have pushed Japan toward, although it is not there yet, the same institutional category as the United Kingdom – a highly centralized government, strong parties, and single-member districts.[38] Second, it offers a novel model of welfare politics by integrating insights from electoral studies and veto player theories. This new model of welfare politics explains why some countries are more likely than others to adopt social welfare programs and why other states employ functional equivalents targeted at specific groups or regions.

Third, this book contributes to the varieties of capitalism (VOC) studies.[39] VOC studies are based on the idea that different institutional frameworks give rise to distinctive types of market economy, in which key economic actors such as corporate managers, workers, and capital providers behave differently. The VOC literature distinguishes two general types of such market economies: coordinated market economies (CMEs); and liberal market economies (LMEs). CMEs are characterized by long-term relationships among key economic actors, in which employers and workers, firms and their capital providers cooperate with one another to increase their collective long-term gains. The VOC literature has identified a long list of institutions present in CMEs that enable economic actors to make long-term commitments. CMEs contrast sharply with LMEs, which lack such institutions. The VOC literature argues that it is precisely the absence of

---

[38] There are a number of scholars who also see such a centralizing trend (Estévez-Abe 2006; Hiwatari 2006; Noble 2006a, 2006b; Reed and Thies 2001; Takenaka 2006; and Tatebayashi 2004). Few studies, however, pursue structurally based explanations of policy outcomes. For important exceptions, see Rosenbluth and Thies (2001) and Rosenbluth and Schaap (2003). My position is closer to Rosenbluth and her collaborators than to others. For a position that sees no major change in Japanese politics after the electoral reform, see Christensen (1998, 2006).

[39] Although Hall and Soskice (2001) have popularized the term "varieties of capitalism," the debate about different organizational and institutional features of capitalist systems precedes their volume. Earlier work includes Albert (1993); Boyer (1988, 1991); Crouch and Streeck ed. (1997); Dertouzos et al. (1989); Dore (1973, 1986, 1987); Hall (1986); Hollingsworth and Boyer (1997); Piore and Sable (1984); Streeck 1992; and Zysman (1983), among others.

institutional prerequisites that make long-term commitments in LMEs unsustainable. Existing studies in the VOC literature consider the welfare state to be part of these institutional prerequisites. Nonetheless, they adhere to a rather crude understanding of the role of the welfare state in defining a model of market economy. They typically focus, for instance, solely on social spending programs. Recent VOC studies have thus tended to eliminate Japan as an example of a CME, because of its "small social spending."[40] This book offers a better account of the institutional prerequisites of CMEs than those that focus merely on social spending.

The argument of this book proceeds in nine chapters. Chapter 1 situates the Japanese social protection system in a comparative perspective. Chapter 2 presents the structural model of welfare politics, upon which later chapters will draw. At this stage, however, the chapter presents the model in general terms. Chapter 3 applies the model to Japan to identify particular recurrent patterns of welfare politics that were present in different historical periods in postwar Japan. The remaining chapters provide evidence to demonstrate the effectiveness of the structural logic approach in accounting for actual patterns of policy development under specific institutional contexts. Except for a preliminary comparative application of the structural logic approach at the end of Chapter 2, this book presents a series of historical cases from Japan.[41]

The book starts with the Allied Occupation of Japan in the immediate postwar years and covers the most recent period under Prime Minister Junichiro Koizumi. The goal of the historical analysis is to contrast different periods in Japan when politics took place in different institutional environments. The task here is twofold. First, I show that, in each historical period, political actors acted consistently in accordance with specific expectations derived from the institutional model of welfare politics put forth in this book. Second, I show that policy shifts occurred when the key institutions changed. This book reveals why bureaucrats and politicians chose one form of social protection rather than another. To this end, the book relies on newspaper articles, memoirs of policy makers, and historical studies to identify relevant policy makers' incentives. Fortunately, there are volumes of recorded interviews and memoirs of bureaucrats on the major policy issues. Most of these interviews and memoirs were recorded upon their retirement, which allowed for frank discussions of the legislative process under question. This book also relies on interviews with bureaucrats and Liberal Democratic Party (LDP) politicians conducted by the author.

Chapters 4 and 5 provide historical evidence to demonstrate how the actions of the actual policy makers match the expectations derived from the structural logic. These two chapters together explain why postwar Japan came to depend on

---

[40] Although Japan has been treated as an important prototype of a CME in David Soskice's earlier studies, Japan has been dropped in the more recent studies that focus on the size of social spending as a prerequisite of CMEs (see Iversen and Soskice 2002, for instance).

[41] This book explains the historical development on the basis of a deductive structural logic. In this sense, it is akin to the Analytic Narrative approach advocated by Bates, Greif, and Levy, et al. (1998).

work-based and savings-oriented welfare programs. Chapter 4 covers the early postwar period to demonstrate how politicians in the ruling party quickly took to using public policies as distributive incentives to court organized groups. Chapter 5 covers the welfare expansion period (the 1960s and early 1970s). Chapter 6 changes gears and examines the role that the Japanese welfare system played in the development of Japan's distinctive form of capitalism. It identifies how the Japanese social protection system helped create and sustain a coordinated market economy in the absence of generous social security programs for wage earners. Chapter 7 covers the late 1970s and the 1980s, when some of the vulnerabilities embedded in the Japanese social protection system began to surface. Chapters 8 and 9 deal with the contemporary period (from 1989 to 2007). They provide evidence of policy shifts in the direction predicted by the structural logic. Changes in institutional components of the structural logic ought to lead to changes in welfare politics. This indeed was the case. Chapter 8 attributes the shift of government resources to the middle-class wage earners that occurred after 1989 to the rise of new veto player configurations. Chapter 9 argues that the electoral and legislative rule changes in the latter half of the 1990s fundamentally changed the distributive calculations of political actors. As a result, Japan's social protection system began to change.

I

Rashomon

The Japanese Welfare State in a Comparative Perspective

Existing descriptions of the Japanese welfare state call to mind Akira Kurosawa's movie *Rashomon*, a murder mystery in which the main witnesses all disagree on the basic facts. Scholars of comparative welfare states report that Japan possesses a small welfare state much like the Anglo-American countries (Huber and Stephens 2001; Wilensky 1990, 2002). Scholars in Japan agree – and often lament – that their country has not caught up with the generous welfare states in northern European countries (Kaneko 1991; Osawa 2006, 2007; Shinkawa 1993; Watanabe 1990, 1991; Yokoyama 1976a). Western scholars familiar with the Japanese welfare system, however, disagree – albeit for different reasons. Many industrial relations scholars, for instance, claim that Japan possesses generous welfarist corporations that make a Western-style welfare state unnecessary (Dore 1973; Rose and Shiratori, eds. 1986). Many scholars of Japanese politics, in contrast, contend that Japan's welfare state – far from being small or unique – is actually not much different from the large welfare states of the continental European countries (Anderson 1993; Calder 1988; Campbell 1992; Campbell and Ikegami 1998; Kasza 2006). These scholars all capture part of the truth, but they miss the forest for the trees.

Once we take both social security programs and their functional equivalents into consideration, the initial puzzle presented at the very beginning of this book can be solved. Japan provides a much greater degree of social protection than its small social spending would indicate. Japan's functional equivalents have effectively sustained a coordinated market economy (CME) in Japan, despite the fact that Japan lacks the large welfare state of other CMEs. This chapter demonstrates, however, that Japan is not the only country to rely on functional equivalents. In fact, many of the functional equivalents that Japan relies on are also important in other CMEs. Japan, however, differs from most CMEs in important ways. When compared to other countries, the Japanese social protection system stands out for its emphasis on (a) work-based protection; and (b) savings-oriented programs controlled by the state. "Work-based" protection does not simply mean employer-provided fringe benefits. Instead, by "work-based," I mean two things. First, "work" mediates *both* private and public welfare provision in Japan. Even the eligibility for most public welfare benefits is tied to one's job – that is, one's occupation, the firm size of one's employer, and whether one's work is full- or part-time. Second, protection and creation of "work" is itself seen as a form of welfare provision.

This chapter situates Japan in a comparative context to highlight these two features. Unless otherwise noted, this chapter uses the early 1990s as a reference point for cross-national comparison to capture how different advanced industrial countries looked before many of them embarked on welfare reforms in the 1990s. Recent changes in Japan will be the topic of a later chapter. The remainder of the chapter describes the social protection system in Japan from a comparative context. Rather than selecting a few program areas for comparison, it looks at all major welfare areas including (a) income maintenance programs (public assistance and family allowance); (b) social services; (c) housing; (d) unemployment; (e) pension; and (f) health care. Section 1 illustrates and explains the work-based features of Japan's social security programs. Section 2 turns to functional equivalents. Section 3 describes Japan's savings-oriented features. Section 4 concludes by summarizing the limits of existing notions of the welfare state in capturing the real varieties of welfare capitalism and raises new causal questions in light of the new cross-national variations identified in this chapter.

JAPAN'S WORK-BASED SOCIAL PROTECTION[1]

Japan is often described as a small welfare state. Not all small welfare states, however, are the same.[2] As Figure 1.1 shows, Japan allocates its social spending very differently from other small welfare states. The percentage of social spending going into disability, family allowance, unemployment, and social services is much smaller in Japan than in other welfare states.

Comparing spending figures without controlling for unemployment rates or demographic structure, however, is not very useful. The replacement ratios of typical social security benefits relative to average wages/salaries provide more direct measures of the generosity of different welfare states. Table 1.1, therefore, ranks countries according to their benefit generosity: the more generous countries are ranked on the top and generosity declines in descending order. (The actual figures and the details about the data sources and calculations can be found in Appendix 1.A at the end of this chapter.)

Japan compares favorably to other welfare states in standard pension for a married couple and the public provision of health care.[3] Japan, however, is "meaner"

---

[1] Unless otherwise noted, this chapter uses 1990 as the base year to capture the status quo before new policies were introduced. More recent changes will be the subject of Chapters 8 and 9.

[2] Some scholars, for instance, have challenged Esping-Andersen's category of liberal welfare regimes – that is, Anglo-American small welfare states – on the grounds that the United States was so different from the rest of the pack (the United Kingdom, Australia, and New Zealand). See Esping-Andersen (1990), Castles and Mitchell (1991).

[3] Lynch (2001) has a fascinating study of age bias in welfare states. Japan and the United States rank among the top in her scores.

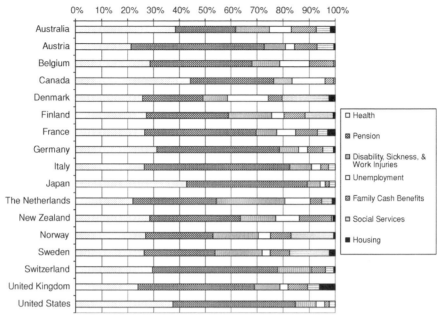

FIGURE 1.1 Ratios of Social Spending Items in Seventeen OECD Countries in 1990. *Source:* OECD online database.

than its fellow small welfare states when it comes to transfers (such as unemployment benefits, family benefits, and sickness benefits) to working-age individuals and their families.[4] The aforementioned *Rashomon* mystery is thus rooted in an asymmetry of benefit generosity in Japan. Japan is as generous as large European welfare states when one looks at health care and pension, but it is even more miserly than other small welfare states when one looks at income benefits for working-age people.

Japan's aversion to cash transfers is also evident in its strict means testing for public assistance.[5] While all other small welfare states simply require that individual applicants to public assistance fall under a certain income threshold, Japan requires income information of the applicants' close kin.[6] The stigma of getting family members involved deters many Japanese people from applying for

---

[4] Although Esping-Andersen (1990) categorizes all English-speaking countries together in his category of "liberal welfare regimes," the figures presented here demonstrate variations within this group of countries (see Castles and Mitchell 1991). While Japan and the United States stand out for their meager provision of support for families, other English-speaking countries offer more to low-income working families.

[5] See Goodman (2000) and Milly (1999) on Japan's public assistance programs.

[6] Japan's means testing is not strictly individual or based upon household. The Japanese civil law considers a broader kinship beyond the nuclear family as immediate family, and considers the family to be primarily responsible for the welfare of its members. Means-tested benefits come in when economic conditions of the immediate family prevent it from providing welfare. In other words, means testing for benefit eligibility evaluates the economic situation of the extended family.

TABLE I.I. *Benefit Generosity Ranking of Seventeen OECD Countries*

Standard Pension	Unemployment	Sickness	Family Benefits	Health Care
United States	Denmark	Germany	Austria	Sweden
Belgium	Netherlands	Norway*	Belgium	United Kingdom
JAPAN	Belgium	Belgium	Norway	Denmark
Austria	Finland	Finland	Sweden	Norway*
France	Norway*	Sweden	Netherlands	New Zealand
Italy*	France	Switzerland	Finland	Finland
Sweden	Austria	Austria	France	Italy
New Zealand	Sweden	Italy	Italy	**JAPAN**
Canada	Canada	Netherlands*	United Kingdom	France
Denmark*	Germany*	Denmark	Switzerland	Germany
Finland*	Australia	Canada	Denmark	Canada
Germany	New Zealand	France	Germany	Austria
Norway	Switzerland	**JAPAN**	Australia	Australia
Netherlands	United Kingdom	New Zealand	Canada	Netherlands*
United Kingdom	United States	Australia	New Zealand	Switzerland
Switzerland	**JAPAN**	United Kingdom	**JAPAN**	United States
Australia	Italy	United States	United States*	

Note: (*) means that the country is ranked the same as the one just above.
Source: Appendix 1.A. The Japanese standard pension benefits are based on earnings-related Employee Pension benefits.

public assistance.[7] Even low-income mothers are no exception to the rule – that is, Japan's aversion to income transfers. The treatment of low-income mothers offers an additional contrast between Japan and the United States as well as between Japan and the United Kingdom. The Japanese welfare state possesses no *maternalist* tendencies like the U.S. welfare state.[8] Instead of paying cash benefits to low-income mothers so that they can stay home to care for their own children – as the United States used to do until the welfare reforms in 1994 – Japan makes low-income mothers work.[9] In fact, Japan introduced public child care quite early in the postwar period, so that low-income mothers and widows could work outside their home.[10] Japan thus deviates significantly from other small welfare states

[7] Tachibanaki (2000) reports that the percentage of citizens under the poverty line in Japan is roughly the same as in the United Kingdom, yet Japan spends a significantly smaller percentage of its budget on poverty.

[8] For the American maternalist welfare state, see Skocpol (1992).

[9] A number of studies in Japan show high rates of labor force participation by single mothers. See Shirahase (2005) for a review of the literature.

[10] The Child Welfare Law of 1947 introduced a need-based (and means-tested) public child care in Japan (see Peng 2002). Until the means testing was removed in the 1990s, mothers who applied for public child care slots for their children were required to prove that they needed to work outside

and from continental European welfare states, both of which provide transfer payments to mothers with children rather than forcing them to work. Japan, however, has been rather restrictive in its provision of social services – child care and elderly care – to middle-class families, as its relatively small spending in social services indicates (Figure 1.1).[11] While the state expects low-income wives and mothers to work, middle-class wives and mothers are expected to stay home to provide care for their children and old parents (see Gottfried and O'Reilly 2002). As Esping-Andersen (1999), MacFarlan and Oxley (1996), and Wilensky (1990; 2002) have shown, Japan's overall provision of social services has remained meager for most of the postwar period. In recent years, however, Japan has been actively expanding social services for middle-class families.[12] In 1995, Japan introduced paid child care and family care benefits to provide 40 percent of workers' wages for up to a year when they take a leave to care for an infant or an old parent who needs care. In 1997, Japan introduced a new social insurance system, Long-term Care Insurance, mainly for the care of the frail elderly. Public child care is now also available to middle-class families.

Japan further stands out from other small welfare states in its benefit eligibility requirement. When compared to Anglo-American welfare states (Australia, Canada, United States, United Kingdom, and New Zealand), Japan links benefit eligibility to one's work to a much greater degree. Despite their low levels of social spending, Anglo-American welfare states tend to provide more universalistic benefits (Castles and Mitchell 1991). Table 1.2 demonstrates that the gap between minimum public pension and standard public pension is narrower in small welfare states except in Japan. In fact, Japan is one of the countries where the gap is greatest. This happens because Japan sorts citizens into different occupational pension schemes, whereas other small welfare states tend to enroll all private-sector workers into one national scheme.[13] In this regard, Japan resembles continental European welfare states. Both Japan and the continental European countries possess highly fragmented social insurance schemes in old-age pension and health care. Table 1.2 reproduces Esping-Andersen's measure of fragmentation of social insurance schemes (see Column 2).

What is noteworthy about Japan is a strong link between a person's work and social security benefits. The Japanese welfare state is highly fragmented along occupational lines. Japan permits a greater degree of "opting out" than most

the home to support their children and that there was no alternative child care giver (such as a grandmother living in the same household or nearby).

[11] Because Japan's public child care provision was strictly means-tested, the overall supply of public child care in Japan has been rather meager from a comparative perspective (see Wilensky 1990; Esping-Andersen 1999).

[12] Chapters 8 and 9 provide details of the policy developments since the 1990s.

[13] Esping-Andersen (1990) has measured fragmentation on the basis of the number of social insurance schemes that exist. The larger the number the more fragmented it is. Countries he calls "conservative welfare regimes" all possess highly fragmented schemes. In contrast, liberal welfare regimes in Anglo-American countries and social democratic welfare regimes in Scandinavia similarly possess fewer social insurance schemes. Japan thus deviates from other liberal welfare regimes.

TABLE 1.2. *Fragmentation and Pension Gap*

	Pension Gap	Fragmentation
Germany	4.17	6
JAPAN	3	7
Italy	2.67	12
Belgium	2.16	5
Austria	2.05	7
Finland	1.68	4
United Kingdom	1.52	2
Sweden	1.51	2
France	1.5	10
Norway	1.47	4
United States	1.37	2
Canada	1.29	2
Denmark	1.06	2
Australia	1	1
Netherlands	1	1
New Zealand	1	1
Switzerland	1	2

Notes: Pension Gap is calculated as a ratio of standard pension for a single person to minimum pension for a single person (see Appendix 1.A). Fragmentation is measured as the number of occupationally distinct public pension schemes (source: Esping-Andersen 1990, 70, and the U.S. Social Security Administration ed. *Social Security Around the World*, 1999 version).

other welfare states.[14] As a result, insofar as salaried workers are concerned, social security benefits appear largely indistinguishable from voluntary corporate fringe benefits. Moreover, the Japanese welfare state treats citizens very differently depending on their occupation. What might be termed "a patchwork of inconsistent benefit principles" characterizes Japan's social security system, whereby different benefit designs apply to different occupational groups. To show how the welfare state discriminates between different groups of citizens, I now want to describe Japan's public pension and health care programs in greater detail.

Figure 1.2 illustrates the fragmented public pension system in Japan.[15] The Employee Pension Scheme covers workers employed in firms with more than five regular employees. The Employee Pension Scheme levies a legally determined percentage of workers' income as social security contributions – to be split evenly between workers and their employers – and provides earnings-related benefits.

[14] Perhaps Italy and Germany come closest to Japan in terms of the degree of fragmentation. It is not a coincidence that Japan, Italy, and Germany are the countries that record the widest gaps between minimum pension and maximum pension (See Palme 1990).

[15] Scholars point out that contributory earnings-related pension schemes are potentially highly inegalitarian (Esping-Andersen 1990; Palme 1990). Indeed, although the overall replacement rate is relatively generous in Japan, the gap between actual pension benefit levels is quite wide. Palme (1990) reports that the gap between the minimum pension and maximum pension is widest in Japan, Germany, and Italy compared to other major OECD countries.

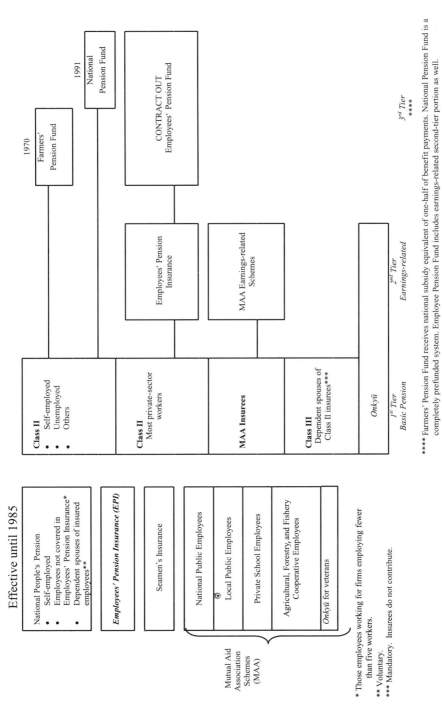

FIGURE 1.2 Japan's Fragmented Public Pension System. *Source:* Shakai Hosho Nenkan, *Social Security Yearbook.*

Effective until 1985

National People's Pension
- Self-employed
- Employees not covered in Employees' Pension Insurance*
- Dependent spouses of insured employees**

Employees' Pension Insurance (EPI)

Seamen's Insurance

Mutual Aid Association Schemes (MAA)
- National Public Employees
- Local Public Employees
- Private School Employees
- Agricultural, Forestry, and Fishery Cooperative Employees
- *Onkyū* for veterans

* Those employees working for firms employing fewer than five workers.
** Voluntary.
*** Mandatory. Insurees do not contribute.

1970
Farmers' Pension Fund

1991
National Pension Fund

CONTRACT OUT
Employees' Pension Fund

Employees' Pension Insurance

MAA Earnings-related Schemes

Class II
- Self-employed
- Unemployed
- Others

Class II
Most private-sector workers

MAA Insurees

Class III
Dependent spouses of Class II insurees***

Onkyū

1st Tier
Basic Pension

2nd Tier
Earnings-related

3rd Tier
****

**** Farmers' Pension Fund receives national subsidy equivalent of one-half of benefit payments. National Pension Fund is a completely prefunded system. Employee Pension Fund includes earnings-related second-tier portion as well.

25

In contrast, the National Pension Scheme covers farmers, the self-employed, and workers employed in small enterprises that are exempted from enrollment in the Employee Pension Scheme.[16] Like the Employee Pension Scheme, the National Pension Scheme is also a contributory scheme, but it only levies flat-rate contributions in exchange for flat-rate benefits.[17] Seamen and public-sector employees, in turn, possess their own earnings-related social insurance schemes.[18] Furthermore, veterans and their survivors are entitled to noncontributory pension called *Onkyu*.[19]

   The government also strengthens the link between one's work and public pension benefits by permitting some groups of workers to opt out of the broader social insurance schemes. Large firms – and consortia of firms in the same trade – are allowed to opt out of the Employee Pension Scheme and set up their own independent fund called the Employee Pension Fund, which provides better benefits than the more general Employee Pension System.[20] Legally speaking, the Employee Pension Fund remains part of the social security scheme and is subject to an intricate web of regulations.[21] Nonetheless, in reality, the Employee Pension Fund feels more like a corporate pension as retirees receive their statutory public pension topped by corporate supplementary benefits from their former employers. Even in Germany, which otherwise possesses a work-based pension system like Japan, large companies are not permitted to opt out of the broader occupational pension. This corporate dimension of the public pension system is further strengthened by the long vesting period and the lack of portability of

---

[16] The cut-off point for compulsory enrollment in the Employment Pension Scheme is whether a firm employs more than five regular employees or not. All firms with fewer than six regular employees are exempt.

[17] The cohorts that were too old to earn pension entitlement under the Japanese contributory pension schemes receive small sums of noncontributory and means-tested transitional benefits called welfare benefits. As of 1990, 1.2 million elderly received noncontributory pension benefits (Ministry of Health and Welfare, Minister's Secretariat, Statistics and Information Department ed. 1996: 288).

[18] In the early 1990s, the Employee Pension had the largest number of enrollees – 33 million workers. In descending order, 31 million people were enrolled in the National Pension; 12 million were enrolled in Employee Pension Funds; 3.3 million and 1.6 million people were enrolled in the Municipal Civil Servants' Mutual Association and the National Civil Servants' Mutual Association, respectively; the other occupational schemes enrolled less than half a million people. The numbers are based on Kenko Hoken Kumiai Rengokai 1995, 14–15.

[19] Two million people received Onkyu. The information about Onkyu recipients is based on the Diet minutes recorded for the Cabinet Committee meeting on April 26, 1990, at the Lower House.

[20] Firms employing more than five hundred workers qualified. Workers' consent was required to set up an Employee Pension Fund.

[21] Legally speaking, the government considers the EPF to be part of the social security contribution and subjects it to an intricate web of regulations. One regulation concerns the levels of EPF pension benefits. The government legally requires EPF to provide better pension benefits than EPS. By opting out, firms thus become responsible for providing pension benefits that would be 30 percent higher than what employees would have received if they had stayed within the national EPS. As we shall see in a later section of this chapter, EPF is also subject to strict regulations over its investments. In exchange for these regulations, the EPF enjoys a special tax status. Like other public pension funds, the EPF is completely tax exempt. In this, it differs from other "purely private" pension plans.

Employee Pension Fund benefits. I shall come back to this point in the section on corporate pension later in this chapter.

Japan links employment status to public pension eligibility in yet another way. The Japanese welfare state treats part-time workers very differently from full-time regular workers. The Japanese government exempts employers from enrolling their part-time workers in otherwise mandatory social insurance schemes – such as the Employee Pension Scheme.[22] Because women constitute the majority of part-time workers, such an exemption affects women most. As the feminist scholarship on welfare states has shown, any strict contributory requirement generally hurts women, because women frequently interrupt or withdraw from the labor market (Orloff 1993; Sainsbury ed. 1994, 1999). Notwithstanding this feature, the most interesting gender bias in the Japanese pension system is that it treats women differently depending on to whom they are married.[23] As of 1985, wives of men enrolled in the Employee Pension Scheme became entitled to their own pension benefits without having to contribute anything. They are the only group of citizens entitled to noncontributory pension.[24]

Health care offers a very similar picture: it is fragmented; it applies a patchwork of benefit principles; and it permits opting out (Figure 1.3). The Government-Administered Health Insurance (Seifu Kansho Kenko Hoken) covers workers (and their families) who work for firms of more than six workers. Firms employing more than one thousand workers can opt out of the Government-Administered Health Insurance and set up their own health care insurance cooperatives called *kempo*. Public-sector workers, in turn, have their own mutual aid associations (*kyosai*). The rest of the nation is covered by the National Health Insurance (Kokuho), which is administered by municipal governments as municipal schemes.[25] The government also permits some independent occupations – such

[22] As a result, the flat-rate National Pension Scheme is the only pension scheme that part-time workers can enroll in. Even if employers were to enroll part-time workers into the same social schemes with full-time core workers, part-time workers are unlikely to receive adequate pension anyway, because of Japan's very strict contributory requirement. Although other countries that adopt contributory pension schemes only impose a long period of contribution for citizens to qualify for full pension benefits, Japan imposes a long contributory period for citizens to even qualify for minimum pension. In other words, marginal workers with unstable interrupted work histories face a tremendous difficulty in earning pension entitlements. This is also true of other countries with fragmented contributory social insurance schemes like Germany.

[23] Brinton (1993) and Osawa (1992) offer excellent accounts of how Japan's postwar economy reveals the highly gendered nature of Japan's model of capitalism. Gottfried and O'Reilly (2002) compare Japan to Germany to argue that their economic models both stand on a gendered social contract.

[24] Except for the older generation of citizens who were too old to qualify for the contributory pension that was introduced in the postwar period. They receive meager benefits called Fukushi Nenkin (welfare pension). See Campbell (1992: chapter 5).

[25] In the mid-1990s, Kokuho covered the largest number of people – 39.8 million working-age people and their family members plus 4 million retirees. In descending order: Seifu Kansho covered about 19.3 million workers and 18.5 million dependent family members; Kenpo covered 15.5 million workers plus 17 million dependents; Kokuho Kumiai covered 4.6 million; the National Civil Servants' Mutual Association covered 1.7 million workers and 2.5 dependents; the Municipal Civil Servants' Mutual Association covered 3 million workers and 3.9 million dependents; the Private School Teachers and Staff Mutual Association covered 430,000 teachers and staff plus

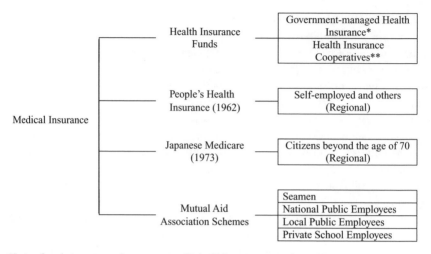

*System for private-sector employees not covered in health insurance cooperatives.
** Only for workers employed by firms employing, in most cases, more than 1,000 workers.

FIGURE 1.3 Japan's Fragmented Health Care System. *Source:* Shakai Hosho Nenkan, *Social Security Yearbook.*

as medical doctors – to opt out of the respective municipal schemes in an ad-hoc manner to set up their own National Health Insurance Cooperatives (*kokuho kumiai*).[26] It is important to note that "opting out" does not mean opting out of the social security system and going into a private arrangement. In Japan, "opting out" means creating a separate social insurance scheme with restrictive work-based eligibility in order to offer better benefits than would otherwise be available.

Benefit principles vary from one scheme to another. *Kempo*, mutual assistance associations, and the Government-Administered Health Insurance all levy certain percentages of workers' wages as social security contributions to be evenly shared by employees and employers. The National Health Insurance (NHI), however, charges a fixed monthly sum irrespective of enrollees' income levels. Not only do benefit levels vary from one scheme to another, but also the amount of government subsidies varies.[27] The government subsidizes health care schemes for small firms and the self-employed more generously than for employees in large firms. While *kempo* receives almost no government subsidies, the Government-Administered Health Insurance for workers and National Health

380,000 dependents; and the Seamen's Mutual Association covered 120,000 seamen and 230,000 dependents. These figures are based on Kenko Hoken Kumiai 1995, 12–13.

[26] It is fragmented into about 5,200 regional and occupational schemes.

[27] Two types of workers – those working in the public sector and those working in large companies in the private sector – were entitled to receive 100 percent health care coverage, meaning they paid no copayment. They also enjoy health care coverage for their dependents at no extra cost. In contrast, the self-employed get inferior coverage; and have to pay extra to get their dependents covered.

Insurance Cooperatives receive respectively 13 percent and 50 percent of their spending from the central government.[28]

The quasi-corporate nature of social security benefits in Japan is also evident in health care. Company-based schemes (*kempo*) typically offer their employees and their dependent family members better benefits than what is legally required.[29] Moreover, it is optional for employers to contribute more than their legal share (50 percent) of social security contribution on behalf of their employees.[30] In fact, a large number of large firms do so. Corporate generosity, however, only extends to current employees and their families. Corporate paternalism does not apply to those who have retired. *Kempo* coverage terminates as soon as a worker retires from the company. Retirees thus enroll in the National Health Insurance in their respective municipalities of residence. Given that *kempo* offers better benefits than the National Health Insurance Cooperatives, upon retiring, workers typically lose access to better health care coverage.[31] In this sense, old American large companies – such as auto makers – are more generous toward their employees: many of them offer corporate-sponsored health care benefits to retirees.

Although Japan's occupationally fragmented contributory health care links benefit eligibility to work, one exception exists. The only exception to the rule is health care for the elderly – defined as those beyond the age of seventy. Elderly citizens enjoy the only truly universalistic benefit in Japan. While younger citizens pay patients' copayments, elderly patients pay nothing (although this situation changed in recent years).[32] The national government, the respective municipal NHI cooperative, and levies from the occupationally based health care schemes cover the copayments for the elderly.[33]

---

[28] It is noteworthy that employers in certain industries are exempt from enrolling in Seifu Kansho. These industries include agriculture and fishery.

[29] Legally, *kempo* was only required to pay for 70 percent of the health care cost of the dependents. Yet many large firms whose *kempo* is financially sound offer better coverage for dependents. Furthermore, large firms typically add extra benefits such as free health checkups – not covered in Japanese statutory health insurance – turning the social insurance schemes into quasi-corporate fringe benefits.

[30] Legally, employers are required to shoulder at least 50 percent of the social security contributions on behalf of their employees. In health care, large firms often pay more than 50 percent, thus reducing their employees' contributions.

[31] Until the 2001 health care reform that equalized patients' copayments across all schemes, *kempo* (and Seifu Kansho) enrollees paid smaller copayments than NHI enrollees. NHI enrollees always have been required to pay 30 percent copayments, whereas *kempo* enrollees originally paid no copayments. Once copayments were introduced to *kempo*, they gradually increased from 10 percent, to 20 percent and more recently up to 30 percent. In addition, *kempo* and Seifu Kansho offered better benefits for dependent family members (although family members were required to pay copayments). These two schemes covered dependents with no additional contributions, whereas NHI charged additional contributions to cover family members.

[32] This benefit for older citizens is what is generally referred to as the Free Medical Care for the Elderly.

[33] Since 1982 all social insurance schemes – such as *kempo* and the Government-Administered Health Insurance for workers – have been required to pay special levies to finance the medical cost of the elderly enrolled in NHI.

To summarize, the Japanese social security system is work-based in a dual sense. In one sense, contributory benefits tie citizens' benefits very closely to their occupations. In another sense, the paucity of cash benefits and services for average working families mean that "work" is the only means of sustenance for most families. A closer examination of benefit structures reveals that Japan offers relatively generous benefits only when social security programs are fragmented into work-based schemes, as in the case of health care and pension. In other words, when benefit eligibility is restricted to employees of a particular firm or a member of a particular occupational group, benefit levels tend to be high. When the benefit eligibility is more comprehensive or universalistic, benefits are either nonexistent or meager. Public assistance and family allowance constitute comprehensive programs in the sense that they apply to all citizens with need regardless of their occupation. Similarly, Japan's unemployment insurance constitutes one national scheme for everyone who is enrolled.[34] In all these programs, Japan lags behind other countries in terms of benefit generosity.

JAPAN'S FUNCTIONALLY EQUIVALENT PROGRAMS

Japan's social spending and its paucity of income transfers to working-age population does not mean that Japan can be described as a laissez-faire state. When we consider functional equivalents to orthodox social security programs, it becomes evident that Japan relies on a variety of functional equivalents especially in areas where its social security benefits remain meager. Following the earlier theoretical discussion of the concept of functional equivalents, we can now distinguish two dimensions in which functional equivalents may vary.[35] On the first dimension, functional equivalents can be (i) policies that promote private welfare provision – such as market-based and employer-based welfare; (ii) policies that protect jobs and income by curtailing or regulating market competition; or (iii) policies whereby the state directly creates jobs and training positions. On the second dimension, the direct beneficiary of a particular functional equivalent can be an individual citizen or a firm or producer. A cross-national comparison of different types of functional equivalents to income transfer programs for working-age citizens reveals two things. One, Japan favors functional equivalents whose beneficiaries are firms and producers, rather than direct benefits for individual workers. Two, Japan favors functional equivalents that protect jobs by regulating competition. In other words, Japan again stands out for its emphasis on "work."

Let me begin by examining how different countries combine different types of functional equivalents with orthodox unemployment benefits.[36] Table 1.3 compares the following functional equivalents: (i) active labor market policy (ALMP); (ii) employment protection legislation; (iii) public sector employment; (iv) wage

---

[34] Unlike continental European welfare states, Japan offers no noncontributory unemployment assistance after unemployment benefits run out.

[35] For detailed discussions of the concept of functional equivalents, see the Introduction.

[36] For a discussion of unemployment benefits and their functionally equivalent – although the authors do not use this term – public benefits, see Blöndal and Pearson (1995).

TABLE 1.3. *Functional Equivalents for Unemployment Benefits (Expressed as Country Rankings)*

ALMP	Employment Protection	Public-Sector Employment	Wage Subsidies	Public Works	Administrative Intervention	State Control
Sweden	Italy	Norway	Finland	**JAPAN**	Italy	Italy
Finland	France	Sweden	Belgium	Finland	France	Norway
Germany	Norway	Denmark	**JAPAN**	Italy	Belgium	Finland
Norway	Germany	Finland	Sweden	Norway	**JAPAN**	France
United Kingdom	**JAPAN**	Canada	Norway	France	Switzerland	Belgium
France	Austria	Belgium	Germany	Austria	Germany	Denmark
New Zealand	Netherlands*	United Kingdom	New Zealand	Sweden	Finland	Netherlands
United States	Sweden*	Australia	Austria	Netherlands	Sweden	Austria
Denmark	Belgium	United States	Australia	Canada	Austria	Switzerland
Canada	Finland*	Austria	France*	Australia	Netherlands	Germany
Austria	Denmark	Netherlands	United Kingdom	United Kingdom	Norway	New Zealand
Netherlands	Switzerland	Switzerland	Denmark	Germany	Denmark	Sweden
JAPAN	Australia	New Zealand	Netherlands*	Denmark	United States	Canada
Italy	New Zealand	Germany	United States*	United States	New Zealand	**JAPAN***
Belgium	Canada	**JAPAN**	Canada	Belgium	Australia	Australia
Switzerland*	United Kingdom				Canada	United States
Australia	United States				United Kingdom	United Kingdom

Note: An asterisk (*) means that a country ranks the same as the country just above.
Source: See Appendix 1.B.

31

subsidies; (v) public works; (vi) administrative intervention into the market; and (vii) direct state ownership of enterprises. These functional equivalents differ in terms of direct beneficiaries and in terms of their relationship vis-à-vis the market. The first three measures directly benefit workers. An active labor market policy involves government-provided training programs for displaced workers. This policy offers training and financial support directly to individual workers during the training period. Employment protection legislation also protects individual workers' jobs. Public sector employment also provides individual workers with jobs and directly pays workers wages and salaries without benefiting any intermediaries. Yet each of these three policies relates to the market differently. ALMP facilitates labor mobility whereas employment protection legislation does not. Public sector employment may absorb extra manpower but it potentially creates a large sector outside the market.

The remainder of the functional equivalents in Table 1.3 targets firms as direct beneficiaries of protection. Wage subsidies are paid to employers to hold onto redundant workers during the downturn in the business cycle. Public works spending props up overall demand in the economy, helping firms, which, in turn, can retain more workers than would otherwise be possible. Public works also directly benefit construction firms and related industries. Administrative intervention captures the degree to which the government intervenes to control market competition by means of licensing and permits, and lax enforcement of antitrust regulation.[37] These policies all protect existing private sector firms and their profits. High levels of administrative intervention thus indicate higher state capacities to shield private sector companies from competition. State ownership, in contrast, means state intervention into a product market by replacing profit motivations with policy considerations (See Appendix 1.B for the details of the data and calculations used for Table 1.3.) A state-owned firm, when the state thus decides, need not lay off workers regardless of the market conditions.

As a way of making visual comparisons easier, Table 1.3 ranks countries on the basis of their reliance on different types of functional equivalents. We observe that Japan emphasizes functional equivalents targeted at employers to a greater degree than those targeted directly at individual workers. Viewed comparatively, Japan ranks very high on its reliance on wage subsidies, public works, and administrative intervention into the market. Yet it ranks very low when it comes to those functional equivalents that offer direct benefits to individual workers such as ALMP and public sector employment – with the exception of relative strong employment protection legislation. It is noteworthy that the Japanese state mostly

---

[37] Here I am using the index on "barriers to entrepreneurship" developed by Nicoletti et al. (1999) as a subindex to measure the degree of product market regulation. This subindex is constructed based on measures of licenses and permits, sector-specific administrative burdens, and antitrust exemptions. The summary measure, "product market regulation index," however, also includes direct state control such as ownership of companies. For the purpose here, administrative intervention is more adequate and precise than the aggregate product market regulation index.

relies on administrative intervention to protect firms and ranks among the lowest when it comes to direct ownership.[38]

Japan has probably the strictest rules about layoffs in large companies of all advanced industrial societies. These rules are not a component of the labor standards law, but are based on the accumulation of case law.[39] The Japanese courts have accumulated case laws that defined "a justifiable layoff" so narrowly that they virtually make it impossible for employers to lay off their workers unless their companies are under severe financial distress. In cases of unjustified dismissals, the Japanese courts order employers to reinstate the dismissed workers to their original jobs. In contrast to most other advanced industrial countries, Japanese employers are not permitted to settle financially with their dismissed workers in lieu of reinstatement. The difficulty of dismissal makes employment protection extremely important not just for workers but also for employers in Japan. Japan's unemployment insurance program, appropriately called Employment Insurance, provides firms with wage subsidies to hold onto their workers during hard times.[40] Industrial policy and lax antitrust regulation offer tools to prevent layoff by reducing competition in specific product markets.

Table 1.3 captures these policy tools with the administrative intervention index taken from an OECD study of product market regulation (see Appendix 1.B for details). The so-called convoy system (*gososendan hoshiki*) in Japan offers a classic example of the use of industrial policy as means of delivering social protection.[41] The convoy system refers to the way in which the Japanese government has used its regulatory powers to control entry to and exit from a product market. In many product market sectors, once allowed in, companies are not allowed out. The convoy system is a government-orchestrated safety net for specific industrial sectors. Japan's regulation of financial institutions provides perhaps the best example of the convoy system. In postwar Japan, the Ministry of Finance (MOF) strictly regulated new entry into different financial markets. The MOF also made sure that no bank or insurance company failed. Until the financial Big Bang in the latter half of the 1990s, the number of firms in financial markets remained

---

[38] By looking at energy industries, Samuels (1987) explores why Japan, otherwise famous for its developmental state, owns so little of its economy compared to other countries.

[39] Although the OECD's index of employment protection records relatively strict labor regulations concerning firing in Japan, the OECD Job Study (1994) notes that the real hurdle against firing in Japan lies in the accumulation of court rulings unfavorable to employers (see Chuma 1998; Otake and Fujikawa 2001). Hiroyuki Chuma (2002) sees Japan's employment policy and employment regulations basically as social policy.

[40] These benefits are exclusively funded by employers' contributions, in contrast to unemployment benefits that are jointly funded by contributions of workers, employers, and the state. Because of rather involved administrative requirements, mostly large firms qualify for receiving such wage subsidies rather than smaller firms.

[41] Japanese scholars have long been aware of the use of industrial policy for protective purposes. The frequently used term, "convoy system," has been around for decades to refer to the safety net provided by means of regulation. Uriu (1996), in his critique of Chalmers Johnson, discusses the use of industrial policy for protective purposes in detailed case studies. For a recent general discussion of the convoy system in English, see Schoppa (2006).

the same. The other important economic ministry, the Ministry of International Trade and Industry (MITI), also frequently resorted to legal cartels to control competition and to prevent corporate bankruptcies in industries such as steel, textiles, and coal.[42] Protection of employment was frequently one of the main goals of such cartels. Aside from these policies, legal barriers against mergers and acquisitions have stabilized employment levels in Japan by successfully preventing hostile takeovers.

Table 1.3 demonstrates that Japan is not unique in its use of administrative intervention into the market. Many European countries rely on similar measures. In fact, an OECD study by Nicoletti et al. (2000) shows a high correlation between employment protection legislation and product market regulation. Coordinated market economies (CMEs) generally fall into this category of countries with strong employment protection and product market regulation. Hall and Gingrich (2004) argue that CMEs also possess a number of restrictions such as legal barriers to merger and acquisition that protect existing companies. Despite Japan's small welfare state, Japan also falls into the CME category, once we extend the taxonomy to include functional equivalents.

In addition to protecting jobs by means of administrative intervention, Table 1.3 shows that the Japanese government also intervenes to prop up demand for manpower by means of public works spending. Interestingly, Scandinavian welfare states – except for Denmark – also rely on public works spending when compared to other countries (Huber and Stephens 2001). Japan's heavy reliance on public works spending, however, contrasts sharply with its small public sector employment. Japan differs greatly from Scandinavian welfare states that also rely on the public sector for job creation. Recall that, while public sector employment directly pays wages to individual workers, public works projects channel money primarily to construction and related firms, which pay the wages of otherwise unemployed workers. Yet again, the contrast between Japan and Scandinavian countries is indicative of Japan's aversion to direct benefits for workers.

Let me now turn to functional equivalents that protect household income of working-age citizens in lieu of family transfers and public assistance. Table 1.4 compares minimum wage levels, tax expenditures for families, and occupationally targeted policies for income protection.[43] A minimum wage, while not typically treated as social policy, can be considered as a regulatory functional equivalent of public assistance, because its goal is to prevent poverty among low-income workers. Tax expenditures for families, such as tax deductions for dependents,

---

[42] There is an abundant literature that describes and analyzes how Japan used industrial policy to manage competition and to protect jobs. Uriu (1996) demonstrates that industrial policy was never only about enhancing national competitiveness but rather it aimed at social protection of workers employed in numerous troubled industries (see also Kume 1998). For Japan's high propensity for cartel formation, see Tilton (1996) and Schaede (2000).

[43] Similarly, private insurance programs such as life insurance policies are also used by families to insure against various contingencies (such as the death of the breadwinner). For this reason, tax expenditures to encourage these private alternatives are also legitimate functional equivalents to publicly provided income protection. I will discuss life insurance products in greater detail later in the chapter.

TABLE 1.4. *Functional Equivalents for Family Benefits/Public Assistance*

	Statutory Minimum Wage (as a ratio of median earner's wages)	Tax Break for Social Purposes Similar to Family Allowance (% of GDP)	Agricultural Subsidy Index[a]
Australia	0.58	0.2	7.3
Austria	0.62	0.4	6.7
Belgium	0.60	0.6	7.1
Canada	0.35	–	28
Denmark	0.54	0	5.1
Finland	0.52	0	16.8
France	0.52	–	9
Germany	0.50	1.9	9.4
Italy	0.55	–	5.5
JAPAN	0.32	0.5	22.75
Netherlands	0.55	0	2.9
New Zealand	0.45	0	4.1
Norway	0.64	0	–
Sweden	0.52	–	8.1
Switzerland			
United Kingdom	0.40	0.3	12
United States	0.39	0.3	18.2

[a] Agricultural Subsidy Index calculated as the percentage of agricultural subsidies over GDP divided by the ratio of the agricultural population in the workforce. (Ten-year averages from the mid-1980s to the mid-1990s are used.)

Source: The data for Australia and Japan from OECD (2001), *Society at a Glance*, 71; the data for other countries are based on Esping-Andersen (1999, 22); tax data are based on Adema (2001); data source of agricultural subsidies is *Eurostat Yearbook: A Statistical Eye on Europe*, various years, and agricultural population ratio calculated from *ILO Yearbook of Labour Statistics*, various years.

can also be considered as a functional equivalent to income transfers to families.[44] Whereas minimum wage and tax expenditures apply to any person who meets the requirement, functional equivalents that are targeted at specific occupational groups can also be included. Table 1.5 only compares targeted protection of farmers as an example of occupationally targeted protection because it is relatively easy to find a proxy variable to measure it.[45] (Here I use the size of agricultural subsidies corrected for the size of agricultural population.) Although we can consider functional equivalents that target other occupational groups, the sheer heterogeneity of all possible policy tools makes creating a systematic summary

[44] Tax experts use the term tax expenditures to refer to special tax measures such as deductions, deferrals, and exemptions designed to forgo portions of tax revenue. The term "expenditure" is used because discounting taxes on someone or some specific item is the same as providing state subsidies. Scholars of the American welfare state have long been aware of the importance of the government's use of tax expenditures as social policy tools; see Howard (1997).

[45] For a fascinating comparative study of agricultural policy in France, Japan, and the United States, see Sheingate (2001). He also takes the view that agricultural policy should be understood as social protection and demonstrates how different countries use agricultural policy to provide social protection.

TABLE 1.5. *Functional Equivalents for Early Retirement*

Disability Benefits	Activity Rates	Social Security Pension	Private Pensions and Annuities
Netherlands	Switzerland	New Zealand	Canada
Sweden	**JAPAN**	Sweden	Australia
Finland	Sweden	Norway	**JAPAN**
Norway*	Norway	Italy	United States
New Zealand	Denmark	Switzerland	Switzerland
Australia	United Kingdom	Denmark	Denmark
Switzerland*	United States	Germany	Netherlands
Belgium	Canada	Finland	United Kingdom
Denmark	Australia	Austria	Germany
United Kingdom*	New Zealand	France	Belgium
Austria	Germany	Netherlands	Norway*
France*	Finland	United Kingdom	France
Italy*	France	United States	Sweden
United States*	Netherlands*	Belgium	New Zealand
Germany	Austria	Australia	Finland
Canada	Italy	Canada	Austria
JAPAN	Belgium	**JAPAN**	Italy

Notes: An asterisk (*) means that a country ranks the same as the country just above.

Disability benefits: The percentage of spending on disability benefits as a ratio of GDP. Based on the OECD online database (base year = 1990).

Activity rates of men between 55 and 64: *OECD Employment Outlook 2002*, Table C.

Social Security Pension: The weight of social security in the overall total of pension and individual annuity programs upon which old people depend. Esping-Andersen (1990, 85).

Private Pensions and Annuities: The weight of private pensions and individual annuities in the overall total of pension and individual annuity programs upon which old people depend. Esping-Andersen (1990, 85).

index a very difficult task. For the purpose of this chapter, I will simply refer to existing studies on protective policies for small family enterprises as evidence of occupationally targeted income protection in a number of OECD countries including Japan.

The first column in Table 1.4 ranks OECD countries in terms of their levels of minimum wage. Some countries rely on statutory minimum wage, whereas others set the wage floor through collective wage bargaining – or an equivalent like the Italian *scala mobile* (Bonoli 2003). Because countries with collective wage bargaining compress wage structure, they produce favorable ratios of real minimum wage relative to average wages. Table 1.4 shows that Japanese minimum wage is the lowest of the advanced industrial societies. Table 1.4 also shows that Japan, in lieu of generous cash benefits to families, provides tax relief for families. When it comes to tax relief, Japan actually is among the most generous of the advanced industrial countries. Note that the OECD tax expenditure figures used in Table 1.4, however, underestimate the real scope of Japan's dependence on tax expenditures for families, because it excludes tax breaks for spouses and elderly parents.[46] Japan's tax relief for families is thus much more generous than suggested by Table 1.4. Here again, we see that Japan emphasizes "work" and "work income" rather than income transfers or regulatory intervention to protect workers' wages directly. In addition to tax expenditures for dependent family members, most Japanese firms provide corporate "family allowances" (that is, wage supplements for dependents) as a functional equivalent of public family allowance. Corporate family allowances compose nearly 4 percent of the monthly wages for workers in firms employing more than 1,000 workers, whereas they make up less than 2 percent of wages for workers in companies that employ between 30–99 workers.[47]

   The fact that Japan is so averse to direct transfers to individual workers does not mean that Japan provides no transfers. As Table 1.4 illustrates, Japan relies heavily on agricultural subsidies. A large bulk of the subsidies is aimed at small-scale rice producers. Japan's price support of rice is nothing other than a mechanism for delivering direct cash benefits to rural families. Any rural family with however tiny a rice field qualifies for this support. Japan's agricultural policy hence is a social policy in disguise.[48] Just as governments resort to agricultural subsidies to protect farmers' livelihood, so they use industrial and financial policy to protect household income of small-business owners (and their family workers). Many advanced industrial countries use such policy tools to protect small family business.[49] Japan has restricted entry of large-scale retail stores into the retail market by special regulation such as the Large-Scale Retail Stores Law (Upham 1987; 1993). Some European countries like Germany use restrictive regulation over the hours of operation for retail shops to prevent competition from large retail stores. Many European countries also use licenses to protect specific businesses such as pharmacies and liquor stores. Japan provides small-business owners with a web of special public loans to keep their business afloat in difficult times.[50] Public loans to small business tend to be more developed in European countries that have traditionally relied on indirect financing such as France and Germany,

---

[46] The OECD narrowly conceives the scope of functional equivalents and underestimates the overall size of tax expenditures in Japan. The Japanese tax authorities consider nonworking spouses (and also spouses who work part-time) and nonworking parents in the same household as dependents and grant the head of the household generous tax deductions. Nonetheless, the OECD only considers tax deductions for dependent children as functional equivalents of public cash benefits for families (see Adema 2001, 21, for why the OECD takes this view). In other words, if we adopt the Japanese definition of dependents, the scope of tax expenditures in Japan increases significantly. Yasushi Iino, a public finance expert at Keio University, calculates that Japanese personal tax deductions amounted to 3 percent of GNP in 1995 (Iino 1996, 99–101).

[47] These are 1985 figures from the Ministry of Labor, Rodo Daijin Kanbo Seisaku Chosabu ed. 1988, 17. Since the majority of the Japanese workforce is employed in firms with fewer than 100 workers, the gap among workers is actually much higher than what these numbers suggest.

[48] Many scholars in Japan see agricultural policy as such (Honma and Hayami 1991; Honma 1994; Itsumi and Kato 1985).

[49] A number of Japanese scholars note the aspect of "social protection" in policies toward small businesses in Japan. Calder (1988, chapter 7) provides a very useful overview of Japanese policies for small firms.

[50] See Iwamoto (1995); Schaede (2004); and Tsuchiya and Miwa (1989); among others.

rather than the United Kingdom and the United States.[51] Even in the absence of systematic comparative data, these examples suffice to show that governments use functional equivalents to protect the jobs and income of small family business owners.

Although not included in Table 1.4, housing policy should be mentioned. Few people would dispute that the provision of affordable housing is an important concern for any welfare state, since the cost of housing is the largest household expenditure for most citizens. Most governments in advanced industrial societies combine multiple policy tools to provide affordable housing.[52] Typically, the menu of policy tools includes rent control; housing allowance; publicly financed rental housing construction; publicly subsidized rental housing; and homeownership programs. Japan stands out for its public support of corporate housing. Japan has provided very generous tax concessions to both employers and employees on corporate housing. (Unfortunately, the OECD data on tax expenditures for social purpose does not include tax expenditures for housing.) Whereas most other advanced industrial countries treat the monetary value of employer-provided housing as taxable income, Japan does not (Tamakuni 1995). The tax code also offers generous tax breaks for employers who build corporate housing. In the early 1990s, 13 percent of the rental housing in Japan was corporate housing (Kokuritsu Shakai Hosho Jinko Mondai Kenkyujo ed. 1996, table 317). Since only large firms have the financial resources to build corporate housing, tax benefits for corporate housing are much less comprehensive than tax breaks for dependents. These policies can thus be seen as policies targeted at large companies.

Japan also stands out for its emphasis on homeownership. As in the United States, which relies on quasi-public financial institutions – Fanny Mae and Freddie Mac – to promote the private mortgage market, Japan relies upon quasi-public mortgage agencies – the Housing Finance Corporation (Jutaku Kinyu Koko) and the Pension Welfare Corporation (Nenkin Fukushi Jigyodan). Unlike in the United States, the actual implementation of loan programs in Japan has involved employers to a much greater degree. In the case of the Pension Welfare Corporation, the employer borrows the money from the Corporation, and the employees then, in turn, borrow from their employers. Furthermore, as Housing Financial Corporation mortgages require relatively large down payments, most applicants need to save up before they apply for mortgages. Japan has tax-deferred corporate homeownership savings plans – called *zaikei* – so that wage earners can save the necessary down payments through an interest-deferred account. *Zaikei* plans resemble various tax-deferred savings plans that are available to American workers via their workplace, but unlike Individual Retirement Accounts (IRA), workers can only take advantage of the tax benefits if their employer has the

---

[51] Zyman 1983. See Calder (1988, chapter 7) for an excellent discussion on the same point.
[52] See Heidenheimer, Heclo, and Adams (1990) for a concise qualitative comparison of housing policies in Europe, Japan, and the United States.

zaikei plan. The Postal Savings System offers options for homeownership savings accounts (*jutaku tsumitate*) for those who have no access to *zaikei*. The Japanese government also promotes various types of life insurance plans as "private welfare products" by making insurance premiums tax deductible.

The discussion so far has focused on functional equivalents to those social security issue areas where Japan has lagged behind other welfare states. This does not mean that Japan has no functional equivalents in areas such as health care and pension. Like many other countries, Japan, too, has private health insurance companies. Yet the scope of the private insurance sector has been small in Japan, as the public sector covers most of the health expenditure (see Table 1.1 and Appendix 1.A). Here let me consider functional equivalents to public pension. Tax-deferred savings accounts, individual pension plans, and corporate pension plans all constitute such functional equivalents. Private pension plans, however, are not the only functional equivalents to public pension. Some scholars have long noted that some countries use disability benefits and early retirement pension to push older workers out of the workforce.[53] Although welfare state studies that focus on social rights do not consider "work" to be a source of social protection, a quick look at recent policy debates in the OECD and various national governments makes it clear that policies that encourage "employment of older citizens" are crucial functional equivalents to pension.[54] Table 1.5 thus compares the size of private pension programs relative to the overall pension, the relative reliance on disability benefits and the activity rate of older men and the activity rate of men between the ages 55–65.

Table 1.5 illustrates how little Japan relies on cash benefits like disability benefits to "retire" older workers. Instead, Japan boasts a very high activity rate of older men (55–65). Campbell (1992) has noted Japan's policy makers' interest in using "work continuation" as a source of old age income aside from pension. In other words, yet again, Japan demonstrates a strong emphasis on work rather than income transfers. Interestingly, Scandinavian countries, too, possess high levels of activity rate of older men. Given the fact that Japan and Scandinavian countries both rank high on job-producing functional equivalents as shown in Table 1.3, these similarly high activity rates of older men suggest a common emphasis on work.

Table 1.5 also demonstrates the degree to which OECD countries rely on corporate pension, individual savings, and annuity programs, which constitute an important share of old-age pension. Although not indicated in Table 1.5, most of the private pension and savings in Japan comes from individual sources rather than corporate pension plans. Because corporate pension is only available to core workers in relatively large firms, the coverage of corporate pension is relatively

---

[53] In the sense that disability benefits and early retirement provide ways for manpower adjustments, they can also be considered as functional equivalents to unemployment benefits. As far as situating Japan into a comparative perspective, it makes no difference either way. For comparative studies, see Rein and Freeman (1988); and Esping-Andersen (1995).

[54] Note that I am not making a normative judgment as to the relative moral value of social wages versus wages from the market.

low in Japan compared to other countries.[55] According to a government survey, 11 percent of Japanese respondents say they have a private corporate pension, compared to 39 percent in the United States, 22.7 percent in Germany, and 14.8 percent in Sweden (Cabinet Office, Government of Japan 2000).

Let me say a few words on the characteristics of corporate pension plans. The benefit structure of private corporate benefits is as important as the benefit structure of public benefits.[56] Corporate pensions are, by definition, all work mediated. Yet some pension plans are more labor-market neutral than others (that is, some plans explicitly penalize job hoppers, whereas others do not). As discussed in the Introduction, a pension plan can take the form of a defined benefit plan (DBP) or a defined contribution plan (DCP). The DBP promises pension benefits that are determined on the basis of workers' final salary and years of service. Unlike the DCP (e.g., the 401k in the United States), the DBP lacks portability. The DBP is designed to reward loyal workers: benefits get better the longer the enterprise tenure. Moreover, employers normally impose a long vesting period (a predetermined number of years for a worker to earn his pension right), so that those workers who quit prematurely forgo part of what they would have received if they had stayed. In contrast, the DCP is not strictly speaking a pension, as employers do not promise to pay pension benefits but simply promise to contribute annually a fixed percentage of their workers' wages into their individual retirement plans. This design makes it a lot easier for workers to take their pension funds with them when they change jobs. This is why the DCP is more labor-market neutral than the DBP.

Japan is one of the countries that emphasize the DBP (see Table 1.6). It should also be mentioned that Japanese corporate pension schemes typically impose very long vesting periods by international standards.[57] Until a major reform of corporate pension in 2002, the Japanese government did not grant any tax concessions on the DCP. In other words, the government only provided tax concessions for corporate pension plans that favored loyal workers and penalized mobile workers. Although corporate pension plans are limited to relatively large firms in Japan, most employers provide one-time lump sum payments when workers quit. In addition to tax breaks for employers, the Japanese government provides extremely generous "tenure-rated" discounts on the income tax on retirement lump sum payments: the longer the enterprise tenure, the lower the tax rate on one's retirement lump sum payment. Although the United States also possesses a highly work-based welfare system in which employers provide health insurance and occupational pension, public policy in the United States does not link social protection to long enterprise tenure as Japan does.

---

[55] See also a useful overview of Japanese corporate pension by Katsumata (2004).

[56] Immergut (1986) makes an excellent point about the importance of the benefit structure of private programs in her study of private corporate sickness benefits in Germany.

[57] Workers who quit before the vesting period is fulfilled lose their claim to corporate pension. In Japan the vesting period has been about fifteen years compared to a few years in the United States. In Germany – another country that imposes a long vesting period – it is about ten years. Hence Japan stands out in its very explicit bias in favor of corporate loyalty.

TABLE 1.6. *The Size of Welfare Funds as Percentage of GDP and Pension Plan Types*

% of People in Defined Benefit Plans	% of People in Defined Contribution Plans		Private Pension & Life Insurance	Social Security Reserves	
2004	2004		2001	2001	
–	–	Australia	82		
25	75	Austria	23		
100	0	Belgium	37		
		Canada	69	1	
50	50	Denmark	95		
79	21	Finland	25	4	
60	40	France	57	1	
95	5	Germany			
8	92	Italy	22		
94	6	**JAPAN**	49	30	+64% (postal system)
95	5	Netherlands	129		
–	–	New Zealand	2		
–	–	Norway	31	40	
50	50	Sweden		25	
–	–	Switzerland	186		
84	16	United Kingdom	128		
30	70	United States	81	12	

Source: OECD Comparative Data Insurance 1993–2000 (online); OECD (2005); the data on Japanese postal savings and insurance from www.japanpost.jp.

So far this chapter has demonstrated how closely Japan has linked its safety net to its citizens' position in the workforce. The Japanese welfare state only provides generous social security benefits when they are delivered as occupationally fragmented benefits. It barely offers any comprehensive universalistic income transfer benefits. Insofar as social protection for the working-age population and their families is concerned, Japan relies heavily on work-mediated protection. As in the case of social security benefits, Japan also tends to favor occupationally targetable functional equivalents to a greater degree than other countries. In other words, Japan does not provide functional equivalents that involve paying cash compensation directly to workers who qualify. Instead, Japan provides protection that is more specific to occupations and to product markets. The next section turns to the financial dimensions of the welfare state.

SAVINGS-ORIENTED SOCIAL PROTECTION

Despite its small tax extractive capacity, the postwar Japanese state has controlled huge reserves of "welfare funds." In lieu of income transfers financed from general tax revenue, Japan promotes contributory social security programs and functional equivalents that accumulate money. Let me begin by looking at the social security programs and then proceed to functional equivalents.

When we look at social security programs, we find that Japan has adopted a unique partially funded pension system rather than a more typical "pay-as-you-go (PAYG)" system.[58] A regular PAYG system annually levies social security contributions (or taxes) needed for that fiscal year's pension payments. A funded system, in contrast, accumulates a surplus balance every year until the pension scheme reaches maturity. By the mid-1990s, Japan's social security pension had accumulated reserves equivalent to five years of pension benefits. Until the recent wave of pension reforms, very few advanced industrial countries built up public pension reserves of this magnitude. Today, Japan's reserves (30 percent of its GDP) rank second only to Norway's (40 percent), followed by Sweden (25 percent).[59] While the United States and Finland also have pension reserves – 12 percent and 4 percent of the GDP respectively – other advanced industrial countries possess purely pay-as-you-go pension schemes that accrue reserves the size of about 1 percent of the GDP.[60] While Japan always favored fund accumulation, some of the other countries that possess pension reserves today adopted fund-accumulating design more recently. The United States, for instance, began accumulating reserves only after the reforms undertaken by President Ronald Reagan. Sweden moved to a more market-based, partially funded public pension system in 1998.

In Japan, the Trust Fund Bureau of the Ministry of Finance has managed the pension reserves for most of the postwar period, while some money has been set aside for use by the Ministry of Health and Welfare. The Trust Fund Bureau invests the money in the governmental Fiscal Investment and Loan Program, which, in turn, finances a large number of public corporations (Tokushu Hojin).[61] Fund management in Japan thus is totally independent of the market, as the allocation of funds to public corporations is determined through political channels. Japan's fund management style stands in sharp contrast to those of Sweden and the United States. Sweden invests its pension reserves in equities, whereas the United States invests its reserves in Treasury Bonds. In neither case is the government directly involved in the investment of the funds as in Japan.

In addition to vast public pension reserves, Japan also relies on other capital-accumulating programs such as corporate pension, life insurance plans, and other savings programs. The government provides tax benefits for these programs in

---

[58] As Kato (1991a, 1991b) and Campbell (1992) argue, postwar Japan's public pension system shifted from a funded system toward a pay-as-you-go system. Nonetheless, it continued to raise reserves.

[59] The figures are based on OECD (2005).

[60] See Patashnik (1995) for the importance of social security funds in the United States in financing the fiscal deficit. In the United States, a similar arrangement occurs between some state employees' pension funds and their governments. The figures are based on the OECD newsletter cited above.

[61] See Calder (1990) for a concise discussion of the FILP. The public pension system was not the only social security program that accumulated money. The Employment Insurance and Work Injuries Insurance also frequently ran surpluses.

the name of "welfare." Promotion of savings itself is not uniquely Japanese. As I already mentioned, countries other than Japan also accumulate public pension reserves. Countries such as the Netherlands, Switzerland, the United Kingdom, and the United States also possess huge private pension funds, which they promote by means of generous tax expenditures.[62] As Table 1.6 shows, as of 2001, many of these countries possess much greater private pension funds than does Japan. Some continental European countries with small private pension reserves do have their equivalents in the form of life insurance plans that are similar to private pension programs.[63] The OECD figures on private pensions and life insurance equivalents, however, underestimate the importance of life insurance products in postwar Japan's welfare system. In Japan, most of the life insurance plans were not private pension plans but were long-term savings plans combined with insurance against death.[64] Japan always provided generous tax deductions for life insurance premiums, and by the mid-1980s, Japan's life insurance industry surpassed its U.S. counterpart in asset size. According to the Household Economy Survey (Kakei Chosa) by the government, an average wage earner's family in the early 1990s would spend about 5 percent of the monthly wage on life insurance premiums. When the magnitude of the overall life insurance industry (rather than private pension components) is considered, the significance of Japan's life insurance industry becomes more evident (Table 1.6).

Japan has also offered tax deductions and exemptions for the following: corporate in-house savings programs (*shanai yokin seido*); a special savings account for the elderly (*rojin tokubetsu maru yu*); and various tax-deferred *zaikei* accounts. As discussed earlier in the section on housing-related policies, Japan initially introduced a savings program called *zaikei* to help workers accumulate the down payments for homeownership. In an effort to promote workers' welfare, *zaikei* was later expanded to include savings for supplementary old-age income and educational funds for children. In addition to promoting private financial products, the Japanese government also participated actively in the financial markets as a player. The Japanese government competed against private life insurance companies and banks by selling life insurance and pension products through its

[62] According to the OECD statistics on tax expenditures for social purposes, these countries provide the largest sums of tax expenditures for private pension products.
[63] As an OECD report notes, countries with the tradition of indirect financing tend to have larger insurance sectors (OECD 2005).
[64] Up until the 1960s, a large bulk of life insurance products was long-term savings accounts. Since the 1970s, close to 60 percent of those who purchased life insurance policies said that they purchased the policies to insure their families against loss of income in the event of the death of the breadwinner. Consumers' preference for particular types of life insurance products varies depending on their age and sex. Prime-age men predominantly use life insurance as a way of protecting their family income. Others primarily see life insurance policies as long-term savings accounts. Seimei Hoken Bunka Senta (Life Insurance Culture Center) carries out surveys. See its periodic publications, *Seimei Hoken Fakuto Bukku* and *Seimei Hoken ni Kansuru Jittai Chosa*, for these trends. For the historical macrotrend, see the survey results cited in Tachibanaki (2000, 59); and Nihon Hokengyoshi Hensan Iinkai (1968a, 582).

thousands of post offices across the country.[65] The Postal Insurance (*kampo*) and the Postal Savings (*yucho*) both dwarf their private sector counterparts. *Yucho* and *kampo*, while they competed against their private sector counterparts in the market, were nonetheless very peculiar public financial institutions whose funds were managed by the Trust Fund Bureau just like the public pension reserves. The funds were allocated by political rather than economic considerations (Anderson 1990; Calder 1990). Certainly, Japan is not the only country that relies on public financial institutions. Before private banks turned to consumer finance, most countries relied on public or nonprofit financial institutions such as postal savings accounts and building societies. Countries such as the United Kingdom and the United States, however, shrank the role of public agencies as direct players in the market as the financial market developed and diversified. Continental European countries whose capital markets remained smaller, however, tended to preserve public financial institutions to a greater degree. Germany, France, and Italy all have sizable public finance sectors that consist of postal banks and savings associations.[66]

As can be observed from Japan's vast public pension reserves under state control and its reliance on public financial institutions, Japan generally avoided market mechanisms in mobilizing and allocating capital. This tendency can also be observed in its mode of regulating corporate pension programs. Instead of protecting workers' pension rights or legally stipulating fiduciary responsibilities of private program administrators (that is, employers and financial institutions), Japan has restricted competition. The Employee Retirement Income Security Act (ERISA) in the United States provides a good example of regulation focused on pension rights and fiduciary responsibilities. Japan lacks any equivalent of ERISA. Until a recent reform, the Japanese government did not require employers to reinsure their pension liabilities. Instead, Japan opted for controlling the fund management process directly. It would be useful here to describe how Japan regulated private welfare programs by referring to the case of corporate pensions.

Prior to the Corporate Pension Reform in 2002, Japan only permitted three types of corporate pensions: (i) the retirement lump-sum payment (*taishokukin*); (ii) the tax qualified pension (*zeisei tekikaku nenkin*); and (iii) the Employee Pension Fund (*kosei nenkin kikin*). The retirement lump-sum payment – the most popular form of corporate pension in Japan – was not really a pension, since it was just a lump-sum payment granted upon retirement.[67] Experts also called it a "book-reserve pension," because the sponsoring employer was allowed to set aside part of its pre-tax earnings on the company books without having to really

---

[65] See Rosenbluth (1989) for an account of the perpetual conflict between private sector financial institutions and the postal system.

[66] See Aizawa and Hirakawa (1996) for detailed comparisons of public and nonprofit savings institutions in Germany, France, Italy, Japan, the United Kingdom, and the United States.

[67] Nearly 80 percent of the workers receive a retirement lump-sum payment, although the actual sum varies depending on the firm size, final salary, and the tenure.

fund future payment liabilities.[68] Meanwhile, employers were allowed to use the money for reinvestment within the company.

The other two types of corporate pensions were legally mandated to set up pension funds outside the sponsoring companies. The government "protected" these corporate funds by restricting which financial institutions were licensed to manage them and by restricting their investment portfolio. Until the 1990s, only life insurance companies were licensed to manage the tax qualified pension, whereas trust banks and life insurance companies were licensed to manage the Employee Pension Funds. Note that these two financial sectors – life insurance and trust banks – were heavily regulated for most of the postwar period. Until the "Financial Big Bang" in the late 1990s, only a handful of life insurance companies and trust banks existed, as their numbers were actually controlled by the financial authorities. The Ministry of Finance had successfully created and maintained an oligopolistic financial market by means of licensing and administrative guidance.[69] Furthermore, the government legally determined the projected rate of return (to be used for actuarial calculations) on both Employee Pension Fund and tax qualified pension.[70]

Table 1.7 lists different sources of Japanese welfare funds to estimate the real scope of savings-oriented welfare programs in Japan. Whereas corporate savings accounts and the book-reserve pension helped companies retain capital within for reinvestment, the other types of programs created vast amounts of capital under state control. In sum, one can argue that a *quasi-socialization* of capital occurred through Japan's savings-oriented welfare programs. The Japanese welfare state *socialized* capital both directly and indirectly. It directly socialized capital via its huge public pension reserves. It indirectly socialized capital by leaving private welfare funds in the hands of heavily regulated financial institutions highly susceptible to pressures from the regulatory agency (the Ministry of Finance).

THE REAL VARIETIES OF WELFARE CAPITALISM

At the start of this chapter, I said that the Japanese welfare state calls to mind Kurosawa's movie, *Rashomon*, because every scholar disagrees about what it looks like. The orthodox approach to the welfare state treats Japan as a typical small welfare state. Scholars of Japanese politics point to Japan's relatively generous pension and health care programs and argue that Japan resembles European countries rather than the United States. This chapter solves this mystery by reconceptualizing the very concept of the welfare state.

---

[68] More precisely, employers were allowed to set aside 40 percent of the sum equivalent to the total of retirement lump-sum payments they would owe if all of their workers were to quit that year. This rate was reduced to 20 percent in the late 1990s. For a concise English-language account of Japanese retirement payments, see Clark (1990).
[69] For Japanese financial regulations, see Rosenbluth (1989) and Vogel (1996).
[70] For details, see Estévez-Abe (2001).

TABLE 1.7. *Japan's Welfare Funds*

	1994
Postal Savings	181,780
Postal Insurance	94,000
Employee Pension	104,532
National Pension	6,371
Zaikei	16,537
Corporate Savings Accounts	3,020
Mutual Assistance Association	37,911
Employee Pension Fund	39,000
Tax Qualified Pension	17,000
Retirement Payment Book Reserve	13,934
Life Insurance	177,966
% of GDP	144%
(in billion yen)	

Source: Fukushima, Yamaguchi, and Ishikawa (1973), Japan Long-term Credit Bank (1996), *Fukuri Kosei Handbook* (1994), a Government Tax Committee document, www.japanpost.jp, Ministry of Welfare's *Kosei Tokei Yoran 1995*, *Seimei Hoken Fakuto Bukku 1995*.

This chapter has argued that the Japanese social protection system possesses two salient characteristics. First, Japan ties the social safety net to one's work to a much greater degree than occurs in other countries. Japan shies away from comprehensive universalistic income transfers to working-age citizens. Instead, it relies upon more occupationally targeted means of intervention to deliver protection. Japan stands out for its emphasis on social security programs and functional equivalents that are targeted at firms and producers rather than individual workers. Second, Japan favors welfare programs that accumulate capital and it places welfare funds under state control to a greater degree than do other countries. A close look at its welfare system reveals that postwar Japan actually socialized capital while keeping most of its economy in private hands. These characteristics of the Japanese social protection system are vital in understanding the specific model of capitalism that developed in postwar Japan. These contradictions have profound implications for labor incentives, labor relations, and the flow of capital within the economy, as will be discussed in Chapter 6.

Although the primary goal of this chapter was to portray Japan's social protection system accurately, the implications are comparative. The cross-national comparisons presented in this chapter challenge the orthodox notions of welfare states and welfare politics. Let me emphasize three major points.

The first point worth emphasizing is that distinctions such as "universalistic versus fragmented" and "generous versus meager" that focus solely on orthodox social security programs fail to capture the ways in which welfare states vary. Existing studies of welfare states typically are only interested in highlighting differences between – the normatively superior – social democratic welfare states, on the one hand, and other types of welfare states (conservative and liberal welfare states), on the other. This chapter has emphasized the importance of functional equivalents to round out the picture. By looking at the full range of social security programs and their functional equivalents, we can overcome taxonomies of welfare capitalism that are often more normative than analytical.

What one might call a social democratic bias has prevented scholars from considering a full range of functional equivalents. When existing studies discuss functional equivalents, they only consider market-based private welfare programs as "liberal" alternatives to public welfare programs.[71] In contrast, welfare state scholars consider active labor market policy (ALMP) to be part of the "public" welfare state activity, although it is clearly a functional equivalent to unemployment benefits.[72] The fact that social democratic welfare states rely on ALMP makes it easy for welfare state scholars to accept it as a legitimate policy to study. Generally, if a social democratic welfare state does something, it becomes part of the definition of welfare state activities. Let me present a few more examples of conceptual bias. When the Swedes used supplementary pension schemes to accumulate capital, it was automatically perceived as an important step to economic democracy (Esping-Andersen 1985; Pontusson 1984). But when Japan does the same, no welfare state scholar would think of it as an advancement of economic democracy.[73] Huber and Stephens (2001) point out that social democratic governments use public works to boost the economy to create jobs. Japan does this too, but it is treated as a different thing all together.

The second point is that Japan is not the only country to use industrial policy to intervene into the market for the purpose of social protection. Many of the CMEs – including some social democratic countries – also rely on administrative intervention in the market as a functional equivalent of the more orthodox social protection programs. Furthermore, Japan shares some similarities with social democratic countries in its emphasis on job creation via public works spending. The real question hence is not which countries rely more or less on functional equivalents, but what types of social security programs and functional equivalents a particular country combines to deliver protection. Just like social security programs vary qualitatively (for example, universalistic versus occupationally fragmented), functional equivalents vary qualitatively, too. Some functional equivalents provide comprehensive benefits to all citizens that qualify – such as tax expenditures for families – whereas others are more targeted. Functional equivalents also vary in their orientation toward the market. Some functional equivalents promote welfare provision via the market, whereas others restrict or replace the market. Understanding how different welfare states combine qualitatively different policy tools is crucial for understanding the real varieties of welfare capitalism.

---

[71] See Esping-Andersen (1990); Hacker (2002); Howard (1997); Rein and Rainwater eds. (1986); and Shalev ed. (1996). For important exceptions, see Sheingate (2001) and Skocpol (1992).

[72] See Esping-Andersen (1990).

[73] Pontusson (1991) argues that social democratic countries use social policy as industrial policy in order to intervene in the market, whereas countries where organized labor is weak do not.

The third point worth emphasizing is that the cross-national variations identified in this chapter reveal different sets of similarities that cannot be readily explained by existing theories of welfare states. Although a thorough comparative study is beyond the scope of this book, let me nonetheless point out a few sets of similarities that unsettle the conventional wisdom in welfare state studies. Most existing comparative studies of welfare states – statistical studies, in particular – treat Japan as a typical "small" welfare state (Huber and Stephens 2001; Iversen and Soskice 2006; Wilensky 2002, among others). This chapter has, however, provided ample evidence to suggest that Japan is not as market oriented as other small welfare states. Japan uses very different types of functional equivalents when compared to other small welfare states.

This chapter has also brought out some important similarities between Japan and countries such as Italy and Finland. Japan and Italy, for instance, rank similarly in Table 1.1 and Table 1.3. They both offer meager unemployment benefits but rely on very similar functional equivalents (such as strong employment protection, public works spending, and regulatory intervention) to cope with unemployment. Neither the power resources model, which attributes policy outcomes to the political clout of Social Democrats, nor its corollary, which focuses on the role of Christian Democrats, can explain why Japan and Italy should be similar in this dimension. Furthermore, contrary to the welfare state literature that generally treats all Scandinavian welfare states as similar, this chapter has revealed that Finland shares commonalities with an unusual set of countries. Finland has a more fragmented social security system than other Scandinavian countries and resembles Italy and Japan in its reliance on public works. Finland and Japan are also among the top spenders on agricultural subsidies. These two countries both rely on wage subsidies and employment protection as well. None of the standard causal models of politics in advanced industrial societies explain these similarities between Finland and Japan. The next chapter develops a new institutional model of politics that can fill this and many other gaps in our knowledge of the welfare state.

APPENDIX I.A. *Detailed Data and Explanations for Table 1.1*

	Standard Pension	Unemployment	Family Benefits	Health Care
Australia	32 (49)	27	3.6	67
Austria	82 (70)	31	14.2	74
Belgium	80 (77)	43	13.1	
Canada	54 (64)	28	2.8	75
Denmark	54 (64)	52	5.6	83
Finland	67 (64)	39	6.6	81
France	60 (69)	37	7	77
Germany	75 (62)	28	4.4	76
Italy	72 (69)	3	6.5	79
Japan	51 (73)**	9	0	78
Netherlands	48 (58)	51	7.3	67
New Zealand	41 (65)	26	2.2	82
Norway	63 (61)	39	10.2	83
Sweden	65 (68)	29	8.7	90
Switzerland	39 (51)	22	6	52
United Kingdom	47 (56)	18	6.1	84
United States	56 (78)	11	0	40

Standard Pension Levels: Replacement rate for the year 1990 reported in Lyle Scruggs (2004), Welfare State Entitlements Data Set: A Comparative Institutional Analysis of Eighteen Welfare States, Version 1.0.

**The Japanese figures reflect Employee Pension benefits.

Unemployment Benefits Levels: An index of generosity that takes into consideration replacement rate and duration. Blöndal and Pearson (1995).

Family Benefits: Percentage of family benefits as a ratio of an average worker's earnings based on *OECD Tax/Benefit Position of Production Workers Annual Report 1990–1993*.

Health Care: Percentage of public spending on health care as a ratio of total health care spending. OECD Health Data 2003.

	ALMP	Employment Protection	Public-Sector Employment	Wage Subsidies	Public Works	Administrative Barriers to Business	State Control of Economy
Australia	6	1.1	18.7	5	2.32	1.13	1.26
Austria	11.5	2.4	14.6	6	3.18	1.6	2.11
Belgium	7	2.1	19.2	30	1.35	2.55	2.78
Canada	12	0.6	19.8	1	2.51	0.8	1.29
Denmark	16	1.5	31.2	2	1.95	1.32	2.46
Finland	38	2.1	26.3	71	3.58	1.93	2.68
France	25	3.1	20.5	5	3.21	2.73	2.63
Germany	33	2.8	13.4	13	2.23	2.1	1.76
Italy	8	3.3	18.5		3.28	2.74	3.92
Japan	9	2.6	8	29	5.03	2.33	1.29
Netherlands	10	2.4	13.9	2	2.65	1.41	2.28
New Zealand	24	1	12.5	9		1.21	1.66
Norway	31	2.9	32	15	3.24	1.33	3.19
Sweden	80	2.4	31.8	24	3.03	1.8	1.51
Switzerland	7	1.3	12.6			2.24	2.08
United Kingdom	28	0.5	18.8	3.5	2.3	0.48	0.55
United States	18	0.2	15.6	2	1.69	1.26	0.85

Active Labor Market Policy: Percentage of spending on active measures as a ratio of all unemployment-related spending; calculation based on OECD figures.

Employment Protection: Based on the OECD index of the strictness of employment protection legislation. Nicoletti et al. 2000.

Public Sector Employment: Percentage of civil public employment as a ration of the workforce. ILO Labour Force Survey, 1995–2003 (1995 figures for all countries except for the United States. The U.S. figure is from 2000).

Wage Subsidies: Percentage of wage subsidies as a ratio of unemployment spending. Calculation based on OECD figures.

Public Works: Government's Gross Fixed Capital Account as a ratio of GDP for years closest to 1990. National Accounts of OECD Countries: 1988–1998. Vol 2. 2001.

Administrative Barriers to Business: Based on the index for "Barriers to Entrepreneurship" in Nicoletti et al. 2000.

State Control of the Economy: State ownership of the economy as in Nicoletti et al. 2000.

2

Structural Logic of Welfare Politics

Some countries provide universalistic social security benefits, whereas others provide more fragmented social security benefits. Similarly, some countries rely on functional equivalents that allow for occupational targeting, whereas others emphasize geographical targeting. This chapter employs an institutional model of welfare politics to explain why certain policy choices are more likely in a specific institutional context. I use the term *structural logic* to describe my approach, because political institutions have been known to "structure" politics (Steinmo, Thelen, and Longstreth eds. 1992). Political institutions structure politics by defining the rules of the game (Hall and Taylor 1996; Kato 1996). In so doing, they shape incentives and thereby affect the likelihood of certain actors triumphing over others in the political game. This means that when the structure of the political system changes, so political outcomes are likely to change. The task of this chapter is to identify the institutions that structure welfare politics and to specify the ways in which they do. While the rest of the book applies the structural logic to explain welfare development in postwar Japan, this chapter develops the logic in ways that are applicable to all advanced industrial countries.

This chapter constructs a structural logic of welfare politics in two steps by focusing on institutional factors that affect (a) veto player configurations; and (b) veto players' distributive incentives. Veto players, by definition, are those actors whose consent is required for successful legislation. The veto player configuration in a specific country tells us which political actor is likely to prevail in that country. Once we determine who the veto players are, we know that policies in that country can never deviate from the veto players' preferences. The idea behind this structural logic approach is that by identifying the vital preferences of the veto players, we can predict the policy orientation of that country.

There are three kinds of veto player: (i) constitutional; (ii) parliamentary; and (iii) nonparliamentary veto players. Different types of veto players affect welfare politics – and politics more generally – differently. Constitutional veto players arise from the constitutional structure of a democracy. Federalism, strong bicameralism,[1] a strong judiciary, a practice of referendum, and a presidential system all give rise to separate institutions with mutual veto powers, and thereby increase the number of veto players. Conversely, unified, unicameral parliamentary systems have fewer veto players. Constitutional veto players are, however, not the only veto players. By parliamentary veto players, I have in mind political parties and politicians in the parliament capable of blocking parliamentary decisions. By nonparliamentary veto players, I refer to bureaucratic and societal actors such as corporatist actors with the ability to control the legislative agenda or veto legislative proposals. These three types of veto players ultimately make up the real configuration of veto players in a specific polity.[2]

For the sake of presentational simplicity, I primarily focus on the number and preferences of parliamentary veto players – politicians and political parties with seats in the parliament – in constructing the structural logic of welfare politics. I assume that the constitutional structure remains centralized and that the parliament remains the single constitutional veto player. This strategy makes sense, because parliamentary veto players are the most important for two reasons. First, regardless of the constitutional structure, any successful legislation ultimately has to be acceptable to parliamentary veto players. Second, the presence of nonparliamentary veto players is largely a function of the specific configuration of parliamentary veto players for reasons to be discussed later in this chapter.[3] Assuming that politicians seek reelection and that political parties seek to expand their influence in the parliament, we can reasonably assume that politicians and political parties will allocate resources in ways that maximize their electoral chances. This assumption makes it possible to identify the types of welfare programs most suitable for improving a party's electoral prospects under different electoral systems.

The core of my argument is the following: district magnitude and the importance of the personal (or party) vote together determine (i) what electoral strategies are likely to be most appropriate in a specific polity; (ii) the likely configuration of parliamentary veto players; and (iii) when nonparliamentary veto players are likely to emerge. The first two dimensions determine the overall characteristics of the social protection system in a specific country, and the third adds additional details. Needless to say, an actual application of the structural logic approach requires that we pay attention to the constitutional structure,

---

[1] Not all second chambers are veto players. Not every bicameral system endows the second chamber with veto power. Even if the second chamber is constitutionally endowed with veto power, bicameralism can, in fact, be weakened when the two chambers of the parliament are elected by a similar electoral rule. When the composition of interests represented in the two chambers is similar, there is little reason for the second chamber to veto the decision of the first chamber. However, when the two chambers are elected very differently, preferences of the two chambers are more likely to diverge. See Tsebelis (2002).

[2] Existing studies of veto players also recognize multiple types of veto players, although they may not always agree on whether they produce different political outcomes (see Birchfield and Crepaz 1998; Crepaz 1998; Huber, Ragin, and Stephens 1993; Tsebelis 2002).

[3] Nonparliamentary veto players such as bureaucratic actors and interest groups only arise when agenda setting and/or legislative power is delegated to them by parliamentary veto players. As will be discussed later in this chapter, electoral calculations of politicians are primary factors that determine the terms of the delegation. In other words, these nonparliamentary veto players operate within the constraints of the strategic calculations of the parliamentary veto players.

since a divided structure gives rise to many constitutional veto players. There is ample literature on the effect of constitutional veto players on welfare politics.

The argument of this chapter proceeds in four sections. Section 1 presents a deductive model of politicians' distributive strategies on the basis of district magnitude and the strength of the personal vote. Section 2 builds upon the preceding section to construct different patterns of a structural logic of welfare politics. Section 3 applies the structural logic put forth in this chapter to explain some of the cross-national variations identified in Chapter 1. Section 4 adds more layers by identifying when and why bureaucrats and interest groups arise as veto players and identifies the institutional basis of bureaucratic preferences.

PARLIAMENTARY VETO PLAYERS' ELECTORAL CALCULATIONS

Assuming that the goal of politicians is to maximize their chances of (re)election, the rules of the electoral game are likely to shape their strategies. Politicians will seek the support of those voters and groups necessary for their (re)election by promising them "distributive advantages." These distributive advantages might include anything from public pension benefits to tax expenditures on savings programs. Depending on the nature of the electoral institutions, politicians in a particular country will favor one or more of the following: (a) organized voters (as opposed to unorganized voters); (b) geographically specific benefits; and (c) particularistic rent-seeking groups. These "biases," as they might be termed, are very useful in thinking about welfare politics, because they shape what one might call the "distributive preferences" of politicians.[4] These biases, in short, mean that, independently of societal actors' preferences, electoral systems influence the way in which politicians and political parties respond to the same demand for social protection. For instance, a politician who needs localized votes is likely to advocate geographically targeted forms of social protection even if a universalistic program might have addressed the same problem. Likewise, a politician who seeks support from a well-organized occupational group is likely to push for an occupationally targeted form of social protection. A politician seeking to raise political contributions, in turn, is likely to favor forms of social protection that best generate rent for special interests.

Building upon existing studies of electoral systems, this section constructs a logic of electorally motivated preferences for social protection based on two factors: (i) district magnitude – that is, the number of seats allocated to an electoral district; and (ii) relative importance of personal vote. Combinations of these two factors allow us to predict likely representational and distributional biases.

District Magnitude

There exists an abundant literature – both empirical and formal – on the representational and distributional biases inherent in different electoral systems. Scholars

---

4 Katzenstein (1985) was the first to draw attention to the importance of proportional representation in the development of large welfare states in Europe.

generally consider proportional representation (PR) systems to favor organized groups, whereas single-member districts (SMD) using the plurality rule – that is, "first-past-the-post" systems – favor unorganized voters (Downs 1957 and Powell 1982; see Bawn and Thies 2003 for a slightly different argument). The main intuition behind this assumption is that the smaller the vote share required for winning a seat, the greater the incentive on the part of politicians (or political parties) to cultivate the support of an organized group (Cox 1990, 1999; Krauss 1993; Lijphart, Pintor, and Sone 1986; Myerson 1993; Reed 1990; Taagepera and Shugart 1989). Even when the vote/seat conversion rule is not proportional, when the district magnitude – the number of seats assigned to an electoral district – is large, the pursuit of a minority of reliable voters becomes a successful electoral strategy.[5] The narrowness of the constituency group of a winning candidate is a function both of (a) the number of candidates running in a district, and (b) district magnitude. Preexisting cleavages and other factors sometimes have an independent effect on the number of candidates, but the impact of district magnitude is critical in predicting politicians' behavior. As Myerson (1993: 857) argues, "electoral systems that encourage candidates to advocate the interests of existing minorities may also incite candidates to use narrow campaign strategies that create favored minorities even in situations where all voters are initially the same."

For the purpose of simplification, for the rest of this section I will assume that when the district magnitude is large, the number of candidates in a district will also become large, and that when the district magnitude is one – for example, single-member districts as in the United Kingdom and the United States – only two serious contenders are likely to arise. This choice of district magnitude as a variable to predict politicians and political parties' behavior is justified on two grounds.[6] First, there is a consensus among scholars of electoral systems that district magnitude correlates strongly with the number of candidates.[7] Second, existing formal theories of electoral systems produce more stable results when the cases under consideration are more straightforward, such as a two-candidate race in a single-member district rather than a three-candidate race.[8]

At the simplest level, therefore, we can assume that a large district magnitude encourages candidates to seek the support of organized groups. This strategy can be expected to be more effective if the group is well organized and is

---

[5] By reliable voters, I mean societal groups closely aligned with political parties that promise higher turnouts than other groups to deliver votes (see discussions in Cox and McCubbins 1986).

[6] Both Cox (1990) and Myerson (1993) also examine the implications of different ballot structures such as differences in the number of votes per voter, the presence of cumulative voting, partial abstention, single transferable vote (STV), and single nontransferable vote (SNTV). Although these factors are important, here I try to simplify the insights from existing studies of electoral studies to better manage broad categorical comparisons. Transferability of votes will be dealt with in relation to the other variable used in this section, the relative importance of the personal vote.

[7] On the relationship between proportionality, effective number of parties, and district magnitude, see Cox (1990, 1997); Lijphart (1984); and Taagepera and Shugart (1989), among others.

[8] See Cox (1990) for instance. His prediction for a two-candidate race in a SMD is more straightforward than his prediction for a three-candidate SMD race.

capable of mobilizing its members' votes (Cox and McCubbins 1986). Granted these assumptions, it follows that politicians and political parties competing in multimember districts (MMD hereafter) can be expected to prefer forms of social protection that help strengthen their ties with organized constituency groups. The aim of these politicians and parties is to turn these groups into reliable support groups in exchange for favorable policies and benefits. Targeted forms of protection that single out specific societal groups thus become highly desirable from politicians' perspective.[9] Highly occupationally fragmented social insurance schemes, for instance, serve as more convenient conduits of benefits targeted at specific groups of voters. Similarly, market-restricting regulations serve as tools to protect very specific socioeconomic groups.

In contrast, when the district magnitude is one – as in single-member districts – the pursuit of organized groups becomes a suboptimal strategy. The winner-take-all nature of electoral competition under SMD means that candidates are more vulnerable to decisions by unorganized voters.[10] A small percentage point difference in vote share can potentially translate into a huge gap in the allocation of seats. As a result, the relative importance of unorganized voters increases in SMD systems. Unlike in MMD systems, the relative importance of unorganized voters in SMD systems makes it very costly – electorally speaking – for politicians to advocate market-restricting regulations as means of social protection. This type of functional equivalent protects well-organized groups at the expense of unorganized voters such as consumers, who will be forced to bear the cost of the regulations in the form of higher prices (see Rogowski and Kayser 2002).

District magnitude also affects the relative importance of distributive benefits that can be targeted geographically (Weingast, Shepsle, and Johnsen 1981). When all other factors are equal, the smaller the district magnitude the more important are geographically targeted benefits. In SMD systems, where each district is represented by only one politician, politicians seeking election need to win the majority of votes in their respective districts to secure seats. It thus makes more sense for these politicians to advocate geographically targeted distribution that benefits their own districts.[11] Obviously, malapportionment of votes and

---

9 See Milesi-Ferretti, Perotti, and Rostagno (2002) for a similar argument. Although most agree that large district magnitudes – PR systems being notable examples – favor groups of voters that share similar attributes rather than geographical location, some scholars have erroneously interpreted this group orientation as an orientation for broad comprehensive benefits such as social security benefits and educational spending (see, for instance, Persson and Tabellini 1999, 2000). These scholars overlook the fact that ruling parties may use programs targeted at specific groups for electoral purposes.

10 Based on the idea of different seat-vote volatilities in different electoral systems, Rogowski and Kayser (2002) also come to a similar conclusion about the relative unimportance of organized voters in SMD.

11 Weingast, Shepsle, and Johnsen (1981) illustrate that SMD motivates politicians to support programs that benefit their districts while spreading their costs across the nation. They follow Theodore Lowi's classification of public policy types in defining "distributive" programs as particularistic spending that encompasses "projects, programs, and grants that concentrate benefits in geographically specific constituencies, while spreading their costs across all constituencies through generalized taxation."

fiscal centralization make geographically targeted programs even more attractive to politicians.[12]

To summarize, the existing literature on electoral systems generates two specific expectations for what types of social protection are most likely to be favored in democracies with different district magnitude sizes. Politicians running for office in MMD systems are more likely to advocate forms of social protection that are targeted at their constituent groups.[13] These programs can take the form of either (a) highly fragmented social security programs; or (b) market-restricting regulations. Politicians in single-member districts, in contrast, are more likely to advocate geographically targetable programs and *less* likely to advocate market-restricting regulations.

So far the presentation of this model employs the terms *politicians* and *parties* interchangeably; however, they are not the same actors. Nor do their interests always converge. Earlier, it was argued that weak party discipline gives rise to intraparty veto players. To put it briefly, when politicians rely on the personal vote for their (re)election – as opposed to the party vote – they are most likely to develop electoral strategies independent of their party leaders' strategies (Bawn and Thies 2003; Grossman and Helpman 2005; McGillivray 1997, 2004; Myerson 1993). For this reason, we need to consider those rules of the game that promote the personal vote as opposed to the party vote.

Party Vote vs. Personal Vote

Aside from potential variations in district magnitude, electoral systems also vary in the relative importance of the party and personal reputation at the polls. The personal vote becomes important in those systems where individual politicians face intraparty electoral competition and need to cultivate more personalized support against their intraparty competitors.[14] According to Carey and Shugart (1994), this happens when (i) party leadership does not control access to the party label – as in the U.S. primaries; (ii) voters cast their votes for specific candidates rather than parties; and (iii) there is no sharing of votes among candidates from the

---

[12] Malapportionment of votes, another feature of the electoral rules, also affects the extent of geographical distributive bias (Rodden 2005; Samuels and Snyder 2001). Any gap in the vote-seat ratio gives strong incentives for political parties to distribute to districts where "one seat is cheaper." In any case, the smaller the district, the more vulnerable is the electoral system to potential malapportionment. No malapportionment is possible, for instance, when there is only one nationwide electoral district. Degree of fiscal centralization also is a critical factor in promoting geographical targeting (see footnote 11 and also Besley and Coate 1999; Diaz-Cayeros et al. 2002, among others).

[13] My position is close to Milesi-Ferretti, Perotti, and Rostagno (2002) and differs from Persson and Tabellini (1999, 2000), who assume that large district magnitude favors broad-based spending rather than targeting. Note that many quantitative studies that explore the distributive implications of electoral systems assume that targeting is generally geographical in nature. In my view, they erroneously associate large district magnitude (or PR) with "comprehensive" redistributive programs. Also see footnote 9. While building on the insights of this literature, my emphasis and application thus varies.

[14] See Cain, Ferejohn, and Fiorina (1987) for effects of the personal vote.

same party. Single nontransferable votes (SNTV) in prereform (pre-1994) Japan and the preference voting system in prereform Italy provide good examples of electoral systems that produce intraparty competition. Both types of votes permit voters to select specific individual candidates from among the multiple candidates from the same party running in the same district.[15] At the opposite end of the spectrum, there are proportional representation systems that adopt closed party lists, which produce very little intraparty competition. In these systems, party leaders nominate candidates and rank them on the party list in a specific order. Voters cast their vote for a particular party, and candidates get elected in the order in which they are listed, so that the party's vote share and its seat share match. Many northern European countries use this system.

For politicians who rely on the personal vote, it is more rational to focus on delivering benefits to their individual constituency groups even at the expense of the rest of their party or country. This is not a trivial point, because what is electorally desirable for an individual politician may be at odds with what is good for the party as a whole.[16] More specifically, the personal vote intensifies the importance of individual politicians' "core constituencies."[17] Individual politicians will have strong incentives to prevent the party leadership from shifting resources away from their own core constituencies in favor of other groups of voters, whose support might benefit the party as a whole. The party leadership, which does not control access to the party label, is in a weak position to discipline intraparty opposition. The predominance of the personal vote thus means that – all things being equal – the party becomes weaker (Cox 1987; Grossman and Helpman 2005). When the party vote is important, in contrast, it is the electoral strategy of the party that matters rather than the actions of individual politicians. The party leadership decides who runs on the party ticket, what the party platform is, and what the party's electoral strategy is.

A strong personal vote exacerbates some of the effects that district magnitude produces.[18] It has been argued that politicians running in MMD systems seek the support of organized groups of voters. When the personal vote is strong, individual politicians will seek ever more narrowly organized groups in their attempt to carve out their own niche of support groups.[19] Similarly, it has been argued that SMD systems favor geographical targeting. Strong parties and weak parties in a SMD system, however, develop different types of geographic bias. The goal of the party leadership under SMD systems is to win enough seats to govern. Party

[15] SNTV means that votes cast for specific candidates only count toward their election and they cannot be passed on to elect their fellow party candidates in the same district (Cox 1997; Myerson 1993).

[16] When personal vote is important, the politician's primary loyalty goes to her constituency rather than to the party itself.

[17] Golden (2003) and McGillivray (2004) make similar arguments.

[18] Carey and Shugart (1994, 418) note that when there is intraparty competition, the value of personal reputation increases as the district magnitude increases.

[19] These groups may or may not be geographically concentrated. For instance, consider groups such as farmers. Although this is a socioeconomic group that shares a particular attribute (that is, occupation), its members are likely to be concentrated in some areas.

leaders thus care greatly about marginal districts, whereas individual candidates care about their districts. When the party is strong, public policy is likely to benefit marginal districts.[20] When the party is weak, in contrast, electoral districts of influential individual politicians are likely to benefit more than others. In SMD systems, swing voters can make a critical difference to whether a party can seize power or not. A politics based on the personal vote requires more money (Chang and Golden 2007; Cox and Thies 1998; Golden 2003, Golden and Picci 2005). When a politician has to differentiate herself from her fellow party members, she needs to deliver her personal message to the electorate directly. Personalized campaigns and constituency services are much more costly to individual politicians than are party-based campaigns and constituency services. The greater the fund-raising needs, the greater the politicians' incentives to advocate policy decisions that "generate money." Policies catering to the needs of special interest groups fit this bill nicely, because these groups can return the favor with money and votes.[21] In the context of social protection, providers of welfare goods and services – for example, physicians, nurses, pharmaceutical companies, insurance companies, or housing developers – are likely to be primary beneficiaries. Mutually beneficial relationships can develop between these providers and financially strapped individual politicians.[22]

Here it is important to emphasize that the strength of the personal vote is not solely a function of electoral rules. Institutional factors such as the degree of power concentrated in the prime minister's office – and in her Cabinet – only help to strengthen the party leader in relation to her party and increase her electoral importance.[23] Obviously, the stronger the party leader's control over policy decisions – and hence the more important the party platform – the less relevant the personal vote.[24] This means that parliamentary systems are more likely to strengthen the party to a much greater degree than presidential systems do when there is a SMD (see Cox 1987; Haggard and McCubbins eds. 2001; Tatebayashi 2004). Legislative rules such as a strong committee system and unanimity rules, in contrast, decentralize the decision-making process – especially when the personal vote is important. A strong committee chairman can wield power independent of

[20] Bawn and Thies (2003) correctly point out that individual politicians' desire to appeal to unorganized voters in their single-member districts declines when the party vote is more important. This happens because individual candidates' effort in their local constituencies matters little. They thus conclude that there is little political incentive to cater to the needs of unorganized voters when politicians are elected on the basis of the party vote. Their formal model of politicians' behavior, however, does not take into consideration party leaders' strategic calculations. In SMD systems, a party leader has a strong desire to appeal to unorganized swing voters in competitive districts in order to seize or maintain power. See McGillivray 2004.

[21] See Noll and Rosenbluth (1995) for a similar logic.

[22] Of course, other institutional arrangements such as the strictness of the electoral campaign law and how well it is implemented make a difference in terms of the real degree to which politicians seek financial support in exchange for favorable policy decisions.

[23] For the sake of presentational simplicity, this chapter does not provide an account of the full range of institutional varieties in terms of these legislative arrangements. The next chapter, however, provides a detailed discussion of the legislative rules in postwar Japan.

[24] See Cox (1987) on the importance of concentration of power in the Cabinet for a strong party to emerge under a SMD. I have discussed Cox's work at length elsewhere (Estévez-Abe 2006).

TABLE 2.1 *Preferences of Parliamentary Veto Players*

		The Importance of the Personal Vote	
		Weak **(= Strong Party)**	**Strong** **(= Weak Party)**
District Magnitude	**Small**	**Type I** Unorganized voters matter. Geographical location of support matters for political parties. Little need for individual politicians to raise money. →Universalistic programs. →Targeting is more likely to be geographical than occupational. →Few programs that are manipulated to produce rent for particularistic groups.	**Type II** Unorganized voters matter. Geographical location of support matters greatly for individual politicians. Money matters for individual politicians. →Targeting is more likely to be geographical than occupational. →Numerous programs that are manipulated to produce rent for particularistic groups.
	Large	**Type III** Organized voters matter greatly. Fragmented social security programs and targeted functional equivalents are likely. Geographical location of support matters least for political parties. Little need for individual politicians to raise money.	**Type IV** Organized voters matter greatly. Fragmented social security programs and targeted functional equivalents are most likely in this configuration. Geographical location of support matters for individual politicians. Money matters for individual politicians.

his party and emerge as a veto player. Unanimity rules in committees similarly equip dissenters in the party with veto power. Some legislative rules, however, have the opposite effect – namely, strengthening the party leader.

On the basis of a few simplifying assumptions, the preceding sections offer an institutional micrologic of the distributive programs most rewarding to politicians and political parties. Based on such a micrologic, it is possible to identify the kinds of social protection programs likely to be favored by politicians and political parties in different systems. Table 2.1 summarizes specific types of social protection most likely to be preferred in four different institutional contexts depending on how district magnitude and the relative importance of the personal vote combine.

STRUCTURAL LOGIC OF WELFARE POLITICS

Formulating a set of expectations about the preferences of parliamentary veto players is, however, different from formulating expectations about the final policy outcomes. In addition to parliamentary veto players' preferences, their configurations produce important political effects (Bonoli 2000; Weaver and Rockman 1993). In order to construct a structural logic of welfare politics, it is necessary that we simultaneously take into consideration parliamentary veto players' "preferences" and their "configurations." Configurations of parliamentary veto players, in turn, are determined by (i) specific government types; and (ii) the degree of party discipline. The first factor determines the number of political parties with veto power. The second factor determines the presence of intraparty veto players. What appears to be a complex process of simultaneously combining preferences and configurations can be done by looking at three factors: (i) government types (majoritarian, coalition, or minority governments); (ii) district magnitude (MMD versus SMD); and (iii) the relative importance of the personal vote (strong versus weak). Theoretically, twelve possible institutional combinations exist – $3 \times 2 \times 2$. In reality, the number of likely combinations is much smaller, because district magnitude is closely related to government types (Cox 1997; Grossman and Helpman 2005; Lijphart 1984; Taagepera and Shugart 1989).

Government Types and Distributive Implications

The numbers of veto players matter in thinking about political outcomes. Political scientists agree that they affect the likelihood of policy shifts: the greater the number of veto players, the more difficult it is for everyone to agree on a policy. A consensus exists that the number of *constitutional* veto players negatively affects the legislative capacity of a political system: the greater the number of constitutional veto players, the less likely is the passage of a universalistic social security program or a new tax policy (Immergut 1992; Maioni 1998; Steinmo and Watts 1995). There is no consensus, however, about the precise effects of *parliamentary* veto players. Some scholars argue that the number of veto players – whether constitutional or not – simply makes any shift from the status quo more difficult (Huber, Ragin, and Stephens 1993; Tsebelis 2002). Others argue just the opposite: the number of parliamentary veto players positively affects the growth of the welfare state and the state's tax capacity (Birchfield and Crepaz 1998; Crepaz 1998). This section takes a position closer to the latter group of scholars, albeit for very different reasons.[25] The claim here is the following: under specific conditions, multiple parliamentary veto players facilitate legislative compromise and make tax increases possible in ways that multiple constitutional veto players do not. Let me explain why.

The number of constitutional and nonconstitutional veto players affects politics in different ways. The concepts of *party identifiability* and *accountability* are instructive here.[26] Identifiability refers to the ease by which voters can identify the legislation of a particular policy as the responsibility of a specific party.

[25] Crepaz simply attributes the much more cooperative nature of *collective* – those located in the same institutional arena – to the presence of "face-to-face" interaction among this type of veto players.
[26] For the concept of party identifiability, see Mark Hallerberg (2002); for accountability, see Whitten and Powell (1993). Also see Strøm (2003).

Accountability refers to the ease by which voters can penalize a party. When identifiability and accountability are both high, political parties perceive the risk of introducing an unpopular policy to be very high, because the penalty of an electoral backlash is greatest. Identifiability is highest when the ruling party is the sole veto player – in both the constitutional and parliamentary sense. Identifiability is lowest in coalition governments with numerous political parties. Accountability is highest in SMD systems, because voters can vote out the ruling party. A big swing in the seat share that results in SMD systems increases the chance of electoral backlash against unpopular policies. In contrast, accountability is lower in MMD systems. When the district magnitude is large, the seat share of a party is more resilient.[27] Moreover, MMD systems are more likely to produce coalition governments, reducing voters' control over which parties should rule.

Paradoxically, as a result, the sole parliamentary veto player in a SMD system, who has the power to introduce any policy, operates within the confines of a very credible threat of an electoral backlash.[28] For this reason, Westminster-style democracies – political systems with one sole veto player – can only introduce taxes that are clearly earmarked to support broad-based comprehensive programs that benefit the majority.[29] In comparison, ruling parties in a coalition government – under MMD systems – find it much easier to introduce an unpopular policy such as a tax increase, because there is little need to worry about a possible electoral backlash.[30] Furthermore, political parties in a ruling coalition expect that they are likely to retain veto power over the use of increased tax revenue.[31] This expectation makes it more likely for coalition partners to agree on tax increases. The importance of the personal vote is also relevant. When individual politicians seek the personal vote, they face greater levels of accountability even under MMD systems. This creates a stronger incentive for them to block tax increases that might affect their core constituency groups or to provide tax loopholes and tax expenditures for their constituency groups. As a result, the overall tax capacity declines.

In sum, all things being equal, we can expect MMD systems with frequent coalition and minority governments to possess greater tax-extracting capacity

[27] See Rogowski and Kayser (2002) for a similar point.

[28] A good example is Margaret Thatcher's poll tax. As prime minister in a highly centralized Westminster system, she was capable of introducing a new poll tax. When she realized how unpopular it was, fearing electoral repercussions, she withdrew the new tax.

[29] Moe and Caldwell (1994) use a version of veto player theory to explain why Westminster-style democracies are likely to produce more universalistic programs. Their reasoning is different from mine. I'd like to thank Terry Moe for his comments on this point.

[30] Bawn and Rosenbluth (2006) develop an interesting argument about spending by coalition governments. They argue that coalition governments can spend more because each political party is less fiscally responsible than the single ruling party that has to internalize the cost of spending. Their argument mostly concerns spending and not taxation.

[31] Or at least, they expect the continuity of the status quo over the use of the new revenue; even they themselves lose veto power because of the likelihood that there would always be multiple parliamentary veto players.

than Westminster-style democracies.[32] Tax capacities are important in thinking about social protection, because they are likely to affect the generosity of public benefits. Indeed, as already shown in the Introduction, social spending levels and tax capacities strongly correlate. Furthermore, if Westminster-style democracies were to introduce new taxes for social protection purposes, the revenue would likely be used for universalistic programs. The same is not true in MMD systems due to the absence of credible threats of electoral backlash.

One qualification is the effect of the relative importance of the personal vote. As discussed already, the personal vote makes individual politicians the unit of distributive calculations rather than the party. The personal vote strengthens the tie between individual politicians and voters by making politicians highly dependent on their constituents (see Mitchell 2000). When politicians running in MMD systems seek the personal vote, they are likely to be averse to advocating policies that are unpopular with their constituent groups for fear of losing their support.

Predicting Different Patterns of Structural Logic of Social Protection

As mentioned earlier, theoretically speaking, we can think of twelve possible institutional combinations of different government types, district magnitude size, and the importance of the personal vote.[33] The actual number of likely combinations is much smaller. SMD systems, for instance, almost never produce coalition or minority governments (Cox 1997; Lijphart 1984; Taagepera and Shugart 1989). As a result, possible institutional combinations in SMD systems are (i) SMD/Majority Party Government/Strong Party (= weak personal vote); and (ii) SMD/Majority Party Government/Weak Party (= strong personal vote). MMD systems, in contrast, produce coalition and minority governments more frequently than majority party governments. For MMD systems, we need to consider all three government types. Because each government type can be combined either with strong party or weak party, six different combinations can exist in MMD systems. They include (iii) MMD/Minority Government/Strong Party; (iv) MMD/Minority Government/Weak Party; (v) MMD/Coalition Government/Strong Party; (vi) MMD/Coalition Government/Weak Party; (vii) MMD/Majority Party Government/Strong Party; and (viii) MMD/Majority Party Government/Weak Party.[34]

(i) SMD/Majority Party Government/Strong Party. A Westminster-style democracy falls into this category. Both identifiability and accountability are

[32] Certainly, when the number of constitutional veto players is large, even coalition governments might face difficulties in introducing an unpopular policy. For instance, a constitutional arrangement such as national referendum can vote down a new tax policy.
[33] In order to simplify the argument, I will assume that the parliament is the only constitutional veto player.
[34] For the reasons identified later in this section, of the seven configurations, the following two sets of configurations share similar effects. The first set consists of three configurations that share weak party – (ii), (v), and (vii). The second set consists of (iv) and (vi).

highest in this combination. In spite of its monopoly of veto power in the parliament, the ruling party needs to be aware of the electoral consequences of unpopular policies. New taxes, tax increases on the majority, and any market-restricting policies that protect particularistic interests at the expense of unorganized consumers can backfire at the polls. In sum, the ruling party in this combination is most likely to refrain from new taxes, tax increases, and market-restricting functional equivalents. It also means that any increases in taxes can only be justified when they provide benefits for the majority. For this reason, governments in this category are likely to possess (a) relatively small tax capacities; (b) universalistic social security programs; (c) relatively meager social security benefits; and (d) more comprehensive and market-based functional equivalents (rather than market-restricting ones).[35] Strong party also means that the ruling party will be more responsive to demands from competitive districts rather than safe seats.

(ii) SMD/Majority Party Government/Weak Party. When the party is weak, the ruling party becomes more like a coalition of parties than a unified party due to the rise of intraparty veto players. The capacity of the ruling party to make bold policy shifts decreases drastically. While resembling a coalition government in this sense, the high degree of identifiability and accountability in this combination reduces the tax-extractive capacity of this type of government. As for the distributive bias, intraparty players tilt the overall social protection system to the advantage of (a) groups that pay off individual politicians; and (b) safe seats (= influential senior politicians' districts). Social security benefits are likely to be meager, whereas geographically targeted benefits for safe seats will be abundant.

In spite of its SMD system, the weak party in this configuration creates a lot of similarities with two other configurations that also include the weak party: (vi) MMD/Coalition Government/Weak Party; and (viii) MMD/Majority Party Government/Weak Party.

(iii) MMD/Minority Government/Strong Party. Party identifiability is high while accountability is low in this configuration. Although a high degree of identifiability results due to the fact that there is only one ruling party, low accountability means that, with the consent of some opposition parties, this government can implement unpopular policies such as tax increases. Similarly, low accountability and the distributive bias in favor of organized groups – two characteristics of MMD systems – make it possible for ruling parties in this category to use market-restricting regulations as functional equivalents to protect their core constituent groups even when such regulations lead to higher consumer prices.

Although all parties in this system cater to the needs of organized constituent groups, the minority position of the ruling party prevents it from only benefiting

---

[35] For instance, tax benefits for private welfare are more comprehensive and market based than regulatory control over the number of pharmacies to protect the livelihood of small business owners.

its own core constituent groups. This happens in two ways. The minority position forces the ruling party to offer benefits to the core constituent groups of
the opposition parties. It can also counteract the tendencies for fragmented and
targeted forms of social protection that arise from MMD when the ruling party is
likely to propose more comprehensive forms of social protection whose benefits
extend to supporters of some of the opposition parties. In other words, generous universalistic benefits can emerge in this category in spite of the fact that
MMD systems do not by themselves favor universalistic programs. Governments
in this category also enjoy stronger tax capacity compared to governments in the
SMD/Majority Government/Strong Party category. And, as a result, they can
finance more generous universalistic benefits.

(iv) MMD/Minority Government/Weak Party. A weak party basically makes
this configuration similar to the MMD/Coalition Government/Weak Party configuration. A weak party makes the ruling party a coalition of individual politicians, each of whom is accountable to their own core constituency groups.
The weak party perpetuates the orientation toward fragmented social protection schemes, whose costs are passed on to unorganized voters. The minority
position of the ruling party, however, forces it to seek compromise from the
opposition parties. Core constituent groups of at least one opposition party get
to be included in the coalition of interests that support the government. Although
the possibility of introducing more comprehensive benefits increases, tax capacity
is likely to be lower than in the previous configuration due to the weak party. Any
cost increases that affect core constituency groups of the ruling party politicians
are thus likely to be difficult to legislate.

(v) MMD/Coalition Government/Strong Party. Identifiability and accountability are both low. Assuming that all other factors are equal, tax and social
security contribution levels are likely to be high. As a result, governments in
this category can finance generous public benefits. Political parties in the ruling coalition all have incentives to provide forms of social protection targeted
at their constituent groups. As a result, social security programs are likely to be
fragmented along occupational lines. Market-restricting regulations as functional
equivalents targeted at specific constituent groups are highly likely. Not only do
political parties have the incentives to adopt such functional equivalents, but they
also face little chance of electoral backlash from unorganized voters who bear the
cost of such regulations.

(vi) MMD/Coalition Government/Weak Party. Although party identifiability
is low, individual politicians face high levels of accountability due to the importance of the personal vote. The personal vote means that individual politicians
rely heavily on the support of particularistic groups. Individual politicians in
the ruling coalition are likely to oppose any policy that imposes costs on their
constituent groups for fear of being voted out in favor of someone else from
their party. (Remember they face intraparty electoral competition.) The need to

finance one's own campaign also creates strong incentives for politicians to trade policy favors with money.

As a result, this combination is likely to produce distributive advantages for even more narrowly organized groups than in the previous combination. The degree of fragmentation in the social security system is likely to be much greater than under the same combination with strong parties. Likewise, the use of market-restricting functional equivalents is even more likely than in the previous combination. Groups aligned with influential individual politicians in the ruling coalition are expected to get the most out of the government. Tax capacity is likely to be lower than coalition governments with stronger parties.

(vii) MMD/Majority Party Government/Strong Party. In this configuration, the party leadership is the sole veto player. This configuration, nonetheless, differs from the first configuration – a Westminster-style system: identifiability is as high as in the first configuration but accountability is lower. Since there are more political parties in MMD systems, the ruling party can stay in power by forming a coalition with other parties even when it loses its absolute majority. As a result, tax capacity is likely to be higher than in the first configuration.

As with other MMD systems, this configuration is biased in favor of organized groups of voters. When the ruling party relies on the support of multiple organized groups, a highly fragmented social security system and the reliance on market-restricting functional equivalents are possible outcomes. In this case, the pattern of politics will resemble that of coalition governments with strong parties – the (v) configuration. When the ruling party relies on a few large organized groups, the degree of fragmentation is likely to be significantly lower. Even in that case, market-restricting policies are likely to be used to provide protection.

(viii) MMD/Majority Party Government/Weak Party. This configuration produces a result very similar to the one in the (vi) configuration – MMD/Coalition/Weak Party. Although a single party holds the absolute majority in the parliament, the party itself is fraught with intraparty veto players. The distributive bias favors highly particularistic groups closely linked to individual politicians – especially the influential ones in the party. Social security programs are likely to be highly fragmented. The ruling party is also likely to advocate market-restricting functional equivalents to deliver targeted forms of protection. As explained in (vi), intraparty veto players are likely to block any policy that negatively affects their core constituent groups and those groups that pay them off. Tax capacity is likely to be even lower than the (vi) configuration because individual politicians in the ruling party rely on the personal vote.

ACCOUNTING FOR CROSS-NATIONAL VARIATIONS IN SOCIAL
PROTECTION: PRELIMINARY EVIDENCE

This chapter has argued so far that the number and the type of veto players, district magnitude, and the relative strength of the personal vote can predict patterns of welfare politics. This section applies the micrologic presented in this chapter to account for the qualitative variations observed in Chapter 1.

Table 2.2 shows how advanced industrial countries compare on all of the institutional dimensions relevant in predicting the pattern of social protection.[36] Although this chapter has identified eight possible institutional configurations, most advanced industrial countries more or less cluster into four types of institutional configurations. These four clusters, this section demonstrates, roughly explain the cross-national variations in the degree of fragmentation of social security programs, the use of market-restricting functional equivalents, and geographical targeting.

SMD/Majority Party Government/Strong Party

The first institutional category consists of SMD systems with governments ruled by a single party with an absolute parliamentary majority. This category is what scholars often call a Westminster-style democracy. Based on Table 2.2, we can identify Australia, Canada, the United Kingdom, and the United States as SMD systems (Column I).[37] Only Canada and the United Kingdom fulfill the definitions of the Westminster democracy – that is, very few constitutional veto players, government ruled by a single party with the absolute majority.[38] Australia comes close enough to be included in the group, although Australia typically has more than one ruling party due to its strong bicameralism. The United States does not belong to this group because of its weak parties and a highly decentralized political structure – in other words, many constitutional veto players. Germany has a median district magnitude of one but is not a SMD system. Germany has a mixed system of SMD and MMD (PR). In Germany, the MMD-based tier is the dominant one.[39]

---

[36] The figures used here are the averages during the postwar years – roughly from the late-1940s through to the mid-1990s – as a way of capturing the institutional characteristics that were dominant for most of the postwar years rather than on the most recent characteristics. In other words, in the case of Japan, this means focusing on the electoral system in place until the reform in 1994 rather than the current system. France is omitted from the figure because the French electoral system changed so frequently that it cannot be captured with one set of figures.

[37] I do not have all the data necessary to include New Zealand in the comparison.

[38] Although 13 percent of all Canadian postwar governments were minority governments, this figure is not high.

[39] Postwar Germany has adopted a mixed electoral system, whereby some parliamentary seats are allocated through single-member districts while the remainder is allocated via proportional representation system that uses closed party lists. Although the median district magnitude of the lower chamber – Bundestag – equals one in Germany, it is fundamentally different from other pure SMD systems. Unlike pure SMD systems, where all representatives are elected in SMD districts, only half of the German lower house representatives are elected in SMD. The other half are elected in PR-based Länder districts. The PR tier uses closed party lists, and most candidates who run for SMD are also listed on the PR party lists. The overall seat allocation is designed to reflect the vote share in the PR tier. This feature of the German electoral system makes it much more like other MMD systems that produce more proportional results. The local-level party nominates SMD candidates, and party convention at the Länder level determines how PR candidates are

TABLE 2.2 *A Comparative Table on Institutional Dimensions*

	I Number of Parties in Government	II Frequency of Majority Party Government	III Frequency of Minority Government	IV Constitutional Veto Players	V Mean District Magnitude	VI Strength of Personal Vote
Australia	1.6	36	0	3	1	4
Austria	1.8	33	2	1	13	5
Belgium	2.21	6.3	3	1	5	5
Canada	1	100	13	2	1	6
Denmark	2.1	29	82	0	9	5
Finland	3.5	0	7	1	13	4
France 4				0		
France 5				1		
Germany	2.36	0	0	4	1	5
Italy	2.78	8	20	1	17	3
Japan	1.3	84	10	1	4	1
Netherlands	3.3	0	0	1	150	5
Norway	1.55	67	50	0	7	6
Sweden	1.55	63	69	0	11	6
Switzerland	3.74	0	0	6	6	5
United Kingdom	1	100	0	0	1	6
United States	1.64	36	0	5	1	1

Column I: Number of parties in government, based on online data from Robert Franzese's website.

Columns II and III: Percentage of majority and minority governments as yearly average (based on data from George Tsebelis's web site).

Column IV: Huber, Ragin, and Stephens (1993).

Column V: Cox (1997).

Column VI: Rankings on the basis of Carey and Shugart (1994), Iversen and Soskice (2002), and Tatebayashi (2004).

The empirical data presented in Chapter 1 offer evidence for the validity of the predictions derived in this chapter. As predicted, this group of countries – Australia, Canada, and the United Kingdom – possesses universalistic social security programs (see Table 1.2 in Chapter 1). Also as predicted, tax capacity of countries in this group is relatively small and so are the benefit levels of social security programs (see Figure 0.1 in the Introduction and Table 1.1 in Chapter 1). The United States differs from this group in its lack of a national health care program. In addition to its numerous constitutional veto players, weak parties in the United States decentralize the political system by giving rise to intraparty veto players (see Columns V and VI in Table 2.2). Indeed, scholars of comparative welfare states have attributed the absence of national health care in the United States to its decentralized political system by means of careful comparative case studies (Immergut 1992; Maioni 1998; Steinmo and Watts 1995).

As suggested by the structural logic, functional equivalents based on market-restricting regulations are much rarer in this group of countries than in MMD-based countries (see Table 1.3 in Chapter 1). Functional equivalents favored by SMD systems tend to be market-expanding programs, as seen in the relatively large shares of private health care and private pension market (Table 1.6). Compared to private pension products in MMD systems, private pension products in SMD countries tend to be managed competitively by the market principle.[40] There is not much occupationally targeted protection, in contrast to that found in many MMD-based countries.

The structural logic suggests that in SMD systems we can expect geographic targeting in lieu of the occupational targeting of social protection. SMD systems with strong parties can be expected to deliver more social protection to marginal districts, whereas SMD systems with weaker parties can be expected to divert more benefits to regions where the intraparty veto players – whether individual politicians or intraparty factions – get their votes. The comparative data on social protection provided in Chapter 1 are not sufficiently detailed to say anything conclusive about geographical targeting.[41] It is nonetheless noteworthy that, despite

---

ranked on the list. As a result, organized groups within Länder gain influence over political parties. Distributive incentives of political parties thus will be oriented toward organized groups as in other MMD systems. This means that fragmented social insurance schemes are likely to result. Indeed, Germany is one of the countries whose pension and health care insurances schemes are most fragmented. Note that because of the strong bicameralism in Germany, the upper chamber – Bundesrat – is also a constitutional veto player in Germany. Because the Bundesrat is based on regional representation, it serves as another layer of institution that empowers groups that are organized well in Länder. In other words, no welfare program has a chance of legislative success in Germany unless such organized groups give their consent.

[40] This is not unrelated to the fact that financial regulations differ between MMD systems and SMD systems. The logic is the same as the one developed for the likelihood of market-restricting regulations. Organized groups with influence over political parties are capable of securing "insider protection" in MMD systems. See Gourevitch and Shinn (2005).

[41] Quantitative figures on the size of public works, public sector employment, and agricultural subsidies per se do not really tell us if they have been used for the purpose of geographical targeting or more occupational group–specific targeting associated with MMD systems. A definitive answer requires a careful in-depth study of these programs, which is beyond the scope of this book. It is

the fact that SMD countries generally spend less on social security items and offer relatively meager benefits, they are among the most generous providers of agricultural subsidies. Certainly, Canada, the United Kingdom, and the United States spend more per capita on agricultural workers than the OECD average (Table 1.4). The structural logic approach developed here suggests that in a SMD with a strong party system as in the United Kingdom, the presence of rural districts with swing voters may have led to high levels of agricultural subsidies. In fact, McGillivray (2004) has shown in the British case that a "SMD system combined with strong party" provides more protection to marginal districts regardless of which party is in power. In contrast to a country like the United Kingdom with a highly centralized polity and strong party, the United States is highly decentralized and its party is weak. Pork provided by influential individual politicians from rural districts or the president's electoral calculations are likely to be behind high figures for agricultural subsidies in the United States.[42]

MMD/Coalition Government/Strong Party

This category includes countries such as Austria, Belgium, Germany, the Netherlands, and Switzerland. Of this group, we might expect Switzerland to differ from the rest of the countries because Switzerland has a very different constitutional structure. Indeed, it possesses the largest number of constitutional veto players of all advanced democracies (Column IV, Table 2.2). My structural logic predicts that for those countries other than Switzerland, we can expect occupationally fragmented social security programs and market-restricting functional equivalents. The structural logic also predicts that the social security benefits in these countries are likely to be generous, because their low levels of identifiability and accountability make it easier to raise state revenue to pay for the benefits. In fact, as shown in Table 1.1 and Table 1.2 in Chapter 1, this group of countries provides (i) the most generous public welfare benefits; (ii) the most fragmented social security systems; and (iii) market-restricting functional equivalents. (The exception here is the Netherlands, which, for idiosyncratic reasons, has a universalistic pension scheme.[43])

MMD/Minority Government/Strong Party

This category consists of minority governments in MMD systems. Table 2.2 identifies Denmark, Norway, and Sweden in this institutional category. They all have large district magnitude, few constitutional veto players, and a strong

precisely because the seemingly similar programs can be used for different electoral purposes that detailed country-specific information is necessary for a proper comparison.

[42] Obviously, malapportionment is another possible explanation. If rural areas hold more votes, their votes become cheaper for politicians and parties to "purchase." Some studies indicate the SMD system leads to an overrepresentation of rural votes (Rodden 2005).

[43] Lynch (2006) provides an excellent account of the development of pension programs in the Netherlands.

party vote (Columns V, IV, and VI in Table 2.2, respectively). They also stand out for the frequency of minority governments (Column III). As the structural logic predicts, they all have highly universalistic programs of social protection. Existing case studies also support my structurally induced micrologic. Huber and Stephens (2001) provide an excellent account of how the social democratic minority governments had to propose universalistic social security programs in order to entice the Agrarian Parties in their respective governments to sign onto their legislative proposals for social security expansion. Swenson (2002) in turn, reveals that many of the legislative initiatives by the Social Democrats enjoyed the consent of the employers – and hence the Conservative Parties. They all have universalistic pension schemes and national health care systems, and also allocate their social spending fairly evenly to different program areas (see Chapter 1). Their public benefits are among the most generous.[44]

What my analysis highlights is the following. As a subcategory of MMD-based systems, these countries also share similarities with other MMD-based systems in their use of direct state involvement in protecting and providing jobs through a variety of functional equivalents. In contrast to other MMD systems, this group of countries relies less on anticompetitive regulation as a means for social protection, but it relies more than SMD systems, as predicted by my structural logic.

MMD/Coalition or Majority Party Government/Weak Party

For reasons identified earlier, the two combinations of MMD/Coalition Government/Weak Party and MMD/Majority Party Government/Weak Party are similar. Finland and Italy fall into the former category and Japan falls into the latter category. (Unless otherwise noted, I will refer to Italy and Japan prior to electoral reforms in the 1990s, because the cross-national comparisons are based on welfare programs developed prior to the reforms.) Japan provides an unambiguous case where the personal vote is important (Column VI, Table 2.2). Finland and Italy also rely on the personal vote albeit not to the same degree as Japan.[45] The party is much weaker in Japan than it is in the other two countries, making Japan *the* prototype of a country that combines MMD and a weak party system.[46] As expected, these three countries possess fragmented social security programs along occupational lines, which are associated with MMD systems

---

[44] Clearly, the predominance of the Social Democratic Party is relevant. Of interest here is that the Labor Party in SMD countries has not been able to offer as generous public benefits because of the structural constraint on their tax capacities due to their high identifiability and accountability.

[45] It is reasonable to think that the party is weaker in Italy than in Finland, although the measurements developed by Carey and Shugart (1994) do not capture it. The electoral rules in Italy make it possible for candidates from different parties to form an electoral alliance. It is not controversial to assume that such an arrangement weakens the party. See Katz (1986) on Italy and Raunio (2006) on Finland. See Kitschelt (2000) for discussion of clientelistic parties.

[46] Japan's medium-sized districts and the need for personalized electoral campaigns – exacerbated by Japan's single nontransferable vote (SNTV) – motivated individual politicians to seek benefits for their political machines. The Japanese electoral institutions will be discussed in greater detail in Chapter 3.

without minority governments. Table 1.2 in Chapter 1 has shown that Finland's social security pension, in fact, is much more fragmented than that of other Scandinavian countries with which it is normally grouped in comparative studies. The social security programs in Japan and Italy are among the most occupationally fragmented. The importance of the personal vote in this category makes it important for individual politicians to provide favors to societal groups in exchange for money and votes. It is noteworthy that, as Chapter 1 reported, these three countries scored relatively high on public works and anticompetitive administrative intervention, both of which enable the selective provision of social protection. As argued earlier, both public works and administrative intervention provide good conduits of "rents" for constituent groups. Finland and Japan also score high on their use of agricultural subsidies. Agricultural subsidies permit the ruling parties to target benefits at specific occupational groups (that is, farmers) either in specific locations or by crop types.[47]

As for state revenue capacity, the fact that both Italy and Japan are notorious for chronic fiscal deficits indicates their difficulty in raising revenue. It is also noteworthy that although Finland's tax capacity is much higher, Finland's revenue capacity is lower than those of Denmark and Sweden. (Norway, due to its oil wealth, is not really comparable, strictly speaking.)

Four Types of Welfare Capitalism

Most importantly, my structural logic approach reveals four institutional clusters of advanced industrial societies and explains why each of these clusters has a distinctive welfare system. The structural logic approach explains cross-national variations in the fragmentation in social security programs as well as qualitative differences in functional equivalents. By including a full range of functional equivalents into the scope of comparison, my study illuminates the presence of four types of welfare capitalism. The four institutional configurations identified in this section correspond to these four worlds of welfare capitalism. They might be

---

[47] Due to its districting, Finland rewards political parties that win strong localized support rather than those that attract support evenly across the nation, unlike in other Scandinavian MMD systems. Furthermore, unlike in other Scandinavian systems that possess strong parties, individual candidates are much more important in the Finnish system. The national party leadership plays no role in candidate nomination, and voters vote for individual candidates on an open party list. As a result, candidates run personalized campaigns and rely on personally raised funds. The relative representation merit of rural regions and the weakness of parties provide a viable explanation as to why agricultural subsidies in Finland are much more significant than other MMD systems and other Scandinavian countries, in particular. Agricultural votes were highly organized votes in most constituencies, and the importance of the personal vote in Japan made individual politicians seek agricultural support. A large number of politicians in the ruling conservative party thus acted as agricultural lobbyists, making the dynamics of politics over social protection distinctively different from other MMDs where strong parties formed coalition or minority governments. Unlike in governments with strong parties as coalition partners, where parties aggregate intraparty distributive preferences and negotiate with one another over the allocation of benefits and costs, Japan's majority government headed by a weak party was more vulnerable to lobbying from intraparty veto players.

called, in the order discussed in this section: (a) universalistic pro-market welfare states; (d) fragmented generous welfare states; (c) market-conforming generous universalistic welfare states; and (d) fragmented statist welfare states.

Certainly, the evidence provided here remains preliminary. Nonetheless, this preliminary comparison suggests that my structural logic captures an important aspect of the distributive politics in advanced industrial societies. A fuller analysis requires a careful collection of both quantitative and qualitative data. Consider agricultural subsidies. They can be used either as a distributive tool for geographical targeting or as a tool for occupational targeting. A more precise analysis thus requires in-depth case studies that determine how different policies are implemented and the political intentions behind the introduction of specific tools.

ADDITIONAL LAYERS OF COMPLEXITY: NONPARLIAMENTARY
(CORPORATIST AND BUREAUCRATIC) VETO PLAYERS

Under specific configurations of parliamentary veto players, the third type of veto players – "nonparliamentary veto players" – can arise. Nonparliamentary veto players consist of interest groups and bureaucratic actors. In order to understand who prevails in a specific polity, it is necessary that we understand when and how interest groups and bureaucratic actors gain veto power. Let me begin by discussing interest groups first, and then proceed to discuss bureaucratic actors.

Interest Groups as Corporatist Veto Players

Political scientists have noted that some governments invite representatives from peak-level interest groups such as labor federations and business organizations to formally take part in the policy process. The direct participation of interest group representatives is generally referred to as corporatism or neocorporatism (Schmitter and Lehmbruch eds. 1979). This kind of interest representation can be labeled as "extraparliamentary" participation, to be contrasted with interest representation by political parties. Whether a country adopts a formal extraparliamentary mode of representation is a function of district magnitude. Direct participation of interest groups is most likely to occur when the district magnitude is large. As I have already discussed, politicians and parties seek the support of well-organized groups under multimember districts. On matters that are vital to their core constituency groups, parliamentary veto players might "delegate back" the legislative and regulatory functions to their core constituency groups.[48]

The relative importance of the personal vote, in turn, influences the type of interest groups most likely to participate via extraparliamentary channels. Peak-level encompassing associations – to use Mancur Olson's term – rather than particularistic groups are likely to gain direct access to policy process when the

---

[48] The delegation literature characterizes voters as principals and politicians as voters' agents. Direct participation by core constituent groups thus consists of the principals taking important matters into their hands.

personal vote is unimportant – and thus the party is strong. For the reasons already specified earlier in this chapter, the personal vote emboldens particularistic rent seekers capable of "buying" the support of individual politicians – under both MMD and SMD systems. When politicians rely on the personal vote, they have more incentive to grant particularistic groups direct access to the policy process. Furthermore, strong parties can legislate whatever agreements the key encompassing associations reach, but weak parties cannot. When the party is weak, intraparty veto players can veto the party leaders' pursuit of collective interest on behalf of particularistic interest groups.

In short, peak associations such as a national labor federation and employers' associations most likely emerge as veto players under the combination of MMD systems and strong party. In other words, what political scientists call neocorporatism is much more likely to develop in countries with MMD systems and strong party (see Katzenstein 1985).[49]

Bureaucratic Veto Players

Institutionally speaking, bureaucrats lack any formal veto power. However, when ruling parties delegate legislative tasks to bureaucrats – as happens frequently in some parliamentary democracies – bureaucrats draft actual legislative proposals.[50] Bureaucrats gain agenda-setting power – which is akin to veto power[51] – when the ruling parties lack legislative capacities and delegate legislative tasks to bureaucrats.[52] Bureaucrats, as first movers, thereby gain agenda-setting power to eliminate undesirable policy options from the draft proposals. Certainly, the ruling parties have the legal authority to veto bureaucratic proposals that they do not like. Yet insofar as political parties lack the ability to draft alternative legislative proposals, the bureaucrats' advantage as first mover remains.[53]

Bureaucratic agenda-setting power is more likely to be effective when (a) there are multiple "principals" (see Hallerberg 2002; Strøm 2003; Tsebelis 2002); and (b) institutional checks such as referendum, strong judiciary, and information disclosure laws are absent. When there are multiple principals and/or the means

---

[49] In coalition and minority governments that are likely to emerge under MMD, delegation of power to encompassing associations also increases the likelihood of legislative compromise on matters upon which the encompassing associations agree. In minority governments, such extraparliamentary mechanisms to build compromises can be very efficient.

[50] Most of the American politics literature on delegation concerns the policy implementation process, because the United States is unique in that individual legislators do the legislating.

[51] Agenda setters present the first proposal, taking into consideration all the other veto players' preferences. An agenda setter "can consider the winset of the others as his constraint, and select from it the outcome he prefers" (Tsebelis 2002, 34).

[52] The existence of party-affiliated policy think tanks and the number of staff available to each politician, for instance, serve as indicators of the level of legislative capacity of parliamentary actors.

[53] Although the principal-agent literature discusses numerous ways in which the principal (politicians) might monitor and punish the agent (bureaucrats), it generally sees information asymmetry between the principal and the agent as beneficial to the latter. See the rational choice literature cited in footnote 55.

of oversight is underdeveloped, however, bureaucratic power increases: weak parties – associated with the personal vote – enhance bureaucratic power by eroding the capacity of the ruling party (or parties) to act as effective principals with veto power over bureaucrats.[54]

Bureaucratic Preferences

In countries where bureaucrats enjoy such conditions, it is necessary to understand how bureaucratic actors define their organizational interests and preferences.[55] Existing theories of societal actors' preferences are simply not applicable to bureaucratic organizations. Just as we made some simplifying assumptions about politicians, we can do the same with bureaucrats. Certainly, individual bureaucrats might have different reasons for joining the bureaucracy. Some of them may have been attracted to employment security or the idea of public service, whereas others may have been attracted to the prestige and power associated with elite bureaucracy. Regardless of the original motivations of individuals, it is reasonable to assume that most of them seek higher returns from their investment in their bureaucratic careers – be that higher lifetime earnings or better job opportunities after their bureaucratic career.[56]

The best way to make predictions about bureaucratic behavior is to identify the structure of personnel management practices in bureaucratic organizations.[57] Personnel management practices for career officials vary from country to country. Some countries fill senior government positions with career civil servants, whereas others rely primarily on a revolving door of political appointees. Even

---

[54] Coalition governments increase the number of veto players within the government, but, as far as political parties are strong cohesive parties, each ministry is supervised by one principal.

[55] The rational choice approach tends to be less interested in bureaucratic policy preferences per se than the question of effective delegation (Bawn 1995, 1997; Calvert, McCubbins, and Weingast 1989; Epstein and O'Halloran 1994, 1995, 1996, 1999; Horn 1995; Huber and Shipan 2000; Huber, Shipan, and Pfahler 2001; Lupia and McCubbins 1994; McCubbins, Noll, and Weingast 1987, 1989). Rather than asking how specific characteristics of bureaucratic organization might shape their policy preferences, the literature tries to identify the institutional arrangements that best align the behavior of bureaucratic agents with the wishes of their "principals." Or alternatively, it tries to attribute any feature of the bureaucratic organization to principals' preferences. The public choice school has been more interested in bureaucratic preferences but has had little to say about cross-national differences (Brennan and Buchanan 1980; Niskanen 1971). There also exist studies of bureaucratic attitudes and ideologies (Aberbach, Putnam, and Rockman 1981; Aberbach et al. 1990; Suleiman 1974). This group of studies do not seek an organizational basis of bureaucratic preferences as this study does. Heclo (1974) pays close attention to how specific missions define bureaucratic goals and policy preferences. I agree that specific missions assigned to career bureaucracy are important. I build upon Heclo (1974) by also looking into self-interested behaviors of bureaucratic actors as a result of intended or unintended incentives built into the personnel management practice.

[56] Income incentives are important motivations of individual bureaucrats (Arnold 1979).

[57] I take a view that what we consider interests or behavior of the bureaucratic organization is rooted in individual-level incentives within the organization. In this vein, organizational culture, for instance, can be viewed as a function of the organizational structure of the bureaucracy (Hall 1986, 9). Also see Carpenter (2001).

among those that rely on career civil servants, recruitment methods can further differ. Some countries recruit their staff based on highly selective and competitive civil service examinations, whereas others do not. Some countries hire people with adequate specialized training and background for specific jobs, whereas other countries hire "generalists" and train them internally.[58] Even among bureaucracies that rely on internal labor markets, their internal personnel rotation and promotion practices may differ. In some national bureaucracies, career civil servants experience frequent interministerial transfers, whereas in other bureaucracies such lateral movements are extremely limited.

These distinctions have important implications for the preferences and behavior of civil servants. Political appointees are likely to be influenced by their own partisan commitments and their political aspirations to a greater degree than career civil servants. The fundamental difference between political appointees and career officials lies in the fact that the former need to look for a new job in the near future, whereas the latter do not. Political appointees are more likely to be motivated solely by personal calculations than are career bureaucrats, who are likely to develop collective interests.

Think here, for example, of a senior official who has been appointed by a fiscally conservative ruling party and who aspires to be appointed to a cabinet position in the future. She knows that she has no chance of staying on if the fiscal conservative party loses in the next elections. But if the party wins, it will appoint officials based on their partisan commitment and competence. The senior official in this example has an incentive to undermine the authority, budget, and jurisdiction of the agency that she oversees in order to advance her partisan reputation. She is not likely to care much about civil servants' pensions and other benefits since she does not plan to stay on the government payroll for all her career.

Senior officials of a bureaucratic organization with a rigid internal labor market develop very different incentives. In such a system, a bureaucrat's future within the government – both promotion and salary – is determined according to internal rules of the bureaucracy. Bureaucrats – high and low – collectively share an interest in improving opportunities for promotion, wages, and benefits for civil servants. Moreover, when salary increases are only possible with seniority-based, rather than performance-based promotions, every member of the organization develops an equal interest in expanding the number of managerial positions. Career bureaucrats in such an organization have an incentive to advocate policy options that increase managerial positions.

Obviously, in order to finance more managerial positions, bureaucrats need to seek more money – hence a greater budgetary allocation. These bureaucrats have an incentive to propose social protection programs that maximize the number of well-paid managerial jobs under their control. Budget maximization per se

---

[58] Obviously, the type of national labor markets matters. When external labor markets for specialists and professionals are underdeveloped, internal labor markets offer the only option for the bureaucracy.

captures little of what bureaucrats might propose as preferred policies (see Blais and Dion eds. 1991). For instance, the creation of quasi-government entities provides ways to increase de facto bureaucratic managerial positions. What might at first appear as an outsourcing of bureaucratic jobs to outside agencies can, in fact, benefit bureaucrats. By retaining jurisdiction and hence oversight over quasi-government agencies, bureaucrats can gain *more* discretion on personnel matters in the new agencies.

In sum, the precise organizational context of recruitment, promotion, and remuneration shapes (i) individual incentives; and (ii) the unit where individual incentives coalesce with collective incentives. Unlike societal actors' preferences, which change as socioeconomic conditions change, bureaucratic preferences remain stable because the organizational features – and their legal foundations – remain relatively stable. For this reason, bureaucratic preferences constitute part of the broad structural logic of a particular polity.

CONCLUSION

This chapter has presented the core argument of this book. My structural argument, while building upon the rich literature on electoral systems and their effects, offers a framework to explain qualitative differences in both orthodox social security programs and their functional equivalents. As demonstrated in this chapter, this framework does a better job of situating Japan in a broader comparative context. In so doing, it also explains previously neglected sets of similarities and differences among advanced industrial societies. Most importantly, this chapter has shown that there are some consistent patterns in which different countries resort to targeted or market-restricting methods of social protection rather than universalistic or market-conforming methods of social protection.

3

Historical Patterns of Structural Logic in Postwar Japan

Chapter 2 has demonstrated that it is possible to construct a structural logic of social protection by identifying the configuration of veto players and the specific institutional constraints on their preferences (that is, district magnitude and the relative importance of the personal vote). This chapter applies my structural logic approach to explain welfare state development in Japan. In contrast to the more comparative orientation of the previous chapter, this chapter claims that my structural logic approach can explain two sets of variations in policy outcomes within the same country: (i) cross-policy variations during the same period; and (ii) historical variations. To put it simply, cross-policy variations can be understood as a reflection of the relative power of different actors and their preferences. In other words, programs sought by influential actors have a better chance of being adopted, whereas programs they oppose have a worse chance. My structural logic explains cross-policy variations by predicting which actors have the most power in a specific institutional context. Granted this approach, it follows that policy shifts in social protection happen when (i) the veto player configuration changes; and/or (ii) veto players' preferences change. Historical shifts in welfare politics can be understood in terms of the shifts in the power distribution within a polity and the changes in the preferences of the veto players.

This chapter proceeds in four sections. Section 1 chronicles historical shifts in the government type, district magnitude, and the relative importance of the personal vote that occurred in postwar Japan. By doing so, it identifies four different combinations that roughly correspond to four distinctive historical periods: (i) from 1951 to 1989;[1] (ii) from 1989 to 1993;[2] (iii) from 1993 to 1996;[3] and

---

[1] From the time when the end of the Allied Occupation was determined until the LDP lost its absolute majority in the Upper House in the Upper House elections in 1989.
[2] From the LDP's loss of the absolute majority in the Upper House in 1989 until the LDP's fall from power in 1993.
[3] From the formation of the non-LDP coalition government in 1993 until the Lower House elections in 1996.

(iv) from 1996 to the present.[4] Later sections apply my structural logic to explain the characteristics of distributive politics that emerged in each of the four periods. Section 2 describes in great detail how the combination of MMD and SNTV shaped politicians' distributive incentives and decentralized the Liberal Democratic Party (LDP). Section 3 explains how some of the legislative rules further decentralized the decision-making process by granting bureaucrats with agenda-setting power. Section 4 explains how the shifts in the structural logic that occurred in 1989, 1993, and 1996 each pushed Japanese welfare politics in a different direction.

FOUR HISTORICAL PERIODS

Table 3.1 chronicles historical shifts in (i) government types; (ii) district magnitude; (iii) the relative importance of the personal vote; and (iv) legislative rules in postwar Japan. For the sake of simplicity, Table 3.1 omits the information on the constitutional structure – the fifth important institutional dimension – because it remains constant throughout the postwar period.

Historical Shifts in the Government Type

The 1951 decision to end the Allied Occupation within a year marked a key turning point in postwar veto player configuration.[5] During the occupation, the Supreme Commander of Allied Powers (SCAP) had the ultimate say on Japanese legislation. The General Headquarters (GHQ) was involved in every detail of government. In this respect, the GHQ was the ultimate veto player. With the decision to end the occupation, veto power was transferred back to the Japanese Diet. This decision initiated the long conservative party dominance of post-occupation Japan. Before the conservative political parties merged in 1955 to create the LDP, its predecessors, the Liberal Party and the Democratic Party, ruled either alone or in coalition.[6]

Since 1955, the LDP has for the most part ruled Japan alone with an absolute majority. Constitutionally, postwar Japan has always been a parliamentary democracy with a unitary state and a bicameral Diet consisting of the Lower House (Shugiin) and the Upper House (Sangiin).[7] The LDP possessed an

---

[4] From the formation of a new Cabinet after the Lower House elections in 1996 through to the current period.

[5] The Cold War changed the context in which the U.S. government approached Japan. The American occupation of Japan changed its initial pro-labor position to favor conservative parties. This shift is generally referred to as the "Reversed Course" (see Dower 1999; Duus 1998). Chapter 4 offers an overview of the immediate postwar period.

[6] Calder (1988), Kohno (1997), and Thayer (1969) offer brief historical accounts of Japan's party system in the immediate postwar period.

[7] The Japanese Upper House is capable of vetoing decisions by the Lower House. The Lower House can override the Upper House veto with a two-thirds vote. When there is disagreement between the two Houses, the Lower House prevails over budget, foreign treaties, and the appointment of the prime minister. Only the Lower House has the prerogative to call for a no-confidence vote in the government.

TABLE 3.1. *Historical Shifts in Japan's Political Structure*

Years	Government Type	Electoral System	Personal Vote	Legislative Rules		
				Diet/Cabinet	Bureaucratic Delegation	Extraparliamentary Organs
1945–1951	The Allied Occupation of Japan	After 1947, the medium-sized MMD with SNTV/plurality rule	Strong	Moderately strong committees	High	*shingikai*
1952–	Conservative coalition & one-party rule with absolute majority					
1955–1989	LDP founded in 1955 One-party rule with absolute majority (1), (2)	1983 – Upper House adopts closed PR list for its nationwide district				
1989–1993	Partial minority government (3)					
1993–1996	Coalition governments (4), (5)	1994 – Lower House adopts a mixed system (SMD and PR)				
1996–present	Coalition governments (6), (7), (8), (9)	2001 – Upper House PR tier switches to an open-list method	Weaker	2001 – Stronger Cabinet Office	1999 – Partial reduction in legislative delegation	The creation of more top-down councils led by the prime minister

Notes: (1) From 1974 to 1980, LDP loses enough seats to control all Diet committees, and some chairmanships fall into the opposition's hands. (2) From 1983 to 1986 – LDP–New Liberal Club coalition; however, for part of this period, the LDP possessed the absolute majority. (3) From 1989 to 1993, LDP loses the absolute majority in the Upper House. (4) From August 1993 to June 1994 – non-LDP coalition of eight parties. (5) From July 1994 to November 1996 – LDP-led coalition (LDP, Japan Socialist Party, and Komeito). (6) From January 1999 – coalition of LDP and Liberal Party. (7) In October 1999, Komeito joins the coalition. (8) In 2000, coalition of LDP, Conservative Party, and Komeito. (9) November 2003, LDP-Komeito coalition. See Chapters 8 and 9 for more details of each period.

absolute majority in both Houses for most of the period between 1955 and 1989. In the face of the constitutional concentration of power in the Diet, this means that the LDP was the only veto player in Japan during this period.

The LDP did not, however, always have an absolute majority in the two Houses. As Table 3.1 illustrates, post-occupation Japan experienced three government types: (i) majoritarian governments (led by the LDP); (ii) partial minority governments (whereby the LDP lacked an absolute majority in the Upper House); and (iii) coalition governments (with or without the LDP). Shifts from one government type to another, according to my structural logic approach, change the range of the most likely policy choices for social protection. As Chapter 2 argues, whether there is one party that possesses the absolute parliamentary majority determines the degree of party identifiability, whereas the district magnitude determines the degree of accountability. Different combinations of identifiability and accountability, in turn, make costly policies easier or more difficult to introduce.

Changes in the District Magnitude and the Personal Vote

My structural logic assumes that differences in the district magnitude or the relative importance of the personal vote, therefore, change the electoral strategies of politicians. Single-member districts, for instance, empower unorganized voters to a much greater degree than is the case in multimember districts. The importance of the personal vote, in turn, makes politicians focus on personalized campaigns and on fund-raising. A shift away from the personal vote makes the party – rather than individual politicians – the unit of strategic (and also distributive) calculations. As Table 3.1 indicates, Japan's electoral rules changed three times: the rules for the Upper House were changed twice; and the rules for the Lower House were changed once.[8] Here I direct more attention to the 1994 Electoral Reform in the Lower House for two reasons. First, the Lower House is the more dominant of the two in both authority and size (it has roughly twice as many Diet members as the Upper House). Second, the rule changes in the Upper House only affected about one hundred Diet members, whereas the rule change in the Lower House affected all – roughly five hundred – Diet members.[9] From the perspective of my structural logic, the distinction between periods before and after the 1996 Lower House elections is particularly crucial, because the new rules changed both the district magnitude and the relative importance of the personal vote.

The 1994 Electoral Reform introduced a new mixed system in the Lower House, replacing the medium-sized multimember district (MMD) with the single nontransferable vote (SNTV). Voters were given two votes – one for the

[8] For a good historical overview of the Japanese electoral rules, see Soma (1986). For the details of the recent electoral rules, see Senkyo Seido Kenkyu Iinkai ed. (2001).
[9] The precise total number of seats changed from time to time from 466 in the 1947 elections to 511 in the last elections under the old rules. For the electoral reform of 1947, see Soma (1986, 241).

single-member district (SMD) and the other for the multimember district with proportional representation (MMD/PR). Voters cast their vote for a specific candidate in the SMD tier and for a specific party in the PR tier. The PR tier adopted a party list. Of the 480 Lower House Diet members, 300 were to be elected in the SMD tier; the remaining 180 were to be elected in the PR tier, which consisted of eleven regional districts. Although multimember districts persisted, this reform changed the median district magnitude in the Japanese Diet from four to one in the Lower House.

Aside from the median district magnitude, Japan's new mixed system was highly SMD dominant for other reasons, too. The new Lower House rules permitted political parties to "dual list" their SMD-tier candidates on the PR party list.[10] Political parties had two options to construct the list. One option was to rank every candidate on the list. The other option was to rank those candidates who were dual-listed in the SMD tier all the same. (For instance, they would all be listed as rank 1.) In this latter case, dual-listed candidates who won in the SMD tier would be removed from the PR list, and candidates who lost their SMD seats would be elected in the PR tier in the order of their performance in the SMD tier (that is, the smaller the margin of loss, the better the performance). This means that the *real* number of Lower House Diet members who ran from SMDs was actually much higher than 300. In the 2005 Lower House elections, of the 180 Diet members who were elected in the PR tier, 117 had also run in the SMD tier.[11] In short, nearly 90 percent of the Lower House Diet members were SMD candidates. This was indeed a drastic change that was expected to reshape politicians' incentives.

The 1994 Reform also reduced the importance of the personal vote significantly. Japan used to be one of the countries where the personal vote was strongest, because the previous MMD/SNTV system generated fierce intraparty competition at the polls. Every Lower House Diet member was elected on the basis of MMD/SNTV. Intraparty competition was a serious issue for the LDP candidates, because the LDP typically fielded more than one candidate in every district.[12] A SNTV system in a multimember district meant that each of the LDP candidates would be elected on the basis of ballots cast with their names on them. There was no vote sharing among candidates from the same party in the same district. A popular LDP candidate could not share her excess votes with her less popular colleague running in the same district in order that they both be elected. On the contrary, LDP candidates running in the same district were thus forced to compete fiercely against one another over conservative votes. The new electoral rules, in contrast, completely eliminated intraparty electoral competition from the Lower House. Now every candidate ran either as their party's *only* official candidate and/or on their party's PR list.

---

[10] See McKean and Scheiner (2000) and Cox and Schoppa (2002).
[11] *Yomiuri Shimbun*, September 12, 2005, 13.
[12] A broad consensus exists about the harshness of intraparty competition in Japan: see Bouissou (1999); Curtis (1971, 1988); and Ramseyer and Rosenbluth (1993), among others.

Although it is difficult to give post-reform Japan a specific score because of its mixed system, Japan has moved closer to countries like Germany and the United Kingdom (see the country rankings in Table 2.2 in Chapter 2). Let me compare the composition of the whole Diet (both Houses) before and after the 1996 Lower House elections – the first under the new SMD-dominant mixed system – to highlight the overall change. The percentage of Diet members elected in MMD/SNTV declined to 13 percent from 80 percent.[13] In contrast, the percentage of Diet members elected in SMDs jumped to 47 percent from 7 percent. Because of the aforementioned practice of "dual-listing," the percentage of Diet members who ran from a SMD further climbed to about 60 percent of all Diet members.[14]

The electoral rules in the Upper House did not counteract the new tendencies brought about by the 1994 Electoral Reform. When the Lower House changed its rules, the Upper House had already adopted a de facto mixed system since the 1983 elections. On paper, the Upper House adopted multimember districts ranging from two-member districts to a fifty-member district. However, because only half the Upper House was reelected every three years, the two-member districts were in actuality SMDs. This meant that, of the 250 Upper House Diet members, 100 were elected from the nationwide 50-member district, roughly 52 were elected in SMDs, and the rest were elected in medium-sized multimember districts.[15] As of 1983, the Upper House adopted a closed-list PR system in its 50-member district. Prior to this change, the Upper House applied the SNTV to all its multimember districts, just like the pre-reform Lower House. In 2001, the nationwide district in the Upper House switched to an open-list PR system instead of a closed party list system.

Four Distinctive Periods in Postwar Japan

Chapter 2 has identified the structural logic of social protection that emerges out of different combinations of government types, median district magnitude, and the importance of the personal vote. It has argued that different combinations (i) determined the specific forms of distributive benefits that political parties were likely to prefer; and (ii) predicted the likelihood of electoral penalty that ruling parties might face in introducing policies that were costly for the majority. Based on the information provided so far, it is possible to identify four different combinations of government types in post-Occupation Japan. These four combinations include: (i) Majority Party Government/MMD/SNTV; (ii) Partial Minority Government/MMD/SNTV; (iii) Coalition Government/MMD/SNTV; and (iv) Coalition Government/SMD. These four combinations coincide with roughly four different periods in the same chronological order. The first Majority Party

---

[13] Based on my calculations.
[14] The figures are based on the result of the 2005 Lower House election. *Yomiuri Shimbun*, September 12, 2005, 13.
[15] The precise number of the overall seats and the seat allocation changed from time to time for reapportionment.

Government/MMD/SNTV roughly overlaps with the period between the end of the Occupation in 1951 and the loss of the LDP's absolute majority in the Upper House in 1989.[16] Partial Minority Government/MMD/SNTV overlaps with the period between the LDP's loss in 1989 and its ouster from power in 1993. Coalition Government/MMD/SNTV coincides with the period that began with the formation of the first non-LDP coalition government in 1993 and lasted until the first Lower House elections under the new rules in 1996. The final configuration, Coalition Government/SMD, coincides with the period since the 1996 Lower House elections to the 2007 Upper House elections.

The implication of my structural logic is that these four configurations created different structural constraints on welfare politics in each of the aforementioned periods. Regardless of specific events and issues that required policy response, policy outcomes, so my structural logic suggests, should have followed the specific distributive pattern as long as the structural logic remained the same. Broadly stated, the argument put forth in Chapter 2 means that Japan's MMD/SNTV system created a systematic bias in favor of well-organized groups of voters at the expense of unorganized voters from 1951 to 1996. The SNTV also meant that money became important for politicians, who developed strong incentives to favor rent-seeking groups willing to "pay" for policy favors (Cox and Thies 1998; Fukui and Fukui 1999). I argue that the rise in the importance of SMDs and the decline of the personal vote after the 1996 elections, for the first time, systematically tilted the advantage in favor of unorganized voters, leading to a fundamental transformation of Japan's social protection system.

Boldly stated, my structural logic says two things. First, after the decline of the LDP in 1989, Japanese welfare politics came to resemble the welfare politics of many of the northern European countries that possessed MMD and coalition or minority governments. Second, after its electoral reform, Japan's structure increasingly resembled that of a country like the United Kingdom. This means, to follow the logic of my argument, that the Japanese welfare state increasingly resembles the British one. The following sections provide greater detail of what my structural logic implies about distributive politics in each of the four periods.

STRUCTURAL LOGIC UNDER THE CONSERVATIVE DOMINANCE (1951–1989)

Conservatives who had the absolute majority could introduce policies that suited their electoral strategies. The dominance of MMD/SNTV in both Houses meant

---

[16] I say this government type "roughly" corresponded with this period because there was a short interruption in the late 1970s when the LDP's seat share dropped from its comfortable threshold of an absolute majority, which was necessary for the LDP to control the majority of all Diet committees plus their chairmanships. As a result, the latter half of the 1970s is called the period of *yoyato hakuchu* (meaning "close rivalry between the ruling party and the opposition"). The structural logic during this period thus resembles that in the next period, characterized by what I call a partial minority government.

that individual Diet members had strong incentives to deliver social protection in a highly targeted manner to well-organized groups of voters. Even if the voters were homogenous, politicians possessed strong incentives to use targeted benefits as selective incentives to mobilize and organize voters. The importance of money that results as a by-product of personalized campaigns under a SNTV system, in turn, meant that politicians developed strong incentives to engage in a political exchange of policy and money. In addition to organized groups of voters, particularistic rent-seeking groups enjoyed great distributive advantages under the conservative dominance that lasted until 1989.[17] Policy costs were to be passed on to unorganized voters either in terms of greater shares of tax and social security contributions or in terms of higher consumer prices (see Chapter 2).

Prior to the formation of the LDP in 1955, its predecessors, the Liberal Party and the Democratic Party, ruled Japan. In 1955, the conservative parties joined forces to create the LDP in their attempt to establish a united front in response to the merger of the two Socialist parties. The political dynamics, however, changed little before and after the creation of the LDP.[18] The predecessors of the LDP, just like the LDP itself, operated within the same institutional context. The same MMD/SNTV that prevented the LDP from becoming a centralized party had also prevented its predecessors from becoming centralized parties.

I want to emphasize here that my structural logic claims that as long as the structural logic remained the same during this period – covering almost four decades – the distributive implications of social protection programs remained the same. Regardless of drastic socioeconomic changes that Japan experienced, politicians in the ruling party clung to their personal core constituent groups. As this section illustrates, the logic of the personal vote meant that the party leader could do little to reshape the distributive orientation of his party to adjust to the new voter demographics. More specifically, this meant that the LDP remained unresponsive to unorganized urban voters despite the rapid increase in their numbers since the 1960s.[19]

[17] There were some brief interruptions during the otherwise single party–dominated period. Between 1974 and 1980, the LDP's seat share declined below the level necessary to control all Diet committees. The LDP possessed an absolute majority, but this decline increased the bargaining position of the opposition parties. Furthermore, between 1983 and 1986, the LDP ruled in a coalition with the New Liberal Club. The New Liberal Club consisted of former LDP members who broke with the party over disagreements about political ethics. As far as welfare politics was concerned, the LDP-NLC coalition was not very different from governments led by the absolute majority of the LDP.

[18] Prewar conservative politicians ran for office based on their personal reputation under medium-sized, multimember districts with SNTV. Postwar conservative politicians continued to do the same because the Allied Occupation agreed to reintroduce the same medium-sized, multimember districts with SNTV rules in 1947 after the Occupation officials briefly experimented with a new electoral system. As a result, all conservative parties – both prewar and postwar – were basically alliances of senior conservative politicians and their personal followers. These alliances were often reshuffled, leading to the merger of existing parties or creation of new ones. See Kitaoka (1985) and Thayer (1969). Calder (1988, chapter 1) provides a good chronological review of these developments.

[19] In this sense, my structural logic leads to a different interpretation of Japanese politics than that presented in Ramseyer and Rosenbluth (1993). Yoshiaki Kobayashi's empirical analysis of the

Electoral Incentives of Conservative Politicians

Some differences existed between the Lower House (Shugiin) and the Upper House (Sangiin) in terms of the type of organized groups that attracted politicians' mobilizing efforts. If we are to understand the electoral incentives of the conservative politicians during this period, we need to understand the differences between the two Houses.

Whereas all Lower House politicians were elected from medium-sized multimember districts, each covering a relatively small area, the Upper House politicians competed in much larger geographical districts.[20] The contrast is particularly stark between the medium-sized multimember districts (ranging from two to six seats) in the Lower House and the fifty-member nationwide district for the Upper House. For politicians running in medium-sized Lower House districts, geographical location of support was critical. There were about 128 districts in the country, and a politician running in one specific district needed to cultivate a personalized following in that specific location. As Tatebayashi (2004) demonstrates empirically, multiple LDP candidates running in the same medium-sized district often used two different strategies to carve out votes to coexist.[21] One strategy was geographical division of labor, whereby multiple LDP candidates concentrated their vote mobilization in different cities and towns within the same district. The other strategy was a functional division of labor, whereby multiple LDP politicians specialized in different policy areas to divide up votes by the trade and occupation of voters.

For Upper House politicians running in the fifty-member nationwide district, in contrast, the precise geographical location of their constituents was not relevant. Until 1983 when the new nationwide closed party list PR system was adopted, voters voted for a specific candidate. This meant that the candidates' only concern was to secure the support of a well-organized group with the capacity to mobilize the vote on a national scale. The number of votes a particular candidate received served as a gauge of the mobilization capacity of the interest group that backed the candidate. The use of SNTV in the nationwide MMD provided a good opportunity for interest groups to demonstrate their electoral prowess. Under this electoral system, we can therefore expect Upper

historical shifts in the voters who supported the LDP corroborates my interpretation. Kobayashi refutes claims that the LDP became "pro-urban" in the 1980s by showing the persistent rural bias in votes for the LDP. See Kobayashi (1997, 152, 160–161).

[20] The local district tier (*chihoku*) of the Upper House consisted of medium-sized districts – two to four – whose boundaries overlapped with prefectural (*ken*) boundaries and one nationwide district with fifty seats. As of the mid-1970s, a candidate would have needed ten times more votes to win a seat in the local district for the Upper House than in the Lower House. These are my own calculations based on the electoral results in the mid-1970s. I would like to thank Hiroyuki Nagayama from Hiroshima University for his help with the data. Curtis (1976) also notes the same gap between the two chambers.

[21] McCubbins and Rosenbluth (1995) argue that LDP politicians used PARC subcommittees to divide votes within the same district. However, as Tatebayashi (2004) demonstrates, "vote divisions" also occurred along geographical lines within the same district. There is empirical evidence to show that many LDP candidates received most of their votes in their home towns.

House politicians running from the large nationwide districts to act as de facto lobbyists for nationally organized interest groups (Köllner 2002).

These differences tell us that, electorally speaking, the conservative ruling-party politicians in the two Houses expected different levels of "returns" from different kinds of social protection. For the conservative politicians in the Lower House, it made more sense to advocate programs such as public works projects, which were malleable to geographical targeting. In those districts where the Lower House LDP politicians engaged in the aforementioned functional division of labor, they were most likely to find industry- or trade-specific social protection programs to be the effective means to demonstrate their effort to their supporters. The Upper House politicians elected in the nationwide large district, in turn, were most likely to seek policies that protected and augmented "rents" for their specific organized constituent groups.[22]

Given the incentives of the ruling conservative party Diet members, it is not difficult to identify the types of groups with the best political (that is, electoral) leverage vis-à-vis the ruling party. Nationally organized groups with local branches overlapping with Lower House districts could be expected to have fared the best under the conservative rule – both before and after the creation of the LDP – during this period. Such groups could show off their vote-mobilizing capacity at the national level (the fifty-member district in the Upper House elections) as well as form part of the more localized electoral campaigns for specific Lower House candidates. In postwar Japan, groups such as veterans' survivors, special postmasters, physicians, and dentists emerged as powerful interest groups.

It is important to emphasize here that politicians do not merely respond passively to demands of organized groups. Under the electoral rules described here, even if the voter population were initially homogeneous, politicians would still have a strong incentive to cultivate differences in order to organize subgroups of voters for electoral purposes.[23] Any form of targeting of benefits helps to create such differences. Public policies can, in short, create new vested interests where none previously existed.[24] As the following chapter demonstrates, this was precisely the strategy adopted by the LDP (and its predecessors) during the immediate postwar period. This book, therefore, attributes both the fragmented social insurance schemes and the targeted (whether occupationally or geographically) forms of functional equivalents to the active electoral strategies of conservative politicians.

Weak Party Leader and the Decentralized Decision-Making Process

Chapter 2 has argued that the personal vote makes individual politicians' electoral strategies prevail when there is a conflict between individual politicians' interests and the party's as a whole. This happens because the personal vote weakens the

---

[22] This means that these politicians would have advocated not merely bigger shares of the budget for their core constituent groups but policies that increased their profits and income.

[23] Myerson (1993) makes this point. See Chapter 2.

[24] For this aspect of policy feedback, see Paul Pierson (1994).

party leader. The personal vote creates a strong incentive to decentralize the decision-making process within the party. And at the same time, when formal legislative rules decentralize decision-making power – as in the case of the strong committee system in the United States – they further weaken the party and its leadership. This section briefly presents how the personal vote has actually decentralized the policy-making process within the LDP government. Paradoxically, Japan's single-party-dominant democracy did not lead to a high degree of concentration of power.[25] On the contrary, postwar Japanese governments were all highly decentralized because of the electorally motivated incentives and the legislative rules that went with those incentives.

Intraparty competitions at the polls created strong incentives: (i) to build personalized political machines; and (ii) to form intraparty factions (*habatsu*). It is well documented how LDP politicians relied on personalized machines called *koenkai*.[26] *Habatsu*, in turn, served as "support mechanisms" for individual politicians who competed against their fellow LDP candidates. The LDP candidates running from the same district belonged to different *habatsu*. Once elected, *habatsu* ensured that individual politicians could "aggregate" their votes to exercise influence over allocation of resources – that is, budget and posts within the party and the Cabinet. *Habatsu* leaders, senior politicians aspiring to become prime minister, had their own reasons to form intraparty groupings. As far as these leaders were concerned, *habatsu* offered them a way to hoard LDP Diet members' votes for the selection of the party president – basically synonymous with prime minister in a country where the LDP ruled uninterruptedly.

The LDP was more of a coalition of these factions than a cohesive party with discipline (Bawn, Cox, and Rosenbluth 1999; Cox and Rosenbluth 1995, 1996). Indeed, the personalized nature of electoral campaigns made it difficult for the LDP leadership to control even the candidate nomination process.[27] Furthermore, soon after the creation of the LDP, power brokers within the LDP – that is, *habatsu* leaders – developed an elaborate system of "checks and balances" to keep an eye on the prime minister.[28] One such scheme was called *yoto shinsa*, which refers to a practice requiring all legislative bills to gain prior approval from the General Affairs Committee (Somukai) before the Cabinet can submit them to

[25] Richardson (1997) offers a very similar interpretation. He also thinks that Japan's political system under the LDP was highly decentralized.

[26] For a great account of how *koenkai* operated, see Curtis (1971, 1988) and Grofman et al. (1999). Even some Socialist candidates, who did not face intraparty competition, began to develop *koenkai* around 1960 (Kitaoka 1985). Masaru Kohno (1997, chapter 6) identifies the electoral basis of the LDP intraparty politics.

[27] From time to time, coordination problems occurred, whereby too many LDP politicians ran from the same district – some bearing the status of official party nominees whereas others were forced to run as "conservatively leaning" independents (*hoshukei mushozoku*). When "unofficial" LDP candidates won – even at the expense of official party candidates in the same district – the LDP always embraced them as full party members.

[28] As of the mid-1980s, Cabinet-level appointments began to reflect the power balance of *habatsu*. *Habatsu* leaders rather than the prime minister determined Cabinet positions; see Junko Kato (1997, 262).

the Diet.[29] It is important to note that Somukai is not a governmental committee, but merely a committee within the LDP whose raison d'être is to undermine the power of the Cabinet, a formal governmental organ. Somukai consists of thirty-one LDP Diet members: fourteen selected by LDP Diet members in the Lower House; six selected by Diet members in the Upper House; and the remaining eleven appointed by the party president. Somukai membership was to reflect the factional composition of the two Houses while permitting the party president to choose about a third of the members on his own. The fact that Somukai adopted a unanimity rule rather than majority rule further constrained the LDP party president – that is, the prime minister – by emboldening intraparty veto players.[30]

In addition to Somukai, the Policy Affairs Research Committee (Seichokai) played a crucial role to ensure a bottom-up process of decision making, whereby individual politicians' electoral concerns could be reflected in the party's official decisions.[31] The Policy Affairs Research Committee (PARC) consisted of subcommittees (*bukai*) that corresponded to each ministerial jurisdiction. LDP Diet members joined different subcommittees reflecting a functional division of labor with their colleagues in the same district and the most urgent needs of their personal machine (McCubbins and Rosenbluth 1995). All potential legislative proposals first needed to be approved unanimously by a respective subcommittee and then by the whole PARC meeting before they were submitted to Somukai.

Despite the fact that the LDP was the single party that possessed veto power in the Diet, in reality its internal structure emboldened intraparty veto players. The uncodified rules described here decentralized the decision-making process by creating intraparty veto players. In Japan, therefore, chairs of key LDP committees – who had no legal authority – had a greater say on their respective policy issues than the relevant Cabinet minister. The collective nature of the decision-making process in the LDP severely limited the prime minister's authority during the period of the LDP dominance.

Needless to say a decentralized decision-making process created numerous intraparty veto players. As a result, it reduced the LDP leader's capacity to aggregate internal demands.[32] This aggregation mechanism worked much better in

---

[29] The need for Somukai's approval was institutionalized in 1960, just about when competition among faction leaders for the prime ministerial post was intensifying. See Iwai (2002), Kitaoka (1985), and Masumi (1988) for detailed accounts of intraparty politics during this critical period. To my knowledge, Campbell (1992) offers the best account of the intraparty committees and their roles in the legislative process.

[30] The LDP internal rulebook states that the majority rule suffices. Yet, by convention, Somukai always adopted consensus rule.

[31] See Ramseyer and Rosenbluth (1993) for a detailed description of PARCs.

[32] Krauss and Pekkanen (2004) argue that *habatsu* served as a mechanism to aggregate interests within the LDP. I, however, think that it was a limited role. *Habatsu* leaders' reputation and power depended upon their capacity to meet their followers' distributive requests rather than to discipline them to vote for the collective good of the party as a whole. Thus although *habatsu* leaders possessed power over their members, their coordinating capacity was more suited to distributing benefits rather than imposing costs. Moreover, *habatsu* leaders, whose power rested on how many votes they controlled in the party presidential election, were not interested in supporting policies that

allocating particularistic benefits than in making costly decisions or pursuing the collective goal of the party. For instance, even if the LDP's long-term electoral success hinged on reaching out to new groups of voters, any move that imposed a cost on existing core constituent groups would be vetoed. Intraparty veto players within the LDP would most likely prevent the leadership from pursuing such a shift. This means that, structurally, it was very difficult for the LDP leadership to adopt policies to appeal to new groups of voters even in the face of its perpetually declining vote share.[33] Based on the electoral need of LDP members, we can estimate the relative power of different constituent groups. Nationally organized groups with well-developed municipal branches stood to gain most, as they could mobilize the largest number of LDP Diet members. Such groups possessed greater leverage over the LDP government than encompassing organizations such as Keidaren (the peak-level big business association) or Nikkeiren (the peak-level employers' association).[34]

Decentralization occurred in yet another dimension. A lot of legislative power was actually delegated to the bureaucracy. The scope of delegation granted the bureaucracy strong agenda-setting power. The existence of multiple veto players within the LDP government helped bureaucrats transform their agenda-setting power into veto power. As mentioned earlier, the LDP's PARC subcommittees were organized along ministerial lines. Members of these subcommittees worked in close alliance with respective ministries. The LDP politicians relied on bureaucrats to come up with schemes to benefit their constituent groups, and the bureaucrats relied on their LDP allies to push for new legislation on their behalf and to veto undesirable changes. Insofar as the decision-making process within the ruling party remained decentralized, this politico-bureaucratic alliance remained highly effective in fending off any attempts to reduce the ministry's jurisdiction.

Although scholars such as Sato and Matsuzaki (1986) have argued that the LDP politicians accumulated policy expertise by becoming members of PARC subcommittees, it is unclear what kind of legislative capacity such "expertise" produced. PARC subcommittee members continued to rely on bureaucrats for

---

might cost their members' reelection. Policy decisions that involved a zero-sum game among LDP constituent groups were, as a consequence, likely to be blocked.

[33] Calder (1988), Pempel (1982), and Ramseyer and Rosenbluth (1993) consider that the LDP was capable of a strategic move. Certainly, senior politicians did influence the preference aggregation process at the *somukai* level. (Note that ministers played a very small role in this process.) Unlike individual LDP politicians, who only cared about their own reelection, the central leadership was responsible for the electoral fortune of the party as a whole. Aside from the party president, the formal central leadership consisted of the following characters of the Board of the Party Executives (Yakuinkai): (i) the general party secretary (*kanjicho*); (ii) the chairman of the General Affairs Committee, or *somukai*; and (iii) the chairman of the Policy Affairs Research Committee, or *seichokai*. The formal leadership relied on the power of the informal leaders – that is, *habatsu* leaders. It was the task of *habatsu* leaders to aggregate diverse policy demands that arose from within the party, because only they had the power to punish the rank and file in their own factions. Yet for the reasons identified earlier, *habatsu* leaders were far from omnipotent: see footnote 32.

[34] See Richardson (1997) for a similar view.

policy ideas. More often than not, even the demands that PARC subcommittee members made of the party were drawn up by bureaucrats.[35] In the absence of either independent or party-affiliated think tanks, the Japanese bureaucracy possessed a monopoly on policy expertise and policy-relevant information.

Certainly, LDP politicians, as principals, supervised their agents (Ramseyer and Rosenbluth 1993). But PARC members were principals who only cared about very limited aspects of policy decisions. More specifically, they only cared about the distributive implications of a particular policy decision for their own reelection. In other words, insofar as bureaucratic preferences were aligned with the distributive interests of the respective PARC subcommittee members, bureaucrats possessed the ability to mold policies in ways that were more compatible with their organizational interest.[36] The legislative decentralization under the MMD/SNTV system thus gave rise to an alliance of PARC subcommittees and different bureaucratic units – I call this alliance a politico-bureaucratic alliance.[37]

Furthermore, as I shall explain in greater detail, legislative routines such as applying the unanimity rule in *jimu jikan kaigi* (a regular pre-Cabinet conference attended by all bureaucratic vice ministers) and using extraparliamentary consultation councils called *shingikai* both served as effective tools for the bureaucracy to veto undesirable policies and to insert their favored policies into legislative bills. The specific personnel management and remuneration rules within the Japanese bureaucracy, in turn, explain the peculiar preferences that Japanese ministries developed in crafting social protection programs. The next section is devoted to this issue.

LEGISLATIVE RULES, BUREAUCRATS, AND THEIR PREFERENCES

Japan's prime minister possessed limited power over his own Cabinet for most of the postwar period. The old Cabinet Law – effective until the reform in the late 1990s – permitted Cabinet ministers to submit proposals to the Cabinet without allowing a similar prerogative to the prime minister.[38] Cabinet ministers, in turn, represented the policies articulated by the politico-bureaucratic alliances discussed earlier in relation to the role of the PARC subcommittees in the LDP. Here let me focus on why the legislative rules in Japan provided bureaucrats with an ample scope of agenda-setting power, which permitted them to insert their favored policy options into the legislative process.

---

[35] Based on my observations as a participant observer in the LDP's Tax Committee meetings in December 1996. I would like to thank Mr. Yoshiro Hayashi, chairman of the LDP Tax Committee at the time, who briefly appointed me to his staff so that I could sit through the closed meetings.

[36] Noll and Rosenbluth (1995) specify conditions under which politicians support a greater degree of bureaucrats' regulatory discretion.

[37] Muramatsu and Krauss (1984, 1987) have also observed such alliances and characterized Japan's political process as "patterned pluralism." For a good discussion of the corporatism-pluralism debate to characterize Japan, see Pempel and Tsunekawa (1979) and Schwartz (1998).

[38] Iio (2004) and Tanaka and Okada (2000) provide detailed explanations of the changes that occurred.

Rules of Delegation – Bureaucratic Agenda-Setting Power

Certain institutional conditions gave rise to bureaucratic veto players. Chapter 2 argues that bureaucrats gain veto power when (a) the scope of the legislative delegation is large; (b) the legislative capacity of the ruling party (or parties) is low; and (c) there are multiple principals. Japan fulfilled all these conditions unambiguously throughout much of the postwar period. The key aspects of the terms of delegation in postwar Japan can be summarized in three points.

First, the scope of bureaucratic delegation in Japan was extensive. The Japanese Cabinet did not simply delegate policy implementation to the bureaucracy; it also delegated a substantial portion of its own legislative work. Bureaucrats came up with policy ideas and did the drafting, because the ruling party lacked legislative capacity. Japanese legislators typically had no legal training, and no expert staff or party-affiliated think tanks that would assist them. The scope of legislative delegation was so immense that Japan even appointed bureaucrats to be "government commissioners" (*seifu iin*) to answer Diet members' questions in lieu of their often policy-ignorant ministers during the formal Diet sessions. (Compare this to another parliamentary system such as that of the United Kingdom, where only parliamentary members are allowed in the Parliament!)

Second, Japan adopted a legislative procedure called the *jimu jikan kaigi. Jimu jikan kaigi* refers to a conference of bureaucratic vice ministers (*jimu jikan*) – that is, the top civil service posts – that meets prior to every Cabinet meeting. During most of the postwar period, by convention, all the legislative proposals that the Cabinet approved for Diet submission first needed to be unanimously approved at this conference. Neither Cabinet meetings nor *jimu jikan kaigi* meetings themselves entailed heated debates, because most political negotiations happened at the level of Somukai. The importance of *jimu jikan kaigi* lay in its unanimity rule, which made it possible for bureaucratic vice ministers to veto proposals from other ministries that trespassed upon their "turf." This rule encouraged ministries to give up legislative proposals that infringed on the jurisdictional turfs of other ministries.[39]

---

[39] When there is enough support from the ruling party, a particular ministry can craft a legislative proposal without having to go through interministerial negotiations. This takes the following form. Instead of the Cabinet submitting a legislative proposal to the Diet as a government-sponsored bill, which requires both Cabinet approval and the approval of the bureaucratic vice ministers, a particular LDP Diet member sponsors the submission of the bill to the Diet as his own bill (in the United States, individual legislators typically sponsor bills). Legislative proposals that are not Cabinet proposals do not go through the layers of scrutiny open to veto players. A proposal thus can be taken directly to the Diet floor for deliberation by Diet members and a vote. The existence of this method indicates how costly interministerial negotiations are and how real the threat of veto from other ministries is. It is noteworthy that Kakuei Tanaka, a big-time faction leader who also served as prime minister, was known for resorting to nongovernment bills to circumvent bureaucratic resistance and the opposition from his allies within the LDP. Generally speaking, the likelihood of individually submitted bills becoming legislated has been much lower than the likelihood of passage of government bills. Non-Cabinet proposals are typically submitted by the opposition parties that are without sufficient number of votes to legislate anything.

Third, *shingikai* offered another important mechanism for bureaucrats to exercise agenda-setting and veto power.[40] *Shingikai* was an extraparliamentary policy
deliberation body, which allowed representatives from occupational groups and
trade associations to come together to "deliberate" on policies that affect them.[41]
Ministries had the authority to set up a *shingikai* and appoint its members.[42]
Each ministry possessed a fair number of *shingikai* to cover all the policy areas
within its jurisdiction.[43] Bureaucrats used *shingikai* for two major purposes: (i)
to generate a consensus over their own legislative proposals in order to preempt
any opposition from the parliamentary veto players; and (ii) to legitimate their
legislative proposals by inviting well-respected individuals from academia and
societal organizations to "approve" them (Schwartz 1998).

Depending on the bureaucratic objective, the nature of *shingikai* thus varied.[44]
On the one hand, some *shingikai* brought together representatives of all vested
interests to negotiate with one another over the terms of policy changes. On
the other hand, some *shingikai* had no interest representation or deliberation.[45]
Interest groups that participated in the former type of *shingikai* gained quasi-veto
power by holding up the pre-legislative process by refusing to take part in deliberations.[46] Yet even in this case, ultimately, an interest group's capacity to veto
an unwanted policy depended on their influence over the vote of parliamentary
veto players. In other words, as long as the LDP had an absolute majority in the
Diet, an interest group only gained veto power via its capacity to mobilize an
intraparty veto player within the LDP.

In either case, *shingikai* strengthened bureaucratic power over the legislative agenda.[47] Bureaucrats decided which groups were to be represented in the
shingikai, which itself as a body had no formal authority to draft, approve, or
reject a legislative bill. The *shingikai* merely "deliberated" on the content of
the legislative draft prepared by the respective ministerial bureau and made a

[40] Schwartz (1998) provides a thorough analysis of *shingikai* and *shingikai* politics in the key policy
areas.

[41] It has no formal authority to pass, reject, or even to draft a legislative bill, but it "deliberates" on
the content of the legislative draft prepared by the respective ministerial bureau. At the end of the
deliberation, it makes legislative recommendation for the government.

[42] The Prime Minister's Office – the former Sorifu – and ministerial bureaus also have the authority
to set up *shingikai*.

[43] The Japanese government publishes the list of all *shingikai* and their members annually. See
Shingikai Yoran, various years.

[44] Sone Kenkyukai's survey result of *shingikai* develops an objective method to distinguish different
types of *shingikai* on the basis of frequency of actual meetings and membership composition (Sone
Kenkyukai 1985).

[45] In Japan, this type of *shingikai* is referred to as *kakuremino* (a literal translation is "disguising robe").

[46] This is the tactic the Japan Medical Association is known for using. While less publicized, this tactic
was used by other participants as well (from my personal communications with Junko Takashima,
who has served as labor representative – from Rengo, the peak-level labor association – in a number
of labor policy–related deliberation councils).

[47] Ehud Harari argues that interest representation by means of *shingikai* only occurs when bureaucrats
are trying to co-opt societal actors in order to legislate something (Harari 1974). I share his view.

"recommendation" (*toshin*) to the government. Since only bureaucrats set the agenda for *shingikai* deliberations as a rule, their agenda-setting power gave them de facto veto power. Policies that bureaucrats opposed did not enter into the debate in *shingikai*. Bureaucrats were also capable of influencing the content of the *shingikai*'s final policy recommendation by handpicking the committee chairman. Typically, ministries appointed academics sympathetic to their policies to chair their *shingikai*. The chair's role was to carve out a compromise so that the legislative process could go forward.[48] Bureaucrats could capitalize on any disagreements among committee members to stall unwanted legislative changes and to push for their preferred policy as a compromise option.

Bureaucratic Preferences and Social Protection

At first glance, Japan's civil service was not too different from the career civil service in most European countries.[49] Japan's personnel management rules for career bureaucrats gave rise, however, to very specific bureaucratic preferences for social welfare programs in Japan. A very rigid internal labor market governed bureaucratic agencies in Japan throughout the postwar period.[50] Like Japanese large firms, these agencies only hired young school leavers for entry-level positions. Applicants who had passed the highly competitive civil service exams were then sorted into different ministries. Lateral movements within the bureaucracy were extremely limited, and a very strict seniority system applied to promotions. Unlike European bureaucracies that guaranteed employment until retirement age, Japanese elite bureaucrats had very truncated careers, because they were required to leave the ministry well before their retirement age. By convention, when someone was promoted to the position of bureau chief or vice minister – the highest possible rank for civil servants – everyone else in the same or older cohort had to resign. Many bureaucrats were thus required to leave in their early fifties. Even those bureaucrats who made it to the very top did not escape this practice. Job rotation came every other year, and even vice ministers had to relinquish their positions to the next cohort.[51]

Assuming that bright ambitious people care about the material well-being and prestige associated with their status, then ministries could only recruit the best and the brightest when they could offer some compensation for the truncated

---

[48] Public interest representatives are selected by bureaucrats and tend to be expert academics. Bureaucrats choose academic experts on the basis of their seniority in academia and for the position they hold. Bureaucrats rarely choose academics who are critical of their ministry.

[49] Unlike in the United States, there is almost no political appointment outside the Cabinet (that is, ministers and vice ministers). In other words, intra-agency routine promotions staff almost all managerial positions in government agencies.

[50] See Hayakawa (1997) and Inatsugu (1996). Aoki (1988) notes a parallel between the personnel management practice in the Japanese bureaucracy and that in large Japanese private firms.

[51] This contrasts sharply with what happens in large Japanese firms: someone who makes it to the top management position becomes exempt from the mandatory retirement age that applies to everyone else.

public service career. In a flexible labor market like the one in the United States, public officials could secure good post–public service jobs in the private sector. However, in a rigid internal labor market like the postwar Japanese labor market, where entry to good jobs took place at the bottom of the job ladder, the American option did not exist.[52] For this reason, ministries themselves assumed the role of a post-retirement job placement agency.[53] Ministries used the promise of post-retirement earnings as a reward for their top bureaucrats in order to retain the ministerial prestige and attract the best and the brightest into the civil service. This institutional practice was known as *amakudari*, which literally means "descent from Heaven."

Amakudari was a very systematic business: each ministry orchestrated post-retirement career paths for its career officials depending on their final position in the ministry. In order to maintain the integrity of the personnel practice – and the ministerial prestige – ministries needed a sufficient number of good, high-paying post-retirement positions. Ministries thus used their regulatory authority and the discretionary allocation of subsidies to their own advantage. Many private sector firms, hoping to be in good stead with their regulators, offered special seats to retired officials (Calder 1989; Colignon and Usui 2003; Inoki 1995; Schaede 1995). More to the point, every ministry spent considerable time and energy seeking to secure these special seats.

Although social policy appeared to have nothing to do with this idiosyncratic personnel practice, some types of welfare programs helped create *amakudari* positions. Welfare programs that involved licensing, social security contributions, and savings were, in this respect, the most suitable programs. If licensing requirements were sufficiently vague, applicants had more reason to curry favor with the licensing authorities by offering post-retirement jobs to bureaucrats.[54] Contributory welfare programs that accumulated money, in turn, were administered by bureaucrats in the form of "special accounts" or "mutual assistance cooperatives."[55] The legal language over the terms of bureaucratic administration was vague enough to permit ministries to use the money in special accounts under their jurisdiction for their own purposes. Through this access to an "independent" source of money, ministries financed projects that created post-retirement

---

[52] Unlike in the United States, even private employment agencies were prohibited by law in Japan until recently.

[53] Aside from the practice of early retirement, other personnel management decisions and rules have been relevant: (i) a few rounds of bureaucratic downsizing that occurred in the postwar years; and (ii) the ceiling on the number of national civil servants. These decisions created a need to help reemploy "laid-off" bureaucrats. See Colignon and Usui (2003, chapter 2).

[54] When a particular welfare service is contracted out to a nongovernment entity, some form of bureaucratic scrutiny if not licensing occurs in most countries. Estévez-Abe (2003) talks about how this process takes place in Japan and situates Japan into a comparative perspective.

[55] Money is pooled in the form of special budget accounts (*tokubetsu kaikei*) or mutual assistance cooperatives (*kyosai kumiai*). Unemployment insurance, children's allowance, and old-age pension – are all set up as special accounts.

jobs for their members.[56] For instance, money in special accounts was used to set up public corporations (*tokushu hojin*) or other quasi-government nonprofit organizations.[57] Ministerial officials then "descended" to head these organizations. These organizations, in turn, had very poor governance structure. They were not legally required to make their balance sheets publicly available. Despite the fact that they were financed by public money, their balance sheets were not even submitted to the Diet. In short, these organizations provided almost heavenly opportunities for bureaucrats and their political allies to use public funds in ways that served their interests.

Job placements in these semipublic agencies and facilities were particularly valuable for ministries, because of the two-year ban on the *amakudari* of high-ranking bureaucrats to private firms that they used to regulate. In order to circumvent this ban, ministries needed positions in quasi-public organizations. For ministries that did not possess licensing authorities or discretionary spending – both of which created rents for private firms – public corporations and nonprofit organizations provided precious opportunities for *amakudari*.

The organizational features described here made the Japanese bureaucracy very different from the elite bureaucracies in other countries. For instance, Germany's elite bureaucrats – the Beamten – have always enjoyed high levels of remuneration both during their job tenure and afterwards (in the form of noncontributory, generous pensions). They thus have no need for post-retirement jobs. In contrast, France and the United States are similar to Japan in that high-ranking public officials expect post-retirement employment in the private sector. Yet unlike in the United States, where each official fends for herself in the external labor market, the French elite take advantage of the fact that so many of the private sector firms are actually owned by the state. Japan's distinctiveness lay in the fact that ministries themselves have to be highly entrepreneurial in securing post-retirement jobs for their own members.[58]

[56] This kind of money improves a ministry's position in relation to the budgeting authority (Ministry of Finance). When the overall revenue falls short, the MOF often "borrows" money from surplus special accounts. This gives ministries with their own money leverage in their negotiations with the budgeting authority to finance their pet projects. Interview at the Ministry of Finance 1995.

[57] Public corporations (*tokushu hojin*) and especially those nonprofit organizations called *gaikaku dantai* are set up by ministries to carry out policy objectives and are financed by different sources of public money – primarily loans from the government's Fiscal Investment and Loan Program (FILP) and special accounts that specific ministries control. Chalmers Johnson (1978) provides an excellent historical account of Japan's public corporations. See Estévez-Abe (2003) for more on *gaikaku dantai* and the process through which these nonprofit organizations used to be licensed in Japan.

[58] The French equivalent of *amakudari* is called *pantouflage*. Yet the number of elite bureaucrats is much smaller in France and the prominence of state-owned enterprises creates a different situation. In the United States, the extensive external market and the constant "revolving door" between public- and private-sector careers make a highly organized system of reemployment of bureaucrats after their retirement unnecessary. Potential rent-seeking incentives exist both in France and the United States, but they do not take on the "organized" efforts of Japan.

In short, the organizational structure of the Japanese bureaucracy produced very specific preferences. Bureaucrats developed strong preferences for contributory benefits that accumulate money; they also had a strong desire to retain administrative control over welfare programs in their hands. Each ministry, even those without jurisdiction over social welfare programs, was eager to justify a welfare program – or a functional equivalent – under its own jurisdiction. Likewise, ministries had a strong incentive to expand their regulatory discretion. While some legislation was better than none, bureaucrats generally opposed any reform that reduced their control over money and personnel.

STRUCTURAL SHIFTS SINCE 1989

Structurally speaking, three important shifts have occurred since 1989. The first shift occurred in 1989 when the loss of the LDP's absolute majority in the Upper House elections led to the emergence of what I call "partial minority government." The second shift occurred when the LDP was ousted from power in 1993, thereby initiating a period of coalition governments. The third shift occurred when the 1996 Lower House elections changed the profile of a median Diet member.

Post-1989 "Partial Minority Government": New Universalistic Tendencies

The emergence of what I call "partial minority government" in 1989 changed the parameters of politics by affecting the configuration of parliamentary veto players. Despite the continuity in the electoral system – the MMD/SNTV system – the new partial minority government introduced a new political dynamic associated with minority governments (see Chapter 2). For the first time, the LDP governments became more willing to introduce universalistic social protection programs with a broader appeal. This is not to say that Japan became a universalistic welfare state. The electorally motivated incentives of LDP politicians remained the same under the same MMD/SNTV system. The persisting importance of the personal vote meant that the LDP continued to be a highly decentralized party just as in the previous period. With the LDP still in charge of the Lower House, the median LDP Diet member continued to favor highly targeted social protection programs. The emergence of a partial minority government did, however, increase the number of parliamentary veto players, which now included part of the opposition parties. The upshot was that policies that extended benefits to wage earners and their families – constituent groups of the opposition parties – were now more likely than during the 1951–1989 period.

The increase in the number of parliamentary veto players benefited social and labor policy bureaucrats. Recall that the politico-bureaucratic alliance that emerged in the previous period meant that bureaucrats had a lot of leverage to introduce policies that promoted their organizational interest insofar as those policies also benefited the key players in the LDP – such as the members of the PARC subcommittees in the LDP. The emergence of the partial minority government meant that bureaucrats could now push for public programs whose benefits extended to wage earners and their families – a group of voters neglected during the previous period of LDP dominance.

The Post-1993 Coalition Governments: Becoming like a Continental European Welfare State

The defection of a group of LDP Diet members to form a separate party and their successful bid to bring down the LDP government in 1993 opened a new era of coalition governments in Japan. Here I summarize the structural logic in place during the period between 1993 and the 1996 Lower House elections, which changed the face of the median Diet member in Japan. During this period, Japan was ruled by coalitions of parties running in a MMD system. This configuration is very similar to that in many European coalition governments. In spite of some differences that result because of a strong personal vote in Japan, the configuration of coalition governments in the context of a MMD system made decisions to increase taxes easier – just as in the case of European coalition governments. (As Chapter 2 argues, the emergence of a multi-party coalition reduces party identifiability, making it easier to introduce unpopular policies.) Also, coalition governments under MMD are expected to introduce policies that benefit a wider range of organized groups than a single-party government under a MMD system, like that of the 1951–1989 period.

As for the electorally motivated incentives of the ruling-party politicians, nothing much changed. The MMD/SNTV system meant that political parties were better off pursuing organized groups of voters. In this sense, just as in the period of the partial minority government, the emergence of coalition governments merely expanded the range of organized interests to be rewarded. One deviation from this structural constraint was the mini-parties that emerged with the support of disgruntled unorganized voters. These parties, when in the ruling coalition, challenged the vested interests on behalf of the unorganized voters who were shouldering the cost of benefits to the organized groups. The fact that these parties could never sustain their electoral fortune attests to the importance of the structural logic presented here. Under a MMD/SNTV system, political parties that pursue unorganized voters should not do well, because it is not the optimal strategy.

A series of coalition governments gave Japanese unions a direct voice on policy making. At least one of the political parties in the ruling coalition drew on the support of organized labor. For the first time, organized labor gained veto power on the Diet floor via their surrogates – that is, political parties. The new configuration of parliamentary veto players since 1993, just like that in the post-1989 partial minority governments, also increased the leverage of social and labor policy bureaucrats. These bureaucrats could now count on the legislative support of non-LDP parliamentary veto players. In fact, under the coalition governments of this period, we see the introduction of a comprehensive welfare program whose benefits went beyond the usual LDP's core constituent groups. In short, my structural logic provides an explanation as to why the Japanese welfare state began to resemble the European welfare state during this period. As Chapter 1 demonstrates, Japan used to stand out for its paucity of public benefits and services to wage earners and their families. This aspect of Japan's welfare state began to change as the structural logic shifted.

The Post-1996 Structural Logic: Becoming like a British Welfare State?

In 1994, Japan introduced a new SMD-dominant mixed electoral system for the Lower House. A critical shift occurred in 1996 when the first elections under the new electoral rules took place. The new electoral rules completely eliminated the intraparty competition prevalent under the previous MMD/SNTV system. Under the new SMD-dominant system, electorally desirable forms of social protection changed. In addition to the elimination of intraparty electoral competition, a series of legislative rule changes swung the pendulum in the direction of the stronger party and the party leader (especially in the case of the ruling party). These changes included (i) the elimination of government commissioners (*seifu iin*) and the expansion of Cabinet positions (that is, the creation of junior ministers) in 1999; (ii) a revision of the Cabinet Law; and (iii) the reorganization of the government, which included the expansion of the Cabinet Office.[59] The last two reforms were approved in the Diet in 1997 and implemented as of January 2001.[60] To put it briefly, the Electoral Campaign Reform concentrated more financial resources in the hands of the party leadership by introducing tax-financed subsidies for political parties, which were to be paid to the party rather than to individual politicians. The other changes concentrated power in the hands of the prime minister. The reforms in 1999 increased the number of Cabinet positions that the prime minister could allocate, and the reforms in 2001 increased the prime minister's agenda-setting power.

To put it boldly, one can say that Japan has been moving toward a Westminster system.[61] The combination of the new electoral rules and the enhanced power of

---

[59] For the details of changes during this period see Estévez-Abe (2006), Hikotani (2004), Iio (2004, 2006), Ishihara (2001), Takenaka (2002, 2006), and Tanaka and Okada (2000).

[60] These reforms were carried out by the LDP government under Prime Minister Ryutaro Hashimoto. Tanaka and Okada (2000) provide the details of the legal changes that occurred as part of the Administrative Reforms. They point out that the fourth clause of the old Cabinet Law did not clearly state the superior position of the prime minister in relation to his ministers. This clause specified individual ministers' prerogative to submit proposals to the Cabinet but did not specify the prime minister's power to do so. The tasks of the Cabinet secretaries have also been expanded to include policy-making functions in addition to their traditional administrative and coordinating functions (Tanaka and Okada 2000, 72–84).

[61] Some critics might argue that the persistence of coalition governments in Japan should disqualify Japan as a Westminster system. A Westminster system is a type of democracy where the power is most centralized: in the hands of the sole party with an absolute majority and in the hands of

the LDP leader – in his capacity as prime minister – meant a fundamental shift in the power relations within the LDP. The greater centralization of power in the hands of the LDP leader has made it possible for the leader to shift the distributive orientation of his party for the first time.[62] At the same time, the new SMD-dominant system has changed the electoral calculations of both leaders and the rank and file. Just as it is expected of a SMD system with a strong party, a newly emboldened prime minister is most likely to favor programs for swing voters in competitive electoral districts. Such a strategy would have been impossible under the decentralized government caused by the former MMD/SNTV system, where the prime minister had no power to override his party members' desire to protect the vested interests of their core constituent groups. Furthermore, under the new SMD-dominant system, an electoral strategy to seek the support of specific organized groups at the expense of unorganized voters was no longer as successful as it once was.

Following the structural logic articulated in the previous chapter, institutional changes described here mean that Japanese welfare politics is also likely to change. More specifically, on the basis of the structural logic, we can expect Japanese welfare politics to become more like that in the United Kingdom. The weakening of the logic associated with MMD systems reduces political pressure in support of fragmented social security programs and their functional equivalents targeted at the core constituent groups. The new policy orientation – while retaining a bias in favor of geographical targeting to deliver more to competitive electoral districts – is likely to favor unorganized voters more than ever in Japanese politics. The increasing importance of unorganized voters is also likely to favor more universalistic programs. The irony here – just like in the United Kingdom again – is that the new political configuration developed in the post-1996 period is likely to weaken the government's capacity to impose new burdens – such as new taxes – on the majority of voters. This occurs because the SMD-dominant electoral system increases the level of accountability, while the greater concentration of power increases the level of identifiability. Political systems with high identifiability and accountability are expected to have more difficulty in introducing costly policies such as tax increases in spite of the greater power of the government

its party leader, who is the prime minister. The nature of coalition government under Japan's SMD-dominant mixed system nonetheless has differed from that under MMD systems during the previous period (or in many European countries). Under a SMD system, multiple ruling parties possess a strong incentive to act like a single party to avoid electoral competition in the SMD tier. The presence of multiple candidates from the ruling parties can cause a big loss of SMD seats for the ruling parties only to benefit the largest opposition party. As a consequence, an electoral alliance is likely to accompany stable coalition governments under SMD-dominant systems. In other words, electorally speaking, coalition parties increasingly act as one party. This, in turn, means that using the analogy of a Westminster-style democracy to describe a coalition government under a SMD-dominant system is not too far-fetched. Chapter 9 comes back to this point.

[62] Pekkanen, Nyblade, and Krauss (2006) report a fact that is compatible with the argument put forth here. They find that politicians in competitive seats are assigned to more explicitly "distributive" policy issues when the LDP allocates intraparty positions.

(see Chapter 2). In short, Japan seems to be on a path to a more universalistic but "not-so" generous welfare state.

The post-1996 changes are also likely to erode the basis of bureaucratic veto power and politico-bureaucratic alliances. Alliances between bureaucrats and groups of LDP politicians relied on the decentralized power structure to be effective. The greater centralization of power thus challenges the bureaucratic agenda-setting power as well as the power of their political allies (such as PARC subcommittees within the LDP). While bureaucrats continue to possess the same organizational interests, because the recruitment and promotion procedures remain the same as before, politicians now have new preferences. Structurally, as a result of the SMD-dominant electoral system, politicians are more eager to appeal to unorganized voters rather than to seek the support of organized groups in exchange for policy favors. In stark contrast to politicians under the old MMD/SNTV system, politicians and political parties today possess strong incentives to attack "special interests" on behalf of unorganized voters. Electorally speaking, bureaucratic rent-seeking activities are likely to be the easiest target.

CONCLUSION

This chapter has applied the structural logic developed in Chapter 2 to identify four distinctive patterns of structural logic in postwar Japan. Following the structural logic, this chapter has presented what policy outcomes were most likely under each of the four patterns of structural logic. Throughout this chapter, I assumed that Japan had a centralized constitutional structure in order to facilitate the application of the structural logic approach to Japan. Although Japan could potentially possess a strong bicameral system, it has more or less functioned as a unicameral system for most of the period covered in this book. This happened because the same party, the Liberal Democratic Party, completely dominated both Houses of the Diet for most of the postwar period. Even after the Upper House election in 1989, when the LDP lost its absolute majority in the Upper House, the LDP remained the largest party in the House and maintained its absolute majority by forming coalitions with smaller parties. Given this reality, we lose nothing by simplifying the story by assuming that postwar Japan possessed a centralized constitutional structure. (The concluding chapter will discuss the implications of the LDP's defeat in the 2007 Upper House elections, whereby the LDP lost control of the Upper House.)

The following historical chapters demonstrate the validity of the structural logic as a narrative of the postwar welfare state development in Japan. Chapter 4 zeroes in on the critical postwar moment when the electorally motivated politics was unleashed in Japan after the Allied Occupation. Chapter 5 contrasts the structural argument against the backdrop of the existing explanations of the welfare expansion in the 1960s and the early 1970s in Japan. Chapter 6 examines the role of the social protection system in Japan's distinctive model of capitalism.

Chapter 7 then turns to the issue of how Japan failed to reform its social protection system when problems began to emerge as early as the mid-1970s because of the structural constraints on politics. Chapter 8 demonstrates how policy shifts only began to occur when the government type changed in 1989. Chapter 8 also compares differences in the kind of policy shifts that were made possible in two different periods – the period between 1989 and 1993 and the period between 1993 and 1996. Chapter 9 examines the effects of the post-1996 centralization of politics on Japan's welfare system.

4

The Rise of the Japanese Social Protection
System in the 1950s

This chapter turns to the historical sequence of events that led to the emergence of Japan's distinctive welfare system. This chapter focuses on the transition from the period of the Allied Occupation of Japan, which lasted from 1945 to 1951, to the period after sovereign power was returned to the Japanese Diet in 1952. A big policy shift occurred after 1951. During the Occupation, universalistic welfare programs developed for the first time. Yet as soon as the Japanese Diet regained its full legislative power, Japan abandoned the universalism introduced by the Americans.[1]

More specifically, this chapter carries out three tasks. First, this chapter attributes this policy shift to the new structural logic of politics that emerged in the early 1950s. The Allied Occupation placed a number of stringent constraints on Japanese politicians. It was only after the Occupation ended that the electoral motivations associated with multimember districts and the personal vote began to shape Japan's welfare state. Second, this chapter accounts for the cross-policy variations during the same historical period. Despite the fact that welfare issues were a political priority during the late 1940s and the 1950s, governmental action was highly selective. Simply put, programs in line with the preferences of the veto players had a much better chance of being enacted and expanded. Thus during the occupation period, welfare programs reflected the preferences of the occupying Allied Forces – the veto player at the time – whereas, after 1951, they reflected the preferences of conservative politicians – the new veto player. Third, this chapter provides evidence that politicians and bureaucrats possessed the preferences predicted by the structural logic. This is important because my structural logic offers a micrologic of incentives and behaviors of politicians and bureaucrats in different contexts.

---

[1] The Allied Powers and Japan finally signed a peace treaty (the San Francisco Peace Treaty) in September 1951. The Occupation forces were to withdraw from Japan in the following year. See Masumi (1983b) and Duus (1998).

JAPAN'S NASCENT UNIVERSALISM UNDER THE ALLIED OCCUPATION (1945–1951)

Before pursuing these tasks, however, it might be useful to provide a brief overview of Japan's political history in the postwar era.[2] (Readers familiar with this history can skip this overview.) In 1945, Japan, like Germany, was occupied by the Allied Forces. The Allied Occupation government called the first postwar elections in 1946. (Japanese women voted for the first time.) Although the democratically elected politicians elected the prime minister, who then formed the government, the General's Headquarters of the Allied Forces (hereafter GHQ) held both agenda-setting and veto power.[3] The GHQ remained the ultimate governing authority in Japan until the return of full sovereignty to the Japanese government in 1952.

The main objective of the Allied Forces was to democratize every aspect of Japanese society, including its economy and its political system. To this end, the GHQ disarmed Japan; it dismantled a dozen family-owned industrial concerns that controlled about 80 percent of the Japanese economy and it closely supervised Japan's legislative process. Although there was still a Japanese government and all legislation was passed by the Japanese Diet, the GHQ regularly issued memoranda and directives to guide Japanese policy making. The GHQ also controlled policy debate outside the government by censoring every means of communication (such as newspapers, books, and magazines) to suppress criticism of GHQ policy. No less important, the GHQ also carried out measures to weaken the conservative forces within Japan. Thus the GHQ pursued an extensive purge of Japanese Imperial military personnel, conservative party politicians, and business leaders. Altogether about 210,000 people were purged from government or other positions of power. Some of the most senior conservative leaders – politicians who were later to play prominent roles in postwar Japanese governments, such as Prime Minister Nobusuke Kishi – were purged and jailed in Sugamo Prison. Unlike the business and political leaders who were purged, the Japanese bureaucracy was kept more or less intact. Although the wartime Ministry of Home Affairs was dismantled, it was simply broken into smaller ministries with all their officials in place.[4]

---

[2] Dower (1999), Duus (1998), and Masumi (1983a, 1983b) provide thorough accounts of political events during the immediate postwar period.

[3] This does not mean, however, that the Japanese Diet members and bureaucrats were powerless. The political process of this period was characterized by constant negotiations between bureaucrats and their counterparts in the GHQ and the ruling party and the GHQ leadership. Still, the GHQ possessed the ultimate authority to make decisions on any issue of great concern to them. The GHQ, for instance, rejected the constitution that the Japanese had drafted and imposed their draft; when the United States decided that the Japanese economy needed a "shock therapy" in order to put an end to the wartime "control economy," the GHQ drafted an austerity budget and simply handed it over to the Japanese government.

[4] The new ministries included the Ministry of Health and Welfare (Koseisho), Ministry of Labor (Rodosho), Ministry of Construction (Kensetsusho), and Ministry of Home Affairs (Jichisho).

The GHQ also considered it an imperative to nurture countervailing powers to those of the reactionary conservatives. The GHQ released imprisoned communist and socialist leaders, legalized unions, and encouraged worker mobilization. The GHQ also banned, at least initially, employers from organizing themselves nationally, while, in contrast, it helped workers to organize themselves. Thanks to the GHQ's policy, Japanese unions rapidly organized workers during the Occupation period and reached nearly 50 percent, a postwar peak, in 1950. Indeed, the first Socialist-led coalition government in Japan – a rarity not to be repeated until 1995 – was formed in 1947 under the Allied Occupation.

Notwithstanding the GHQ's anticonservative policy, conservative political parties remained the dominant forces in the Japanese Diet during and after the Occupation. In all postwar elections under the Allied Occupation – 1946, 1947, 1949, and 1950 – conservative political parties gained more seats than socialists and communists. Given the conservative dominance in the Diet, the GHQ forbade the Japanese government from passing any legislation that benefited groups associated with the military regime. In this way, the GHQ ensured that conservatives would not use their dominance in the Diet to legislate policies that helped them mobilize reactionary societal groups. The beginning of the cold war, however, altered the GHQ's stance toward Japan's conservative parties. In the new geopolitical situation, U.S. policy sought to turn postwar Japan into a loyal and prosperous capitalist economy. In its new attempt to prevent Japan from falling into the hands of communists, the GHQ "reversed course" and abandoned many of its previous pro-union and socialist-friendly policies.[5] By the early 1950s, all of the purged senior conservative politicians had been rehabilitated.

Thus when the Allied Occupation ended in 1952, Japan was governed by one of the conservative parties, the Liberal Party led by Prime Minister Shigeru Yoshida.[6] Until 1955, Shigeru Yoshida's Liberal Party and Ichiro Hatoyama's Democratic Party alternatively shared power. In that year, all conservative parties joined forces to form a new party. It is worth mentioning here that social welfare was an extremely important issue for conservative parties throughout the 1950s. At every election, promises of more welfare provision played prominent roles in each party's campaign.[7] And even more importantly, the ruling conservative party used its position in power to mold Japan's social protection programs to maximize electoral gain.

The political dominance of the conservatives continued throughout the Allied Occupation and after it. The merger of all conservative parties to create the

---

[5] The Japanese called this shift in the U.S. policy toward Japan the "Reversed Course." The American occupation authorities lifted the purge in 1950, and many of the conservative senior politicians resumed their political careers.

[6] Otake (1986) provides an excellent study of politics under Yoshida and contrasts immediate postwar Japanese politics to that in Germany.

[7] The existing literature on Japanese politics argues that Japanese conservatives became "pro-welfare" converts in the mid-1960s in their attempt to appeal to the ever-increasing number of disgruntled urban voters. A close look into the electoral politics of the early 1950s, however, presents a very different picture.

Liberal Democratic Party in 1955 did not change welfare politics. The continuing use of the same electoral rules consisting of the multimember districts and single nontransferable vote (MMD/SNTV) meant that the new Liberal Democratic Party continued to pursue similar electoral strategies. Since its creation in 1955, the LDP maintained an absolute majority until 1989. During this period, the LDP used its power to shape Japan's social protection system to its advantage. Many of the social protection programs were targeted either at rural districts or at specific societal groups that contributed votes and money to the LDP.

The transition period between the Occupation and the conservative rules that followed is critical. Japan embraced universalistic principles in its social policy for the first time during the occupation period. The GHQ successfully prevented the electoral calculations of politicians – particularly the conservative politicians in the ruling party – from shaping the postwar welfare state. Once the artificial constraints imposed on conservative politicians by the GHQ disappeared, distributive effects of Japan's electoral rules came out in full force. The occupation period, therefore, contrasts sharply with the post-occupation period, during which the ruling conservative party – finally free from constraints imposed by the GHQ – almost immediately began to fragment Japan's welfare state. The postwar development of Japan's distinctive welfare system cannot be understood without looking at this period. To grasp the development of the postwar Japanese welfare system, we need to understand why and how the Allied Occupation introduced universalistic programs and why and how Japan's independent postwar governments replaced them with targeted programs.

Public Assistance and Unemployment Insurance[8]

Public assistance and unemployment insurance provide, as we shall see, the best examples of universalistic programs that came into existence during the occupation of Japan. The Second World War devastated Japan. About 65 percent of all residences in Japan were destroyed. The loss of life amounted to 2.5 million deaths (one-third of the deaths consisted of civilians). Only Germany experienced greater damage than Japan. The destruction of the physical infrastructure (dwellings, factories, roads, and ports) disrupted people's lives and destroyed the economy. Productive capacity in 1946 fell to less than one-third of the 1940

---

[8] This section and later sections rely on a number of excellent collections of welfare bureaucrats who actually were involved in all major social policy legislations in the 1940s, 1950s, and 1960s. Koseidan ed. (1988), Koyama ed. (1985), The Ministry of Health and Welfare, Pension Bureau, and the Employee Pension Fund Association (1979), Nenkin Fukushi Jigyodan (the Pension Welfare Corporation) ed. (1972), and Omoto (1991) collectively provide long interviews of about fifty social policy bureaucrats. Two volumes put together by the reporters of a weekly economic journal record long interviews of bureaucrats, union leaders, and business leaders who were involved in politics during the 1950s, 1960s, and 1970s (Mainichi Shimbunsha Ekonomisuto Henshubu ed. 1984a, 1984b). Hirata et al. (1979a, 1979b) provide interviews of Ministry of Finance officials on tax-related policies during the early postwar period.

level. Millions of people lost their jobs.[9] As a result, postwar Japan suffered from dangerous levels of poverty.

The GHQ, in its attempt to bring order to the postwar chaos, ordered the Japanese government to address citizens' pressing welfare needs. In its directives concerning social welfare programs, the GHQ demanded that laws and policies treat all citizens equally rather than as members of various privileged groups – especially those groups associated with the old military regime.[10] Thus the GHQ abolished veterans' pension in 1945 and strictly prohibited any differential treatment of veterans or their families (see Murakami 1987; and Nishikawa 1991). In 1945, the GHQ issued a directive demanding the introduction of comprehensive income assistance for the poor (rather than targeted programs for specific groups). The following year, the GHQ also issued a report that suggested that the Japanese government study the feasibility of an unemployment insurance program.[11]

The Public Assistance Law was legislated immediately under the conservative Liberal Party government in 1946. In drafting the law, the Japanese government had to satisfy three conditions imposed by the GHQ's directive SCAPIN 775: (i) equal treatment of all citizens; (ii) governmental responsibility to provide welfare; and (iii) a guaranteed social minimum (Tada 1991, 72–73). Although this new program was means-tested, it was quite a departure from the prewar poor relief law. The new law did not link eligibility to inability to work like the old law did.[12] Under the new law, the national government assumed a new responsibility to guarantee a social minimum. This approach was in line with the spirit of the new American-drafted Constitution that stipulated that it was the state's responsibility to protect the basic rights of citizens, including their rights to livelihood.[13] A former bureaucrat in the Ministry of Health and Welfare (hereafter Ministry of Welfare), who helped draft the Public Assistance Law, later acknowledged that

---

[9] The number of workers who lost jobs in military factories and veterans added up to more than 12 million people. This number did not even include workers who were laid off from private enterprises, those who lost their livelihood due to damages of the war, and Japanese civilians returning from the colonies. See Ministry of Labor, *The Twenty-Year History of Unemployment Measures Projects* 1970.

[10] Murakami (1987) provides the details of the making of social policy under the GHQ. Koyama (1950) provides a detailed account of the GHQ directives concerning the new Public Assistance Law.

[11] The same report also ordered the Japanese government to create an insurance program for workers' injuries. The prewar health care insurance schemes for workers covered workers' injuries. Under these schemes, the cost of medical treatment for workers' injuries and other related expenses was carried by both workers and employers because the health care schemes were financed by employers and employees. The GHQ argued that providing medical treatment and wage compensation for workers' injuries was solely the responsibility of the employer. The Japanese government reformed the preexisting health care insurance (Nishikawa 1991, 119).

[12] For a detailed analysis of the postwar development of public assistance in Japan, see Milly (1999).

[13] Nonetheless, there were loopholes in the new law. The governmental responsibility in the law was cast in terms of the citizens' constitutional right to livelihood. Furthermore, the actual implementation of the Public Assistance Program was delegated to *minsei iin* – private citizens appointed as volunteer social workers prying into neighbors' lives (see Tada 1991, 73).

the GHQ was crucial in securing the necessary budget to implement the new public assistance program.[14]

The unemployment insurance program introduced in 1947 was also surprisingly universalistic compared to most programs introduced after the Occupation.[15] Here it is important to recall that electoral incentives based on MMD/SNTV – the electoral system in place from the end of the Allied Occupation until 1996 – make fragmented programs much more likely than universalistic ones. Although the new unemployment insurance was a contributory program, its coverage was broad and included special measures to take care of marginal workers. It stands out when compared to most of the postwar social and labor policies, because employers had a very limited say during the legislative process. Employers generally argued that it was premature to introduce comprehensive unemployment insurance in Japan. The government nonetheless implemented the new program swiftly over the employers' objections. The benefit structure was much more favorable to workers than anything the employers would have liked: for instance, the new program guaranteed benefits for workers who voluntarily resigned and provided a progressive benefit formula guaranteeing higher replacement ratios for low-paid workers.[16] The government even provided noncontributory unemployment allowances to those workers who were unemployed before they had contributed long enough to the unemployment insurance to qualify for benefits. As part of its concessions to employers, the government exempted small firms with fewer than six workers and seasonal workers from compulsory enrollment; furthermore, the benefit period was kept short (six months). Even taking these concessions into consideration, the new unemployment insurance can still be counted as a comprehensive program. It included workers in most sectors that were employed in companies with more than five regular employees; and it also covered women.

It is worth noting how the legislative process that led to the unemployment insurance program minimized the influence of core male workers' unions and large firms. Thus some of the demands made by two of the more radical labor federations trumped the opposition of the moderate labor federation and employers. A radical labor federation, Zensanbetsu, and the similarly left-wing public sector union federation, Kankoro, demanded that all workers be treated the same, regardless of age, sex, and the size of the enterprise. They also demanded that

[14] This is based on the statement of Kasai Yoshitsugu, a Ministry of Welfare official directly involved in the legislative process of the Public Assistance Law (Koyama ed. 1985, 52). Kasai recalls how easy it was to receive necessary funding for the new program while also recalling how strongly the GHQ prohibited any benefits for veterans and related groups.

[15] A center-left coalition government, which included the Socialist Party, was in place at the time of the legislation of the Unemployment Insurance. As it will be discussed in this section, core male workers' unions did not support a universalistic unemployment insurance system.

[16] For the content of various legislative options and the record of statements by all the major unions and employers' groups, see Ministry of Labor ed., Unemployment Insurance Section, Employment Stabilization Bureau, 1960, 210–234.

seasonal workers be included.[17] In contrast, the Sodomei (a more moderate labor federation consisting of politically moderate private sector workers) advocated the exclusion of female workers, seasonal workers, and those working in enterprises employing fewer than five workers. Trade associations of highly skilled work-ers such as the Japan Machine Tools Association shared Sodomei's preference for earnings-related benefits as well as family supplements. Sodomei advocated a three-way split of insurance costs between the worker, the employer, and the state. Many trade associations of employers held the same view.[18] In fact, Sodomei had more in common with the employers than with Zensanbetsu.

Such an outcome was an important anomaly that became possible only under the peculiar conditions of the Occupation. During the Occupation, groups whose views were close to those of the GHQ – the veto player during this period – received favorable representation in the legislative process.[19] In contrast, those groups that were out of the GHQ's favor were excluded from the policy process. During the legislative process leading up to the introduction of the unemploy-ment insurance program, the pro-universalism camp received favorable represen-tation in the policy deliberation process in ways that the relevant interest groups did not. In postwar Japan, any policy deliberation for a social protection program that exclusively affected wage earners – such as unemployment and employees' public pension – would take place in a tripartite *shingikai*.[20] The membership in such a *shingikai* would consist of academic experts and representatives from the peak-level employers' association, Nikkeiren, and two of the labor federations – one moderate, Sodomei (Domei), and one more radical, Sohyo. This type of tripartite deliberation ensured that business and labor – exclusively representing core male workers – had a chance to block undesirable policy changes.

Under the Allied Occupation, which favored universalistic benefits, the gov-ernment deviated from the conventional practice and put together a special com-mittee to discuss various options for unemployment insurance. Significantly, this committee only included one business representative and one union representa-tive among its thirteen members.[21] The rest of the members consisted of aca-demics and bureaucrats, including scholars such as Makoto Suetaka, who was influenced by the universalistic Beveridge Plan in the United Kingdom. In other

---

[17] They also demanded that young school leavers who failed to find jobs be eligible for benefits. This section relies on the preferences stated by unions and trade associations at the public hear-ings held in November 1946. The relevant statements are reproduced in Ministry of Labor ed., Unemployment Insurance Section, Employment Stabilization Bureau, 1960, 210–234.

[18] Given the Japanese dual labor market, male workers in large firms enjoyed more job security than marginal workers in the secondary labor market. As a result, they preferred to exclude high-risk groups from the insurance pool. Furthermore, highly paid workers benefit more from contributory earnings–related benefits than flat-sum benefits for everyone, which are more progressive by design. These observed preferences in Japan are in accordance with Isabela Mares's theory of social policy preferences (Mares 1997, 2003).

[19] Zensanbetsu's more radical demands to make employers shoulder the whole cost of unemployment benefits were not supported (ibid.).

[20] For the history of Japan's "corporatism," see excellent accounts by Garon (1987) and Gordon (1989).

[21] For the list of the members, see Ministry of Labor (1969, 1127).

words, bureaucrats, albeit with the support of the GHQ – the key veto player during the occupation – had the opportunity to create a more universalistic program, even in the absence of employers' and unions' support. Without going into the same degree of detail, it suffices here to mention that the Workers' Injury Insurance was enacted in the same period and in much the same way. The Workers' Injury Insurance also increased financial burdens on the employer on behalf of workers. These two programs would have been more difficult to introduce had it not been for the unusual circumstance of the Allied Occupation.

The Ministry of Labor, which was to administer both the Unemployment Insurance and the Workers' Injuries Insurance, was a major beneficiary of the Allied Occupation. The power of the Ministry of Labor bureaucrats was greater during this period than at any time between 1951 and 1989. It is no coincidence that the final outcome was a statewide insurance scheme administered by the new Ministry of Labor, which, as a result, gained access to funds accumulated in the new contributory Unemployment Insurance and the new Workers' Injuries Insurance. The GHQ's labor section was a strong ally of the Ministry of Labor, which itself was a GHQ creation. Rather than creating one ministry that dealt with welfare issues, the GHQ opted for creating a separate ministry devoted solely to the protection and promotion of workers' rights when it dismantled the Naimusho (the wartime Home Ministry) to create smaller ministries.[22]

Limits of Bureaucratic Initiatives

The legislative opportunities that social policy bureaucrats enjoyed under the GHQ, however, also placed limits on what they could do.[23] Such opportunities were largely based on a congruence of interest with the ultimate veto player, the GHQ. When Japanese social policy bureaucrats pushed for policies that the GHQ was against or uninterested in, those ideas went nowhere. The GHQ, for instance, struck down Japanese social policy bureaucrats' proposals to create family allowance and public housing. The GHQ considered family allowance unnecessary for a country like Japan, which, in their view, suffered from excess population.[24] Similarly, rather than the public provision of affordable rental housing as preferred by social policy bureaucrats, the GHQ promoted private construction

[22] This is why postwar Japan ended up with two separate ministries related to welfare issues: the Ministry of Labor and the Ministry of Health and Welfare. These two ministries only finally merged in January 2001 as part of the governmental reorganization. Just as a reminder, I use the old terminology – Ministry of Labor and Ministry of Welfare – in referring to labor and social policy bureaucrats' activities prior to 2001.

[23] Social policy bureaucrats and other bureaucrats thus tried their best to introduce new programs in their jurisdiction within the confines of the GHQ's general policy. Often, one ministry's loss was another ministry's gain, as ministries often competed on similar policy terrains. Various interviews recorded in Omoto (1991) illuminate this point. For instance, although the Welfare Ministry's idea to expand the state's responsibility to deliver rental housing as a welfare good did not gain the GHQ's support, the Construction Ministry's officials managed to create a new big program for housing as a homeownership promotion program more in accordance with the GHQ's policy.

[24] See Ministry of Health and Welfare White Papers (Kosei Hakusho) 1965, 32.

of homes to stimulate the Japanese economy and get it back on its feet again soon.[25] The Ministry of Construction, in turn, took advantage of the policy orientation of the GHQ to successfully create a new public housing mortgage company, Japan's Housing Financial Public Corporation (Jutaku Kinyu Koko).[26] This public corporation was created with government funding to combat the lack of money for the private construction of homes.

It should also be pointed out that the highest priority for the Ministry of Welfare in the years following the defeat was the revitalization and continuation of the preexisting social insurance schemes under its jurisdiction – that is, old-age pension and health care. Postwar Japan had inherited social insurance schemes in health care and old-age pension. The social insurance schemes for health care were two tiered: one tier was occupationally fragmented; the other was geographically fragmented.[27] The Employee Pension, which covered industrial workers, however, consisted of one national program.[28] All these programs were in a dire financial state as a result of the war. The Social Insurance Systems Research Council (set up by the Ministry of Welfare) issued a report in 1947 calling for a comprehensive pension system financed from general government revenue. Around the same time, officials in the health care section of the Welfare Ministry were developing ideas for a national health care system.[29]

The GHQ was more forthcoming in supporting new measures for health care than for pension, which it did not see as a priority issue. The GHQ officials saw nothing wrong with the preexisting national health care cooperatives set up by municipal governments.[30] They actually considered them democratic – and hence desirable – because they did not require compulsory insurance and were administered by local governments. For this reason, the GHQ approved the infusion of state subsidies to rescue the preexisting health care cooperatives set up

---

[25] Hayakawa and Tsunohashi (1985, 51). Omoto (1985, 421–425) talks about how the GHQ even closed down a preexisting public corporation (Jutaku Eidan), whose task was to provide public housing. The GHQ was extremely suspicious of state agencies created during wartime.

[26] Mitsuyoshi Maeda was a construction ministry bureaucrat at the time of the creation of this financial corporation. See his recollections recorded in Omoto (1991), especially pages 237–247.

[27] Japan was the fourth country to introduce compulsory health care in 1922. It consisted of company-based social insurance schemes (*kempo*). Unlike their postwar reincarnations, the pre-war health insurance schemes covered non-work-related illnesses and accidents alongside work injuries (Saguchi 1957, 226). The wartime government expanded health care coverage in 1938 by encouraging municipal governments to set up voluntary health care cooperatives. This expansion is attributed to the wartime state's concern for the deteriorating health of the rural population from which it conscripted soldiers (see Kondo 1963; in English, see Kasza 2002).

[28] The Employee Pension was introduced under the wartime government in 1941. This was a pre-funded program. Wartime social policy bureaucrats used wartime mobilization of capital as a justification to introduce this program. See comments by one official involved in the legislation of this program in 1941 (Takeo Hanasawa's comments in Koseidan ed. 1988, 23).

[29] Hideo Ibe and Kazuo Suzuki, both health care officials at the time, testify that they were already working on what was later called the All Nation Insurance in the latter half of the 1940s. See their interviews recorded in Koyama ed. (1985, 273).

[30] The GHQ commissioned a study group on Japan's social security system chaired by William Wandell. The Wandell Report was more pragmatic than the idealist report issued by the Social Insurance Systems Research Council. See Koyama ed. (1985, 56–59).

by municipal governments. The GHQ's attitude toward the preexisting occupational schemes was not so favorable. Although the GHQ did not abolish the preexisting occupationally fragmented health care cooperatives or the Employees' Pension System, as it did veterans' benefits, the GHQ did not consider these programs as top-priority issues. This meant that the Ministry of Welfare officials could not rely on budgetary resources to revitalize the occupational health care cooperatives and the Employees' Pension System. Any measures to bring these programs back to life had to involve increases in social security contributions levied from employers and workers. In contrast to the Unemployment Insurance, the Ministry of Welfare officials could not count on the GHQ's support to impose new financial burdens on employers and workers.

THE EROSION OF THE NASCENT UNIVERSALISM IN THE 1950S

The end of the Occupation and the return of full governing power to the Japanese Diet brought about a structural shift in the logic of welfare politics. This new period – which lasted, more or less, from 1951 to 1989 – saw conservative politicians using welfare programs to mobilize and organize subgroups within MMDs. Conservative politicians, who were previously constrained in their political activities, found themselves in 1951 playing catch-up with socialists and communists, who the Americans had allowed (at least initially) to organize supporters. With the constraints imposed by the anticonservative policy of the GHQ over, conservative politicians began using public policies for electoral purposes. Conservative politicians quickly latched onto targeted welfare programs as a way of creating differences among an otherwise homogeneous voter population. These targeted benefits created selective incentives for societal groups to form and organize. Negotiations for benefit hikes opened ways for the development of a political exchange between groups seeking favorable policy decisions and politicians seeking votes. Here it is important to bear in mind that the combination of MMDs and SNTV rewarded individual conservative politicians for organizing such groups. In short, the electoral motivations of postwar conservative politicians began to shape, step by step, different aspects of the welfare system. Under the auspices of these conservative politicians, Japan came to abandon many of the universalistic programs put in place by New Dealers in the Allied Occupation.

A key episode in this story is the close relationship that developed between conservative politicians and the association of deceased veterans' families (Izokukai), because it provides both the clearest and the most important example of the type of welfare politics that dominated in this period. The development of Izokukai is both fascinating and highly revealing. There were close to 8 million dependents of deceased veterans (of which 2 million were war widows) in Japan. Postwar conservative politicians were led to create highly targeted benefits, largely for their own personal political gain, for veterans' families and repeatedly expand those benefits. These politicians showed no corresponding desire to create comprehensive public assistance programs, which covered all families in need, because such programs lacked the necessary personal political payoff. The case study of benefits for veterans' families provides a classic example of welfare politics during this period. This section also touches upon other societal groups such as the special postmasters, the Japan Medical Association, and construction companies. All these groups became loyal conservative constituent groups by mechanisms very similar to those that developed with respect to Izokukai.

Welfare Benefits as Selective Incentives for Voter Mobilization and Organization

By the time the end of the Allied Occupation was negotiated in 1951, various constraints imposed by the GHQ on Japan's legislative process had been lifted. In the new context of the cold war, the American home government wanted to ensure that socialists would not gain too much power in Japan. The GHQ thus lifted the previously imposed restrictions on the Japanese conservative politicians.[31] Welfare politics changed immediately. Social policy – among other things – was used as a vehicle to deliver targeted benefits to various societal groups that conservative politicians were courting. The fact that there were elections almost every year exacerbated the competition to mobilize and organize specific groups of voters. National elections took place almost every year: 1952, 1953, 1955, 1956, 1958, 1959, 1962, 1963, and 1965. In addition, general local elections took place in 1951, 1955, 1959, and 1963. Because national-level politicians depended on local politicians for their own campaigns, the general local elections had crucial implications for Diet members under the MMD/SNTV system. In fact, survivors' benefits for widows and families of deceased soldiers surfaced as a major issue during the electoral campaign for the general local elections in 1951, the final year of the Occupation. As mentioned earlier, the GHQ had forbidden any form of welfare benefits that singled out military personnel, their survivors, and families. With the end of the Occupation in sight, however, the political parties brought up the issue again. Prime Minister Shigeru Yoshida – leader of the Liberal Party – as well as his Finance Minister Hayato Ikeda campaigned around the country promising welfare benefits for the dependents of soldiers killed in the war (*izoku* or "survivors," as I will call them here).[32] These benefits became the first targeted programs introduced by the newly independent Japanese government.

Benefits for survivors were perceived as neither an ideological nor a partisan issue. Socialists and conservatives both supported the idea of special benefits for surviving families of veterans.[33] Here it is important to recall that regardless of party ideology, the combination of multimember districts and single nontransferable vote (MMD/SNTV) made it imperative for politicians to seek the support of organized groups in their electoral bid by promising special benefits targeted

[31] Because the Americans reversed their previous support of the left in favor of the right, this period is typically referred to as the "Reversed Course" (Dower 1999; Masumi 1983b).

[32] *Nihon Izoku Tsushin*, May 1, 1951, 1.

[33] Various issues of *Nihon Izoku Tsushin* (Japan Survivors' Newsletter) report the major political parties' position regarding special welfare benefits for wives and old parents of the deceased soldiers. See *Nihon Izoku Tsushin*, March 1, 1951, 2; September 1, 1951, 1.

at those groups. Even the socialists, in their attempt to court this specific group, promised targeted benefits rather than universalistic family benefits, which included all families that lost breadwinners. The sheer number of survivors turned them into an extremely attractive group of voters for a political party to court. In fact, the Japan Survivors' Association (Izokukai) had already demonstrated its electoral potential in 1950,[34] when the president of Izokukai ran quite successfully as a Liberal Party candidate in the Upper House elections.[35]

The (conservative) Liberal Party government legislated – and thus earned credit for – the Survivors' Protection Law (Engo Ho) in 1951. The new law introduced pensions and lump-sum payments for deceased soldiers' families. Prime Minister Yoshida, Finance Minister Ikeda, and Welfare Minister Ryogo Hashimoto all personally met with representatives of Izokukai to promise special benefits.[36] The fact that the Liberal Party (LP) was in power when the occupation ended gave it an enormous advantage in using public policy as a selective incentive to organize voters. The LP gained a first mover's advantage in mobilizing and organizing support by promising and delivering benefits to specific groups. Thus while all the political parties supported benefits for survivors, it was the Liberal Party, which at the time held all the relevant cabinet positions, that actually delivered the promised policies.[37] Interestingly, Izokukai was not initially committed to supporting the LP. Izokukai simply wanted compensation for survivors and used their numbers to influence political decisions. In the 1952 Lower House elections, Izokukai endorsed candidates from different political parties – including even a socialist.[38] Izokukai's strategy was to campaign in favor of those candidates committed to providing generous benefits to Izokukai.[39] Their partisan loyalty to the Liberal Party – and later the LDP – was primarily due to the fact that the Liberal Party was the ruling party capable of delivering specific benefits. In turn, the LP had to earn Izokukai's support by delivering the "promised goods." In 1952, for instance, Izokukai demanded greater benefits for survivors, and the Liberal Party responded by agreeing to a lump sum payment per deceased soldier.

The political exchange of benefits and votes between the Liberal Party and Izokukai developed and deepened throughout the 1950s. Through repeated exchanges of benefits and votes, the tie between party and group was solidified. After the Liberal Party merged with other conservative parties to create

34 Initially, Izokukai was called Izoku Renmei. In order to avoid confusion, I will simply refer to them as Izokukai.
35 Tanaka, Tanaka, and Hata (1995, 198–200).
36 *Nihon Izoku Tsushin*, July 1, 1951, 1; *Nihon Izoku Tsushin*, August 1, 1951, 2; *Nihon Izoku Tsushin*, January 1, 1952, 2; *Nihon Izoku Tsushin*, February 2, 1952, 3.
37 *Nihon Izoku Tsushin* (September 1, 1951, 1) reports how every political party was sympathetic to their demands.
38 The president of Izokukai, Ginzo Nagashima, who had become an Upper House member, invited over a dozen Diet members to found a pro-Izoku association of Diet members. This group even included a socialist, Tsuruyo Tsutsumi. *Nihon Izoku Tsushin*, March 1, 1952, 2
39 *Nihon Izoku Tsushin*, November 15, 1950, 2. During this period, issues such as politicians' visit to the Yasukuni Shrine had not yet become important.

the Liberal Democratic Party, the same tie continued between Izokukai and the LDP. After the introduction of survivors' pensions and lump-sum payments, the Izokukai lobbied the Liberal Party for the reintroduction of veterans' pensions, which had been abolished under the Allied Occupation.[40] In 1953, the Liberal Party reinstated veterans' pensions and also reduced the penalty on war widows who had remarried so that they could continue receiving survivors' benefits.[41] In 1954, the Liberal Party introduced special public loans to survivors allowing them to use their future payments of survivors' pension as collateral.[42] In the same year, the government provided new lump-sum payments for survivors while, at the same time, it defined "survivors" more expansively – by including survivors of civilians mobilized for war efforts.[43] These policy decisions reflected the Liberal Party's desire to court the votes of Izokukai members.[44] These annual improvements of benefits occurred in large part due to the nearly annual elections taking place in this period.

During the electoral campaign in 1955, all parties yet again competed with one another to court Izokukai. They all promised to increase survivors' pensions to match civil servants' pensions, and to broaden the eligibility criteria.[45] The socialists called for an expansion of benefit eligibility to survivors of civilians such as students who were mobilized during the war to work in factories and lost their lives in air-raids. This proposal was soon adopted by the conservatives as well.[46] In other words, at every election, promises were made for some combination of new benefits, benefit hikes, or an expansion of eligibility rules. Although the opposition parties often supported benefit expansion, it was the ruling party – who was in the best position to deliver these benefits – that won the electoral support of the Izokukai leadership.

The case of Izokukai provides a useful illustration of the mechanism by which specific electoral rules shaped politicians' behavior as well as the strategies of societal groups. Izokukai leaders functioned as critical brokers of this exchange of benefits and votes. Highly targeted welfare benefits not only consolidated survivors' support for the conservatives, they also helped the Izokukai to recruit members. The Izokukai leaders needed to organize as many survivors as possible and to persuade them to vote for officially endorsed candidates, because the political influence of these leaders rested on their capacity to deliver votes. They did this by using information as a selective incentive to increase members. New benefits for survivors required that they apply for benefits. Izokukai used its

[40] *Nihon Izoku Tsushin*, September 1, 1952, 1–2; *Nihon Izoku Tsushin*, October 1, 1952, 1.
[41] *Nihon Izoku Tsushin*, August 1, 1953, 1.
[42] *Nihon Izoku Tsushin*, February 1, 1954, 1; *Nihon Izoku Tsushin*, April 1, 1954, 1.
[43] *Nihon Izoku Tsushin*, April 1, 1954, 1; *Nihon Izoku Tsushin*, June 1, 1954, 1; *Nihon Izoku Tsushin*, July 1, 1954, 1. The qualifying conditions to receive benefits as a survivor continued to expand. See *Nihon Izoku Tsushin*, April 30, 1959, 1.
[44] The policy changes reflected Izokukai's demands. See *Nihon Izoku Tsushin*, November 1, 1953, 2; *Nihon Izoku Tsushin*, January 1, 1954, 2; *Nihon Izoku Tsushin*, April 1, 1954, 2.
[45] *Nihon Izoku Tsushin*, February 1, 1955, 1.
[46] *Nihon Izoku Tsushin*, October 1, 1956, 1; *Nihon Izoku Tsushin*, December 1, 1956, 1.

organizational newsletter to provide information about how to apply for new benefits.

This process was facilitated by the fact that the Ministry of Welfare designated Izokukai as the sole channel of communication between the ministry and survivors. Izokukai, in turn, informed its members about benefit eligibility changes and other important benefit information. As a result, many survivors came to closely associate state-sponsored benefits with their Izokukai membership. In other words, the "official" status accorded to the Izokukai transformed public benefits into selective incentives to recruit and organize members.[47] Such a quasi-official status obviously would not have been granted, had Izokukai not been a political machine for the ruling party.

Izokukai leaders also strengthened local branches in the late 1950s and the early 1960s. By the early 1960s, Izokukai had established a more sophisticated electoral strategy to maximize its impact on the LDP.[48] To this end, it concentrated its support on one or two LDP candidates in the Upper House national district for the express purpose of showing off its vote-mobilizing power. Indeed, Izokukai leadership was keenly aware of the political advantage that the large multimember district generated for a well-organized group like theirs.[49] At the same time it endorsed about forty LDP members in the rest of the Upper House's MMD districts (called "prefectural districts"). While using the Upper House as a useful instrument of power, it also endorsed more than two hundred Lower House members to cultivate a sufficient number of LDP politicians in both Houses. During electoral campaigns, Izokukai rallied their members to vote for specific candidates, making an explicit link between votes and future benefit hikes.

Izokukai's strategy of cultivating close ties with individual conservative politicians – both senior leaders and rank and file – paid off. When any opposition to survivors' benefits arose, the LDP's senior politicians would weigh in on behalf of Izokukai. When, for instance, the Ministry of Finance and the Ministry of Welfare opposed Welfare Minister Hashimoto's plan to provide more to survivors in 1959, Hashimoto even resigned his post in protest. Later when Izokukai demanded favorable treatment of survivors under the new National Pension System introduced in 1960, a number of intraparty veto players ruled in Izokukai's favor.

The bureaucrats in the ministries strongly opposed this kind of selective expansion of the welfare state. The Ministry of Welfare officials objected to the very idea

---

[47] This also indicates that the Welfare Ministry, originally opposed to status-based benefits, had come around to use its jurisdiction over survivors' benefits as a way of building a close tie with the group of conservative politicians that "represented" Izokukai within the party.

[48] Izokukai's pre- and post-election analyses become increasingly sophisticated in the early 1960s. See *Nihon Izoku Tsushin*, October 30, 1960, 1, for an example of how the group times its annual meeting to coincide with the government's final stage of budget negotiations (it always happens toward the end of the year).

[49] An issue of *Nihon Izoku Tsushin* very explicitly mentions that the national district in the Upper House is the measure of their power (April 30, 1962, 2).

of status-based benefits, such as the ones given to veterans' survivors. The Welfare officials believed that benefits should be need-based – and thus more broadly available – rather than status-based.[50] The Ministry of Finance also opposed such attempts, because of the fiscal pressures they created.[51] Insofar as ruling party politicians were concerned, however, the targeting of benefits paid off electorally, especially for individual LDP politicians who relied on Izokukai's vote mobilization abilities. In contrast, universalistic benefits such as family allowance for single mothers – something social policy bureaucrats had wanted – would not have been useful in mobilizing and organizing a subgroup of voters.[52] Without the GHQ as a critical ally, however, social policy bureaucrats were no longer able to resist the distributive incentives of politicians.

Izokukai illustrates nicely the way that targeted benefits oiled the wheels of the postwar conservative political machine. Izokukai became a core constituent group for many LDP politicians. By regularly raising the benefit levels, the vows of political exchange could be renewed. Thus following the death of Ginzo Nagashima, the first president of Izokukai, LDP politicians always filled this position, further consolidating Izokukai as a major LDP support group. The LDP also gradually expanded the eligibility rules for survivors' benefits to boost the membership of Izokukai – again over the opposition of the Welfare Ministry. Even as recently as 2000, veterans and survivors still constituted one of the largest support groups for the LDP.[53] It is important to emphasize here that Izokukai had ties not merely to the LDP in general, but to specific LDP politicians, whom they would endorse in MMD competitions.

Political Exchange and Other Societal Groups

The case of Izokukai provides a good example of how electoral strategies can shape the welfare state. A similar political exchange of votes and benefits occurred between the Liberal Party and other societal groups, including post masters (represented by the National Association of Special Postmasters) and physicians (represented by the Japan Medical Association). Insofar as public policy could generate targeted benefits, a quid pro quo developed between the targeted group and

---

[50] The position of the welfare officials is clear from the Ministry's White Papers (Kosei Hakusho) for 1956. Chapter 1 of the Papers devotes one whole section (section 4) to the plight of single mothers. The section claims that benefits for veterans' survivors were inefficient means to address the problem associated with the rise of single mothers after the war. Not all these mothers were widows of fallen soldiers; many were regular widows who lost their husbands to illness and accidents. Also see Campbell (1992, 57).

[51] *Nihon Izoku Tsushin*, April 1, 1956, 1.

[52] The development of this tie between Izokukai and the LP (and the LDP after 1955) does not mean that the conservative party as a whole embraced Izokukai. Some party members had reservations about the generous treatment of veterans and survivors. They feared it would set a precedent for other groups (Campbell 1992, 57).

[53] If one takes into consideration that there was no supply of new veterans in Japan since 1945, the prowess of the Izokukai is quite intriguing as well as impressive. The LDP managed to inflate the number by expanding the definition of survivors eligible for benefits.

the ruling party. Occupational groups whose income and profits could be augmented by public policy were ideal candidates for this type of political exchange.

The timing of the mobilization and organization of these groups coincided with the cultivation of Izokukai. The years immediately following the end of the Allied Occupation were the period when conservative politicians were frantically trying to catch up with socialists and communists who had stolen a lead in organizing supporters. These mobilization efforts were led by different senior conservative politicians rather than coordinated at the party level. Different senior politicians thus cultivated ties with different groups. In the case of Izokukai, a number of senior Liberal Party politicians such as Okinori Kaya developed very close ties with the group. In fact, Izokukai supported Kaya's electoral comeback following his release from the Sugamo Prison, where all the purged politicians had been jailed. (Like other conservative politicians, Kaya joined the new Liberal Democratic Party in 1955.)

Other conservative politicians such as Shigemasa Sunada turned their attentions to the special postmasters (*tokubetsu yubin kyokucho*), whom they transformed into a highly politicized national organization, the National Association of Special Postmasters (Zentoku) in 1953.[54] Here it is important to note that Japan has two kinds of postmasters. The "unspecial" postmasters are civil servants who gain promotion to the top managerial positions in their respective post offices. Special postmasters, in contrast, are former local notables who are appointed by the government as postmasters. The origin of this distinction lies in the late nineteenth century, when the Japanese state recruited local notables to serve as postmasters to expand the reach of the state-run postal services – and also to give credibility to the newly created postal system (see Maclachlan 2004; Westney 1987).

Like Okinori Kaya, Shigemasa Sunada was a Liberal Party member, who later joined the Democratic Party, and then the Liberal Democratic Party. Sunada targeted special postmasters to counter the organizational offensive by the socialists. As was the case with veterans' survivors, public policy could create "rent" paid by special postmasters to the government; because of their status, their remuneration and perks were all decided by the government. As civil servants, these postmasters were legally prohibited from campaigning for specific political parties or individual candidates. Sunada even tried (albeit unsuccessfully) to change the legal status of special postmasters to "political appointees," so that they could freely campaign for conservative politicians. However, Sunada was successful in incorporating the family members of the special postmasters – who were free to engage in political activities – into the conservative political machine. The conservative government further rewarded postmasters by allowing them to sell financial products and life insurance policies at their post offices.[55]

---

[54] Calder (1990, 47) and Wada (1997, 120–123) refer to the importance of Sunada's role. For an overview of the political exchange that developed between conservative politicians and the special postmasters, see Maclachlan (2004).

[55] For instance, the Liberal Party government devised a system whereby survivors' pensions would be paid at post offices in a clear attempt to bring business to special post offices. *Nihon Izoku Tsushin*, October, 1, 1952, 1.

The conservative political machine also found a way of recruiting doctors. In the early 1950s, the Japan Medical Association (JMA) had not yet become a solid conservative constituent group. During this period, the JMA even endorsed some members of the Socialist Party at elections (Koyama ed. 1985, 253). To understand the transformation of the JMA into a loyal wing of the conservative party, we first need to understand a few things about the postwar Japanese medical system. Postwar Japan inherited the prewar health care system, whereby the fees for physicians were negotiated between the physicians' association and the compulsory company-based health care insurance schemes (*kempo*). Although Japan had introduced compulsory health care insurance relatively early (1922), the Japanese state never socialized medical services. Most of the physicians in Japan were doctors with their own private practice. Physicians had not been happy about the level of the fees set by the social insurance schemes. The financial deterioration of many health care insurance schemes made matters worse – to the point that many physicians were not willing to see patients. In 1951, when the new round of negotiations over medical fees – a negotiation involving Ministry of Welfare bureaucrats, the representatives of the health care cooperatives, and the Japan Medical Association – ground to a halt, conservative politicians intervened to settle the issue in the physicians' favor.[56] The Liberal Party leaders promised physicians a generous level of income tax deduction on the income they received from the health care cooperatives. By doing so, the Liberal Party turned what was a relatively modest raise in medical fees into a significant net gain for physicians.[57] In 1954, the Democratic Party government – another conservative government – turned this temporary tax deduction into a permanent provision.[58] As soon as the physicians realized the amount of "rent" that they could extract from the government, they began to offer their political support to the ruling party. From 1955 on, the new LDP could count on the loyal support of the JMA. Just like Izokukai, the Japan Medical Association ran its own candidates – typically

[56] Taketo Tomono, a welfare official who served in both the wartime and the postwar years, recalls how conservative politicians became involved in the fee-setting process for physicians as early as 1946. Yet until the early 1950s, Tomono states, physicians themselves were not very interested in the reimbursements from the social insurance schemes, because most of their income was coming from non–social insurance sources. It was in the early 1950s that physicians realized that the reimbursements from the social insurance schemes would be lucrative if they played the game right (see Koyama ed. 1985, 38, 43).

[57] See Kazuo Imai's account of the process. Imai was a Welfare Ministry official at the time (Koyama ed. 1985, 186–187).

[58] To prevent any veto by the Tax Bureau of the Ministry of Finance, the Liberal Party did not involve them at all in the negotiation. In 1954, the Liberals successfully legislated an income tax reform bill in order to institutionalize huge permanent income tax deductions for physicians. The Liberal Party circumvented the MOF by submitting the bill to the Diet as one sponsored by individual legislators rather than a government bill. Although the MOF would have been able to block or negotiate a government bill, which would have been drafted by them, the MOF had much less control over individual legislators' bills. Retired MOF officials recall their futile efforts to persuade conservative politicians not to grant such tax deductions to physicians (Hirata et al. 1979a, 464–465). For an excellent account of all the major tax policy decisions during this period, see Sato and Miyajima (1990).

physicians – as LDP candidates in the Upper House elections and mobilized support for particular LDP candidates in the Lower House elections.[59]

Small construction companies were another group that was mobilized by conservative politicians. Japanese construction companies tended to be small, which meant that there were numerous company owners who could be mobilized by the strategic use of public policy.[60] Public works were an effective means of increasing the business income of construction companies. Although construction companies typically were paid only after the completion of projects, the Liberal Party government introduced a law that enabled the prepayment for contractors of public projects.[61] Public works projects were likewise designed to benefit companies, both big and small, that provided construction materials.

All these exchanges between conservative politicians and various interest groups – each an exchange of benefits for electoral support – were perfected by the Liberal Democratic Party when they took over in 1955. Hikes in compensation for veterans and survivors, fees for physicians, public works spending, and regulatory advantages over postal products were all benefits purchased by loyal support for the ruling Liberal Democratic Party.

FRAGMENTATION OF PENSION PROGRAMS[62]

As we have seen, the distributive strategies of the parliamentary veto players (that is, the conservative politicians in the LDP and its forerunners) involved the cultivation of various occupational and other groups. These distributive strategies had the effect of fragmenting the preexisting public pension schemes. What happened to the public pension system in the 1950s provides yet another piece of evidence of the impact of the structural logic in Japan during this period. According to the structural logic, politicians under the MMD/SNTV system are more likely to pursue benefits targeted at their own organized constituent groups. The structural logic also claims that bureaucratic agenda-setting power is effective insofar as bureaucratic preferences are congruent with the parliamentary veto players' distributive priorities. In other words, we can expect

---

[59] See Campbell and Masuyama (1994) for an overview of the politics of physicians' fee setting.

[60] Even in 1980, 78.3 percent of construction firms in Japan consisted of small firms with capital of roughly fifty thousand dollars (at $1 = 100 yen) or less (see Ministry of Construction 1984, 354). The LDP government encouraged the formation of enterprise cooperatives among small- and medium-scale construction companies so that they could contract public works projects for which they would not be eligible due to their small size (Ministry of Construction 1960, 231).

[61] See Kohno and Nishizawa (1990, 159). The number of guaranteed prepayments increased from 1,590 to 28,076 in 1960 and 162,562 in 1975 (Ministry of Construction 1984, 367–370).

[62] Campbell (1992) offers a fascinating account of how the public pension scheme became fragmented in the 1950s. I wholly agree with his analysis in terms of the political forces at work in the process. I differ from Campbell in two ways, however. First, I emphasize that the same type of politics behind the fragmentation of Japan's Employee Pension System was also behind other aspects of the Japanese welfare state. Second, although Campbell's analysis focuses on technocratic (selfless) intentions of welfare bureaucrats, I also highlight the importance of their selfish organizational motivations.

bureaucrats to succeed when they propose policies that benefit the constituent groups of the ruling-party politicians. By the same token, we can expect bureaucrats not to succeed when their proposed policies primarily benefit either unorganized voters or the constituent groups of the opposition parties. Indeed, this is exactly what we observe in the period under review here. The result is the steady fragmentation of welfare provision, including, most importantly, public pensions.

Fragmentation of public pensions generally occurred in two steps. First, pension bureaucrats in the Ministry of Welfare were desperate to fix and expand the Employee Pension System. Big business – an important contributor to conservative parties – successfully thwarted the pension bureaucrats' efforts. Second, the low levels of Employee Pension benefits, in turn, motivated groups with ties to conservative politicians to seek superior benefits by setting up occupationally fragmented social insurance schemes. The result was a highly fragmented system of old age provision.

Failure to Expand the Employee Pension Benefits

Throughout the late 1940s and the 1950s, the Ministry of Welfare bureaucrats were determined to protect and expand the preexisting social insurance schemes in health care and pension under their jurisdiction. But their efforts were hopeless as they conflicted with the vital interests of constituents of ruling conservative politicians. Employers, a loyal conservative constituency group, opposed any expansion of the Employee Pension benefits and successfully blocked it.

Political negotiations to reform the Employee Pension System began in earnest in 1953 as the first cohort of beneficiaries began to draw benefits (Koseidan ed. 1988; Yamazaki 1985). The Employee Pension had been introduced during the war as a pre-funded pension in an effort to mobilize capital for the war effort.[63] The devastation by the war and the postwar inflation had completely eroded the sustainability of the pension system. Although the Employee Pension had been designed to provide earnings-related benefits, benefit levels were extremely meager. The pension bureaucrats in the Ministry of Welfare wanted to maintain the earnings-related benefit design and to improve benefit levels.[64] They also wanted to maintain part of the pre-funding of benefits in order

---

[63] This program was called Workers' Pension. To be more precise, this was the rationale that welfare officials used to persuade the Ministry of Finance in 1941. Welfare officials wanted a new fund-accumulating program in their jurisdiction and proposed that such a program would counteract the rising wartime inflation as well as raise additional funds for the war efforts. See Takeo Hanazawa's comments in Koseidan ed. (1988, 17). Hanazawa was personally involved in the legislation of Workers' Pension in 1941.

[64] The welfare ministry bureaucrats considered it crucial to maintain an earnings-related design if they were to create a public pension system that would be attractive to core male workers. Katsutsugu Hisashita, a welfare official, discusses in great detail what the ministry's preferences were (Koseidan ed. 1988, 80–93).

to accumulate money.[65] The pension bureaucrats had strong organizational interests at stake here. They thought that without relatively high earnings-related benefits, it would be impossible to get well-paid workers on board. And they favored a pre-funded pension system, because it would accumulate a pot of money that they themselves could control.[66] Welfare bureaucrats feared – rightly, it turned out – that unless they improved the Employee Pension benefits, alternative pension arrangements would develop at the expense of their jurisdictional control over the money that accumulated in the pension account.

Pension bureaucrats understood very well that if they wanted to reform the Employee Pension, they needed to get the employers' consent. As a loyal constituency group of the conservatives, the employers could count on the ruling party, the Liberal Party, to block undesirable changes. The Liberal Party had no interest in using the general budget to finance generous benefits for wage earners, who tended to vote for the opposition parties, at the expense of employers, one of their core constituent groups. The published statements of pension bureaucrats who were involved in the legislative processes reveal that they were extremely worried about employers' opposition for this very reason.[67]

The employers, however, opposed any expansion of the public pensions system that would increase their own financial burden.[68] As far as employers were concerned, private corporate benefits were much preferable to public schemes for labor management reasons. Labor relations in the early 1950s were fractious, and employers relied on company-based benefits to pacify their workforce.[69] For this reason, Nikkeiren – the peak-level federation of employers' associations – argued that the earnings-related component of the pension should be left to the

[65] Under the arrangement at the time, the Trust Fund Bureau of the Ministry of Finance controlled the reserves. The Welfare Ministry officials wanted a way to tap into the funds directly. See recollections of welfare officials in Pension and Welfare Corporation (Nenkin Fukushu Jigyodan ed. 1972).

[66] I will discuss this point in much greater detail later in this chapter.

[67] Pension officials (Shigetaka Ozaki and Takeji Kato) involved in the Welfare Ministry's attempt to increase contributions for the Employee Pension recall that, in their understanding at the time, they thought that unless Nikkeiren consented, the LDP government would not have signed onto a reform opposed by big business. Their detailed recollections of the policy process are recorded in Koseidan (1988, 130–133).

[68] For employers' position in the occupation period, see *Nikkeiren Times*, March 17, 1949. Once the negotiations for the Employee Pension began, employers continued their opposition. See *Nikkeiren Times* dated January 28, 1954; February 11, 1954; February 25, 1954; March 4, 1954; April 1, 1954; April 22, 1954. Also see Yamazaki (1985).

[69] The issues of the *Nikkeiren Times* during 1948, 1949, 1950, and 1951 are full of articles about actual cases of corporate fringe benefits that had been introduced in leading companies. The main theme of all these articles – and the intentions behind institutional changes presented in the articles – is how to construct cooperative and peaceful labor relations at work. This was a painful lesson learned by employers as a result of extremely violent confrontations with labor in the years following the war. Militant unions demanded economic democracy and had even seized control of the production process in some instances. The economic austerity program – the Dodge Line – implemented by the GHQ in 1949, for instance, produced massive waves of layoffs and escalated labor conflicts. There is a vast literature on labor relations during the immediate postwar period. See Gordon (1985, 1993), Hiwatari (1991), and Nishinarita (1992, 1994) for excellent overviews.

discretion of individual companies and that public pension should offer only meager flat-rate benefits (that is, the same for everyone).[70] They were also particularly
incensed by the fact that bureaucrats controlled the pension reserves at a time of
extreme capital shortage. Nikkeiren demanded that they should have access to the
reserves.[71] To appease employers, the Ministry of Welfare provided employers
with loans using the pension reserves in the Employee Pension.[72] Employers were
not satisfied and continued to oppose any expansion in the Employee Pension.
The employers ultimately prevailed.

Pension officials feared that unless the Employee Pension provided earnings-
related benefits, its programmatic expansion in the future would be closed off
by the growth of earnings-related private corporate pension schemes.[73] Indeed,
Nikkeiren lobbied the government for favorable tax provisions for employer-
provided functional equivalents to public pensions.[74] Thus in 1951 the Tax
Bureau in the Ministry of Finance introduced corporate tax deductions to facilitate payments of retirement lump-sum payments (RLSP) – which served as functional equivalents for severance and pension payments. Employers were thus
allowed to keep up to the 50 percent of all the RLSP required to pay if all of
the workforce were to quit that year.[75] In 1954, Nikkeiren secured tenure-rated
income tax deductions on the receipt of RLSP as a way of providing more RLSP
for loyal workers for less money.[76] Similarly, the tax authorities offered tax provisions for corporate savings plans.[77] All these tax expenditures greatly contributed
to easing the capital shortage that large firms faced in the 1950s, while, at the

---

[70] For Nikkeiren's demand, see Nikkeiren (1958: 183, 194, 210, and 216); *Nikkeiren Times*, September
16, 1952; December 17, 1953; December 25, 1953. Under a broad-based social insurance scheme,
large firms would have to subsidize benefits for workers in smaller – and more volatile – firms
(see Ministry of Health and Welfare, Pension Bureau et al. 1979, 55–56; Yamazaki 1985). Instead,
Nikkeiren, on behalf of large firms, demanded government support for corporate functionally
equivalent programs – typically in the form of tax support. It is worth noting that the same
labor management and risk/benefit calculations meant that large firms were less hostile to the
preexisting company-based health care cooperatives (*kempo*) – company-based social insurance
schemes indistinguishable from corporate benefits.

[71] Nikkeiren officially demanded that the pension reserves should belong to employers and workers.
They demanded "recycle loans" (*kangen yushi*), where they would be able to borrow from the
pension reserves (see *Nikkeiren Times*, September 30, 1948; February, 17, 1949; and April 20,
1950; Nikkeiren's demand dated September 16, 1952 recorded in Nikkeiren 1958, 183). Nikkeiren
continued to make similar demands; see, for instance, *Nikkeiren Times*, January 28, 1954. Employers
wanted to borrow money to invest in corporate fringe benefits.

[72] The following articles detail the content of the loans: *Asahi Shimbun*, October 12, 1952; *Nikkeiren
Times*, October 16, 1952.

[73] See pension officials' recollections in Koseidan ed. 1988, 80–93.

[74] For Nikkeiren's demands for tax deductions, see *Nikkeiren Times*, February 7, 1952 and January
29, 1953. Also see Nikkeiren (1958), which includes the records of all their policy demands during
this period.

[75] Ministry of Finance (1997, 56).

[76] Hirata et al. (1979a, 577); Kokuritsu Kokkai Toshokan Chosa Rippou Kousakyoku 1972, 55–56).

[77] Employers were allowed to create internal savings accounts for their employees. Employees
received higher than the market rate interest rates, while employers could "borrow" from their
workers at rates lower than the market rates.

same time, helping employers to use fringe corporate benefits as instruments to control workers' behavior.[78]

Generally speaking, employers were very successful in gaining tax concessions under the conservative rule in the 1950s and 1960s. Instead of supporting public welfare benefits for wage earners, employers asked for tax concessions on corporate fringe benefits as well as tax deductions on wage income to ease wage pressures (see chronology of tax deductions in Appendix 4.A).[79] It is also noteworthy that the government promoted the sale of life insurance policies in the name of welfare by providing generous deductions on the premiums paid to life insurance products (Sato and Miyajima 1990, 32; see Appendix 4.A). Some of the life insurance products were group products for employers; many were for individuals. These were all market-based functional equivalents to public welfare programs.[80] The government periodically increased life insurance deductions as well as heavily protecting the industry. This policy enabled the ruling party to establish a form of political exchange with the life insurance industry, while also allowing the regulators in the Ministry of Finance a great degree of control over the industry.

Most tax concessions came in the form of administrative orders (*tsutatsu*) issued by the Tax Bureau of the Ministry of Finance (MOF), which did not require any approval by the Cabinet or the Diet.[81] Furthermore, within the context of the pro-business Liberal Party government, direct negotiations between employers and the tax authorities did not even become politicized.[82] The pension bureaucrats, who were not party to any of the negotiations over the aforementioned tax expenditure programs, had no means to prevent the development of functional equivalents, which were likely to inhibit the development of generous earnings-related Employee Pension benefits in the future.

Electoral Calculations and Fragmentation

The employers' successful opposition to pension hikes also cost the Welfare Ministry in other ways. As the Employee Pension System continued to promise only meager pensions, conservative politicians began to intervene to help their core constituency groups set up more favorable occupational pension schemes. In

[78] Chapter 6 offers a detailed account of how Japan's social protection system shaped industrial relations in postwar Japan.

[79] A number of Nikkeiren's official policy statements are reproduced in Nikkeiren ed. (1958). According to Nikkeiren ed. (1958), Nikkeiren made demands for tax deductions to contain wage pressures almost every year since 1948.

[80] As later chapters will show, Japanese conservatives were never keen on introducing public welfare programs for unorganized urbanites. In the absence of public welfare programs for wage earners' families, the Japanese came to rely heavily on life insurance products.

[81] Decisions over *tsutatsu* took place in a nonpoliticized way and did not involve politicians. See the recollections of Jiro Yoshikuni, who was in the Tax Bureau of the Finance Minister at this time, in Ito and Ekonomisuto Henshubu ed. (1977, 28). Also see Hirata et al. (1979a, 1979b).

[82] Generally speaking, during the 1950s, there was very little understanding that tax concessions like regular budgetary items involved a zero-sum game. All this changed in the 1970s when the fiscal situation tightened. See Sato and Matsuzaki (1986).

1953, the LP government allowed private school teachers to establish the Private Schools' Teachers and Staff Mutual Aid Association (MAA). Under the law at the time, only civil servants possessed their own MAA. This allowed civil servants an exemption from enrolling in the more broad-based social insurance schemes for pension and health care and provided them with significantly better benefits than most private sector workers. Private school teachers were the first group to realize that they would be better off creating their own MAA like the civil servants than being absorbed into the Employee Pension (Shiritsu Gakko Kyoshokuin Kyosai Kumiai ed. 1965, 28). With their ties to conservative politicians, private school teachers gained sufficient support within the Diet to override the opposition of Welfare Ministry officials. To the chagrin of pension bureaucrats in the Welfare Ministry, other groups followed suit. In 1954, employees of municipal governments broke off from the broad-based social insurance schemes for workers to create their own MAA; the Mutual Assistance Association for Local Government Employees was thus created in 1954. Conservative politicians always intervened in favor of fragmented programs rather than a comprehensive one.[83]

The same trend in favor of fragmentation continued under the LDP government formed in 1955. In 1958, the LDP permitted the creation of an independent mutual assistance cooperative for the employees of the agricultural cooperatives, *nokyo*, so that *nokyo* employees would receive better benefits.[84] Since the conservatives had still not consolidated support in rural areas, building close ties with *nokyo*, which was beginning to emerge as the key organization representing farmers, was extremely critical at the time. Yet many in the LDP leadership also worried about further fragmenting the public pension system (Campbell 1992, 78–79). These worried leaders were simply overridden. Ichiro Kono was the key force behind the creation of this separate social insurance scheme for the *nokyo* employees. Kono, a former Minister of Agriculture with close ties to farmers and *nokyo*, was the chair of one of the critical intra-party committees, Somukai, and thus possessed control over the legislative agenda of the party (Campbell 1992, 78–79). As a result, he was able in 1958 to negotiate the inclusion of his "pet project" in the party's policy agenda. Needless to say, special treatment for *nokyo* employees was not something that the rank and file from rural areas would oppose. It should be emphasized here that the Allied Occupation had prohibited precisely this kind of cooptation of *nokyo* by the government. The GHQ wanted *nokyo* to be purely a voluntary association independent from the political authorities (Calder 1988, 252).

Electorally speaking, any preferential treatment to potential support groups was a worthwhile investment for any politician. Under the MMD/SNTV system, individual politicians cared more for their individual elections – and hence

---

[83] See Campbell (1992, 57); Ikuo Soneda, a former pension official, recalls that the Welfare Ministry was powerless against the political decisions to fragment the pension system, see Koseidan (1988, 113).

[84] The argument this time was that *nokyo* employees often worked alongside municipal public workers doing similar kinds of work, but municipal employees enjoyed better benefits – partly thanks to the 1954 decision to let them create their own MAA (Koseidan ed. 1988, 115).

catering to their own constituent groups – than the collective interest of their party or consistency of public programs. The importance of the personal vote under the MMD/SNTV system weakened the party leadership to such an extent that the LDP leaders could not themselves preserve the integrity of the social insurance scheme. They had to give way to powerful LDP politicians whose personal electoral interests took precedence. In short, the fragmentation of the pension system was largely a function of the decentralized nature of the Japanese political system under the MMD/SNTV system as detailed in Chapter 3.

FAVORING FUNCTIONAL EQUIVALENTS: UNEMPLOYMENT AND HOUSING

The same electoral dynamics that fragmented the pension system also affected other areas of social protection. The MMD/SNTV system encouraged parliamentary veto players to pursue targetable programs that benefited their respective constituent groups. By the same token, unorganized voters and the support groups of the opposition were squeezed out of government programs. Politicians had little incentive to advocate universalistic and comprehensive welfare programs, whose benefits extended to unorganized voters. Furthermore, the ruling conservative party had very little incentive to offer benefits that extended to wage earners, who did not constitute part of the conservative political machine – and worse still, the organized wage earners tended to vote for the opposition. The benefits that wage earners received in this institutional configuration were, as expected, employer-provided benefits rather than government-subsidized ones. Employer-provided benefits, in turn, reflected employers' labor management strategies, rather than the parliamentary veto players' electoral strategies. What happened to Japan's policy to cope with unemployment and housing illustrates how the structural logic under the MMD/SNTV was responsible for more fragmented forms of social protection that benefited particularistic groups.

Targeted Functional Equivalents Rather than Generous Unemployment Benefits for Every Worker

The Korean War boom that pulled the Japanese economy out of recession also generated excessive competition in some sectors of the economy. Many firms expanded their productive capacities, creating an oversupply of products that led to a downward spiral in their prices. The end of the Korean War boom endangered the survival of many small and medium-sized firms.[85] Rather than letting such firms fail and providing unemployment benefits to displaced workers, Japan introduced functional equivalents aimed at selectively rescuing specific industries.

In 1952, the government introduced a new law called "Provisional Procedures for the Stabilization of Special Small and Medium Enterprises" to set up "adjustment cooperatives," which were legalized forms of production cartels. The textile

---

[85] The U.S. government, in its effort to stimulate Japanese economy, used Japanese products for its military procurements. As a result, the Japanese economy picked up.

industry was one of the industries that suffered from overcapacity in the aftermath of the Korean War. Adjustment cooperatives were formed in the textile
industry.[86] Other product markets dominated by small firms followed suit and
set up their own adjustment cooperatives. These cooperatives provided a strong
incentive for small firms to organize themselves along industrial and geographical
lines to enjoy the benefits of the new law.

These adjustment cooperatives served conservative politicians' electoral need
to get small businesses organized.[87] Organizing small businesses was particularly
important to politicians given Japan's economic structure. Compared to other
advanced industrial societies, a large share of enterprises in Japan consisted of –
and still consists of – very small firms with fewer than ten employees. Many of
these firms were family businesses with a very politically vocal group of small
business owners – similar to those of France.[88] Conservative politicians curried
favor with small business owners for three reasons. First, small businesses were
likely to be responsive to favorable public policies targeted at them. Second,
small businesses were not, as of the early 1950s, part of the conservative political
machine.[89] Third, the fact that small businesses could be mobilized along different
product markets provided perfect tools for conservative politicians running from
the same medium-sized multimember districts who needed to "divide" votes.

In another effort to protect small and medium-sized firms, the conservative
government introduced legislation in 1954 that restricted the development of
large retail shops. This was a reversal of the GHQ's decision that repealed the
old department store law that restricted the opening of large stores.[90] Preferential
credit policies for small firms also reflected the desire on the part of ruling politicians to win their electoral support.[91] Capital for loans for small firms came from
public financial institutions financed by the Fiscal Investment and Loan Program,
which, in turn, was financed from welfare funds such as pension reserves, Postal
Savings, and Postal Insurance.

While a number of functional equivalents to unemployment benefits developed during the 1950s, the Unemployment Insurance itself did not become
any more generous. The electoral incentives in favor of particularistic forms

---

[86] Uriu (1996) has an excellent detailed account of textile industry politics. His comparative study of
how the Japanese government responded to the cries for help from different industries reveals a
story highly compatible with my structural logic. To summarize briefly, Uriu argues that industries
with numerous smaller firms did better than highly concentrated industries in receiving help from
the government.

[87] Tatebayashi (2004) provides case studies to demonstrate how this happened. Kozo Watanabe,
one of the politicians Tatebayashi focuses on, talks about how hard he tried to get adjustment
cooperatives organized as means of mobilizing small businesses.

[88] For comparative dimensions, see Berger ed. (1977, 1981), Berger and Piore eds. (1980), and Calder
(1988).

[89] Calder (1988, 338–340) offers a great overview of conservative politicians' efforts to mobilize and
organize small business. On political activities of small business owners, see Krauss (1980).

[90] Calder (1988, 340); for a historical development of the Retain Law, see Upham (1987).

[91] As Calder mentions, there were hundreds of unions being formed in small firms every month as of
1956. The LDP began organizing smaller firms into conservative organizations (see Calder 1988,
338–342).

of social protection meant that industries with political influence could seek special protection in the form of industrial policy or public spending. Whenever the economy slowed down, large firms typically lobbied the government for public works spending to boost overall demand rather than to improve unemployment benefits.[92] Politicians were happy to oblige, if only because public works spending permitted geographical targeting in their own electoral interests. The availability of this form of targeted protection made employers averse to shouldering the cost of unemployment benefits. As far as employers were concerned, functional equivalents were preferable to the Unemployment Insurance. Functional equivalents never levied employers' contributions like the Unemployment Insurance did.

In fact, by the mid-1950s, the character of Japan's Unemployment Insurance changed. The 1955 reform of the Unemployment Insurance added a merit-based component, whereby core male workers who held the same job for a long time received better unemployment benefits.[93] Since unemployment benefits were provided regardless of the reason for leaving employment, this reform meant that core workers who worked in the same firm until retirement age received the most generous benefits. This 1955 reform thus transformed the Unemployment Insurance into a form of additional retirement income for core male workers in large firms. The ruling party, LDP, had no reason to oppose this shift, which was demanded by the employers' association. The special circumstances under the Allied Occupation, which had enabled the labor policy bureaucrats to introduce a program favorable to marginal workers, no longer existed.

Responding to Particularistic Groups: Japan's Housing Policy

Under the structural logic of MMD/SNTV, particularistic groups that swayed the intraparty veto players tended to get more than encompassing groups in a zero-sum situation such as in budgetary politics.[94] This meant that encompassing groups such as Nikkeiren, the national federation of employers' associations, and Keidanren, the peak big business association, were disadvantaged in budgetary politics. Keidanren's close ties with the party leadership, for instance, meant little in the context of a weak party, where individual politician's electoral needs came

---

[92] See Kitayama (2003) and Richardson (1997) on how business demanded public works spending. Kohno and Nishizawa (1990) show how most industries benefited greatly from public works investments.

[93] On the legislative change, see Suganuma (1991, 113). Private sector unions' attitudes were similar to those of their employers. Labor mobility was thus always one-way: from large firms to smaller firms, but never the other way around (see a study conducted by Kanagawa Prefecture Government in 1956). Since large companies offered better wages and benefits, which were often tenure-rated for labor management reasons, core male workers in large firms cared more about job protection than unemployment insurance.

[94] To this day, Campbell (1977) has the best account of budgetary politics in Japan. Campbell notes that, when it came to their influence over politicians, big business did not fare as well as electorally crucial groups. The weakness of big business is also noted by Curtis (1975) and Richardson (1997).

before those of the party. The policy developments in housing provide evidence for this pattern.

Housing surged as one of the major items in the electoral campaign in the 1950s.[95] As the Japanese economy began to expand in the 1950s, many large firms – particularly manufacturing firms – needed cash to build housing near their offices and factories. Nikkeiren thus demanded subsidies for "industrial housing."[96] Prime Minister Shigeru Yoshida, the leader of the Liberal Party – then the ruling party – responded immediately by announcing industrial housing construction as one of his Cabinet's top priorities in 1952.[97] Similarly, when Ichiro Hatoyama, the leader of the Democratic Party – one of the two major conservative parties at the time – formed a government in 1954, the Ministry of Construction set out to create a new public corporation, the Housing Corporation.[98]

Under both governments, the Ministry of Construction, sensing an opportunity to expand its influence, acted quickly. In 1952, the Ministry immediately allied itself with Nikkeiren to propose a new law, the Industrial Workers Housing Supply Law (Sangyo Rodo Shayo Jyutaku Kyokyu Hoan).[99] Likewise in 1954, the Ministry prepared legislation for the creation of the Housing Corporation (Harada 1985, 366–367). In both instances, the lack of interest on the part of conservative politicians frustrated the construction bureaucrats' efforts. The Construction Ministry, for instance, was only granted 2 billion yen instead of the 15 billion yen it had requested for Industrial Workers' Housing.[100] Instead, the government used the Housing Financial Corporation – created in 1950 to promote homeownership by individuals – to offer employers loans for the construction of corporate housing.[101] Employers were not happy at all. Nikkeiren complained that the interest rates charged by the Housing Financial Corporation were too high.[102] When the Construction Ministry began to prepare for a new Housing Corporation, they could not entice conservative politicians even to attend the Construction Committee in the Diet, which met to discuss the idea of the Housing Corporation.[103]

---

[95] The headline of the front page news in a major newspaper, *Asahi Shimbun*, in January 27, 1955, reads "The Democratic Party and the Liberal Party Compete Over Housing Policy." Also see *Asahi Shimbun*, January 8, 1955. *Mainishi Shimbun* and *Jiji Shimbun* also ran op-eds on the need for more housing in Japan (*Jiji*, January 3, 1955; *Mainichi*, October 24, 1954).

[96] *Nikkeiren Times*, January 3, 1952; *Tokyo Shimbun*, September 10, 1952; Nikkeiren ed. 1958, 143–144, 190. Also see Tetsuya Nambu's recollections (Omoto 1991, 347). Nambu was a construction official at the time.

[97] *Nihon Keizai Shimbun*, November 6, 1952.

[98] Sumitaka Harada 1985, 360. Nambu's comments in Omoto 1991, 352–358.

[99] *Tokyo Shimbun*, February 5, 1952; *Tokyo Shimbun*, September 10, 1952. *Nikkei Shimbun*, August 15, 1952.

[100] *Asahi Shimbun*, September 15, 1952 (evening edition).

[101] The government reformed the Housing Financial Corporation Law to offer employers loans (Harada 1985, 336–337). Originally, the Housing Financial Corporation was created under the Allied Occupation with the purpose of helping individual citizens purchase homes. The government changed the law to make employers eligible for loans to build corporate housing (Jutaku Kinyu Koko ed. 1970, 84–88).

[102] *Nihon Keizai Shimbun*, August 15, 1952.

[103] This committee only had one member from the ruling party. See Nambu's interview in Omoto 1991, 352–358.

It was only when Construction bureaucrats began to lobby executives in specific industries for support – rather than simply allying themselves with an encompassing organization such as Nikkeiren – that the legislative ball began to roll.[104] Executives in construction and financial companies immediately understood the merits of the new policy proposal for their business. In contrast to Nikkeiren's demand for workers' housing, specific industries had a lot to gain from this new policy. Construction companies and related industries that produced construction materials welcomed the new policy that would boost demand for their services and products. At the time, Japan was going through an economic downturn after the Korean War boom, and business leaders badly needed a boost. Financial institutions came on board, because they were looking for good investments during the economic downturn. Life insurance companies and other financial institutions were eager to lend money to the new Housing Corporation. Banks, in particular, were keen on becoming subcontractors for the Housing Corporation by being the loaners of their money.[105] The construction bureaucrats thus succeeded in mobilizing particularistic interest groups, which, in turn, lobbied the ruling party for their own self-regarding interests. The legislation to create a new Housing Corporation was thus successfully passed in 1955.

This example shows that the conservative ruling party was much more responsive to demands from particularistic groups than to the collective interests of big business. Thus was the general need for more housing translated into a policy that conservative politicians could manipulate for votes and money. Ideas such as European-style housing allowance programs and public housing fell flat, despite the eager support of officials in the Ministries of Welfare and Construction.[106] Tetsuya Nambu, a construction official at the time, recalls that conservative politicians were never interested in using public money to subsidize housing for wage earners, whom they saw as "socialist sympathizers."[107] Ultimately, only those policy ideas that appealed to the ruling-party politicians' interests materialized.

It is noteworthy that Nikkeiren was more successful in gaining tax concessions through direct negotiations with the tax authorities than in receiving government subsidies for corporate housing. Corporate housing, in particular, received lucrative tax concessions.[108] Companies were permitted to write off the interest paid

---

[104] Tetsuya Nambu offers detailed accounts of the process based on his involvement in the legislative process, Omoto 1991, 352–358.

[105] Ibid.

[106] The Ministry of Construction had originally been part of the old Naimusho like the MOW and MOL. Naimusho's more welfare-oriented housing section thus had been moved into what became the MOC. One of the more welfare-oriented officials in the new MOC, Goro Ito, was a vocal critic of the government housing policy. Mr. Ito advocated housing allowances and German-style social housing. See his op-ed in *Asahi Shimbun*, February 4, 1955.

[107] Tetsuya Nambu recalls how conservative politicians were not eager to provide affordable public rental housing for "socialists" (in the words of the politicians quoted by Nambu). See Nambu's comments in Omoto 1991, 353.

[108] On Nikkeiren's demands for tax deductions on corporate fringe benefits, issues of *Nikkeiren Times* dated January 30, 1952; April 24, 1952; July 10, 1952; September 11, 1952; and September 18, 1952; Nikkeiren (1958) lists Nikkeiren's official policy statements dated January 30, 1952 and July 30, 1952. Also see Harada (1985, 382).

on loans to construct company housing. Furthermore, an accelerated depreciation rate was applied to the value of corporate housing (and other "corporate
welfare facilities"). Employees, in turn, paid a fraction of the market rate on the
rent – tax free. In contrast to Nikkeiren's ease in gaining tax concessions, getting the government to pay for the cost of corporate housing from the general
budget proved almost impossible.[109] Unlike budgetary politics, which pitched
large firms directly against the LDP's other core constituent groups, tax politics
did not. As mentioned earlier, tax policies during this period were not yet politicized, and conservative politicians saw tax policies as nonzero-sum issues.[110] The
relative weakness of encompassing organizations vis-à-vis particularistic groups
observed in the case of housing policy confirms the structural logic as presented
in Chapters 2 and 3.

BUREAUCRATIC PREFERENCES AND POWER

The earlier sections have demonstrated how limited were bureaucratic legislative
abilities when they were not aligned with the electoral calculations of ruling-party
politicians. The conservative ruling party – the veto player – had no incentive
to expand benefits for wage earners – unorganized voters at best, and organized
constituent groups for the opposition at worst – by levying more social security
contributions from employers, an important conservative constituency. Thus the
pension bureaucrats could not expand the Employee Pension as they had wished
unless they could get the employers' consent. The same happened in the case
of unemployment and housing policies. Unemployment benefits did not expand,
because the ruling conservatives had nothing to gain from such an expansion.
Universalistic housing programs such as housing allowance failed for the same
reason. In contrast, particularistic functional equivalents flourished. Bureaucrats,
in fact, were quite successful in pushing for particularistic programs that bolstered
the electoral interests of conservative politicians.

   Bureaucratic preferences also played a big role in fragmenting the Japanese
social protection system. As Chapter 3 explained in detail, Japan's distinctive
personnel management practice produced intense bureaucratic preferences for
resources, both jurisdictional and financial, to finance post-retirement positions.
Contributory social insurance programs – pensions, for instance – provided ideal
vehicles for such an objective, because they "raised" money in a special account
(*tokubetsu kaikei*) that was then earmarked for a specific use.[111] Such a special

---

[109] Harada (1985, 382) observes that the government was not forthcoming concerning employers'
      demands for subsidies for company housing at the time.
[110] Once the economy slowed down, however, gaining tax concessions became an important part
      of the distributive struggle. Big tax concessions for large firms were cut back and replaced with
      numerous tax expenditure programs for smaller firms (based on the historical trends of tax expen-
      ditures provided by the Tax Bureau, MOF to the author; an interview with the LDP Tax Com-
      mittee Chairman, Yoshiro Hayashi, 1996). Also see Sato and Matsuzaki (1986).
[111] Multiple Pension Bureau officials whose statements are recorded in Koseidan ed. 1988 very
      explicitly admit the usefulness of having a pot of money like pension funds to create *amaku-
      dari* positions. One of them, Takeo Hanasawa, a welfare official involved in the creation of the

account was independent of the general budget and created an autonomous source of money for the ministry that possessed jurisdiction over that special account. For instance, the Ministry of Welfare had jurisdiction over the Employee Pension Special Account, while the Ministry of Labor had jurisdiction over the Unemployment Insurance Special Account and the Special Account for the Workers' Injuries Insurance. The legal terms of the policy objectives for a specific special account were typically loosely defined, so that the overseeing ministry could use the money relatively freely. Both ministries had a big stake in ensuring that money accumulated in their own special accounts. For this reason, pension bureaucrats were always keen on retaining some form of pre-funded design. In the case of the Unemployment Insurance and the Workers' Injuries Insurance, the Ministry of Labor always set the contributory rates high enough to maintain reserves in the respective special accounts. Such "discretionary funds" quickly caught the attention of nonwelfare ministries, who then became themselves interested in pension programs.[112]

When conservative politicians voted to set up new occupationally targeted pension schemes – such as the new mutual assistance associations for private school teachers, municipal government employees, and *nokyo* employees, some ministries made great gains at the expense of the pension officials in the Ministry of Welfare. Ministries overseeing respective occupations such as the Ministry of Agriculture, Forestry, and Fishery (referred to as Ministry of Agriculture hereafter) and the Ministry of Education seized jurisdictional control over the reserves built up in the new pension schemes. Legally speaking, the pension funds could be used for anything that promoted "the welfare," broadly conceived, of those enrolled in the pension scheme. Thus soon after the creation of a mutual

Employee Pension in 1941, admits that he was aware of the advantages of having an independent source of money and that he used that to get the Ministry of Finance – overseer of the budget as a whole – interested in supporting the legislation of the Employee Pension. He also says that his ministry was not happy that the Trust Fund Bureau of the Ministry of Finance invested all the money in the pension reserves, which, in the eyes of welfare ministry officials, belonged to the Ministry of Welfare. They thus made arguments about the need to use the reserves to promote the welfare of the enrollees of the Employee Pension in the hope of having direct access to the reserves (Hanasawa's comments in Koseidan 1988, 23). Hanasawa specifically mentions how such an independent source of money would be useful for financing *amakudari* positions.

[112] As formulated in Chapter 3, Japanese bureaucrats possessed a strong interest in fund-accumulating programs whose funds were at their discretion. As the Ministry of Welfare tried to expand their control over the pension reserves, other ministries tried to make claims. The Welfare Ministry tried to use the discontent of employers and workers over the fund-accumulating design of the Employee Pension to justify new schemes for them to spend the money for "the welfare of workers." Initially, the Welfare Minister used the money for hospitals and corporate welfare facilities (health care issues were within its own jurisdiction). As employers began demanding more money for housing, the Welfare Ministry decided to use the pension reserves to provide housing loans. The Ministry of Construction, which had been borrowing from the FILP to finance housing intervened – unsuccessfully – to claim that money for all housing-related projects should be its task (see recollections of Katsutsugu Hisamoto and Kazuo Okamoto in Koseidan 1988, 67–68, 105–106). The recollections of bureaucrats recorded in Pension and Welfare Corporation (Nenkin Fukushu Jigyodan ed. 1972) also illustrate how other ministries such as the Ministry of Post and Telecommunications and the Ministry of Finance were all keen on savings-oriented programs.

assistance cooperative for *nokyo* employees, the Ministry of Agriculture tapped the funds to build a brand new facility in Central Tokyo.[113] Needless to say, the facility served to create jobs for retired Ministry of Agriculture bureaucrats. It is quite amusing to read the recollections of the pension officials in the Ministry of Welfare, who watched other ministries erode the foundation of their Employee Pension. They saw nothing wrong with the Ministry of Agriculture's misman-agement of the pension reserves per se.[114] Instead, the pension officials in the Ministry of Welfare were more irritated by the fact that the Ministry of Agricul-ture was enjoying new perks at their expense. These pension officials were also very angry at the higher echelon of their own ministry for losing the political battle over the jurisdictional control of the new occupational schemes for school teachers, municipal government employees, and *nokyo* employees.[115]

The pension bureaucrats in the Ministry of Welfare lost the jurisdictional bat-tle to the Ministry of Education and the Ministry of Agriculture, because the latter ministries had formed alliances with conservative politicians whose constituent groups were private school owners and *nokyo* members and employees. As far as these politicians were concerned, discretionary funds at the disposal of education and agricultural bureaucrats simply meant more money for them to distribute benefits to their constituent groups. In other words, the politico-bureaucratic alliances undermined the real interests of future pension beneficiaries who would have been served better if politicians and bureaucrats had not used their pension reserves for their selfish purposes. In an institutional environment where unor-ganized interests mattered little, such interests had no political significance. It is not surprising that the mismanagement of pension funds was never revealed or politicized as long as the LDP dominance and the MMD/SNTV system contin-ued. It was only recently that the decades-long mismanagement of pension funds and employment insurance funds hit the headlines.

Employers and unions always opposed the accumulation of reserves that could be used by bureaucrats.[116] Although bureaucrats depended on their political allies to change the status quo in their favor, they could also use their own agenda-setting power to protect the status quo. Employers and unions had little capacity in *shingikai* to take these programs away from the bureaucrats. The *shingikai* pro-cess, as we saw in Chapter 3, primarily served the interest of bureaucrats. *Shingikai* participants are simply asked to discuss the specific items on the agenda prepared by bureaucrats. Representatives of employers and unions had no authority to add new items to the deliberation agenda. In this way, the bureaucrats' agenda-setting

---

[113] Ikuo Soneda's statement in Koseidan 1988, 114. Soneda worked in the Pension Bureau during the period of pension fragmentation.

[114] Soneda's comments in Koseidan 112–113. Also see Hanasawa's comments in Koseidan 1988, 23.

[115] See Soneda's statement in Koseidan 1988, 113.

[116] For a good collection of official positions of Nikkeiren and the major unions (Sohyo and Sodomei) in the early 1950s, see Shakai Hosho Kenkyujo ed 1975a. (This volume contains reproductions of all the policy positions issued by groups participating in *shingikai* on social policy issues.) Also see *Nikkeiren Times*, January 28, 1954; Ohara Rodo Mondai Kenkyujo 1960, 399–400; Ohara Rodo Mondai Kenkyujo 1961, 415–419; and Yamazaki 1985.

power generated de facto veto power.[117] Throughout the 1950s, unions and employers complained about excessive amounts of pension reserves, but this issue was never included in the *shingikai* deliberations. The employers' association was also wary of the excess administrative costs caused by the existence of multiple social insurance schemes in different ministries.[118] When it called for the integration of all social insurance, nothing happened.[119] No ministry put the issue of administrative cost on the agenda for policy deliberations.

The bureaucrats' regulatory power over specific industries was also used to "raise" discretionary funds. The Ministry of Finance bureaucrats, for instance, benefited from a very generous tax provision that they granted large firms. Japan's generous tax expenditures for retirement lump-sum payments allowed large firms to create internal book reserve pensions. Employers were permitted to tap into this money without penalty for corporate investments. The Ministry of Finance required employers to deposit 25 percent of the RLSP book reserve in banks, thereby boosting the capital flow of banks.[120] The MOF officials controlled the banks and used the banks to place post-retirement MOF officials. Similarly, the Ministry of International Trade and Industry, which oversaw adjustment cooperatives and controlled entry into various product markets by licensing, often used their regulatory position to create a raft of post-retirement positions.[121]

It is striking how entrepreneurial Japanese ministries were when it came to finding resources to create new post-retirement jobs. Given the highly decentralized nature of Japanese conservative governments, individual politicians saw little problem in various ministries possessing control over governmental resources. Conservative politicians had no choice but to build their own individualized political machines. Decentralized control over government resources facilitated the formation of an alliance between specific politicians, specific occupational groups, and the bureaucratic branches that held jurisdiction over the pertinent product markets. The Ministry of Post and Telecommunication offers yet another good example here. Although the Ministry of Finance possessed jurisdiction over financial matters, the Ministry of Post and Telecommunication retained some control over the money raised from Postal Savings. A small portion of the savings was earmarked for the welfare of residents in the region where the money was raised. The regional offices for the Ministry of Post thus came to possess construction departments, which used the money for public works (Maeno 1994, 44). It is not

---

[117] Nikkeiren managed to get its view reflected during the negotiations in the Lower House. The legislative bill was modified to expand the scope of the "recycle loans." *Nikkeiren Times*, April 29, 1954 and July 15, 1954.

[118] The Unemployment Insurance and the Workers' Injuries Insurance were administered by the Ministry of Labor, whereas the Employee Pension was administered by the Ministry of Welfare.

[119] For Nikkeiren's repeated demands to integrate all the social insurance schemes, see *Nikkeiren Times*, August 9, 1949; February 19, 1953; February 26, 1953; and September 10, 1953, among others.

[120] Nikkeiren did not like this aspect of the tax arrangement for RLSP and complained. *Nikkeiren Times*, January 30, 1952; February 7, 1952.

[121] See Estévez-Abe (2003).

difficult to see how such ministerial control over construction budgets served to attract individual politicians to become allies of the ministry.

This chapter has provided historical evidence for three claims made in the earlier theoretical chapters. First, this chapter has shown that the combination of MMD/SNTV in postwar Japan led to the development of fragmented social security programs and targeted forms of functional equivalents. Second, it has shown that under the conservative rule, benefits were targeted at the groups that contributed money to the conservatives in return for policy favors. Third, this chapter has provided evidence that Japanese bureaucrats favored, for reasons of their own personal gain, savings-oriented programs.

Appendix 4.A Chronology of Tax Expenditures

1950 New Income-Based Taxation System, devised by the Shaup Commission, was introduced. It included various deductions:

Personal basic deduction, Kiso Kojo (25,000 yen).

Deductions for wage earners, Kinro Shotoku Kojo (15 percent of their income and less than 30,000 yen).

Dependents' deductions, Fuyo Kazoku Kojo (12,000 yen per head).

Fifteen-percent deductions from retirement income. Special measure to tax retirement income over the course of five years.

Medical cost deductions, Iryoshi Kojo (when the medical cost incurred during the fiscal year exceeded 10 percent of the annual income, up to 100,000 yen of the amount that exceeded 10 percent was deducted from the taxable income).

Handicapped deductions, Fugusha Kojo (12,000 yen).

1951 Increases in personal deductions (basic up to 50,000, dependents 20,000).

Deductions for life insurance premiums (up to 2,000 yen) were reintroduced. (They used to exist before the Occupation.)

Book reserve system was introduced for retirement lump-sum payments (RLSP).

Nonprogressive tax rate was partially applied for interest income to stimulate savings.

1952 Increases in personal deductions (basic up to 60,000 yen, and 35,000 yen for the first of the dependent family members). Deductions for wage income were also increased to 45,000. Life insurance deductions were raised up to 4,000. Retirement income was taxed as a separate type of income to reduce progressivity of taxation on it.

Deductions for social security contributions were introduced.

1953   Increases in deductions for life insurance premiums (up to 8,000 yen from 4,000 yen). For other income deductions, the temporary increases introduced in 1952 were made permanent measures.

Income from interests was exempt from income tax. A nonprogressive separate tax rate was created for interests.

1954   As a measure to reduce tax burdens on lower- and middle-income groups, various deductions were expanded. Basic deduction→70,000 yen. Dependents→40,000 yen for the first member, 20,000 yen for the second and the third dependents. Life insurance→12,000 yen.

Deduction for social insurance–related incomes, Shakai Hoken Shinryo Hoshu (special income deductions for physicians), formerly based on administrative order, was legislated.

1955   As a further measure to reduce taxes on lower- and middle-income groups, basic deduction and wage income deduction were raised to 80,000 yen and 60,000 yen respectively. Life insurance deductions→15,000 yen.

A new deduction for widows was created.

1956   Book reserve allowance for RLSP was limited.

1957   Income Tax Reform. Progressivity was reduced for lower- and lower-middle-income groups. Personal deductions and deduction for the first dependent member were raised to 90,000 yen (from 80,000) and 50,000 yen (from 40,000) respectively.

1958   New tax deductions for long-term savings (bank deposits, trust bank accounts, life insurance packages, etc.). Three percent of the annual savings (up to 6,000 yen a year) was deducted from income taxes.

1959   Increased emphasis on deductions for dependents to alleviate taxes on families. Deductions for the first dependent member increased to 70,000 (from 50,000 yen), for additional dependents, 30,000 yen each (currently, 25,000 for the second and the third, and 15,000 for the fourth member).

1961   Increases for the existing personal and dependent deductions. Basic deduction increased to 90,000 yen. For dependents older than 15 years of age, deductions were raised to 50,000 yen each.

Introduction of income tax deduction (90,000 yen) for dependent spouse, Haigusha Kojo.

Ceiling for retirement income deductions (1 million yen) was abolished, and differential treatments according to the age and seniority of the retiree were expanded.

1962   Deductions for widows, working students, elderly, and handicapped were raised from 5,000 yen to 6,000 yen. Personal basic deduction and deduction for dependent spouse were both raised to 100,000 yen. Life insurance deductions were raised to 50,000 yen.

Tax Qualified Pension Plan was established.

1963 Basic deduction increased by 10,000 yen. Deductions for spouse and dependents under the age of 15 were all increased by 5,000 yen each.

Introduction of small tax-free savings accounts (up to half a million yen).

1964 Personal deductions were raised. Basic→120,000 yen. Spouse→110,000 yen. Dependents (older than 13 years of age)→50,000 yen. Dependents (younger than 13 years)→40,000 yen. Wage earner's deduction was raised too. Its fixed deduction was now 20,000 yen, income up to 400,000 yen was further subject to 20 percent deduction, and the rate of 10 percent applied to the amount that exceeded that limit (overall ceiling for the amount of deduction was 140,000 yen). Deductions for RLSP income abolished age discrimination, and introduced standardized seniority-based system (every year of tenure qualified for a 50,000-yen deduction). Deductions for life insurance premiums were raised to 35,000 yen.

New deduction for insurance premiums paid to insure housing→2,000 yen.

1965 Personal deductions were raised. Basic→130,000 yen. Spouse→120,000 yen. Dependents (older than 13 years of age)→60,000 yen. Dependents (younger than 13 years)→50,000 yen. Wage earner's deduction was raised too. Its fixed deduction was now 30,000 yen, income up to 500,000 yen was further subject to 20 percent deduction, and the rate of 10 percent applied to the amount that exceeded that limit (overall ceiling for the amount of deduction was 150,000 yen).

1966 The minimum taxable income was raised, consequently reducing the number of tax payers by nearly 10 percent. Personal deductions were also raised. Basic→140,000 yen. Spouse→130,000 yen. Wage earner's deduction was raised too. Its fixed deduction was now 40,000 yen, and the overall ceiling for the amount of deduction was raised to 180,000 yen.

1967 Personal deductions were raised. Basic→150,000 yen. Spouse→150,000 yen. Dependents →70,000 yen. Wage earner's deduction was raised too. Its fixed deduction was now 80,000 yen, and the overall ceiling for the amount of deduction was 220,000 yen. Tax exemption for retirement was hiked. Up to 5 million yen was now exempted from income taxation.

Introduction of savings toward home ownership. Up to 4 percent of annual savings set aside for down payment became deductible (10,000-yen limit applied).

1968 Minimum taxable income was raised. Personal deductions were raised. Basic→160,000 yen. Spouse→160,000 yen. Dependents→80,000 yen. Wage earner's deduction was raised too. Its fixed deduction was now 100,000 yen, income up to 800,000 yen was further subject to 20 percent deduction, and 10 percent deduction for up to 1 million yen. Deductions for elderly, widows, and working students were raised to 80,000 from the current 70,000 yen per person. For those heavily handicapped, personal deductions were further raised to 120,000 yen. Dependent deduction was raised to 100,000 yen for those families where spouse deductions did not apply (that is, single-parent families).

1969   Minimum taxable income was raised again. (Its generosity surpassed that of the United Kingdom and Germany, close to U.S. levels.) Personal deductions were also raised. Basic→170,000 yen. Spouse→170,000 yen. Dependents→100,000 yen. New rates for wage earner's deduction were introduced. Income up to 1 million received 15 percent deduction (the rate for the first 800,000 yen remained the same), 5 percent for 2 million and 2.5 percent to 3 million yen. The eligibility for home ownership savings was expanded.

1970   Minimum taxable income level was again raised. Deductions for the handicapped, elderly, widows, and working students were increased to 100,000 yen. For regular personal deductions, dependent deductions were raised more (by 20,000 yen) than basic and spouse deductions (by 10,000 yen each). Ceiling for wage earner's deduction was raised to 4 million. Deduction rates were improved for income up to 2 million and 4 million yen respectively (10 percent and 5 percent respectively). Medical deductions were raised. Medical cost beyond 5 percent of income (or 100,000 yen, whichever was smaller) became deductible (1 million yen limit for all deductions).

1971   All personal deductions were increased by 10,000 yen. Ceiling for Small Savings exemption was raised.

Source: Diet Library Legislative Research Bureau, ed. 1972, *Wagakuni no Shotokuzei no Hensen*, Special report; Ministry of Finance Fiscal History Commission Group, ed. 1997. *Showa Zaiseishi* vol. 15; Ministry of Finance Fiscal History Commission Group, ed. 1977. *Showa Zaiseishi* vol. 8; Sato and Miyajima 1990.

5

Economic Growth and Japan's Selective Welfare Expansion

Japan's economic takeoff coincided with the expansion of its welfare state. In 1961, Japan extended old-age pension and health care coverage to include, at least potentially, all citizens. Indeed, the Ministry of Welfare proudly announced that Japan had achieved All Nation Insurance (Kokumin Kaihoken), alluding to the universalistic ideal associated with Sir William Beveridge's famous report. In the mid-1960s, the government also began to increase steadily the levels of pension benefits, and this trend continued well into the 1970s. Furthermore, during the early 1970s, Japan introduced two new programs – the Children's Allowance (Jido Teate) and health care for the elderly. The two new programs were universalistic, unlike any other programs that had been previously introduced in Japan. In 1973, Prime Minister Kakuei Tanaka famously proclaimed that year as Fukushi Gannen, meaning "the first year of the welfare calendar."

These developments, at first glance, appear to contradict my structural logic. The institutionally constrained micrologic of welfare politics put forth in this book holds that distributive implications of welfare politics are only expected to change when either electoral rules change or the configuration of parliamentary veto players changes. Neither type of change occurred during the welfare expansion period in the 1960s and the early 1970s. This means that the same kind of political dynamics described in the previous chapters continued to shape welfare politics during the welfare expansion period. If this is true, we should observe a continuing bias in favor of social protection programs that can be targeted both geographically (such as public works) and functionally (such as protective regulation for specific industries and occupational welfare schemes). The welfare expansion period, however, gave rise to what appeared to be comprehensive rather than specific programs – expansion of pension and health care coverage and the introduction of two universalistic programs (the Children's Allowance and the Free Health Care for the Elderly). These two programs, in particular, offer tough cases for my structural argument. This chapter will demonstrate that even these toughest cases actually provide the exceptions that prove the rule. All the cases of comprehensive programs introduced during this period were initiated at the local level and only later adopted at the national level. By extending the analysis to the institutional context of local elections, this chapter meets an apparent challenge to my structural logic approach.

BEYOND THE EXISTING EXPLANATIONS

Existing studies of the development of the welfare state in postwar Japan emphasize the role of electoral threats from the opposition parties in creating *pro-welfarist moments*. Indeed, during the 1960s and the early 1970s, the LDP faced two such challenges. First, the conservative rural constituency was declining in numbers: it went down from 32 percent of the total workforce in 1960 to 17.4 percent in 1970.[1] Hideo Ishida, a LDP labor minister in the early 1960s, urged his party to steer a course in favor of the growing number of wage earners (Ishida 1963). He predicted that failing to do so would cause the party to lose its governing position. Second, urban voters were increasingly dissatisfied with the LDP's "economic growth first" policy. This dissatisfaction manifested itself most starkly in the elections of governors and mayors.[2] In the latter half of the 1960s, the opposition forces successfully seized a number of metropolitan governments.[3] For instance, the Socialist Ryokichi Minobe won the election to head the Metropolitan Government of Tokyo in 1967.[4]

Standard accounts of Japanese politics attribute welfare expansion in the 1960s and the early 1970s to the LDP's strategy to transform itself into a "catchall" party to win the support of urban voters.[5] Facing the rise of the opposition, so the argument goes, the LDP became pro-welfarist by preemptively adopting the opposition parties' policy platform in order to limit their further electoral advancement. Existing studies point to improvements in pension benefits for wage earners and the introduction of the universalistic Children's Allowance and Free Health Care for the Elderly as evidence for a shift of the LDP's position in favor of wage earners and other unorganized voters.

A close look at multiple policy areas – rather than exclusively looking at those policy areas where public benefits expanded – reveals important patterns of policy outcomes that are left unexplained in the conventional account of welfare expansion. First, the LDP's "copying" of the opposition parties' welfare policies was highly selective. Typically, the LDP government continued to be averse to using budgetary resources for wage earners' benefits. All social security benefits for wage earners continued to be financed by their own contributions and their employers' contributions. Second, even during the time of the expansion

[1] These figures refer to the size of the agricultural workforce as a percentage of the total workforce.
[2] There exists a solid body of English-language studies on this phenomenon. See Allinson (1979), McKean (1981), and Steiner, Krauss and Flanagan eds. (1980).
[3] The fact that mayoral and gubernatorial elections took place in single-member districts had a lot to do with big swings in the electoral outcome. In urban local governments where the opposition could put up viable candidates, unorganized voters could swing the outcome.
[4] Kakuei Tanaka, a famous – notorious, some might say – postwar prime minister and LDP leader, himself envied the strength of the opposition parties (Tanaka 1967).
[5] See, for instance, Anderson (1993), Calder (1988), and Pempel (1982).

of comprehensive social security programs, Japan continued to introduce highly fragmented programs. Third – and most important – universalistic programs were only adopted at the national level after being adopted at the local government level. Some existing studies note that local programs were often forerunners of national welfare programs, but do not explain why. The structural logic approach fills this gap.

This book argues that distributive policies only fundamentally change when the institutional components of what I call a structural logic change. During the period under consideration, neither the electoral rules nor the government type changed. The electoral rules were based on the combination of MMDs and SNTV; and the LDP continued to hold an absolute majority in both Houses. As argued in Chapter 3, the use of SNTV weakened the LDP as a party, creating a highly decentralized policy-making process. Under such a system, the party leader has little power to steer his party's distributive orientation away from the core constituent groups of incumbent politicians to court new voters. When voters under question are unorganized voters, the shift becomes even more unlikely. In other words, the LDP had neither the incentive nor the political capacity to shift distribution in favor of urban wage earners, despite the "crisis" that the party faced. Likewise, the LDP had little incentive to provide universalistic welfare programs for unorganized voters.

Notwithstanding the constraints of the structural logic imposed by the MMD/SNTV system under LDP dominance, there remained two possible scenarios for the expansion of benefits for wage earners and introduction of universalistic benefits. The first scenario involved changes in employers' preferences. Expansion of public benefits for wage earners came about only when employers – an important constituent group of the LDP – developed preferences for public benefits and were willing to pay for them. This type of welfare expansion, in short, was not based on the electoral calculations of the LDP. Indeed, the LDP had no objection to employer-financed public benefits. By the same token, the LDP resisted the urge of employers to shoulder part of their labor costs.[6]

The second scenario involved local politics. All other comprehensive welfare programs introduced during this period can be explained by extending the structural logic to local politics. As discussed in Chapter 2, politicians elected in single-member districts (SMDs) pursue different strategies from those elected in multimember districts. Politicians who are campaigning on the basis of the personal vote in SMDs, in particular, are likely to seek unorganized voters in their districts. Mayors and governors in Japan were elected in SMDs. Mayoral and gubernatorial candidates thus needed to appeal to unorganized voters in addition to organized groups. Noncontributory universalistic benefits – whether old-age pension, health care benefits, or benefits for children – provided great tools to appeal to unorganized voters. Mayoral and gubernatorial elections created

---

[6] As already shown in the previous chapter, employers' demands were only effective when they did not conflict with LDP politicians' electoral calculations.

political momentum for comprehensive benefits. Due to Japan's fiscal centralization mayors and governors, however, only possessed very limited fiscal resources at their discretion. As a result, conservative mayors frequently lobbied the national government for subsidies.[7]

The close electorally mediated relationship between conservative local politicians and conservative national Diet members generated an intriguing "trickle up" process, whereby the national government would adopt popular universalistic public welfare benefits first introduced at the local level. National Diet members relied heavily on local politicians at election times. Many LDP Diet members had to coexist with their fellow party members within the same district under the MMD/SNTV system. These members used their ties with specific local politicians to carve out different niches – typically geographic niches (see Chapter 3).[8] Diet members relied on local politicians for votes, and the local politicians relied on their Diet members for subsidies for their district. Heads of local governments – mayors and governors – were particularly important in this network. "Trickling up" was possible when conservative mayors and governors mobilized the LDP intraparty veto players to legislate new national subsidies to finance programs provided by local governments. This was most likely to happen when conservative mayors and governors (i) needed financial help to maintain or improve benefits they currently provided at the local level; or (ii) wanted the national government to provide benefits offered by other local governments.

THE IRONY OF THE ALL NATION INSURANCE (KAIHOKEN)[9]

Japan's All Nation Insurance in health care and pensions was enacted in 1958 and 1959 respectively and implemented in 1961.[10] It is, however, misleading to consider the All Nation Insurance system as universalistic. The expansion of coverage did nothing to integrate the occupationally fragmented social insurance schemes; it merely added new contributory social schemes for those groups, like the self-employed, who were not covered in the preexisting occupational groups. All Nation Insurance did nothing to shift Japan to a universalistic welfare state like the British or Swedish welfare states. Both programs developed as part of the LDP's strategy to win the support of very specific groups of voters – farmers and small business owners.

---

[7] Note that urban areas, where the LDP was weaker, tended to have more revenue collected at the local level. Scheiner (2006) provides a very interesting account of the political effects of Japan's fiscal centralization.

[8] See Tatebayashi's excellent work on the dual strategy of LDP candidates to divide votes within the same district (Tatebayashi 2004).

[9] For the rest of the chapter, I have consulted published interviews of welfare officials, who were personally involved in the policy process at the time.

[10] This was quite an accomplishment. Japan was only the fourth country to establish such a broad health care coverage among industrial countries – and was the twelfth to introduce extensive pension coverage.

The Creation of the National Pension System: The "Trickling Up" from Local to National[11]

A comprehensive public pension emerged as a policy issue only as the LDP tried to fend off attempts by the Japan Socialist Party (hereafter JSP) to mobilize rural voters against the LDP.[12] Rapid economic growth had widened the gap between different sectors of the economy.[13] Agricultural income fell behind industrial wages.[14] Workers in very small firms, unlike their counterparts in larger firms, had no access to health care, because their employers were exempted from enrolling their workers in social insurance schemes. The JSP took advantage of this widening gap to criticize the LDP for being overly pro–big business, and tried to mobilize rural voters and workers in small firms. Not only were unions rapidly spreading to workers in small firms, but small firm owners, in protest at what they saw as the ruling party's pro–big business attitude, had started to organize themselves.[15] The LDP hit upon the strategy of using various welfare programs to develop and consolidate ties to farmers and small business owners.

Although we now think of rural voters as the core constituent group of LDP politicians, their support was still up for grabs in the 1950s. Given the fact that more than half of the electoral districts were rural districts – where the majority of voters engaged in agriculture – no party could assume power without organizing part of this group as its constituent group.[16] When the two Socialist Parties joined forces to create the Japan Socialist Party in 1955, the new party formulated its social security policies, which included an idea for comprehensive pension coverage for farmers and fishermen. The JSP brought up the issue of comprehensive pension in an aggressive campaign to attract farmers, because Japan's occupationally fragmented pensions did not cover farmers. In the 1956 Upper House elections, both the LDP and the JSP promised to introduce a comprehensive public pension system that extended coverage to farmers.

[11] See Campbell's excellent detailed analysis of the policy process leading to the introduction of the National Pension (Campbell 1992, 62–88). I agree with the basic facts of the legislative process. My analysis differs from his in its application of structural logic to explain the policy process and the outcome.

[12] Based on the recollections of Ozaki Shigetaka, who was a welfare official involved in the introduction of the National Pension (Koseidan 1988, 119).

[13] The Economic Planning Agency was concerned with this issue (Economic Planning Agency 1958, 368 and 379, for instance).

[14] By the early 1960s, agricultural income fell below 68 percent of nonagricultural income (Hayami 1991, 101).

[15] About one hundred unions that organized workers in small firms were emerging per month. See Calder (1988, 338). Calder also provides a succinct story of small business movements during this period. Communist, socialist, and independent drives to organize small business were becoming increasingly salient in the mid-1950s. Ginnosuke Ayukawa, a famous small business activist, founded his non-party-affiliated organization (Chuseiren) in 1956 (Hiwatari 1991; Krauss 1980).

[16] According to Yoshiaki Kobayashi's calculations, about 47 percent of the electoral districts in Japan were "heavily rural," 22 percent "rural," and 11 percent "somewhat more rural" in 1960. In contrast, even when all types of urban districts combined (heavily urban, urban, and somewhat urban), they only made up about 16 percent of all districts. (The numbers do not add to 100 percent, because Kobayashi has a category that is neither urban nor rural.) See Kobayashi (1985).

The LDP did not, however, follow up on its own promise once the election was over. It was only after the Lower House election in 1958 that the LDP got on its feet to introduce a new pension program. This time lag can only be explained by the "trickling up" mechanism presented earlier. Soon after, local governments in Oita, Iwate, Saitama, and Fukuoka prefectures – all of which were rural prefectures – had introduced universalistic cash benefits for the elderly in 1956 (see Campbell 1979, 1992). These benefits, called "old people's pension" (Keiro Nenkin), entailed small sums of noncontributory cash transfers to the elderly (older than 85 or 90, depending on the locality). While the national parties debated the introduction of a comprehensive pension program, these "old people's pensions" proved so popular that, by the end of 1957, 222 localities had introduced such benefits.[17] The introduction of universalistic cash benefits at the local level can be explained in terms of the electoral incentives facing mayors described earlier. The growing popularity of these benefits led to the resurgence of comprehensive pension as a topic in the Lower House elections in 1958. Recall that mayors had an incentive to adopt popular programs because they run in single-member districts. They also had an incentive to demand national subsidies for those programs.

The LDP was pressed to introduce some benefits that were explicitly pro-farmer by emulating the popular local pension benefits. So at the time of the Lower House elections in 1958, the LDP pledged to introduce comprehensive pension benefits by 1959. After the Lower House election in 1958, the LDP immediately ordered the Ministry of Welfare to produce a draft proposal quickly.[18] The LDP faced two more rounds of elections in 1959 – the Upper House and the general local elections.[19] With two elections coming up, the LDP needed to respond to the Socialists' charge that the LDP was pro–big business and cared little for farmers. The LDP had no grand pension plan. The preexisting local benefits affected the kind of benefits the LDP wanted to adopt at the national level. All they wanted was noncontributory pension benefits for the rural population just like the local "old people's pension benefits." According to pension bureaucrats who took part in the legislative negotiations, the LDP instructed them to come up with a legislative proposal for "candy pension" (*amedama nenkin*). The LDP just wanted to give the elderly in rural areas "pocket money" so that they could buy their grandchildren some candy.[20]

---

[17] Ministry of Health and Welfare Pension Bureau ed. 1962, 13.

[18] Shigetaka Ozaki and Kazuo Okamoto, both of whom were welfare ministry officials involved in the creation of the National Pension, both state how the LDP took up the issue with an urgency after the 1958 elections (Koseidan 1988, 122, 125).

[19] For those not familiar with Japanese politics: the timing of the Upper House elections and the general local elections is predetermined, but the Lower House elections are not. Half of the Upper House is up for reelection every three years, whereas all local politicians are up for reelection every four years. In contrast, the Lower House can be dissolved at any time by the prime minister to call for elections.

[20] See recollections of Masatoshi Yamamoto, another welfare ministry official involved in the legislative process (Koseidan 1988, 148–149).

The LDP's electoral calculations and the bureaucratic preferences, however, were not in synch. The pension bureaucrats in the Ministry of Welfare were single-mindedly focused on the Employee Pension. They were more interested in expanding the coverage of the Employee Pension, which accumulated reserves, than in creating a noncontributory pension program. They also feared that a non-contributory scheme might hinder the future expansion of the Employee Pen-sion (Koseidan 1988, 123–124). The LDP's desire for a noncontributory pension scheme was also opposed by the Budget Bureau of the Ministry of Finance, which, wary of the budgetary cost of noncontributory welfare programs, advocated a contributory pension scheme (Koseidan 1988, 122).

The LDP's electorally motivated preferences nonetheless prevailed. In 1959, the LDP government introduced the Welfare Pension (Fukushi Nenkin) and the new National Pension to fulfill its campaign promise. The Welfare Pen-sion was a noncontributory pension for those citizens who were already too old to meet the contributory requirements of the new National Pension. In other words, the LDP did manage to introduce noncontributory benefits targeted at the self-employed, most of whom were farmers. The National Pension, in turn, was a compulsory national scheme for citizens not enrolled in the Employee Pension or in the existing MAAs. Although the National Pension was introduced as a contributory scheme, it differed from the Employee Pension in three ways. First, the National Pension benefits were heavily subsidized from the general tax revenue. Second, the National Pension was not an earnings-related benefit like the Employee Pension. The National Pension promised an equal (and meager) benefit in exchange for a fixed sum of contributions. The self-employed con-stituencies of the LDP never liked reporting their full income to the authorities. As a result, earnings-related pensions for the self-employed were not feasible and were not a good political idea either.[21] Third, although the National Pension was a compulsory social insurance, enrollment was, in fact, voluntary since there was no punishment for not enrolling.[22] In contrast, wage earners had no real choice as their employers withheld their social security contributions from their pay checks. The compliance problem of the National Pension System was to cause a serious "hollowing out" problem down the road.[23]

---

[21] The government explained this difference in terms of the difficulty of assessing personal income of the self-employed. However, a quick look at the postwar development of tax policy suffices to demonstrate how the LDP was quick to provide tax loopholes for the self-employed. The distinc-tion between business income (and expenses) and personal income (and expenses) was therefore blurred to the advantage of the self-employed. See Sato and Miyajima (1990).

[22] Unlike employees whose employers enrolled them in compulsory social insurance schemes and withdrew employees' share of social security contribution from their paychecks, in the case of a self-employed person, the "compulsory" nature was weaker. Even if he did not pay the required contributions, the state never really forcibly levied them.

[23] When the number of irregular workers increased beginning in the late 1990s, many of these workers, who were not enrolled in the Employee Pension, chose not to contribute to the National Pension. As a result, one in every four people who were legally obligated to contribute to the National Pension did not comply with the law, eroding the very basis of the social insurance system.

Nonetheless, the Ministry of Welfare did gain something after all. In order to administer a new National Pension, a whole new agency, the Social Insurance Agency (Shakai Hokencho), was created under its jurisdiction. The top positions were to be filled by career officials from the Ministry of Welfare. Furthermore, the Ministry of Welfare created the Pension and Welfare Corporation using the pension reserves in 1961.[24] Statements of the Welfare Ministry officials show how keen they were on creating a new organization.[25] The historical evidence makes it clear that the ministry officials were not solely seeking more money to control but more post-retirement positions for the ministry.[26] This confirms my interpretation of bureaucratic behavior presented in Chapter 3. In short, bureaucratic pursuit of organizational interest basically went unchecked unless it conflicted with the LDP's distributive strategy. Japanese bureaucratic organization first and foremost sought post-retirement positions rather than maximization of budget.

Delivering Targeted Benefits to Farmers

Ironically, as it turned out, rural voters were not happy with the National Pension. Against the expectations of the LDP politicians, farmers complained bitterly about its contributory design: they hated it (Otake 1991, 182). In addition to the complaints of farmers, two other events in 1960 prompted the LDP to consider noncontributory benefits targeted at farmers. The first event was the loss of some rural seats in the Lower House elections. The JSP increased its seats in rural areas at the expense of the LDP.[27] The second event was Prime Minister Ikeda's projection – shocking to LDP Diet members – that the agricultural population would rapidly decline.[28] The first event pushed the rank and file in the LDP – most of whom were from rural electoral districts – to demand direct subsidies for rural households. As with the Izokukai, the rank and file considered it necessary

---

[24] This corporation was created when the government introduced the National Pension system. There was a lot of concern about what to do with the pension reserves. Neither unions nor employers had been happy about all their contributions going into the FILP. The Ministry of Welfare took advantage of this general discontent to build a special corporation that would manage part of the pension reserve on behalf of the program enrollees.

[25] See comments by Kenji Kato and Tetsuya Nakano in Koseidan 1988, 135–139, 156. Also see a roundtable discussion with seven former welfare ministry officials involved in the creation of the Pension Welfare Corporation (Nenkin Fukushi Jigyodan ed. 1972, 527–555).

[26] This is evident from Kenji Kato's statement that what the Welfare Ministry worried most about was whether their demand for access to the pension reserve might prompt the Ministry of Finance to suggest the integration of all preexisting corporations that the Welfare Ministry had created using social security contributions. (For instance, they had created an organization using the money in the Seamen's Insurance.) See Kenji Kato in Koseidan 1988, 141.

[27] Nihon Shakaito (Japan Socialist Party) Nosei Giindan ed. 1981, 6–13.

[28] Another senior LDP politician and former labor minister, Hirohide Ishida, wrote an article in 1963 predicting that the reversal of numbers in farmers and industrial workers would cause the LDP to decline in the future (Ishida 1963). Prime Minister Ikeda's statement preceded that of Ishida. For Ikeda's statement, see Mainichi Shinbunsha Ekonomisuto Henshubu ed. 1984a, 393.

to establish a clear case of political exchange. The second event led to demands
for policies that would reduce the outward migration from rural areas.[29]

In 1960, the LDP reversed its earlier agricultural policy, which hitherto had
emphasized increasing agricultural productivity. Prior to 1960, Japan was heading
in the direction of a more liberalized agricultural market. Throughout the 1950s,
the conservative governments – whether ruled by the Liberal Party, the Democratic Party, or the Liberal Democratic Party – were all in favor of repealing the
Food Control Law.[30] The wartime government had introduced this law to control the prices of agricultural products. Big business advocated policies to enhance
agricultural productivity in order to reduce the cost of food, which was linked
to workers' demands for wage increases.[31] Agricultural associations insisted on
retaining price supports. The post-1960 electoral calculations, however, made
such a productivity-oriented policy undesirable. The LDP rank and file came to
fear that any policy that promoted productivity necessarily involved the integration of small-scale farms (Sorai 2000). Such a policy would inevitably reduce the
number of farmers. Instead, the LDP government began to take advantage of
the Food Control Law. In 1960, the LDP began to manipulate the price-setting
process – of rice in particular – to provide de facto income support for rural
households.[32] In other words, given the unpopularity of contributory benefits
such as the National Pension System, the LDP shifted to a functional equivalent
whose cost was to be born by consumers and tax payers. Yet again, as seen earlier,
big business failed to mobilize the LDP to push for a more efficiency-oriented
agricultural policy, because their demand conflicted with the LDP politicians'
more immediate electoral concerns.

The Agricultural Basic Law introduced in 1961 reflected the importance of
electoral calculations. By stipulating government responsibility for improving
agricultural infrastructures, the law opened ways for the national government
to spend on public works projects in rural areas. This meant that the ruling
party politicians gained a bigger pot of money to spend on public works in their
constituencies. In fact, Ichiro Kono, an influential senior LDP politician who
was serving at the time as agriculture minister, stated that he would only provide
public funding to those districts that elected LDP candidates.[33] This kind of
distributive strategy only made sense in a medium-sized multimember district
system, where politicians needed the support of a particularistic group in their
respective districts. The link between pork and votes was therefore very clear.
Similarly, the LDP also strategically "distributed" funds to small construction

---

[29] On the LDP's policies to contain migration out of rural districts, see Watanabe (1998, 245).

[30] Ohara Rodo Mondai Kenkyujo 1953, 522–3.

[31] Two peak-level business associations, Keizai Doyukai and Keidanren, submitted policy recommendations for more efficient agriculture. See an interview of Fumio Aoba, a former Nikkeiren
executive recorded in Mainichi Shinbunsha Ekonomisuto Henshubu ed. 1984b.

[32] Mulgan (1988) offers a fascinating detailed account of how "rice politics" operated in postwar
Japan. Also see Schwartz (1998, chapter 6).

[33] Nakamura (2000) provides a vivid account of the process of *kosho-zuke* (siting decisions for public
works projects) based on episodes collected during his career as a journalist.

companies in rural areas in addition to farmers. Empirical studies show that rural areas – in particular those districts where there were LDP politicians – received disproportionate shares of the public works budget (see Ihori and Doi 1998).

Both construction companies and farmers quickly became very reliable supporters of the LDP. In fact, in 1963, the LDP government legislated a quota system for public works, which required that all public works projects involve local small construction firms. The LDP's policy helped create jobs and subsidize household income in rural areas. In short, both rice producer support and special quotas for small construction firms were types of social protection clearly targeted at specific occupational groups. In the case of public works, it also permitted geographical targeting. The cost of these programs, in turn, was passed on to unorganized voters, such as consumers and general tax payers. These social protection programs were precisely the types of social protection that made most sense under the MMD/SNTV system.

In short, what appeared like a shift to a more comprehensive pension system did not imply any change in the political dynamics. Certainly, the "trickling up" mechanism did lead to a comprehensive program. Nonetheless, the LDP's strategy to target benefits to rural voters demonstrates that no change had occurred in the overall dynamics of welfare politics in Japan. It continued to be constrained by the logic of the MMD/SNTV system.

All Nation Insurance in Health Care in 1961

Japan introduced compulsory health care insurance for industrial workers as early as 1922 and voluntary people's health care cooperatives in 1938 to cover the rural population.[34] Voluntary people's health cooperatives were set up by municipal governments. However, nearly 32 percent of the Japanese population did not have any health coverage as of the mid-1950s.[35] A number of reports issued in the 1950s – by deliberation groups formed by the Ministry of Welfare – called for a more extensive health care system.[36] In fact, in contrast to their lack of interest in the creation of the National Pension System, the Ministry of Welfare bureaucrats were much more eager to expand health care coverage during this period.[37] Nonetheless, the Ministry of Welfare bureaucrats considered it totally

---

[34] See Garon (1987) for an excellent account of the prewar development of Japan's social insurance system. For the wartime period, see Kasza (2002).

[35] See the Ministry of Welfare's White Papers 1956, 170, and Koyama ed. 1985, 274.

[36] These reports included the 1956 report by the Social Security System Deliberation Council and the report by the so-called Seven-Member Committee. These reports reflected the Welfare Ministry's view by suggesting (i) the creation of a special occupational insurance scheme to enroll workers employed in very small firms – those with fewer than five workers – which were exempt from compulsory occupational healthcare schemes (that is, *kempo* and Seifu Kansho); and (ii) the expansion of the preexisting national health care cooperatives. For the details, see Koyama ed. (1985, 275).

[37] The welfare ministry officials were already considering a comprehensive health care plan to cover the whole nation. In the ministerial five-year plan issued in 1956, the National Health Insurance Bureau of the Welfare Ministry specifically referred to a plan for "all nation health coverage."

beyond their capacity to extend health insurance coverage to those 30 million citizens (Koyama ed. 1985, 276).

All Nation Insurance for health care appeared in the policy agenda during the budgeting process for the fiscal year 1957 under Prime Minister Ishibashi (Zaisei Chosakai ed. 1957, 864). All Nation Insurance for health care provides a classic case of the "trickling up" effect. The timing of politicization of the issue had a lot to do with demands from conservative mayors, who were responsible for the existing municipal health care insurance schemes – that is, the people's health care cooperatives. The general assembly of the Central Association of National Health Cooperatives voted to demand All Nation Insurance one month after the Upper House elections in 1956.[38] Mayors from cities, towns, and villages provided the political muscle behind the Central Association of National Health Cooperatives. Mayors – almost all of them conservative in those days – possessed a great deal of influence over conservative Diet members in their capacity as key players in the latter's personal political machines. All Nation Health Care Insurance had become an issue for mayors because of financing problems in the preexisting people's healthcare cooperatives administered by municipal governments. Mayors were directly responsible for health care provisions and hence had great political stakes in the fiscal state of these programs.

Welfare Ministry officials involved in health care policies attest to the political power of mayors.[39] The source of their power fits the expectation derived from the structural logic approach. Evidence shows that mayors exerted influence on the basis of their personal ties to individual Diet members.[40] This means that those mayors who were part of the political machine of senior LDP Diet members exerted a lot of influence over national policy. The final push for the actual legislation of the All Nation Insurance again came from lobbying from influential mayors. In spite of the opposition from the Japan Medical Association – another

---

See statements by Hideo Ibe, a welfare ministry official involved in the all nation health insurance coverage (Koyama ed. 1985, 273).

[38] Based on the recollections of Kazuo Suzuki, a welfare ministry official involved in the process. Recorded in Koyama ed. (1985, 279).

[39] Hideo Ibe's statements in Koyama ed. (1985, 277).

[40] Hideo Ibe and Kazuo Suzuki confirm the critical role played by specific mayors in swaying the LDP to subsidize national health care cooperatives. One case is the politics leading up to the national government's decision in 1952 to provide grants to promote national health care cooperatives, which at that point were still voluntary programs. The Central Association of National Health Cooperatives asked Zenichi Tamenari to personally persuade Finance Minister Hayato Ikeda to provide subsidies for National Healthcare Cooperatives. Tamenari was a mayor in Ikeda's district in Hiroshima prefecture. Tamenari's influence over Ikeda was based on his ability to round up votes for Ikeda. Although Ikeda had been categorically rejecting any subsidies for health care, Kazuo Suzuki recalls that Tamenari's personal request was a decisive factor in Ikeda's change of heart. Ikeda's switch was critical because of his position as finance minister. Emboldened with this success, mayors' associations also pushed for subsidies equal to 20 percent of their costs. The conservative government complied and legalized subsidies to cover 20 percent of the cost of National Healthcare Cooperatives in 1955. It should be noted here that 1952 and 1955 were both election years when Diet members needed the help of local politicians most. See statements by Hideo Ibe and Kazuo Suzuki in Koyama ed. (1985, 279 and 277 respectively).

conservative lobby group – those mayors with close ties to the intraparty veto players pushed the LDP to submit the proposal to the Diet and vote favorably on it. Ichiro Kono, the chairman of Somukai (the LDP General Affairs Committee) and Ryogo Hashimoto, the Welfare Minister, were among those politicians who were intensely lobbied by their mayors.[41] The new National Health Insurance Law was successfully enacted in 1958.

The Japan Medical Association (JMA), which also had ties to LDP politicians, however, did not lose out completely.[42] One important aspect of Japan's social insurance schemes for health care was that most physicians owned private practices. To the extent that physicians were seeing fee-paying patients, they controlled how much they charged for each procedure. This was not the case for patients enrolled in social insurance schemes. For this group of patients, respective social insurance schemes reimbursed physicians according to predetermined fees. The JMA, which primarily represented privately practicing physicians, feared the loss of their autonomy to the growing public health care insurance sector.[43] Physicians thus feared that the growing public insurance would socialize medicine by allowing the government to set the price of medical procedures. The LDP nonetheless protected the JMA's interests by making sure that the JMA had a say over the fee schedule of reimbursements by the public health care insurance schemes. The JMA – along with other medical providers – was represented in the governmental committee that set the fee schedule. The committee was called the Central Medical Social Insurance Council (Chuo Shakai Hoken Iryo Kyogikai, Chuikyo).[44] In 1959, when the Ministry of Welfare brought up the topic of the "socialization of medicine," the JMA strongly resisted.[45] In 1960, the Japan Medical Association withdrew its representatives from the aforementioned Council (Chuikyo) to hold up the process of deliberations unless its interests were preserved.[46] The LDP intervened on behalf of the JMA. The physicians' pressure on the LDP led in 1961 to an increase in the number of representatives of physicians' interests.[47] The decision-making system for setting the fee schedule, therefore, effectively gave the JMA a veto power.[48]

---

[41] Juro Suzuki, the mayor of Odawara City, in Ichiro Kono's district, was one of the mayors who used his influence. See Kazuo Suzuki's recollections of the legislative process in Koyama ed. (1985, 283–284).

[42] A number of former welfare ministry officials – Hideo Ibe, Kazuo Imai, and Yoshimi Furui – describe the details of the JMA's lobbying efforts vis-à-vis the LDP (Koyama ed. 1985, 185–241, 252, 255–258, 285).

[43] See the recollections of the welfare ministry officials cited in footnote 38.

[44] For good studies of the political mechanism determining the medical fees, see Campbell and Masuyama (1994), Hiroi (1994), and Nishimura (1996).

[45] This was supported by representatives of the company-based health insurance schemes (*kempo*) and business.

[46] For the specific confrontations involving the JMA during this period, see Koyama ed. (1985, 5–6).

[47] See the interview of Imai Kazuo, Ministry of Welfare official in charge of the health care issues at the time, recorded in Koyama ed. (1985, 185–241).

[48] Various issues of the *Nikkeiren Times* complain about the status quo of the health care system from the perspective of the lack of cost control measures. See, for instance, *Nikkeiren Times*, March 30, 1955.

The Ministry of Welfare, in its attempt to get the JMA and the other associations of medical service providers to sign on to the All Nation Health Care Insurance, agreed to create separate, more advantageous social insurance schemes for them. Physicians, dentists, and pharmacists were permitted to opt out of their municipal national health care cooperatives to set up their own.[49] The LDP government also permitted a whole range of other trades (with small businesses), such as tofu makers, to do the same. The same pattern observed in the previous chapter thus persisted. Groups with electoral influence always managed to gain targeted benefits in ways that fragmented Japan's social protection system.

What is noteworthy is that although fragmentation occurred in health care just as in pension, functional equivalents to public health care insurance – that is, private health care insurance – did not develop in Japan (see Chapter 1). In the postwar decades, the JMA came to see the public provision of health care as more compatible with its interests.[50] If the fees were set politically, the JMA could continue benefiting its core members by influencing the price-setting process. Private health care insurance, however, might have threatened their control over the pricing of medical services since insurance companies would be involved in setting the fees in ways that generated more profits for them rather than for physicians. Indeed, health care is the only issue area where no functional equivalent developed in Japan.

THE UNEVEN EXPANSION OF BENEFITS FOR WAGE EARNERS (MID-1960s TO 1974)

If the coverage expansion of pension and health care is the story of the late 1950s, the expansion of public benefits for wage earners is the key story of the period between the mid-1960s and the mid-1970s. The standard account of Japanese welfare politics holds that the LDP improved public benefits for wage earners in an attempt to become a "catchall" party. Upon closer look, however, an uneven pattern of welfare expansion becomes evident. Despite dramatic benefit expansion in public pensions, for instance, income transfers and services to working-age wage earners (and their families) did not develop. The standard analysis fails, in other words, to account for the cross-policy variations in the pattern of welfare expansion. The growing share of wage earners among the voting population did not bring about a distributive shift in favor of wage earners.

A structural logic explanation that focuses on features of the electoral system can explain this outcome. The combination of MMD and SNTV made it imperative for individual LDP politicians to cater to the needs of particularistic organized groups. For the reasons identified in Chapter 3, the importance of the personal vote weakened the capacity of the LDP prime minister to pursue

---

[49] Hideo Ibe talks about how the Ministry of Welfare offered physicians, dentists, and pharmacists their own health care cooperatives to appease them (Koyama ed. 1985, 280).

[50] See statements by Taketo Tomonori, another welfare ministry official who served during the wartime and early postwar periods (Koyama ed. 1985, 42–43).

the collective interest of the party as a whole. In other words, even if the LDP prime minister were aware of the need to shift the distributional orientation of the party to capture new urban voters, the structural logic prevented him from prevailing over his own party. The structural logic in place during this period thus implied that the areas/types of benefits most likely to expand continued to be those that benefited the individual LDP politicians' constituents rather than unorganized wage earners. Any expansion of benefits for wage earners would have only come about when employers demanded them.

This section demonstrates that when wage earners' benefits expanded, it happened only because of shifts in their employers' preferences rather than because of the LDP's electoral calculations. Moreover, benefit expansions for wage earners took place in ways that further fragmented Japan's social protection, as large firms were only willing to finance public programs that targeted their workforce. This section also shows that such benefit expansions were financed by employers' (and workers') contributions rather than by the general budget. This was the case precisely because the budgetary resources were primarily allocated to the LDP's particularistic organized constituency groups. By means of a comparison of developments in pension, unemployment, housing, and income transfers to families, this section provides evidence that the structural logic indeed accounts for the uneven pattern of welfare expansion.

New Labor Market Conditions and Employers' New Preferences

By the early 1960s, employers faced wage pressures due to three socioeconomic conditions: (i) tight labor markets; (ii) increases in workers' living expenditures; and (iii) improvements in enterprise tenure and life expectancy. The wage and fringe benefit system that became a common practice in the postwar period among large firms exacerbated wage pressures. It would be helpful to explain how each of these socioeconomic conditions created problems for employers.

First, tight labor market conditions caused an acute shortage of young workers in the 1950s and continued into the 1960s. In the 1950s, Japanese large firms uniformly adopted the practice of recruiting young school graduates. In their bid to attract young workers, employers continued to raise the starting salary. Under Japan's seniority wage system, the rise in the starting salary led to demands from older workers to increase their wages to maintain the seniority curve in the wage structure. As a result, employers were seeking ways to adjust the whole wage structure to their new needs.

Second, just as employers were trying to modify the wage structure, they faced greater obstacles. During the immediate postwar period, unions had imposed a need-based wage formula on their employers, whereby a significant portion of the wages reflected neither the productivity of the worker, nor the firm, but the worker's need (see Gordon 1985; Urabe and Omura 1983). The majority of employers, therefore, provided family allowances to employees with families (Oshio 1996). Employers were keen on reducing the need-based component of the overall wage structure. Changes in the pattern of educational investment by working-class families, however, were causing greater demands for higher wages and family allowances.[51] Japan's *seikatsukyu* (livelihood wages) system exacerbated the wage pressure from older workers with families.

Third, improvements in enterprise tenure and life expectancy also produced an upward spiral in labor cost. Improvements in life expectancy (that is, longevity) led company unions to demand an extension in the mandatory retirement age (set at fifty-five). In 1962, leading industry unions – such as the Union of Electronics Workers (Denki Roren) – began to pressure their management to extend the mandatory retirement age.[52] Moreover, as employers and company unions developed cooperative relations, the average length of enterprise tenure became longer. Under seniority wages, extending the mandatory retirement age and longer enterprise tenure immediately increased the overall labor cost. Furthermore, the benefit level of the largest corporate welfare item – the retirement lump sum payment – was typically linked to a worker's enterprise tenure and his final salary. In other words, the wage and fringe benefit structure of Japanese firms created serious problems in coping with workers' demands for an extension in the retirement age.[53]

Small and large firms faced slightly different problems. Tight labor market conditions made it much more difficult for smaller firms to hire young workers. Large firms could outbid smaller firms by offering generous corporate fringe benefits in addition to better wages. Smaller firms with limited resources simply could not compete on the labor market. Large firms, however, faced their own problems. Because the seniority wage curve was steeper in larger firms and they offered more benefits, the last two socioeconomic conditions hit large firms particularly hard.

By the late 1950s, both small firms and large firms were lobbying the LDP government for some kind of public policy to help them cope with their rising labor costs. By the early 1960s, large firms changed their attitude toward public welfare benefits. In the early 1960s, representatives of big business in various government *shingikai* began referring to a European-style family allowance

[51] The cost of supporting a family was increasing as more children stayed longer at school before they entered the labor market (more children continued schooling until the age of 18 rather than 15, which had been the case for most working-class people). Middle-aged workers' cost of sustaining their family thus was growing, leading to greater demands for wage increases (Yokoyama 1976b). Another reason why there was a serious shortage of young workers was that more people began to pursue more advanced degrees (for example, a senior high school diploma rather than a junior high school diploma, or a college degree rather than high school degree). Shakai Hosho Kenkyujo (1975a, 420) presents the analysis by the Ministry of Welfare at the time, which identified that the disposable income of families with multiple children was becoming ever tighter.

[52] The following article records an informal discussion among personnel managers and union leaders comparing different company cases and the experience of recent union-management negotiations. Personnel managers were from a leading electronics company (Toshiba) and a textile company (Mitsubishi Rayon); union leaders were from the respective industry unions. See "Zadankai Teinensei no Saikin no Doko to Mondaiten" ("A Roundtable on the Recent Trends and Problems of the Mandatory Retirement System") recorded in *Nihon Rodo Kyokai Zasshi*, no. 93, 1966, 40–55.

[53] The steel industry – the key sector of the economy during the growth period – reports all these problems mentioned here. See Nihon Tekko Renmei (1969, 543–545, 549).

as a way of reducing wage pressures from middle-age workers with families.[54] What employers had in mind was a noncontributory universalistic income transfer program. Employers thought that such a public welfare benefit could help them restructure wages to reflect workers' jobs rather than their needs. To this end, they hoped to shift the cost of the need-based portions of the wages onto the public welfare program.

Similarly, by the mid-1960s, employers changed their attitude toward public pensions. Continuing increases in labor costs led the peak-level employers' association, Nikkeiren, to issue a report in 1965 titled "Rationalization of Corporate Welfare." This report highlighted the need for governmental action in old-age pension and housing. After all, retirement lump-sum payment and corporate housing were the two largest fringe benefits. More specifically, Nikkeiren called for policy provisions that would permit employers to harmonize public and corporate pensions and to reduce their spending on company housing.[55] By the mid-1960s employers were willing to support the expansion of the Employee Pension. Employers also wanted the government to do more to alleviate their cost of corporate housing.

The employers' change of heart did not, however, mean that they had become favorable to all kinds of public benefits. Their attitude toward Unemployment Insurance remained hostile at best. The Japanese labor market at the time faced labor shortages. During this period, unemployment was a problem only in specific declining industries such as coal mining and textiles. A disproportionate share of unemployment benefits, however, went to seasonal workers and female workers who quit work to get married. Large firms generally saw Unemployment Insurance as wasted on these groups and as also building too big a reserve of contributions for no good reason.[56] In this context, not only did employers oppose improvements in unemployment benefits, but they also demanded reductions in their own contributions to Unemployment Insurance. Interestingly, employers' attitude changed after the first oil crisis in the mid-1970s when the macroeconomic conditions rapidly deteriorated. Here what is noteworthy is that even when they changed their attitude toward Unemployment Insurance, large firms were

---

[54] These *shingikai* included the MITI's Keizai Shingikai (Shingikai on the Economy), MOL's Koyo Shingikai (Employment Shingikai) and the Jinko Mondai Shingikai (Population Problem Shingikai), among others. In the Economy Shingikai in 1960, employers raised issues of correcting the wage structure. In 1963, the same *shingikai* also mentioned the need to consider a family allowance as one option of policy intervention to solve the chronic shortage of young workers. For the reproductions of *shingikai* reports and policy requests issued by labor and employer organizations on social policy issues during this period, see Shakai Hosho Kenkyujo ed. (1975a).

[55] Nikkeiren (1963) records all of the policy-related demands issued by the organization since the late 1950s. See its statement dated December 9, 1963, for its view on coordinating its private corporate pension costs and its social security costs. Its statement dated October 22, 1953, concerns its demands for policy assistance in the area of housing.

[56] Nikkeiren (1973) records all of the policy-related demands issued by the organization since the late 1960s. Nikkeiren's statement issued on December 26, 1968, summarizes employers' view of the Unemployment Insurance.

more interested in soliciting governmental assistance in protecting jobs than simply paying more to laid-off workers. This was largely due to the compromise that developed between Japanese large firms and their unions in the aftermath of the tumultuous labor conflicts in the late 1940s and the early 1950s. This compromise primarily rested on the employers' commitment to the employment security of core male workers.[57]

The LDP's Continuing Unwillingness to Pay for Wage Earners' Benefits

Of these new policy demands from employers, only those demands that did not conflict with the LDP's electorally motivated distributional calculations materialized. Hikes in wage earners' benefits were supported as far as employers and workers themselves financed such expansions. The LDP government continued to be unwilling to allocate budgetary resources to finance benefits for wage earners. In contrast, it was much more forthcoming with tax expenditures for corporate fringe benefits. Just as Chapter 4 observed, when employers' demands for governmental assistance were framed in ways that permitted favoring particularistic groups, the LDP responded swiftly. In other words, the cross-policy variations reflect the overall constraints of the structural logic under LDP dominance. The rest of the section compares the LDP's distributive decisions in four areas that affected wage earners: (i) family allowance, (ii) housing, (iii) pension, and (iv) unemployment.

(i) Income Transfers to Wage Earners' Families. Universalistic family allowance benefits never materialized in the 1960s despite employers' interest in such benefits. When a universalistic family allowance – called Children's Allowance (Jido Teate) in Japan – was finally introduced in 1971, it happened *not* as a response to employers' demands but as a "trickling up" effect of local electoral competition. (I will come back to this case later in the chapter.) Here, it suffices to point out that the LDP did not allocate budgetary resources to finance Children's Allowance benefits for wage earners. Yet again, the structural logic of the MMD/SNTV system explains the distributive outcome. The LDP government decided to pay for Children's Allowance benefits for the self-employed – its constituency – out of the general tax revenue. In contrast, it decided to levy employers' contributions to pay for wage earners' benefits.

Although the LDP was not keen on financing family allowance benefits for wage earners, this does not mean that the LDP ignored employers' demands. Just like Chapter 4 observed, employers' demands for tax benefits were met relatively easily. Nikkeiren annually asked for tax deductions to ease wage pressures.[58] The

---

[57] See Chapter 6 for the reasons why employment security was so important for Japanese workers in large firms. Also see Andrew Gordon (1985, 1998).

[58] Nikkeiren (1958) records all of the organization's policy demands since the late 1940s. Nikkeiren asked for income tax deductions for wage earners almost every year. Its statement dated September

LDP government was forthcoming with periodic increases in income tax deductions for dependent family members (see Chronology 5.1). By increasing the take-home pay, these policies helped relieve part of the wage pressure on large firms. Such firms benefited, because the effect of tax deductions was greater for better-paid workers in large firms. LDP politicians were not yet worried about the forgone tax revenue as a form of spending. Large firms, which were big contributors to the LDP, therefore found it easier to gain tax-concession expenditures to subsidize their labor cost. Once the fiscal conditions tightened in the 1970s, however, the LDP's attitude changed.[59] A greater awareness of the zero-sum nature of tax expenditures – if someone gets a tax cut, someone else gets less of the budget – made the LDP much less willing to approve tax expenditures for big business. More locally based constituent groups, which formed part of the political machines of individual LDP politicians, did much better in the distributive struggle over tax expenditures.

Chronology 5.1 also reveals an almost constant hike in the tax deductions for premiums paid into life insurance policies by individuals. Obviously, the LDP government, while not keen on providing income transfers to wage earners' families, encouraged their purchase of private plans to protect themselves against various contingencies such as the death of the breadwinner. It should be emphasized that these tax deductions mattered greatly to the life insurance industry. In other words, these deductions can be considered highly particularistic distributive benefits for the life insurance industry. Because of Japan's stringent financial regulation, there only existed about a dozen life insurance companies, which profited handsomely from the LDP's favorable tax policy for their industry. As we shall see, these tax deductions were not the only ones enjoyed by the life insurance industry. The LDP government also created a highly protected niche market for the industry.

(ii) Housing for Wage Earners. We can observe the same pattern in housing, pension, and unemployment. Any successful new housing program had to be compatible with the LDP politicians' distributive calculations.[60] Even when the large firms sought ways to contain the cost of corporate housing in the 1960s, the LDP government continued to show little interest in affordable housing for wage earners in urban areas. LDP politicians were particularly averse to the idea of providing public housing, which only benefited non-white-collar workers,

---

5, 1951, specifically mentioned the objective of containing both wage pressures and inflation as a justification for greater tax deductions.

[59] For the historical shift in the tax politics as a result of the shrinking overall pie, see Murakawa (1985); Sato and Matsuzaki (1986); Sato and Miyajima (1990). Indeed, the overall sum of tax expenditures that large corporations received decreased drastically between 1956 and 1976. In 1956, 20.7 percent of possible revenue from corporate taxes was lost as a consequence of tax expenditure programs. The figure dropped to 5.1 percent in 1976. These figures are based on the data provided by the Ministry of Finance, Tax Bureau.

[60] An interview of a former Ministry of Labor official, Tatsu Hashizume, is very insightful (Omoto 1986a, 30–40; and 1986b, 58–64).

who voted for the opposition parties.[61] As employers became increasingly interested in homeownership for their workers, the LDP found more common
ground.[62] The LDP government was receptive to homeownership programs that
also benefited particularistic groups willing to engage in political exchange with
the LDP.[63]

The new program called Workers' Asset Formation Program (*zaikei*) was
introduced in 1972. It was a tax-deferred corporate savings account to help workers save for their down payments. The Ministry of Labor officials had been keen
on introducing this program ever since they learned that Germany had introduced policies to bolster workers' assets in 1961.[64] It was only when employers
and the economic ministries grew highly concerned about the rise in labor cost
and its inflationary pressure in the early 1970s that the idea for a homeownership
savings plan made it to the policy agenda.[65] The Ministry of Labor successfully
persuaded the Ministry of Finance that a new savings plan would be a good tool
with which to combat inflationary pressures.[66]

Zaikei was also designed to generate particularistic benefits. *Zaikei* accounts
had to be opened in designated types of financial institutions. Not surprisingly, the
LDP government permitted its constituent groups to qualify as licensed financial
institutions to deal with *zaikei* accounts. For this purpose, the Postal Savings and
the Norin-Chukin (a savings bank established by the agricultural cooperatives,
nokyo) gained approval in addition to city banks.

Here it is worth noting a very "selfish" behavior on the part of some ministries. Those ministries overseeing fund-accumulating social insurance schemes
saw in employers' chronic demand for cheap capital for housing – initially to
build corporate housing and later to finance homeownership of their workers – a
great opportunity to create new post-retirement jobs. So the Ministry of Welfare
and the Ministry of Labor both took advantage of employers' desire to cut their
corporate housing costs and offered to assist. The Ministry of Labor created
the Workers' Welfare Corporation in 1957 using the reserve in the Workers'
Injuries Insurance.[67] The Ministry of Welfare created the Pension and Welfare

---

[61] See similar discussions in Chapter 4.
[62] See Nikkeiren (1968, 74) and Nihon Romu Kenkyukai (1963, 330).
[63] Housing developers organized an association a year after the creation of the *zaikei* program to
demand more tax benefits and public loans for housing. Toshi Kaihatsu Kyokai Somu Iinkai ed.
(1985) compiles all the policy requests made. Similarly, life insurance companies and trust banks
began lobbying the government annually to grant *zaikei*-related policy requests (see various issues
of the trade journal *Zaikei*). The LDP stood to gain from any policy favors they extended to these
related industries. Here the exchange was money for policy favors.
[64] The Ministry of Labor began preparing a plan as early as 1966 (Romu Kenkyujo ed. 1990,
314; Omoto 1986a, 30–40). Also see the Ministry of Finance Zaiseishitsu ed. (1997, 293–
296).
[65] The Economic Planning Agency issued a warning about an inflationary trend in 1970. By 1973,
unions were achieving a 30 percent increase in wages, adding to the inflationary pressures.
[66] See comments by Hashizume recorded in Omoto 1986a. Hashizume was involved in the legislative
process for *zaikei*.
[67] The Ministry of Labor also created another corporation called the Employment Promotion Corporation in 1961 using the reserves in the Unemployment Insurance. The Ministry also tapped
into this source of money to provide money for housing.

Corporation using the pension reserves in 1961.[68] These corporations opened ways for employers to borrow money from the social insurance reserves, thus deflating employers' criticism.[69] More importantly, they provided ideal destinations for retired bureaucrats. The two ministries also used these corporations to finance various building projects. It is interesting that union demands for more adequate fund management to seek higher returns on the pension reserve were completely ignored. It was only in the late 1990s that policy makers began to think about this issue after many cases of bureaucratic mismanagement of social insurance reserves became evident.

(iii) Old-Age Income for Wage Earners. In contrast to family allowance and housing issues, we observe a big expansion in public pensions during the same time period (from the mid-1960s to the mid-1970s). As implied in the structural logic, the expansion in wage earners' pensions had little to do with the LDP's electoral calculations. To reiterate, under the MMD/SNTV system, LDP politicians had very little interest in allocating funds to finance benefits and services for organized and unorganized wage earners. Instead, the expansion in pension benefit levels was largely due to employers' new preferences and the effort on the part of the Ministry of Welfare to capitalize on the employers' new attitude. By the mid-1960s, Nikkeiren, the federation of employers' associations, had become more receptive to the idea of better public pension benefits under a specific condition. More specifically, Nikkeiren demanded a special measure so that large firms could opt out of the statutory Employee Pension and set up their own pension funds.[70] The objective was to streamline their private and public pension costs to economize. The Ministry of Welfare accommodated employers' wishes in 1964 by creating a scheme called the Employee Pension Fund. Employee pension benefit levels began to improve significantly after the 1964 Employee Pension Reform, but only when employers, for the first time, consented to such improvements.

Until employers became favorable to the idea of public pensions – and willing to accept hikes in their contribution rates – the Employee Pension remained meager. Prior to the 1964 Employee Reform, employers continued to demand tax concessions for their corporate programs. The LDP government was quite happy to provide employers with various tax provisions to help them reduce their labor costs – particularly when LDP politicians saw an opportunity to benefit some particularistic groups on the side. Large firms already enjoyed a favorable tax arrangement for retirement lump-sum payments. Nonetheless, this tax arrangement did not allow them to prepare for future pension payments by building up a pension reserve.[71] Large firms now wanted tax deductions so that they

---

[68] The Ministry of Welfare created this corporation when the new National Pension was created.

[69] Employers always demanded access to these reserves. Nikkeiren (1958) reproduces all of its official policy requests. (For instance, see its statement dated July 19, 1954.)

[70] Shintaro Tanaka from Oji Seishi, who was representing Nikkeiren during the negotiations, articulated this demand (Koseidan ed. 1988, 152–153). Also see Yamazaki (1985).

[71] The tax code permitted a book-reserve pension to finance retirement lump-sum payments. Companies were allowed to set aside money for possible retirement payments that they might need to pay that year. (I will not go into the basis of the calculations. It suffices here to point out

could create real pension funds.[72] In 1958, they gained a tax concession from the government to set up an externally funded pension fund called Tax-Qualified Pension (Zeisei Tekikaku Nenkin). Under this scheme, companies with more than five hundred employees could set up corporate pension funds, whereby their contributions to the fund and capital gains that accrued enjoyed tax exemptions. Importantly, the LDP government mandated that all the Tax-Qualified Pension (TQP) be managed by the life insurance industry. Needless to say, such a policy created a big market for about a dozen life insurance companies.

The Ministry of Welfare officials had been against the TQP but were powerless. They feared two possible consequences. First, they feared that the development of corporate pensions would hinder the development of the Employee Pension. Second, they feared that the Ministry of Labor would expand their jurisdiction by claiming control over corporate pension programs.[73] When Nikkeiren became interested in a new "opt out" scheme, the Ministry of Welfare was very conciliatory.[74] The Welfare officials much preferred a new scheme under their jurisdiction than an alternative scheme created by the Ministry of Labor.[75] Although the Ministry of Welfare had been powerless to block new programs such as TQP, it was very successful in manipulating policies within its jurisdiction. When it prepared for the creation of a new Employee Pension Fund, it also created a new nonprofit organization called the Federation of Employee Pension Funds. Like all the other nonprofit organizations and special corporations created by this ministry, this too was to provide lucrative post-retirement positions. Indeed, the pension officials involved in the legislative process decided on the salary levels of the top positions of the new organization to be filled by their colleagues.[76]

The 1964 Pension Reform was the turning point. The Ministry of Welfare's decision to introduce a new "opting out" scheme – the Employee Pension Fund – fragmented the pension system even further. Large firms and consortia of firms – with more than one thousand employees – were allowed to set up their own company-based pension fund called the Employee Pension Fund (EPF). These employers, by managing their contributions (and their workers' contributions) independently, could offer better benefits than otherwise possible if they had stayed within the Employee Pension pool.[77] In short, this arrangement turned

---

that it was set in a favorable way to employers. See Clark 1990 for a good description of the system.)

[72] See Nikkeiren's statements in August 1957 recorded in Nikkeiren 1958. Also see Koseidan ed. (1988, 153).

[73] See statements by Kenji Kato and Tetsuo Nakano, welfare ministry officials involved in pension politics during this period (Koseidan ed. 1988, 141–142, 154).

[74] The welfare ministry officials concluded that unless they accepted the employers' demands they would never be able to persuade them to pay more contributions. See Masatoshi Yamamoto's statements in the Ministry of Health and Welfare and Kosei Nenkin Kikin Rengokai eds. (1979, 23–24).

[75] Kenji Kato's comments illustrate the position of the Ministry of Welfare at the time (ibid.).

[76] See Hideo Ibe's statement in Koseidan ed. (1988, 202).

[77] By law, EPF was required to provide better benefits than the statutory Employee Pension benefits. This was no hardship, because the opting out enabled companies with a relatively young workforce to offer much better benefits for less anyway. See Murakami (1979).

part of the public pension into a de facto corporate pension. It is noteworthy that, just like the TQP, specific sectors of the financial market were to gain significantly from the new Employee Pension Fund. By law, these funds had to be managed by either life insurance companies or trust banks. (Initially, it was just going to be the life insurance industry, but successful lobbying by trust banks led to the inclusion of the latter.[78])

The LDP's lack of interest in the Employee Pension casts light on how the structural logic constrained LDP politicians. As far as wage earners' benefits were concerned, the LDP let Nikkeiren take care of them. Most of the negotiations took place between Nikkeiren, unions, and the Ministry of Welfare (or the Ministry of Labor in the case of Unemployment Benefits, for instance). The LDP would have intervened to block the legislative process if smaller companies had been against the reform. But that was not the case. This was a rare moment when even the smaller companies did not oppose the rise in the contributions. Recall that during this time, the tight labor market was forcing smaller companies to catch up with their larger competitors in terms of remunerations. In this particular environment, improvements in public pension benefits offered one solution by leveling the playing field to a degree. Furthermore, importantly, for the very small firms, joining the Employee Pension remained a voluntary option.[79]

For the very small firms that were exempt from compulsory enrollment in the Employee Pension, the LDP had already created a separate program, the Mutual Assistance Program for the Retirement Bonus for Small and Medium-Sized Enterprises in 1959. Small firms now could provide their workers with retirement benefits by contributing to the Mutual Assistance Program. Unlike TQP, this program was subsidized from the general budget. Importantly, this program primarily aimed at helping small-scale employers cope with their labor market and labor management needs.[80] The Program basically subsidized small-scale employers' payment of retirement lump sum payments.[81] The political motivation for this new program came from LDP politicians' desire to help small shop owners. Small shop owners were finding it increasingly difficult to hire new workers in the tight labor market of the 1950s.[82] The new program made it possible for them to promise corporate retirement benefits when recruiting workers. Small shop owners' associations represented highly reliable, organized groups of voters in urban electoral districts where organized groups were relatively scarce. Small shop owners, however, were not necessarily always supportive of conservative parties. Indeed, as Calder (1988) and Krauss (1980) point out, many small

---

[78] For the details of the lobbying by the related industries, see Koseidan ed. (1988, 196, 200–201).

[79] These were companies with fewer than five employees.

[80] Arrangements such as retirement bonuses are classic tools used to control workers' behavior. Although labor relations in large firms improved, smaller firms were plagued with labor unrest. See Ohara Rodo Mondai Kenkyujo (1960, 354).

[81] The peak-level employers' association, Nikkeiren, welcomed this policy as something that helped small employers to fight against unionization attempts by radical unions. (The unionization rates in small firms were rising rapidly in the 1950s.) It is noteworthy that the new program permitted ample scope for employers to penalize disloyal workers (Nikkeiren 1963, 54). Unions, for this reason, were against this program (Ohara Rodo Mondai Kenkyujo 1959, 405).

[82] Ministry of Labor 1982, 391–391; Ohara Rodo Mondai Kenkyujo 1959, 405.

business owners felt discontented with the Liberal Democratic Party's pro–big business stance. The 1959 decision to set up a special program for small- and medium-scale enterprises was one example of how the LDP tried to court this group of voters. Again, the Ministry of Labor, which was to oversee the new mutual assistance program, created a special corporation to administer it.[83]

Once the Employee Pension benefits started to improve, the LDP government also began raising National Pension benefits for the self-employed. The LDP government was much more generous to the self-employed than to wage earners. Benefit hikes for the Employee Pension were financed by the contributions of employers and workers, while benefit hikes for the National Pension System were heavily subsidized. Benefit hikes continued into the 1970s. Furthermore, in 1971, the LDP government also introduced a new Farmers' Pension to help an older generation of farmers to pass on their farms to the next generation. This new pension program was treated as an agricultural policy and hence mostly subsidized.

(iv) Coping with Unemployment. Policy developments in Unemployment Insurance were not much different. Throughout the 1960s, employers – except for those in declining industries like coal – were preoccupied with labor shortages rather than with redundancies. As with Employee Pension benefits, any improvements in unemployment benefits were only possible with the employers' consent. The LDP had no reason to impose costs on employers on behalf of unemployed workers or to allocate budgetary resources to wage earners who were unemployed. The Ministry of Labor officials, just like the pension officials, were eager to expand the Unemployment Insurance program, but remained unsuccessful.

Rather than improvements in unemployment insurance benefits, big business tended to ask for public works investments.[84] For companies committed to employment security, counter-cyclical policies were more favorable than passive measures.[85] A wide array of core materials industries (steel, cement, and so forth) stood to benefit from public works. In some product markets, public works accounted for more than 50 percent of demand (Ministry of Construction 1984, 59). Public works provided "free" and "noncontributory" functional equivalents to the more orthodox unemployment benefits based on contributions. For LDP politicians, public works spending was more desirable for both electoral and fund-raising reasons.[86] In addition to their geographical advantages, public works permitted the LDP government to manipulate profits for specific sectors of the economy – something very useful in fund-raising.

The particularistic approach to the problem of unemployment also crops up in the retrenchment of workers in declining industries during the 1960s.

---

[83] Ohara Rodo Mondai Kenkyujo 1960, 405.

[84] For business demands for public works, see Richardson (1997).

[85] See Kitayama (2003) for a similar argument.

[86] Kohno and Nishizawa (1990) demonstrate how the LDP government used public works to match their electoral goals.

Unemployment benefits lasted for a very short period of time and failed to provide an adequate social safety net for displaced workers. Rather than seek an overhaul of the Unemployment Insurance, Japan's company unions cooperated with their employers to lobby the government for industry-specific solutions.[87] The precise response here was a function of the electoral importance to the LDP of the industry. Industries with ties to influential LDP politicians were generally better off in gaining favorable policy support, including subsidies. Influence was not a function of the largesse of the industry per se. As Uriu (1996) shows, labor-intensive industries with small firms – such as in coal and textile industries – were more successful in getting the government to protect them.

The Ministry of Labor officials hoped to include more active measures, such as financing the relocation and retraining of redundant workers in declining industries to the growth sector of the economy.[88] Facing employers' ire, the labor officials acquiesced to their demands for contribution cuts and tighter eligibility rules in order to fend off more serious attacks on the Unemployment Insurance.[89] It was only when the economic conditions drastically changed following the first oil crisis in 1973 that employers' attitude changed.

In 1974, the government announced an austerity package to contain inflation. The drop in macroeconomic demand caused acute manpower adjustment problems especially in manufacturing firms.[90] Employers suddenly demanded reform of Unemployment Insurance so that new active measures could be implemented. Large firms were particularly interested in wage subsidies to hold on to redundant workers.[91] In 1974, Unemployment Insurance was finally reformed and renamed Employment Insurance. Employment Insurance sought to prevent job losses by providing wage subsidies during economic downturns. Here, again, wage earners' benefits were financed by the employers.[92] (Chapter 7 will further discuss the 1974 Employment Insurance Reform.)

---

[87] Industries that began to have problems, such as textile and steel, early on developed industry-level formal consultative bodies between labor and management to discuss industrial policy.

[88] *Nihon Keizai Shimbun*, May 2, 1971, reports various initiatives of the Ministry of Labor, which aimed at expanding the role of the Unemployment Insurance.

[89] Frequently, employers publicly doubted the significance of the Unemployment Insurance. A number of case studies chronicle the consistent pattern whereby the Ministry of Labor reduced contribution rates in exchange for employers' consent to expand the range of tasks that the Ministry could carry out using the Unemployment (and later Employment) Insurance (see Miura 2002, among others).

[90] For specific numbers of manpower adjustment during this period, see Dore (1986).

[91] Unions were against the reform of the Unemployment Insurance to introduce active policy measures. They argued that such a reform would facilitate layoffs. Once the post–oil shock downturn in the economy became real and the prospects for layoffs rose, private unions retracted their opposition. Like their employers, core male workers' unions supported a new insurance program that would provide large firms with wage subsidies to hold on to their redundant workforce.

[92] More than 60 percent of manufacturing firms used the new wage subsidies program to avoid layoffs. These wage subsidies were used to pay wages during "temporary layoffs." Many Japanese firms resorted to temporary layoffs to cope with manpower redundancy (the Ministry of International Trade and Industry ed. 1981, 52–53).

In sum, benefit expansion was far from uniform in all welfare issue areas. Importantly, there is no evidence to suggest that the LDP was changing its distributive orientation to become a "catchall party." Wage earners' benefits, as shown here, only expanded when employers were willing and able to finance such expansions.

THE "TRICKLING UP" OF UNIVERSALISTIC PROGRAMS: THE CHILDREN'S ALLOWANCE AND THE FREE MEDICAL CARE FOR THE ELDERLY

The structural logic implies that under Japan's MMD/SNTV system, universalistic social policy moments are only likely to arise by means of the "trickling up" mechanism. The only two universalistic noncontributory benefits in Japan – the Children's Allowance in 1971 and the Free Medical Care for the Elderly in 1972 – provide evidence for the effect of "trickling up." Both programs emerged first as local initiatives and were then thrust into the national policy agenda when the LDP government stepped in to eliminate legislative competition at the local level.[93]

Children's Allowance

Although employers' desire for a tax-financed family allowance program went nowhere in the 1960s, a new political context emerged in the late 1960s. Newly elected mayors and governors in so-called progressive local governments (*kakushin jichitai*) began introducing new social welfare programs that proved very popular among residents.[94] Among the two most popular programs were noncontributory children's benefits and free medical care for the elderly.

Some of the progressive municipalities – including the Metropolitan Government of Tokyo – began to provide noncontributory children's benefits to large families in 1967.[95] In 1969, Musashino City, one of the progressive municipalities, announced the expansion of their children's benefits.[96] The issue of children's benefits quickly became one of the campaign topics for the Lower House elections in 1969 (Kenko Hoken Kumiai Rengokai ed. 1971, 143–145). Most of these progressive local governments emerged in wealthy urban areas with their own revenue sources capable of initiating new benefits without subsidies from the national government. Fiscal autonomy allowed the new progressive mayors and

---

[93] Although existing studies of social policy developments note that these programs were both introduced by local governments, none of them identifies the structural logic behind how single-member districts created political incentives for mayors and governors to introduce universalistic programs at the local level.

[94] For more detailed accounts of progressive local governments, see Allinson (1979), Krauss (1980), and McKean (1981), among others.

[95] Musashino City in the outskirts of Tokyo was the first to introduce noncontributory benefits to families with children. See *Mainishi Shimbun*, February 18, 1967.

[96] Initially, only families with more than four children were eligible. (Cash benefits were provided depending on the number of children, excluding the first three children in the family.) Musashino City extended the benefit to the third child in the family. *Asahi Shimbun*, September 18, 1969.

governors to initiate programs. In contrast, local governments that were more dependent on transfers from the national government had less room for their own initiatives. It was very important, therefore, for the LDP government to do something at the national level to head off criticism by conservative mayors and governors.

A brief look at the failed legislative attempts prior to 1967 highlights the importance of the "trickling up" effect. Ever since the 1959 United Nations' declaration for children's welfare, the Ministry of Welfare tried to introduce benefits for single-parent families.[97] Employers' interest in a family allowance program had created an opening for a more comprehensive family benefit in the early 1960s. Employers, wary of growing wage pressures, became interested in tax-financed family allowances as a way of shifting part of their wage costs onto the government.[98] In 1960 the Ministry of Welfare began considering family benefits that extended to ordinary families with children.[99] In spite of the fact that the Ministry was contemplating financing the new benefits on the basis of employers' contributions, the Ministry excluded employers from policy deliberations.[100] As soon as the deliberation council on children's welfare – the Central Children's Welfare Deliberation Council – began its deliberations in 1964, levies from employers and the self-employed were brought up as possible funding sources of the new program.[101] Nikkeiren immediately opposed new levies on employers, making it clear that employers would only support tax-financed benefits.[102] In the face of the employers' opposition, welfare officials – knowing that the LDP would oppose it – dropped the policy.

The "trickling up" mechanism brought the issue back into the policy agenda. This happened in 1969 – the year of the Lower House elections. On the order of the ruling party, the Ministry of Welfare reactivated the policy deliberation process over a new children's allowance program. The Ministry of Welfare officials requested the participation of Nikkeiren and peak unions from the

[97] *Tokyo Shimbun*, February 6, 1960.
[98] Shakai Hosho Kenkyujo ed. (1975a, 1975b) reproduces the recommendations of every *shingikai* deliberation related to social security programs as well as formal statements by all the relevant organizations. The documents related to the Economic Shingikai (Keizai Shingikai) dated November 1960 and December 1963 are particularly relevant (Shakai Hosho Kenkyujo ed. 1975a, 230, 255, 260–361, 369). Export-sector firms were also preoccupied by accusations that Japan's small welfare benefits were enabling them to export cheaply. Business and part of the bureaucracy were also worried about the falling fertility rates as it meant slower growth of manpower supplies in the future. See Ministry of Health and Welfare ed. 1963, 291.
[99] It was reported in a major national newspaper that the Ministry of Welfare began considering different funding options; see *Asahi Shimbun*, May 4, 1960, and September 19, 1960.
[100] This only happened because employers were not represented in this *shingikai*. This *shingikai* typically dealt only with issues concerning children from poor families – something considered irrelevant to employers. See *Mainichi Shimbun*, August 20, 1964.
[101] See *Mainichi Shimbun*, August 20, 1964.
[102] See *Nikkei Shimbun*, July 9, 1964. Employers calculated the cost of their current corporate family allowance programs to average around 3 percent of the labor cost. To replace this program with a public program that would cost them between 4 and 4.5 percent of the labor cost made no sense, as far as they were concerned (*Nikkei Shimbun*, Januaury 17, 1965).

beginning.[103] The Ministry of Welfare sought a contributory scheme and correctly understood that unless Nikkeiren was party to the deliberations, it would be difficult to get employers to contribute to the new program. The Ministry of Welfare's preference accords with the prediction spelled out in Chapter 3: a contributory scheme creates a pot of money at the discretion of the overseeing ministry.

Nikkeiren wanted the new benefit to be primarily financed by the general tax revenue.[104] Business opposition to a contributory scheme was so intense that Keidanren, the peak-level association of big business, began to lobby the LDP leadership directly.[105] This was a rare occurrence because of the division of labor between Keidanren and Nikkeiren. In dealing with the government, Keidanren normally delegated all social and labor policy issues to Nikkeiren to specialize on economic policy issues. Keidanren leaders, as the biggest financial contributors to the party, had easy access to the leadership. They argued that if employers were to be forced to contribute to the new program, the self-employed must contribute too. The LDP leadership acquiesced and created a new plan to mandate that the self-employed contribute.[106] The LDP rank and file, however, were adamantly opposed to levying contributions from the self-employed. The LDP leaders, for reasons explained by my structural logic, were not able to impose new burdens on the core constituent groups of their own rank and file. The rank and file mobilized to repeal the new contributory plan and prevailed.[107] The final policy reflected the position of this intra-party opposition group rather than the party leadership. The LDP leadership, as a sop to business, reduced the overall scope of the program, and limited eligibility to families with more than three children.[108]

The new Children's Allowance was introduced in time for the local elections and the Upper House election in 1971. Despite its shortcomings, the creation of such a comprehensive benefit whose eligibility extended to wage earners was nonetheless quite remarkable in the context of the LDP dominant politics. This kind of program would never have been introduced if it had not been for the "trickling up" effects due to the single-member districts that elected mayors and governors.

---

[103] *Nihon Keizai Shimbun*, May 5, 1969.

[104] Nikkeiren was willing to compromise if the government were to introduce a tax-based benefit by agreeing to a special corporate tax, for instance. They were nonetheless against a contributory scheme (*Nihon Keizai Shimbun*, September 18, 1969, and October 24, 1969).

[105] According to Nikkeiren's November 1, 1969, memo, employers considered children's allowance to be part of the national population policy and hence the whole nation should equally share its cost. It criticized the government's plan to use employers' contributions to meet 40 percent of the program cost. *Mainichi Shimbun*, October 24, 1969, reports a statement by a Nikkeiren representative. This representative (Takeshi Sakurada) hinted that employers might be willing to compromise as long as the government shouldered the bulk of the program cost.

[106] *Asahi Shimbun*, September 17, 1970, reports this decision by the LDP leadership.

[107] See *Asahi Shimbun*, October 29, 1970.

[108] Although the new program was means-tested, the majority of families with more than three children qualified.

Free Medical Care for the Elderly

The political process that led to the introduction of the Free Medical Care for the Elderly was very similar to that for the Children's Allowance in that both programs were initiated locally, then adopted nationally for the same reasons. The first local government to cover the elderly's health care costs was Sawauchi Village in Iwate Prefecture in 1960. Sawauchi Village's experiment was, however, an isolated event, which did not lead to any major legislative changes, whether in other localities or at the national level (Campbell 1979, 330). While such an isolated event did not merit the LDP's Diet members' attention, the situation changed when a larger group of local governments began to waive the elderly's out-of-pocket copayments in 1969. These local governments included those in metropolitan centers such as Tokyo and Kanagawa. Such waivers surfaced as local initiatives due to the number of the elderly who could not afford the copayments. While these copayments were affordable for healthy young working-age people, the sicker and poorer elderly found them onerous.[109]

As mentioned earlier, mayors and governors possessed strong incentives to introduce popular comprehensive benefits lest they lose office. The local elections in 1971 accelerated the increase in the number of local governments that offered waivers for the elderly. By 1972, all prefectures in Japan – except for three – were offering some kind of financial subsidies to the elderly. At the same time, local governments – mayors and governors – began pressuring the national government in an effort to shift the rising cost of the waiver program onto the national government. The LDP government at the national level was forced to take some action.[110]

The Free Medical Care for the Elderly that was legislated in 1972 was thus a very generous program. The new program was to cover all the copayment portion of patients beyond the age of seventy. Furthermore, the benefit eligibility was so extensive that 90 percent of those over seventy were eligible. The cost of the coverage was to be split among the national government (two-thirds), the prefectural government (one-sixth), and the local government (one-sixth). This program did, however, run the risk of creating immense moral hazards by removing any cost constraint on elderly patients seeking medical care. Since this program only subsidized the copayment portion, the higher demand for medical services by the elderly was to translate immediately into higher burdens on the existing health care cooperatives that actually paid for the non-copayment portions of the health care.[111]

---

[109] See Campbell (1979) for an excellent account of how policy makers perceived these problems.

[110] See Campbell's account of this policy process (Campbell 1992, chapter 4). He captures the atmosphere of the policy process in all of its details.

[111] This was likely to most affect the National Health Insurance run by local governments, because the NHI had older enrollees than other schemes. In Japan, retirees leave their occupational health insurance schemes to join the National Health Insurance.

There are, nonetheless, some important differences between the Free Medical Care for the Elderly and the Children's Allowance. The contrast helps illuminate the importance of the LDP's electoral calculations in determining the policy outcome. The Ministry of Welfare officials had always been hesitant about the Free Medical Care for the Elderly.[112] Even in mid-1971, the Ministry of Welfare officials had not finalized the details of the program. The ministry's lack of enthusiasm contrasts sharply with their decade-long effort to introduce the Children's Allowance. In both cases, however, it was intra-LDP committees that made the final decisions about the shape of the program. The LDP acted much more favorably to the idea of the Free Medical Care for the Elderly than to the Children's Allowance.

In the case of the Free Medical Care for the Elderly, the LDP easily reached a consensus to finance the program from the general budget. The LDP Executive Council, for instance, wanted the national scheme to be exactly the same as the one introduced by the Tokyo Metropolitan Government. Unlike in the case of Children's Allowance, the beneficiaries were more likely to be supporters of the LDP than the opposition. The elderly were much more likely to vote for the LDP when compared to younger cohorts, and the Japan Medical Association, another constituent group of numerous LDP Diet members, stood to gain from a big infusion of government money into health care (Ihori and Doi 1998, 160). In the case of the Children's Allowance, in contrast, the LDP never even considered using the general budget to finance cash benefits to wage earners' families, although the party was quite willing to cover the cost of cash benefits to children of the self-employed.

CONCLUSION

This chapter has demonstrated the limits of the conventional explanation of the welfare expansion in Japan. Electoral challenges from the opposition certainly affected the timing of the introduction of some of the programs during this period. As far as the distributive content of social protection programs was concerned, however, the structural logic mattered more than the electoral competition per se. As this chapter has shown, welfare expansion was not a consequence of the LDP leaders' systematic efforts to court urban voters. At the national level, the LDP politicians continued to seek social protection programs that permitted targeting in exchange for votes and money. Wage earners, despite their increasing numbers as voters, only gained better benefits when their employers were willing to pay for them, and they rarely got their share of the budget under the LDP dominance. Those rare universalistic programs that came into existence only did so because of the "trickling up" mechanism compatible with my structural argument.

[112] Different bureaus within the Ministry feared – for different reasons – that such a program would be damaging to their pet programs and projects. For the details of different preferences within the Ministry of Welfare, see Campbell 1979, 334.

Bureaucrats continued to depend on the willingness of the LDP to introduce new social protection programs. As we have observed in the previous chapter, bureaucrats were more protective of preexisting social protection programs that accumulated money. They were also more eager to push for new programs that accumulated money.

6

Institutional Complementarities and Japanese Welfare Capitalism

Japan poses a theoretical puzzle for the varieties of capitalism debate.[1] For Soskice (1990a, 1990b, 1994, 1998), Japan represents a prototype of a coordinated market economy (CME). In his view, long-term mutual commitments among key economic actors characterize CMEs, whereas a more explicit reliance on the market principle characterizes liberal market economies (LMEs). According to Hall and Soskice (2001), CMEs include Austria, Belgium, Denmark, Finland, Germany, Japan, Luxembourg, the Netherlands, Norway, Sweden, and Switzerland. LMEs, in turn, include Anglo-American countries: Australia, Canada, New Zealand, the United Kingdom, and the United States. Some scholars consider large welfare states to be a definitional requirement of a CME, whereas others consider small stock markets and concentrated corporate ownership patterns to be additional requirements of a CME.[2] Japan, however, provides a problematic case, because its "orthodox" welfare state is not as generous as welfare states in other CMEs (see Figure 0.1 in Introduction). Japan also looks different from other CMEs in its large stock market and diffused corporate ownership structure (Table 6.1).[3]

To summarize briefly, certain types of welfare states and stock markets are considered as institutional requirements to support CMEs, because employers

---

[1] Hall and Soskice (2001) have conveniently labeled the debate on institutional differences among advanced industrial economies as the varieties of capitalism debate. This literature owes a lot to studies preceding the volume edited by Hall and Soskice. For earlier studies that contributed to the debate, see Aoki (1980, 1988, 1994); Aoki and Dore ed. (1994); Aoki and Patrick ed. (1994); Berger and Dore eds. (1996); Boyer (1988, 1991); Dertouzos et al. (1989); Matzner and Streeck (1991); Maurice, Sellier, and Silvestre (1986); Zysman (1983); among others.

[2] For the first view, see Iversen and Soskice (2001) and Huber and Stephens (2001); for the latter, see Gourevitch and Shinn (2005). Scholars have been aware for some time that certain types of stock market regulations promote insider protection (Pagano and Volpin 2001; Roe 1994a; Shleifer and Summers 1988; among others).

[3] A number of studies show Japan's similarity to LME countries (La Porta et al. 1998; La Porta, Lopez-de-Salinas, and Shleifer 1999). Shleifer and Vishny (1997) puzzle over why Japan has a large equity market despite its weak protection of minority investors.

TABLE 6.1. *Market Capitalization of Listed Domestic Equity Issues as Percentage of GDP*

	1975	1985	1995
(LMEs)			
Australia	22	37	70
Canada	30	45	66
New Zealand	–	39	53
United Kingdom	37	77	122
United States	48	57	98
(CMEs)			
Austria	3	7	14
Belgium	15	26	37
Denmark	11	26	33
Finland	–	–	35
Germany	12	29	24
Japan	28	71	69
Netherlands	21	47	72
Norway	–	16	30
Sweden	3	37	129
Switzerland	30	91	129
(Mixed Cases*)			
France	10	15	33
Italy	5	14	19
Spain	–	12	27

* Hall and Soskice (2001) consider France and Southern European countries to be mixed cases that share some of the institutional characteristics of CMEs.
Source: Stilpon Nestor and John K. Thompson, "Corporate Governance Patterns in OECD Economies: Is Convergence under Way?" (table 3) http://www.oecd.org/dataoecd/7/10/1931460.pdf

and workers in CMEs engage in human capital investment strategies based upon long-term employment relationships (see Dore 2000; Hall and Gingrich 2004). When compared to LMEs, employers in CMEs – knowing their workers will be around for a long while – are more involved in the skill acquisition process of their workers. Similarly, workers in CMEs – knowing their jobs are safe – are more willing to invest in skills specific to particular crafts or trades as well as in firm-specific skills (Estévez-Abe et al. 2001). Job security is critical for investments in specific skills, because of their limited portability. Relatively small stock markets and highly concentrated corporate ownership patterns mean that corporate managers are not constantly under pressure from stockholders. Corporate managers in such systems face little risk of takeovers. For this reason, small stock markets and highly concentrated corporate ownership are more compatible with CMEs, because they protect insiders, that is, managers and workers, rather than outsiders, that is, minority stockholders.[4] In other words, jobs are more secure when stockholders are weaker. Large welfare states, in turn, offer greater levels of compensation to workers when their jobs are lost. Generous unemployment benefits serve as an insurance scheme to protect the loss of workers' specific skill investments (Iversen and Soskice 2002). For this reason, large welfare states are more complementary to CMEs, where workers are expected to lose more when they lose their current jobs because of their specific skill investments.

Japan, while being one of the most important examples of a CME, possesses a small welfare state, relatively large stock markets, and diffusely owned corporations. In fact, Japan looks more like a LME in this regard. This chapter solves this apparent puzzle. The welfare state, as reconceptualized in Chapter 1, is critical. One cannot understand how Japanese capitalism – or any other capitalism – operates without looking at its social security programs and their functional equivalents. A complete picture of institutional complementarities that sustain a particular type of market economy is only possible by understanding different sets of institutions that might be producing similar effects.[5] This chapter demonstrates that Japan's work-based and savings-oriented social security programs and their functional equivalents sustained its more coordinated model of capitalism by offsetting Japan's small welfare state and large equity market. A new puzzle emerges, however, once we take into consideration the full scope of Japan's social protection system. Paradoxically, the distinctive shape of postwar Japan's welfare system can make it appear more like a socialist than a capitalist economy. Indeed, a comparison between Japan and Sweden reveals that social democratic Sweden has always been, in many ways, much more capitalist and pro-market than Japan. The structural logic of welfare politics can explain the second puzzle. The historical chapters to follow reveal how Japan's specific institutional configuration consistently led politics to triumph over the market. Japan's small welfare state, thus, by no means implies the unbridled triumph of market forces.

In short, this chapter identifies the most important ways in which Japan's social protection system shaped Japan's brand of capitalism. In so doing, this chapter takes the view that many of the firm-level practices that constitute the Japanese model of capitalism became more common during the early postwar decades – the 1950s and the 1960s. The rest of the chapter is organized into four sections. Section 1 discusses the relationships between work-based welfare programs and lifetime employment. Section 2 discusses the role of Japan's social protection system in creating cooperative industrial relations. Section 3 explains the specific ways in which Japan's savings-oriented programs socialized capital in Japan and influenced Japan's economy. Section 4 concludes by comparing Japan to other CMEs.

---

[4] As Shleifer and Summers (1988) argue, takeovers constitute a major threat to the long-term mutual commitment between a firm and its workforce.

[5] For a discussion of institutional complementarities, see Aoki (1988), Freeman (1995), Milgrom and Roberts (1994, 1995), and Okuno (1984).

LIFETIME EMPLOYMENT AND JAPAN'S WORK-BASED
SOCIAL PROTECTION

One of the trademarks of the postwar Japanese model of capitalism has been its *lifetime employment.*[6] Although the nature of employment relations began to change recently, for most of the postwar period, Japan's large firms and their core male workers were committed to a long-term relationship, whereby workers were recruited as young school leavers, received vocational training within the firm, and moved up the job ladder until their mandatory retirement age.[7] For employers to invest safely in human capital, low labor turnover is absolutely crucial. In fact, counter to the famous argument by Becker (1964) that employers only invest in firm-specific skills, new theories suggest that low labor mobility makes it worthwhile for employers to invest even in general skills – that is, skills that are portable to other employers.[8] In other words, institutional limits to labor mobility can motivate employers to pay for their workers' skill acquisition. Employees' commitment manifested itself in terms of internationally low rates of voluntary change in employment in Japan; the employers' commitment to job security was observed in their aversion to layoffs.[9] Despite numerous culturalist interpretations of the Japanese employment system, historians such as Gordon (1985) have revealed that Japanese workers and employers were not always committed to either long-term or harmonious industrial relations.[10] This chapter identifies the institutional foundation of Japan's lifetime employment and the firm-based skill training system associated with it.

[6] The widely used term, lifetime employment, is misleading. It means "employment guarantee until one's corporate retirement age."

[7] Until recent changes in labor management practices, new hiring almost exclusively took place at the bottom of the job ladder (see Ono 1989, Hisamoto 1998). On the Japanese vocational system, see Sumiya and Koga eds. (1978) and Odaka (1993b). For an insightful comparison of Germany and Japan, see Thelen and Kume (1999); Thelen (2004).

[8] Becker (1964) argues that employers only invest in firm-specific skills that are not portable to other employers. The same logic means that only workers would invest in general skills. Critics specify conditions under which employers will invest in general skills (Acemoglu and Pischke 1999; Katz and Ziderman 1990; Pichler 1993).

[9] Although Japan is not the only country that boasts low turnover rates, Japan is one of the countries with longest enterprise tenure. There exists an abundant literature on Japan's lifetime employment (see Hashimoto and Raisian 1985; Koike 1988, 1990; Ono 1989). *OECD Employment Outlook 1993* provides detailed comparisons of enterprise tenure and mobility of different age cohorts of workers in major OECD countries. Japan stands out for low turnover rates of young workers. Germany displays a similar pattern to Japan.

[10] Abegglen and Stalk (1985) probably offer the best known example of a culturalist argument. Morishima (1982) also develops a culturalist interpretation of the Japanese system, calling it "Confucian capitalism." In a similar vein, see Dore (1973, 2000). Despite the fact that some scholars attribute lifetime employment to Japan's cultural traditions, internal labor markets and employer-provided vocational training per se are not uniquely Japanese. Similar firms can be found in other countries as well. Gordon (1985) refutes a facile cultural explanation that attributes Japan's cooperative industrial relations to the Confucian culture of harmony. Gordon provides a convincing account of how Japan gradually built cooperative industrial relations out of tumultuous relations in the 1920s. He provides evidence that Japanese employers bitterly complained about their unruly skilled workers and how much they used to envy American employers for having a wonderfully disciplined workforce (Gordon 1985). Moriguchi (2003) provides an equally convincing comparative study of Japan and the United States that supports Gordon's argument.

The lifetime employment system relied on a number of conditions to function properly. First, commitment to long-term employment security – on the part of both employers and employees – had to be credible for employers to safely invest in their workforce.[11] Second, employers needed to make sure that they recruited high-quality workers, since the return on their human capital investment depended on the quality of individual workers. Third, employers needed to ensure workers' effort and cooperation.[12] In other words, Japan's lifetime employment required very specific incentive structures to fulfill these conditions. Seniority wages perhaps offer the best-known example of material incentives complementary to internal labor markets.[13] Under a seniority wage system, for instance, workers agree – implicitly or explicitly – to work for less during the earlier part of their working lives in exchange for wages exceeding their productivity later in their career. The seniority wage system thus strongly motivates workers to stay in the same company to collect the promised rewards when they are older. Indeed, Japan has been known for its steep seniority wage curve in large firms.[14] Like seniority wages, this chapter demonstrates, Japan's combination of fragmented social insurance schemes, its paucity of income transfers to working-age people, and its work-based functional equivalents provided an incentive structure highly compatible with the firm-based vocational training system that developed in postwar Japan. Japanese social security programs and their functional equivalents made it very costly for core male workers to switch jobs.

As for historical timing, Japan's lifetime employment emerged as a response to labor unrest and technological requirements in the decades immediately following the war.[15] Welfare programs that developed in the 1950s and the 1960s

---

[11] Without such a commitment, employers are likely to underinvest in their workers' skill formation because they run the risk of high turnover rates or poaching by other employers.

[12] Economists discuss the need to avoid the "hold-up" problem. See Glick and Feuer 1984 and Feuer, Glick, and Desai 1987.

[13] Edward Lazear (1979) explains how labor management practices such as seniority wages and mandatory retirement are complementary to internal labor markets.

[14] Koike (1990) uses comparable data from the mid-1970s to compare wage curves in Japan, Europe, and the United States for both blue-collar and white-collar workers. He finds that the seniority wage curve for white-collar workers is also steep in other countries, although not as steep as in Japan. He also finds that the seniority curve for blue-collar workers in Japan is exceptionally steep compared to wages of blue-collar workers in other countries, which tend to be flat.

[15] Although some large firms began to offer lifetime employment to a few workers in the prewar period, the practice of lifetime employment as a common practice in large firms only became widespread in the postwar years. Although some scholars – such as Hazama (1964) – trace the "historical origin" of Japan's lifetime employment to the prewar period, I agree with those who emphasize the importance of postwar events in shaping the postwar employment practices (see Gordon 1985, 1998; Hisamoto 1998; Ono 1989; Sugayama 1995). Hisamoto (1998), in particular, offers a very strong argument in favor of the postwar origin of the Japanese lifetime employment system by carefully examining the timing in which the most salient features of the lifetime employment system, such as *shukko* in lieu of layoffs, emerged. He argues that the Japanese lifetime employment as it is commonly known was only "perfected" after the first oil crisis. Taking into consideration high levels of layoff during the immediate postwar period well into the 1950s, it makes more sense to think that the emergence of lifetime employment succeeded – not preceded – the postwar waves of layoffs. Noguchi (1995), in turn, emphasizes the wartime origin of the key postwar institutions.

provided material incentives to help create and sustain Japan's lifetime employment system. As this chapter shows, Japanese social protection programs (i) encouraged long enterprise tenure; (ii) indirectly subsidized "efficiency wages" of large firms; (iii) promoted workers' cooperation with the management; and, finally, (iv) made job security more credible. This section focuses on the first three issues. The next section delves into the fourth issue of job protection.

Penalty against Job Hoppers

The goal in this section is to identify how the old pension plans influenced the distinctive industrial relations that developed in postwar Japan. The old system of corporate pensions consisted of three types of defined benefit plans: (i) retirement lump-sum payment (RLSP), which was a book reserve pension (more explanation about this term will follow later in the chapter); (ii) Tax-Qualified Pension (TQP); and (iii) the Employee Pension Fund (the opted-out portion of the compulsory Employee Pension Scheme). None of these was labor-market neutral. On the contrary, they all provided very specific incentives in favor of building cooperative, long-term employment relations.

Table 6.2 shows that the RLSP spread widely during the immediate postwar period. Strictly speaking, RLSP was not a corporate pension. It was a lump-sum payment that most workers received when leaving their employer – voluntarily or not. Three factors determined how much a departing worker received: the final salary, the length of service, and the cause of separation. Every additional year of enterprise tenure used to sharply increase a worker's RLSP until he (rarely she) accumulated about thirty years of enterprise tenure. A study reports a general postwar trend of such a tenure bias: the level of RLSP that a worker with thirty years of enterprise tenure received was close to one hundred times higher than the sum paid to someone with three years of tenure (Maruyama 1995, 95). Workers who were laid off were also treated generously. According to *The Survey of Retirement Lump Sum Payment System* conducted by the Ministry of Labor in 1956, on average blue collar workers who quit voluntarily within three years of service only received half the sum of someone with the same tenure who was laid off.

It is noteworthy that a very clear penalty was imposed on young and mid-career workers who left employment voluntarily. Penalties against voluntary resignations generally decreased as the worker got past a certain age. The aforementioned survey results indicate that if we take the amount of RLSP paid to workers who voluntary left as 100 and compare it to what laid-off workers with the same tenure received, the ratios look like the following: 200 for three years of tenure, 165 for those with five years, 138 for those with ten years, 128 for those with fifteen years, and 109 for those with thirty years.[16] These ratios demonstrate that employers were mostly interested in suppressing turnover rates of young and mid-career workers to avoid losing the hiring and training costs. In addition to

[16] The content of *The Survey of Retirement Lump Sum Payment System* conducted by the Ministry of Labor in 1956 is reproduced in Ministry of Finance ed. 1997.

TABLE 6.2. *Timing of the Introduction of RLSP by Sector and Size*

	Total # of Firms Surveyed	Pre-WWII	1945–1950	1951–1952	1953–1954	1955–1956
All Sectors	21,759	21.1	34.5	17.2	14.8	11.3
Mining	711	36.6	29.7	17.2	8.2	8.4
Manufacturing	11,395	8.3	39.9	19.2	17.5	13.7
Wholesale & Retail	3,154	10.5	40.1	16.8	17.9	12.7
Finance, Insurance, Real Estate	3,399	52.9	20.0	14.2	7.8	4.2
Transportation, Telecommunications, & Utilities	3,100	40.4	26.0	13.3	10.9	9.2
Construction	1,080	21.2	36.7	15.5	13.3	11.1
More than 500 employees	1,353	31.5	38.9	12.7	6.4	10.0
100–499	6,353	23.3	36.7	16.4	13.6	9.0
30–99	14,053	19.1	33.1	17.9	16.1	12.4

Source: Ministry of Labor 1956 Survey reproduced as table 2.2 in Kiyoshi Yamazaki (1988) *Japan's Retirement Payment Systems.*

lowering turnover rates of mid-career workers, retaining new recruits was critical for the kind of systematic in-house vocational training system that developed in large Japanese firms. Japanese large firms immediately began training their new recruits in-house by incorporating them into their long-term human management plans. Not only did Japanese employers need to retain the human capital they had invested in, but unless they could count on high retention rates of new workers, it would have been difficult for employers to implement systematic multi-year training programs to build up the required human capital. In contrast to younger workers, as older workers got close to the mandatory retirement age, the RLSP gap between voluntary resignations and layoff disappeared. This was due to the fact that, by this age, employers had already recouped their investments and preferred that their older workers quit. (As mentioned earlier, Japan's seniority wage meant that younger workers worked cheaply in return for wages that would be beyond their productivity as they grew in seniority. In this system, older workers became very expensive workers.)

The material rewards and punishments mentioned so far possessed real effects. As Maruyama (1995) demonstrates, workers who switched jobs suffered from significant losses in their overall lifetime earnings when RLSP benefits were taken into consideration.[17] Existing economic studies using data from different times – the early 1970s and the 1990s – indicate that the presence of RLSP reduced turnover rates at the enterprise level.[18] From the early 1950s until very recently, public policy continued to reinforce loyalty-enhancing incentives embedded in RLSP by granting loyal workers big tax cuts upon their receipt of RLSP.[19]

Tax-Qualified Pension (TQP) and Employee Pension Funds, introduced in 1959 and 1964 respectively, also possessed clear incentives in favor of long enterprise tenure. They were both corporate pension schemes with almost no portability: those who left their employer prematurely lost their pension claim. This happened because, unlike American corporate pension schemes, the vesting period of Japanese corporate pensions was notoriously long. This meant that workers became eligible for corporate pension only after about fifteen years of service at the same company. This was even true of the Employee Pension Fund, which was, legally speaking, part of the social security

---

[17] Maruyama (1995) compares the levels of RLSP received by workers who have changed jobs and those who have stayed in the same company for all their working lives, controlling for individual attributes such as age and education. His study shows a drastic reduction in the overall RLSP received by workers who have changed their jobs.

[18] Matsukawa (1978) uses data from 1973 to show the turnover-reducing effects of corporate benefits. Nishikubo (1998) carried out a similar calculation using data from the 1990s and found negative effects of corporate benefits on turnover.

[19] The Diet approved reductions of income taxes on RLSP in 1952. As discussed in Chapter 1, Japanese workers receive bigger tax cuts upon receiving their RLSP the longer the workers' enterprise tenure. Since large companies provide bigger sums of RLSP (equal to about thirty months of salary), we are talking about huge tax savings. Not only do retirees pay little income tax but they also do not pay social security contributions on the RLSP. (For details, see Sato and Miyajima 1990; Tomiyasu 1963; Yamazaki 1988).

system.[20] As Chapter 1 describes, the postwar Japanese government only provided tax benefits to corporate pension plans that were designed as defined benefit plans (see footnote for a quick reminder of what defined benefit and defined contribution plans are).[21] Defined benefit plans are generally less portable from one employer to another. In this respect, defined contribution plans are more labor-market neutral. It was only as recently as 2002 that the Japanese government finally created legal provisions to make defined contribution plans possible.

Programs such as corporate homeownership programs also affected workers' ability to switch jobs, because workers who had taken advantage of company-provided housing mortgages and loans had a strong financial incentive to stay. These programs were not uniquely Japanese. In the same period, U.S. firms also provided a wide range of corporate fringe benefits to retain and reward their workers. What was very distinctive in Japan was the degree to which public policy had favored corporate loyalty-enhancing benefits. Generally, U.S. tax policy was more labor-market neutral concerning corporate benefits, and its social security more universalistic than Japan's.[22]

Attracting Better Workers for Less

As Japanese firms imported the latest technologies and upgraded their production facilities during the 1950s and 1960s, they increasingly became dependent on new school leavers – young workers without prior work experience – as a major source of manpower.[23] Upon hiring new school leavers, large firms offered them

---

[20] Recall that Employee Pension Funds were something that firms that opted out of the statutorily mandated Employee Pension System *had* to set up (see Chapter 1). This option was only permitted of firms and groups of firms that had more than one thousand employees. When a worker left his job in a large firm with an Employee Pension Fund to get his next job in a smaller firm not qualified to have its own Employee Pension Fund, the worker lost any supplementary pension benefits that he would have otherwise received from the fund had he stayed in the first firm.

[21] Companies that offer defined benefit plans promise a predetermined level of pension benefits for the future, bearing any investment and demographic risks themselves. For defined contribution plans, employers only promise how much they are going to contribute to their employees' retirement accounts without any promise of future benefit levels. In the latter, employees bear all possible risks – such as living longer than their money can support their old age and investment risks.

[22] For instance, the United States has provided tax benefits for defined contribution plans, which are by design more labor-market neutral.

[23] Three factors are particularly responsible for this shift. First, the manufacturing sector was growing very rapidly and overall labor demand was expanding. Second, the new technologies adopted in modern large-scale factories made skills of older skilled workers redundant. A higher level of general skills such as basic knowledge of science and math became more valuable to employers. Employers thus began to hire more senior high school graduates rather than junior high school graduates even for blue-collar jobs. Third, large firms preferred to hire young people fresh from rural areas not previously tainted with radical socialist ideas in order to prevent radical union movement. The 1954 study conducted by Kanagawa Prefecture – *Keihin Kogyo Chitai Chosa Kenkyu Hokokusho (A Survey of the Keihin Industrial Zone)* – very clearly records that large firms generally recruit young workers from rural areas without any previous industrial experience, whereas small firms rely more on experienced industrial workers. Tojo (1995) provides an interesting account of how the wartime mobilization of students into factories may have shown some employers the desirability of young school leavers as good recruits.

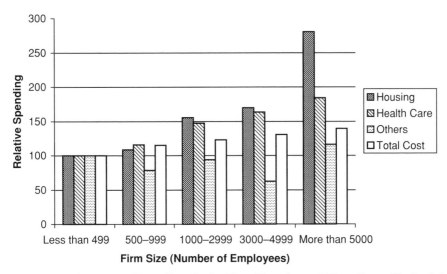

FIGURE 6.1. Corporate Fringe Benefits by Firm Size. *Source:* Nihon Romu Kenkyukai 1975. *Romu Nenkan 1975.*

systematic on-the-job and off-the-job training.[24] In order for firms to make the most out of their human capital investments, it was crucial that they recruited "high quality" workers, since actual return on their human capital investment varied depending on workers' intellectual abilities and efforts.[25] The best way to ensure high-quality new entrants was to make the recruitment process competitive: the more people wanted to work for the firm, the more selective the firm could be in its recruitment process. Japanese large firms made themselves more attractive by offering better material rewards (that is, efficiency wages).[26] Workers in large firms received better short-term and long-term real wages when compared to the rest of the workforce primarily because of the extra non–wage benefits they enjoyed. As Figure 6.1 shows, the size of the fringe benefits always varied significantly based on the firm size. For instance, a blue-collar worker retiring from a large manufacturing firm (with more than one thousand employees) after thirty years of service received a RLSP approximately equivalent to fifty months of his final salary in the 1980s, whereas retirees from smaller firms received much less.[27]

---

[24] Hisamoto (1998), Sumiya and Koga eds. (1978), and Odaka (1993b) provide a detailed history of the transformation of the Japanese vocational training system both in and out of the firm. They note that the technological transformation in the 1950s and after led large manufacturing firms to adopt new hiring and training practices.

[25] In fact, employers' motivations behind the provision of fringe benefits vary according to firm size. A survey of firms conducted by the Life Insurance Association reports that large firms (those hiring more than one thousand workers) provide fringe benefits explicitly in order to recruit and retain good workers (Nishikubo 1998, chapter 4).

[26] Peter Swenson refers to Japanese large firms as "segmentalists" (Swenson 2002).

[27] See Ministry of Labor 1982. Taishokukin Shikyu Jittai (The Survey of the Situation of Retirement Payments).

While an economist might attribute the better material rewards provided by large firms to their superior productivity (or the better quality of workers), such an economic explanation only captures part of the reality. In Japan, public policy played an important role in "subsidizing" labor management practices of large Japanese firms. Japan's social security benefits and tax provisions for corporate benefits greatly reduced the actual cost of "efficiency wages" offered by large firms. In the early 1950s, the Japanese government introduced very favorable tax policies for three of the largest corporate fringe benefits – corporate housing, RLSP, and corporate savings accounts.[28] Japan's tax policies generated significant financial benefits for employers as well as for employees of large firms.

The Japanese tax authorities, in fact, exempted "wage payment in kind" in the form of corporate housing from income taxes. Given the fact that large firms typically charged their employees almost one-tenth of the market-rate rent, corporate housing increased the disposable income of workers in large firms.[29] Tax treatment of corporate housing also provided a great incentive for large firms to invest in real estate. The tax provision allowed employers to treat as losses all the interest payments on the money they borrowed for the purchase of real estate and construction of "welfare facilities" for their workforce. Employers could also depreciate the value of these welfare facilities annually. Meanwhile, the value of real estate appreciated steadily and rapidly throughout the postwar period until the burst of the bubble economy in the early 1990s. Corporate provision of housing, therefore, also meant that employers were enjoying lucrative tax deals that helped them invest in properties. It was no coincidence that a large proportion of the precious metropolitan real estate came to be owned by large companies.

Tax treatment of RLSP had a similar effect. The tax authorities permitted firms to set aside a portion of pre-tax earnings for the annual payment of RLSP and to use the money as internal capital for reinvestments.[30] Since large firms were more likely to take advantage of the favorable tax treatment of internal capital, the taxation for the RLSP guaranteed large firms easy access to capital.[31]

---

[28] For the role corporate savings played in the economic growth period, see Narita (1997). For the benefits of RLSP for sponsoring companies from the perspective of raising internal capital, see Tomiyasu (1963, 1333).

[29] For the details of the tax code concerning corporate housing, see Kimoto (1996, 96–98). Although I do not go into specific details here, it suffices to point out that the tax code for fringe benefits uses an archaic asset evaluation formula that dates back to the 1940s, consequently grossly underestimating the actual income gains from subsidized corporate housing, rendering those income gains tax exempt.

[30] The actual definition of how much could be set aside was extremely generous. When the book reserve scheme was approved in 1952, firms were allowed to set aside 100 percent of the hypothetical RLSP they would be required to pay if all current workers were to retire in that fiscal year. In 1956, the tax allowance was reduced to 50 percent of the hypothetical RLSP total; then down to 40 percent in 1980 and further down to 20 percent more recently. See Sato and Miyajima (1990); Yamazaki (1988, 97–98); and interviews with Keidanren officials, 1997 and 2001.

[31] Unlike in the case of corporate housing, the taxation for RLSP benefited more profitable firms. (The more profitable the firms, the more tax savings the book reserve of RLSP payments provided them.)

Yashiro (1997) estimates RLSP typically amounted to one-sixth of the real assets of large corporations, on average.

Corporate savings programs were also similar in that they, too, benefited workers and employers alike. Just like corporate housing and RLSP, corporate savings programs enjoyed special tax treatments. These savings programs offered workers above-the-market rates of interest, and, at the same time, provided employers with extra capital. Higher-than-market interest rates that employers offered their workers were not taxed. Large companies actually offered convenient "banking services" in the early postwar decades when commercial banks offered few consumer services. Workers not only deposited their savings with their employers, but could withdraw and borrow money from their employers. A survey of large firms conducted in 1961 revealed that about 76 percent of employees worked for firms that offered corporate savings accounts (Nihon Romu Kenkyukai 1963, 337). During the years when very few financial means existed for ordinary workers, corporate savings plans offered very important economic opportunities for workers. Again, employers who offered these benefits gained a lot themselves, because they could take advantage of their workers' savings as an additional source of capital. Since capital was so scarce in Japan in the postwar period, corporate savings programs generated in-house capital despite the above-the-market interest that employers paid on their workers' deposits. A survey by the Western Japan Employers' Association (Kansai Keieisha Kyokai) published in 1963 indicated that a large number of employers set up corporate savings systems in order to raise capital within the firm and not merely for human resource management reasons.[32] During the economic growth period, the total balance on corporate savings accounts continued to grow, as large firms borrowed from their workforce.[33]

In the 1970s, the government introduced a new corporate savings scheme called *zaikei* (this is a Japanese abbreviation for a rather long-worded "Workers' Asset Formation Plan"). Like corporate savings plans, *zaikei* was an employer-sponsored savings program.[34] Initially *zaikei* accounts aimed at helping employees save for the down payment of their home purchase. The timing coincided with employers' attempt to reduce their corporate housing costs by encouraging homeownership.

Aside from long-term gaps in lifetime earnings and in asset formation that they produce, corporate housing benefits also served a short-term goal of attracting and retaining young workers in a tight labor market. Corporate housing enabled large firms to offer younger workers much higher salaries in real terms than nominal starting salaries suggest. The role of corporate housing as a recruitment

---

[32] The survey results are reproduced in Nihon Romu Kenkyukai (1963, 340).

[33] Once the nature of the financial market changed in the mid-1970s when the sources of capital for large Japanese firms increased and diversified, the relative importance of corporate savings accounts began to decline. Popularity of corporate savings accounts peaked around 1976 (Narita 1997, 6).

[34] Unlike the old corporate savings accounts, employers did not administer the accounts directly, but simply had banks administer them.

tool is evident on examining its historical trend. Once the shortage of young school leavers became a chronic problem in the 1960s, construction of new corporate housing began to rise annually, reaching a peak of around ninety thousand units in 1970.[35] The numbers dropped immediately after the first oil crisis: in 1974, new construction dropped to about forty thousand units; it eventually fell to twenty thousand in 1984. Labor shortages during the bubble era again reversed the trend: after 1988, the construction of new corporate housing units increased, recovering to forty thousand units a year in 1991.[36]

The preferential tax treatment of corporate fringe benefits only affected core male workers employed in large companies – less than one-third of wage earners. A number of existing studies provide strong evidence of the important economic effects of these benefits. According to some studies conducted by Japanese economists, workers who have lived in corporate housing tend to possess more assets (savings and homeownership) than others; and those with access to corporate housing loans are more likely to own houses (Kido 1990; Nishikubo 1996; Ota 1994). Core workers in large firms thus enjoyed real perks not generally captured in wage data. In other words, thanks to the government's tax policy, Japanese large firms could offer their workers more remuneration in real terms, while maintaining a nominally compressed wage structure. It is important here to remind the reader again that employers benefited greatly from the government policy. None of these generous tax policies were introduced for the sake of workers. On the contrary, it was precisely the absence of public benefits for wage earners that increased the material importance of fringe benefits, perpetuating a dual labor market.

In the same way that tax policy for fringe benefits aided large firms, so too did the social security system. The way in which employers' and employees' social security contributions were calculated benefited large firms and their core male workers. Despite the seemingly progressive formula for the levying of social security contributions, the government applied it in ways that advantaged high-earning core male workers in large firms.[37] Furthermore, until recently, the government exempted biannual bonus payments from social security contributions.[38] Japanese biannual bonus payments were part of the regular package that linked workers' compensation to corporate performance. Large firms tended to pay a larger share of the overall wages in bonuses. For this reason, the exemption of bonuses from social security taxes lowered the labor cost of large firms. Japan's generous policy of permitting large firms to opt out of the respective broader

---

[35] During this period of scarcity of young workers, employers referred to them as "golden eggs." The figures for the construction of corporate housing are reported in the Japanese Government's Construction Statistical Annual (Kenchiku Tokei Nenpo).

[36] Economic Planning Agency 1990, chapter 3, section 3; Toyo Keizai ed. 2002, 92; Sumitomo Trust Bank website, http://www.stbri.co.jp/café/no7–1/7–1–1.html (downloaded 5/21/03).

[37] At the higher end of the wage scale, the government applied one rate rather than a more progressive rate. See Takayama (1992, 165–166).

[38] In 1974, the government began to levy a special social security contribution for health care from bonus payments (1 percent of the bonus payments). More recently, the government began to include bonuses into the basis of social security contributions for pension.

social insurance schemes (that is, company-based health insurance cooperatives, *kempo*, and company-based Employee Pension Funds) also benefited core workers in large firms. Company-based social insurance schemes enabled large firms in growth industries, in particular, to promise their workers superior benefits for less.[39]

In short, public policy in Japan enabled large firms to provide welfare benefits in excess of what their productivity per se would have allowed. It is also important to note that Japanese large firms did not provide corporate housing out of goodwill and paternalism.[40] Large American firms generally spent a much greater percentage of their overall labor cost on fringe benefits when compared to their Japanese counterparts.[41] The specific public policy configuration in Japan, nonetheless, subsidized "efficiency wages" in Japanese large companies, thereby helping to create a segmented labor market of insiders (core male workers in large firms) differentiated from other marginal workers (primarily women and workers in smaller enterprises).[42] The policy support for increasing material returns to careers in large firms also played an important role in transforming radical unions into cooperative unions, as we shall see next. It is further important to note that government "subsidies" for core workers' benefits came in the form of tax expenditure rather than direct subsidies from the general budget. And, as already noted, they often came in a form that greatly benefited companies. Furthermore, to reiterate yet again, the absence of public programs for wage earners increased the value of employer-provided benefits – and the value of a career in a large firm – tremendously.[43]

COOPERATIVE INDUSTRIAL RELATIONS AND JOB PROTECTION

Japan's social protection system had a lot to do with the development of cooperative industrial relations. Some work-based welfare programs functioned as

---

[39] Many large firms benefited from opting out, particularly during the high economic growth period. During this period, large firms in growth industries hired large numbers of young school leavers every year. Since large Japanese firms imposed a relatively early mandatory retirement age (initially at 55 and gradually raised to 60), these companies possessed a much younger composition of workers than the rest of the workforce.

[40] Initially, the rebuilding and subsequent expansion of factories during the 1950s and 1960s made it necessary for large firms to provide affordable housing close to work. Employers also saw company housing, where subordinate workers often lived close to their supervisors, as a good way to monitor workers' participation in undesirable activities (radical unionism). In addition, the practice of frequent transfers of white-collar employees to different company branches made corporate housing an important part of labor management practice in Japan.

[41] In fact, U.S. firms saw this gap as their serious disadvantage. Japanese automobile companies spend a fraction of what U.S. automobile companies pay on the health care cost of their workers.

[42] See Swenson (2002) for an excellent analysis of how certain types of welfare benefits and wages are compatible with segmented labor markets.

[43] Many women, who worked part-time, were not eligible for the same corporate and social security benefits that their full-time male colleagues were. For these women, marriage became the means to social protection (see Brinton 1993; Gottfried and O'Reilly 2002). Obviously, men with careers in large firms became the most desirable ones for young women to marry.

effective profit-sharing schemes between workers and their employers, while the absence of non-work-based benefits made workers highly dependent on their work. These profit-sharing schemes stood on the premise of credible long-term employment contract.

Creating Cooperative Workers

Japanese labor unions were extremely radical in the immediate postwar period. Indeed, their radical demands for economic democracy (that is, workers' control of the firm and need-based wages) were, in many instances, quite successful.[44] In the years immediately following the war, employers were completely on the defensive. The economic austerity package imposed by the U.S. Occupation Government in 1949 – called the Dodge Plan after the name of the Texan banker who devised the plan – finally changed the situation. The Dodge Plan terminated price controls and loans from the Reconstruction Financial Corporation that kept many large firms financially distressed.[45] Corporate managers were cornered into confronting radical unions to carry out necessary layoffs or going bankrupt. The massive layoffs that resulted intensified labor conflicts. Employers' struggles to reestablish their control over the workforce persisted into the early 1950s.

In their struggle to reestablish their control over the workforce, employers used corporate welfare benefits as important bargaining chips.[46] Large firms reintroduced corporate RLSP – banned by the wartime regime in 1941 – in lieu of severance payments to provide compensation to workers who were laid off after the economic rationalization plan imposed by the Dodge Plan.[47] Employers used

---

[44] In some companies, unions succeeded in seizing control of the company in the midst of the postwar economic chaos. In Yahata Steel, for instance, even the CEO had to attend labor-management councils to consult unions on issues ranging from labor management to general corporate management during the period 1947–1949. For details, see Yahata Steel Company History (Shashi Hensan Iinkai, ed. 1981). In 1946, unions also successfully imposed a "humane" wage schedule called *densangata chingin*, whereby the wage was determined by the needs of the worker rather than his or her job or performance. There exists an abundance of history books on the union movement during this period; for good accounts of major labor disputes during the immediate postwar period, see Fujita and Shiota (1963a and 1963b). For a general picture of the historical context of the radical labor movement and its significance, see Gordon (1985, 1998) and Odaka (1993a, b), for instance.

[45] Odaka (1993a) offers an account of why corporate managers gave in to unions' radical demands in the immediate postwar period. At the time, the market was not functioning yet; the wartime control economy persisted as the postwar government maintained price control. Since the government set the price, corporate managers could simply pass the increased labor costs on to the price. Furthermore, large firms in core industries depended on lending from the public Reconstruction Financial Corporation (called the Fukkin) for their operating costs. In short, the condition of soft budgeting that existed for large firms during this period facilitated the success of Japan's radical labor movement.

[46] The official ten-year history of Nikkeiren (Japan's peak employers' association) compiled in 1958 evokes the sense of crisis felt by corporate managers in the 1940s and the early 1950s.

[47] Large firms in the prewar period also used corporate RLSP to mold the behavior of their core workers. The wartime regime banned RLSP when it introduced a social insurance pension scheme for industrial workers in 1941.

RLSP as "carrots" to get unions to accept layoffs and mandatory retirement at age fifty-five.[48] Employers also used generous RLSP as an incentive for unions to sign the revised labor agreements. These new labor agreements aimed at curtailing radical labor movements by limiting union membership to the employees of the firm.[49] The government's decision in 1952 to provide favorable tax deductions on RLSP facilitated formal agreements between unions and management over the conditions of corporate RLSP. Once the government required some form of labor agreement as a condition for firms to qualify for generous tax benefits to create a book reserve for RLSP payments, employers' attitude toward signing labor agreements became very positive.[50] By 1953, most large firms in key sectors signed new labor agreements while formalizing their RLSP (see Table 6.2).[51] Most firms succeeded in reversing in their favor the labor agreements imposed by radical unions in the 1940s.[52] All major unions (such as the unions of railway workers, miners, and steel workers) concluded their negotiations over labor agreements and RLSP around this time. They accepted mandatory retirement and layoffs, although conditionally, while corporate management promised to compensate loyal workers for their service in return.[53] The government policy

---

[48] Mandatory retirement at fifty-five as a corporate practice diffused among large companies between 1947 and 1949 (Kudo 1979, 207; Kurosumi 1966, 55–65).

[49] In the early days of the Allied Occupation, the American occupiers promoted labor movements as a counterbalance to the reactionary conservative forces within Japan as part of their broader goal to democratize Japanese society and economy.

[50] A newsletter of the company union for a leading bank at the time, *Nihon Kangyo Ginko*, reports how employers' attitude toward RLSP and the signing of new labor agreements became more positive once the tax policy changed. See their newsletter dated September 25, 1953, reprinted in *Nihon Kangyo Ginko*, Jyugyoin Kumiai ed. *Hado Shukusatsuban* 1:241. This newsletter acknowledges the importance of corporate fringe benefits and income tax deductions as alternatives to wage increases. Yahata Steel began including RLSP in their wage negotiations (Shashi Hensan Iinkai ed. 1981, 663).

[51] The Kansai Keikyo (Western Japan Federation of Employers' Associations) conducted a survey of RLSP benefits (more than half of the respondents were from large firms with more than one thousand employees). According to this survey, most firms formalized the benefit formula and eligibility rules of their RLSP in the past year or were in the process of doing so (*Rodo Jiho*, no. 1228, March 27, 1953, 2–17). Typically, the company's mandatory retirement age served as the reference point to set the corporate benefit formula.

[52] *Nihon Rodo Nenkan (Japan Labor Almanac)* compiled by the Ohara Rodo Mondai Kenkyujo (Ohara Institute of Labor Issues) keeps very detailed records of annual labor-management negotiations. The 1953 issue contains specific sectoral and company cases that demonstrate how the content of the new labor agreements signed during this period strengthened the managerial prerogatives at work. In other words, the new labor agreements were more beneficial to the employers than the previous agreements signed during the immediate postwar period. See Ohara Rodo Mondai Kenkyujo 1953, 380–388. Also see *Rodo Jiho*, no. 1258 (November 13, 1953, 2–25) for a survey of the details of RLSP programs in major companies. *Rodo Jiho (Labor Report)*, a chronicle of labor legislations and labor issues published for personnel managers in corporations, provides detailed accounts of negotiations in major firms and sectors during this period.

[53] Shitetsu Roren (Federation of Private Railway Workers' Unions) also consented to layoffs in exchange for improvements and formalization of the RLSP (see Ministry of Labor ed. 1953, 41–42; *Rodo Jiho*, no. 1241, July 3, 1953, 37–38). For miners, see *Rodo Jiho*, no. 1252, September 25, 1953, 2–15. Zen-nittsu Rodo Kumiai (Zen-nittsu Union), for instance, accepted the management's demand to institutionalize corporate mandatory retirement as a way of getting rid of the redundant

for RLSP thus helped resume confrontational negotiations over layoff and other work conditions. Furthermore, the precise design of the RLSP benefit formula in the majority of firms also turned core male workers into "stakeholders." To put it simply, financially speaking, the RLSP was a scheme that "forced" workers to invest their retirement income in their employer.

Aside from the RLSP, other company-based benefits expanded during this period. The percentage of company housing – another big item – in the overall housing supply in urban areas rose from less than 3 percent before the war to 8.2 percent by the end of 1953 (Ariizumi 1956, 49, 79). Large companies also developed corporate homeownership programs in the 1960s.[54] In the early 1950s, the government introduced preferential treatment for company housing. As in the case of RLSP, large firms and their employees enjoyed generous tax concessions on all kinds of corporate housing assistance, including rental corporate housing and corporate loans for homeownership.[55] In 1955, the government introduced new legislation, Sangyo Jutaku Yushi Ho (Industrial Housing Loan Act), to channel public funds into the construction of "industrial housing" (Jutaku Kinyu Koko Nijunenshi Hensan Iinkai ed. 1970, 84–89).

Company-based welfare provision and wages had a lot to do with the rise of company unionism and cooperative industrial relations in Japan.[56] Provision of welfare benefits as corporate benefits rather than universalistic social security benefits during the formative period of postwar industrial relations reoriented unions' goals. In the decade and a half following the war, attempts at strengthening industrial unions failed. Instead, company unions established themselves as the dominant force of Japan's labor movement. Notwithstanding the attempts by the industrial unions to standardize wages and nonwage costs within sectors, decisions over corporate welfare benefits remained highly company based. In the absence of universalistic benefits, unions relied heavily on employers for both wages and employer-provided safety nets. Company-based welfare benefits served as a *profit-sharing* mechanism between employers and workers in large firms. Company-level negotiations between unions and management thus became the most important locus of negotiation. By the early 1960s, company unions in the private sector increasingly became cooperative toward their management.[57] The organizational continuity of the firm became the most

workforce. In exchange, unions negotiated in order to improve RLSP benefits for their members (see Ministry of Labor ed. 1953, 94). Steel companies and unions began including RLSP as part of wage negotiations as of 1953 (Shashi Hensan Iinkai ed. 1981, 663).

[54] For instance, during this period, Hitachi expanded its housing supply as well as programs for homeownership. Between 1960 and 1970, Hitachi helped ten thousand of its workers purchase their homes (see Hitachi Seisakujo 1971.) Hitachi was not an exception: also see *Rodo Nenkan* (various issues) and Romu Kenkyujo ed. (1994).

[55] Employers could subsidize their employees by bringing up interest rates on their savings and lowering their interest rates on borrowing without their employees being liable for income taxes on the monetary benefits received. See Yamamoto (1996).

[56] For a similar view, see Kaneko (1991) and Watanabe (1990) among others.

[57] Scholars of labor relations in Japan agree that the founding of the IMF-JC – the Japanese branch of the International Metalworkers Federation – in 1964 marked a decisive shift. See Kume (1988), Shinoda (1989), and Watanabe (1990).

important concern for core male workers. Large private-sector unions – particularly in export-sector manufacturing firms – chose to cooperate with their management in dealing with regular cyclical problems as well as manpower adjustment problems caused by rapid technological changes during the 1950s and onward.

By the mid-1960s, both employers and unions realized that a new kind of cooperative industrial relations had emerged with emphasis on the company-level alliance between workers and the management (see Garon and Mochizuki 1993; Gordon 1998). An executive of Nikkeiren, Japan's peak employers' association, complained that the management of the leading firms were too eager to maintain cooperative industrial relations at the company level and neglected the collective interests of capitalists as a whole.[58] Looking back on the transformation of private unions, Yoshiji Miyata, one of the most influential union leaders in postwar Japan,[59] noted in an interview that:

> We were facing a situation where technological advancements were making, say, two out of ten workers redundant, creating a need to transfer the redundant to other tasks. This really was the first experience of this sort for (blue-collar) workers. Yet given the way the technology was going, we came to realize we had to accept it. In other words, we thought that improving the return on capital investment would lead to more corporate profits. This would increase overall production, there would be more value added, and the firm would prosper. Then, it becomes a matter of linking it (that prosperity) to the improvement of our working conditions, and increasing our wages. So the idea was that, insofar as the distribution of the pie was fair, we were ready to cooperate.[60]

To reiterate, Japanese welfare programs – both orthodox social security programs and their functional equivalents – ensured that the distribution of the growing pie was "fair" for core male workers in large firms.

Protecting Job Security

Some scholars have noted that Japanese core workers were more willing to sacrifice their short-term gains in favor of long-term interests by restraining their wage demands when their employers were having hard times. This happened because Japanese core workers cared deeply about their job security for selfish reasons. Japanese core workers' skills were mostly acquired via employer-provided training. Job security was particularly important for such workers because they did not possess any certified skills that made it easy for them to find an equivalent job elsewhere. The fact that so much of their lifetime earnings – in terms

---

[58] See comments by a Nikkeiren official reported in *Rodo Nenkan 1968 (Labor Almanac 1968)*, 14–15. Maeda is particularly troubled by the lack of cooperation among employers to contain wage levels.

[59] Miyata, the Steel Union Federation leader, played an important role in the foundation of the IMF-JP. His cooperation with the government and business was crucial in orchestrating economy-wide wage constraint in the aftermath of the first oil crisis. Shinkawa (1984) offers an excellent analysis of this process.

[60] See Miyata's interview published in a two-tome volume of collected interviews of key political players during the rapid economic growth (Ekonomisuto Henshubu ed. 1984, 253).

of both wages and welfare benefits – was tied to their enterprise tenure increased the cost of layoffs. Even the most generous unemployment benefit imaginable could not compensate for the loss of a good job in a large firm, because there was little hope for the laid-off worker to ever find a comparable job in the context of a rigid internal labor market. As a consequence, layoffs always led to costly confrontations between companies and their unions. Japanese large firms, for this reason, typically went out of their way to hold onto redundant workers.

Credible job protection was the linchpin of Japan's cooperative and long-term employment relations in large firms. Without credible job security, workers would not have consented to cooperate with their employers to adjust to technological changes during the 1950s, 1960s, and 1970s out of fear of losing their jobs. Likewise, young workers would not have consented to seniority wages, which redistributed from the young to the old within the same company.[61] In fact, by the time of the oil crisis, the Japanese courts had accumulated extremely restrictive case laws against dismissal.[62] Japan also introduced the Employment Adjustment Fund (Koyo Choseikin), which provided wage subsidies to employers in trouble. Likewise, Japan's frequent use of market-restricting policies – cartels and the convoy system – reflected the government's role in protecting jobs.

Japan's social protection system thus focused on protecting and creating jobs rather than paying generous unemployment benefits to workers. Public works spending – one of the most important functionally equivalent policies to orthodox social security programs – was used to protect and create jobs (see Kitayama 2003). In addition to its macroeconomic effect, public spending directly increased demand for the construction industry and related industries such as nonmetal mining, lumber and wood, cement, glass, metal products, and steel, well into the 1980s.[63] All these industries were considered core industries in Japan and controlled a large share of the overall employment.

Japan's financial regulation also made it easier for large firms – even those in competitive sectors – to protect job security. Postwar Japan developed a highly stable pattern of corporate ownership through the practice of reciprocal shareholding, *mochiai*.[64] Publicly traded firms agreed to buy each other's shares with

---

[61] Indeed, there was evidence to suggest that young workers actually thought in this way. The results of a survey of young people ranging from the ages 15 to 24 demonstrated that they placed a lot of emphasis on the stability of their future or current employers (these survey results are presented in Hazama 1971, 165–166).

[62] Sugeno (1988) explains the details of the postwar development of the case laws on layoff in Japan.

[63] According to the Construction White Papers (Kensetsu Hakusho) for 1984, 82.5 percent of demand for nonmetal mining products, 71.2 percent of demand for "glass, cement, and stone" products, 65.8 percent of demand for lumber, 56.6 percent of demand for metal products, and 50.3 percent of demand for steel came from investments in construction projects (Ministry of Construction 1984, 59).

[64] Gerlach (1992) provides useful comparative figures on this score. In the United States, market investors held close to 95 percent of stocks, whereas less than 5 percent of the stocks were in the hands of inside investors. In other words, 95 percent of the U.S. stocks were "on the market." In Japan, only 25–30 percent of stocks were "on the market" to be sold and purchased by market investors. Although only inside investors held less than 5 percent of the stock market, amazingly high percentages (70–75 percent) of the stocks were held by "stable investors" (Gerlach 1992, 55).

the understanding of long-term holding, forming interfirm networks known as *keiretsu*.[65] To put it briefly, this practice reduced shareholders' pressures on corporate management, thereby making it possible for corporate managers to hold onto their workforce longer in two ways. First, *keiretsu* groups devised something called *shukko*, whereby a company suffering from redundant workers "lent" them to another firm in the *keiretsu*. Second, the relative lack of monitoring that resulted from *mochiai* enabled Japanese large firms to create special subsidiaries whose sole raison d'être was to hire away redundant workers – typically the more expensive older workers – from their parent companies. These subsidiaries were called *koreisha kogaisha*, literally translated as "subsidiary companies for old people"). These subsidiaries emerged as a response to the first oil crisis, and their numbers increased well into the 1980s.[66] The Employment Management Survey conducted by the Ministry of Labor reports that, after the first oil crisis, 26.4 percent of firms with five thousand workers or more created "subsidiaries for old people" (Ministry of Labor 1982). It is difficult to imagine American investors tolerating corporate investment in subsidiaries whose purpose was to hire redundant workers. Japan's financial regulation made possible a practice such as *mochiai*, which systematically weakened the impact of market pressures on corporate managers.[67] In this respect, Japan's social protection played a crucial role in changing the nature of Japan's capital market. Let me turn to this issue in greater detail in the next section.

Socialization of Capital

Japan's savings-oriented welfare programs raised two kinds of money: (i) capital accumulated in private financial institutions; and (ii) capital accumulated in various governmental accounts. The government controlled the former indirectly while controlling the latter kind of capital directly.

Creating Patient Capital: Uncapitalist Capital?

The Japanese government promoted specific types of corporate and individual pension products. The government did so by means of regulation and tax benefits. When the Tax-Qualified Pension system was introduced in 1959, only life

Financial institutions controlled nearly two-fifths of all shares in 1985 (Gerlach 1992, 59). Also see Sheard (1994).

[65] Scholars have given different names to corporate groupings that result from *mochiai*, depending on the nature of relationships among firms, such as "manufacturing *keiretsu*" and "financial *keiretsu*." See Gerlach (1992); Kato (1996); Kikkawa (1992).

[66] A study conducted by the Labor Economic Bureau of the Tokyo Metropolitan Government in 1983 indicates that most of these subsidiaries were introduced after the first oil crisis (Koreisha Shuro Jyukyu Mondai Kenkyukai 1983). Also see Ministry of International Trade and Industry (Industrial Policy Bureau Enterprise Behavior Section) ed. 1981.

[67] Some scholars see Japanese practices such as *mochiai* as economically highly efficient, whereas others are skeptical about the idea of market-restricting practices ever being efficient. For the former see Aoki and Patrick (1994), among others. For the latter view, see Miwa and Ramseyer (2006).

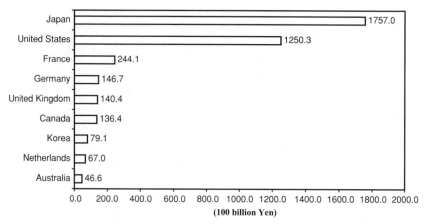

FIGURE 6.2. Assets of Life Insurance Companies (1991). *Source:* Seimei Hoken Senta, ed. 1992. *Seimei Hoken Fakuto Bukku.*

insurance companies were licensed to manage it. This was not difficult, because all new financial products had to be licensed by the Ministry of Finance throughout the entire postwar period until very recently. Similarly, when the government decided in 1964 to permit large firms to opt out of the Employee Pension Scheme to set up their independent pension funds – that is, Employee Pension Funds – only trust banks and life insurance companies were licensed to manage them. These measures created captive markets for existing life insurance companies and trust banks (Ministry of Finance 1974, 174–179). As a result, the industry grew steadily throughout the 1960s, eventually making Japan one of the largest life insurance countries, as shown in Figure 6.2 (Usami 1984, 341).

Japan chose to "manage" market pressures in the private pension and insurance markets in the name of protecting the welfare of its citizens, instead of adopting a U.S.-style "Prudent Man Rule" or ERISA – Employee Retirement Income Security Act – for private pension programs.[68]

ERISA, for instance, legally obligates overseers of pension products to make prudent decisions on behalf of pension plan holders. In Japan, entry into the trust banking and life insurance industry was strictly controlled by the government.[69] Market-restricting regulations permeated the investment portfolio of life insurance companies. For instance, in the case of the Employee Pension Fund, the government determined the expected rate of return. As a consequence, the number of trust banks and life insurance companies was kept small – seven and twenty-five respectively. The United States, in contrast, has always had a few

[68] Until the mid-1990s, not only did the Japanese government reduce competitive pressures on life insurance companies and trust banks by creating niche markets for them, but it also reduced competition within the life insurance industry and trust banking sector respectively by the convoy system. In other words, the government did not allow new entry or exit from these financial sectors and allowed very little product differentiation. Imagine a stricter form of the Glass-Steagall Act that prohibits banks from entering into the brokerage business by creating a firewall.

[69] The financial regulation was drastically changed in the late 1990s.

thousand companies. This means that the vast assets accumulated by the Japanese life insurance industry (as shown in Figure 6.2) were controlled by twenty-two companies until the late 1990s. Government policy thus helped accumulate large reserves of money into a few companies, while shielding them from market pressures. The absence of market competition in the life insurance industry and in trust banking meant that investment decisions did not need to be made based on typical risk/return calculations. In the case of life insurance companies, the lack of monitoring was conspicuous. Life insurance companies as mutual companies did not even have shareholders.[70] Since life insurance products promised a predetermined rate of payment and the government made sure that no life insurance company went under, policyholders lacked an incentive to monitor investments by life insurance companies. Japan thus accumulated very uncapitalist capital.

This uncapitalist capital turned life insurance companies and trust banks into very lenient capital providers for Japanese firms and major city banks. This uncapitalist capital meant a lot for Japanese corporations – and for the government (which will become clear later in this chapter). Life insurance companies and trust banks became critical shareholders and capital providers in the postwar period. Indeed, they became the largest shareholders of major corporations in Japan.[71] Moreover, Japanese life insurance companies devoted a much larger share of their assets to shareholding and loans than their counterparts in other countries (Yamanaka 1982, 6). Life insurance and trust banking sectors also played a critical role as providers of long-term capital supplementing the capital provided by banks (that is, city banks, semi-public, long-term credit banks).

Reinforcing *Mochiai*

As already mentioned, trust banks and life insurance became the largest shareholders during the postwar period. Nihon Seimei, for instance, by the end of the 1980s, was the largest shareholder of more than one hundred of the largest corporations in Japan (Komiya 1994, 380–381). Shareholding by life insurance companies and trust banks proved critical for the development of the *mochiai* practice. A typical *mochiai* included a city bank, a trust bank, a life insurance company, and a whole range of other companies that have business dealings with these financial institutions. All these companies and financial institutions held one another's shares to create a stable majority of shareholders to prevent hostile takeovers. Although observers emphasize the role of city banks as the linchpin

---

[70] Policyholders are the de jure owners of life insurance companies. Yet in the heavily regulated environment, individual policyholders had little incentive to monitor.

[71] In the late 1980s, twenty-five life insurance companies came to hold 12.8 percent of the stocks of the major corporations. Although the figure is smaller than the total stockholding by the banking sector, 22.2 percent, when the smallness of the number of companies in the life insurance sector is taken into consideration, the size of each life insurance company as a stockholder becomes significant (Komiya 1994, 365). Even the medium-sized life insurance companies are usually the largest – or at least among the top ten largest – shareholders of a significant number of large corporations (Komiya 1994, 365–366).

of reciprocal shareholding, for most of the postwar period, city banks were prevented from owning more than 5 percent of a single firm (Asahi Seimei Sogo Kikakubu ed. 1986, 81). In contrast, regulations covering shareholding by trust banks and insurance companies were much more lenient.

Anticompetitive regulations over corporate pensions –Tax-Qualified Pension plans and Employee Pension Funds – and group insurance plans created incentives for trust banks and life insurance companies to take part in *mochiai*. Although trust banks and life insurance companies competed for clientele, the de facto cartels reduced the scope of competition for their services, products, and performance. Instead, competition among rival insurance companies and trust banks took on a different form. In a nutshell, private welfare products such as group life insurance plans, Tax-Qualified Pension plans, and the semi-corporate, semi-public Employee Pension Funds prepared the ground for a form of barter and exchange between life insurance companies and their client firms (Nihon Hokengyoshi Hensan Iinkai 1968b, 293). Hiroshi Yamanaka, president of Meiji Life Insurance, confirms that corporate clients usually asked life insurance companies to invest in their stocks or give them loans in exchange for contracts for corporate pension fund management or group insurance plans (Yamanaka 1982, 36). According to Yamanaka, this type of investment was referred to as "sales-related investments" (*eigyo toshi*).[72]

Funded corporate pensions were introduced during the mid-1960s, when Japanese firms prepared for the first phase of financial liberalization. The timing proved critical. Japanese business leaders feared the acquisition of Japanese firms by foreign capital and sought ways to prevent this (Ministry of Finance ed. 1991, 682–684; Kasahara 1968, 385–386). As Table 6.3 demonstrates, the overall weight of the life insurance industry as shareholders of all publicly traded firms in Japan increased by 3 percent in two years from 1964 to 1966 – a period of intense concern about impending financial liberalization. This is the biggest increase recorded by the life insurance industry during the entire period between 1961 and 1986. No other category of shareholders recorded such a big increase. Considering that there were only fourteen life insurance companies, this 3 percent jump in the weight of the life insurance industry meant that each one of those fourteen life insurance industries enormously increased its profile as one of the largest shareholders for many of the publicly traded companies. Let me demonstrate this with an example.

Just within a year from 1965 to 1966, life insurance companies increased their holding of Toyota shares by 33 percent, to own more than 10 percent of the overall Toyota shares. Similarly, they increased their holding of Nissan shares by almost 20 percent within the same period, also collectively owning more than

---

[72] Yamanaka worked for and later served as chairman of Meiji Life Insurance during the critical postwar years. Life insurance companies call this type of deal an *eigyo toushi* (sales-related investment). This has been a very common practice even for the largest life insurance companies. The same has happened with non–life insurance companies, which sold products for corporate clients. There are reports that suggest that a large decrease in the shareholding of a particular client would translate to a reduction of sales to that particular corporation. See Komiya (1994, 445).

TABLE 6.3. *Distribution of Shareholding (by Shareholder Types)*

	Government	Total	Banks & Trust	Investment Trust	Pension Funds	Life Insurance	Non-Life Insurance	Securities Financial Companies	Others	Securities Companies	Nonfinancial Corporations	Individuals & Others	Foreigners
					Financial Institutions								
1961	0.20	29.97	8.91	9.94	—	7.19	3.53	3.40		2.79	18.70	46.68	1.66
1962	0.21	30.73	8.98	11.03	—	7.29	3.35	3.94		2.45	17.68	47.13	1.80
1963	0.25	30.85	9.23	11.17	—	7.58	3.30	3.55		2.24	17.89	46.68	2.10
1964	0.21	29.50	9.32	8.89	—	7.88	3.33	3.27		4.45	18.38	45.55	1.91
1965	0.20	28.95	9.86	6.54	—	8.73	3.34	4.09		5.81	18.43	44.79	1.82
1966	0.25	29.83	10.85	4.29	—	10.91	3.47	3.91		5.39	18.61	44.10	1.82
1967	0.26	30.56	12.75	2.43	—	10.24	3.51	1.61		4.43	20.54	42.36	1.85
1968	0.27	32.01	13.50	1.67	—	10.80	3.71	2.33		2.09	21.42	41.92	2.30
1969	0.26	31.91	13.84	1.19	—	11.02	3.91	—	1.93	1.39	22.05	41.11	3.29
1970	0.24	32.34	13.99	1.38	—	11.11	4.03	—	1.83	1.19	23.09	39.93	3.22
1971	0.25	33.91	15.05	1.30	—	11.26	4.41	0.88	1.01	1.45	23.63	37.19	3.58
1972	0.23	35.13	15.71	1.27	—	11.29	4.61	1.08	1.18	1.82	26.58	32.71	3.52
1973	0.24	35.08	16.20	1.25	—	11.12	4.58	0.88	1.06	1.48	27.53	32.71	2.96
1974	0.22	35.46	16.29	1.59	—	11.17	4.60	0.80	0.10	1.28	27.12	33.45	2.47
1975	0.23	36.04	16.42	1.58	—	11.47	4.69	0.82	1.06	1.43	26.28	33.46	2.56
1976	0.22	36.50	16.76	1.40	—	11.84	4.74	0.74	1.01	1.36	26.45	32.92	2.55
1977	0.20	37.83	16.93	1.97	—	12.15	4.78	0.87	1.01	1.51	26.17	32.02	2.27
1978	0.21	38.79	17.38	2.16	—	12.38	4.87	2.00	1.12	1.76	26.29	30.81	2.14
1979	0.22	38.85	17.15	1.92	0.48	12.33	4.87	2.10		2.01	26.11	30.36	2.45
1980	0.22	38.85	17.31	1.52	0.40	12.48	4.91	2.23		1.73	25.96	29.21	4.03
1981	0.21	38.65	17.29	1.32	0.41	12.58	4.90	2.15		1.72	26.33	28.45	4.65
1982	0.21	38.90	17.59	1.22	0.37	12.66	4.90	2.16		1.79	25.98	28.04	5.09
1983	0.20	38.98	17.92	1.01	0.43	12.70	4.85	2.07		1.91	25.88	26.78	6.25
1984	0.20	39.62	18.35	1.08	0.51	12.72	4.77	2.19		1.90	25.94	26.29	6.05
1985	0.75	42.22	19.57	1.34	0.71	13.51	4.50	2.59		1.96	24.11	25.22	5.73
1986	0.91	43.50	20.50	1.80	0.92	13.28	4.42	2.57		2.51	24.46	23.87	4.75

Compiled from data in Research Dept., Nikko Securities Co., Ltd., *Toushi Geppou* (Tokyo: Nikko Securities Co., Ltd.).

10 percent of Nissan shares. The largest two life insurance companies, Nihon Seimei and Dai-ichi Seimei, both became the largest shareholders of these two automobile companies.[73] The role of life insurance companies in consolidating *mochiai* during the mid-1960s was critical. Although corporations that were formerly part of the same prewar *zaibatsu* groups – family-owned industry conglomerates – had developed mutual corporate shareholding practices prior to the mid-1960s, this had not yet become a generalized practice. As a result, the postwar shift of emphasis from individual shareholders to institutional shareholders was accelerated in the mid-1960s, and life insurance companies had emerged as important institutional shareholders thanks to preferential policies (Ministry of Finance ed. 1991, 683).

Furthermore, as Table 6.4 illustrates, life insurance companies and trust banks also emerged as the largest owners of Japanese city banks around the same time. Savings-oriented welfare funds were used to contain the impact of a large stock market to sustain a more bank-based financial system. Welfare funds in the hands of trust banks and life insurance companies were "patient capital" in the dual sense: first, they made little demand on the management of the companies whose shares they owned; and, second, they held onto the shares as long-term investors. Individuals who purchased life insurance products, in turn, had little say over the investment portfolio of their own assets. It is important to emphasize that this patient capital was used not only to shield nonfinancial corporations but also to shield banks from market pressures.

In sum, despite Japan's relatively large stock market and the diffuse ownership structure of Japanese large firms, public policies that promoted and regulated private welfare products changed the nature of Japan's stock market. Instead of following the more liberal (market-based) pattern, Japan developed ways to contain market pressures arising from its large stock market and diffuse ownership structure.[74] Although Japan's largest firm continued to be diffusely owned, as we have observed, Japanese firms found ways to protect insiders from market pressures. Japan's savings-oriented welfare programs, I have shown, were important means by which Japan accumulated very uncapitalist capital in the hands of life insurance companies and trust banks. This uncapitalist capital made it easier for Japanese firms – and banks – to commit to long-term relationships by systematically weakening the role of stockholders. The next section discusses how the Japanese state took advantage of the savings-oriented welfare programs.

Socialization of Capital and Japan's Small Tax State

The Japanese government also raised money directly for its own accounts via social protection programs. The Japanese state has always scored among the

[73] Detailed data are available in Kasahara (1968, 533) and *Yuka-shouken Houkokusha* (Tokyo: Ministry of Finance).

[74] It is important to point out here that it was the Allied Occupation that was responsible for Japan's diffuse ownership structure. One of the first things that American occupiers did was to dismantle the prewar *zaibatsu* groups. Prior to this reform, the Japanese economy was almost completely dominated by a handful of *zaibatsu* groups, which were family-owned industrial conglomerates.

TABLE 6.4. *Life Insurance Industry and Ownership of Banks*

A. Mitsui Bank Shares

	% Held by Mitsui Life Insurance	% Held through Mutual Holding
1964	10.00%	31.16%
1965	10.60%	31.92%
1966	11.32%	31.77%
1967	11.30%	32.32%

B. Mitsubishi Bank Shares

	% Held by Meiji Life Insurance	% Held through Mutual Holding
1964	17.00%	27.85%
1965	16.80%	28.83%
1966	19.40%	28.64%
1967	18.67%	30.30%

C. Sumitomo Bank Shares

	% Held by Sumitomo Life Insurance	% Held through Mutual Holding
1964	5.77%	34.64%
1965	5.53%	36.14%
1966	6.33%	35.90%
1967	8.77%	38.44%

D. Fuji Bank Shares

	% Held by Yasuda Life Insurance	% Held through Mutual Holding
1964	0.00%	20.85%
1965	9.50%	23.92%
1966	10.19%	22.29%
1967	10.52%	22.47%

E. Dai-ichi Bank Shares

	% Held by Asahi Life Insurance	% Held through Mutual Holding
1964	6.56%	27.29%
1965	7.36%	24.33%
1966	11.98%	24.53%
1967	10.66%	17.23%

F. Sanwa Bank Shares

	% Held by Daido Life Insurance	% Held through Mutual Holding
1964	0.00%	22.48%
1965	5.92%	23.82%
1966	6.53%	24.00%
1967	7.59%	24.93%

Source: Keizai Chosa Kyokai, ed., *Nenpo Keiretsu no Kenkyu*, 1965, 1966, 1967, 1968.

lowest in terms of tax revenue as a percentage of GNP. Yet its financial capacity defied its otherwise valid description as a small tax state. Until recently, the Japanese state possessed direct control over public welfare funds – based on social security contributions – and over capital reserves in state-run financial services such as Postal Savings and Postal Insurance. Moreover, as discussed earlier, the Japanese state also exercised indirect control over private welfare funds mostly in the hands of life insurance companies and trust banks – including individual and group insurance plans, Tax-Qualified Pension, Employee Pension Fund, and *zaikei*.

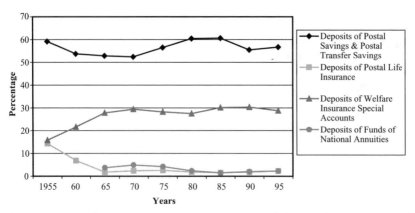

FIGURE 6.3. Employees' Pension Assets as Sources of the Fiscal Investment and Loan Program.

The Ministry of Finance (Trust Fund Bureau) directly managed the public pension reserves. After the Employee Pension Scheme was expanded in the 1960s, it became an especially important source of capital for the Fiscal Investment and Loan Program (FILP) overseen by the Ministry of Finance (See Figure 6.3).[75] The Postal Savings system provided the largest single source of funds for the FILP. The reserves of the Employee Pension Scheme and the Postal Savings together funded most of the FILP. The FILP itself was almost one-third of the size of the general budget and financed a wide range of policy activities.[76] Throughout the postwar period, the FILP financed numerous public corporations such as the Housing Financial Corporation, the Japan Export Import Bank, the Japan Development Bank, and the Small and Medium Enterprise Financial Corporation, among others (Miyawaki 1995, 33; Johnson 1978). During the early postwar period, the FILP used special public corporations to divert capital to the four core industries, namely, steel, maritime, coal, and electricity (Ishikawa and Gyoten eds. 1977, 193). A large portion of capital needed by industries in the 1950s came from the FILP. Table 6.5 shows, however, that the targets of the FILP diverged. In the 1960s, there was a shift from a heavy emphasis on financing

[75] The GHQ, although initially determined to restrict the role of the Savings Bureau, the predecessor of the Trust Fund Bureau, became increasingly aware of the urgent need to inject capital into the economy for development. During the immediate postwar period, the Economic Reconstruction Finance Corporation (ERFC) channeled funds into the economy. The GHQ shifted to a fiscal austerity policy called the Dodge Line in 1949 – the Japanese equivalent of Erhart's fiscal policy in West Germany during the same period – and stopped loans from the ERFC. Industry still needed capital. The Korean War increased the capital demand, and the GHQ conceded that the money accumulated in the Savings Bureau was the only alternative source. See Takehara (1988, 102–103); Nishimura ed. (1994, 56–72). In 1951, the Savings Bureau was reorganized in its current form and renamed the Trust Fund Bureau (Anderson 1990; Calder 1990).

[76] See Calder's insightful article on this issue (Calder 1990). Anderson (1990) discusses the role of the Postal Savings in the FILP. Whereas Calder and Anderson evaluate the role of the FILP positively, many Japanese scholars are highly critical of it (see Takehara 1988; Miyawaki 1995; among others).

TABLE 6.5. *Allocation of Funds by the Fiscal Investment and Loan Program*

Year	(1) Housing	(2) Residential Infrastructure	(3) Welfare	(4) Education	(5) Small Medium Firms	(6) Agriculture Fishing	(7) Natural Disaster Prevention	(8) Roads	(9) Transportation Communication	(10) Regional Development	(11) Core Industries	(12) Trade	Sum of (1)–(6)	Sum of (7)–(10)	Sum of (1)–(3)
1953	5.2	7.8	1.6	4.5	7.9	11.2	14	3.7	11.3	3.7	29.1	n.a.	38.2	32.7	14.6
55	13.8	7.7	2.1	4.5	8.1	8.9	7.7	3.7	12.2	8.5	15.8	7	45.1	32.1	23.6
60	12.6	9.1	1.7	3.4	12.5	7	6.4	4.4	14.6	7	13.4	7.7	46.5	32.4	23.4
65	14.4	11.5	3.3	2.7	12.8	5.8	3.8	8	13.9	6.4	8.9	8.5	50	32.1	29.2
70	19.3	11.6	2.8	2.2	15.4	5	1.6	8.6	13.2	4	5.7	10.6	56.3	27.4	33.7
75	21.4	16.7	3.4	2.9	15.6	4.1	1.2	8	12.7	3.3	3	7.7	64.1	25.2	41.5
80	26.2	14.1	3.5	4.4	18.7	4.9	1.7	5.7	9.6	2.6	3	5.6	71.8	19.6	43.8
85	25.4	15.7	2.8	3.6	18	4.3	2.3	8.8	8.4	2.4	2.9	5.4	69.8	21.9	43.9
93	29.5	16.6	3.8	1.8	14.6	2.5	1.4	9.9	7.9	2.7	3.5	5.8	68.8	21.9	49.9

Source: Fukushi Kokka vol. 5, MOF, Zaisei Tokei (1985), 144.

industrial projects to financing the building of the social infrastructure. Loans
for items such as housing and road construction came to surpass those for industrial technologies. Furthermore, loans to small- and medium-scale enterprises
increased as well.

The welfare funds greatly enhanced the financial capacity and hence the policy capacity of the Japanese state beyond what its modest tax/GDP ratio would
suggest.[77] In many ways, the Japanese government used FILP money for what
other governments normally do with their general tax revenue or with money
borrowed from the market (that is, treasury bonds). The FILP has been appropriately nicknamed the "second budget."[78] Furthermore, just as the FILP was
used as the "second budget," life insurance money was used as the "third budget" during the early postwar period. As regulator of the life insurance and trust
banking industries, the Ministry of Finance possessed a great deal of influence
over these two highly cartelized financial segments. In the early 1950s, the Bank
of Japan coordinated life insurance loan syndicates to fulfill capital demands not
met by banks (Yamanaka 1982, 27). The money from the FILP by itself was not
enough, and the government also instructed life insurance companies to provide
loans to the four core sectors – electricity, steel, maritime, and coal (Yamanaka
1982, 30). Life insurance companies committed nearly a third of their outstand-
ing loans to these strategic industries.[79] The government not only requested that
the life insurance industry invest in core industries, but also requested its cooperation in other policy-related projects. Upon request from the government, the
life insurance industry responded positively by loaning large sums to the Japan
Housing Public Corporation (Nihon Jutaku Kodan) in 1955, for instance (Usami
1984, 346–347). As barter for this cooperation in 1955, the life insurance industry
received a hike in tax-deductible life insurance premiums (Nihon Hokengyoshi
Hensan Iinkai ed. 1968b, 447; Seimei Hoken Kyokai ed. 1973, 365). When the
Ministry of Finance began to issue deficit bonds in the early 1960s, it again
solicited help from the life insurance industry to purchase bonds and also to
divert its capital into the FILP (Nishikawa 1994). As a consequence, the size of
loans due to various governmental requests amounted to more than 40 percent
of loans made by the life insurance industry as a whole during the early postwar
period. Governmental influence on investments and loans made by the life insurance industry continued until the regulatory framework itself was overhauled in
the late 1990s. (The most notorious case is the PKO – price keeping operation –
whereby the government asked the life insurance industry to heavily invest in
domestic corporate stocks to boost the sluggish stock market in the 1990s.)

In short, a large pool of welfare funds enabled the Japanese state to borrow
from its citizens while completely bypassing the capital market. Through its

[77] The United States – another small-tax state – does use its social security funds to finance its deficit,
but does so via the market by purchasing treasury bonds.
[78] Some critics of this tendency used the term "FILPization" of the general budget. For a debate on
this topic, see Wada (1979), Takehara (1988), and Kono (1993).
[79] Kasahara (1968, 390–391). Also see Komiya (1994, 464).

control over welfare funds, the Japanese state thus drastically expanded its financial capacity.

JAPAN'S WELFARE CAPITALISM

This chapter has shown the specific ways in which Japan's social protection contributed to the building and sustaining of long-term relationships between workers and their employers, and those between companies and their capital providers. In doing so, this chapter has solved the puzzle stated at the beginning of the chapter. Japan's functional equivalents worked in the absence of generous public welfare benefits to sustain long-term and cooperative relations between workers and employers in large firms. The findings in this chapter also illuminate the importance of the financial dimensions of the welfare state. Although political scientists rarely pay attention to the financial design of welfare programs, this chapter has identified the specific ways in which savings-oriented welfare programs might affect the nature of financial markets.

More broadly, this chapter has demonstrated the usefulness of going beyond a narrow focus on a few orthodox social security programs in thinking about different types of welfare capitalism. The findings in this chapter are relevant beyond Japan. Other CMEs, too, rely on similar functional equivalents and market-restricting financial regulations to protect long-term relationships. Indeed, Germany, another important example of a CME, has also used corporate pension programs to tie core male workers to their employers while at the same time increasing capital at the employers' disposal. The role that social protection programs play in a market economy is much broader than what is generally assumed in the welfare state literature or in the varieties of capitalism literature.[80]

The findings in this chapter give rise to another puzzle. Japan's postwar experience offers an interesting contrast to that of Sweden. The Japanese experience, in fact, presents a mirror image of Swedish experience. What the mirror image reveals is highly counterintuitive: social democratic Sweden was more capitalistic than conservative Japan. To put it bluntly, the Swedish welfare state used social policy as industrial policy. Its policy mix favored large, capital-intensive, and publicly traded firms and prompted shifts of employment distribution away from small, family-owned firms. Just as Sweden used social policy as industrial policy, Japan used its industrial policy as social policy. The direct effect was to perpetuate Japan's dual economy, whereby the majority of the workforce remained in small – and often family-owned – enterprises. The mirror image analogy does not end here. Sweden used social policy as industrial policy to facilitate manpower adjustments of export-sector firms by externalizing the cost of adjustment via the welfare state. For instance, Sweden used an extensive active labor market program to absorb redundant workforce. The Swedish welfare state – with its collective wage bargaining and high levels of universalistic benefits – shifted manpower away

---

[80] Edwards and Fischer (1994, 53–58); Hauck (1994); Kubler (1994). For a comparison between Germany, Japan, and the United States, see Roe (1994b).

from low-wage sectors of the economy (Davis and Henrekson 1997, 2000; Edin and Topel 1997). In addition, Sweden's tax policy favored large firms financed by institutional investors to the disadvantage of small and family-owned firms (Davis and Henrekson 1997). As a result, the Swedish state effectively shaped the national distribution of employment in favor of large, capital-intensive firms.

The Japanese welfare state did just the opposite. Japan used industrial policy as social policy.[81] Instead of aiding firms to shed their redundant workforce, the Japanese welfare state subsidized employment of excess labor – in both large and small firms. Rather than creating a large public sector – which would have benefited the opposition parties – or an extensive active labor market to pool and train redundant workers, Japan subsidized private sector employment instead. Japan's "socialization" of capital was a crucial piece that made the system work. It allowed the state to invest in public works beyond its tax revenue. It also permitted private firms to function as primary welfare providers by shielding them from financial pressures. In short, Japan's small social welfare spending and its weak organized labor did not yield a form of laissez-faire capitalism. On the contrary, postwar Japan pursued a brand of capitalism, where economic units – that is, firms – were very much treated as units of welfare provision as if under a socialist regime. Furthermore, state intervention to protect businesses in Japan perpetuated the presence of a large number of inefficient firms.

The puzzle of why a country dominated by the pro-business LDP became more socialist than a country long dominated by the Social Democrats can only be solved by understanding the structural logic of welfare politics. The combination of MMD and strong party and the frequency of minority governments in Sweden meant that employers' associations and unions representing competitive sectors of the economy could form an alliance to bind their political parties. This might explain why Sweden sometimes appears to be more "liberal" than Japan despite its large public-sector employment. More generally, the political weight granted to "encompassing organizations" – to use Mancur Olson's term – within the Swedish political system more effectively prevented rent-seeking by particularistic groups. The combination of MMD, the personal vote, and the majority party government in Japan encouraged rent-seeking by particularistic groups. Japan's state intervention, which often went against the market, can only be interpreted in terms of the political power of particularistic groups and their bureaucratic allies.

---

[81] Pontusson (1991) develops a very interesting argument about how and why social democratic countries use social policy in lieu of industrial policy.

7

The Emergence of Trouble in the 1970s

By the 1970s Japan was gaining recognition in the West for its successful "model of capitalism," from which other countries had a lot to learn. Lifetime employment and close interfirm relationships – *mochiai* and *keiretsu* – were seen as keys to Japan's corporate success.[1] Behind these plaudits, however, lurked serious institutional vulnerabilities in Japanese welfare capitalism. Japan's postwar welfare capitalism rested on a couple of assumptions.[2] The first assumption was that the economy would continue to expand at a rapid pace. The second one was that the demographic structure would remain relatively young. The Japanese system of social protection was particularly vulnerable to any changes in these two assumptions. The oil crisis of 1973 challenged the first assumption by abruptly ending Japan's high economic growth. A shortfall in corporate profits and the tax revenue led the Japanese government to issue "deficit bonds" worth 2.9 trillion yen to finance its budget in 1975. Since then, the Japanese state has depended on "borrowing" to make ends meet.[3] Furthermore – to mention changes in the second assumption – not only was life expectancy increasing, but so was the average age of employees of large firms.

Numerous reform attempts followed in the aftermath of the first oil crisis. The government tried to reform Japan's unemployment insurance, health care, pension, children's allowance, agricultural subsidies, and taxation system. Scholars

---

[1] The global success of Japanese manufacturing in the 1980s stimulated a huge body of literature. See Aoki (1980, 1988); Aoki and Dore eds. (1994); Aoki and Okuno eds. (1996); Aoki and Patrick eds. (1994); Dertouzos, Lester, Solow, and the MIT Commission (1989); Dore (1973, 1986, 1987); Gerlach (1992); Kenny and Florida (1988); Koike (1981, 1987, 1990, 1991); Milgrom and Roberts (1995).

[2] All welfare states in advanced democracies were created on two assumptions: that the demographic structure would remain roughly the same, and that the economy would continue to grow. Japan was no exception.

[3] The bubble economy during the latter half of the 1980s provided a temporary respite. Rapid increases in tax revenue made it possible for the government to postpone drastic reforms of the welfare state. This bubble economy, however, solved no problems. When the bubble burst, the ever-present problems came back with a vengeance.

of Japanese politics generally agree that attempts to cut back benefits in the latter half of the 1970s failed, whereas similar efforts in the 1980s were more successful.[4] Most scholars also agree on the importance of the ad hoc Research Council on Administrative Reform (Rincho) in the early part of the 1980s.[5] The Rincho was set up by the LDP prime minister to guide policy discussions to reform public enterprises and public spending programs. Scholars nonetheless disagree as to whether the reforms in the 1980s were "welfare retrenchments" or merely "welfare adjustments" to make the Japanese social security system more sustainable. Those who see the reforms in the 1980s primarily as "welfare retrenchments" emphasize the importance of the rise of a form of Thatcherite neoliberalism in Japan during this period.[6] During this period, the LDP senior leadership, big business, and the Ministry of Finance came together to reduce the size of the welfare state in Japan. Those who interpret the subsequent reforms as "welfare adjustments" that stabilized Japan's social security system tend to emphasize the role of welfare bureaucrats, who, it is believed, were committed to protecting the two big programs under their jurisdiction – health care and pension.[7] The Ministry of Welfare bureaucrats themselves considered pension and health reforms in the 1980s as *bappon kaisei* (major reforms) that solidified the foundation of Japan's welfare state. They refer to the 1985 Pension Reform, in particular, as an important step on the path to a more universalistic public pension. Either way, scholars agree that the 1980s was a time of successful reforms.

This chapter provides an alternative account of what happened after the oil crisis. Put simply, this chapter claims that even the supposedly successful reforms of the 1980s failed to bring about fundamental change. Japan's social protection system continued to be work based and savings oriented. Japan's reliance on functional equivalents persisted. All the institutional vulnerabilities of the system remained. This chapter explains the limited nature of the reforms in terms of the structural logic. Most of the institutional vulnerabilities of Japan's social protection system had political roots. The combination of MMD and SNTV had given rise to social protection programs targeted at specific organized groups. Moreover Japan's social protection system rested on institutional arrangements open to profiteering by particularistic groups that supported the LDP. The real costs of these programs were passed on, in turn, to unorganized voters – urban tax payers and consumers, in particular.

Welfare politics thus remained the same throughout the 1951–1989 period, because the basic structure of politics remained the same. The LDP government was guided by the same distributive incentives in favor of electorally important organized groups at the expense of unorganized voters. The dominance of the

---

[4] See Aoki (1988); Campbell (1992); Eguchi (1985); Junko Kato (1991a, 1991b); Hiwatari (1995); Hayakawa (1991a, 1991b); Hayakawa et al. (1986); Nakano (1986, 1989).

[5] Campbell (1992); Kambara (1986); Kato (1991b); and Otake (1997).

[6] Kambara (1986) and Shinkawa (1993), for instance, see the policy developments since the 1980s primarily as welfare retrenchments.

[7] Campbell (1992), Nakano (1989), and Kato (1991b) emphasize the role of welfare bureaucrats' commitment to salvage the social security system.

MMD/SNTV system continued to weaken the party leadership and shape the distributive incentives of individual LDP Diet members. Even when the prime minister identified a necessary if painful reform, intraparty veto players blocked him. Any attempt to reduce the benefits of the core constituent groups of LDP Diet members faced insurmountable hurdles. Nor was it an easy option for the LDP leadership to reach out to new urban voters. Despite the fact that some LDP leaders were becoming aware of the need to cultivate the electoral support of such voters, individual LDP Diet members, preoccupied with their immediate reelection, did not share these long-term concerns. Under the MMD/SNTV system, it made more sense for individual politicians to focus their attention on highly organized and reliable groups of voters. As a result, efforts to reform the existing perks and benefits of conservative constituent groups were extremely difficult.

The decentralized nature of the LDP government, which was primarily caused by the combination of MMD/SNTV, also granted bureaucrats ample room for discretion. Bureaucrats, as we have seen, often used their power to mold Japan's social protection programs to serve their own organizational interests. In the context of the LDP dominance under the MMD/SNTV system, bureaucrats continued to expand and protect their organizational turfs in alliance with their political allies, who wanted to expand and protect policy favors for their core constituent groups.

THE UNRAVELING OF INSTITUTIONAL VULNERABILITIES

During the rapid economic growth period – from the mid-1950s until the first oil crisis – the Japanese model of welfare capitalism appeared to possess all manner of economic strengths. At the microlevel, Japan's work-based social protection gave large firms enormous advantages in hiring and managing their workers. It tied core male workers to the company and served as a profit-sharing mechanism to help create peaceful labor relations based on long-term cooperation. Public policy actively assisted large firms' use of welfare benefits as labor management tools. Not only did tax exemptions and deductions reduce the cost of fringe benefits, but the government also permitted large firms to turn social security benefits into quasi–fringe benefits. Public policy thus created a gap in real lifetime earnings between core male workers employed in large firms and others employed in smaller firms. As a result, large firms were better able to attract high-quality workers and to hoard them in rigid internal labor markets.[8]

Likewise, at the macro level, Japan's mode of social protection seemed to yield benefits. Functionally equivalent programs such as income support for

---

[8] By high quality, I mean young school leavers with good school credentials. Japan had developed a fairly systematic school-to-work transition, whereby high-ranking schools developed close ties with large firms to facilitate placement of their students. See Dore and Sako (1989) and Kariya (1991). Hence, it is important to note that Japan's employer-provided vocational training system is based upon the recruitment of young workers with high levels of general skills. For a general argument about the relationship between school systems and labor markets, see Jutta Allmendinger (1989).

agricultural families and public works spending – in lieu of more comprehensive family allowance programs and unemployment benefits, respectively – made a lot of macroeconomic sense during the high economic growth period. As industrial wages rose rapidly, rural incomes lagged behind. Income support for farmers redistributed income from growing industrial sectors to declining agriculture (Honma 1994). Public works spending, particularly in rural areas, had the same effect of redistributing funds to regions that were left out of the rapid economic growth. Both types of policies functioned more or less as tools of Keynesian policy to boost the purchasing power of rural residents and overall domestic demand. The paucity of income transfers to the working-age population meanwhile ensured that reservation wages remained low, which benefited employers.

During the economic growth period, neither employers nor unions felt the burden of Japan's Keynesian policy. Nor did employers or unions care much about the fact that the government heavily subsidized welfare benefits for non–wage earners in the form of both social security benefits and various functional equivalents. Strange as it may sound, the Japanese state continued to cut tax rates almost every year during the economic growth period. The government granted large firms big tax breaks and reduced personal income taxes (see chronology of tax cuts in Appendix 4.A). Thanks to rapid economic growth, Japan had the luxury of piling up natural increases in the overall tax revenue while reducing the tax rates.[9] Potential conflicts of interest between industrial actors and farmers remained latent. Even after the two oil crises, Japan still performed better than most other advanced industrial societies.[10]

Below the surface, however, a more fundamental institutional dissonance was emerging. First, the labor cost structure of large firms was highly sensitive to the average age and tenure of workers.[11] Second, the revenue structure of the Japanese welfare state was particularly vulnerable to economic fluctuations. Third, Japan's social security system for pensions and health care was particularly vulnerable to demographic aging. Fourth, many of Japan's functionally equivalent social protection programs consisted of market-restricting regulations. To make matters even worse, the economic downturn caused by the two oil crises and structural

---

[9] The following two sources contain a good overview of Japanese taxation: Sato and Miyajima (1990); Kokuritsu Kokkai Toshokan Chosa Rippo Kosakyoku (1972).

[10] Japan maintained relatively low inflation and unemployment rates; even after the first oil crisis, the Japanese unemployment rates remained between 2.0 and 2.5. Indeed, Japan's successful wage coordination and manpower adjustment policies challenged the conventional wisdom in comparative political economy. See Shinkawa (1993). Dore (1986) marveled at Japan's upholding of its internal labor market (its lifetime employment) and its simultaneous success in actually downsizing its industrial workforce in the aftermath of the oil crises. He coined a term "flexible rigidities" to describe manpower management practice in Japan.

[11] Nikkeiren issued a systematic study about the need to overhaul corporate practices to streamline corporate fringe benefits as early as 1965. Reflecting business demands, the Industrial Structure Shingikai in the Ministry of International Trade and Industry also issued a recommendation to rationalize corporate fringe benefits in 1968. A trade journal titled *Fringe Benefits (Fukuri Kosei)* reports case studies as well as surveys of large corporations to describe widespread labor problems and to suggest solutions. See for instance, *Fukuri Kosei*, November 18, 1975.

changes of the economy began to unravel institutional vulnerabilities embedded in the Japanese welfare system. In short, the way in which social protection was institutionalized in Japan created specific problems.

Problems of Older Workers

By the mid-1970s the successful institutionalization of an internal labor market in large firms and improvements in life expectancy led to a rise in both the average years of employees' tenure and their age (see Table 7.1). Workers' demands for extensions of the mandatory retirement age intensified throughout the 1970s. Given Japan's seniority-based promotion and wage structure, such extensions involved an immediate increase in labor costs.[12] Wages and nonwage benefits designed to reward seniority had been necessary components of internal labor markets. However, this type of remuneration system, when combined with the aging of the corporate workforce, boosted labor costs. The very fact that the benefit formula for major corporate benefits such as retirement payments was explicitly linked to the length of workers' service made Japanese large firms especially vulnerable to the "lengthening" of the enterprise tenure. The real cost of internal labor markets was thus beginning to dawn on both business leaders and policy makers.

The two oil crises hit Japan just as it was trying to cope with the extension of the mandatory retirement age.[13] The economic slowdown brought on by these oil crises further exacerbated the "intrafirm aging process." Typically, Japanese large firms would react to a downturn in the business cycle with a hiring freeze. But this created an irregular age structure within the firm: boom years created large cohorts of new young hires; lean years led to small cohorts. Large cohorts of new young hires reduced the overall average tenure and age of the workforce, while small cohorts increased them. Because of wages and promotions based on tenure and age, the unevenness in cohorts also sowed the seeds of even larger problems.[14]

---

[12] Seniority wage itself is not uniquely Japanese. As Koike (1991) demonstrates, Japan stands out for the steepness of the seniority curve and for applying seniority wages to blue-collar workers. While white-collar wages do increase with enterprise tenure in most other countries too, blue-collar wages tend to be flat. Also, Japanese wages reflect more than enterprise tenure, they reflect workers' actual age.

[13] Some unions – electronics and textile – began to demand extension of the mandatory retirement age in the early 1960s (*Rodo Kyokai Zasshi* 1966). Other unions soon followed suit. The Ministry of Labor adopted the extension of company mandatory retirement age as its policy goal and began to offer employers some grants to extend the retirement age in 1972. However, the oil crisis set back the bureaucratic policy objectives. Also see Campbell (1992) for an account of how the MOL perceived old workers' problems and tried to expand their programs into a new area to address them.

[14] In particular, the aging of a large cohort hired during the rapid economic expansion in the 1950s and the 1960s, drastically increased cost pressures on their employers. The Institute of Labor Affairs compiled a volume about how large firms were coping with the problems described here (Romu Kenkyujo 1975).

TABLE 7.1. *Demographic Aging of Workforce by Industry*

	Industry Breakdown of Average Age of Workforce					
	1955	1960	1970	1975	1980	1990
Metals	33.1	33.5	32.1	33.7	32.5	40.2
Electronics	31.1	28.1	26.2	31.5	27.6	35.3
Transportation Machinery	26.5	35.3	29.3	33.4	32.1	37.6
Precision Machinery	32	28.5	27.8	30.4	28.4	35.7
General Machinery			30.4	32.7	30.9	37.5
Paper & Pulp	32.8	33.9	34.6	37.2	30.8	40.3
Chemicals	30.2	31.4	33.7	33.9	33.2	38.9
Rubber			28	32.6	26.3	39.2
Cement	33.2	35.5	35.3	36.3	33.5	38.8
Textile	26	26.8	25.5	31	24.5	37.1
Printing	34.5	33.9	29.4	33.4	30.4	35.8
Food Processing	29.2	28.3	26.8	31.2	29.4	40.1
Mining	34.7	36.3	38.7	41	38.1	39.2
Construction		35.2	33.1	30.2	32.7	40
Utilities	36.1	36.4	38.6	37.2	37	36.8
Transportation	35.7	32.6	34.7	35.4	31.1	38.6
Telecommunications			32.8	35.8	32.8	41.2
Finance and Insurance	29.3	28.3	30.3	30.7	30.3	37.4
Trading and Other Services	27.6	28.5	25.7	30	33.4	36.3

Source: Nikkeiren, Welfare Cost Survey, various years.

	Average Enterprise Tenure (# of years) by Industry					
	1955	1960	1970	1975	1980	1990
Metals	8.8	7.7	10	11.8	9.7	19.1
Electronics	10	7.7	6.7	10.7	7.7	14
Transportation Machinery	9.8	12.1	8.4	10.2	9.9	16
Precision Machinery	9.8	8	11	9.2	7.4	13.4
General Machinery			9.1	9.8	8.4	15.6
Paper & Pulp	9.9	10.5	14.1	16	12.8	19.2
Chemicals	9	10.1	11.4	12.5	11.4	17.2
Rubber			7.7	10.4	6.3	17.5
Cement	9.7	11.3	13.4	14	11.2	17.2
Textile	7	7.6	8	11.5	7.5	16
Printing	9.7	10.3	7.5	11.3	7.8	13.2
Food Processing	8.9	10.9	9	10.8	8.1	18.8
Mining	10.5	11.6	14.7	15.9	14.5	16.2
Construction	9.7	11.2	8.2	7.9	7.5	16.6
Utilities	12.5	13.6	17.5	17.5	15.3	17
Transportation	9.4	10.8	11.9	13.9	9.7	15.8
Telecommunications			10.1	13.2	8.7	18.4
Finance and Insurance	7	6.9	10.5	9.2	8.1	10.9
Trading and Other Services	6.6	7.5	5.9	8.7	8.2	14.1

Source: Nikkeiren, Welfare Cost Survey, various years.

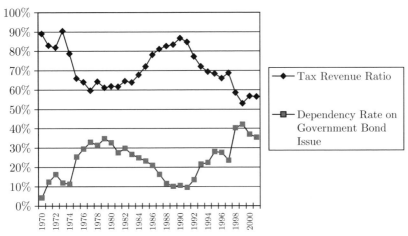

FIGURE 7.1. Fluctuation in Tax Revenue and Government Debt (as percentage of the Government Expenditure). *Source*: Ministry of Finance, *Zaisei Tokei* (*Fiscal Statistics*), various years.

Problems in the Revenue Structure

There existed four different problems in the Japanese revenue structure. First, the Japanese welfare state was always underfunded. Political decisions since the mid-1960s to raise future pension benefits and expand medical services were all based on highly optimistic future revenue forecasts. Functional equivalents such as public works spending and agricultural subsidies also cost the Japanese government enormous sums of money. The earlier decades of economic expansion and rapid increases in tax revenue had masked the gravely underfunded state of Japan's social protection. The Japanese government was, however, quite innovative. It controlled vast reserves of welfare funds, which it used to finance policy objectives. Nonetheless, borrowed money had to be returned one day with interest. The economic downturn in the 1970s made evident an uncomfortable fiscal fact of life: there was a huge gap between the government's tax extractive capacity and its spending commitments. The two oil crises exacerbated the problem by ending the era of "easy financing." The continuous growth of government revenue caused by rapid economic growth came to an abrupt end. Tax revenues plummeted, and the revenue growth of social security contributions slowed down (see Figure 7.1). In order to provide the promised levels of benefits, additional sources of revenue were necessary. This meant that the government had to revise its tax structure, borrow money, or raise social security contributions.

The second problem with Japan's revenue structure lay in its susceptibility to market fluctuations – a problem that stemmed from the dependence of taxes and social security contributions on income. Wage earners and their employers paid a certain percentage of their salary as social security contributions. The growth of revenue from social security contributions was a function of wage growth and the increase in number of wage earners. Since these two factors were affected by the state of the economy, Japan's overall tax revenue was also linked to income

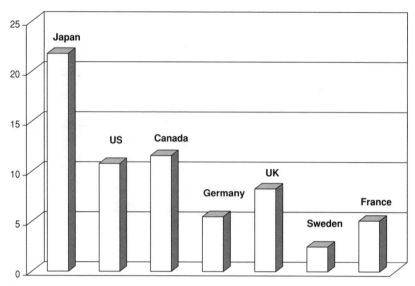

FIGURE 7.2. Japan's Dependence on Corporate Tax Revenue in 1980 (as percentage of overall tax revenue). *Source:* OECD Revenue Statistics 1965–1995.

growth. This problem was exacerbated by Japan's reliance upon personal and corporate income taxes rather than indirect taxes. Japan relied heavily on corporate taxes in particular (Figure 7.2). In short, government revenue fluctuated widely depending on the economic climate.

A third problem was that the Japanese revenue structure lacked equity. The fiscal burden of Japan's social protection system was allocated very unevenly between different groups. Wage earners did not fare as well as others. The absence of any equivalent to U.S. social security numbers to monitor the flow of money from one source to another made it very difficult for the Japanese tax authorities to track down the real taxable income of the self-employed. It was thus easy for farmers and the self-employed to underreport their income when filing their tax returns. Although there are no definite numbers, tax experts estimate that the self-employed and farmers only reported about 50 percent and 30 percent, respectively, of their income. (In contrast, employers had to report 100 percent of the salaries they paid their employees.) The same flaw existed in the collection of social security contributions. Earnings-related social security contributions were automatically deducted from wage earners' paychecks. In contrast, farmers and the self-employed only paid flat-rate contributions, since it was difficult to levy earnings-related contributions from these groups. The actual collection of social security contributions from these groups was a matter of voluntary compliance – never the most reliable revenue-raising method. Wage earners – the largest single tax-paying group – also shouldered more than their fair share when it came to the financing of Japan's functional equivalents. Their taxes paid for public works and agricultural subsidies, and they footed the bill for myriad market-restricting regulations in the form of grossly inflated prices.[15]

---

[15] Katz (1998) provides a useful comparison of consumer prices in major cities to demonstrate how inflated Japanese prices were.

TABLE 7.2. *Speed of Aging in Japan and Selected OECD Countries*

Country	Year when the ratio of population over 65/total population reached:		Duration of transition from 7% to 14% threshold (years)
	7%	14%	
Japan[a]	1970	1995	25
United States	1945	2015	70
United Kingdom	1930	1980	50
Germany	1930	1975	45
France	1865	1995	130
Sweden	1890	1975	85

[a]Japan is projected to be one of the oldest countries by 2025, when those above the age of 65 will be over 26 percent of the population.
Source: Ministry of Health and Welfare (1997, 8).

The fourth problem with Japan's revenue structure was that its occupationally based, fragmented social insurance schemes were vulnerable to demographic changes. Under Japan's work-based social insurance schemes, citizens were insured in different schemes depending on their occupation. For instance, farmers and the self-employed were enrolled in the National Pension Scheme (NPS), whereas salaried workers were enrolled in the Employee Pension Scheme (EPS).[16] Public sector workers, in turn, had their respective mutual aid associations (MAAs). The revenue structure of these fragmented schemes was highly susceptible to structural shifts in the workforce. Industrialization, for instance, reduced the number of new entrants into agriculture. This affected the demographic balance within the National Pension Scheme. In other words, the ratio of pensioners to younger premium-paying contributors rose. Similar actuarial problems plagued some of the MAAs for public sector employees. For instance, when Japan National Railways reduced its workforce, it undermined the long-term financial basis of its pension scheme.

Rising Welfare Costs

While any welfare state is vulnerable to cost increases induced by an aging society, Japan's welfare state was particularly so. Not only was Japan's demographic aging proceeding at a historically unprecedented pace (see Table 7.2.), but Japan's welfare state was designed in such ways that demographic aging accelerated the rise in social spending. Recall that the Japanese state offers very little in terms of income transfers and social services for working-age citizens and their families. The two major social security items – health care and pensions – dwarfed any other social spending items. This meant that the rise in social spending in Japan was closely linked to the growing size of the elderly. Moreover, the way in which the health care system was set up generated moral hazards that were particularly linked to demographic aging.

---

[16] See Chapter 1 for details of the social insurance schemes for pension and health care.

In health care, the fragmented social insurance schemes meant that the risk incidence varied quite significantly from one scheme to another. In Japan, the percentage of members beyond the age of sixty-five varied widely among different schemes. Health insurance schemes for salaried workers only insured active workers – the young and healthy. National health insurance cooperatives (*kokuho*), which were administered by each municipal government, had to cover all the retirees in addition to farmers and the self-employed. As a result, the elderly (those above sixty-five) composed about 70 percent of *kokuho* compared to about 15 percent in company-based social insurance schemes (*kempo*). Since age is the best predictor of the risk of illness and other ailments, the expenditure levels of *kokuho* were much higher than for *kempo*. In other words, while employers and their workers economized on their insurance costs by only insuring the young and the healthy, sicker elderly citizens were dumped on the *kokuho*. Because the municipal schemes were heavily subsidized, the increase in the number of elderly enrollees in these schemes led to a rapid rise in the fiscal responsibilities of the government.

The Japanese health care system was also rife with moral hazards on the part of both patients and physicians. The Free Medical Care for the Elderly introduced in 1972 was particularly bad. It removed any cost constraint on the part of elderly patients. After the introduction of the Free Medical Care for the Elderly, spending on elderly medical care grew exponentially, from 400 billion yen in 1973 to 800 billion yen in 1975 to 1.8 trillion yen in 1979 (Tsuchida 1991, 280). As a result, the frequency of visits to physicians in Japan in this period was more than double the OECD average.[17] Furthermore, since the health care system covered prescription drugs, no cost awareness applied to drug prescriptions either. Physicians overprescribed medications and received hefty sums of commissions from the pharmaceutical companies. As a result, more than 40 percent of Japan's social security spending for health care went for prescription drugs. This compared to 12 percent in the United Kingdom; 23 percent in Germany; and 18 percent in France (Kubono 1994a, 75). Physicians – an influential constituent group of the LDP – thus benefited enormously from the lack of cost constraints. By 1981, for instance, the average income of physicians relative to salaried employees was much higher in Japan than in other OECD countries.[18]

---

[17] According to Shigeharu Kubono's calculation based on OECD and World Bank data, the Japanese visited physicians fourteen times a year per person between 1981 and 1983 (Kubono 1994a). The same figures for other countries were as follows: Australia (6.4), Belgium (7.1), Canada (5.5), Denmark (8.4), Finland (3.4), France (4.7), Ireland (6.0), Italy (8.3), Japan (14.2), the Netherlands (3.2), New Zealand (3.8), Norway (4.5), Sweden (2.7), United Kingdom (4.2), and the United States (4.6).

[18] Only Germany and the United States possessed similarly high figures well above the OECD average. In most other advanced industrial societies, doctors make roughly twice as much as salaried employees. The ratios of physicians' income to average income of salaried employees for selected OECD countries are as follows: Australia (2.5), Belgium (1.8), Canada (4.1), Denmark (2.8), Finland (1.8), France (3.3), Germany (4.9), Ireland (1.2), Italy (1.1), Japan (4.7), New Zealand (2.5), Norway (1.7), Sweden (2.1), United Kingdom (2.4), and the United States (5.1). See OECD, 1987, *Financing and Delivering Health Care*. Japanese physicians also enjoyed lucrative tax exemptions, as discussed earlier in this book.

"Market-Restricting" Mode of Social Protection

By the early 1980s, it appeared as if Japan was proving successful in combating problems that all advanced industrial societies faced after the two oil crises. Dore (1987), for instance, lauded Japan for adjusting its manpower levels without causing unemployment. Manufacturing firms certainly did reduce their workforce, at no obvious cost to national employment levels. It is not difficult to understand why Japan's record of near full employment gathered so much praise. Japan along with the Scandinavian corporatist systems was one of the few success stories at the time. Both Sweden and Japan avoided the pitfall of "welfare without work" – yet by different means. Paradoxically, the conservative "pro-business" Japan adopted "market-restricting" ways to a much greater degree than social democratic Sweden.[19]

The Swedish government helped private firms shed redundant workers by publicly retraining displaced workers through its active labor market policy. Sweden's collective wage bargaining also set wage levels in ways that encouraged the movement of labor from inefficient to efficient sectors.[20] In contrast, the Japanese government subsidized employment in inefficient sectors such as in agriculture and the construction industry. As a measure of the relative efficiencies of the two countries, it is worth noting that the average Swedish construction firm continued to increase in size in the postwar period, whereas the average Japanese construction firm remained very small.[21] Agriculture and construction industries were not the only ones that enjoyed government protection in Japan. Market-restricting regulations, cartels, industrial subsidies, and the presence of "patient capital" helped a wide range of Japanese industries. The benefits of such policies fell as generously on the inefficient as the efficient (See Uriu 1996; Tilton 1996).

REFORM ATTEMPTS IN THE LATE 1970S

Solutions to Japan's problems required an overhaul of Japan's social protection system. Benefits to vested interest groups had to be trimmed. Policy measures to cope with economic adjustments had to become more market conforming. The rising cost of an aging society and economic adjustment had to be shared by different groups of citizens in an equitable way. Nonetheless, my structural logic implies that a fundamental reform would have been impossible as long as the LDP remained in power under the MMD/SNTV system. Under this system, the only kinds of reforms that would have been possible were benefit cuts and cost increases for groups other than the core organized support groups of the LDP. Big policy shifts, in other words, had to wait until Japan adopted institutional configurations

---

[19] Sweden increased women's activity rate higher than that of Japan. Sweden did so by hiring women in the public sector. The largesse of the public-sector employment in Sweden – in contrast to Japan's small public sector – implies that the Swedish political economy has never been all market based. Nonetheless, to exaggerate the point for the sake of drawing a contrast, Sweden kept the market-based sector (private sector) and the public sector apart, whereas Japan blurred the distinction.

[20] This is part of the Rehn-Meidner Model. See Pontusson (1992).

[21] See Davis and Henrekson (1997, 2000) on the Swedish data.

more permissive of drastic changes. It was only during later periods after 1989 (to be explored in Chapters 8 and 9) that power and preferences within the Japanese government made fundamental reform possible. In the late 1970s and the 1980s, the only reforms possible were those that *did not* affect the LDP's core constituent groups. The cost of any reforms had to be shouldered by nonconstituent groups.

Before I proceed to demonstrate how limited the reforms in the 1980s actually were, it is necessary to explain why the reforms in the 1980s appear more successful than the reforms in the 1970s. Simply stated, a specific political context of the latter half of the 1970s temporarily inhibited the LDP government's capacity to shift the cost of reforms onto nonconstituent groups. During the latter half of the 1970s, the LDP's control over the legislative process weakened while the opposition parties gained greater power. As a result, the LDP government was not capable of retrenching wage earners' benefits. It was only capable of doing so after they regained their full political capacity in the Lower House and Upper House elections in 1980. This is why reform attempts in the 1980s appear more successful than those in the 1970s.

The Emergence of the Hakuchu *Period (1974–1980).* During the 1960s, the LDP leadership was extremely preoccupied with the electoral advancement of the opposition parties. In the mid-1970s, their preoccupations materialized. After the 1974 Upper House elections, the gap between the LDP and the opposition party narrowed to a mere seven seats in the Upper House. While the LDP maintained an absolute majority in the Diet, its overall seat share nonetheless fell short of the number necessary to dominate all Diet committees.[22] The LDP experienced similar electoral losses in the Lower House elections held in 1976 and 1979, and also in the Upper House election in 1977. As a result, during the latter half of the 1970s, the LDP lost control of the Diet committees on social and labor issues, giving the opposition parties more bargaining power. An era generally referred to as the years of the "close gap" (*hakuchu*) began. This era lasted until 1980. That year, the LDP regained enough seats in excess of the absolute majority to control all Diet committees in both the Lower and Upper House elections.[23]

During the *hakuchu* period, the bargaining power of the opposition increased.[24] As a result, the organized constituent groups of the opposition

---

[22] In order to control all Diet committees and seize chairmanships, the ruling party needs the absolute majority plus the number of seats equal to the number of committees.

[23] There was a brief moment of coalition government between 1983 and 1986. During these three years, the LDP formed a coalition with the New Liberal Club in its attempt to secure enough seats to control all Diet committees in addition to having an absolute majority in the Diet. The New Liberal Club consisted of a small group of former LDP Diet members, who had parted ways over the Lockheed Scandal involving Prime Minister Kakuei Tanaka. Aside from the issue of political ethics, however, there was not much difference between the LDP and the NLC. In fact, most of the NLC Diet members rejoined the LDP in 1986. For this reason, it makes more sense to treat the NLC as another LDP faction than to treat the LDP-NLC as a genuine coalition government. The reason why some Diet members left the LDP to form the NLC is not pertinent to the analysis here. For a good discussion, see Gerald Curtis (1999).

[24] Needless to say, the loss of the LDP's full control over all Diet committees cannot be equated with the loss of its absolute majority in the Upper House in 1989, which gave rise to a "partial

parties – most importantly, the unions – gained greater leverage than before. Yet this did nothing to aid the cause of welfare reform. Now unions and conservative constituent groups both resisted any attempts at reform. Unions blocked reforms affecting their members, and conservative constituent groups blocked reforms affecting theirs. The upshot was that reforms became even more difficult during this *hakuchu* period. Given the electoral constraints, the LDP government's only viable option, if it was to reduce its fiscal problems, would be to increase burdens on unorganized voters such as wage earners. In the *hakuchu* period, even this option was difficult due to the greater influence of the unions.

Given Japan's fiscal and demographic challenges, reforms of public pension and health care were the most urgent reform items on the agenda. The Ministry of Finance, which oversaw the budgeting process, was deeply preoccupied with what they called "fiscal sclerosis." They worried that the rapid increases in entitlement programs such as pension and health care expenditures, which were rising rapidly, left the government with very little discretion over the budget. In addition to carrying out reforms of pension and health care schemes, the Ministry of Finance also considered it necessary to introduce a new indirect tax.[25] Japan's tax system relied heavily, as we have seen, on income taxes (taxes on corporate profits and wage income). The Tax Bureau of the Ministry of Finance viewed a new indirect tax as a solution to deficiencies in an income tax–based revenue system.[26]

For electoral reasons, however, LDP politicians were in no mood to support benefit cuts or new burdens on their core constituent groups, particularly in the late 1970s when they were doing relatively poorly at the polls. Given the fact that elections took place in 1976, 1977, and 1979, the intraparty dynamics within the LDP, if anything, supported benefit expansions rather than benefit cuts (See Mabuchi 1994, 260–288). In addition, the greater bargaining power of the opposition parties, especially on social and labor policy issues during the *hakuchu* period, meant that unions were well placed to gain more policy concessions from the LDP government than usual. In particular, the Democratic Socialist Party (Minshato), the most moderate of the parties on the left, gained more leverage than others as the LDP sought its cooperation in the Diet. By extension, the organized constituency groups of the Democratic Socialist Party – most of the private sector unions – also benefited. In short, the LDP government now found

minority" government. The opposition parties nonetheless could still delay the legislative process by using their chairmanship of several Diet committees. Since the LDP had to compromise with the opposition parties to a greater degree, the legislative process during the latter half of the 1970s was similar to the "partial minority" that emerged in 1989.

[25] While some scholars attribute the MOF's advocacy of indirect taxes to their technocratic expertise, others see more self-serving motivation. For the former position see Kato (1994), and for the latter view, see Hatsuta (1994).

[26] We can trace the MOF's preference for a VAT-like indirect tax to several reports published by the Government Taxation Research Council – see reports for 1956, 1970, and 1977 (Mabuchi 1994). A well-known former Tax Bureau official, Makoto Utsumi, also states that the MOF's interest in a VAT-type tax goes way back. The MOF officials – including Utsumi – became interested when France devised VAT. France, with its small businesses *patrons*, had a chronic problem of taxing them, just as Japan did.

it difficult to impose costs not only on its own organized constituency groups but also on organized labor. As a result, none of the attempted reforms took place.

In health care, the government's effort to reform the existing system failed due to the opposition from within the LDP. The Ministry of Welfare tried to increase patients' copayments as a way of controlling cost – particularly in relation to the health care cost of the elderly – but failed. In 1976, health care reform failed to introduce copayments for elderly patients (Hiwatari 1995, 91). The Japan Medical Association, an influential constituent group of the LDP, opposed all measures that enhanced cost consciousness on the part of patients and any bureaucratic attempt to change the fee schedule or limit physicians' autonomy. The steady decline in the LDP's vote shares only made individual LDP Diet members emphasize distributive benefits for their core constituency groups such as physicians.

The government also faced opposition from unions. Facing the worsening financial situation of the Government-Administered (Seifu Kansho) Health Insurance Program – the scheme for wage earners not in *kempo* – the Ministry of Welfare tried to impose a new cross-subsidization scheme. Under this new scheme, *kempo*, mostly adopted by large firms, was to subsidize the Government-Administered Program.[27] (Here it worth recalling that most unionized workers in Japan were either employees of large private firms or public sector employees and thus had little incentive to support cross-subsidization even among workers.) Organized labor also succeeded in blocking unfavorable changes in health care. Unions – together with their employers – successfully blocked cross-subsidization among different health insurance schemes (Hiwatari 1995, 79). As a result, the Ministry of Welfare was only able to introduce a modest change in the Government-Administered Program.[28] Planned cutbacks in health care benefits for wage earners either failed to pass or were significantly reduced.

Likewise, attempts to retrench pension benefits failed as well. LDP politicians, instead, successfully endorsed improvements in veterans' and survivors' pensions rather than cut them as the Ministry of Welfare had recommended. Organized labor also successfully blocked pension cuts. The Ministry of Welfare's plan to raise the eligibility age for the Employee Pension from sixty to sixty-five did not materialize due to strong opposition from business and labor.[29] Many corporations were still in the process of raising their mandatory retirement age from fifty-five to sixty. Given this reality, organized labor opposed any increase in

[27] As explained in Chapter 1, the national Seifu Kansho scheme covered wage earners working in firms too small to set up *kempo*, which were company-based health insurance schemes. For an overview of the health care system, see Chapter 1. For a more thorough account, the best sources are Campbell (1992) and Campbell and Ikegami (1998).

[28] The modest reform was the introduction of special levies on biannual bonus payments. Despite the fact that the biannual payments, which made up about 30 percent of the annual salary, were an integral part of workers' wages in Japan, the government previously had excluded them from the base salary when calculating social security contributions. The new arrangement was to withhold 1 percent of the bonuses as a special levy for the health care schemes in which workers were enrolled.

[29] See Nakano (1989, 135). Campbell (1992, 218–222) also notes that no reform happened in the late 1970s despite the willingness of the Ministry of Welfare. Also see Kato (1991a, 1991b).

the pension eligibility age beyond sixty. Employers were opposed to this reform, on the grounds that any discrepancy between the pension eligibility age and the corporate mandatory retirement age would lead to union demands for interim jobs or additional income. The rise in the power of moderate unions such as Domei, upon whose support the Democratic Socialist Party relied, meant that bureaucrats found it difficult to impose any changes on core male workers in large firms.

Interestingly, the greater bargaining power of the opposition parties – and unions – led to both cost reductions and benefit expansions for wage earners in some areas. In 1974, Unemployment Insurance was significantly expanded to become Employment Insurance once unions and employers became interested in benefit expansions. The new insurance now provided benefits such as wage subsidies during the economic downturns in addition to passive measures like traditional unemployment benefits. The new Employment Insurance formally integrated active policy measures. It introduced new special levies from employers to finance measures to prevent layoffs and facilitate labor mobility. An expansion of Unemployment Insurance was something that the Ministry of Labor officials had been trying to do since the 1960s. The Ministry of Labor began its legislative preparations in the late 1960s.[30] The Ministry of Labor feared that, in the context of full employment during the economic growth period, they would be forced to lower the contribution rates unless they expanded Unemployment Insurance to include active measures.[31] (Large firms were always against any increases in their social security contributions to Unemployment Insurance.)

Initially, both employers and unions had been opposing the expansion of Unemployment Insurance albeit for different reasons.[32] Large firms were generally hostile to Unemployment Insurance given the fact that they provided employment security to their workers. They argued that new active labor market policies should be financed from the general revenue. Unions, in turn, suspected that the reform of Unemployment Insurance to expand active policy measures might make it easier for employers to lay off workers. They also argued that the funds in Unemployment Insurance should be primarily used for income compensation and not for broader labor market policies. The Employment Insurance Bill was submitted to the Diet in early 1974, but failed to be legislated before the Diet sessions concluded. Employers and unions changed their attitudes after the labor market conditions worsened as a result of the first oil crisis.[33] They also

[30] For the Ministry of Labor's legislative efforts and failures, see *Asahi Shimbun*, July 29, 1968; October 27, 1968; January 23, 1969; July 2, 1969.
[31] *Nihon Keizai Shimbun* (December 13, 1971) reports how employers' opposition had made it difficult for the Japanese government to build up reserves in the Unemployment Insurance during good years to prepare for bad years. For a view of the Ministry of Labor's political difficulty, see Naka (1990) and also Chapter 5.
[32] Endo (1975, 257–277) provides the details of the policy positions of employers and unions.
[33] The government implemented an austerity policy to combat high inflation, which led to a contraction of overall demand in the economy. See the following newspaper articles for the new preferences of employers and unions (*Nihon Keizai Shimbun*, November 21, 1974; November 25, 1974).

demanded the reform of the benefit structure. The bill was resubmitted and subsequently legislated. Reflecting the demands of unions, the benefit structure was changed to favor core male workers. These were the very same demands that the opposition parties had made on the Diet floor earlier in the year. After the July Upper House elections, the opposition parties had more clout in the Diet. Employment Insurance was legislated with the modifications that unions had requested.[34] New wage subsidies for employers in distress were particularly popular and were widely used.[35]

Many Japanese scholars attribute the formal integration of active measures to unions' greater bargaining power during this period.[36] They also note that only employers bore the cost of the 1974 reform as further evidence of the political clout of organized labor. In fact, workers' contribution declined from 0.65 percent of their wages to 0.5 percent, while employers' contributions were raised from 0.65 percent to 0.8 percent of the wages. My interpretation based on the structural logic is that the new bargaining power of unions helped them avert unfavorable changes but not enough to impose new costs on their employers. The LDP was still the ruling party with an absolute majority. Although it was forced to seek compromise with the opposition parties on social and labor policies, the LDP was not so vulnerable as to be compelled to impose greater costs on employers for the sake of wage earners. Although the employer's share increased, this occurred in the overall context of a concerted effort between unions, Nikkeiren, and the government at the time to contain the overall wage increases. Just as Nikkeiren, the unions, and the Ministry of Labor negotiated on the terms of the Employment Insurance Reform in late 1974, they also negotiated to suppress wage demands. In November 1974, Domei – the federation of moderate private sector unions – had already consented not to demand more than a 20 percent wage increase. Labor had achieved a nominal wage increase of 32.9 percent during the previous year's *shunto*, or spring wage offensive, as the annual springtime wage negotiations are known. In other words, Nikkeiren knew that a 0.15 percent increase in employers' contribution to the new Employment Insurance was negligible given the scope of wage constraints they were negotiating with labor. (The actual wage increase in 1975 was only 15 percent.)[37]

---

[34] See *Asahi Shimbun*, evening edition, December 13, 1974.

[35] In 1975, the electronics industry received 90 trillion yen in wage subsidies; the general machinery industry, steel industry, and other metals received 97 trillion, 77 trillion, and 58 trillion yen, respectively (Hayakawa, Okoshi, and Aida 1984, 44). A survey by the Ministry of International Trade and Industry provides the record of manpower adjustment strategies of firms during the oil crisis (MITI 1981).

[36] Kume (1998), Tsujinaka (1987), Ito (1988), Shinoda (1989). More broadly, these authors think that the demographic decline in the LDP's constituent groups and the formation of a cross-class alliance between export sector firms and unions had brought about a structural change in the political position of labor in Japan. I disagree. As I have shown in Chapter 4, there was little divergence of preferences between moderate unions of private sector workers and their employers even during the earlier periods. Moreover, as will be shown in this chapter, organized labor did not enhance its power in relation to the LDP. If any factor benefited workers and urban voters, it was the relative weakness of the LDP in the Diet during the latter half of the 1970s.

[37] For an excellent account of the negotiations leading up to the 1975 *shunto*, see Shinkawa (1984).

In 1975, the LDP Minister of Labor Hasegawa responded favorably to requests by the two labor federations, Sohyo and Domei, to extend the duration of unemployment benefits for middle-age and older workers. The LDP government extended the benefit duration for fifty-five- to sixty-four-year-olds by sixty days as a special time-limited measure.[38] In 1977, the Ministry of Labor used union pressure from depressed industries as a reason to create the Employment Stabilization Fund.[39] Employers of structurally depressed industries and their unions had also been lobbying, respectively, the Ministry of International Trade and Industry and the Ministry of Labor for special measures for their industries. Both the LDP and opposition parties initially proposed their own legislative bills, but agreed on jointly sponsoring a bill to introduce the Provisional Measures for Laid-Off Workers in Targeted Depressed Industries Law. Such a rare joint attempt can be attributed to the specific political dynamics at work under *hakuchu*.[40]

In 1978, the government further expanded its involvement by enacting the Provisional Measures to Stabilize the Targeted Depressed Industries in order to help industries such as textile and ship building.[41] The LDP government also expanded its assistance to smaller firms – a key LDP support group. Contribution rates for Employment Insurance were thus increased for the first time.[42] Employers protested; they held that increases in employers' social security contributions should be avoided during a time of recession. In contrast, Sohyo, the most important organizational constituency of the Japan Socialist Party, was in favor of increasing contribution rates – those of both workers and employers – in order to finance special measures for depressed regions. The fact that some of the textile and ship-building unions were members of the Sohyo was an important factor.[43] In 1979, the Ministry of Labor also succeeded in expanding Employment Insurance. The expansion consisted of more subsidies for employers who hired older workers; it also increased the benefit duration for workers in retraining programs and those who failed to find work immediately upon completing retraining. It is also worth noting that constituent groups of the LDP also benefited from the government's greater involvement in unemployment policies. In the face of worsening economic conditions and demands from both business and unions, the LDP government even increased spending from the general budget. The LDP, for instance, extended special benefits to groups such as fishermen.[44]

[38] *Nikkei Shimbun*, December 17, 1975; *Nikkei Shimbun*, April 8, 1976. The expiration date of this measure was further extended in 1977 (*Asahi Shimbun*, January 28, 1977).
[39] What used to be part of the Employment Insurance was turned into a separate account that promotes active measures. This new account was financed by the new levies on employers that had been introduced in 1974.
[40] Miura (2002, 280) also notes that this kind of legislative attempt was rare. However, she does not link it to the specific configuration of parliamentary veto players at the time.
[41] Ohara Rodo Mondai Kenkyujo 1978, 542–548.
[42] *Nikkei Shimbun*, August 23, 1978; *Asahi* (evening edition) September 29, 1978; *Asahi* (evening edition) February 9, 1978.
[43] *Nikkei Shimbun*, August 23, 1978.
[44] Based on *Kuni no Yosan* (various years from 1973 to 1978). Not all the budget for unemployment was for industrial workers.

REFORMS IN THE 1980s

Unlike the latter half of the 1970s, the 1980s saw big benefit cuts in health care, pensions, children's allowance, and unemployment. The 1982 reform of the Health Care for the Elderly Law introduced patients' copayments for those older than seventy years; it also created a new cross-subsidization scheme to reduce the government spending on elderly health care (Campbell 1992, chapter 9). The 1984 Health Care Reform reduced health care spending by 620 billion yen by introducing new copayments to be paid by wage earners (previously, they did not pay any copayments).[45] The 1985 Pension Reform reduced benefits by 20–30 percent by extending the required contributory period to qualify for full pensions as well as cutting future benefits (Kato 1991a, b). The 1983 and 1984 reforms of the Employment Insurance brought about cutbacks in state subsidies and benefit cuts. Children's Allowance benefits were cut back, too. Social security programs were not the only programs that were scaled back in the 1980s. The price of rice set by the government annually was also frozen.[46] And public enterprises (the Japan National Railways, Japan Tobacco, Nippon Telecommunications and Telegraph) were privatized.[47]

Campbell (1992, 218–222) suggests that the LDP's electoral victory in 1980 – and the end of the *hakuchu* period – created the political will for benefit-cutting reforms in the 1980s.[48] Scholars disagree as to whether the reforms in the 1980s were welfare retrenchments or not. Those who see reforms in the 1980s as retrenchments interpret them in the context of a rise in neoliberalism in Japan.[49] Nonetheless, they do agree on the importance of the ad hoc Research Council on Administrative Reform (Rincho). Rincho recommended cutting pension and health care expenditures, reforming the system of supporting food prices (especially rice), and privatizing public enterprises.[50] By the early 1980s, as Junko Kato vividly describes it, the LDP leadership was becoming anxious about Japan's fiscal deficits.[51] In many ways, Rincho was a mechanism devised by the LDP leadership

[45] There is an extensive literature on this reform; see Aoki (1988); Eguchi (1985); Hayakawa (1991a, 1991b); Hayakawa et al. (1986); Kato (1995); Nakano (1989); and Otake (1997, chapter 7); among others.

[46] Mulgan (2000, chapter 7) and Schwartz (1998, chapter 6) offer fascinating accounts of the process. As far as agricultural politics is concerned, trade issues also provided another layer of politics. Structurally speaking, farmers possessed great power over the LDP; certain kinds of policy issue linkages in trade negotiations weakened farmers' influence. For this dynamic, see Davis (2003).

[47] On the process of privatization during this period, see Iio (1993), Kusano (1989), Otake (1994).

[48] This does not, however, explain why the LDP continued the reform process even after suffering electoral losses in 1983.

[49] See Kanbara (1986), Otake (1994), and Shinkawa (1993). Tsujinaka (1986, 1987) takes a different view. He sees that the LDP has become more favorable to labor, making Japan look more like a corporatist country.

[50] The Rincho was set up to draft recommendations for administrative reforms by Prime Minister Zenko Suzuki and it continued under Prime Minister Yasuhiro Nakasone. Central themes of the Rincho consisted of "fiscal reconstruction without tax increases" and "the greater use of private sector vitality" (*minkatsu*). See Kanbara (1986).

[51] Junko Kato (1991b, 1994) suggests that the calculations of the LDP leaders may have changed during this period. She argues that, since a growing fiscal constraint left a smaller budgetary pie to

and the Ministry of Finance to isolate the policy agenda from intraparty veto players.[52] The MMD/SNTV system had created strong incentives within the LDP to decentralize the decision-making process within the LDP government. As a result, politico-bureaucratic alliances between groups of LDP Diet members and different branches of the bureaucracy were de facto veto players capable of blocking unfavorable changes. Any significant reform to cut government spending thus would have only been possible by containing the influence of such politico-bureaucratic alliances. In other words, the formation of Rincho was an effort to empower the prime minister by enhancing his agenda-setting power. A real concentration of power in the hands of the prime minister did not occur until Japan adopted a SMD-dominant electoral system and carried out related political reforms in the late 1990s.

Without major changes in the electoral or legislative rules, however, even an innovative device like Rincho could not fundamentally alter the logic of distributive politics, which had remained the same since 1951. Benefit cuts for the LDP's constituent groups remained minimal. To put it more precisely, the 1982 Health Care for the Elderly Law shifted the program cost onto wage earners, while leaving the existing cost structure intact.[53] The Ministry of Welfare did succeed in introducing elderly patients' copayments, but strong opposition from the Japan Medical Association diluted the plan significantly. The elderly were thus charged only a minimal sum and only for their first visit to the doctor. The new copayment was hardly enough to eliminate the moral hazards identified earlier. The more important aspect of the 1982 reform was a cross-subsidization scheme. Before the reform, the National Health Insurance Cooperatives administered by municipal governments covered 70 percent of the elderly's medical costs, while the national government picked up the remaining 30 percent. The new law mandated all health insurance schemes to cover collectively 70 percent of the medical costs for the elderly. All occupationally based health insurance schemes were to contribute to this cross-subsidization scheme – the younger the pool of enrollees in an occupationally based insurance scheme, the more it had to contribute. The new cross-subsidization shifted the large bulk of health care costs onto wage earners and their employers.

The 1984 Health Care Reform introduced benefit cuts by imposing copayments on those enrolled in *kempo* and Seifu Kansho. The aim was to instill more cost consciousness in patients.[54] Since the Japan Medical Association was always opposed to any increase in patients' copayments, the 1984 Reform appeared as

distribute, LDP leaders came around to thinking that something needed to be done. She argues that this motivation led them to reduce the budgets for the largest social spending items, such as health care and pension, and to consider a new tax.

[52] On the Rincho process, see discussions by two of the participants, Hiroshi Kato and Yoichi Sando (Kato and Sando 1983).

[53] For detailed case studies of the health care reforms during the early 1980s, see Aoki (1988); Eguchi (1985); Hayakawa (1991a, 1991b); Kato (1991b); Nakano (1989); and Otake (1997, chapter 7); among others.

[54] Wage earners did not pay copayments, but their dependent family members did.

if the Ministry of Welfare had finally triumphed over the doctors. On closer scrutiny, however, it becomes clear that the success of the 1984 reform rested on a compromise.[55] While the Ministry of Welfare had planned a 20 percent copayment, the actual reform imposed only a 10 percent copayment on wage earners as a result of strong opposition from the Japan Medical Association and organized labor. Given the political power of the Japan Medical Association, no fundamental cost control was introduced. Physicians' fees continued to be set politically and individual health insurance providers had no capacity to negotiate with medical service providers. Again, what occurred at the aggregate level was "cost shifting" onto wage earners. The introduction of copayments for wage earners benefited employers because increases in copayments were expected to reduce the expenditures of *kempo* and the Government-Administered Program, financed by employers' and employees' contributions. Thus this reform, if anything, reduced employers' future costs.

Similarly, the 1985 Pension Reform also introduced de facto cross-subsidization among different social insurance schemes, while cutting wage earners' future pensions. Because of the decline in primary sector employment, the National Pension ran the risk of a deteriorating financial balance. Without cross-subsidization, the government would have had to raise social security contributions for the National Pension. Yet since the LDP's constituent groups were enrolled in the National Pension Scheme, the LDP was not likely to favor this policy. The 1985 cross-subsidization scheme was a political solution to the problem. It alleviated fiscal pressures on the National Pension by yet again shifting the cost onto the wage earners' social insurance scheme.[56] This was done by the creation of a new basic pension. Let me explain why this new basic pension shifted the cost onto the wage earners' social insurance scheme. The 1985 reform promised to provide the same flat-rate pension for all qualifying enrollees in any of the existing public pension schemes. To do this, Employee Pension benefits were to be split into two tiers: the basic tier flat-rate pension and the earnings-related second tier. The basic tier of the Employee Pension Scheme was to offer the same flat-rate pension as the National Pension. Recall that the National Pension only provided a flat-rate pension for every qualifying pensioner, so this reform did not change the benefit structure of the National Pension. By calling it a basic pension, however, the government devised a new more "solidaristic" financing method. Under the new scheme, all social insurance schemes were jointly responsible for the cost of basic pension payments. Since there were more pensioners in the National Pension Scheme, this arrangement meant that the Employee Pension Scheme ended up subsidizing the National Pension benefits.[57]

Cuts also occurred in other benefit programs for wage earners, including child allowance and unemployment benefits. Child allowance benefits were cut by

[55] For details of the trade-offs, see Aoki (1988).
[56] Whether the 1985 reform reduced the total amount of the government subsidies was a contentious point during the Diet session. For details, see Yamazaki (1988).
[57] After this "merger," the pension reserve for the NP grew, indicating that the NP was indeed saving money thanks to subsidization from the EP.

enforcing stricter means testing to reduce the number of families that qualified.[58] Unemployment benefits were cut in both the 1983 and 1984 Employment
Insurance reforms.[59]

Throughout the *hakuchu* era and the Rincho era, the LDP government proved
incapable of rectifying Japan's skewed revenue structure by introducing a new
broadly based indirect tax. In spite of the LDP leaders' willingness to reform the
revenue structure, no broadly based indirect tax was introduced. Any discussion
of such a tax was thwarted by the intraparty opposition (Kambara 1986, 164–183;
Kato 1994; Uchida, Kanazashi, and Fukuoka 1988, chapters 1–9). In its attempt
to introduce a new indirect tax, the Tax Bureau of the Ministry of Finance, which
considered a new indirect tax an absolute necessity, had consented to huge cuts in
personal income taxes as a political compromise with the LDP government. The
Ministry of Finance had hoped this concession would persuade the LDP leaders
to endorse a new indirect tax. When the LDP failed to endorse the new indirect
tax in 1979, the previous reduction in personal taxes proved detrimental to the
fiscal health of the government.[60] For LDP politicians, a broad indirect tax was
undesirable as it affected their constituents, too. Without any parliamentary veto
players on their side, however, there was little that the Ministry of Welfare and
the Ministry of Finance bureaucrats could do.

The same political situation continued throughout the 1980s. Meanwhile, the
LDP government resorted to hikes in corporate taxes. Under Japan's market-
restricting regulatory regime, these hikes were ultimately picked up by unorganized consumers.[61] Corporate tax rates were raised from 36.75 percent to 40
percent in 1974, from 40 percent to 42 percent 1981, and up to 43.3 percent
in 1984. At the same time, tax expenditures for corporations were significantly
cut back. In 1972, tax expenditure programs produced a revenue loss equivalent
of 9 percent of the revenue from corporate taxes; the same figure had fallen to

[58] Ohara Rodo Mondai Kenkyujo 1981, 511, 1984, 498, 1985, 446.
[59] The 1984 reform reduced the replacement rates of unemployment benefits by changing the definition of the base salary.
[60] Many observers of Japanese politics wonder why the MOF had consented to huge tax cuts in the
midst of what they called a "fiscal crisis." Under Prime Minister Kakuei Tanaka, Japan implemented
a tax cut of 2 billion yen; Prime Minister Takeo Fukuda implemented a cut of one billion yen. While
some attribute these decisions to the political clout of LDP prime ministers vis-à-vis bureaucrats,
the high-ranking MOF official, Fumio Takagi, who negotiated the 2-billion-yen tax cuts under
Prime Minister Tanaka, explained that he saw drastic cuts of personal income taxes as a strategy
to pave the way for a new indirect tax. He also says that thanks to the plunge in the revenue
caused by his big tax cut, his ministry was capable of reducing the public works budget. In the face
of the later developments, Takagi's justification does not stand. Ando (1987) includes interviews
with Masataka Ookura and Fumio Takagi, two Ministry of Finance officials with direct knowledge
of tax politics during this period (see Ando 1987, 100–120, 157–168). Also see Mabuchi (1994);
Shiota (1985).
[61] It is worth noting that, during the period when the government raised corporate taxes, large
corporations in protected sectors of the economy became the largest tax payers in the corporate
tax payer rankings. Large banks rose to the top of the rankings, whereas large manufacturers went
down. To the extent that the burden was shifted onto unorganized consumers, it did so silently
and invisibly.

2.2 percent by 1982.[62] Although the cost of corporate taxes was ultimately passed
on to consumers, business leaders were not happy at all. The fact that big business's political influence was based on its financial contribution to the LDP as
a whole weakened its position in a game of musical chairs over who would bear
the cost of spiraling government expenditure.[63] Individual LDP politicians cared
more about pleasing their key constituency groups in their electoral districts
than big business. This is why the business representatives took an active role in
Rincho discussions to emphasize spending cuts above all else.

Beyond reducing payouts from the general revenue and making wage earners pick up the difference, the "welfare reforms" of the 1980s did not constitute
much of a change in the overall pattern of distribution in Japan. What little was
achieved was a function of weak organized labor, which no longer possessed the
bargaining power of the *hakuchu* period. The LDP government could thus shift
the costs of reforms onto the group of voters about whom they cared the least.
The reforms basically cut wage earners' benefits while increasing their social
security contributions. Although a major reform of the health care system was
an important policy goal, the vested interests of physicians meant that this goal
remained an aspiration rather than a reality. Likewise, functional equivalents for
farmers remained largely intact despite the fact that a reform of rice subsidies
had been one of the major goals of Rincho politics. It is true that there were
some setbacks for the Japan Medical Association, such as increases in employees'
copayments. Nonetheless, a fundamental overhaul of the reimbursement system
never took place. Similarly, while rice prices were frozen for a year, the existing
distributive system was left untouched.[64] This was due to the high accountability
that the MMD/SNTV generated. As demonstrated by Aurelia George Mulgan
(1990, 117) and Hemmi (1982, 236), farmers effectively "unelected" LDP politicians. In a MMD/SNTV system, farmers could switch their support from a specific LDP member to another. In the Upper House, many of the rural districts
were de facto single-member districts that allowed disgruntled farmers to punish
the LDP more effectively. Most of the market-restricting regulations remained
intact despite calls for the need to unleash private (that is, market) vitality and
slash market-restricting regulations. The successful privatization of public enterprises – such as the Japan National Railways – was a political strategy to weaken

[62] Based on documents provided by the Tax Bureau, Ministry of Finance (1996).
[63] Campbell (1977) makes the same observation. It should be noted here that the only taxes introduced
    in the 1970s were both special indirect taxes. One was a tax on automobiles, and the other a tax on
    office automation equipment. Both were introduced by Prime Minister Kakuei Tanaka to increase
    the pie for distribution. Note here that in neither case were fundamental electoral interests violated.
[64] Although the Rincho had also recommended a reform of the Japanese agricultural policy to intro-
    duce the market mechanism to increase agricultural productivity, no significant reform was intro-
    duced. See an interview of Taro Yayama by Otake (1997). A member of the Rincho, Yayama says
    that there had been a sense all along that agricultural reform would be difficult, and participants
    had focused on issues on the agenda other than agriculture (Otake 1997, 201). Also see Kanbara
    (1986, 152–159) for the same point.

organized labor rather than a fundamental change in the nature of the Japanese economy.[65]

CONCLUSION: LIMITS OF REFORM

For all the sound and fury, the "successful" reforms in the 1980s did little to alter the nature of Japan's social protection system. Most of the successful reforms in the 1980s involved shifting costs onto wage earners and their employers. The LDP's constituent groups did not lose much in the process. As the structural logic would predict, under a system like that of the LDP-dominated Diet, potential losers in the distributive game would continue to be unorganized workers and consumers. And this is indeed what happened. Some of the benefit cuts that organized labor had successfully resisted during the *hakuchu* period were carried out when the LDP regained its dominance in the Diet. Despite business leaders' effort to reduce their share of welfare costs in the Rincho Council, their efforts did not succeed (see Figure 7.3).

Bureaucratic organizational interests mostly went unchecked too. When ministries tried to implement policies that conflicted with the vital interests of intra-party veto players in the LDP, bureaucratic political capacity was indeed limited. When bureaucrats pursued an organizational interest in ways that did not conflict with the LDP's electoral concerns, their activities went largely unchecked. Limits of reform in the 1980s led the Ministry of Finance to resort to a fiscal gimmick to create – just nominally – a bigger amount of budgetary savings. The Budget Bureau of the Ministry of Finance arranged with the Ministry of Welfare and the Ministry of Labor to temporarily "borrow" money. The arrangement consisted of suspending portions of the subsidies that the government was legally required to pay into the Pension Special Account and the Employee Insurance Special Account. This was "borrowing" off the books. In 1983, the Ministry of Labor and the Ministry of Finance agreed on a "temporary" reduction of state subsidies into the Employment Insurance from one-third of the expenditure to 25 percent.[66] At the time of the 1985 pension reform, the Ministry of Finance suspended its payment into the pension reserves. The Ministry of Welfare, in exchange for this favor, was allowed to manage a bigger part of the pension reserves through its Pension and Welfare Corporation (Nenkin Fukushi Jigyodan).[67] Very little

---

[65] For the process of privation, see Iio (1993) and Kusano (1989). Otake (1997) provides an interview of Hiroshi Kato, one of the key players on the Rincho.

[66] Recall that when Japan introduced the Unemployment Insurance in 1947, the government promised a generous state subsidy: one-third of unemployment insurance benefits was to be covered by the general revenue. This was later changed to subsidies of "one-quarter to a third" of the program cost. In 1983, the Ministry of Labor and Ministry of Finance agreed to reduce the subsidies below 25 percent. Ministries with independent sources of revenue into their special accounts often "lent" the MOF what the government "owed" their accounts. The Ministry of Welfare frequently "lent" money to the MOF by agreeing to forgo annual subsidies from the general revenue until a later date.

[67] See Ohara Rodo Mondai Kenkyujo 1987, part 4, 1:3.

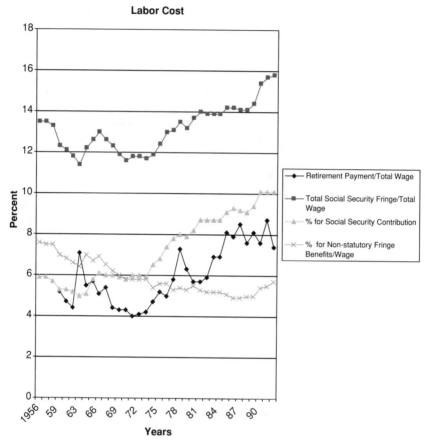

FIGURE 7.3. Labor Cost Increases.

substantive debate took place about whether such a decision represented sound management of pension reserves. The Ministry of Labor, in turn, was allowed to expand the activities of its Employment Promotion Corporation funded by the Employment Insurance Special Account.[68] The lack of proper oversight in the appropriation of welfare funds by different ministries came back to haunt the Japanese government years later.

The shrinking of the pie eventually led to the introduction of a new consumption tax in 1989. Junko Kato (1994) shows that both the LDP's leaders and its rank and file changed their mind about a new tax. She argues that, since a growing fiscal constraint left a smaller budgetary pie to distribute, LDP leaders may have come around to do something about the fiscal balance. She says that this motivation led them to support the introduction of a new tax. Unlike the previous failed attempts to introduce a consumption tax, Prime Minister Noboru Takeshita, the leader of the largest intraparty faction, managed to build a consensus within the LDP to legislate a new tax. Very cleverly, Takeshita devised a

[68] See Ohara Rodo Mondai Kenkyujo 1983, 467–472; 1985, part 3, I:5.

scheme to appease the most vocal opposition from small business owners, one of the LDP's core constituency groups, who were allowed to pocket the consumption taxes that they charged their clients. (This arrangement was called *eki-zei*.) Yet again, a shift to an indirect tax that was supposed to resolve inequities among different types of tax payers resulted in benefiting the LDP's constituency groups at the expense of unorganized voters. As we shall see in the next chapter, this new tax was to cost the LDP its absolute majority in the Upper House.

8

Policy Shifts in the 1990s

The Emergence of European-Style Welfare Politics

This chapter is about change. The LDP's loss of its absolute majority in the Upper House in 1989 marked the dawn of a new era. This chapter covers the second and third periods identified in Chapter 3 – the period between the 1989 Upper House elections and the emergence of the non-LDP government and the period between the emergence of the non-LDP government and the 1996 Lower House elections. From the perspective of the structural logic approach, the second and the third periods share two similarities. First, in both periods, multiple political parties possessed veto power. Second, the electoral system remained the same MMD/SNTV system. This chapter demonstrates that, as a result of the emergence of multiple political parties with veto power and the persistence of a multimember district system, Japanese welfare politics during this period came to resemble welfare politics in northern Europe, as expected on the basis of the structural logic.

Three changes that bear on the Japanese welfare system can be identified here. First, the increase in the number of parliamentary veto players under the MMD/SNTV system meant that the core constituency groups of non-LDP parties gained a new foothold for securing policy favors. Second, the emergence of non-LDP parties as parliamentary veto players opened up new legislative possibilities for welfare-friendly bureaucrats. Social services and benefits for wage earners were now a genuine option. Third, the emergence of coalition governments, just as in European coalition governments, made it easier to raise taxes.

Indeed, reforms undertaken during the 1989–1996 period began to alter the nature of Japan's social protection system. The new public programs introduced during this period all shared a common feature: they focused, for the first time, on the needs of working-age wage earners and their families. Despite continuing fiscal problems, there was less welfare retrenchment in the 1990s than in the 1980s. Instead, Japan's welfare state even expanded during this period. New public programs included (i) child care leave – first introduced as a leave without pay and subsequently turned into a paid benefit; (ii) family care leave; (iii) the Angel Plan (a ten-year plan to combat low fertility rates); (iv) work continuation benefits for elderly workers; and (v) the new long-term care insurance.[1]

Certainly, there were new socioeconomic conditions that demanded new policy responses. In 1989, for instance, the fertility rate fell to a record low of 1.57 – below the replacement ratio. Japan was also already in the midst of an unprecedented level of demographic aging. Japan's demographic problems might initially appear to offer the most straightforward explanation for these policy shifts. Policy needs, however, do not automatically determine specific policy responses. It quickly emerged that some solutions to these demographic problems elicited more political support than others.

It has been claimed throughout this book that the structure of politics narrows the range of possible policy responses. The general claim to be defended in this chapter is that it was not new socioeconomic conditions that determined the development of new types of social protection programs in the 1990s, but a change in the structural logic. More specifically, the emergence of multiple political parties with veto power enabled social and labor policy bureaucrats to introduce new programs and expand old ones. As the structural logic would predict, programs that promoted parliamentary veto players' electoral calculations were more likely to be introduced than those that negatively affected veto players' interests. The rest of this chapter lends support to this claim with evidence drawn from the key policy cases of the 1990s.

This chapter further divides the third period into two subperiods to facilitate a clearer narrative. The two subperiods are (i) the non-LDP coalition period (August 9, 1993–June 30, 1994); and (ii) the LDP-led coalition period (June 30, 1994–November 7, 1996). The first subperiod began when a group of LDP politicians broke off from the LDP to form the first non-LDP government in coalition with seven opposition parties. For convenience, I call this subperiod "the non-LDP coalition period." The second subperiod began when the LDP successfully maneuvered its comeback by forming an alternative coalition government with two other parties. I call this period "the LDP-led coalition period." The rest of the chapter proceeds in chronological order.

THE NEW PRO-WELFARE ENVIRONMENT UNDER THE PARTIAL MINORITY GOVERNMENT

The LDP lost its absolute majority in the Upper House in 1989. As a result, although it continued to govern alone, it did so without an absolute majority in the Upper House between July 24, 1989, and August 9, 1993. I call this type of government a "partial minority government" because the ruling party was in the minority in the second chamber, which possessed veto power over the first

---

[1] The Long-term Care Insurance was legislated after the 1996 Lower House elections. Although the Japan Democratic Socialist Party (formerly Japan Socialist Party) and Sakigake had no representation in the Cabinet, the coalition continued. The LDP relied on their cooperation to enact bills. In a nutshell, the Long-term Care Insurance was legislated in a context very similar to the subperiod between 1994 and 1996. I will come back to this point later in the chapter.

chamber. During this period, a number of very important policy shifts occurred. The government, for the first time, explicitly committed to the idea of increasing public provision of social services, such as frail elderly care and child care. It also finally introduced a statutory child care leave.[2]

The LDP's defeat in the Upper House in the 1989 elections was a direct consequence of strong popular discontent over the consumption tax introduced by the LDP government. Anticipating a backlash against the new tax, in 1988, prior to the introduction of the tax, Prime Minister Takeshita's government released a report, called *Welfare Vision*. The aim of the report was to portray the tax as a necessity for Japan to meet the challenges created by its aging population (Campbell 1992, 245). Unorganized voters, however, perceived the new tax as yet another effort by the LDP to impose costs on them in order to finance pork for LDP constituents. So they punished the LDP by voting for opposition parties – especially the Japan Socialist Party, the largest opposition party. The fact that the Upper House used a de facto mixed system of SMD and MMD increased the volatility of seats.[3] The protest vote was very effective in electoral districts, where only one seat was up for reelection.[4]

The new balance of power in the Upper House forced the LDP to make compromises. The emergent "partial minority government" meant that a smooth legislative process required cooperation of the opposition parties in the Upper House, which could veto decisions by the Lower House.[5] As a result, it led the LDP to (i) initiate comprehensive programs difficult for the opposition parties to oppose; and (ii) trade distributive favors for opposition parties' constituents in exchange for votes on the Diet floor. The core constituent groups of the opposition parties – the unions, in particular – benefited directly from this shift of power. By this time, the formerly divided union federations had developed a united front in the newly created Rengo (founded in 1987).[6]

More immediately, however, the LDP needed to ensure that the voters' discontent over the new consumption tax would not spill over to the upcoming Lower House elections. The timing of the introduction of the consumption tax in 1989 could not have been worse. The next round of the Lower House election was to take place in 1990, if not sooner.[7] Damage control had to be done

---

[2] It had taken the Japanese government an extremely long time to introduce child care leave. The Working Women's Welfare Law (Kinro Fujin Fukushi Ho) legislated in June 1972 contained a clause stating employers' duty to make efforts to provide child care leave. It had little actual impact on employers. It was the introduction of the Childcare Leave for Female Teachers at Compulsory Education School, Nurses, and Licensed Childcare Professionals (*hobo*) at Social Welfare Institutions in 1975 that led to a spike in the number of women taking the leave. See Iino (1992).

[3] Chapter 3 explains why I interpret the electoral rules in the Upper House as a mixed system.

[4] Chapter 2 explains why single-member districts make it easier for disgruntled voters to penalize incumbents.

[5] Japan has relatively strong bicameralism, see Chapter 3.

[6] Shinoda (1989) provides the details of politics within organized labor leading up to this unification.

[7] In Japan, the prime minister dissolves the Lower House to call a new round of elections. This means that an election can take place any time during the four-year term of Lower House politicians. Because the last Lower House elections had taken place in 1986, the four-year term of the incumbents was nearing its end. In contrast, Upper House elections follow a predetermined cycle. The term is six years; half the Upper House is up for reelection every three years.

quickly.[8] Soon after its electoral defeat in the Upper House elections in the summer of 1989, the LDP leadership instructed the Ministry of Welfare to prepare
for a major policy announcement to expand welfare services. The LDP government needed a specific plan to justify the consumption tax. By the end of the year,
they came up with the *Gold Plan* (The Ten-Year Strategy for the Promotion of
Elderly Citizens' Health and Welfare).[9] The Gold Plan focused on the expansion of care services for the frail elderly and stated very specific – but ambitious –
goals. It promised drastic improvements in public elderly services for the middle classes – augmenting, for instance, the number of personal caregivers from
twenty thousand to one hundred thousand in ten years. Under the existing policy
framework, most of the public services for the elderly were strictly means-tested
and not available to middle-class families. It also vowed to eradicate the problem
of the "bedridden elderly" *(netakiri rojin)* – something that happened frequently
in Japan as a result of the lack of proper care for the frail elderly. The Gold
Plan urged municipal governments to draw up an action plan to implement these
measures. The LDP government approved a ten-year budget in the amount of
60 trillion yen.[10]

In 1990, the government reformed the welfare laws (the Shakai Fukushi Kankei
Happo) that regulated different types of social services. The reform gave more
autonomy to municipal governments, so that they could provide welfare services
reflecting their residents' welfare needs. Meanwhile, the national government
allocated greater sums of money for elderly services to be provided at the local
level. The reform of the Elderly Health and Welfare Law in 1991 – the year
of general local elections – increased government subsidies for the nonmedical
portion of the elderly care.[11] Simultaneously as the government increased its
fiscal commitment for elderly care, it reduced the share of the elderly care cost
shouldered by employers and wage earners in the form of compulsory levies
on wage earners' health care cooperatives.[12] This pattern is very different from

[8] Furthermore, general local elections, which occur every four years, were to take place in 1991.
Conservative local politicians were worried, because their electoral fortunes were tied to those of
the individual LDP Diet members with whom they were aligned.

[9] More specifically, it was Finance Minister Ryutaro Hashimoto who instructed the Ministry of
Welfare to come up with a plan to justify the new tax. Hashimoto was not only a former welfare
minister but was also a senior member of the LDP "welfare tribe" (LDP Diet members in the
PARC on social and labor policy issues). As a result, he was familiar with social policy issues. See
Campbell 1992, 246–247; Okuma (2005).

[10] This sum was nowhere near the revenue generated by the new tax, which was expected to be about
60 trillion yen per year. Ritsu Futaki points out that the actual sum of money spent during the
1989–1992 period on the Gold Plan amounted to less than 3 percent of the revenue from the
consumption tax (Futaki 1995). He thus suspects that elderly care was simply used as a justification
for the new tax.

[11] Ohara Rodo Mondai Kenkyujo 1990, 425; 1991, 399.

[12] In their attempt to persuade employers to support the creation of new long-term care insurance,
the welfare bureaucrats used to tell employers that the new care insurance imposed no additional
costs. They argued that the new insurance scheme, if anything, would save costs by moving elderly
patients out of the more expensive medical and institutionalized care facilities to cheaper options.
Based on interviews with Ken Shimomura at the Association of Kenpo Health Care Cooperatives
(Kenporen) on June 10, 1997, and with Akira Takanashi at Nikkeiren, July 1997. Reducing the
burden on workers and employers in 1991 appears highly strategic on the part of the ministry.

the reforms in the 1980s, in which most solutions consisted of shifting greater burdens onto wage earners (see Chapter 7). It is worth noting that the LDP partial minority government also resorted to a new way of financing periodic hikes in physicians' fees. Instead of raising employers' and wage earners' social security contributions, the government cut prescription drug prices in 1990 and then used the savings to pay for hikes in physicians' fees (Ohara Rodo Mondai Kenkyujo 1991, 401).

In stark contrast to its earlier policies, the LDP partial minority government even improved services and benefits to families with children. While the LDP had supported cuts in the Children's Allowance in the 1980s, it now accepted an expansion in the same program.[13] Under the LDP partial minority, national government spending on public day care centers also increased.[14] It should be emphasized that these developments were not automatic responses to the big fertility decline. The political motivation for the expansion of benefits for working mothers and families with children came from the opposition forces. The LDP itself was more focused on the expansion of social services for the elderly than on policies for working mothers for three reasons. First, social services for the elderly appealed to a broader segment of the population – including the LDP's rural base. Second, policies for working mothers had much less appeal to the LDP because they only affected a minority of households in Japan, where most mothers stayed home. The fact that care givers in public child care centers were all unionized workers who supported either the Japan Socialist Party or the Japan Communist Party only made the LDP more averse to the idea of significantly expanded public child care provision. Third, an expansion of elderly services involved perks for the ruling party, because a good share of the spending for such an expansion consisted of subsidies for building facilities. At least, part of the spending for elderly care operated like public works.[15] Improvements in benefits for working mothers thus can only be interpreted in the context of concessions to the opposition parties.

In contrast to the Ministry of Labor, eager to expand benefits for wage earners including working mothers, the Ministry of Welfare had relatively little interest in policies for working mothers.[16] The Ministry even cooperated with the budgeting authorities in the Ministry of Finance to reduce the national government spending on public child care by shifting the cost onto local governments; the effort was unsuccessful. Opposition from both the Ministry of Home Affairs – on behalf of local governments – and public day care center employees thwarted this joint

---

[13] Children's allowance benefits were extended to the first child too. The benefit amount was increased as well. See Ohara Rodo Mondai Kenkyujo 1992, 385.

[14] *Kuni no Yosan* (various years) shows a relative increase in public child care spending under the partial minority government.

[15] Interview at the Ministry of Welfare, June 30, 1997.

[16] A council set up by the Ministry of Welfare, the Council on the Future of Family and Child Rearing (Korekara no Katei to Kosodate ni Kansuru Kondankai) released a report emphasizing the need for supportive programs for working women (*Nikkei*, February 1, 1990, 34). Yet the Ministry remained much less interested in working mothers' issues; it mostly emphasized elderly care.

effort. As constituent groups of the parties of the left, these employees could take advantage of the LDP's minority position in the Upper House (Ohara Rodo Mondai Kenkyujo 1991, 315). In fact, the number of legislative items passed with affirmative votes by the Japan Socialist Party, the Democratic Socialist Party, and Komeito increased dramatically. Nearly half of the new laws passed by the Diet had support from every party except the Japan Communist Party. This was a much higher percentage than preceding years (Ohara Rodo Mondai Kenkyujo 1991, 316). In short, without the political power that the opposition parties had gained in 1989, Japan would not have introduced all the policies it did in the post-1989 period. The rest of this section explains in greater detail why some legislative attempts were successful but others were not.

Opportunities for the Ministry of Welfare under the New Veto Player Configuration

Whatever the real motives, the LDP's new interest in expanding welfare services for the elderly provided a great opportunity for the Ministry of Welfare. The Ministry of Welfare had been trying to contain the rise in medical expenditures for the elderly for some time. The "free health care for the elderly" policy was not only expensive, it involved moral hazards. The Japanese state provided little in terms of care services for the elderly; most of what it did provide was strictly means-tested, institutionalized care in public nursing homes. (The Japanese call this means-tested system the *sochi* system.) In light of the lack of affordable nonmedical care services for the elderly, the middle classes simply used hospitals to deposit their frail elderly parents.[17] The Ministry of Welfare saw the expansion of care services as a solution to this problem.

The Ministry of Welfare also had organizational reasons for devising a new program for elderly care. It was forecasted, for instance, that the number of private nursing homes would expand fourfold between 1985 and 1990.[18] In realizing that it was in a position to regulate this potential new growth sector of the economy, the Ministry eagerly promoted this "silver industry" in the hope of becoming like the Ministry of International Trade and Industry.[19] Thus in 1987 it quickly created the Organization for Silver Service Promotion (Shiruba Sabisu Shinkokai), a nonprofit organization that was to carry out the Ministry's policy objectives.[20] The ostensible role of the new organization was to grant "silver marks" to private manufacturers and service providers as a stamp of official approval.[21] But the organization also provided the Ministry with *amakudari*

---

[17] Chapter 7 describes this problem in greater detail.

[18] Industrial Bank of Japan 1993, 275–281.

[19] Campbell (1992, 234–239) reports that government officials and business people widely shared interests in the market for the aged.

[20] The Ministry of Welfare's White Paper (*Kosei Hakusho*) for 1991 provide the details.

[21] Japanese bureaucrats have long resorted to nonprofit organizations as arms and legs without much oversight from the elected officials (see Estévez-Abe 2003).

positions both on its own staff and in the private companies that it regulated.[22] In 1991, the Ministry of Welfare created the Elderly Welfare Promotion Section (Rojin Fukushi Shinko-ka) within the ministry. The task of this new subministe-rial unit was to promote the silver service industry. The Ministry of Welfare was no less interested in the creation of a new contributory social insurance scheme. A study group assembled by the vice minister of welfare issued a report in late 1989, which suggested using this scheme to fund the expansion of social services for the frail elderly.[23] Such a scheme was more desirable than a tax-financed sys-tem, because insurance revenue could be directly controlled by the Ministry of Welfare.

However, under LDP rule – even under a partial minority government – there was no political will for a new social insurance scheme at the time. Recall that the LDP government favored comprehensive social services as the justification for their new consumption tax. Otherwise, the LDP politicians would not have favored a scheme that delivered benefits to the likes of urban wage earners and their families. With Upper House elections due in 1993 and Lower House elec-tions looming in 1993 or 1994, the LDP had no desire to impose a new contrib-utory scheme on voters. Yet without a commitment from the LDP government, welfare bureaucrats could not introduce a new program.

Nonetheless, the welfare bureaucrats kept busy with various internal efforts. In 1992, the Ministry of Welfare prepared another internal document, titled "The Elderly Total Plan Study Group Report." The report noted the limita-tions of means-tested care services that excluded the middle classes. The report also referred to the importance of socializing the cost of frail elderly care and thus the need for a new social insurance scheme. In the same year, the Ministry "upgraded" the Department of Elderly Health and Welfare from a sub-bureau to a full bureau. In April 1993, the Ministry called for a joint meeting of the three *shingikai* under its jurisdiction – each in charge of different aspects of elderly care – with a view to creating one single *shingikai*.[24] Welfare bureaucrats needed a new *shingikai* to gather representatives from all vested interest groups related to the new care insurance scheme to thrash out a consensus. Although the weakening of the LDP's position had opened a new window of legislative opportunities for the Ministry of Welfare, ultimately the Ministry's room for maneuvering was still constrained by the electoral calculations of the parliamentary veto players. These veto players now included both the LDP and a subsection of the opposition parties. For this reason, welfare bureaucrats added such new participants as the

[22] As a regulating authority of the pharmaceutical industry, the Ministry of Welfare regularly "sent" its retired career officials to pharmaceutical companies for their post-retirement careers.

[23] The Vice Ministry of Welfare – the highest administrative position for career bureaucrats – put together the Study Group for Measures to Address Elderly Care (Kaigo Taisaku Kentoukai). See Futaki (1995).

[24] In April 1993, the Ministry of Welfare had even started the process of merging the three preexisting *shingikai* that each addressed different aspects of elderly care into one *shingikai* on Elderly Health and Welfare. The Ministry called for a special discussion group consisting of members of the three *shingikai* to agree that there should be a more integrated *shingikai* to deliberate on systematic solutions to the problem facing the frail elderly. See *Shakai Hoken Junpo*, October 21, 1993, 15; and the Ministry of Health and Welfare's White Papers for 1993.

Municipal Government Employees' Union (Jichiro), a major constituent group of the Japan Socialist Party. Given the weight of the Socialists in the Upper House, Jichiro itself exercised veto power. This example shows clearly how bureaucrats employed *shingikai* to prenegotiate the terms of a legislative bill by inviting the core constituent groups of parliamentary veto players.

The emergence of the opposition parties as veto players provided the Ministry of Welfare officials with new opportunities to introduce programs and to expand the existing ones. At the same time, however, it also constrained policy options available to the Ministry of Welfare. Benefit cuts were more difficult now that welfare officials faced a broader range of societal groups with potential veto power. Most notably, the enhanced position of the Japan Socialist Party and the Democratic Socialist Party in the Upper House gave unions greater bargaining power over legislation. The Ministry's failed attempt to cut back on pension benefits provides an example of the unions' new bargaining power. The unions were more capable of blocking unfavorable changes in 1989 than in the previous round of pension revisions in 1985. In that earlier round, which took place under the LDP's absolute majority, the Ministry of Welfare had succeeded in significantly cutting back on the future pension benefits of wage earners (see Chapter 7). The 1985 reform also stipulated that the pension eligibility age would be raised to sixty-five. Given the fact that most firms implemented corporate retirement age at sixty, however, a special pension payment from the age of sixty had been permitted for enrollees in the Employee Pension (Ohara Rodo Mondai Kenkyujo 1990, 419). The Ministry of Welfare was very keen on terminating this special arrangement and raising the eligibility to sixty-five across the board. Unlike in 1985, organized labor was more capable of blocking unwanted policy changes in 1989. The Ministry's attempt was indeed thwarted in the Upper House, where union-affiliated political parties possessed more power (ibid.).

Reviewing policy developments since 1989, the preponderance of evidence shows, as in these cases, that the parliamentary veto players' calculations and bureaucratic interests mattered more than socioeconomic changes. True, these changes provided the context for political action. But the Ministry of Welfare's attempts to cope with demographic aging and declining fertility were successful only when not blocked by parliamentary veto players.

Opportunities and Constraints for the Ministry of Labor

The Ministry of Labor also tried to take advantage of the new socioeconomic context and introduce programs. Unlike the Ministry of Welfare, whose jurisdiction reached all aspects of the health and welfare of the population, the Ministry of Labor had legal jurisdiction only on policies and programs that touched upon industrial relations and workers' welfare. Typically, the Ministry of Labor modus operandi involved regulatory interventions on behalf of workers' welfare. Such interventions invariably cost employers autonomy and money. The Ministry of Labor could intervene easily when both employers and unions supported it; when only one supported it, interventions were difficult, and when neither group supported it, impossible. Under LDP dominance, new regulatory intervention was impossible without, at least, employers' tacit consent, because they could persuade the LDP to veto the Ministry of Labor's policy proposals. Small and medium-sized firms, in particular, opposed costly regulations. Because these firms were important constituents of numerous LDP Diet members, the LDP would always veto any cost increases on them. While the LDP held power, any benefits for wage earners were thus hard to come by.

The emergence of non-LDP parliamentary veto players – especially political parties that relied on unions as their organized constituencies – improved the Ministry of Labor's legislative capacity. The enhanced power of the pro-labor parties generated favorable conditions for bureaucrats keen on introducing new benefits for workers. The successful introduction of the Childcare Leave in 1991 is a case in point. The opposition parties took the initiative to introduce the Childcare Leave.[25] A successful passage of an opposition-sponsored legislation, which placed a new burden on employers, would have been unthinkable just some years before. In this respect, this new legislation demonstrated what was now possible legislatively.

In 1987, the four opposition parties – the Japan Socialist Party, the Democratic Socialist Party, Komeito, and the Social Democratic Alliance (Shaminren) – jointly sponsored a bill to introduce a child care leave. This legislative effort failed, because the LDP refused to cooperate. Employers – one of the LDP's core constituent groups – were vehemently opposed to the opposition's proposal. The LDP's electoral defeat in 1989, however, changed the political dynamics in the Diet. In April 1990, the four opposition parties, yet again, jointly submitted a child care leave bill in the Upper House, where the LDP lacked an absolute majority. While not opposed to the idea of a statutory leave itself, the LDP nonetheless opposed specific items in the bill. The opposition parties demanded (i) cash benefits equivalent of 60 percent of workers' wages preceding the leave; (ii) reinstatement of workers to their original jobs upon returning from the leave; and (iii) penalties for employers who violated the law. The LDP was concerned with the excessive burden that a statutory leave would impose on small and medium-sized enterprises. Here the LDP stood by the employers' association, Nikkeiren, in upholding the "no work, no pay" principle. Negotiations between the opposition parties and the LDP in the appropriate committee in the Upper House failed to reach any conclusion. Both sides then agreed to hand the matter over to the Ministry of Labor, which promptly summoned the tripartite *shingikai*, Women and Youth Issues Deliberation Council. Representatives from Rengo, Nikkeiren, and the National Association of Small- and Medium-Scale Enterprises sat down to negotiate the terms.[26]

---

[25] Junko Takashima, who was in charge of women-related policies at Rengo, observed that this legislation was very special and owed its passage to the strength of the opposition parties in the Upper House (interview July 20, 1995).

[26] By the early 1990s, about 40 percent of firms employing more than one thousand workers offered some kind of child care leave. This means that many of the active corporate members of Nikkeiren already had corporate leave programs. Yet as a peak-level association of employers representing all

The Ministry of Labor drafted a compromise plan in February 1991, which required employers to provide workers with an unconditional leave until their children reached the age of one. Although the LDP government initially had only mothers in mind here, the Ministry of Labor's plan included fathers too. The Ministry argued that the Japanese government had already ratified the ILO's agreement on eradicating gender-based discrimination, which precluded a female-only statutory leave. The compromise plan, however, included no paid benefits. Moreover, it allowed a lengthy grace period for small-scale enterprises before they were required to implement the new statutory leave.

Interestingly, the *shingikai*'s final recommendation was no different than the Ministry's earlier compromise plan, which suggests that the bureaucrats had controlled the agenda.[27] In an attempt to persuade employers and unions to accept the compromise plan, the Ministry of Labor tried to appease both sides. For the employers, the Ministry of Labor offered to deregulate restrictions against temporary employment contracts, which would enable employers to hire replacements for workers on leave.[28] For the unions, the Ministry offered to use the surplus in the Employment Insurance account to provide paid benefits. Employers, who were contributing more into the account than their workers, argued that any surplus in the account should be set against further contributions. At this point, the Ministry of Labor and the opposition parties gave up on paid leave merely to get the child care leave bill signed.[29]

It is noteworthy that the Ministry of Labor had a strong interest in introducing a paid child care leave. A long period of economic expansion in the 1980s and Japan's stable industrial relations made it appear as if the Ministry of Labor had outlived its usefulness.[30] The large surplus in the Employment Insurance Special Account, in particular, drew perennial calls from employers to cut the contribution rates.[31] In search of a new mission, labor bureaucrats settled on two issues: working women and older workers.[32] They hoped that paid statutory leaves would compensate women who took time off from work to look after children and elderly parents. The idea of paid statutory leave matched the organizational interest of the Ministry of Labor bureaucrats in general. They wanted to use the surplus in the Employment Insurance to finance paid benefits. In the face of

employers regardless of size, Nikkeiren stood by the representatives from the National Association of Small- and Medium-Scale Enterprises. (Interview with Akira Takanashi at Nikkeiren, July 1997.)

[27] *Nihon Keizai Shimbun*, March 6, 1991, 5.

[28] Nikkeiren, the employers' peak association, demanded deregulation of labor regulation restricting temporary contracts (*Nikkei Sangyo Shimbun*, February 22, 1991, 2). From an interview in 1995 with Junko Takashima, who served as the Rengo's representative in the *shingikai* during this process.

[29] Many details of the new program were to be left to administrative orders and guidance at the time of policy implementation (*Nihon Keizai Shimbun*, May 6, 1991, 5; May 11, 1991, 7).

[30] Naka (1990) provides details of the atmosphere in the late 1980s, during which some even argued that the Ministry of Labor was no longer necessary.

[31] In fiscal year 1989, the Employment Insurance account had revenue of 1,320 billion yen, whereas its benefit payments only amounted to 980 billion. The accumulated surplus exceeded 2 trillion yen (*Nihon Keizai Shimbun*, March 10, 1991, 1).

[32] The newly created Women's Bureau, in particular, was interested in introducing measures to support working women.

declining unemployment rates, they hoped that such benefits would allow them to maintain the Employment Insurance Special Account.[33] Although their plan to use the account initially failed (in 1991), they did not give up on the idea and, as we shall see, eventually prevailed.

Although no drastic policy shift occurred in relation to older workers, this policy area also offers a good look at how Japanese bureaucrats set their organizational goals. The Ministry of Labor interpreted demographic aging as a labor market issue – because that was the Ministry's jurisdictional mission – and focused on policy support for older workers, including a delay in the retirement age.[34] The Ministry began encouraging private firms to postpone their mandatory retirement age until workers reached sixty-five years. In 1990, it introduced a law, which stipulated employers' "duty to make an effort" (*doryokugimu*) to raise their corporate retirement age (Nihon Romu Kenkyukai 1990, 141). With this objective, the Ministry began to offer subsidies to employers from the Employment Insurance Account (Nihon Romu Kenkyukai 1990, 133–134).

To summarize, the policy developments under the partial minority government of July 24, 1989, to August 9, 1993, were different from politics as usual under LDP dominance. The LDP had to compromise with the opposition parties and, as a result, was forced to consider comprehensive programs as well as programs for wage earners. Without the veto power that the opposition parties had gained in the Upper House, the LDP government would have never introduced a child care leave policy benefiting wage earners. In the context of partial minority government, however, a new kind of legislative alliance emerged between the Ministry of Labor and the opposition parties. The result was a statutory child care bill. The general lesson here is that shifts in the political structure are necessary if new policies are to be enacted, regardless of the socioeconomic factors at work.

THE NON-LDP COALITION GOVERNMENTS UNDER THE MMN/SNTV SYSTEM

In 1993, a further change in the structural logic occurred. On August 9, a group of LDP politicians led by Ichiro Ozawa left the party and, together with seven other opposition parties, formed a non-LDP coalition government. The coalition included the Japan Socialist Party; the Democratic Socialist Party; Komeito; Shinseito (Japan Renewal Party); the Japan New Party; Social Democratic League; Sakigake (Harbinger); and the Democratic Reform Alliance.[35]

---

[33] In fact, as early as 1990, the Ministry of Labor unsuccessfully tried to use the Workers' Injuries Insurance Program to cover cash benefits to family members who care for workers who became handicapped due to work injuries (*Asahi Shimbun*, February 21, 1995, 7).

[34] The Ministry of Labor's *Longevity Society Employment Vision* reflects this tendency (see Nihon Romu Kenkyukai 1990, 136–138). Campbell (1992) notes Japan's distinctive reaction to its aging society in terms of doing more to keep older workers employed. Although he does not explicitly specify, Japan's distinctive path cannot be explained fully without the presence of a ministry with exclusive jurisdiction on labor market issues.

[35] To be precise, the Democratic Reform Alliance is not a party but a political group (*kaiha*). All parties form their own political groups within the Upper House for procedural reasons. Various procedural

Morihiro Hosokawa, a handsome leader of the Japan New Party, became the new first non-LDP prime minister in decades. His government lasted from August 9, 1993, to April 28, 1994, when he abruptly resigned over rumors about his possible involvement in a political scandal. Tsutomu Hata, who succeeded Hosokawa to lead the coalition government, had a rocky ride navigating his minority government after the Japan Socialist Party and Sakigake abandoned ship. His government lasted for only four months. The non-LDP coalition ended on June 30, 1994. (Appendix C provides the chronological list of prime ministers during the period covered in this chapter.)

The ouster of the LDP meant that beneficiaries of the old form of distributive politics also changed. The organized core constituent groups of the coalition partners now stood to gain from public policy instead of LDP constituent groups. Although the new political parties such as the Japan New Party drew support from unorganized urban voters, the established parties (such as the Japan Socialist Party, Democratic Socialist Party, and Komeito) relied upon certain organized constituent groups.[36] Unionized workers formed the core constituencies of the Japan Socialist Party and the Democratic Socialist Party; and Soka Gakkai (a religious group) formed the core constituency of Komeito. Soka Gakkai members were primarily drawn from the low-income and lower-middle-income urban population. Reflecting this membership, Komeito tended to favor redistributive public welfare benefits, which it used in lieu of targeted benefits for its members alone.

The emergence of a coalition government in 1993 quickly led to a range of tax-and-spend policy proposals.[37] Prime Minister Morihiro Hosokawa was quite eager to create a new consumption-based tax. The People's Welfare Tax (Kokumin Fukushi Zei) was to be a tax whose revenue would be earmarked for social spending. The prime minister also intended to use this tax as a way of correcting Japan's heavy reliance on income tax. As already discussed in Chapter 7, the cost of Japan's welfare state fell primarily upon the shoulders of wage earners, whereas the main beneficiaries of Japan's welfare benefits were rural voters and the old. A new consumption tax – to be accompanied by reductions in income tax – offered a remedy to these imbalances by spreading the tax burden to everyone regardless of age or job. The Ministry of Finance was, in principle, averse to any earmarked taxes, which reduced their discretion. Yet, desperate for new sources of taxes, the Ministry of Finance went along with the new coalition government's desire to specify the use of new revenue. This development is hardly

---

privileges in the Diet such as time for questioning ministers on the Diet floor or committee assignments are allocated to political groups, not to individual politicians. The Democratic Reform Alliance is a *kaiha* formed by independents to access full benefits as legislators. Curtis (1999, 173) offers a detailed account of the use of *kaiha* in the Diet.

[36] Although new parties emerged to seek the support of disgruntled unorganized urban voters, the fate of these parties was often short lived as it was very difficult to rely on unorganized voters. This is consistent with the theory that explains that political parties are better off pursuing organized groups of voters under MMD systems.

[37] Curtis (1999, chapter 2) provides a fascinating detailed account of political developments during this period.

surprising given the expectations of the structural logic approach: coalition governments under MMD systems find it easier to increase taxes than noncoalition governments and governments in SMD systems. Export sector business leaders and unions were in favor of the new indirect tax.[38]

Prime Minister Hosokawa's plan fell through partly because of his alleged involvement in a bribery scandal and partly because he alienated two of the coalition partners – the Japan Socialist Party and Sakigake.[39] The lesson of his brief premiership should not, however, be lost: coalition governments of multiple parties in MMD systems perceive the risk of a new tax as much lower than other types of governments.[40] This is because both party identifiability and accountability are lowest in this government type. The Hosokawa government's willingness to consider tax increases contrasts starkly with the LDP governments' aversion during the period of its single-party rule. As we shall see, the LDP was less averse to tax increases when it came back to power in June 1994 by forming a coalition government. Even the JSP and Sakigake, who protested against Prime Minister Hosokawa for failing to consult them properly on the idea of the Welfare Tax, were not against a new tax. In fact, they agreed to an increase in the consumption tax rate as soon as they joined the LDP to form an alternative coalition government (Kato 1997, 287–289). Just as Hosokawa did, the JSP and Sakigake made the LDP promise that the new tax revenue be spent for welfare purposes (ibid.). And my structural logic approach explains why: to reiterate, multiparty coalition governments find it easier to raise taxes than single-party dominant governments.

Prime Minister Hosokawa's non-LDP coalition governments differed significantly from the LDP governments in its emphasis on benefits and services for wage earners and their families. The non-LDP coalition governments, in particular, shifted the distributive focus toward wage earners and urban voters, and away from rural voters. The non-LDP government also cut back on public works

[38] Export sector companies such as Toyota had been arguing for some time that social security benefits should be financed by the general tax revenue. See comments by Shoichiro Toyota, Toyota's CEO, in *Asahi Shimbun*, August, 22 1992, 9. Toyota favored consumption tax hikes for this purpose. Toyota company unions expressed the same view in *Asahi Shimbun*, May 24, 1994, 11.

[39] The fact that the Japan Socialist Party was unhappy with Hosokawa's idea for a consumption-based welfare tax appears to defy the logic put forth here. Leading up to the Upper House elections in 1989, the Japan Socialist Party had strongly criticized the LDP's introduction of the consumption tax to its electoral advantage. The Japan Socialist Party thus did not find it easy to shift its position rapidly. The real reason behind why the JSP and Sakigake were not happy with Hosokawa's tax plan had deeper roots. The two parties were not happy about the ever closer relationship between three of the other coalition partners – Komeito, Ichiro Ozawa's Shinseito, and Prime Minister Hosokawa's Japan New Party. They saw Hosokawa's plan as a symbol of the new political dynamics within the coalition whereby they were left out of the loop. See Eto (1998, 77) and Curtis (1999, chapter 2).

[40] Junko Kato compares the failure of the People's Welfare Tax to the failure of the General Sales Tax in 1979 (Kato 1997, 274). In my view, Kato misses an important difference between the two processes. In the earlier case, it was the electoral concerns of the LDP rank and file that killed the LDP leaders' legislative attempt. In the case of the People's Welfare Tax, electoral issues were not the primary reason for opposing the new tax. Rather, the power struggle among the coalition partners shot down the new tax.

spending, in favor of policies that aided urban voters.[41] It also decided to partially liberalize rice imports.[42] This was a big break from the LDP rule. Under the LDP rule, urban voters had to pick up the cost of distributive benefits for rural areas – public works, agricultural subsidies, and higher consumer prices for agricultural products such as rice. Without the LDP in power, the political influence of the agricultural cooperatives (*nokyo*) – one of the most important LDP core constituents – was severely limited.[43] The presence of multiple parliamentary veto players allowed social and labor policy bureaucrats to pursue policies that would have been very difficult to pursue otherwise.

New Bureaucratic Opportunities under the Non-LDP Coalitions

The previous section has demonstrated that, in spite of the "1.57 fertility shock," the LDP was not very eager to help working mothers. Certainly, despite the LDP's lack of interest, the budget for public child care was augmented and the Children's Allowance benefits were slightly expanded. The LDP government's effort in elderly care services dwarfed anything it did for working mothers. As discussed earlier, the Childcare Leave in 1991 only came about thanks to the efforts of the opposition parties and the Ministry of Labor. By 1993, the opposition parties that had earlier pushed for a paid leave were now the ruling parties. Not surprisingly, the new non-LDP coalition emphasized the need for a comprehensive policy package to help urban dual-career families with children. Again, as under the LDP partial minority government, social and labor bureaucrats tried to take advantage of the new parliamentary veto player configuration to advance their organizational agenda.

The Angel Plan

In 1993, the non-LDP government came up with an idea to introduce an ambitious ten-year plan called the Angel Plan to increase public support for working mothers and families with children.[44] The government introduced the Angel Plan Prelude as a preparatory measure for the larger ten-year plan. Both the Ministry of Welfare and the Ministry of Labor were involved in drafting the Prelude,

---

[41] See Ito (2000). Ito notes a policy shift that occurred under coalition governments using language very similar to that of this book.

[42] This decision was reached as Japan's compromise in the Uruguay Round. See Mulgan (2000, 642–643). Agricultural politics also have an important international dimension because of international negotiations. Increasingly in the 1980s, international negotiations over agricultural protection in Japan were linked to other economic and trade issues. As Davis (2003) demonstrates, certain kinds of issue linkages weakened the agricultural lobby's power. This introduces a political dynamic not captured in my structural logic approach.

[43] See Mulgan (2000, 642–643).

[44] Because the power switched back to the LDP-led coalition government at the very end of June 1994 in the midst of the budgetary negotiations for the fiscal year 1995, the actual Angel Plan was approved by the LDP-led coalition government. The Angel Plan was to allocate 60 billion yen over a ten-year period to improve regulatory and public service infrastructure for working parents.

which consisted of the following four elements: (i) expansion of public provision of childcare; (ii) provision of more flexible and convenient child care services; (iii) improvements in cash benefits for households headed by single mothers; and (iv) arrangements to reduce the cost of having children, including an exemption from social security contributions while on child care leave and a special lump-sum payment at the birth of a child (see Kubono 1994b, 92–93). Put all together, the Plan amounted to a benefit for wage earners' families.[45]

The emergence of a non-LDP government interested in policies for wage earners and their families created a favorable political climate for the Ministry of Labor and the Ministry of Welfare to advance programs and services for wage earners – precisely the kinds of benefits hitherto neglected by the LDP. The Ministry of Labor tapped into the Employment Insurance Special Account to subsidize employers willing to set up corporate child care facilities. The Employment Insurance, which was funded by employers' contributions, had an abundant surplus; and the labor bureaucrats had long had their eyes on it as a way of financing new programs. In contrast, the Ministry of Welfare had no special account readily available for child-related programs. In order to solve this problem, the Ministry used the Angel Plan Prelude – and the new climate of concern for families – to justify the creation of a Children's Future Foundation (Kodomo Mirai Zaidan) in 1994.[46] The objective of the foundation, which was to be funded by levies on employers, was very broadly defined as supporting families with children. Under the old LDP rule, this foundation would never have been created, and never at the expense of employers. Furthermore, as a nonprofit organization under the Ministry of Welfare's jurisdiction, the foundation had carte blanche to spend the funds on whatever it wanted. Clearly, one thing the Ministry wanted was to create more jobs for its own staff – and this it did. Generally speaking, the Ministry of Welfare was relatively uninterested in policies for working mothers and families. In the words of a Ministry of Welfare official, they saw child care services as a declining industry – because the number of babies was rapidly decreasing (interview at the Ministry of Welfare, June 30, 1997)!

Employment Insurance Reform

The Employment Insurance Reform in 1994 provides still further evidence of the change in distributive politics as the LDP partial minority government gave way to a non-LDP coalition. Earlier it has been mentioned that the Ministry of Labor, which oversaw the Employment Insurance Special Account, had been wary of employers' perennial demands to cut down on their contribution rates

---

[45] Young families in rural areas were much more likely to live in multigenerational households and thus depended less on public child care.

[46] The Ministry of Labor official whom I interviewed referred to the creation of the Children's Future Foundation as being motivated by "the welfare bureaucrats' envy for the autonomous source of money we have with the Employment Insurance Special Account." Bureaucrats really do think in terms of organizational resources that they can use freely for the reasons this book claims. Interview at the Women's Bureau, Ministry of Labor, 1995.

now that the account was in surplus. The Employment Insurance Special Account was an important "independent" source of money for the Ministry of Labor; and the labor bureaucrats were very eager to look for policies that justified the surplus. While it tried unsuccessfully to introduce paid childcare leave benefits in 1991, the Ministry of Labor found life much easier with the LDP no longer in power. Taking the lead on the Employment Insurance Reform in 1994, the Ministry introduced two new cash benefits: (i) paid benefits for child care leaves; and (ii) wage subsidies for older workers. Both types of benefits were to be financed by the surplus in the Employment Insurance Special Account. This time, the Ministry managed to override the employers' opposition.

How did the Ministry circumvent the employers' opposition in 1994, when they were unable to do so in 1991? Issue linkage and the weaker political position of employers provide the answer. The 1994 Employment Insurance Reform, which introduced new wage subsidies for older workers, coincided with the periodic review of the public pension system.[47] Although lateral coordination among ministries rarely happens in Japan, the Budget Bureau of the Ministry of Finance offered a crucial bridge between the welfare bureaucrats' efforts to cut back on pension responsibilities and the labor bureaucrats' desire to provide benefits for older workers. The Ministry of Labor, therefore, proposed to compensate older workers (those between sixty and sixty-four) for any decrease in wages just as the Ministry of Welfare was trying to raise the pension age.[48] The Employment Insurance was thus reformed, so as to eliminate incentives to retire and increase incentives to continue to work. As the labor market situation was beginning to worsen in 1993, employers were quite happy to use the surplus in the Employment Insurance Special Account to subsidize older workers' wages.[49]

What is interesting is that the Ministry of Labor used the new cash benefits for older workers to justify a new paid benefit during child care leave. The Ministry of Labor thus applied the same level of wage subsidies set for older

[47] Note that, because Japanese companies adopt seniority wages, they impose a specific retirement age. (Unlike in the United States, where age-based mandatory retirement is illegal, it is still a common practice in Japanese firms.) Older workers undergo drastic wage reductions when they seek new jobs elsewhere. The new wage subsidies for older workers encourage the reemployment of post-retirement workers by offering partial compensation to offset reductions in their wages. The new benefit covers up to 25 percent of the older workers' wages when their wages fall by more than 15 percent compared to their "pre-retirement" wage. See Kubono (1994b, 114–115, 239).

[48] The Budget Bureau of the Ministry of Finance had been very keen on reducing the fiscal burden of welfare entitlements and containing the unavoidable rise in the pension cost as the direct cause of societal aging. Although the Budget Bureau is normally against any kind of new cash benefits, budget officials saw great merit in providing cash benefits for older workers to remain in the workforce. The budget officials considered such material incentive a good bartering tool to get social partners to agree to raise the eligible age for pension. (Interview with a budget bureau official who was in charge of the Ministry of Welfare and Ministry of Labor budgets during the period under discussion, June 1, 1995).

[49] This subsidy greatly helped manufacturing firms subsidize their manpower costs. Unlike white-collar workers, older skilled workers were a category of employees that manufacturers benefited from beyond the corporate retirement age. The national subsidies enabled them to hire these workers more cheaply than otherwise. As the Japanese yen appreciated rapidly, hurting the export sector, this subsidy offered important assistance.

workers (25 percent) to younger workers on child care leave. Workers expected to take child care leave were mostly female workers, and this time the employers accepted the same treatment of female workers without much complaint.[50] Without the presence of the LDP in the government, employers' political position was weaker. While the Ministry of Labor also cut the rates of employers' contribution to the Employment Insurance as a way of appeasing employers, it nonetheless succeeded in expanding the content of the Employment Insurance significantly.[51] The Ministry of Labor was even granted a rare expansion of its personnel to deal with new administrative tasks related to the new cash benefits during child care leave.[52] An official I interviewed referred very proudly to this expansion (interview July 24, 1995).

In 1993, the non-LDP government also introduced a new employment promotion program called the Employment Promotion Total Program. This program consisted of subsidies to employers who hired disadvantaged workers (such as recently retrenched older workers) and funds to support regional employment development programs. The eligibility criteria for firms to qualify for these wage subsidies were also significantly expanded. Likewise, the Reform of the Elderly Employment Stabilization Law in 1994 expanded the range of jobs for which employers could hire older workers without a permanent contract (Shimada 2000, 123). This reform aimed at creating incentives for employers to hire older workers.

Interestingly, one aspect of Japan's social protection did not change even under Hosokawa's non-LDP coalition government. The government continued to emphasize work rather than welfare. This can be observed in the new wage subsidies for older workers as well as pro-work regulation. While Prime Minister Hosokawa had no trouble introducing protective policies such as wage subsidies, his effort to deregulate the Japanese economy was not very successful. Prime Minister Hosokawa advocated deregulation as an economic policy to stimulate the economy. This was a departure from the social protection under the LDP, where the primary goal was protection of enterprises. Prime Minister Hosokawa's hostility to vested interests reflected his party's electoral dependence on urban unorganized voters. Nonetheless, some of his coalition partners – those traditional political parties with their organized constituents in the MMD/SNTV system – had a lot to lose from possible deregulation. As the structural logic identifies, MMD systems embolden organized constituent groups. Limits of deregulation even under the non-LDP coalition thus can be explained in the context of the structural logic at the time.[53]

---

[50] Interviews with Junko Takashima at Rengo on July 24, 1995, and at the Women's Bureau, Ministry of Labor, on July 20, 1995.

[51] Interview at the Women's Bureau, Ministry of Labor, July 20, 1995.

[52] *Nihon Keizai Shimbun* (December 24, 1994, 3) reports that the Ministry of Labor was granted forty additional positions.

[53] Vogel (1999) offers an excellent account of how losers and winners in the market are intricately connected to one another, making pro-market reforms difficult. Vogel, however, does not refer to the nature of the electoral system. My argument is that even when the societal conditions remain

New Initiatives for Frail Elderly Care

Earlier it was mentioned that welfare bureaucrats were interested in developing elderly care insurance. The Ministry of Welfare bureaucrats were particularly keen on the idea of shifting elderly care from medical facilities to nonmedical care facilities. They hoped such a shift would help them circumvent the politically powerful Japan Medical Association. The LDP government, however, had little interest beyond the Gold Plan. The LDP leaders had been aware of the moral hazards built into the current health care system. Yet their hands were tied to carry out a real overhaul of the system. The "free health care for the elderly" was a lucrative cash cow for physicians with private practices (key members of the Japan Medical Association). The Japan Medical Association mobilized intraparty veto players within the LDP to block any attempt to reform the current health care system.[54]

Only with the emergence of a non-LDP coalition was the "socialization of elderly care" put on the actual policy agenda.[55] Just like the Ministry of Labor, the Ministry of Welfare benefited from the new configuration of parliamentary veto players. When Prime Minister Hosokawa abruptly announced his intention to introduce a welfare tax in February 1994, his government had to quickly produce a systematic plan for welfare expansion. The task fell to an existing ad hoc committee that Minister of Welfare Keigo Ouchi had assembled in October 1993.[56] As a member of the Democratic Socialist Party, Ouchi had long been interested in benefits and services for wage earners.[57] This ad hoc committee issued a policy document named *Welfare Vision for the 21st Century (21 Seiki Fukushi Bijon)*, which reiterated the need to socialize the costs of caring for the frail elderly.[58] The committee favored a new elderly care system. It also called for a new Gold Plan to expand the infrastructure of care provision. The Ministry of Welfare set up a special team to prepare the New Gold Plan in April 1994.

Although it was the Ministry of Welfare that eventually introduced a long-term care insurance program for the frail elderly, it is important to note that the Ministry of Labor was also keen on developing something similar under its jurisdiction. The Ministry of Labor was eager to claim a stake in the new area

constant, when the rules of the political game change, possibilities for reform change too. My views thus differ from Vogel's.

54 For great studies of how JMA influenced LDP politicians, see Iwai (1990, 166–195); and Takahashi (1986).

55 Eto (1998) similarly thinks that it was not until the emergence of the Hosokawa Cabinet that socialization of elderly care became a political goal.

56 Minister Ouchi had also set up a different group earlier in August called the Discussion Group to Consider Elderly Welfare from General and Multiple Angles (Koreisha Fukushi wo Sogoteki Rittaiteki ni Kenko suru Kondaikai). The Ministry of Welfare, too, had set up a private discussion group under the auspices of the chief of the newly created Elderly Health and Welfare Bureau. (This bureau was created in July 1992.)

57 The Democratic Socialist Party issued a proposal in July 1992 calling for a social insurance scheme that reimburses family members who take care of the elderly at home as well as a statutory one-year leave for workers to look after old parents (*Asahi Shimbun*, March 22, 1992).

58 See *Shakai Hosho Junpo* (October 21, 1993, 4) for the details of this ad hoc committee.

of elderly care. Labor bureaucrats wanted to introduce paid family care leave (*kaigo kyugyo*) to compensate workers for time spent caring for elderly parents. The Ministry of Labor had been promoting family care leaves in private corporations – something that unions supported – since 1990. As a first legislative step, the Ministry wanted to introduce statutory family leave. As with Childcare Leave, the emergence of the non-LDP coalition government was extremely helpful for the Ministry of Labor. The Democratic Socialist Party and the Komeito – both members of the non-LDP coalition government since August 1993 – had proposed family care leaves even before joining the coalition.[59] The new minister of labor in the Hosokawa government happened to be Chikara Sakaguchi, a member of Komeito. At a Cabinet meeting in December 1993, Minister Sakaguchi announced his ministry's intention to have a family care leave bill ready for the Diet session in 1995.[60] Such a receptive reaction to yet another generous leave for wage earners would have been unthinkable under the LDP's single-party rule. Generous leaves for wage earners were not the sort of policy that LDP politicians would have rallied behind. Meanwhile, labor bureaucrats consulted the representatives of unions, the peak-level employers' association, Nikkeiren, and the association of small and medium-sized enterprises about the timetable of policy deliberation in the *shingikai* on Women and Youth Issues. The representatives agreed to put family care leave on their agenda.[61] The non-LDP coalition, however, collapsed in June 1994 before a bill was submitted to the Diet.

In sum, evidence shows that it was Hosokawa's non-LDP coalition government that steered the policy course toward wage earners. The coalition government also made it more difficult for bureaucrats to propose cuts in the benefits of organized labor. The short life of the non-LDP coalition, however, meant that this coalition could not complete its major policy initiatives. Interestingly, most of the policy initiatives were carried over to the next LDP-led coalition government and were legislated. Even with the LDP back in power, a coalition government had a dynamic of its own, creating some continuity in policies.

THE LDP-LED COALITION GOVERNMENTS UNDER MMD/SNTV
(JUNE 1994–NOVEMBER 1996)

The non-LDP coalition government prematurely collapsed on June 30, 1994. The LDP, desperate to come back to power, successfully lured the Japan Socialist Party (hereafter JSP) and Sakigake to leave the non-LDP coalition and join them. The period under the LDP-led coalition government thus began. As a

[59] The Democratic Socialist Party issued a proposal in July 1992 (*Asahi Shimbun*, March 22, 1992). Komeito, in turn, had submitted a family care leave bill to the Upper House in March 1993 (*Asahi Shimbun*, March 13, 1993, 1).

[60] *Asahi Shimbun*, December 21, 1993, 2.

[61] The Women's Bureau of the Ministry of Labor had two policy items in mind. The other item was the reform of the Equal Employment Opportunity Law. The Rengo and Nikkeiren representatives in the *shingikai* believed that having two controversial items simultaneously on the table would lead to a stalemate. Interview at the Women's Bureau, Ministry of Labor, 1995.

way of enticing the JSP to join the coalition, the LDP offered the premiership to Tomiichi Murayama, the JSP leader at the time.[62] This third subperiod continued until the first Lower House elections under the new rules took place in November 1996.

From the perspective of the structural logic, the LDP-led coalition government period was very similar to the non-LDP coalition government period. In spite of their different partisan compositions, the coalition governments during the two periods shared the same "structure": (i) multiple parliamentary veto players within the government; and (ii) the MMD/SNTV system. The fact that the JSP and Sakigake participated in both the non-LDP and the LDP-led coalition governments added another layer of continuity between the two subperiods. The return of the LDP to power, therefore, did not necessarily mean a return to the old style of politics. Certainly, the LDP was able to distribute favors to its constituents, but so were the Japan Socialist Party and Sakigake.

Many of the legislative projects initiated by the non-LDP coalition governments (Hosokawa and Hata governments) were carried over to Murayama's LDP-led coalition government. These legislative initiatives included (i) the Angel Plan; (ii) the Family Care Leave (Kaigo Kyugyo); and (iii) the new insurance scheme for elderly care, the Long-Term Care Insurance (Kaigo Hoken). The continuing participation of the JSP in power ensured favorable policies for unionized workers. Soon after the new LDP-led coalition was formed, it decided on special exemptions of social security contributions during child care leaves.[63]

Similarities between the non-LDP and LDP-led coalitions can also be observed in tax policy. As already discussed in relation to the Hosokawa Government's proposal of the Welfare Tax, my structural logic stipulates that coalition governments under MMD systems find it easier than other types of governments to introduce costly policies such as tax increases. Indeed, the experience of the new LDP-led coalition government attests to this. As soon as the LDP, the Japan Socialist Party, and Sakigake agreed to form a government together, they also agreed to raise the consumption tax from 3 percent to 5 percent. It is also not a coincidence that the idea to introduce a compulsory social insurance for the elderly appeared on the legislative agenda under the coalition governments – both the non-LDP and the LDP-led coalitions.[64] Potential revenue from the new tax was to subsidize the program. The program also planned to levy contributions from a broad segment of the population – including the elderly. Needless to say these broad-based contributions themselves were very much like a new tax.

[62] The participation of the Japan Socialist Party in the LDP-led coalition government was indeed as important an event as the ouster of the LDP in 1993 in its historic meaning, marking the closure of a political era known as the 1955 Regime. The 1955 Regime refers to the long rule by the LDP that began in 1955 when the party was founded. Under this regime, the Japan Socialist Party was the largest opposition party. Postwar Japanese political history thus developed in terms of conflict and compromise between these two parties.

[63] *Nihon Keizai Shimbun*, December 24, 1994, 3; December 31, 1994, 3.

[64] Although the Long-term Care Insurance was not legislated until after the first Lower House election under the new rules, this program should nonetheless be considered as a result of the politics characterized by the coalitions.

Nonetheless, the return of the LDP to power in June 1994 also brought back distributive pressures from individual LDP members. The LDP-led coalition government under Prime Minister Murayama was more willing to dispense pork to rural areas than the non-LDP coalition. Major public works spending projects that had been suspended under the Hosokawa government were restarted. The Murayama government also approved a huge multiyear agricultural budget. This budget was intended to compensate farmers for the partial liberalization of rice imports included as part of the Uruguay Round Agreements under the Hosokawa government (Ito 2000, 222). Under the MMD/SNTV system, both conservative and socialist politicians from rural districts had high stakes in distributive benefits for rural areas. The government also bailed out the financial arm of the agricultural cooperatives (*nokyo*), covering its losses from an exposure to housing loan (*jusen*) problems. Japan's agricultural cooperatives still constituted one of the most important political machines for the LDP.[65]

It is noteworthy that, in spite of the continuing flow of money to rural areas, the regulatory scheme for agriculture was reformed. The 1995 Law for Stabilization of Supply, Demand, and Prices of Staple Food reversed the previous policy and adopted a market mechanism (Mulgan 2000, chapter 8). The absence of market mechanisms in many agricultural product markets had been costing urban voters a lot in terms of both higher consumer prices and tax revenue spent on rural subsidies. Sakigake was the only coalition partner oriented toward unorganized urban voters, and it generally pushed the LDP-led coalition to pay attention to urban voters' needs. Although Sakigake was an extremely small party compared to the LDP, its influence was magnified by its veto power. The LDP-led coalition negotiated on every policy area in what they called "project teams." The membership composition in each project team was equitably allocated to all three coalition partners, thereby allowing each party power to veto.

Family Care Leave: An Unusually Swift Legislation

The legislative processes for the Family Care Leave and the Long-term Care Insurance underscore the dynamics in the LDP-led coalition. They both illustrate how, just as in the case of the non-LDP coalition, the presence of multiple political parties benefited wage earners to a much greater degree than under the old LDP rule. Furthermore, as veto players increased, the scope of bureaucratic agenda-setting power increased.

The successful introduction of the Family Care Leave came as a surprise even to the Ministry of Labor bureaucrats themselves, due to the unprecedented speed with which the initial idea of a family care leave became law.[66] This anomaly was

---

[65] Mulgan (2000, chapter 6) provides a thorough account of Japanese agricultural politics. She shows how the legal foundation and the role of *nokyo* provided two key pillars of Japanese agricultural politics.

[66] Labor bureaucrats themselves state that they would not have been able to introduce a new statutory program so swiftly had it not been for the presence of parliamentary veto players interested in family care leave. Interview, Women's Bureau, Ministry of Labor, July 24, 1995.

a direct consequence of the emergence of coalition governments with pro-labor parties. When the LDP held an absolute majority, the introduction of any statutory benefit for workers usually took an extremely long time. Often it took several years after a particular legislative issue came onto the agenda. For instance, even after precursors to the statutory Childcare Leave had been around for more than a decade, a mandatory leave policy emerged only in 1991 when the LDP was forced to compromise with the opposition. As mentioned earlier, the LDP's aversion to statutory leaves was due to employers' opposition. Most importantly, the LDP was very sensitive to opposition from small and medium-sized firms, which constituted part of the political machine of many individual LDP Diet members. Small enterprises were generally against increases in their social security contributions and any new labor regulations, whether mandatory leaves or regulations about work conditions. Given the LDP's hostility, the Ministry of Labor adopted a very long-term strategy. Labor bureaucrats would typically not even try to impose a statutory program from the beginning. They would first educate employers and promote a corporate version of whatever program they were interested in. Once a critical mass of large firms adopted the program at the enterprise level, then the Ministry of Labor would propose turning it into a statutory program, while giving a multiyear moratorium for smaller employers. During this moratorium, employers were simply asked to "make efforts" (*doryoku gimu*) to introduce a specific benefit. Only after the program was accepted by most companies would the program become legally binding.

The Family Care Leave did not follow the usual pattern, precisely because the LDP was no longer the sole ruling party. Recall that Hosokawa's non-LDP coalition government had promised to submit a family care leave bill by the 1995 Diet session. Although the non-LDP coalition broke down, Murayama's LDP-led coalition government kept family leave on the agenda. Murayama's Japan Socialist Party had a stake in introducing a family care leave. Its biggest organized supporter, Rengo, the peak labor association, was keen on introducing a statutory family care leave. In 1993, about 81,000 workers quit their job to look after an old parent (or an in-law). That number was estimated to rise to 219,000 by 2025.[67] In contrast to Rengo, Nikkeiren generally preferred the expansion of public care services rather than a statutory paid family care leave.[68] Under the Murayama government, the Socialists in the Upper House – where they possessed more seats than in the Lower House – demanded the introduction of statutory family care leave, and eventually the Murayama Cabinet submitted a bill to the Diet in 1995 – just as the Hosokawa government had planned.[69]

As for the content of the new statutory leave, it had to be acceptable to all coalition partners – and by extension their core constituents. The first round of negotiations took place in the relevant *shingikai*, the Women and Youth Issues Council.

---

[67] *Asahi Shimbun*, December 10, 1994, 4. Rengo leaders considered family care more urgent and important than child care leave.
[68] *Nikkei Shimbun*, November 7, 1994, 13; an interview at Nikkeiren, 1997.
[69] *Asahi Shimbun*, October 8, 1994, 7; *Nikkei Shimbun*, June 2, 1995, 2.

The representatives from Rengo and Nikkeiren, however, failed to reach an agreement in the *shingikai*. Rengo wanted a one-year leave with paid benefits and also demanded a broad definition of family care. Employers wanted a three-month leave, no benefits, and a narrow definition of family care. As far as small firms were concerned, they wanted a long grace period. Ultimately, the Ministry of Labor drew up a compromise plan and submitted it to the *shingikai* for the social part-ners in the *shingikai* to consider.[70] Rather than creating a separate law, the labor bureaucrats chose to reform the Childcare Leave to include additional conditions and terms of the new leave, to be called the Childcare and Family Care Leave (Ikuji Kaigo Kyugyo). The compromise draft primarily reflected the employ-ers' concerns. Strong employer opposition – especially from smaller firms – would have led to a veto by the LDP.[71]

In recognizing the importance of the LDP's core constituents' needs, the labor bureaucrats (i) limited the length of the leave to three months; (ii) defined family care narrowly as care of family members in the same household; (iii) did not create paid benefits; and (iv) provided a long grace period for small firms by pushing back the implementation of the new statutory leave to April 1999.[72] Despite the efforts of Rengo to force the Japan Socialist Party to modify the bill in ways that were more favorable to workers, the Socialist Prime Minister Murayama was bound by the possible veto of his coalition partner, LDP.[73] The Cabinet-sponsored bill ultimately submitted to the Diet was the same as the compromise draft prepared by labor bureaucrats. The government also promised to make it easier for employers to hire replacement workers during the statutory leaves of their employees by further deregulation of labor contracts.

Although Rengo did not get everything it demanded, the swift legislation of yet another statutory leave was quite remarkable. Employers really were against the introduction of another statutory leave, and such legislation would have been unthinkable under the old LDP rule.[74] Indeed, the increase in the number of

[70] *Asahi Shimbun*, January 11, 1995, 2; *Asahi Shimbun*, evening edition, January 24, 1994, 2.
[71] During the summer of 1994, the labor bureaucrats visited more than one hundred business leaders in their prelegislative attempt to get the leaders to understand the need for statutory family care leave. It had taken painstaking efforts by the labor bureaucrats to get the employers to accept.
[72] For more detail, see *Shakai Hosho Junpo*, no. 1877, June 21, 1995, 21.
[73] Rengo was more politically assertive than usual. Not only did it possess strong influence over the Japan Socialist Party in the government, but it also possessed power over the largest opposition party, Shinshinto (New Frontier Party). (The Democratic Socialist Party, which had close ties with many private sector unions, had dismantled itself to create the Shinshinto together with the New Japan Party, Ichiro Ozawa's group, Social Democratic League, and part of Komeito. See Curtis 1999, appendix 1, for a succinct mapping of party realignment during the period between 1955 and 1999.) Both the Japan Socialist Party and Shinshinto, therefore, were competing to appease Rengo. Rengo convinced Shinshinto to submit a more generous alternative legislative bill, hoping to gain more concessions on the Diet floor (*Asahi Shimbun*, March 15, 1995, 7; April 16, 1995, 2; May 14, 1995, 3; June 5, 1995, 1). Nonetheless, Prime Minister Murayama, the Japan Socialist Party leader, was not happy with Rengo's strategy. In his view, Rengo was rocking the foundation of the Socialist-LDP-Sakigake coalition (*Nihon Keizai Shimbun*, March 20, 1995, 2).
[74] A Labor Ministry official involved in the legislative process recalls that employers really were against this statutory leave. By 1995, the economic situation had worsened and employers were not in the mood to tolerate labor cost increases. (The timing coincided with the general economic

parliamentary veto players clearly expanded the range of constituent groups that stood to gain from public policy. The Ministry of Labor seized the opportunity to expand other programs for wage earners under their jurisdiction. They succeeded in expanding the existing Workers' Asset Formation Program (the *zaikei*), which was a tax-deferred employer-sponsored savings account.

Bureaucrats' success in implementing their favorite policies was largely contingent on the desire of parliamentary veto players. In spite of the labor bureaucrats' success in introducing a new statutory leave and expanding existing ones, its plan to create something resembling a new care insurance scheme went nowhere.[75] The labor bureaucrats were also interested in creating paid family care benefits to pay for elderly care services. Recall that elderly care services were a big growth sector of the economy. Because the Labor Ministry oversaw public personnel dispatching services, the idea was to put the two together to venture into a "new business." Politicians did not have any interest in such an insurance scheme, and the idea did not make it onto the policy agenda.[76] This failure of the labor bureaucrats contrasts with the success of the welfare bureaucrats in introducing a major new insurance scheme. The difference, in the words of a Labor Ministry official, was that the Ministry of Welfare's plan involved dispensing money to build physical infrastructure – more care-providing facilities – which created lucrative distributive opportunities for politicians to take advantage of. The Ministry of Labor's plan only involved dispatching workers registered in public employment agencies to those who needed their services – something that did not generate a financial stake for politicians.

Long-term Care Insurance

Like the Family Care Leave, it was also the Hosokawa Cabinet that initially got the ball rolling on Long-term Care Insurance. By the end of 1993, the welfare bureaucrats had come up with a basic blueprint for a new elderly care insurance scheme. When power changed hands, the Ministry of Welfare was in the midst of preparing a revised Gold Plan (the New Gold Plan) as well as preparing to introduce a care insurance scheme.[77]

As far as the Ministry of Welfare was concerned, the continuing presence of the Japan Socialist Party and Sakigake in the ruling coalition was beneficial, because these parties had already agreed on the socialization of elderly care. When the LDP returned to power, the coalition partners supported the efforts

---

downturn related to the bursting of the bubble as well as the rapid appreciation of the yen, which hurt the manufacturing sector.) Interview at the Women's Bureau, Ministry of Labor, 1995.

[75] A Labor Ministry official involved in the legislative process for the statutory family care leave stated that the ministry was interested in creating paid family care benefits to pay for care services. Interview at the Women's Bureau, Ministry of Labor, 1995.

[76] Interview at the Ministry of Labor, 1995.

[77] The Ministry of Welfare created a special team for elderly care policies in April 1994. On the last day of the non-LDP Hata Cabinet, it created another study group (June 30, 1994). All the ministerial activities continued despite changes in power.

by the Ministry of Welfare to introduce a new care system for the elderly.[78] The Ministry of Finance, which typically opposed any costly new programs, supported the creation of a program as a necessary quid pro quo to justify the hike in the consumption tax. Needless to say, in their capacity as the budgeting authority, they also had a stake in remedying the moral hazards in the health care system for the elderly.

In fact, in September 1994, the new coalition partners created a project team dedicated to the issue of socialization of elderly care. During the old LDP rule, bureaucrats sought the consent of the PARC members to ensure a successful legislative process; now bureaucrats had to gain approval from Sakigake and JSP members of the project team as well. The welfare bureaucrats opted for creating a *shingikai* with much broader membership to get all vested interest groups to deliberate – and more importantly agree – on their basic blueprint. In October 1994, the Ministry of Welfare called for the first meeting of the newly created *shingikai* on the Elderly Health and Welfare to set a timetable for deliberations on the creation of a social insurance scheme for frail elderly care. The *shingikai* membership consisted of representatives from (i) providers of medical services;[79] (ii) providers of welfare and social services;[80] (iii) municipal governments;[81] (iv) Nikkeiren, Rengo, and the Federation of Health Care Cooperatives (Kenporen); and (v) the public sector union of municipal government employees (Jichiro). Jichiro made it into the council primarily because it was one of the major organized constituencies of the Japan Socialist Party. In short, the Ministry hoped to get pre–Diet approval from the core constituent groups of parliamentary veto players in the *shingikai* by the end of 1995 and to submit a legislative bill in the Diet sessions in early 1996.[82] This timeline was set with a view to implementing the new insurance as of April 1997 when the consumption tax rate was to be increased to 5 percent. The Ministry of Finance, too, was eager to have the new program coincide with the tax hike.

Opposition from within the *shingikai*, however, thwarted the timetable planned by the welfare bureaucrats. No final agreement emerged by the end of 1995 as

[78] Based on interviews with politicians and welfare bureaucrats, Mikiko Eto (1998, 79) reports that the coalition partners did not oppose a new system devised by bureaucrats, but they did not actively push for it either.

[79] This group, in turn, included the Japan Medical Association, the Japan Dentists' Association, and Japan Pharmacists' Association.

[80] Representatives of the existing nonprofit welfare organizations that provide social services for municipal governments.

[81] As administrators of the fiscally strained National Health Care Cooperatives, municipal governments had a large stake in reducing the medical cost for the elderly. Although municipal governments potentially gained from a new elderly care scheme that would reduce the cost pressure on municipal health care, they were wary of any attempt by the Ministry of Welfare to make them the responsible administrative units of the new elderly care scheme.

[82] In July 1995, the Social Security Systems Council issued its first recommendation in thirty-three years to increase social services for middle-class citizens. It recommended that the government provide a broader range of choices of services in exchange for an adequate level of users' fees, granted that the bulk of the service costs be covered by social insurance revenue and general tax revenue. For the details of the discussions and the content of the recommendation, see an article written by one of the committee members, Kotani (1995).

planned, and negotiations continued into 1996. The major opposition came from municipal governments rather than the Japan Medical Association or Nikkeiren. This came as a surprise to the welfare bureaucrats. In anticipating opposition from employers and the Japan Medical Association, the welfare bureaucrats had been working with them for quite some time. "Social hospitalization" was an important source of income for privately owned small hospitals, whose owners were vocal members of the Japan Medical Association (JMA) and vital members of LDP politicians' political machines. These hospital owners vehemently opposed any new policy that placed elderly patients away from their facilities. The Ministry of Welfare, therefore, had agreed to designate such small hospitals as eligible to be reimbursed from the new care insurance. Instead of applying a strict separation of medical and nonmedical care providers, these small hospitals were to be licensed to care for the elderly who required nonmedical care. As a result, the JMA was in principle supportive of the new insurance scheme. Nikkeiren, however, was unhappy about the levies on employers introduced by the new social insurance scheme.[83] The Ministry's plan hoped to collect insurance contributions from residents above the age of twenty although only those above the age of sixty-five were eligible to receive care services. Employers wanted the age of compulsory enrollment to be raised in order to minimize their contribution for employees. Big business, in particular, argued that the new care services should be financed by the general tax revenue by increasing the consumption tax.[84]

Unexpectedly, the strongest opposition came from municipal governments. The welfare bureaucrats had assumed that municipal governments would support a new elderly care insurance program. In their thinking, a new insurance would reduce the high costs of "social hospitalization" and thus improve the fiscal conditions of the National Healthcare Cooperatives administered by municipal governments. Municipal governments did not see it that way. Instead they feared two possible outcomes. First, the new care insurance might lead to drastic increases in demand for public services in excess of their fiscal abilities and their infrastructure. Second, they might encounter problems in collecting contributions for the new insurance.[85] For these reasons, municipal governments preferred to offer cash benefits to family care givers as a way of reducing demands for public services.[86]

---

[83] Despite some disagreement, Nikkeiren supported the new care insurance scheme, which unlike the health care insurance, required the elderly themselves to contribute to the insurance as well as pay 10 percent of the costs out of pocket. In any case, welfare bureaucrats explained that employers' overall social security contributions would not change. Interview at Nikkeiren with Takanashi, July 1997.

[84] See *Nihon Keizai Shimbun*, December 10, 1996, 5. The business associations Keidanren and Keizai Doyukai were much more hostile to new social security contributions than was Nikkeiren. Big business – and the Ministry of Finance – grew highly concerned that the planned consumption tax hike was only 5 percent rather than the initially planned 7 percent. It was the emergence of serious financial troubles in housing mortgage companies that created political conditions that led to the moderation of the planned tax hike. See Arioka (1996, 8–9).

[85] Municipal governments had chronic problems collecting contributions from enrollees in the National Health Care Cooperatives. They worried that the new insurance scheme would suffer from the same problem.

[86] Germany, one of the few other countries that provide long-term care insurance, offers cash benefits to family members.

Public interest representatives in the *shingikai*, however, opposed such benefits on feminist grounds. They argued that cash benefits to family members would promote the perpetual role of women as care providers rather than promoting the socialization of the elderly care (Eto 1998).

The Ministry was still very eager to draft a workable compromise so that they could submit a bill to the regular spring Diet session in 1996. Various compromises were attempted but the municipal governments continued to resist. It should be noted here that the Ministry of Welfare's plan included no cash benefits for family members. As we know now, the Long-term Care Insurance Bill that was later legislated did not include such cash benefits. It is difficult to believe that a feminist concern in *shingikai* affected the policy outcome. In fact, some LDP politicians were supportive of such benefits on grounds of rewarding family values. It thus makes more sense to think that the Ministry of Welfare had included a feminist in the *shingikai* for its own purpose. It was not difficult to imagine that the feminist argument would have made it difficult for the Japan Socialist and Sakigake to support cash benefits for the fear of appearing too conservative and "reactionary." Indeed, cash benefits to family members would have hindered the Ministry of Welfare's plan to boost the growth of the silver industry under its own jurisdiction.[87] I want to emphasize here that the Ministry's plan was *not* to expand public care services. *Its aim was to socialize the cost to pay for the services provided by the private sector.* Needless to say, for LDP politicians, growth of a new sector that would be highly dependent on income from a government program meant welcome opportunities for potentially lucrative political meddling.[88]

The timing of the Lower House elections was critical in understanding the delay in the legislative development. The coalition partners' attitudes began to diverge as the Lower House elections approached. Sakigake and Socialists were in favor of legislating some sort of compromise so that they could claim their policy achievement at the polls. Precisely for this reason, some senior LDP politicians were averse to the idea of submitting the bill to the Diet under the coalition with Sakigake and Socialists. Moreover, many LDP Diet members were hesitant to introduce a program so strongly opposed by mayors, especially in an election year. Although the new electoral rules eventually changed the relationship between Diet members and local politicians, the Lower House Diet members still relied at this point on local politicians to campaign for them. The LDP's electoral calculations delayed the legislative process significantly (Eto 1998, 86 and also footnote 19). The LDP politicians finally worked out a compromise plan that reduced the burden on employers and local governments.[89]

---

[87] Since the introduction of the Gold Plan, the number of entrants into the silver industry grew rapidly. As of 1995, it was already a 50-billion-yen industry. See *Nihon Keizai Shimbun*, March 9, 1995, 38; March 27, 1995, 29; April 7, 1995, 27.

[88] A couple of high-ranking Ministry of Welfare officials were arrested on bribery charges. They had both used their discretion over government licensing of elderly care facilities – and related subsidies – for private gains.

[89] This was called the Niwa Plan. This plan, among other things, raised the age of compulsory enrollment in the new insurance from the planned twenty years old to forty-five, thus easing the cost pressure on employers. See Ikeda (1996, 66).

Meanwhile, the LDP-led coalition was beginning to fall apart. Not only did the coalition partners begin to pursue their own electoral strategies, but the realignment of political parties was affecting the party system itself. The opposition parties were uniting their forces to create one large opposition party to position themselves better for their first fight under the SMD-dominant mixed system. The Japan Socialist Party basically split into two groups – one group staying in power with the LDP and the other group joining other opposition parties. The group that stayed in the coalition now called themselves the Japan Democratic Socialist Party. In January 1996, the LDP president Ryutaro Hashimoto succeeded Prime Minister Murayama to head the LDP-Socialist-Sakigake coalition (see Appendix C). The defeat of Sakigake and the Japan Democratic Socialist Party (formerly the Japan Socialist Party) in the October 1996 elections further diminished their importance in the coalition. The two parties lost cabinet positions in the post-election Cabinet reshuffle.

Because the LDP still lacked enough votes in the Diet, however, Sakigake and the Japan Democratic Socialist Party stayed in the coalition. When the new Long-term Care Insurance was finally legislated in 1997, it occurred under this coalition. This is why it makes sense to think of this program as something enabled by the dynamics of the LDP-led coalition government, although I categorize 1997 as a new period from the perspective of the structural logic. Nonetheless, the enhanced LDP's power made it possible for the LDP government to introduce one more concession to employers. The LDP government raised wage earners' health care copayments from 10 percent to 20 percent. Needless to say, this eased the financial state of employer-sponsored health care cooperatives, saving employers considerable money. It is very unlikely that the Socialists and Sakigake would have agreed to such a concession under the terms of their coalition with the LDP prior to the elections.[90]

CONCLUSION

This chapter has demonstrated how policies changed when the structural configurations changed in Japan. Once the configuration of parliamentary veto players in Japan began to resemble that of many European MMD systems, policy outcomes became similar. What used to be structurally difficult became easier. The coalition governments found it easier to raise taxes than the previous LDP governments. The partial minority government and the two different types of coalition governments all pushed the pendulum in favor of more comprehensive benefits so that all veto players had something to gain. The participation of parties of the left in the ruling coalition, in particular, ensured the distributive advantage of wage earners – and unionized workers in particular. For the first time, the government began expanding social services for wage earners and their families.

At the same time, the persistence of a multimember district system meant that core constituent groups of parliamentary veto players continued to enjoy

---

[90] After the 1996 Lower House elections, the seat shares of the two parties declined so much that they could no longer maintain parity in legislative project teams as before.

distributive advantages. Recall that MMD systems favor organized groups of voters rather than unorganized voters. In this sense, some of the old practices of social protection continued. Many of the functional equivalent programs targeted at specific organized groups remained intact during the period discussed in this chapter. In addition, new groups also gained from public policy. Ironically, Jichiro, the public sector union and the core constituent of the Japan Socialist Party, gained most under the LDP-led coalition.[91] Needless to say, expansion in public provision of social services benefited Jichiro. Each parliamentary veto player could block unfavorable changes that might affect its organized constituency groups.

As a consequence, despite Prime Minister Hosokawa's commitment to deregulation as a policy priority, nothing much happened. A very important aspect of Japan's social protection system – whereby the government protected firms by anti-competitive regulation – persisted under both the non-LDP coalition and the LDP-led coalition. Japan's organized groups – whether unions, trade associations, or other occupational groups – all gained from such regulation. Similarly, other functional equivalents such as public works and wage subsidies to deliver protection via one's work also continued for the same reasons. Nor was there any change in the state-controlled savings-oriented welfare programs. Someone like Hosokawa, whose party relied on the support of unorganized voters, clearly wanted to challenge the status quo. Nonetheless, his coalition included established parties that had developed close ties with organized groups under the MMD system. Such parties were intent on maintaining benefits for their core organized groups.

Despite changes in the parliamentary veto player configuration, bureaucrats continued to enjoy high degrees of influence. As Chapter 2 specified, the presence of multiple parliamentary veto players is likely to create more leverage for bureaucrats. During the period under study here, bureaucrats continued to be able to ally themselves with specific veto players to block unwanted changes. Furthermore, welfare and labor bureaucrats found new allies in non-LDP veto players. The emergence of union-affiliated veto players, in particular, opened new legislative possibilities for welfare and labor bureaucrats. The peak-level labor federation, Rengo, had a strong interest in maintaining a channel of direct participation in the policy process via *shingikai*. The persisting role of *shingikai* ensured that bureaucrats retained their agenda-setting power. As demonstrated in this chapter, many new programs for wage earners were introduced, all of which increased the amount of resources available for welfare and labor bureaucrats. Clearly, as implied in the structural logic, bureaucrats could never override vetoes by parliamentary veto players. Bureaucrats were only successful when pushing for a particular program that promoted parliamentary veto players' interests. Nonetheless, they had the capacity to mold the programmatic details of new programs that elicited little interest from the parliamentary veto players.

[91] Shinoda (1996) chronicles how unions benefited from the new political configurations during the period under study in this chapter.

APPENDIX 8.A. *Chronology of Governments (1987–1996)*

Prime Minister	Dates in Office	Why Left Office
Noboru Takeshita	1987.11.6–1989.6.3	Consumption Tax, Recruit Scandal
Sosuke Uno	1989.6.3–1989.8.10	The LDP's Electoral Loss in July (Upper House)
Toshiki Kaifu	1989.8.10–1991.11.5	Partial Minority Government
Kiichi Miyazawa	1991.11.5–1993.8.9	Partial Minority Government, Split of the LDP
Morihiro Hosokawa	1993.8.9–1994.4.28	New Japan Party, Sakigake, Socialists, Clean Politics Party, Democratic Socialists, and Shinsei-to
Tsutomu Hata	1994.4.28–1994.6.30	Non-LDP Coalition Government
Tomiichi Murayama	1994.6.30–1996.1.11	LDP-Socialist-Sakigake Coalition Government
Ryutaro Hashimoto	1996.1.11–1996.11.7	LDP-Socialist-Sakigake Coalition Government

The next chapter turns to the most recent period. This is the period when Japan began to diverge from the northern European path observed in this chapter. The new SMD-dominant electoral rules and a series of legislative rule changes transformed the profile of the median Diet member as well as the relationship between the LDP leadership and its rank and file. These rule changes pushed Japan out of the MMD/Coalition Government category and into the SMD/Coalition Government category. For the reasons already discussed in Chapter 3, this SMD/Coalition Government category is very similar to the SMD/Majority Party category.[92] In other words, the structural logic approach suggests that Japanese welfare politics began moving in the direction of a Westminster-style democracy as in Britain rather than something resembling the coalition governments in many European countries. Chapter 9 shows that such a shift is indeed under way in Japan.

[92] For the sake of simplicity, I am assuming here, as I did in Chapter 3, that the constitutional structure remains the same. In other words, I am assuming that the constitutional structure is centralized as in a unicameral parliamentary system. In reality, Japan has a strong bicameral system, and this changes the dynamics. I will come back to this point in greater detail later.

9

The End of Japan's Social Protection as We Know It

Becoming Like Britain?

The structural logic approach put forth in this book predicts the most likely policy outcomes on the basis of the government type, party strength, and district magnitude. This chapter applies the logic to explain why Japan's social protection system began to change fundamentally in the post-1996 period. At first sight, there appears to be little difference between the pre-1996 and the post-1996 periods: the government type remained the same – that is, coalition governments. This apparent continuity, however, masked a tidal shift in Japanese politics that occurred after the electoral and legislative rules were changed in the latter half of the 1990s. In October 1996 the Lower House adopted a SMD-dominant mixed electoral system, requiring the typical Lower House politician to compete for a single seat in her district. This chapter covers the period from the 1996 Lower House elections through to 2006.

Of critical importance here is the centralization of decision making within the LDP as a consequence of the new electoral rules. The LDP leadership had always found it very difficult to impose its will on the party, due to the weakening of the party that occurred under the MMD/SNTV system.[1] Japan's MMD/SNTV system had empowered intraparty veto players, such as *habatsu* leaders and subcommittees of the Policy Affairs Research Council (PARC), which were allied with different ministries. Under the new electoral rules, the elimination of intraparty competition eroded the basis of the old LDP politics by making it possible for the party leader to centralize the party. A series of legislative rules introduced after the electoral reform further strengthened the LDP prime minister's authority over the party.

---

[1] Chapter 5 has demonstrated how the LDP leadership failed to steer the party away from its rural organized base to capture the newly expanding mass of urban voters. While some scholars – Pempel among others – argue that the LDP had become a catch-all party, Kobayashi demonstrates empirically that the LDP *did not* shift to favor urban voters (see Pempel 1982; Kobayashi 1997, 160–161). The LDP kept its hold on power with a declining vote share, which slipped below 50 percent in 1963 and never recovered (Kobayashi 1997, 152).

These changes pushed the Japanese political structure toward the Westminster system – a greater concentration of power in the hands of the prime minister under a SMD electoral system. Following the structural logic developed in Chapter 2, it is possible to make some predictions concerning the likely impact on Japan's social protection system. In short, we can expect this protection system to resemble that in the United Kingdom. This means four things: (i) a move away from fragmented forms of social protection targeted at organized constituent groups; (ii) a shift toward more universalistic – but meager – benefits; (iii) distributive bias in favor of competitive districts; and (iv) a reduction in bureaucratic discretion.

Let me briefly recapitulate here the argument of Chapter 2. Under a SMD system, there are few electoral benefits to social protection programs targeted at specific occupational groups. The SMD system makes an electoral backlash against the ruling party more likely, because minor shifts in vote shares can lead to a big swing in seats. Under such a system, it is necessary to appeal to unorganized voters. The old tactic of diverting pork and "rent" to particularistic organized groups in exchange for votes and money no longer carries the advantage it did under the MMD/SNTV electoral system. The need to appeal to unorganized voters, in turn, leads political parties to favor universalistic benefits. Some geographical targeting of benefits – frequently observed under the MMD/SNTV electoral system – is likely to occur under the new system, but for different reasons. Under a SMD system with concentrated power, the party leader is likely to allocate more resources to swing districts to maximize the party's overall electoral performance. A greater concentration of power in the hands of the leader of the ruling party (the prime minister) can be expected to reduce bureaucrats' power for two reasons. First, the greater agenda-setting power of the prime minister diminishes the scope of bureaucrats' agenda-setting power. Second, the smaller number of veto players within the ruling party reduces the bureaucrats' capacity to use intraparty veto players against the party leader.[2]

Ironically, however, a greater concentration of power at the center is not likely to boost the state's extractive capacity. Highly concentrated political power combined with a SMD system (or a SMD-dominant system like that of Japan) makes policies such as tax increases on the majority electorally risky (for the reasons why, see Chapter 2). The combination of the greater concentration of power and the SMD electoral system is thus likely to lead to universalistic but meager public benefits – very much like those of the British welfare state.

THE ELECTORAL REFORM AND THE PARTY CENTRALIZATION OF THE LDP

The changes that occurred in the post-1996 period were fundamentally different from the changes that took place during the period following the LDP's electoral loss in 1989 in the Upper House. The post-1996 transformation of Japanese politics was brought about by electoral and legislative rule changes. The

---

[2] The scope of bureaucratic discretion declines as bureaucrats lose the advantage of multiple veto players as their strategic allies (Chapter 2).

centralization of the LDP constituted the most important aspect of this post-1996 transformation. Recall that Chapter 3 discussed the precise ways in which the MMD/SNTV system prevented the LDP from becoming a centralized party. Intraparty veto players such as *habatsu*, Somukai, and PARC all owed their power and continuity to the effects of the MMD/SNTV electoral system.[3] The Lower House elections in 1996, however, dismantled institutional barriers to a more centralized decision-making system within the LDP.

The Lower House elections in 1996 produced the first cohort of politicians elected under the new mixed system. This new system consisted of two tiers – one with single-member districts, the other with proportional representation. In contrast to the MMD/SNTV electoral system, candidates no longer competed against their fellow party members in the same district. Parties nominated one single official candidate per district in the SMD tier. In the PR tier, all candidates shared the votes cast for the party. For the first time, the LDP candidates could campaign on their party's policy platform. This was an enormous shift in Japanese politics. Under the MMD/SNTV electoral system, the LDP did not function as a cohesive party. It was prevented from doing so by *habatsu* leaders, Somukai, and the subcommittees of PARC. The MMD/SNTV electoral system, in short, created and justified the highly decentralized nature of the LDP and its government. The removal of the MMD/SNTV electoral system meant the weakening of the power basis of *habatsu*, Somukai, and PARC subcommittees. The pendulum of power swung in favor of the party label and the party leader.

The disappearance of intraparty competitions at the polls changed the incentives of individual Diet members and the intraparty power dynamics. Three changes are particularly significant in understanding Japanese politics at this time. First, PARC subcommittees lost their raison d'être as a device to divide votes among fellow LDP representatives from the same district. Under the MMD/SNTV system, the *habatsu* leaders used to negotiate on behalf of their members for slots in specific PARC subcommittees. The party also used to compile an official list of its PARC subcommittee members to be distributed. The list was an important instrument for individual LDP politicians to signal to their respective constituent groups the "policy efforts" undertaken on their behalf. After the 1996 elections, the party stopped compiling an official list of the membership of each PARC subcommittee. Politicians' objectives in joining PARC subcommittees changed.[4]

The second key change at the time involved the *habatsu*, whose electoral and financial importance declined precipitously. Without intraparty electoral

---

[3] All the relevant literature has been discussed in Chapter 3.

[4] Pekkanen, Nyblade, and Krauss (2006) argue that PARC membership is still important for distributive purposes and that the LDP appears to be assigning politicians from more competitive districts to more pork-oriented PARC subcommittees rather than high-policy subcommittees. Although the gist of their argument is compatible with my structural logic, social welfare issues do not represent high-policy issues as Pekkanen et al. portray. Policy decisions on health care and elderly care affect "rent" available for service provider groups and have a strong component of "pork."

competition in the MMD/SNTV electoral system, LDP candidates no longer relied on the backing from *habatsu* to run for office. All they needed was official endorsement by the party. Gone were the days when a *habatsu* candidate could run without the LDP endorsement against LDP official candidates. The new reform of the Electoral Campaign Law that accompanied the 1994 Electoral Reform further reduced the importance of *habatsu* for individual politicians. This reform introduced generous government-provided funding (*seito joseikin*) for political parties. The money was paid to the party and the party leadership allocated it to the rank and file. The records show that fund-raising activities of *habatsu* dropped almost immediately after the reform and did not recover.[5] Although the *habatsu* remained as intraparty groupings, their role changed drastically.[6]

The third important change at this time concerned the change in the rank and file politicians' attitude toward their party leader. For the first time, they had a strong incentive to choose a popular leader. In a parliamentary democracy, a SMD-dominant mixed system establishes a direct link between a citizen's vote and the prime minister. As Maurice Duverger famously predicted, SMD systems are more likely to give rise to a two-party system by making it difficult for small parties to gain seats.[7] In Japan, while small parties persisted thanks to the PR tier, the introduction of the SMD tier led to the development of two large parties – which control 85 percent of the seats – as predicted.[8] In this situation, voters know that their votes – even votes cast for a specific candidate at the SMD tier – become de facto votes for a new prime minister, since the leader of the winning party (of the two large parties) becomes the prime minister. It is no coincidence that as electoral competition between the two largest parties intensified, the party leaders began to develop specific policy promises – called *manifestos* – offering voters different choices for a government. Although it was only in 2003 that every party began issuing its own policy manifesto before the elections, the evidence suggests that voters became more policy-oriented from the time the first Lower House elections took place under the new rules (see Figure 9.1).[9]

---

5 Based on *Yomiuri* newspaper reports, Takenaka (2006, 155) illustrates a big drop in *habatsu* factions' financial activities.

6 Today they mostly function as units to rally behind a particular candidate for the LDP presidential election. It is possible to predict on the basis of the structural logic that these groupings will increasingly be based on ideological and policy similarities.

7 Duverger (1954) predicted that the number of parties tends to become "one plus the electoral magnitude." In other words, in single-member districts, the number of political parties is predicted to fall to two.

8 Cox and Schoppa (2002) argue that Japan's mixed system prevents the development of a two-party system.

9 One might ask why voters' attitude changed for the Upper House elections although the electoral rules for the Upper House remained the same since 1983. The answer lies in the dominance of the Lower House in Japanese politics: it is the bigger and more dominant of the two Houses. It was only when the Lower House rules also changed that the overall weight of policy increased in the minds of Japanese voters. The big drop in LDP votes that occurred in 1989 (shown in Figure 9.1 for the Upper House) coincides with the election during which voters penalized the LDP over the introduction of the new consumption tax. For a full discussion of this issue, see Estévez-Abe and Sugawara, unpublished paper.

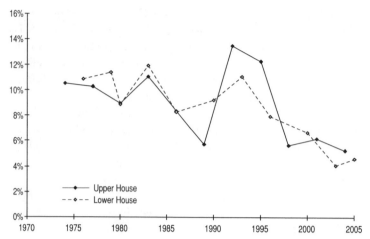

FIGURE 9.1. The Share of Votes Indifferent to Policy Issue at the Polls. *Source:* Akarui Senkyo Suishin Iinkai data, multiple years.

The greater importance of the party ticket, therefore, became interlinked with the popularity of the party leader. The popularity of the party leader affected the electoral fate of individual politicians more than ever before. Given the fact that a winning party has to court unorganized voters in a SMD-dominant system, a popular leader who can reach out to unorganized voters becomes highly valuable to the party members. Especially when the party leader is the prime minister, he enjoys a level of visibility beyond what any campaign ad can buy. The leader hence becomes the single most important deliverer of the party's platform.[10]

New post-1996 developments in the elections of the LDP president offer corroborating evidence of the transformation in the incentives facing the LDP rank and file. Choosing an electorally capable party leader became the new mantra of LDP politicians. In 1995, the LDP began holding public debates among contestants for the leadership, which were broadcast on television. This timing is important. In 1995, the LDP knew that whoever they selected as their leader would be the face of the party in the next round of the Lower House elections – the first elections to take place under the new electoral system. These public debates helped gauge the popular appeal of the candidates and their messages. This practice quickly took root, and the number of televised debates by LDP party presidential contenders has increased steadily. In 1995 and 1998, there were three televised debates; the number increased to five in 2001 and eight in 2003.[11]

[10] The Japanese practice of dual-listing SMD candidates on the PR list has made the popularity of the party and the party leader particularly valuable for SMD candidates who run in competitive districts. These candidates face a greater likelihood of losing their SMD seats. The more popular the party and the party leader, the better the chances of the defeated SMD candidates to gain seats via the PR tier.

[11] This tally of televised debates was collected from the television program schedules published daily in *Yomiuri Shimbun*. The data have been provided by Takako Hikotani.

In sum, an increasing interest in the personal qualities of political candidates emerged.[12]

Ryutaro Hashimoto was the winner of the 1995 race. In 1997, Hashimoto, a popular incumbent, was reelected without any opposition. The 1998 party presidential race, which took place following Hashimoto's resignation, was unprecedented.[13] *Habatsu*, which had always been the most important unit of candidate nomination and voting, lost control of the selection process. Candidates used to be *habatsu* leaders or, at the very least, were backed by their own *habatsu*. Each *habatsu* served as a voting bloc. Yet in 1998 Seiroku Kajiyama left his own faction, the Obuchi faction, to run for party president against his own faction leader, Keizo Obuchi. Something like that had never happened before. Many young Diet members supported Kajiyama, fearing that *habatsu*-based elections were unlikely to turn up the best person for the job.[14] These were a new cohort of politicians who began their career under the new system and were more sensitive to the importance of their leader. Although Kajiyama lost to Keizo Obuchi in the party presidential bid, more than a hundred votes were cast for Kajiyama by his fellow LDP Diet members. Kajiyama's formidable performance revealed that the rank and file were working with a new playbook.

The 2001 party presidential race provides further evidence of the changes afoot. Obuchi's term was brought to an abrupt end by his sudden death in April 2000. The LDP reverted to its old habits: a group of senior LDP party leaders convened by Obuchi's bed and appointed one of their own – Yoshiro Mori – as the new LDP party leader and, by extension, the new prime minister. The behind-the-scenes selection of the party leader proved to be a disaster. Many considered Mori to be unfit as prime minister. He soon resigned as his ratings plummeted. Learning from the mistake, the LDP devised new selection rules for their party presidential race in 2001.[15] The new rules were designed to enhance the voice of the local branches of the LDP as well as the "popular voice" of the fee-paying LDP supporters.[16] They specifically reduced the weight of the LDP Diet members' votes – thus further eroding the capacity of *habatsu* to influence the

---

[12] The television news shows did not use to feature individual candidates during the LDP presidential elections. This changed drastically in the post-1996 period. During the 1993 LDP presidential elections, TV networks used individual candidates' names only four times in their program descriptions. The number increased to sixteen, twenty-six, and fifty-four in 1995, 1998, and 2001 respectively.

[13] Otake (2003) shares the same view about the significance of the 1998 LDP presidential elections.

[14] From personal communications with Miyuki Hokugo, an *Asahi* newspaper journalist covering the story at the time. Taro Kono's web site was extremely insightful. He was one of the first-term LDP Diet members who supported Kajiyama's candidacy, and he depicted his daily interactions with his fellow LDP members very candidly in his web site. The site soon became a great source for journalists who were covering the 1998 LDP presidential election.

[15] Many came to question Mori's ability to serve as prime minister after his numerous blunders. He became famous for misspeaking, and his popularity suffered.

[16] Before 2001, ten thousand votes cast by fee-paying LDP supporters counted as one Diet member's vote. In 2001, the winner-take-all electoral college method was adopted. It was decided that whoever got the largest number of votes in a prefecture would take all votes assigned to the prefectural electoral college. Another important change was that the results of the prefectural

outcome. Junichiro Koizumi, who had never been a faction leader and had never played any leadership role within the LDP, defeated his opponent, Hashimoto, who was the head of the largest *habatsu*. Koizumi's victory was made possible by the new rules.[17] The rules themselves would never have been adopted were it not for the new electoral pressures that called for a popular party leader. The electoral changes set in motion a whole range of other rule changes in the Diet and in the government. All these changes pushed in the direction of a stronger prime minister and more visible party leaders.

LEGISLATIVE RULE CHANGES AND THE STRONGER PRIME MINISTER

Two sets of political reforms took place during the post-1996 period: (i) a strengthening of the prime minister; and (ii) a recalibration of the terms of bureaucratic delegation. Both were related to the electoral rule changes that had occurred earlier. This section, however, does not so much concern the origin of the legislative rule changes in the 1990s as it does their impact on the LDP government.[18]

Prime Minister Ryutaro Hashimoto – the first prime minister in the post-1996 period – carried out the first set of major political reforms. His reform, referred to as the Hashimoto Administrative Reform (Hashimoto Gyosei Kaikaku), was legislated in 1997 with an implementation date of January 2001. This reform consisted of the following four elements: (i) a revision of the Cabinet Law to grant the prime minister much greater agenda-setting power; (ii) an expansion of the Cabinet Secretariat; (iii) the creation of the Cabinet Office; and (iv) a reduction in the number of ministries and *shingikai*.[19] The goal of the new Cabinet Office was to assist the prime minister's legislative initiatives, thereby allowing the prime minister to overstep existing ministerial boundaries. The prime minister gained not only an expanded staff but also new tools to implement top-down policy making. These tools included special ministers that the prime minister could appoint to address specific policy issues. The hope was that such ministers, unattached to any ministries, would not be "captured" by career bureaucrats in their ministries. The Council of Economic and Fiscal Policy (Keizai Zaisei Shimon Kaigi), established within the Cabinet Office, was another important addition to the prime minister's tool box.[20] This council was to be chaired directly

votes came in before the Diet members' votes, preventing the Diet members' preferences from influencing regular LDP supporters' votes.

[17] He was popular among non–Diet members. The new electoral college–style voting method led to Koizumi's landslide. Under the old system where LDP Diet members' vote counted more than the popular vote, Koizumi would not have been elected.

[18] I discuss the process of rule changes elsewhere (see Estévez-Abe and Sugawara, unpublished paper).

[19] For the most thorough account of the Administrative Reform of 1997, see Tanaka and Okada (2000).

[20] Hiroshi Kato recounts that informal policy discussion meetings summoned by Prime Minister Hashimoto must have served as a blueprint for the Economic and Fiscal Council, which Hashimoto introduced as part of his Administrative Reform. Hashimoto regularly held informal policy discussions with the chairs of four critical *shingikai*. The four *shingikai* consisted of the Governmental Tax Council (Seifu Zeisei Chosakai), the Economic Council (Keizai Shingikai), the Fiscal System

by the prime minister and staffed by economic ministers and private experts close to the prime minister. Contrast this council to *shingikai*, which were appointed by bureaucrats. These bureaucrats would decide which organizations (that is, vested interest groups) were to be represented and which "scholars" would join the group to voice the ministry's own conception of "the public interest." In short, the prime minister's new tools not only concentrated power in his hands, they also constrained the power of bureaucrats.

The Hashimoto Administrative Reform was thus an attempt by the LDP leadership – Prime Minister Ryutaro Hashimoto, to be more precise – to centralize power and to enable a more top-down decision-making process. This meant containing the power of intraparty veto players as well as their bureaucratic allies. These reforms took place in the context of the introduction of a SMD-dominant electoral system, which increased competitive pressures on the LDP. LDP politicians recognized that a failure to resolve pressing policy issues might result in a loss of power. These policy issues – financial globalization, nonperforming loans, and others – were not, however, sufficient cause for the Hashimoto Administrative Reform. The rank-and-file LDP Diet members – and the senior politicians holding positions with veto power – would never have relinquished power to their leader, if the electoral logic of the SMD system had not been informing their self-interested calculations.

In 1999, Hashimoto's successor, Prime Minister Keizo Obuchi, also carried out a set of political reforms. The Obuchi Government – in coalition with the Liberal Party and Komeito – recalibrated the terms of bureaucratic delegation.[21] The Obuchi government undertook three key reforms in this area: (i) it abolished the government commissioners (*seifu iin*); (ii) it increased the number of junior minister positions to be staffed by Diet members; and (iii) it introduced a British-style prime minister's question time – *toshu toron* (literally, "party leader's debate.")[22] These changes were intended to make politicians more responsible for policy details to reduce their excessive dependence on bureaucrats. At the

Council (Zaisei Seido Shingikai), and the Social Security System Council (Shakai Hosho Seido Shingikai). These councils were under different ministerial jurisdictions – two were under the Ministry of Finance, one under the former Ministry of International Trade and Industry, and one under the Prime Minister's office. Despite the fact that these councils discussed policy solutions on issues that were deeply intertwined with one another, there was no lateral coordination because of the ministerial boundaries and the highly decentralized nature of the LDP itself. Strange as it may sound, it had been impossible for the Japanese government to concurrently deliberate on social security, taxation, and economic policy. Hashimoto's unofficial gatherings with the chairs thus marked a new willingness on the part of the LDP leader to laterally coordinate policy issues beyond ministerial boundaries and, in so doing, centralize the locus of decision making. Hiroshi Kato, one of the four chairs involved in the informal gatherings, makes this observation in his biography published as a newspaper column (Hiroshi Kato, "Jidai no Shogensha," *Nihon Keizai Shimbun*, February 27, 2007, 15).

21 In January 1999, Prime Minister Obuchi formed a formal coalition with a small conservative party, the Liberal Party (a break-off group from Shinshinto, the New Frontier Party). In October of the same year, Komeito formally joined the coalition, too. Ichiro Ozawa, the leader of the Liberal Party, played a key role in the reforms mentioned here.

22 On the introduction of junior ministers and the abolishment of Seifu Iin, see Takenaka (2002); for the overall changes, see Estévez-Abe (2006), Takako Hikotani (2004), and Takenaka (2006).

time, Japanese politicians were so heavily dependent on the bureaucracy that they had to rely on bureaucrats, appointed as special commissioners (*seifu iin*), to answer questions on the Diet floor. The 1999 reform abolished this practice and created junior cabinet positions as a way of training future ministers. The introduction of the prime minister's question time required party leaders capable of debate. The fact that the debate was televised increased the visibility of the prime minister and other party leaders.

It is also worth pointing out that post-1996 prime ministers resorted to various top-down councils chaired by themselves.[23] This can only be interpreted as the prime ministers' effort to control the policy agenda. These councils typically differed from *shingikai* in their membership compositions. Members were selected on the basis of their ideological proximity to the prime minister rather than their status as representatives of specific trades, sectors, and unions. Prime Minister Hashimoto's reform and Prime Minister Obuchi's reform together enhanced the power and the visibility of the prime minister,[24] although it was not until 2001 that the effects of the reforms were fully apparent. Figure 9.2 indicates that the visibility of the prime minister, measured by media exposure, dramatically increased from 2001 onward.[25] (Prime Minister Mori was in office at the time in 2001.)[26]

Junichiro Koizumi was the first LDP President to be elected on the basis of pure popular vote. Koizumi was able to take advantage of his popularity and the newly expanded position of the prime minister. His predecessors lacked both a popular mandate and the institutional advantages available to Koizumi. The fact that Koizumi did not rely on his fellow LDP Diet members' votes – and particularly *habatsu*-based voting – allowed him a great deal of autonomy. He challenged important unspoken rules in the LDP. First, he appointed his ministers by himself without any consultation with the *habatsu* leaders.[27] This was to break with the tradition of allocating cabinet positions to *habatsu* leaders who, in turn, nominated specific members. Second, Koizumi decided that Somukai's consensus was no longer necessary before his Cabinet could submit a legislative bill to the Diet. For Koizumi, majority rule was sufficient to make collective intraparty decisions. In abandoning traditional consensus rule, Koizumi immediately

[23] Of great importance to the Hashimoto Cabinet were two formal councils: the Administrative Reform Council (Gyosei Kaikaku Kaigi) and the Fiscal Structure Council (Zaisei Kozo Kaigi). As soon as Keizo Obuchi became prime minister in 1998, he created the Economic Strategy Council (Keizai Senryaku Kaigi) in the image of the American Council of Economic Advisers. In 1999, he created another one, Industrial Competitiveness Council (Sangyo Kyosoryoku Kaigi). Prime Minister Mori created the Fiscal Leadership Council (Zaisei Shuno Kaigi). Shimizu (2005) offers detailed descriptions of the political developments during this period of power concentration.
[24] Hikotani (2004) calls these reforms Hashimoto Reform and Ozawa Reform respectively. The second set of reforms – the ones introduced during the Obuchi government – were initiated by Ichiro Ozawa when his party, the Liberal Party, formed a coalition government with the LDP.
[25] Ikuo Kabashima, a well-known expert on electoral analysis in Japan, provides evidence that suggests that the importance of the party leader in affecting voters' choices has increased during this period (Kabashima 2004).
[26] Certainly, there are important differences between Prime Minister Mori and his successor, Prime Minister Koizumi. Koizumi was the first to be elected LDP president by a popular vote, whereas Mori became the LDP president without any proper procedure.
[27] Junior ministers were nominated on the basis of recommendations from *habatsu* leaders.

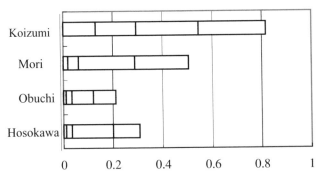

FIGURE 9.2. Visibility of Prime Ministers. *Note:* The relative visibility of prime ministers is calculated on the basis of the daily frequency in which a particular prime minister and his Cabinet were mentioned in the program guides of the four major news shows. *Source:* Data compiled by Ikuo Kabashima's students at Tokyo University and provided to the author by Taku Sugawara.

reduced the number of intraparty veto players. Third, Koizumi also changed the party rules over candidate nominations. He introduced age limits to candidates on the PR party list, thereby purging some senior politicians. All of Koizumi's actions were a function of the enhanced power allowed to the party leader under the new institutional rules.

As a result of these steps, the Koizumi Cabinet consisted of ministers chosen by the prime minister himself. Koizumi also appointed special ministers to carry out top-priority issues. In contrast to the United Kingdom, where Cabinet members typically have an elected seat in Parliament, a Japanese prime minister can appoint anyone to his Cabinet. Indeed, Koizumi appointed Heizo Takenaka, a nonpolitician, as one of his key economic ministers to oversee economic reforms.[28] Koizumi's choice reflected a desire to appoint someone loyal to his agenda, rather than to specific constituency groups or bureaucratic interests.

Koizumi was certainly an extremely able and astute politician.[29] But a large part of his power and strategy was a function of the new institutional context. Absent this context, there would have been no Prime Minister Koizumi. Furthermore, the new institutional context allowed Koizumi's successor, Prime Minister Shinzo Abe – who was neither able nor astute – to appoint his own cabinet and close-knit advisers. The new institutional context creates a much more powerful prime minister than that of the old system. It, however, does not guarantee that every prime minister will be able to use the new powers to his (and hopefully "her" one day) advantage. Certainly, Abe's popularity among ordinary people led LDP party members to elect him as their new president. Like Koizumi, Abe promoted politicians who shared his own policy ideas.[30] Prime Minister Abe thus proceeded to legislate those policies he deeply cared about, such as the highly ideological educational reform and the upgrading of the Defense Agency to the Ministry of

[28] Heizo Takenaka was a professor of Policy Management at Keio University when he was appointed.
[29] For an excellent study that teases out the importance of leadership styles, see Samuels (2003).
[30] Abe even engineered the comeback of those politicians who were forced out of the LDP over their dissent on Koizumi's Postal Reform Bill.

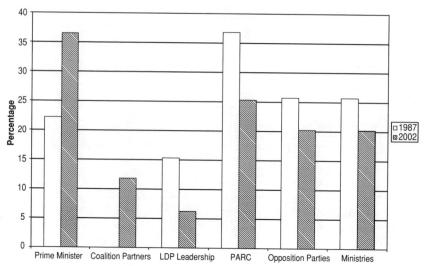

FIGURE 9.3. Various Actors' Perceived Influence in Economic Policy. *Source:* Tatebayashi (2004, 2006).

Defense, among others. However, Abe's bad judgment on both the appointment of his Cabinet and policy priorities cost him dearly. Abe's popularity ratings soon plummeted due to his poor communication skills and bad judgment, leading to a catastrophic loss for the LDP in the Upper House election in 2007.

IS POST-REFORM JAPAN A WESTMINSTER SYSTEM OR NOT?

Ever since the reforms of the electoral and legislative rules, the Japanese political system has taken on many of the features of the British-style Westminster system.[31] Today, the LDP prime minister enjoys more power than at any time in the pre-reform postwar period. A multi-year elite survey conducted by Michio Muramatsu and his collaborators provides evidence of this fundamental shift in Japanese politics.[32] Their survey asks Diet members to evaluate the scope of influence exercised by: (i) the prime minister; (ii) coalition partners; (iii) the LDP senior leadership; (iv) PARC subcommittees; (v) the opposition parties; and (vi) ministries. Figures 9.3, 9.4, and 9.5 summarize their survey results. Economic policy is also of concern here, because in the past Japan relied upon economic regulation as a functional equivalent to orthodox social protection programs. The figures all indicate a rise in prime ministerial influence, and a fall in intra-LDP actors' influence. In economic policy and political reforms, the prime minister

---

[31] Some scholars argue that the nature of the Westminster system has changed since the days of Margaret Thatcher. The British prime minister today possesses more power than in the old days. Some scholars talk about a process of presidentialization that has been occurring in many parliamentary systems (Krauss and Nyblade 2005). Here, it is enough to point out that before and after Thatcher, the United Kingdom always had a much more concentrated power structure than Japan. Institutionally speaking, contemporary Japan, however, has moved in a direction of greater power concentration, moving it closer to the British system.

[32] See Muramatsu and Kume eds. (2006) for the latest wave of surveys. For Muramatsu's earlier surveys, see Muramatsu, Ito, and Tsujinaka (1986).

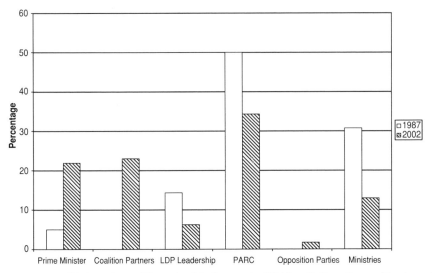

FIGURE 9.4. Various Actors' Perceived Influence in Welfare Policy. *Source:* Tatebayashi (2004, 2006).

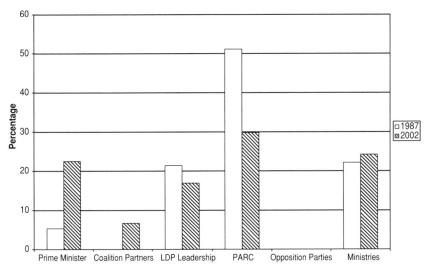

FIGURE 9.5. Various Actors' Perceived Influence in Public Policy. *Source:* Tatebayashi (2004, 2006).

today is the most influential actor. In contrast, in social welfare and public works, PARC subcommittees – while significantly weakened than before – are still the most influential actors. Yet even in these issue areas, the importance of the prime minister has risen by nearly 20 percent. In sum, these figures demonstrate the greater centralization of the policy process.[33]

---

33 Tatebayashi (2004, 2006) has used the Muramatsu et al. survey results to demonstrate the central-ization in the LDP. As indicated below the figures, I have adopted the data reported in Tatebayashi (2004, 2006).

Furthermore, the process of concentration of power, if anything, accelerated after 2002 – the most recent year in Michio Muramatsu's study. It is important here, however, to recognize the institutional obstacles to prime ministerial power that remain. Intraparty veto players (especially PARC) still matter, although much less than they used to, especially in welfare policy and public works. Figures on welfare policy also indicate the importance of coalition partners such as Komeito. Two institutional features are of particular relevance here in understanding the persistence of intraparty veto players and illuminating Japan's differences from the British system. The first feature is Japan's strong bicameralism. The second is the continuing use of multimember districts in the two Houses. Although Japan today can be categorized as a SMD-dominant system, it nonetheless uses mixed systems consisting of single-member districts and multimember districts (see Chapter 3 for detailed descriptions of the Japanese electoral systems both old and new). This second feature, which allows smaller parties to persist, explains why Japan appears more like a proto-Westminster system.[34] A Westminster system with a coalition government might appear oxymoronic. The rest of this section deliberates on why it still makes sense to apply the structural logic of politics associated with a Westminster-style system – that is, a highly centralized government ruled by a strong party in a SMD system – to explain Japanese welfare politics during the period between 1996 and 2007.

Japan's Strong Bicameralism

Japan's bicameralism has always been stronger than that in the United Kingdom, because the Japanese Upper House actually possesses veto power. Furthermore, the prime minister does not have power over the Upper House to the same extent that it does over the Lower House: the prime minister's prerogative to dissolve the Diet applies to the Lower House but not the Upper House. This means that the prime minister cannot control the timing of the Upper House election. The Upper House follows a predetermined calendar to elect one-half of its members every three years. In Japan, more often than not, elections for the Lower House and Upper House take place in different years. Theoretically, there has always been a chance that Japan could end up with a divided government like that of the United States – with the possibility of different parties controlling the two Houses in the Diet.

For most of the postwar period, however, two kinds of symmetries ensured that the veto power of the Upper House remained irrelevant.[35] The first symmetry was that the typical Diet member in the two Houses was elected in a MMD/SNTV system and as such pursued similar distributive strategies to favor

---

34 Small parties, nonetheless, increasingly capture fewer votes in every election cycle. About the persistence of small political parties in Japan, see Cox and Schoppa (2002).

35 What is particularly pertinent is a point made by Tsebelis (2002). He thinks that the upper chamber becomes a constitutional veto player in a real sense when the compositions of the two chambers differ. In Tsebelis' view, bicameralism becomes stronger when the two chambers are elected by different methods.

their core constituents. The second symmetry was that the partisan composition of the two Houses was the same. These two symmetries transformed Japan's de jure bicameral system into a de facto unicameral system. In recent years, these symmetries disappeared, unleashing the decentralizing effects of Japan's strong bicameralism in spite of the otherwise centralizing tendencies. Nonetheless, as it will be explained later in this section, the LDP prime minister still managed to contain the full effect of Japan's strong bicameralism to centralize his party and the locus of decision making. Let me first talk about the new decentralizing tendencies and then elaborate on how the centralizing tendencies of the SMD-dominant electoral system and the stronger prime ministerial office counteracted the decentralizing tendencies in the period between 1996 and 2007.

Today, the typical Diet member in the Lower House is very different from one in the Upper House. At every Lower House election, the number of candidates dually listed in the SMD tier and PR tier has increased. As a consequence, the typical Lower House Diet member competes in the SMD tier. In contrast, the Upper House has continued to use a MMD-dominant mixed system. Moreover, the use of a large multimember district (forty-eight seats) in the Upper House has preserved the importance of well-organized constituent groups. This tendency was even strengthened when the Upper House reintroduced an element of the old electoral rules by adopting an open list method in the PR tier in 2001. The intention here was to motivate vested interest groups to mobilize votes to elect their candidates in the Upper House. The result was that the typical Diet member in the Lower House and that in the Upper House possess rather different distributive preferences.

The partisan compositions in the two Houses have also diverged since 1989. Ever since the LDP lost its absolute majority in the Upper House, the LDP has been unable to regain its dominance and has had to govern in a formal or informal alliance with the opposition parties. The lack of an absolute majority in the Upper House has exposed the LDP prime minister to two vulnerabilities: the increased power of the opposition parties and the enhanced bargaining power of the LDP members in the Upper House vis-a-vis their party leader. The LDP's precarious position in the Upper House has allowed party rebels to side with the opposition parties to veto a legislative bill when the votes are close – as occurred in 2005 when the Upper House voted on Koizumi's Postal Reform Bill.[36] In such cases, the prime minister is relatively powerless, because he has no power to dissolve the Upper House. Furthermore, because the Upper House members have a six-year fixed term, they are more independent from their party leader than their Lower House peers, who face elections much more frequently – once every three years on average.

In short, the Upper House decentralizes the policy process in favor of well-organized interest groups – particularly those with a national mobilization capacity strong enough to make a difference in the large nationwide district. The "classic" constituent groups of the LDP, agricultural cooperatives, special

---

[36] See Estévez-Abe (2006) for the details.

postmasters, veterans, and physicians, still retain influence in this way. The strength of the Upper House thus explains the persistent (if now much weaker) influence of the bottom-up decision making characterized by the PARC within the LDP government. The "forces of resistance" against reforms – to borrow the famous term coined by Prime Minister Koizumi – were strongest in policy areas where the vital interests of the aforementioned groups were at stake.[37] The persisting influence of PARC politicians over welfare issues, for example, reflects the influence of LDP politicians with close ties to the Japan Medical Association (JMA). Even as of 2006, about 18 percent of all LDP Diet members were pro-JMA politicians. Some of these politicians were physicians who ran for office as LDP candidates in order to directly represent the JMA's interests, and others were LDP members who received large sums of the JMA's money.[38] This percentage is much higher still in the nationwide PR district in the Upper House, where about 30 percent of the successful candidates in 2006 were JMA-affiliated candidates.

Despite the decentralizing effects of Japan's stronger bicameralism, in the period between 1996 and the Upper House elections in 2007, the LDP managed to control both Houses with the help of Komeito. The LDP's electoral loss in the Upper House elections in 2007 ultimately unleashed the full impact of Japan's strong bicameralism. After the 2007 elections, the DPJ emerged as the largest party in the Upper House, whereas the LDP-Komeito coalition no longer possesses an absolute majority. In other words, Japan finds itself in a state of a divided government. The concluding chapter will discuss this issue in light of the structural logic approach. This chapter will focus on the period between 1996 and 2007.

Coalition Governments under the SMD-Dominant System

At first glance, the persistence of an LDP coalition government seems to undercut the claim that Japan is moving in a Westminster direction. The continuing use of multimember districts in post-1996 Japan created a situation whereby no party would win the absolute majority in the two Houses. As a result, Japan has been ruled by either a coalition government or "a partial minority government." The Hashimoto Cabinet that was formed soon after the 1996 Lower House elections continued to be a coalition government with the Social Democratic Party and Sakigake, because the LDP lacked an absolute majority in the Upper House.[39] The first Obuchi Cabinet (from September 1997 to January 1999) was "a partial minority government." The LDP ruled alone while relying on Komeito's cooperation in the Upper House, where the LDP lacked an absolute majority. Aside

[37] Again, the whole political saga of the Postal Reform offers a good example; see Patricia Maclachlan's excellent case study (Maclachlan 2006).
[38] Calculated based on the information in Japan Medical Association News (*Nihon Ishikai Renmei Nyusu*, December 25, 2006). See Iwai (1990, chapter 6).
[39] These two parties were so weakened at the polls that they were no longer represented in the Cabinet after the 1996 elections.

from a short-lived coalition in 1999 with a small conservative party, the LDP has governed in coalition with Komeito since October 1999.[40]

Certainly, a coalition government differs from a majoritarian government – the major defining feature of a Westminster system – because the presence of a coalition partner increases the number of veto players. Post-1996 Japan thus found itself caught in a paradox: the centralization of power within the LDP has reduced the number of intraparty veto players, whereas the rise of coalition politics means that the LDP has not become the sole veto player in the Diet. A coalition government under the current SMD-dominant system is likely to be much less decentralizing than a coalition government under the former MMD system. It is important to understand why.

Coalition governments under a SMD-dominant mixed system are very different from coalition governments under a MMD system. Most importantly, under the current SMD-dominant system, electoral cooperation among coalition partners is a prerequisite for maintaining a stable coalition government. This prerequisite constitutes perhaps the most important difference between coalition governments under the SMD-dominant and the old MMD system. Under a MMD system, coalition partners need not worry about electoral alliances with their partners. There are multiple seats in a district, so coalition parties can each field their own candidates. Under a SMD-dominant mixed system, the story is very different. Coalition partners have every reason to avoid competition in the SMD tier. Fielding multiple candidates from the coalition parties in the SMD tier merely splits votes for the existing coalition government. This will only benefit the candidates from the largest opposition party, dramatically enhancing their chance to win. In light of the volatility of seat shares in the SMD tier, it thus becomes critical for the coalition partners to cooperate at the polls.

An electoral alliance also makes a lot of strategic sense for the coalition partners when they consist of one large party and one or two small parties. Such an alliance makes sense for small parties, who would otherwise suffer in the SMD tier. As a result, small parties refrain from fielding their own candidates in those single-member districts where they do not expect to win. In return, they "lend" their otherwise dead votes to the large party in exchange for (i) votes in those districts where the small party has a chance of winning; and (ii) promises that the larger party will support their favored policies. Small parties that can draw upon well-organized voters are the most reliable candidates for such an exchange. These parties can more credibly deliver votes to the large party in the SMD tier. In sum, the form of electoral cooperation required in the current system thus makes coalition partners act as if they were a single party at the polls.

The same logic also implies that a coalition of two large parties is very unlikely under a SMD-dominant system. Even if the two parties were to agree on a grand

---

[40] The small conservative party mentioned here refers to the Liberal Party, led by Ichiro Ozawa. Ozawa, a very influential former LDP politician, was responsible for the vote of no confidence against Prime Minister Kiichi Miyazawa and for splitting the LDP in 1993. In 2000, the Liberal Party withdrew from the coalition while some members formed a new party, the Conservative Party (Hoshuto), to stay in the coalition. The members of the Conservative Party eventually merged back into the LDP.

coalition, every time the next electoral cycle approached, each would try to win enough seats to go solo in the next round of government formation. For two large parties, in contrast to electoral cooperation between a large party and a smaller one, it makes little strategic sense. Unless all SMDs are completely uncompetitive – that is, either one of the large parties completely dominates the district – each of the two large parties is likely to field candidates in every SMD, hoping to capture the majority of seats. The greater seat volatility created by the SMD tier makes the strategy to aim at forming its own government a viable one.

The previous paragraphs describe, in a nutshell, the exchange relationship that currently exists between the LDP (the large party) and Komeito (the small, reliable, vote-delivering party). This explains why Komeito is the ideal coalition partner for the LDP and why the LDP-Komeito coalition has been so much more stable than any other coalition since 1993. The LDP and Komeito have coordinated their electoral strategies in ways unseen before in earlier coalition governments. In fact, the LDP has found Komeito's electoral cooperation indispensable for retaining power in the current mixed system. Komeito can credibly commit their supporters, because they all belong to an extremely well-organized religious group, Soka Gakkai.[41] Furthermore, Komeito is ideologically attractive as a coalition partner. Unlike, for instance, the Japan Communist Party – another well-organized small party – Komeito positions itself around the center on most key policy issues. Its electoral support is also quite useful, because its urban base supplies votes in an area where the LDP remains weak.[42] It is worth noting that the LDP and Komeito actually differ greatly on a number of important policy issues – especially on issues of foreign and defense policy. The stability of their coalition government in spite of their fundamental ideological differences offers the strongest evidence for the stability of electorally motivated coalitions identified here.

A Modified Westminster System in the 1996–2007 Period

Despite the rise in the veto power of the Upper House and the presence of a coalition partner, the centralizing tendencies of the new electoral and legislative rules have nonetheless outweighed these factors during the period between 1996 and 2007. There are three reasons why the effect of these rules has been so decisive. First, Upper House LDP politicians must also rely on a popular party leader. The presence of the SMD districts in the Upper House election increases the volatility of the electoral results in the Upper House. As shown earlier in Figure 9.1, voters have been paying more attention to policy issues in the Upper House elections. The party leader – especially when he is prime minister – is

---

[41] In fact, empirical studies show that about 85 percent of those who voted for Komeito in the PR tier voted for the LDP in the SMD tier.

[42] The LDP, however, did extremely well in urban districts in the Lower House elections in 2005. Many attribute this success to Prime Minister Koizumi's popularity among voters.

the most visible conveyer of the party's message to voters. Upper House candidates running from de facto single-member districts are particularly vulnerable to popularity swings of the party.

Second, the centralizing effects of the rule changes have worked with, rather than against, the effects of the coalition with Komeito. Indeed, Komeito has helped to empower the LDP prime minister in his fight against the "forces of resistance" within his party, not least because it has allowed him to favor unorganized urban voters. This was indeed the case with Koizumi, who challenged highly targeted forms of social protection and state-controlled savings programs. Since Komeito's support draws heavily from low-income urban dwellers, Komeito has long advocated universalistic redistributive welfare programs. Komeito's presence in the coalition, in short, has helped the LDP to shift its policy toward urban residents, even in the face of opposition from LDP members in the Upper House and from rural districts.

Third, and finally, the new legislative rules that concentrate more power in the hands of the prime minister have given the prime minister greater control over the overall policy agenda of the coalition government. A new apparatus (that includes the Council of Economic and Fiscal Policy) has allowed the prime minister to centralize power even in a coalition government. Indeed, there is evidence to suggest that the LDP excluded the Minister of Health, Labor, and Welfare from this Council, because he was from Komeito.[43] The LDP leadership considered it important that their coalition partner was kept outside of the top-down council so as to ensure that the LDP prime minister and his LDP ministers could set the basic policy guidelines for the government. The fact that the prime minister could decide which ministers to include in his strategic council demonstrates how the concentrated power of the prime minister affected the nature of the coalition government during this period.

POLICY OUTCOMES: EVIDENCE OF POLICY CHANGE UNDER THE NEW STRUCTURAL LOGIC

The structural logic predicts that a shift from a decentralized system with a weak party and a MMD electoral system to a more centralized system with a strong party and a SMD electoral system is likely to bring about the following four changes in the social protection system: (i) a move from forms of social protection targeted at well-organized groups; (ii) a shift toward more universalistic – and meager – benefits; (iii) a distributive bias in favor of competitive districts; and (iv) a reduction in bureaucratic discretion. Indeed, recent policy developments in Japan demonstrate that the nature of Japan's social protection system has begun to change in precisely this expected way. These changes have less to do with the personalities or ideological inclinations of particular leaders than they do with a change in the structural logic of the Japanese political system.

---

[43] This occurred as the LDP leaders were preparing for the reorganization of the government structure effective in January 2001 (Shimizu 2005, 236–237).

A fundamental reform of Japan's social protection required much more than mere reforms of orthodox social security programs. Japan long used market-restricting functional equivalents to protect the self-employed and specific industries and their core workers. Japan also relied on a large reserve of savings-oriented programs under state control, which created a flow of capital independent of the market. The following paragraphs demonstrate how the LDP leaders in the post-1996 era began to challenge market-restricting functional equivalents and bureaucratic control over savings-oriented programs in earnest. Certainly, politico-bureaucratic alliances resisted. "Tribal leaders" of such alliances within the LDP resisted the centralization of power by the prime minister, whereas bureaucrats tried to protect the status quo. Reform attempts thus encountered strongest resistance in policy issues where (i) a large number of LDP politicians had electoral and financial stakes[44]; and (ii) bureaucrats monopolized policy-relevant information and expertise.

Retrenchment of Market-Restricting Targeted Protection

There was a clear shift in government policy in 1996 under Prime Minister Hashimoto. The new policy direction emphasized reducing both the scope of bureaucratic involvement in the economy and the targeted protection of particularistic interest groups. Not only was Japan's recession making most voters worse off but the overall fiscal cost of maintaining the same system was rising for the majority of voters. Targeted protection for the few at the expense of the many – a viable strategy under the LDP rule in the context of a MMD/SNTV electoral system – was no longer a good electoral strategy in the new SMD-dominant system. In contrast to the old MMD/SNTV system, the SMD-dominant system provided swing voters with sufficient power to alter – sometimes quite drastically – the final seat share. The new electoral system required the prime minister to appeal to unorganized voters in order to stay in power. The task for the LDP prime minister was to produce policies that were less favorable to particularistic interests and more favorable to urban voters. To achieve this goal, the LDP leader had to destroy old politico-bureaucratic alliances.

Ryutaro Hashimoto, the first LDP prime minister in the post-1996 period, deserves credit for recognizing the importance of the electoral changes and setting bold policy goals.[45] Hashimoto promised "Six Major Reforms" (Roku Dai Kaikaku) – consisting of reforms in the economic structure, fiscal structure, financial system, administrative structure, social security system, and education system.

---

[44] Recall that those LDP politicians elected in prefectures with a MMD/SNTV system or in the open-list PR tier of the Upper House still had a reason to cater to the needs of specific groups.
[45] Prime Minister Hashimoto made more of a contribution to political and economic reforms in Japan than any other prime minister. Despite Hashimoto's contributions, he passed away without the kind of recognition showered upon Koizumi. The Japanese media portrayed Hashimoto as the "don of the forces of resistance against Koizumi." Preceding his premature death, he had to testify in court in relation to an illegal political donation to his faction by the Japan Dentists Association. I consider him one of the best and perhaps the most unappreciated of the postwar prime ministers.

In his attempt to tackle vested interests – both within his own party and within the bureaucracy – Hashimoto used two formal councils as a way of setting his own policy agenda: the Administrative Reform Council (Gyosei Kaikaku Kaigi) and the Fiscal Structure Council (Zaisei Kozo Kaigi).[46] In order to take full charge, Hashimoto himself chaired the Administrative Reform Council by incorporating it within the Prime Ministerial Office. He convened weekly meetings to tackle major issues and set up a subcommittee to identify areas in need of deregulation. On the top of this agenda was the cumbersome licensing used to control new competitors in transportation and other industries. Hashimoto's Fiscal Structure Council also turned a skeptical eye toward public works. To overcome resistance from the agricultural lobby, a prime beneficiary of such works, cuts were sold as part of the picky details of the Uruguay Round of trade liberalization. As a result of such measures, the share of the agricultural budget related to public works fell by more than one-third between 1997 and 2005.[47]

Hashimoto's reform efforts affected the shape of Japan's social protection. Hashimoto's "Financial Big Bang" deregulated financial product markets and opened the doors to new players (Laurence 2001). Banks and insurance companies were no longer to be protected by market-restricting regulation.[48] Given the fact that "protected financial institutions" had been one of the pillars of Japan's work-based social protection, Hashimoto's deregulation brought about a significant change. Nor was Hashimoto's government willing to protect, at least in the old way, the self-employed, even though they formed an important constituent group of the LDP under the old MMD/SNTV system. The Large Scale Retail Store Law of 1974, which had existed to protect small shopkeepers from larger competitors, was eliminated in 1998 (effective 2000).[49] Likewise, the government abolished a whole raft of retail licenses covering the sales of rice, liquor, nonprescription medications, and other goods.[50]

---

[46] The Administrative Reform Council had been created under Prime Minister Murayama (during the LDP-Japan Socialist-Sakigake coalition). Its profile, however, only increased under the Hashimoto Cabinet. Murayama, as the head of the Japan Socialist Party, was not keen on deregulation. He was, in particular, against deregulation of labor standards laws. The Fiscal Structure Council was Prime Minister Hashimoto's creation.

[47] The public works budget as part of the agricultural budget declined from 19.7 billion yen in 1997 to 12.8 billion yen in 2005 (Ministry of Agriculture, Fishery, and Forestry, cited in Davis and Oh 2006).

[48] As Vogel (1996) points out, deregulation does not necessarily mean an absolute reduction in the number of regulations.

[49] As Lincoln (2001, 112–113) notes, the law that replaced the old one provided legal grounds for intervention by small shopkeepers. The new law regulated the opening of large stores on environmental grounds (traffic congestion and noise) and required consultation with local representatives. Lincoln hence concludes that not much has changed. I disagree. The old law, by requiring strict licensing conditions, interfered with every aspect of large-scale store operation even in getting approval to open a large-scale store. Under the new law, local small shops and a large store can work out mutually acceptable terms.

[50] The government used to control the number of stores either in terms of allocating store spaces per number of inhabitants in the vicinity or in terms of geographical distances from one rice (or liquor or drug) shop to the next. The deregulation over rice sales took place in two stages – first in 1996 and then again in 1999. The deregulation of liquor sales also occurred in two stages – first in

The same trend of curtailing targeted benefits for specific industries and trades continued even after Hashimoto left office. In 1999, the Obuchi government decided to terminate wage subsidies for workers in declining industries. Such subsidies typically went to large companies in heavy industries like shipping; the drawback of such policies was that they delayed the shift of workers out of moribund industries. As a component of its Emergency Employment Measures (Kinkyu Koyo Taisaku) to combat rising unemployment rates, the government refocused on the structural transformation of the economy rather than protection of specific industries in the name of employment security per se.[51]

In 1999, under Prime Minister Obuchi, the LDP government introduced the new Agricultural Basic Law, which explicitly affirmed as a policy goal market efficiency in addition to self-sufficiency of the national food supply.[52] Furthermore, in the same year, the government proposed a 30 percent reduction in Farmers' Pension (Nogyosha Nenkin) benefits.[53] Although the agricultural lobby within the LDP reduced the "damage" to 10 percent, the Farmers' Pension was drastically reformed. Under Koizumi, the government made it clear that it would concentrate resources on more efficient large-scale farmers. Agricultural policy, in other words, ceased to be a form of social policy.

Given the newly strengthened Prime Ministerial Office, Prime Minister Koizumi could go even further in challenging intraparty veto players. By the time Koizumi became prime minister, Hashimoto's Administrative Reform had come into full effect. Koizumi used one of the new tools, the Economic and Fiscal Council, very effectively to set policy priorities and impose guidelines for budgeting. This Council took over responsibility for many policy issues that were traditionally the preserve of *shingikai*, where bureaucrats controlled the agenda. The new Council, for instance, set the agenda on social security policies, including health care, pensions, and even labor regulations. The Council brought these issues together with tax issues for the first time.[54] Prior to this, tax policies and social security policies were each isolated in their respective decentralized bureaucratic fiefdoms. Under the old system, bureaucrats used the participation

---

1993 and then in 2000. Deregulation over the sales of nonprescription drugs took place in 1999. It is noteworthy that this kind of licensing still persists in many continental European countries with MMD systems, while the British government under Margaret Thatcher deregulated most of it.

[51] Even during the post-bubble recession, Japanese unemployment rates did not increase much beyond 5 percent. Comparatively speaking, this is not high. Nonetheless, the statistics on unemployment do not capture a whole generation of young workers out of work or those who gave up looking for work. Meanwhile, suicide rates in Japan continued to rise, reaching 30,000 a year at its peak in the early 2000s. In Japan, middle-aged men who lost work were the most likely candidates for suicide, defying the international trend (internationally, the elderly are the most likely to commit suicide).

[52] Some scholars point out that the overall amount of income transfers to farmers did not change during the same period (Davis and Oh 2006). However, this view neglects an important transformation in the way that money was dispensed. Across the board, subsidies to farmers were cut back and replaced with more efficiency-oriented subsidies.

[53] For the content of political negotiations over the reform of the Farmers' Pension, see *Zenkoku Nokyo Shimbun*, December 17, 1999, 1; July 7, 2000, 1; August 11, 2000, 1; August 25, 2000, 2; September 1, 2000, 1; February 23, 2001, 1.

[54] Recall that this was something intended by Hashimoto, the architect of the Administrative Reform.

of representatives of vested interest groups in *shingikai* as a way of protecting their own organizational interest. The *shingikai* system thus was highly effective in maintaining the status quo but not in introducing bold changes. The new Council of Economic and Fiscal Policy, in contrast, involved no "official" representative of specific associations as *shingikai* did. Koizumi handpicked reform-oriented business leaders just as his predecessors Hashimoto and Obuchi had done with their respective top-down councils. These leaders were expected to recommend bold policy ideas independent of the status quo.

Physicians were another group to come under attack. The "old" LDP used the health care budget, as we have seen, to "buy" the support of the Japan Medical Association (JMA), a very powerful lobby. The JMA long exercised control over Japan's health care policy. Nowhere is this more apparent than in the membership composition of the government council (Chuo Shakai Hoken Iryo Kyogikai) that determined the fees for medical procedures to be used in payments from the social security system. Due to their political influence, the JMA was overrepresented in this council and thus could set the fees in ways that promoted their members' interests. Because physicians with their own private practices possessed political power, fees were set in ways that advantaged them. The LDP would periodically raise physicians' fees – particularly before elections. The LDP chose not to do so, however, during the budgetary negotiations at the end of 1999. This reflected a significant shift in the political calculations on the part of LDP politicians. Even LDP politicians close to the JMA accepted this precedent. Facing elections in 2000, LDP politicians worried that voters would punish them for bestowing special favors on physicians.[55]

Again the trend to shift resources away from special interests became even more manifest in Koizumi's Economic and Fiscal Policy Council. Released in 2001, the Council's first budgeting guidelines contained a whole range of new proposals on health care reform. Such proposals would never have seen the light of day under the old system. The guidelines included the standardization of medical procedures, promotion of electronic medical charts, issuing of receipts by clinics, partial deregulation of the health care business, and the creation of a new health care system for the elderly. The JMA had earlier fought tooth and nail against all such proposals for effective cost control and fraud prevention. Although Koizumi could not override intraparty opposition on all counts, he nonetheless cut the rates of governmental reimbursements for physicians' fees, ignoring his party's consensus rule. This was the very first time the physicians' fees were cut in real terms (Ohara Rodo Mondai Kenkyujo 2002, 385–386). This became a highly symbolic episode that made Koizumi's fellow party members realize that their old legislative routines were changing.[56]

By the end of 2005, however, the forces of resistance within the LDP – and those in the respective PARC subcommittee – had crumbled.[57] In 2005, the government reformed the Central Medical Care Council and cut the number of

---

[55] *Yomiuri Shimbun*, December 20, 1999, provides details of the negotiations over physicians' fees and statements of LDP politicians.

[56] Personal communication with Yasuhisa Shiozaki (a LDP Diet member).

[57] *Yomiuri Shimbun*, December 10, 2005.

physicians on the Council. Its power weakened, the JMA had to swallow the bitter pill of reform. Many of the items listed in the 2001 guidelines were introduced.[58] An elderly health care system was also introduced, greatly increasing the financial cost of health care to elderly patients – something that the JMA had always opposed.

Koizumi slashed public works spending, despite protest from old-guard LDP members from rural areas. Koizumi was also reluctant to prop up failing businesses by means of the "old" targeted forms of protection. He argued that it was cheaper to let unsuccessful businesses fail while providing a safety net to workers who lost their jobs (Mulgan 2002). The Koizumi government introduced a new safety net for small business owners, whereby they would be eligible for public loans in the event of losing their business (Uzuhashi et al. 2004). In this sense, the LDP government's policy orientation was drastically changing. All of these examples confirm that the LDP leadership under Koizumi was abandoning the old forms of protection targeted at particularistic groups. The old order was dying; a new one was struggling to be born. In this respect, Koizumi's 2001 campaign phrase, *"Jiminto wo bukkowasu"* ("Smash the LDP"), makes perfect sense.

In addition to challenging the vested interest groups closely linked to the LDP, the post-1996 prime ministers also challenged organized labor by pushing for greater liberalization of the labor market. Paradoxically, in spite of the political weakness of Japan's organized labor, Japan's market-restricting regulation also protected core male workers employed by large companies (see Kume 1998). Core male workers organized into enterprise unions received better benefits and employment security in exchange for their cooperation with management. Given that Japan's unionization rate fell short of 30 percent throughout the 1990s, core male workers in large private companies along with public sector employees constituted the fortunate minority. Prolonged recession, however, was making it very costly for large firms to hire full-time regular workers, who expected to receive company-based social protection and employment security. The fact that even workers' social security benefits were linked to their workplace further increased the labor cost for employers. Employers now wanted much less targeted protection; they wanted to uncouple the strong link between workers' welfare and their workplace.[59] In the latter half of the 1990s, Japan introduced a series of policies aiming at creating a more flexible labor market.

It is no coincidence that policy initiatives for deregulation of labor market regulations came from the prime minister's top-down councils. In stark contrast to existing *shingikai* on labor issues, organized labor was underrepresented in the

---

[58] For instance, physicians long opposed deregulation of health care services: (i) to allow health care providers to offer fee-for-service private health care rather than services determined by the social insurance system; and (ii) to allow companies to own and operate medical facilities. The JMA worried about greater levels of competition in their business. By 2005, the government was capable of achieving partial deregulation in spite of the JMA's resistance.

[59] The employers' position is summarized in the Okuda Vision (released January 1, 2003). This is a document released by Nippon Keidanren when Okuda (Toyota's CEO) was its chairperson. It basically calls for a more universalistic welfare state combined with self-help and private welfare services. Nippon and Keidanren merged in 2002 to become Nippon Keidanren.

prime minister's top-down councils. Post-1996 political leaders saw *shingikai* as a vehicle for bureaucrats to protect their turf using the political muscle of the vested interests. Top-down councils were a way for LDP prime ministers to introduce a more "partisan" agenda rather than bureaucratic agenda. Koizumi's Council of Economic and Fiscal Policy even excluded union representation all together. This clearly had a lot to do with the fact that the unions were core constituents of the LDP's rival, the Democratic Party of Japan (DPJ).[60] Under the SMD-dominant system, where the two largest parties competed for power, a corporatist style of negotiation that involved the rival's core constituents became less attractive. The erosion of Japan's proto-corporatist legislative style also meant that social and labor bureaucrats were losing their agenda-setting power.[61] This trend confirms the implication of my structural logic that corporatist politics requires MMD electoral systems.

In the post-1996 period, the Japanese government became increasingly permissive of irregular employment contracts. It also eliminated restrictions against private employment agencies in an attempt to promote labor mobility. This deregulation allowed employers to hire a flexible labor force without the level of employment protection regular workers received.[62] As we shall see, the same political dynamics that caused a shift away from market-restricting regulations – including labor regulations – also led to a shift for a more universalistic welfare state.

More Universalistic – but Meager – Benefits

The new SMD-dominant system also gave rise to electoral calculations that favored universalistic welfare programs in lieu of targeted forms of social protection. As the DPJ enhanced its electoral presence as the second largest party, it became very important for the LDP government to introduce policies with a greater appeal. It was in this context that the LDP government began to shift its policy. Among new ideas on the table were tax-financed basic pension benefits, an expanded coverage of public pension and employment insurance to irregular workers, and child care insurance.

The LDP, however, faced a real dilemma. On the one hand, electoral competition forced universalistic programs onto the political agenda – they were

[60] In fact, after Rengo fiercely opposed the LDP government's Pension Reform Bill in 1999, the LDP government disinvited Rengo leaders to official top-level meetings with business leaders. Formerly, the LDP used to hold regular tripartite top-level meetings with business and labor. Ohara Rodo Mondai Kenkyujo 2002, 253–254.

[61] An official at the Ministry of Health, Labor, and Welfare expressed irritation at the Economic and Fiscal Policy Council's interference into their jurisdiction and the way they subverted the role of *shingikai* (based on my interview at the Ministry, May 2003). In this sense, the Economic and Fiscal Policy Council was producing effects its architect had intended.

[62] The Japanese government used to restrict terms of employment. Fixed-term contracts were only permitted for a small number of special occupations. Similarly, personnel companies were allowed to dispatch man power to their clients only for a limited range of occupations. Reforms in 1999 and 2003 drastically changed the practice by legalizing the dispatching of workers to all jobs except for a few occupations that for public safety and other reasons should be regulated. See Kume (2000); Miura (2002); Nakamura (2006).

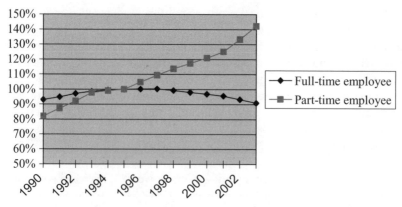

FIGURE 9.6. The Rise in Irregular Workers. *Note:* Year-on-year growth rates (%) with 1995 as a base year (1995 = 100). *Source:* Ministry of Health, Labor and Welfare, *Maitsuki Kinro Tokei Chosa (Monthly Labor Survey)*, various years.

popular with a wide range of voters – yet, on the other hand, the structural logic of the SMD-dominant system made the LDP very hesitant to increase taxes to finance these programs. Broadly based new taxes or tax increases were risky – particularly in a SMD-dominant system with volatility in seat shares. Even the immensely popular former prime minister Koizumi had to promise not to raise the consumption tax. For this reason, Japan's shift away from targeted forms of social protection did not – notwithstanding the new universalistic rhetoric – translate into generous universalistic income transfers. Instead, to make ends meet, the Japanese government retrenched existing benefits by charging more user fees and copayments. Universalistic programs nonetheless did emerge, when they could be financed without tax increases.

A universalistic option for basic pensions emerged on the policy agenda in 1999 under the Obuchi government. The rise of irregular workers and the prolonged recession caused serious actuarial problems in Japan's public pensions (see Figure 9.6). Because irregular workers are exempt from enrollment, the Employee Pension System suffered from a declining number of new enrollees – while the number of pensioners increased. The National Pension System suffered from collection problems, as a larger number of people failed to pay their contributions. This issue loomed large in the periodic round of actuarial revisions of the public pensions scheduled in 1999. Wary of increases in their social security contributions, employers lobbied for a completely tax-financed basic pension (Miyatake 2001, 25). They were joined by unions, the DPJ, and other opposition parties. Employers and some private sector unions were also demanding dismantling of the earnings-related tier of public pension. The Ministry of Welfare, however, was keen on maintaining the contributory social insurance scheme.[63] They favored benefit cuts to avoid a major reform. Like the

---

[63] As of January 2001, the Ministry of Health and Welfare (shortened as the Ministry of Welfare throughout this book) merged with the Ministry of Labor to become the Ministry of Health, Labor,

Ministry, Rengo, the peak-level labor federation, also wanted to continue the current earnings-related contributory pension scheme, although they opposed the Ministry's solution of benefit cuts. Politicians, however, increasingly began to turn in favor of tax-financed basic pensions.[64] The 2000 pension reform was the result of a compromise.[65] Although the earnings-related contributory design was retained by cutting future benefits, the 2000 reform promised to increase the level of government subsidies from one-third to one-half of the total cost of the basic pension by securing fiscal sources by 2004 – when the next round of periodic revisions was scheduled.[66]

Public pension indeed became the main issue of the Lower House election in 2003 and the Upper House election in 2004. From the 2003 election, political parties began releasing "manifestos," whereby they listed their policy promises. The DPJ rallied behind a unified pension system that treated all citizens with the same income and contributions equally – unlike the existing fragmented system. The DPJ also promised a tax-financed minimum pension. Except for Komeito, all the other parties remained vague about how they planned to finance the promised increase in government subsidies. Most of the opposition parties stated they would finance the increase by trimming expenditures in public works, for instance.

Once the negotiations for the 2004 pension reform began – this time under Prime Minister Koizumi – the DPJ called for fully tax-financed basic pensions. Within the LDP too, there was support for this proposal. Both parties realized that tax-financed basic pensions would be a popular universalistic benefit as well as being a good solution for the aforementioned actuarial problem. The LDP, however, was hesitant to commit to a new tax, for fear of provoking an electoral backlash. The new SMD-dominant electoral rules made such a backlash a genuine possibility. Even as late as 2007, the LDP government had still not found a way to pay for the increases in the state subsidy for the basic pension costs promised in the pension reform in 2000. (The law stipulates that subsidies will be raised by 2009.)

Universalistic benefit expansion was possible when it did not involve tax increases. The reforms of the Employment Insurance and Children's Allowance in 2001 and 2004, respectively, provide good examples. As the economy worsened with the prolonged recession, Koizumi's government increasingly talked about strengthening the safety net for individual citizens rather than protecting unproductive businesses. For the first time, the government began to discuss the importance of equal access to social welfare, regardless of position in the

and Welfare as part of the government reorganization planned in Hashimoto's Administrative Reform legislated in 1997.

[64] The Liberal Party (Ichiro Ozawa's party), which was in the coalition government, was very keen on a tax-financed basic pension.

[65] The reform in 2000 actually was supposed to be concluded in 1999, but was delayed. This reform was one of those scheduled revisions of the pension system that took place every five years.

[66] The 2000 reform consisted mostly of benefit cuts: future earnings-related benefits were cut by 5 percent; the pensionable age was raised; automatic slides to adjust pension levels were frozen; and the salary base for the calculations of social security contributions was broadened (to include all the bonus payments). See Miyatake (2001); Otani (2000).

workforce or gender. Japan still relied on contributory social insurance schemes to deliver health care, unemployment insurance, and old-age pension. Employers seldom extended social insurance coverage to workers without permanent employment contracts. With the rise in the number of irregular workers – an inevitable consequence of labor market deregulation – it became increasingly apparent that a more comprehensive social insurance scheme was necessary (see Figure 9.6). Japan's Employment Insurance system used to favor precisely the group of workers who enjoyed job stability. Older male core workers with long tenure who quit voluntarily to retire could still collect unemployment benefits, and their benefits were often more generous than benefits for a laid-off worker with short enterprise tenure. The Employment Reform in 2001 changed the eligibility criterion to allocate more benefits to those who were laid off. It also extended the coverage to part-time workers.[67]

The Children's Allowance was also expanded in 2004. This benefit expansion was financed by the tax revenue generated from reductions in income tax deductions for dependent family members.[68] In other words, the government scaled back on a functional equivalent to augment a universalistic income transfer to children. Nonetheless, when Komeito suggested a plan that involved levying new contributions, Koizumi was less forthcoming. For instance, Koizumi vetoed Komeito's idea to introduce a Childcare Insurance (Ikuji Hoken) (*Yomiuri*, May 23, 2006). This Childcare Insurance policy would have provided family support regardless of occupational status. The Ministry of Health, Labor, and Welfare was eager.

From the perspective of the structural logic approach adopted in this book, it is no surprise that electoral dynamics favored these types of universalistic programs. The initiative for universalistic programs often came from the LDP's coalition partner, Komeito, whose supporters tend to be lower-middle-class urbanites. Nonetheless, these programs were well suited to the interests of Prime Minister Koizumi. Koizumi was eager to court unorganized voters in competitive urban districts. Lavishing more pork on safe rural districts made little sense under the new SMD-dominant system. To be successful, the LDP had to win in competitive urban districts. Obviously, a large number of LDP politicians elected in rural districts did not welcome any shift of resources away from their constituencies to urban areas. This is why Komeito's presence in the government was so crucial for the LDP leader. Universalistic benefits that benefited Komeito supporters and other unorganized urban voters were electorally necessary for the LDP. Whenever it fit his electoral strategy, Koizumi could use Komeito's demand as leverage to get his party to accept benefits for urban voters. In fact, under Koizumi, the LDP drastically increased its appeal to urban unorganized voters.

Nonetheless, ironically, the increased level of accountability and policy identifiability also led to a much more meager welfare state. As the Japanese government

---

[67] According to an official involved in this reform, neither employers nor unions opposed this coverage expansion (interview May 2003).

[68] This was a policy issue about which Komeito felt strongly.

continued to avoid tax increases, it had to cut benefits. Benefit cuts happened not
only in public pensions but also in other programs such as health care and public
assistance programs. In the institutional context where tax increases were difficult,
the government continued to increase patients' copayments in health care and
long-term elderly care. And voters did not perceive copayments as they did taxes –
copayments were more like users' fees. The government raised wage earners'
health care copayments to 30 percent in 2001. In order to make this acceptable, the Koizumi government simultaneously increased the elderly's copayments
while reducing physicians' fees. A tactic of imposing a major loss on a vested interest group such as the Japan Medical Association was deemed necessary to prevent
voter backlash. In 2005, the government shifted more of the cost onto the elderly
themselves by creating a separate contributory insurance scheme for the elderly.
Under the new scheme, they were required to make contributions just like everyone else. And, furthermore, elderly patients with certain levels of income were
required to pay the same amount of copayments as younger people. The government also instructed local governments to tighten eligibility to public assistance
– something not very visible to voters. In short, a shift to universalistic benefits
came with benefit retrenchments.

A Shift to Market-Based Savings Programs

We have seen in Chapter 6 how Japan's welfare state generates savings, which
bureaucratic agencies controlled for their own purposes. The Postal Insurance
(*kampo*), the two public pension schemes (the Employee Pension and National
Pension), tax-deferred corporate pensions, and life insurance policies all provide
examples of policy-supported, savings-oriented programs. They were each either
directly or indirectly controlled by their respective bureaucratic agency. It has
been shown earlier in the book that the Ministry of Welfare and the Ministry
of Finance heavily regulated private savings programs under their jurisdiction in
ways that often influenced how the money should be invested.[69] The vast sums
of welfare funds were also under direct state control. The law stipulated that the
funds in the Postal Savings, Postal Insurance, and pension reserves be managed
by the Trust Fund Bureau in the Ministry of Finance. The Trust Fund Bureau
"invested" the money via the Fiscal Investment and Loan Program (FILP). In
reality, however, the FILP merely loaned the money to numerous special public
corporations (*tokushu hojin*). Most ministries had their own public corporations,
which provided lucrative post-retirement positions (*amakudari*) for bureaucrats.[70]

[69] The Ministry of Finance possessed so much influence over the life insurance industry that it often
requested the industry to make policy-related investments. When the Ministry "requested" the
industry to invest more in the stock market to prop up the Nikkei Index, newspapers called it a PKO
(price-keeping operation). The life insurance industry was vulnerable to political pressure because
it relied heavily on favorable public policy such as tax deductions for life insurance premiums, for
instance. For more, see Chapter 6.
[70] These corporations hired retired high-raking bureaucrats with generous salaries and great second
retirement lump-sum payments. Seiichiro Hayakawa (1997) provides detailed data on the number

Not only was the FILP long exempt from oversight by the Diet, but, legally speaking, special public corporations were not even required to keep proper books for transparency.

Furthermore, some ministries managed all or part of the welfare funds in their jurisdiction on their own. The Ministry of Welfare used part of the pension reserves to set up the Pension Welfare Corporation (Nenkin Fukushi Jigyodan), which then built massive unprofitable resort centers around the country. The former Ministry of Labor played a similar game with funds accumulated in the Work Injuries Insurance and the Employment Insurance. Needless to say, LDP politicians initially welcomed such public works – especially when the resorts were located in their own constituency – and bureaucrats benefited by creating highly paid post-retirement positions in these resort centers.[71]

It was only after the electoral rules changed that politicians showed any interest in the misuse of welfare funds by the bureaucracy.[72] Such a shift in politicians' attitude provides evidence for the argument put forth in this book: as unorganized voters become important, the political cost of benefiting from or neglecting policies that harm the majority drastically increases. For the very first time, politicians became interested in curtailing bureaucratic discretion over these welfare funds. As part of his Administrative Reform, Prime Minister Hashimoto immediately focused on the problem of special public corporations. His focus quickly expanded to include the entire system of the FILP. In 2001, Prime Minister Koizumi completed the FILP reform initiated by Hashimoto. This reform put an end to the flows of money that took place outside of the market. The FILP reform imposed market principles on special public corporations. Under the new scheme, they had to raise their funds in the bond market. As a result, the amount of money going into these public corporations in 2005 fell to one-third of the levels in 1995.[73]

After the FILP reform, the Trust Fund Bureau of the Ministry of Finance (working through the FILP) was no longer the exclusive manager of the money

of *amakudari* to special corporations (*tokushu hojin*) and other nonprofit organizations set up by ministries (*koeki hojin*).

[71] Politicians were not innocent bystanders. LDP politicians were often allied to specific bureaucratic organizations to receive kickbacks for turning a blind eye. A classic case is the scandal known as the KSD Incident in Japan. The former Ministry of Labor had set up a public corporation, which then tried to set up a technological university. The Ministry used funds in the Employment Insurance Special Account to create this university. This corporation bribed a number of senior LDP politicians to receive government subsidies for the university. At the core of the scandal lie the politico-bureaucratic alliances that thrived under the old MMD/SNTV system. The Ministry's misuse of the Employment Insurance Special Account was pervasive. Aside from the aforementioned technological university, the Ministry used the funds in the Special Account to found 26 technical junior colleges, 65 training promotion centers, 47 employment promotion centers, 140,000 housing units, and nearly 2,000 recreational facilities (*Asahi Shimbun*, March 19, 1997, 7).

[72] Even as of 1997, politicians did not think much about *amakudari* that took advantage of pension funds (comment by Mr. Masumoto at Rengo, interview July 23, 1997). One of the first newspaper articles that questioned the misuse of welfare funds by bureaucrats appeared in 1997. *Asahi Shimbun* published a special series titled "On Special Corporations" in March 1997.

[73] For more details, see Noble (2006b).

accumulated in public pensions, Postal Insurance (*kampo*), and Postal Savings (*yucho*). The new reform created three new independent funds, for public pension reserves, Postal Insurance, and Postal Savings, respectively.[74] The new funds were to operate on the basis of investments via the bond and stock markets. In the case of the public pension reserves, the government created a new Pension Investment Fund (Nenkin Unyo Kikin).[75] Simultaneously, the government closed down the Pension Welfare Corporation in 2001 and sold off the resort centers at a huge financial loss. The government did the same thing with unprofitable recreational facilities built by the former Ministry of Labor using the Employment Insurance reserves.

The Koizumi government also tackled the large organizational turf controlled by the former Ministries of Welfare and Labor. (As of January 2001, the Ministry of Health and Welfare and the Ministry of Labor merged to become the new Ministry of Health, Labor, and Welfare.) In 2005, Koizumi decided to dismantle the Social Security Agency, which was founded in 1962 as an arm of the Ministry of Welfare. This agency, too, like many special public corporations, offered the Ministry many *amakudari* positions. Koizumi's idea was to make the agency independent with a proper internal governance structure to prevent such a flow of personnel. The government set a date of 2008 for the dismantling of the agency (*Asahi Shimbun*, May 31, 2005; *Asahi Shimbun*, November 17, 2006). All these changes aimed at cutting back on bureaucrats' discretionary use of welfare funds. While not all efforts by the post-1996 prime ministers to rein in the bureaucratic agencies were successful, the era of complete bureaucratic discretion was over.[76]

While political motivations led to the FILP reform, economic calculations also played a role in the reform of savings-oriented welfare programs set at the corporate level. The major overhaul of the Employee Pension Fund and the legislation of the Corporate Pension Law in 2002 were largely due to financial globalization. The U.S. Generally Accepted Accounting Principles (GAAP) – the U.S. accounting standard – counted as debt the employers' pension commitments. This accounting standard was alien to Japanese firms, all of which had huge pension liabilities. All preexisting corporate pension plans in Japan – the Employee Pension Fund, Tax-Qualified Pension, and retirement lump-sum payments – entailed, from the U.S. accounting perspective, great financial risks.[77] For Japanese firms listed in American stock exchanges and those with large U.S. institutional investors (mostly mutual funds), these huge debts were a matter of

---

[74] The pension reserves, the Postal Savings, and the Postal Insurance were scheduled to gradually shift from FILP-based investments to market-based investments.

[75] The reserve amounted to 140 trillion yen at the time of this reform.

[76] For instance, a Ministry of Finance official involved in the FILP reform commented on how the goal of his ministry was to preserve the framework of the FILP and they succeeded (personal communication). Nonetheless, as this section has shown, the overall size of the FILP had shrunk as intended by politicians.

[77] The U.S. GAAP used a formula that was very unfavorable to employers that (i) provided defined benefit plans and (ii) had a long-term employment relationship with their workforce.

corporate survival.[78] The Corporate Pension Reform in 2002 was designed to adjust Japan's corporate pension regulations, so that Japan's largest firms could satisfy international (that is, U.S.) accounting standards. This reform was an additional factor in leading Japan to adopt marked-based corporate pension plans. Except for the Corporate Pension Reform, which was mainly caused by the application of the U.S. GAAP to Japan's publicly listed firms, other reforms discussed in this section would have been impossible without the new institutional context.

CONCLUSION

Japan's policy process has changed significantly in the post-1996 system. It now resembles, as this chapter has argued, a Westminster-style democracy. To summarize, as a result of the new SMD-dominant mixed electoral system and related political reforms, the LDP became a more centralized party and the prime minister gained agenda-setting power. Nonetheless, even with power concentrated in the hands of the prime minister, some reforms remained difficult. The new institutional configuration certainly allowed the LDP leader to tackle vested interests within the LDP. Many of the functional equivalents aimed at core constituent groups of the LDP were abolished or cut as the LDP prime minister sought to attract unorganized voters. This marked a big change from the politics under the old MMD/SNTV electoral system. Under the impact of the new electoral system, the post-1996 governments were able to adopt bolder reforms than any undertaken by the partial minority and coalition governments during the previous period (1989–1996).

Ironically, just as the universalistic rhetoric became popular, the government began retrenching the welfare state in a way never seen before. Japan's fiscal deficit and demographic aging required either large benefit cuts or even larger tax increases. Neither was a popular option. Increases in copayments thus were the easiest solutions. Many in Japan worry about the choices made by the Koizumi government. One could argue that the undoing of market-restricting functional equivalents to social security programs and of social security benefits happened at the same time. Although the government made attempts to introduce some universalistic benefits, the retrenchments have been bigger than the expansions.

Unlike the MMD/SNTV system, the new SMD-dominant system made possible electoral competition between the two largest parties. The DJP has been positioning itself to take advantage of voters' discontent with Koizumi's policies. The DJP has been accusing the LDP under Koizumi of widening the gap between the wealthy and the poor. Shinzo Abe, Koizumi's successor, was forced to promise new policies to help those who have failed in the market competition by giving them another chance. Whichever party captures the unorganized voters will win urban seats in the next election. It should also be emphasized that

---

[78] Interviews with Shozo Iwakuma and Shinichi Hiraoka at Hitachi Co. Ltd. on January 18, 2001 and Kiyotaka Fujiwara at Keidanren on January 15, 2001.

competitive districts are not always urban ones. We can observe the working of the structural logic in a strategic shift toward rural voters by the Democratic Party of Japan.

As the LDP tilted against its agricultural base, it gave an opening for the DPJ to exploit. In 2004, Naoto Kan, the DPJ leader at the time, pledged his party's commitment to farmers.[79] This was largely due to the DPJ's electoral calculations. The Democratic Party of Japan needed to win in as many single-member districts as possible in the Upper House elections scheduled for 2004. Many of those districts were located in rural areas.[80] The DPJ began to exploit rural voters' discontent with Koizumi's reforms, which, in their view, had impoverished rural areas by cutting back on public works. In 2006, the DJP came up with an agricultural income guarantee system that was much more favorable to small-scale farmers than the LDP's more efficiency-geared agricultural policy (*Asahi Shimbun*, March 16, 2006). This DPJ strategy paid off handsomely in the Upper House election in 2007. The DPJ won in the majority of rural single-member districts, causing a dramatic partisan shift of rural seats.

In short, under a Westminster-style system, regardless of which party controls the Diet, the structurally induced difficulty of raising revenue will persist. In this sense, if Japan continues on its path toward a Westminster-style system, we can predict that it will resemble a country like the United Kingdom where low taxes result in meager benefits. The SMD-dominant electoral system also tilts the political bias away from organized interest groups. As a consequence, we can predict that anticompetitive and other group-specific functional equivalent programs are likely to gradually disappear in Japan like they did in the United Kingdom.

The Upper House election in 2007, however, produced a historic change in Japanese politics. Even after the LDP lost its absolute majority in the Upper House in 1989, it had always continued to be the largest party in the Upper House. Yet in the aftermath of the 2007 elections, the Democratic Party of Japan emerged as the largest party in the Upper House, seizing control of the House Speakership and other crucial positions to determine the legislative calendar of the Upper House. Clearly, such a partisan configuration deviates starkly from the Westminster-style system. Japan's strong bicameralism thus holds the key to predicting Japan's future. The concluding chapter will come back to this issue.

---

[79] He made high-profile speeches in the party's convention in January as well as in the Diet on February 18, 2004.

[80] Remember that Japan's Upper House in reality adopts a mixed system of single-member districts and multimember districts, although officially it only uses multimember districts that range in size from two to fifty. The two-member districts become single-member districts because only half of the Upper House seats are re-elected every three years.

APPENDIX 9.A. *Chronology of Governments (1996–2007)*

Ryutaro Hashimoto	1996.11 ~1998.7	LDP Modified Coalition Government[a]
Keizo Obuchi	1998.7~2000.4	LDP-Led Coalition Government[b]
Yoshiro Mori	2000.4~2001.4	LDP-Komeito Coalition Government
Junichiro Koizumi	2001.4~2006.9	LDP-Komeito Coalition Government
Shinzo Abe	2006.9~2007.9	LDP-Komeito Coalition Government
Yasuo Fukuda	2007.9~present	LDP-Komeito Coalition Government (with a minority position in the Upper House)

[a] Sakigake and the Japan Socialist Democratic Party (formerly the Japan Socialist Party) left the Cabinet but continued to cooperate with the LDP.
[b] With the Liberal Party and then joined by Komeito. A group of the Liberal Party members later left the coalition.

Conclusion

Two Future Scenarios

This book has argued that it is possible to identify likely policy outcomes on the basis of three institutional factors: (i) district magnitude; (ii) the importance of the personal vote; and (iii) the government type. This structural logic approach provides a general analytical framework capable of explaining three different sets of variations – cross-national, cross-policy, and historical. This book has traced the postwar origin and development of electorally motivated distributive politics. Through case studies, it has demonstrated that policy makers actually behave the way predicted by the structural logic and for precisely those reasons identified by the logic.

Japan provides a useful test for an institutional model of welfare politics, because it has experienced major institutional changes. After nearly forty years of institutional stability, both Japan's government type and its electoral rules have changed in the past fifteen years. As a result, broadly speaking, Japan has experienced three very distinctive periods characterized by different institutional configurations. If the structural logic is right, we should be able to show differences in the pattern of welfare politics in Japan in the three periods as predicted by the structural logic. This book has shown that Japanese welfare politics indeed changed according to the structural logic.

The first period – the period of institutional stability from the end of the Allied Occupation of Japan to the Upper House election in 1989 – consisted of conservative dominance in the context of a MMD/SNTV system. The MMD/SNTV favored particularistic organized groups linked to individual conservative politicians. The LDP and its predecessors used public policy to build an elaborate system of political exchange. Japan's distinctive social protection system emerged out of the logic of the postwar MMD/SNTV system. Numerous benefit expansions and cuts took place during this period. Yet the distributive equation remained the same: particularistic groups linked to conservative politicians in power always enjoyed relative advantage whereas unorganized voters suffered disadvantages. Bureaucrats benefited greatly, too, by aligning themselves with

conservative politicians whose electoral interests were compatible with their organizational goals.

The second period (July 1989–November 1996) changed the old distributive
politics by expanding the scope of the organized groups that benefited from public
policy. The increase in the number of political parties during this period – as a
result of the emergence of partial minority and coalition governments – increased
the number of political parties with veto power. Given the continuation of the
MMD/SNTV system, which benefited organized groups, core constituents of
the new parliamentary veto players such as organized labor now stood to gain.
Japan's institutional configuration during the second period resembled that in
many northern European countries. For this reason, I have called this period a
northern European phase.

The Japanese government during this period introduced a whole range of
new programs and services for wage earners and their families. At the same
time, most of market-restricting regulations, which benefited parliamentary veto
players' constituent groups, also continued under the MMD system. Bureaucrats
continued to benefit from the presence of multiple parliamentary veto players
using their power to protect and promote organizational goals. This book has also
shown that a new pattern of tax politics emerged during this period. The Japanese
government during this period enjoyed greater tax capacities. The structural logic
predicts that coalition governments in MMD systems are likely to find it easier to
tax the majority than other types of governments. While the coalition diffuses the
identifiability of the party responsible for the unpopular policy, a MMD system
reduces voters' capacity to punish the ruling parties by voting them out of power.
Indeed, knowing that the electoral risk was contained, the coalition governments
that came into existence between 1993 and 1996 were more forthcoming with
their attempts to raise taxes insofar as they could earmark how to spend the
additional revenue.

The third period – November 1996 to 2007 – involved a more fundamental
distributive shift.[1] The first Lower House election under the new SMD-dominant
electoral rules took place in 1996. The new electoral rules set in motion the
development of a two-party system with greater concentration of power in the
hands of the prime minister and his Cabinet. With these changes, Japan has clearly
moved in the direction of a Westminster-style political system. As predicted
by the structural logic, the unit of electoral strategy has become the party –
even for a formerly decentralized party such as the LDP. The new electoral
strategy no longer favors particularistic groups. Instead unorganized voters and
competitive districts command the attention of the two largest parties. Indeed,
the post-1996 LDP prime ministers have tackled vested interests more earnestly
and effectively than their predecessors. This shift was particularly notable by the
time Junichiro Koizumi came to power in 2001. Strange as it may sound, he ran

---

[1] The Upper House election in 2007 was a historic one in that the LDP lost its position as the largest
party in the Upper House to the Democratic Party of Japan. I will talk about how this should be
interpreted by the structural logic approach.

for the LDP presidential race on an anti-LDP platform ("Smash the LDP"). This can only be understood in the context of the structural change of politics under way since the 1996 election. Koizumi, in order to ensure his party's survival, had to reorient his party toward urban unorganized voters. To this objective, he needed to centralize his party by overriding intraparty veto players.

Koizumi was as fortunate a politician as he was skilled. All the political reforms initiated by the post-1996 LDP governments – under Hashimoto and Obuchi – were fully in effect by 2001 when Koizumi assumed power. The enhanced capacity of the prime minister aided Koizumi in his power struggle with intraparty veto players. His effort to centralize power thus also meant wresting agenda-setting power from bureaucrats. Recall that politico-bureaucratic alliances controlled different policy segments, thereby decentralizing the policy-making process under LDP rule. As shown in Chapter 9, not only Koizumi but all of the post-1996 LDP prime ministers used top-down councils to circumvent veto from the politico-bureaucratic alliances. In the post-1996 period, the bureaucracy came to be characterized as one the major ills to be reckoned with. This was indeed a drastic change in the tone of politics in Japan, where conservative politicians had long maintained a cozy relationship with bureaucrats to their mutual benefit. As the structural logic claims, the MMD/SNTV system provided the foundation for such a cozy relationship to develop and flourish. The MMD/SNTV system made it worthwhile for individual politicians to specialize in a specific policy area of great import to their particularistic constituents. Bureaucrats with jurisdiction in specific policy areas served as great resources and allies for such politicians. In a SMD-dominant system, the electoral calculations of politicians – both the leaders and the rank and file – changed. Bureaucrats were suddenly left in limbo.

Furthermore, ever since the DPJ surged as a major party after the LDP, a more universalistic rhetoric began to dominate welfare politics. Japan's two largest parties, the LDP and DPJ, now very clearly state their universalistic welfare commitments. Indeed, the Japanese government began backpedaling on targeted forms of protection and welfare arrangements that profited particularistic rent-seeking groups. The electoral imperative to appeal to a wider group of voters has prompted the two largest parties to seek the most popular policy mix as their platform. Under the current electoral system, the electoral cost of unpopular policy decisions by the ruling party has increased drastically, while possible payoffs from popular policies also increased. The two parties now both promise more or less the same thing – a better social safety net for everyone, regardless of one's job or age. We can observe the two largest parties jockeying for unorganized voters. While the two parties both advocated economic reforms, the DPJ in the opposition was better placed to criticize the LDP government for producing losers in market competition – such as people who lost their jobs or experienced wage reductions – who had become significantly worse off. The DPJ promised a more egalitarian policy targeted at individual workers and not at specific interest groups as under the former system created by the LDP. The LDP has had to respond. It is noteworthy that Shinzo Abe, who succeeded Koizumi, chose to deemphasize reform and promised to create a new Japan with opportunities for the unsuccessful to retrain and start again.[2]

As predicted by the structural logic, the political importance of competitive districts also rose sharply. As the LDP under Koizumi successfully reoriented itself to appeal to urban unorganized voters to win more urban seats, rural districts have become more competitive. Although the LDP continued to rely on Komeito's help in urban districts, as the LDP's overwhelming landslide in the Lower House election in 2005 shows, Koizumi's LDP drastically increased the number of urban seats in its hands. The DPJ, in turn, used a two-pronged strategy to appeal to urban voters as well as rural voters disenchanted with the LDP as a result of Koizumi's "betrayal." The DPJ's victory in the Upper House election in 2007 partly reflects the success of this strategy. The DPJ won in most of the rural single-member districts without losing its competitive edge in urban districts.

Despite the promises of universalistic benefits, a better social safety net does not come cheaply. Yet both parties tiptoed around the issue of tax increases. This is because a SMD-dominant system makes the ruling party extremely vulnerable to a possible electoral backlash against an unpopular policy. If anything, the LDP government cut back on social security benefits to make ends meet at a time of unprecedented demographic aging. In the name of fair treatment for all generations, benefits for the elderly – health care, long-term care, and pensions – saw the largest cuts. The government improved benefits for working families, but the increases remained minor given the government's fiscal constraints. As a result, social security benefits did not improve, while at the same time Japan's market-restricting functional equivalents were cut back.

Today, many Japanese citizens are deeply concerned with widening inequality. Notwithstanding the scholarly debate on this topic, it is clear that the transition away from the old type of social protection to the new is causing societal anxiety. What will happen in Japan next? Japan's strong bicameralism holds the key to Japan's future. For the sake of simplicity, this book has treated the constitutional structure as a constant and left it out of the discussion. Most of the analytical framework was constructed assuming that the constitutional structure was unicameral. This made it possible to simplify the configuration of partisan veto players. This strategic choice made sense in analyzing Japanese politics until the Upper House election in 2007. As mentioned earlier in the book, even after its loss of the absolute majority in the Upper House in 1989, the LDP government maintained its hold on both Houses with the help of other smaller parties except for a brief period of the non-LDP coalition government. Until the 2007 elections, it also maintained its position as the largest party in both Houses. This means that the LDP government could control the legislative agenda on both floors of

---

[2] Very bizarrely, Abe began emphasizing his party's commitment to economic reform as a major theme of the campaign for the Upper House election in 2007 when voters were clearly more concerned with problems in the public pension administration and with widening inequality. Not surprisingly, Abe's LDP suffered a historic defeat. Abe's failure and the LDP's defeat provide further evidence that unpopular policies can cost dearly in the post-1996 institutional context.

the Diet. The LDP government was thus capable of containing the full impact of Japan's strong bicameralism. As long as these conditions held, it made sense to treat Japan as if it were a unicameral system. The emergence of the DPJ as the largest party in the Upper House changed these conditions, unleashing Japan's strong bicameralism.

Japan's strong bicameralism forces us to think about two possible future scenarios for Japan. In the first scenario, Japan completes its transformation into a Westminster-style democracy. For Japan to transform itself into a Westminster-style democracy, the same party needs to seize control of both Houses of the Diet.[3] If this happens – and continues – Japan's strong bicameralism will be weakened, and we can simply apply the logic of a modified Westminster system to predict the future course of Japan's social protection system. But if the same party does not control both Houses, Japan will deviate from its course to become a Westminster-style democracy. This leads us to the second scenario. In the second scenario, Japan becomes a divided government, whereby two different parties control each of the two Houses. The future of its welfare state will largely depend on which direction Japan takes. The claim of this book is that the structural logic approach can help us predict the future of Japan's social protection system depending on its course.

In the first scenario, it is possible to predict that Japan's welfare state is most likely to resemble that in the United Kingdom. The SMD-dominant electoral system and the strengthening of the prime minister and his Cabinet produce powerful prime ministers capable of big policy shifts. The two largest parties will continue to fight over the support of unorganized voters while offering favors to competitive districts. Universalistic trends are likely to be strengthened, whereas political support in favor of particularistic interest groups is likely to decline. This means that sooner or later, market-restricting functional equivalents will be significantly retrenched just as they were in the United Kingdom. At the same time, as already stated a number of times, the concentration of power in the context of a SMD-dominant system makes unpopular policies highly risky. Regardless of whether the LDP or DPJ is in power, broad-based tax increases that affect the majority will be very difficult to pass, just as they are in the United Kingdom. Universalistic rhetoric notwithstanding, underfunded meager public benefits supplemented by market-based welfare products are likely to be Japan's future.

These changes imply that Japan will find it increasingly difficult to sustain its CME. Japan's anticompetitive regulation and a web of other functional equivalents to the more orthodox social welfare programs helped sustain long-term commitments among key economic actors – such as between an employer and its workers, and between a large firm and its capital providers – despite Japan's official small welfare state. Considering that market-restricting functional

---

[3] As far as the structural logic is concerned, a coalition of one large party and one small one (as in the case of the LDP and Komeito) can be considered as a single party for the reasons identified in Chapter 9.

equivalents will be disappearing, the net level of social protection is expected to decline. When this shift is completed, Japan's market economy itself is likely to become more like a liberal market economy than a coordinated market economy. In other words, a change in the electoral rules can have profound implications for the economy as a whole. Here it might be useful to contrast the future course of Japan with the fate of the welfarist corporations in the United States. Once upon a time, just like many large Japanese firms, many large American firms relied on internal labor markets and tried to instill corporate loyalty by means of generous corporate welfare programs and seniority wages (Jacoby 1997; Moriguchi 2003; Swenson 2002). The absence of protective national institutions made it difficult for American corporations to continue these practices when challenged with socioeconomic changes.

Japan's strong bicameralism gives rise to the second scenario. Indeed, this second scenario came true with the Upper House election in 2007. Although the DPJ does not possess an absolute majority, it is now the largest party in the Upper House. As the largest party, it controls all the key positions in the Upper House that determine the legislative calendar. The DPJ potentially could hold up every legislative bill passed by the LDP that comes to the Upper House.

What does this second scenario mean for Japan's welfare politics? One thing that a divided government can achieve more easily than a Westminster-style system is a tax increase. A divided government, such as that described here, can also function as a grand coalition when the two largest parties come to an agreement. Although the competitive pressures of a SMD-dominant system do not make cooperation an optimal strategy, there is a good chance that the two largest parties will agree on tax increases. Both parties understand that it is very risky for one of them, as the ruling party, to be solely responsible for a tax increase. When both share the responsibility for such a decision, neither gets penalized – or at least, they level the electoral playing field. Something like a welfare tax that is earmarked for a specific use – and hence binds the next government – becomes much easier to introduce than in the first scenario. Under the second scenario, Japan can develop a much better social safety net for the majority of citizens.

Policy-based cooperation between the two largest parties thus partly resembles cooperation among coalition partners in a coalition government under an MMD system and partly resembles the bipartisan cooperation that occurs from time to time in a divided government (such as sometimes occurs in the United States). Cooperation among the largest parties diffuses blame and makes unpopular or costly policy possible. In this sense, a divided government in Japan becomes like coalition governments in Europe, where tax increases are easier than in SMD-based systems. It should be noted, however, that this does not mean the return to a social protection system that favors organized groups. In the second scenario, as in the first one, the SMD-based electoral incentives remain the dominant ones, as each of the two largest parties competes to win in the SMD tier. This means that political parties will generally endorse universalistic programs to capture the support of the median voter. (In both scenarios, some geographic allocation of government resources will always persist because both of the largest parties try to court voters in competitive districts.)

Another decisive difference between Japan's divided government and coalition governments in MMD systems is the different type of cooperation between the two largest parties. Any cooperation between the two largest parties in the current Japanese context is likely to be policy-specific and temporary. Under a SMD-dominant system, each large party's ultimate goal is to form its own government either alone or with one or two of the smaller parties. Each party has an incentive to outdo the other. This creates a basic tension between the two large parties even when they cooperate. In this sense, it differs from the cooperation that occurs in a coalition government under MMD systems. In other words, the constraints imposed by Japan's SMD-dominant electoral system will prevent Japan from forming a grand coalition like the one we see in Angela Merkel's coalition government in Germany. One can say that the policy-specific and temporary nature of bipartisan cooperation in Japan resembles that in the United States – a classic example of a divided government. Yet in Japan, unlike in the United States, bipartisan cooperation is brokered by party leaders rather than powerful individual legislators such as committee chairs.

Some Japanese commentators argue that the current divided government might bring back the old politics, whereby the LDP tries to recruit Diet members from other parties to join the LDP in their attempt to consolidate their dominance in the Diet. The SMD-dominant system, however, makes this a very unlikely scenario.

A divided government will continue for a long while unless the DPJ wins in the next Lower House election. Divided government can persist until 2009 – and beyond. Given the four-year term of Lower House members elected in 2005, Yasuo Fukuda, the new LDP prime minister, has the option not to call for another Lower House election until 2009. Given the fact that the LDP has two-thirds of the Lower House seats, there is no reason for the LDP prime minister to hastily call for an earlier election. If the DPJ wins in the 2009 Lower House elections, it could form a government and set Japan back on its Westminster-style track by dominating both Houses. (Of course, this could happen earlier than 2009, if the prime minister calls for an early Lower House election for whatever reason.) Anything short of a DPJ victory in the next round of the Lower House elections will lead to the continuation of the same divided government. For the LDP to recover its hold on the Upper House, it has to wait until 2013, when the cohort of the Upper House Diet members elected in 2007 complete their six-year term!

The instability of a divided government under a parliamentary system can lead to demands for further institutional reform. Many LDP politicians will have an incentive to bring back the old MMD-SNTV system to prevent the DPJ from seizing power. Under a MMD-SNTV system, as long as it maintains its position as a ruling party, the LDP can probably entice a sufficient number of DPJ members to switch to the LDP – or at least entice them to leave the DPJ to form a separate party and form a coalition government with the LDP. Pressures to go back to the old system are likely to gain force if the DPJ fails in the next Lower House elections. If this happens, Japan will go back to a one-party-dominant democracy.

If the DPJ wins, it is possible that the DPJ and the LDP might agree to complete Japan's transition to a Westminster-style system. This is likely to manifest itself in a possible constitutional revision to weaken Japan's bicameralism, a new measure to synchronize the elections for both Houses, and an electoral reform to further strengthen the SMD tier. As long as there is a built-in potential for a relatively easy shift of power – a more pure SMD system – the two largest parties will gain more from centralizing power than the status quo. For Japan to make this shift, the DPJ needs to seize power and hold it for a while. Right now, the DPJ continues to be as decentralized as the former LDP once was. It still resembles the coalition of mini-parties that came together to create it in the first place. Once the DPJ becomes the ruling party, its leader will have the authority of the prime minister to centralize his party – just as happened in the LDP under Koizumi.

With the possibility of periodic shifts of power, the terms of bureaucratic delegation are likely to change more fundamentally. The introduction of a SMD-dominant mixed system already changes the median Diet member's preference for the ideal terms of delegation. Unlike under the MMD-SNTV system, politicians today do not gain much by granting their bureaucratic allies wide discretion. In the old days, such discretion was mutually beneficial. Bureaucrats gained from it by using tax money to finance their own post-retirement positions. Politicians received handsome kickbacks in the form of distributive favors for their constituent groups and their financial contributors. Under the old MMD-SNTV system, the rewards of such arrangements outweighed the penalty. As explained earlier in the book, politicians and parties are relatively immune to the preferences of the majority of voters in the electoral district. Under the new SMD-dominant system, however, the penalty outweighs any benefit. The electoral volatility of the system makes it too risky to anger voters. In short, the outcome of the next Lower House election will be of historic importance for the future of Japan's democracy.

Finally, I want to end this book with a few words about the importance of socioeconomic changes. The structural logic approach adopted here does not deny the role of socioeconomic changes in producing partisan as well as policy shifts.[4] After all, Japan has experienced a great many socioeconomic challenges in the period covered in this book. In the past fifteen years alone, Japan experienced a prolonged recession in the aftermath of the bursting of the bubble economy; financial globalization; mounting fiscal deficit; and demographic aging. The bubble economy created, when it eventually burst, a severe crisis of nonperforming loans leading to the bankruptcies of a number of financial institutions – something unheard of in postwar Japan. This economic crisis does not itself, however,

[4] For excellent examinations of the role of socioeconomic changes in Japanese politics and economy, see Pempel (1998), Vogel (2006), and Schoppa (2006).

explain the policy responses that later governments adopted.[5] If economic problems defined a government's policy response, the sub-field of comparative politics would have become irrelevant a long time ago. What makes the study of comparative politics fascinating is that some countries adjust policies much faster and better than others.[6] My position is that political institutions hold at least one of the most important clues to explain such differences.

Having said that, I do believe that there is an important way in which socioeconomic changes and institutional changes are interlinked. Unfortunately, this is something that this book has not dealt with. This topic requires a book of its own. It was no coincidence, for instance, that a series of political reforms took place from the mid- to late 1990s in Japan. Political leaders – at least some of them – were aware that Japan faced new policy challenges that the existing political institutions were not suited to solve.[7] They, therefore, set in motion a process of institutional change. In my view, the very fact that socioeconomic problems first required the rewiring of the democratic hardware attests to the structural power of political institutions.

[5] Jennifer Amyx's study of how policy makers reacted – or rather failed to act – in the aftermath of the burst economic bubble drives this point home (Amyx 2004).

[6] Vogel (1999) argues that it is the close ties between winners and losers in the market competition in Japan that make economic reforms very slow in Japan. My institutional argument suggests that the shift from a pure MMD system to a SMD-dominant system weakens the political importance of such close ties. Even if the winners and losers are tied to one another and represented by the same industry associations or unions, the fact that the electoral bias has shifted away from organized interest groups means that their political influence has declined significantly.

[7] I attempt to address some of the questions regarding how socioeconomic and geopolitical contexts bring about political change in Estévez-Abe and Sugawara (2007).

Bibliography

Abegglen, James C., and George Stalk Jr. 1985. *Kaisha, the Japanese Corporation*. New York: Basic Books.

Aberbach, Joel D., Ellis S. Krauss, Michio Muramatsu, and Bert A. Rockman. 1990. "Comparing Japanese and American Administrative Elites." *British Journal of Political Science* 20 (4): 461–488.

Aberbach, Joel D., Robert D. Putnam, and Bert A. Rockman. 1981. *Bureaucrats and Politicians in Western Democracy*. Cambridge, Mass.: Harvard University Press.

Acemoglu, Daron, and Steffen Pischke. 1999. "The Structure of Wages and Investment in General Training." *Journal of Political Economy* 107 (3): 539–572.

Adema, William. 2001. "Net Social Expenditure: 2nd Edition." OECD Labour Market and Social Policy Occasional Paper #52.

Aizawa, Koetsu, and Motoo Hirakawa. 1996. *Sekai no Chochiku Kinyu Kikan*. Tokyo: Nihon Hyoronsha.

Albert, Michel. 1993. *Capitalism against Capitalism*. London: Whurr Publishers.

Allinson, Gary D. 1979. *Suburban Tokyo: A Comparative Study in Politics and Social Change*. Berkeley: University of California Press.

Allmendinger, Jutta. 1989. "Educational Systems and Labor Market Outcomes." *European Sociological Review* 5: 231–235.

Amyx, Jennifer. 2004. *Japan's Financial Crisis: International Rigidity and Reluctant Change*. Princeton, N.J.: Princeton University Press.

Anderson, Stephen. 1990. "The Political Economy of Japanese Saving: How Postal Savings and Public Pensions Support High Rates of Household Saving in Japan." *Journal of Japanese Studies* 16 (1): 61–93.

———. 1993. *Welfare Policy and Politics in Japan: Beyond the Developmental State*. New York: Paragon House.

Ando, Hiroshi. 1987. *Sekinin to Genkai vol. 2*. Tokyo: Kinyu Zaisei Jijo Kenkyukai.

Aoki, Masahiko. 1980. "A Model of the Firm as a Stockholder-Employee Cooperative Game." *American Economic Review* 70 (4): 600–610.

———. 1988. *Information, Incentives and Bargaining in the Japanese Economy*. Cambridge: Cambridge University Press.

———. 1994. "Contingent Governance of Teams: Analysis of Institutional Complementarity." *International Economic Review* 35 (3): 657–676.

Aoki, Masahiko, and Ronald Dore, eds. 1994. *The Japanese Firm*. Oxford: Clarendon Press.

Aoki, Masahiko, and Masahiro Okuno, eds. 1996. *Keizai Shisutemu no Hikaku Seido Bunseki*. Tokyo: Tokyo Daigaku Shuppankai.

Aoki, Masahiko, and Hugh Patrick, eds. 1994. *The Japanese Main Bank System*. Oxford: Oxford University Press.

Aoki, Yasuko. 1988. "Kenpo Kaisei no Seiji Katei." In *Zeisei Kaikaku wo meguru Seiji Rikigaku*, eds. Kenzo Uchida, Masao Kanasahi, Masayuki Fukuoka, 214–244. Tokyo: Chuo Koron.

Ariizumi, Toru. 1956. *Kyuyo/Koei Jutaku no Kenkyu*. Tokyo: Tokyo Daigaku Shuppankai.

Arioka, Jiro. 1996. "Kaigo Hoken Hoan no Kokkai Teishutsu wo meguru Seiji Rikigaku." *Shakai Hoken Junpo* 1913: 6–10.

Arnold, Douglas. 1979. *Congress and the Bureaucracy*. New Haven, Conn.: Yale University Press.

Asahi Seimei Sogo Kikakubu, ed. 1986. *Seimei Hoken Saishin Jijo*. Tokyo: Toyo Keizai Shinpo.

Asanuma, Banri. 1989. "Manufacturer-Supplier Relationships in Japan and the Concept of Relation-Specific Skill." *Journal of Japanese and International Economies* 2 (1): 2–30.

Baldwin, Peter. 1990. *The Politics of Social Solidarity: Class Bases of the European Welfare State 1875–1975*. Cambridge: Cambridge University Press.

Baqir, Reza. 1999. "Districts, Spillovers, and Government Overspending." Macroeconomics and Growth Working Paper 2192, Development Research Group, World Bank.

Baron, David P. 1991. "Majoritarian Incentives, Pork Barrel Programs, and Procedural Control." *American Journal of Political Science* 35 (1): 57–90.

Baron, David P., and Daniel Diermeier. 2001. "Elections, Governments and Parliaments in Proportional Representation Systems." *Quarterly Journal of Economics* 116: 933–968.

Bates, Robert, Avner Greif, and Margaret Levy, et al. 1998. *Analytic Narratives*. Princeton, N.J.: Princeton University Press.

Baums, Theodore. 1994. "The German Banking System and Its Impact on Corporate Finance and Governance." In *The Japanese Main Bank System: Its Relevance for Developing and Transforming Economies*, eds. Masahiko Aoki and Hugh Patrick, 409–449. New York: Oxford University Press.

Bawn, Kathleen. 1995. "Political Control versus Expertise: Congressional Choices about Administrative Procedures." *American Political Science Review* 89: 62–73.

———. 1997. "Choosing Strategies to Control the Bureaucracy: The Statutory Constraints, Oversight, and the Committee System." *Journal of Law, Economics, and Organization* 13: 101–126.

Bawn, Kathleen, Gary Cox, and Frances Rosenbluth. 1999. "Measuring the Ties That Bind: Electoral Cohesiveness in Four Democracies." In *Elections in Japan, Korea, and Taiwan under the Single Non-Transferable Vote: The Comparative Study of an Embedded Institution*, eds. Bernard Grofman, Sung-Chull Lee, Ewin A. Winckler, and Brian Woodall, 300–316. Ann Arbor: University of Michigan Press.

Bawn, Kathleen, and Frances Rosenbluth. 2006. "Short versus Long Coalitions: Electoral Accountability and the Size of the Public Sector." *American Journal of Political Science* 50 (2): 251–265.

Bawn, Kathleen, and Michael Thies. 2003. "A Comparative Theory of Electoral Incentives." *Journal of Theoretical Politics* 15 (1): 5–32.

Becker, Gary S. 1964. *Human Capital: A Theoretical and Empirical Analysis, with Special Reference to Education*. New York: Columbia University Press.

Berger, Suzanne, ed. 1977. "D'Une Boutique à L'autre: Changes in the Organization of the Traditional Middle Classes from the Fourth to Fifth Republics." Comparative Politics 10 (1): 121–136.

———. 1981. "Regime and Interest Representation: The French Traditional Middle Classes." In *Organizing Interests in Western Europe*, ed. Suzanne Berger, 83–101. New York: Cambridge University Press.

Berger, Suzanne, and Ronald Dore, eds. 1996. *National Diversity and Global Capitalism*. Ithaca, N.Y.: Cornell University Press.

Berger, Suzanne, and Michael Piore, eds. 1980. *Dualism and Discontinuity in Industrial Societies*. Cambridge: Cambridge University Press.

Berglof, Eric. 1990. "Capital Structure as a Mechanism of Control: A Comparison of Financial Systems." In *The Firm As a Nexus of Treaties*, eds. Masahiko Aoki, Bo Gustafsson, and Oliver E. Williamson, 237–262. London: Sage Publications.

Besley, Timothy, and Stephen Coate. 1999. "Centralized versus Decentralized Provision of Local Public Goods: A Political Economy Analysis." NBER Working Paper no. 7084.

Birchfield, Vicki, and Markus M. L. Crepaz. 1998. "The Impact of Constitutional Structures and Collective and Competitive Veto Points on Income Inequality in Industrialized Democracies." *European Journal of Political Research* 34: 175–200.

Blais, André, and Stéphane Dion, eds. 1991. *The Budget-Maximizing Bureaucrat*. Pittsburgh, PA: University of Pittsburgh Press.

Blöndal, Svenbjorn, and Mark Pearson. 1995. "Unemployment and Other Non-Employment Benefits." *Oxford Review of Economic Policy* 11 (1): 136–69.

Boix, Carles. 2001. "Democracy, Development, and the Public Sector." *American Journal of Political Science* 45 (January): 1–17.

Bonoli, Giuliano. 2000. *The Politics of Pension Reform: Institutions and Policy Change in Western Europe*. Cambridge: Cambridge University Press.

———. 2003. "Social Policy through Labor Markets: Understanding National Differences in the Provision of Economic Security to Wage Earners." *Comparative Political Studies* 36 (9): 1007–1030.

Bouissou, Jean-Marie. 1999. "Organizing One's Support Base under the SNTV: The Case of Japanese Koenkai." In *Elections in Japan, Korea and Taiwan under the Single Non-Transferable Vote: The Comparative Study of an Embedded Institution*, eds. Bernard Grofman, Sung-Chull Lee, Ewin A. Winckler, and Brian Woodall, 87–120. Ann Arbor: University of Michigan Press.

Boyer, Robert. 1991. "Capital Labor Relation and Wage Formation: Continuities and Changes of National Trajectories among OECD Countries." In *Making Economies More Efficient and Equitable: Factors Determining Income Distribution*, ed. Toshiyuki Mizoguchi, 297–340. Oxford: Oxford University Press.

———, ed. 1988. *The Search for Labour Market Flexibility: The European Economics in Transition*. Oxford: Oxford University.

Brennan, Geoffrey, and James M. Buchanan. 1980. *The Power to Tax*. New York: Cambridge University Press.

Brinton, Mary C. 1993. *Women and the Economic Miracle: Gender and Work in Postwar Japan*. Berkeley: University of California Press.

Burgoon, Brian. 2001. "Globalization and Welfare Compensation: Disentangling the Ties that Bind." *International Organization* 55 (3): 509–551.

Cabinet Office, Government of Japan. 2000. The Summary Results for "Dai-5-kai Koreisha no Seikatsu to Ishiki ni Kansuru Kokukai Hikaku Chosa kekka." http://www8.cao.go.jp/kourei/ishiki/h12_kiso/gaiyou.html.

Cain, Bruce, John Ferejohn, and Morris Fiorina. 1987. *The Personal Vote: Constituency Service and Electoral Independence*. Cambridge, Mass.: Harvard University Press.

Calder, Kent E. 1988. *Crisis and Compensation: Public Policy and Political Stability in Japan, 1949–1986*. Princeton: Princeton University Press.

———. 1989. "Elites in an Equalizing Role: Ex-Bureaucrats as Coordinations and Intermediaries in the Japanese Government-Business Relationship." *Comparative Politics* 21 (4): 379–404.

———. 1990. "Linking Welfare and the Developmental State: Postal Savings in Japan." *Journal of Japanese Studies* 16 (1): 31–59.

———. 1993. *Strategic Capitalism: Private Business and Public Purpose in Japanese Industrial Finance*. Princeton: Princeton University Press.

Calvert, Randall, Mathew D. McCubbins, and Barry R. Weingast. 1989. "A Theory of Political Control and Agency Discretion." *American Journal of Political Science* 33 (3): 588–611.

Cameron, David. 1978. "The Expansion of the Public Economy: A Comparative Analysis." *American Political Science Review* 72 (3): 1243–1261.

Campbell, John C. 1977. *Contemporary Japanese Budget Politics*. Berkeley: University of California Press.

———. 1979. "The Old People Boom and Japanese Policy Making." *Journal of Japanese Studies* 5 (2): 321–357.

———. 1992. *How Policies Change: The Japanese Government and the Aging Society*. Princeton: Princeton University Press.

Campbell, John C., and Naoki Ikegami. 1998. *The Art of Balance: Maintaining Japan's Low-Cost Egalitarian System*. New York: Cambridge University Press.

Campbell, John C., and Mikitaka Masuyama. 1994. "Nihon ni okeru Shinryo Hoshu Seisaku no Tenkai." *Kikan Shakai Hosho Kenkyu*, 29 (4): 359–368.

Carey, John M., and Mathew Soberg Shugart. 1994. "Incentives to Cultivate a Personal Vote: A Rank Ordering of Electoral Formulas." *Electoral Studies* 14 (4): 417–439.

Carpenter, Daniel. 2001. *The Forging of Bureaucratic Autonomy*. Princeton, N.J.: Princeton University Press.

Castles, Francis. 1978. *The Social Democratic Image of Society: A Study of the Achievements and Origins of Scandinavian Social Democracy in Comparative Perspective*. London: Routledge and Kegan Paul.

———. 1982. "The Impact of Parties on Public Expenditures." In *The Impact of Parties: Politics and Policies in Democratic Capitalist States*, ed. Francis Castles, 21–96. Beverly Hills: Sage.

Castles, Francis, and Deborah Mitchell. 1991. "Three Worlds of Welfare Capitalism or Four?" Discussion paper, Australian National University, Graduate Program in Public Policy.

Chang, Eric C. C., and Miriam Golden. 2007. "Electoral Systems, District Magnitude, and Corruption." *British Journal of Political Science* 37 (1): 115–137.

Christensen, Ray. 1998. "The Effects of Electoral Reform on Campaign Practices in Japan: Putting New Wine into Old Bottles." *Asian Survey* 38 (10): 986–1004.

———. 2006. "An Analysis of the 2005 Japanese General Election: Will Koizumi's Political Reforms Endure?" *Asian Survey* 46 (4): 497–516.

Christensen, Raymond, and Paul Johnson. 1995. "Toward a Context-Rich Analysis of Electoral Systems: The Japanese Example." *American Journal of Political Science* 39 (3): 575–598.

Chuma, Hiroyuki. 1998. "Kaikoken Kanyo Hori no Keizai Bunseki." In *Kaishaho no Keizaigaku*, eds. Yoshiaki Miwa, Hideki Kanda, and Noriyuki Yagakikawa, 425–451. Tokyo: Tokyo Daigaku Shuppankai.

———. 2002. "Employment Practices as Social Policy." *World Bank Institute*, no. 37199.

Clark, Robert. 1990. *Retirement Systems in Japan*. Pension Research Council of the Wharton School, University of Pennsylvania.

Cole, Robert. 1979. *Work, Mobility, and Participation: A Comparative Study of American and Japanese Industry*. Berkeley: University of California Press.

Colignon, Richard A., and Chikako Usui. 2003. *Amakudari: The Hidden Fabric of Japan's Economy*. Ithaca, N.Y.: Cornell University Press.

Cox, Gary. 1987. *The Efficient Secret: The Cabinet and the Development of Political Parties in Victorian England*. New York: Cambridge University Press.

———. 1990. "Centripetal and Centrifugal Incentives in Electoral Systems." *American Journal of Political Science* 34: 903–35.

———. 1994. "Strategic Voting Equilibria under the Single Nontransferable Vote." *American Political Science Review* 88 (3): 234–278

———. 1997. *Making Votes Count*. New York: Cambridge University Press.

———. 1999a. "Electoral Rules and the Calculus of Mobilization." *Legislative Studies Quarterly* 24 (3): 387–419.

———. 1999b. "Electoral Rules and Electoral Coordination." *Annual Review of Political Science* (June): 145–161.

Cox, Gary, and Mathew McCubbins. 1986. "Electoral Politics as a Redistributive Game." *The Journal of Politics* 48 (2): 370–389.

Cox, Gary, and Frances Rosenbluth. 1995. "The Structural Determinants of Electoral Cohesiveness: England, Japan, and the United States." In *Structure and Policy in Japan and the United States*, eds. Cowhey and McCubbins. New York: Cambridge University Press.

———. 1996. "Factional Competition for the Party Endorsement: The Case of Japan's Liberal Democratic Party." *British Journal of Political Science* 26:259–297.

Cox, Gary, Frances Rosenbluth, and Michael Thies. 1998. "Mobilization, Social Networks, and Turnout: Evidence from Japan." *World Politics* 50 (3): 447–474.

———. 1999. "Electoral Reform and the Fate of Factions: The Case of Japan's LDP." *British Journal of Political Science* 29: 33–56.

———. 2000. "Electoral Rules, Career Ambitions, and Party Structure: Conservative Factions in Japan's Upper and Lower Houses." *American Journal of Political Science*. 44 (1): 115–122.

Cox, Gary, and Michael Thies. 1998. "The Cost of Intraparty Competition: The Single, Non-Transferable Vote and Money Politics in Japan. *Comparative Political Studies* 31 (3): 267–291.

Cox, Karen, and Leonard Schoppa. 2002. "Interaction Effects in Mixed-Member Electoral Systems: Theory and Evidence from Germany, Japan, and Italy." *Comparative Political Studies* 35 (9): 1027–1053.

Crepaz, Markus. 1996. "Consensus versus Majoritarian Democracy: Political Institutions and Their Impact on Macroeconomic Performance and Industrial Disputes." *Comparative Political Studies* 29 (1): 4–26.

———. 1998. "Inclusion versus Exclusion: Political Institutions and Welfare Expenditures." *Comparative Politics* 31 (1): 61–80.

Crouch, Colin, and Wolfgang Streeck, eds. 1997. *Political Economy of Modern Capitalism: Mapping Convergence and Diversity*. London: Sage Publications.

Curtis, Gerald L. 1971. *Election Campaigning Japanese Style*. New York: Columbia University Press.

———. 1975. "Big Business and Political Influence." In *Modern Japanese Organization and Decisionmaking*, ed. Ezra Vogel, 33–70. Berkeley: University of California Press.

———. 1976. "The 1974 Election Campaign: The Political Process." In *Japan at the Polls: The House of Councillors Election of 1974*, ed. Michael Blaker, 45–80. Washington, DC: American Enterprise Institute.

————. 1988. *The Japanese Way of Politics*. New York: Columbia University Press.

————. 1999. *The Logic of Japanese Politics: Leaders, Institutions, and the Limits of Change*. New York: Columbia University Press.

Davis, Christina, and Jennifer Oh. 2006. "Japanese Agricultural Policy: The International and Domestic Pressures for Reform." Paper prepared for presentation to the Annual Meeting of the Association of Asian Studies, San Francisco, April 8, 2006.

Davis, Christina L. 2003. *Food Fights over Free Trade*. Princeton, N.J.: Princeton University Press.

Davis, E. Phillip. 1995. *Pension Funds: Retirement-Income Security and the Development of Financial Systems: An International Perspective*. N.Y.: Oxford University Press.

Davis, Steve J., and Magnus Henrekson. 1997. "Explaining National Differences in the Size and Industry Distribution of Employment." IUI Working Paper Series no. 482.

————. 2000. "Wage-Setting Institutions as Industrial Policy." Unpublished paper.

Dertouzos, Michael L., Richard K. Lester, Robert M. Solow, et al. 1989. *Made in America: Regaining the Productive Edge*. Cambridge Mass.: MIT Press.

Diaz-Cayeros, Alberto, Kenneth McElwain, Vidal Romero, and Konrad Siewierski. 2002. "Fiscal Decentralization, Legislative Institutions, and Particularistic Spending," unpublished paper.

Dobbin, Frank. 1992. "The Origins of Private Social Insurance: Public Policy and Fringe Benefits in America, 1920–1950." *American Journal of Sociology* 97 (5): 1416–1450.

Dobbin, Frank, and Terry Boychuk. 1996. "Public Policy and the Rise of Private Pension: The US Experience since 1930." In *The Privatization of Social Policy*, ed. Michael Shalev, 104–135. New York: St. Martin's Press.

Dore, Ronald P. 1973. *British Factory, Japanese Factory: The Origins of National Diversity in Industrial Relations*. Berkeley: University of California Press.

————. 1986. *Flexible Rigidities: Industrial Policy and Structural Adjustment in the Japanese Economy 1970–1980*. Stanford: Stanford University Press.

————. 1987. *Taking Japan Seriously: A Confucian Perspective on Leading Economic Issues*. Stanford: Stanford University Press.

————. 2000. *Stock Market Capitalism: Welfare Capitalism: Japan and Germany versus the Anglo-Saxons*. New York: Oxford University Press.

Dore, Ronald P., and Mari Sako. 1989. *How the Japanese Learn to Work*. New York: Routledge.

Dower, John W. 1999. *Embracing Defeat: Japan in the Wake of World War II*. New York: W.W. Norton & Co.

Downs, Anthony. 1957. *An Economic Theory of Democracy*. New York: Harper and Row.

Duus, Peter. 1998. *Modern Japan*. 2nd edition. Boston: Houghton Mifflin.

Duverger, Maurice. 1954. *Political Parties*. New York: Wiley.

Economic Planning Agency. 1958. *Keizai Hakusho 1958*. Tokyo: Okura Insatsukyoku.

————. 1990. *Keizai Hakusho*. Tokyo: Okura Insatsukyoku.

Edin, Per-Anders, and Robert Topel. 1997. "Wage Policy and Restructuring: The Swedish Labor Market Since 1960." In *The Welfare State in Transition: Reforming the Swedish Model*, eds. Richard B. Freeman, Robert Topel, and Birgitta Swedenborg, 155–201. Chicago: University of Chicago Press.

Edwards, Jeremy, and Klaus Fischer. 1994. *Banks, Finance, and Investment in Germany*. Cambridge: Cambridge University Press.

Eguchi, Takahiro. 1985. "Showa 59nendo Kenko Hoken-ho nado Kaisei no Rippo Katei." *Hokudai Hogaku Ronshu* 36 (3): 1091–1193.

Ekonomisuto Henshubu, ed. 1984. *Shogen: Kodo Seichoki no Nihon, vol. 2*. Tokyo: Mainichi Shinbunsha.

Endo, Kimitsugu. 1989. *Nihon Senryo to Roshi Kankei Seisaki no Seiritsu*. Tokyo: Tokyo Daigaku Shuppankai.

Endo, Masao. 1975. *Koyo Hoken no Riron*. Tokyo: Nikkan Rodo Tsushinsha.

Epstein, David, and Sharyn O'Halloran. 1994. "Administrative Procedures, Information, and Agency Discretion." *American Journal of Political Science* 38: 697–722.

———. 1995. "A Theory of Strategic Oversight: Congress, Lobbyists, and the Bureaucracy." *Journal of Law, Economics, and Organization* 11: 227–255.

———. 1996. "Divided Government and the Design of Administrative Procedures: A Formal Model and Empirical Test." *Journal of Politics* 58: 373–397.

———. 1999. "Delegation and the Structure of Policy Making: A Transaction Cost Politics Approach." *Journal of Theoretical Politics* 11: 37–56.

Esping-Andersen, Gøsta. 1985. *Politics against Market: The Social Democratic Road to Power*. Princeton: Princeton University Press.

———. 1990. *Three Worlds of Welfare Capitalism*. Princeton: Princeton University Press.

———. 1994. "Welfare States and the Economy." In *The Handbook of Economic Sociology*, eds. Neil J. Smelser and Richard Swedberg, 711–732. Princeton: Princeton University Press.

———. 1995. *Welfare States without Work: The Impasse of Labor Shedding and Familialism in Continental European Social Policy*. Madrid Instituto Juan March de Estudios e Investigaciones, Centro de Estudios Avanzados en Ciencias Sociales.

———. 1997. "Hybrid or Unique?: The Japanese Welfare State between Europe and America." *Journal of European Social Policy* 7 (3): 179–189.

———. 1999. *Social Foundations of Postindustrial Economies*. New York: Oxford University Press.

Esping-Andersen, Gøsta, and Walter Korpi. 1984. "Social Policy as Class Politics in Post-War Capitalism." In *Order and Conflict in Contemporary Capitalism*, ed. John Goldthorpe, 179–208. Oxford: Oxford University Press.

———. 1985. "From Poor Relief towards Institutional Welfare States: The Development of Scandinavian Social Policy." In *The Scandinavian Model: Welfare States and Welfare Research*, ed. R. E. Eriksson, 39–74. New York: M. E. Sharpe.

Esping-Andersen, Gøsta, Martin Rein, and Lee Rainwater, eds. 1987. *Stagnation and Renewal in Social Policy. The Rise and Fall of Policy Regimes*. Armonk: M. E. Sharpe.

Estévez-Abe, Margarita. 2001. "The Forgotten Link: The Financial Regulation of Japanese Pension Funds in Comparative Perspective." In *The Varieties of Welfare Capitalism: Social Policy and Political Economy in Europe, Japan and the USA*, eds. Philip Manow and Bernhard Ebbinghaus, 190–214. London: Routledge.

———. 2002. "Negotiating Welfare Reforms: Actors and Institutions in the Japanese Welfare State." In *Restructuring the Welfare State: Political Institutions and Policy Change*, eds. Bo Rothstein and Sven Steinmo, 157–183. New York: Palgrave.

———. 2003. "State-Society Partnership in the Japanese Welfare State." In *The State of Civil Society in Japan*, eds. Frank Schwartz and Susan Pharr, 154–172. New York: Cambridge University Press.

———. 2006. "Japan's Shift toward a Westminster System: A Structural Analysis of the 2005 Lower House Election and Its Aftermath." *Asian Survey* 46 (4): 632–651.

Estévez-Abe, Margarita, Torben Iversen, and David Soskice. 2001. "Social Protection and the Formation of Skills: A Reinterpretation of the Welfare State." In *Varieties of Capitalism: The Institutional Foundations of Comparative Advantage*, eds. Peter Hall and David Soskice, 145–183. London: Oxford University Press.

Estévez-Abe, Margarita, and Taku Sugawara. 2007. "The Efficient Secret Revisited: Changing Parties and Votes in Contemporary Japan," unpublished paper.

Eto, Mikiko. 1995. "Fukushi Kokka no Shukusho to Saihen to Kosei Gyosei." *Rebaiasan* 17: 91–114.

———. 1998. "Renritsu Seiken ni okeru Nihonfata Fukushi no Tenkai." *Rebaiasan* Special Issue (Summer) 17: 68–94.

Evans, Peter, Dieter Rueschemeyer, and Theda Skocpol, eds. 1985. *Bringing the State Back In*. Cambridge: Cambridge University Press.

Feuer, Michael J., Henry Glick, and A. Desai. 1987. "Is Firm-Sponsored Education Viable?" *Journal of Economic Behavior and Organization* 8 (1): 121–136.

Freeman, Richard. 1985. "Unions, Pensions, and Union Pension Funds." In *Pensions, Labor and Individual Choice*, ed. David Wise. Chicago: University of Chicago Press.

———. 1995. "The Large Welfare State as a System." *American Economic Review* 85 (2): 16–21.

Freeman, Richard, and M. J. Weitzman. 1987. "Bonuses and Employment in Japan." *Journal of Japanese and International Economics* 1: 168–194.

Fujita, Wakao, and Shobe Shiota 1963a. *Sengo Nihon no Rodo Sogi*, vol.1. Tokyo: Ochanomizu.

———. 1963b. *Sengo Nihon no Rodo Sogi*, vol.2. Tokyo: Ochanomizu.

Fukui, Haruhiko, and Shigeko Fukui. 1999. "Campaigning for the Japanese Diet." In *Elections in Japan, Korea, and Taiwan under the Single Non-Transferable Vote: The Comparative Study of an Embedded Institution*, eds. Bernard Grofman, Sung-Chull Lee, Ewin A. Winckler, and Brian Woodall, 121–152. Ann Arbor: University of Michigan Press.

Fukushima, Ryoichi, Mitsuhide Yamaguchi, and Shu Ishikawa, eds. 1973. *Zaisei Toyushi*. Tokyo: Okura Zaimu Kyokai.

Futaki, Ritsu. 1995. "Koteki Kaigo Hoken Ippento no Giron ni Igi Ari." *Shakai Hoken Junpo* 1868: 9–12.

Gao, Bai. 2001. *Japan's Economic Dilemma: The Institutional Origins of Prosperity and Stagnation*. New York: Cambridge University Press.

Garon, Sheldon. 1987. *The State and Labor in Modern Japan*. Berkeley: University of California Press.

Garon, Sheldon, and Mike Mochizuki. 1993. "Negotiating Social Contracts." In *Postwar Japan as History*, ed. Andrew Gordon, 145–166. Berkeley: University of California Press.

Gerlach, Michael. 1992. *Alliance Capitalism: The Social Organization of Japanese Business*. Berkeley: University of California Press.

Glick, Henry A., and Michael J. Feuer. 1984. "Employer-Sponsored Training and the Governance of Specific Human Capital Investments." *Quarterly Review of Economics and Business* 24 (2): 91–103.

Golden, Miriam A. 2003. "Electoral Connections: The Effects of the Personal Vote on Political Patronage, Bureaucracy, and Legislators in Postwar Italy." *British Journal of Political Science* 33 (2): 189–212.

Golden, Miriam A., and Lucio Picci. 2005. "Pork Barrel and Distributive Politics in Italy, 1952–1992," unpublished paper.

Goodman, Roger. 2000. *Children of the Japanese State: The Changing Role of Child Protection Institutions in Contemporary Japan*. Oxford: Oxford University Press.

Goodman, Roger, Gordon White, and Huck-Ju Kwon, eds. 1998. *The East Asian Welfare Model: Welfare Orientalism and the State*. New York: Routledge.

Gordon, Andrew. 1982. "Why U.S. Wage and Employment Behavior Differs from That in Britain and Japan." *Economic Journal* 92 (1): 13–44.

———. 1985. *The Evolution of Labor Relations in Japan: Heavy Industry, 1953–1955*. Cambridge, Mass.: Council on East Asian Studies, Harvard University.

———. 1989. "Business and the Corporate State: The Business Lobby and Bureaucrats on Labor 1911–1941." In *Managing Industrial Enterprise*, ed. William Wray, 53–85. Cambridge, Mass: The Council on East Asian Studies, Harvard University.

———. 1990. *Labor and Imperial Democracy in Japan*. Berkeley: University of California Press.

———. 1993. "Contests for the Workplace." In *Postwar Japan as History*, ed. Andrew Gordon, 373–394. Berkeley: University of California Press.

———. 1998. *Wages of Affluence: Labor and Management in Postwar Japan*. Cambridge, Mass.: Harvard University Press.

Gottfried, Heidi, and Jacqueline O'Reilly. 2002. "Re-Regulating Breadwinner Models in Socially Conservative Welfare Regimes: Comparing Germany and Japan." *Social Politics* 9 (1): 29–59.

Gould, Arthur. 1993. *Capitalist Welfare Systems: A Comparison of Japan, Britain, and Sweden*. New York: Longman.

Gourevitch, Peter, and James Shinn. 2005. *Political Power and Corporate Control: The New Global Politics of Corporate Governance*. Princeton: Princeton University Press.

Grofman, Bernard, Sung-Chull Lee, Ewin A. Winckler, and Brian Woodall, eds. 1999. *Elections in Japan, Korea, and Taiwan under the Single Non-Transferable Vote: The Comparative Study of an Embedded Institution*. Ann Arbor: University of Michigan Press

Grossman, Gene, and Elhanan Helpman. 2005. "Party Discipline and Pork Barrel Politics." NBER Working Paper 11396.

Gustman, Alan, Olivia Mitchell, and Thomas Steinmeier. 1994. "The Role of Pension in the Labor Market: A Survey of the Literature." *Industrial and Labor Relations Review* 47 (3): 417–438.

Hacker, Jacob S. 2002. *The Divided Welfare State: The Battle over Public and Private Social Benefits in the United States*. New York: Cambridge University Press.

Haggard, Stephen, and Mathew D. McCubbins, eds. 2001. *Presidents, Parliaments, and Policy*. Cambridge: Cambridge University Press.

Hall, Peter A. 1986. *Governing the Economy: The Politics of State Intervention in Britain and France*. Oxford: Oxford University Press.

Hall, Peter A., and Daniel Gingrich. 2004. "Varieties of Capitalism and Institutional Complementarities in the Macroeconomy: An Empirical Analysis." MPIfG Discussion Paper 04/05. Max-Planck-Institut für Gesellschaftsforschung: Cologne.

Hall, Peter A., and David Soskice, eds. 2001. *Varieties of Capitalism: The Institutional Foundations of Comparative Advantage*. New York: Oxford University Press.

Hall, Peter A., and Rosemary C. R. Taylor. 1996. "Political Science and the Three New Institutionalisms." *Political Studies* 44 (5).

Hallerberg, Mark. 2002. "Veto Players and the Choice of Monetary Institutions." *International Organization* 56 (4): 775–802.

Hallerberg, Mark, and Scott Basinger. 1998. "Internationalization and Changes in Tax Policy in OECD Countries: The Importance of Domestic Veto Players." *Comparative Political Studies* 31 (3): 312–352.

Harada, Sumitaka. 1985. "Sengo Jutaku Hosei no Seiritsu Katei." In *Fukushi Kokka*, vol. 6., ed. Tokyo Daigaku Shakai Kagaku Kenkyujo, 336–337. Tokyo: Tokyo Daigaku Shuppankai.

Harari, Ehud. 1974. "Japanese Politics of Advice in Comparative Perspective: A Framework for Analysis and a Case Study." *Public Policy* (22): 536–577.

Hashimoto, Masanori. 1979. "Bonus Payments, On-the-Job Training, and Lifetime Employment in Japan." *Journal of Political Economy* 87: 1086–1104.

Hashimoto, Masanori, and John Raisian. 1985. "Employment Tenure and Earnings Profiles in Japan and the United States." *The American Economic Review* 75 (4): 721–735.

Hatsuta, Tatsuo. 1994. *Shohizei wa Iranai*. Tokyo: Toyo Keizai Shinposha.

Hatsuta, Tatsuo, and Naohiro Yashiro, eds. 1995. *Jakusha Hogo Seisaku no Keizai Bunseki*. Tokyo: Nihon Keizai Shinbunsha.

Hauck, Michael. 1994. "Equity Market in Germany and Its Dependency on the System of Old Age Provisions." In *Institutional Investors and Corporate Governance*, eds. Theodor Baums, Richard M. Buxbaum, Klaus J. Hopt, 555–564. New York: Walter de Gruyter.

Hayakawa, Kazuo, and Tetsuya Tsunohashi. 1985. *Jutaku Mondai to Rodo Undo*. Tokyo: Toshibunkasha.

Hayakawa, Seiichiro. 1997. *Kokka Koumin no Shoshin Kyaria Keisei*. Tokyo. Nihon Hyoron-sha.

Hayakawa, Seiichiro, Yonosuke Okoshi, and Toshio Aida. 1984. *Denki Sangyo ni okeru Rodo Kumiai*. Tokyo: Otsuki Shoten.

Hayakawa, Yoshitaka. 1991a. "Fukushi Kokka wo meguru Seiji Katei (1): 84nen Kenko Hokenho Kaisei Katei no Jirei Kenkyu." *Komazawa Daigaku Hogaku Ronshu* 43: 111–159.

———. 1991b. "Fukushi Kokka wo meguru Seiji Katei (1): 84nen Kenko Hokenho Kaisei Katei no Jirei Kenkyu." *Komazawa Daigaku Seijigaku Ronshu* 33: 33–93.

Hayakawa, Yoshitaka, Yuji Yamaguchi, and Koji Tatsuki. 1986. "21 Seiki no Iryo Hoken wa Tenbo dekitaka: Kenko Hoken-ho Kaisei wo meguru Seiji Katei." *Handai Hogaku* (December): 140–180.

Hayami, Yujiro. 1991. "Institutional Aspects of Agricultural Development." In *The Agricultural Development of Japan: A Century's Perspective*, eds. Yujiro Hayama and Saburo Yamada, 61–108. Tokyo: Tokyo University Press.

Hazama, Hiroshi. 1964. *Nihon Romu Kanrishi Kenkyu: Keiei Kazoku Shugi no Keisei to Tenkai*. Tokyo: Daiyamondosha.

———. 1971. *Nihonteki Keiei: Shudan Shugi no Kozai*. Tokyo: Nihon Keizai Shinbunsha.

Heclo, Hugh. 1974. *Modern Social Policies in Britain and Sweden: From Relief to Income Maintenance*. New Haven: Yale University Press.

Heidenheimer, Arnold J., Hugh Heclo, and Carolyn Teich Adams. 1990. *Comparative Public Policy: The Politics of Social Choice in America, Europe and Japan*. New York: St. Martin's Press.

Hemmi, Kenzo. 1982. "Agriculture and Politics in Japan." In *US-Japanese Agricultural Trade Relations*, eds. Emery N. Castle and Kenzo Hemmi, 219–274. Washington, D.C.: Resources for the Future.

Hendershott, Patrick. 1994. "Housing Finance in the United States." In *Housing Markets in the United States and Japan*, eds. Yukio Noguchi and James M. Poterba, 65–86. Chicago: University of Chicago Press.

Hicks, Alexander. 1999. *Social Democracy and Welfare Capitalism: A Century of Income Security Politics*. Ithaca: Cornell University Press.

Hicks, Alexander, and Lane Kenworthy. 1998. "Cooperation and Political Economic Performance in Affluent Democratic Capitalism." *American Journal of Sociology* 103 (6): 1631–1672.

Hicks, Alexander, and Duane Swank. 1984. "On the Political Economy of Welfare Expansion." *Comparative Political Studies* 17: 81–119.

———. 1992. "Politics, Institutions, and Welfare Spending in Industrialized Democracies, 1960–1982." *American Political Science Review* 86: 658–674.

———. 1999. *Social Democracy and Welfare Capitalism*. Ithaca: Cornell University Press.

Hikotani, Takako. 2004. "Shibirian Kontororu no Shorai." *Kokusai Anzen Hosho* 32 (1): 21–48.

Hirata, Keiichiro, Chu Saichi, and Izumi Minomatsu, eds. 1979a. *Showa Zeisei no Kaiko to Tenbo: vol. 1*. Tokyo: Okura Zaimu Kyokai.

———. 1979b. *Showa Zeisei no Kaiko to Tenbo: vol. 2*. Tokyo: Okura Zaimu Kyokai.

Hiroi, Yoshinori. 1994. *Iryo no Keizaigaku*. Tokyo Nihon Keizai Shinbunsha: 93–126.

Hisamoto, Norio. 1998. *Kigyonai Roshikankei to Jinzai Keisei*. Tokyo: Yuhikaku.

Hitachi Seisakujo. 1971. *Hitachi Seisakujo-shi vol.3*. Tokyo: Hitachi Seisakujo.

Hiwatari, Nobuhiro. 1991. *Sengo Nihon no Shijo to Seiji*. Tokyo: Tokyo University Press.

———. 1995. "55nen Seitosei Henyo no Seikan Kankei." In *Gendai Nihon Seikan Kankei no Keisei Katei*, ed. Nihon Seijigakkai, 77–105. Tokyo: Iwanami Shoten.

———. 2006. "Koizumi Kaikaku no Iso." In *Ushinawareta 10-nen wo Koete II: Koizumi Kaikaku no Jidai*, ed. Tokyo University Social Science Research Institute, 25–72. Tokyo: Tokyo University Press.

Hollingsworth, J. Rogers, and Robert Boyer, eds. 1997. *Contemporary Capitalism: The Embeddedness of Institutions*. Cambridge: Cambridge University Press.

Honma, Masayoshi 1994. *Nogyo Mondai no Seiji Keizaigaku*. Nihon Keizai Shinbunsha.

Honma, Masayoshi, and Yujiro Hayami. 1991. "Causes of Growth and Agricultural Protection." In *The Agricultural Development of Japan: A Country's Perspective*, eds. Yujiro Hayami and Saburo Yamada, 221–239. Tokyo: Tokyo University Press.

Horiuchi, Yusaku, and Jun Saito. 2003. "Reapportionment and Redistribution: Consequences of Electoral Reform in Japan." *American Journal of Political Science* 47 (4): 669–682.

Horn, Murray J. 1995. *The Political Economy of Public Administration*. Cambridge: Cambridge University Press.

Howard, Christopher. 1997. *The Hidden Welfare State: Tax Expenditures and Social Policy in the United States*. Princeton: Princeton University Press.

Huber, Evelyne, Charles Ragin, and John D. Stephens. 1993. "Social Democracy, Christian Democracy, Constitutional Structure, and the Welfare State." *American Journal of Sociology* 99 (3): 711–749.

Huber, Evelyne, and John Stephens. 2001. *Development and Crisis of the Welfare State*. Chicago: Chicago University Press.

Huber, John D., and Charles R. Shipan. 2000. "The Cost of Control: Legislators, Agencies, and Transaction Costs." *Legislative Studies Quarterly* 25 (1): 25–52.

Huber, John D., Charles R. Shipan, and Madelaine Pfahler. 2001. "The Legislatures and Statutory Control of Bureaucracy." *American Journal of Political Science* 45 (2): 330–345.

Hyodo, T. 1971. *Nihon ni Okeru Roshi Kankei no Tenkai*. Tokyo: Tokyo University Press.

Igarashi, Akira. 1985. "Kakushin Seito." In *Gendai Nihon no Seiji Kozo*, ed. Jiro Kamishima, 143–231. Kyoto: Horitsu Bunkasha.

Ihori, Toshihiro, and Takero Doi 1998. *Nihon Seiji no Keizai Bunseki*. Tokyo: Bokutakusha.

Iino, Yasushi. 1992. "Ikuji Kyugyo to Shotoku Hosho." *Kikan Rodoho* 163: 2–6.

———. 1996. "Chu Fukushi/Chu Futan no Genso." *Mita Shogaku Kenkyu* 39 (3): 97–103.

Iio, Jun. 1993. *Mineika no Seijikatei: Rinchogata Kaikaku no Seika to Genkai*. Tokyo: Tokyo University Press.

———. 2004. "Nihon ni Okeru Futatsu no Seifu to Seikan Kankei." *Rebaiasan* 34: 7–19.

———. 2006. "Fukudaijin, Seimujikan Seido no Mokuteki to Jisseki." *Rebaiasan* 38: 41–59.

Ikeda, Shozo. 1996. "Kaigo Hoken wo Tsubushitanowa Dareda." *Ronza* (August): 62–67.

Immergut, Ellen. 1986. "Between State and Market: Sickness Benefits and Social Control." In *Public/Private Interplay in Social Protection: A Comparative Study*, eds. Martin Rein and Lee Rainwater, 57–98. Armonk, N.Y: M. E. Sharpe.

———. 1991. "Institutions, Veto Points, and Policy Results: A Comparative Analysis of Health Care." *Journal of Public Policy* 10 (4): 391–416.

———. 1992. *Health Politics: Interests and Institutions in Western Europe*. New York: Cambridge University Press.

Inatsugu, Hiroaki. 1996. *Nihon no Kanryo Jinji Shisutemu*. Tokyo: Toyo Keizai Shinposha.

Industrial Bank of Japan. 1993. *Nihon Sangyo Tokuhon*. Tokyo: Toyo Keizai Shinposha.

Inoguchi, Takashi, and Yasunobu Iwai.1987. *Zoku Giin no Kenkyu: Jiminto Seiken wo Gyujiru Shuyaku tachi*. Tokyo: Nihon Keizai Shinbunsha.

Inoki, Takenori. 1995. "Japanese Bureaucrats at Retirement: Mobility of Human Resources from Central Government to Public Corporations." In *The Japanese Civil Service and Economic Development*, eds. Hyung-ki Kim, Michio Muramatsu, T. J. Pempel, and Kozo Yamamura, 213–234. Oxford: Clarendon Press.

Ishida, Hirohide. 1963. "Hoshuto no Bijon." *Chuo Koron* (January): 88–97.

Ishihara, Nobuo. 2001. *Kengen no Daiido*. Tokyo: Kanki Shuppan.

Ishikawa, Shu, and Toyoo Gyoten, eds. 1977. *Zaisei Toyushi*. Tokyo: Kinyu Zaisei Jijo Kenkyukai.

Ito, Mitsuharu, and Ekonomisuto Henshubu, eds. 1977. *Sengo Sangyoshi eno Shogen: Vol.1*. Tokyo: Mainichi Shinbunsha.

Ito, Mitsutoshi. 1988. "Daikigyo Roshi Rengo no Keisei." *Rebaiasan* 2 (Spring): 53–70.

———. 2000. "Renritsu Seiken no Seisaku Noryoku." In *Henka wo Do Setsumei Suruka: Seijihen*, eds. Norihito Mizukuchi, Tetsuya Kitahara, and Ikuo Kume, 207–234. Tokyo: Mokutakusha.

———. 2004. "Kantei Shidogata Seisaku Kettei to Jiminto." *Rebaiasan* (April): 7–40.

Itsumi, Kenzo, and Yuzuru Kato, eds..1985. *Kihonho Nosei no Keizai Bunseki*. Tokyo: Meibun Shobo.

Iversen, Torben, and David Soskice. 2001. "An Asset Theory of Social Policy Preferences." *American Political Science Review* 95 (4): 875–893.

———. 2002. *"Political Parties and the Time Inconsistency Problem in Social Welfare Provision,"* unpublished paper.

———. 2006. "Electoral Institutions and the Politics of Coalitions: Why Some Democracies Redistribute More than Others." *American Political Science Review* 100 (2): 165–181.

Iwai, Yasunobu. 1990. *Seiji Shikin no Kenkyu: Rieki Yudo no Nihonteki Seiji Fudo*. Tokyo: Nihon Keizai Shinbunsha.

———. 2002. "Yoto Shinsa wo Haishi seyo." *Ronza* (January): 86–93.

Iwamoto, Yasushi. 1995. "Chusho Kigyo Hogo." In *Jyakusha Hogo Seisaku no Keizai Bunseki*, eds. Tetsuo Hatsuta and Naohiro Yashiro, 11–50. Tokyo: Nihon Keizai Shinbunsha.

Jacoby, Sanford. 1997. *Modern Manors: Welfare Capitalists since the New Deal*. Princeton, N.J.: Princeton University Press.

Johnson, Chalmers. 1975. "Japan Who Governs?" *Journal of Japanese Studies* 2 (1): 1–28.

———. 1978. *Japan's Public Policy Companies*. Stanford: Hoover Institution.

———. 1986. "Tanaka Kakuei, Structural Corruption, and the Advent of Machine Politics in Japan." *Journal of Japanese Studies* 12 (1): 1–28.

Jutaku Kinyu Koko Nijunenshi Hensan Iinkai, ed. 1960. *Jutaku Kinyu Koko Junenshi*. Tokyo: Jutaku Kinyu Koko.

Kabashima, Ikuo. 2004. *Sengo Seiji no Kiseki: Jiminto Shisutemu no Keisei to Henyo*. Tokyo: Iwanami Shoten.

Kahn, Alfred, and Sheila Kamerman. 1983. *Income Transfers for Families with Children: An Eight-Country Study*. Philadelphia: Temple University Press.

Kamerman, Sheila, and Alfred Kahn. 1989. *Privatization and the Welfare State*. Princeton, N.J.: Princeton University Press.

———. 1991. *Government Expenditures for Children and Their Families in Advanced Industrialized Countries, 1960–1985*. UNICEF International Child Development Center, Innocenti Occasional Papers, Economic Policy Series, no. 20.

Kanbara, Masaru. 1986. *Tenkanki no Seiji Katei: Rincho no Kiseki to Sono Kino*. Tokyo: Sogo Rengo Kenkyujo.

Kaneko, Masaru. 1991. "Kaisha Shakai no Keisei to Nihon Shakai." In *Gendai Nihon Shakai* vol. 5., ed. Tokyo University Social Science Research Institute, 125–167. Tokyo: Tokyo University Press.

Kariya, Takehiko. 1991. *Gakko Shokugyo Senbatsu no Shakaigaku: Kosotsu Shushoku no Nihonteki Mekanizumu*. Tokyo: Tokyo University Press.

Kasahara, Nagatoshi. 1968. "Kinyu Shihon Keiretsuka no Sokushin to Hokenkaisha no Yakuwari." In *Nihon Hokengyoshi: Soron*, ed. Nihon Hokengyoshi Hensan Iinkai, 381–575. Tokyo: Hokenkenkyujo.

Kasza, Gregory. 2002. "War and Welfare Policy in Japan." *The Journal of Asian Studies* 61 (2): 417–434.

———. 2006. *One World of Welfare: Japan in Comparative Perspective*. Ithaca, N.Y.: Cornell University Press.

Kato, Hiroshi, and Yoichi Sando. 1983. *Dokosan to Tomoni 730 Nichi*. Tokyo: Keizai Oraisha.

Kato, Junko. 1991a. "Public Pension Reforms in the United States and Japan: A Study of Comparative Public Policy." *Comparative Political Studies* 24 (1): 100–126.

———. 1991b. "Seisaku Kettei Katei Kenkyu no Riron to Jissho: Koteki Nenkin Seido to Iryo Hoken Seido Kaikaku no Kesu." *Rebaiasan* 8: 165–184.

———. 1994. *The Problem of Bureaucratic Rationality: Tax Politics in Japan*. Princeton: Princeton University Press.

———. 1995. "Seisaku Chishiki to Seikan Kankei." In *Gendai Nihon Seikan Kankei no Keisei Katei*, ed. Nihon Seiji Gakkai, 107–134. Tokyo: Iwanami Shoten.

———. 1996. "Review Article: Institutions and Rationality in Politics – Three Varieties of Neo-Institutionalists." *British Journal of Political Science* 26: 553–583.

———. 1997. *Zeisei Kaikaku to Kanryosei*. Tokyo: Tokyo University Press.

Katsumata, Sachiko. 2004. "The Relationship between the Role of the Corporate Pension and the Public Pension Plan in Japan." In *Rethinking the Welfare State: The Political Economy of Pension Reform*, eds. Martin Rein and Winifred Schmahl, 56–80. Northampton, Mass: Edward Elgar.

Katz, Eliakim, and Adrian Ziderman. 1990. "Investment in General Training: The Role of Information and Labor Mobility." *The Economic Journal* 100 (403): 1147–1158.

Katz, Richard. 1986. "Intraparty Preference Voting." In *Electoral Laws and Their Political Consequences*, eds. Bernard Grofman and Arend Lijphart, 85–103. New York: Agathon Press.

———. 1998. *Japan, the System that Soured: The Rise and Fall of the Japanese Economic Miracle*. New York: M. E. Sharpe.

Katzenstein, Peter J. 1985. *Small States in World Markets*. Ithaca, N.Y.: Cornell University Press.

Kenko Hoken Kumiai Rengokai, ed. 1971. *Shakai Hosho Nenkan 1971*. Tokyo: Toyo Keizai Shinposha.

———. 1995. *Shakai Hosho Nenkan 1995*. Tokyo: Toyo Keizai Shinposha.

Kenkyukai, Nihon Romu. 1975. *Romu Nenkan 1975*. Tokyo: Nihon Romu Kenkyukai.

Kenny, Martin, and Richard Florida. 1988. "Beyond Mass Production and the Labor Process in Japan." *Politics and Society* 16: 121–158.

Kenworthy, Lane. 1995. *In Search of National Economic Success: Balancing Competition and Cooperation*. Thousand Oaks, California: Sage Publications.

Kester, W. Carl. 1992. "Governance, Contracting and Investment Time Horizons: A Look at Germany and Japan." *Continental Bank Journal of Applied Corporate Finance* 5 (2): 83–98.

Kido, Yoshiko. 1990. "Jutaku Seisaku Hyoka eno Saihaibunteki Shiten." In *Jutaku Seisaku to Shakai Hosho*, ed. Shakai Hosho Kenkyujo, 75–106. Tokyo: Tokyo University Press.

Kikkawa, Takeo. 1992. "Sengo-gata Kigyo Shudan no Keisei." In *Nihon Keizai no Hatten to Kigyo Shudan*, eds. Juro Hashimoto and Haruto Takeda, 255–304. Tokyo: Tokyo University.

Kimoto, Satoko. 1996. "Fringe Benefit Kazei no Kenkyu." *Zeimu Daigakko Ronshu* 27: 1–135.

King, Desmond. 1995. *Actively Seeking Work? The Politics of Unemployment and Welfare Policy in the United States and Britain*. Chicago and London: University of Chicago Press.

King, Desmond, and Bo Rothstein. 1993. "Institutional Choices and Labour Market Policy: A British-Swedish Comparison." *Comparative Political Studies* 26 (2): 147–177.

Kitaoka, Shinichi. 1985. "Jiyuminshuto: Hokatsu Seito no Gorika." In *Gendai Nihon no Seiji Kozo*, ed. Jiro Kamishima, 25–141. Kyoto: Horitsu Bunkasha.

Kitayama, Toshiaki. 2003. "Doken Kokka Nihon to Shihon Shugi no Shoruikei." *Rebaiasan* 32 (Spring): 123–146.

Kitschelt, Herbert. 2000. "Linkages between Citizens and Politicians in Democratic Polities." *Comparative Political Studies* 33 (6–7): 845–879.

Kobayashi, Yoshiaki. 1997. *Gendai Nihon no Seiji Katei (The Political Process in Contemporary Japan)*. Tokyo: Tokyo University Press.

———. 1985. *Keiryo Seijigaku*. Tokyo: Seibundo.

Kohno, Masaru. 1997. *Japan's Postwar Party Politics*. Princeton, N.J.: Princeton University Press.

Kohno, Masaru, and Yoshitaka Nishizawa. 1990. "A Study of the Electoral Business Cycle in Japan: Elections and Government Spending in Public Construction." *Comparative Politics* 22: 151–168.

Koike, Kazuo. 1981. *Nihon no Jukuren*. Tokyo: Yuhikaku.

———. 1987. "Human Resource Development and Labor-Management Relations." In *The Political Economy of Japan, vol. 1: The Domestic Transformation*, eds. Kozo Yamamura and Yasukichi Yasuba, 289–330. Stanford: Stanford University Press.

———. 1988. *Understanding Industrial Relations in Modern Japan*. London: Macmillan.

———. 1990. "Intellectual Skill and the Role of Employees as Constituent Members of Large Firms in Contemporary Japan." In *The Firm As a Nexus of Treaties*, eds. Masahiko Aoki, Bo Gustafsson, and Oliver E. Williamson, 185–208. London: Sage Publications.

———. 1991. *Shigoto no Keizaigaku*. Tokyo: Toyo Keizai Shinposha.

Kokuritsu Kokkai Toshokan Chosa Rippou Kosakyoku. 1972. "*Wagakuni no Shotokuzei no Hensen*: 1949–1971." Research material #71–3.

Kokuritsu Shakai Hosho Jinko Mondai Kenkyujo, ed. 1996. *Shakai Hosho Tokei Nenpo 1995*. Tokyo: Hoken.

Köllner, Patrick. 2002. "Upper House Elections in Japan and the Power of the 'Organized Vote.'" *Japanese Journal of Political Science* 3 (1): 113–137.

Komiya, Ryutaro. 1994. "The Life Insurance Company as a Business Enterprise." In *Business Enterprise in Japan: Views of Leading Japanese Economists*, eds. Kenichi Imai and Ryutaro Komiya, 365–386. Cambridge, Mass.: MIT Press.

Kondo, Bunji. 1963. *Shakai Hoken*. Tokyo: Iwanami Shoten.

Kono, Koretaka. 1993. *Zaisei Toyushi no Kenkyu*. Tokyo: Zeimu Keiri Kyokai.

Koreisha Shuro Jyukyu Mondai Kenkyukai. 1983. *Koreisha Kaisha ni Kansuru Jittai Chosa Hokokusho.* Tokyo: Tokyoto Rodo Keizaikyoku.

Korpi, Walter. 1978. *The Working Class in Welfare Capitalism: Work, Unions, and Politics in Sweden.* London: Routledge and Kegan Paul.

———. 1980. "Social Policy and Distributional Conflict in the Capitalist Democracies: A Preliminary Comparative Framework." *West European Politics* 3 (3): 296–316.

———. 1983. *The Democratic Class Struggle.* London: Routledge and Kegan Paul.

———. 1985. "Economic Growth and the Welfare State: Leaky Bucket or Irrigation System?" *European Sociological Review* 1: 97–118.

———. 1989. "Power, Politics, and State Autonomy in the Development of Social Citizenship: Social Rights during Sickness in OECD Countries since 1930." *American Sociological Review* 54 (3): 309–328.

Kosei Nenkin Kikin Rengokai, ed. 1979. *Kosei Nenkin Kikin 10 nenshi.* Tokyo: Kosei Nenkin Rengokai.

Koseidan, ed. 1988. *Kosei Nenkin Hoken Seido Kaikoroku.* Tokyo: Shakai Hoken Hoki Kenkyukai.

Koseisho Gojunen Henshu Iinakai, ed. 1988. *Koseisho Gojunenshi.* Tokyo: Kosei Nondai Kenkyukai and Chuo Hoki Shuppan.

Kotani, Naomitsu. 1995. "Koteki Kaigo Hoken no Kochiku ni Mukete." *Insurance* 3638 (January 12, 1995): 12–17.

Kotlikoff, Laurence, and David Wise. 1985. "Labor Compensation and the Structure of Private Pension Plans: Evidence for Contractual vs. Spot Labor Markets." In *Pensions, Labor, and Individual Choice,* ed. David Wise, 55–85. Chicago: University of Chicago Press.

Koyama, Michio, ed. 1985. *Sengo Iryo Hosho no Shogen (Testimonies of the Postwar Medical Insurance System).* Tokyo: Sogo Rodo Kenkyujo.

Koyama, Shinjiro. 1950. *Seikatsu Hogoho no Kaishaku to Unyo.* Tokyo: Nihon Shakai Jigyo Kyokai.

Krauss, Ellis S. 1980. "Opposition in Power: The Development and Maintenance of Leftist Government in Kyoto Prefecture." In *Political Opposition and Local Politics in Japan,* eds. Kurt Steiner, Ellis S. Krauss, and Scott C. Flanagan, 383–424. Princeton: Princeton University Press.

———. 1993. "'Presidentialization' in Japan? The Prime Minister, Media, and Elections in Japan." *British Journal of Political Science* 35: 357–368.

Krauss, Ellis S., and Benjamin Nyblade. 2005. "'Presidentialization' in Japan? The Prime Minister, Media, and Elections in Japan." *British Journal of Political Science* 35: 357–368.

Krauss, Ellis S., and Robert Pekkanen. 2004. "Explaining Party Adaptation to Electoral Reform: The Discreet Charm of the LDP." *Journal of Japanese Studies* 30 (1): 1–34.

Kubler, Friedrich. 1994. "Institutional Investors and Corporate Governance: A German Perspective." In *Institutional Investors and Corporate Governance,* eds. Theodor Baums, Richard Buxbaum, Klaus Hopt, 565–579. New York: Walter de Gruyter.

Kubono, Shigeharu. 1994a. *Kokusai Hikaku kara mita Shakai Hosho Kaikaku.* Tokyo: Nenkin Kenkyujo.

———. 1994b. *Zaisei to Shakaihosho no Shakai Hosho no Shomondai.* Tokyo: Nenkin Kenkyujo.

Kudo, Nobuo. 1979. *Koreika Jidai no Taishokukin Nenkin Seido.* Tokyo: Nihon Keieisha Dantai Renmei.

Kume, Ikuo. 1988. "Changing Relations among Government, Business and Labor in Japan after the Oil Crisis." *International Organization* 42 (4): 659–687.

———. 1998. *Disparaged Success: Labor Politics in Postwar Japan.* Ithaca, N.Y.: Cornell University Press.

———. 2000. "Rodo Seisaku Katei no Seijuku to Henyo." *Nihon Rodo Kenkyu Zasshi* 475 (1): 2–13.

Kurosumi, Akira. 1966. *Teinensei, Taishokukin, Taishoku Nenkin.* Tokyo: Nihon Junposha.

Kusano, Atsushi. 1989. *Kokutetsu Kaikaku.* Tokyo: Chuo Koronsha.

La Porta, Rafael, Florencio Lopez-de-Silanas, and Andrei Shleifer. 1999. "Corporate Ownership around the World." *Journal of Finance* 54 (2): 471–517.

La Porta, Rafael, et al. 1998. "Law and Finance." *Journal of Political Economy* 106 (6): 1113–1155.

———. 2000. "Investor Protection and Corporate Governance." *Journal of Finance Economics* 58: 3–27.

Laurence, Henry. 2001. *Money Rules: The New Politics of Finance in Britain and Japan.* Ithaca: Cornell University Press.

Lazear, Edward. 1979. "Why Is There Mandatory Retirement?" *Journal of Political Economy* 87: 1261–1284.

———. 1989. "Pay Equality and Industrial Politics." *Journal of Political Economy* 97 (3): 561–580.

Lijphart, Arend. 1984. *Democracies: Patterns of Majoritarian and Consensus Government in Twenty-One Countries.* New Haven: Yale University Press.

———. 1994. *Electoral Systems and Party Systems: A Study of Twenty-Seven Democracies, 1945–1990.* New York: Oxford University Press.

Lijphart, Arend, and Markus Crepaz. 1991. "Corporatism and Consensus Democracy in Eighteen Countries: Conceptual and Empirical Linkages." *British Journal of Political Science* 21 (3): 235–246.

Lijphart, Arend, Rafael Lopez Pintor, and Yasunori Sone. 1986. "The Limited Vote and the Single Nontransferable Vote: Lessons from the Japanese and Spanish Examples." In *Electoral Laws and Their Political Consequences*, eds. Bernard Grofman and Arend Lijphart, 154–169. New York: Agathon Press.

Lincoln, Edward J. 2001. *Arthritic Japan: The Slow Pace of Economic Reform.* Washington, D.C.: Brookings Institution Press.

Lizzeri, Alessandro, and Nicola Persico. 2001. "The Provision of Public Goods under Alternative Electoral Incentives." *American Economic Review* 90: 225–239.

Lupia, Arthur, and Mathew D. McCubbins. 1994. "Learning from Oversight: Fire Alarms and Police Patrols Reconstructed." *Journal of Law, Economics, and Organization* 10: 96–125.

Lynch, Julia. 2001. "The Age-Orientation of Social Policy Regimes in OECD Countries." *Journal of Social Policy* 30 (3): 411–436.

———. 2006. *Age in the Welfare State: The Origins of Social Spending on Pensioners, Workers, and Children.* New York: Cambridge University Press.

Mabuchi, Masaru. 1994. *Okurasho Tosei no Seiji Keizaigaku.* Tokyo: Chuo Koronsha.

———. 2006. "Kanryosei no Henyo: Ishuku suru Kanryo." In *Nihon Seiji Hendo no 30-nen: Seijika, Kanryo, Dantai Chosa ni Miru Kozo Henyo*, eds. Michio Muramatsu and Ikuo Kume, 137–158. Tokyo: Toyo Keizai Shinpousha.

MacFarlan, Maitland, and Howard Oxley. 1996. "Social Transfers: Spending Patterns, Institutional Arrangements, and Policy Responses." OECD Economic Studies Working Paper No. 27.

Maclachlan, Patricia L. 2004. "Post Office Politics in Modern Japan: The Postmasters, the Iron Triangle, and the Limits of Reform." *Journal of Japanese Studies* 30 (2): 281–313.

———. 2006. "Storming the Castle: The Battle for Postal Reform in Japan." *Social Science Japan Journal* 9 (1): 1–18.

Maeno, Kazuhisa. 1994. *Yuseisho to iu Yakusho*. Tokyo: Sunashobo.

Mainichi Shinbunsha Ekonomisuto Henshubu, ed. 1984a. *Shogen: Kodo Seichoki no Nihon, vol. 1*. Tokyo: Mainichi Shinbunsha.

———, ed. 1984b. *Shogen: Kodo Seichoki no Nihon, vol. 2*. Tokyo: Mainichi Shinbunsha.

Maioni, Antonia. 1998. *Parting at the Crossroads: The Emergence of the Health Insurance in the US and Canada*. Princeton: Princeton University Press.

Mamiya, Yosuke. 1993. *Hojinkigyo to Gendai Shihonshugi*. Tokyo: Iwanami Shoten.

Manow, Philip. 1997. "*Social Insurance and the German Political Economy*." MPIfG Discussion Paper 97/02, Max-Planck-Institut für Gesellschaftsforschung: Cologne.

Mares, Isabela. 1997. "Interwar Responses to the Problem of Unemployment: A Game-Theoretic Analysis." Paper presented at the 1997 American Political Science Association, Washington D.C., August 28–September 1, 1997.

———. 2003. *The Politics of Social Risk: Business and Welfare State Development*. New York: Cambridge University Press.

Martin, Cathie Jo. 1995a. "Nature or Nurture? Sources of Firm Preferences for National Health Reform." *American Political Science Review*, 89 (4): 898–913.

———. 1995b. "Stuck in Neutral: Big Business and the Politics of National Health Reform." *Journal of Health Politics, Policy, and Law* 20 (2): 431–436.

———. 1997. "Mandating Social Change: The Business Struggle over National Health Reform." *Governance* 10 (4): 397–428.

———. 2000. *Stuck in Neutral: Business and the Politics of Human Capital Investment Policy*. Princeton, N.J.: Princeton University Press.

Martin, Cathie Jo, and Duane Swank. 2004. "Does the Organization of Capital Matter? Employers and Active Labor Market Policies at the National and Firm Levels." *American Political Science Review* 98 (4): 593–611.

Maruyama, Akinori. 1995. "Tenshoku Keiken ni yoru Taishokukin Kakusa no Jittai." *Seimei Hoken Keiei* 63 (6): 94–110.

Masumi, Junnosuke. 1983a. *Sengo Seiji 1945–1955 Vol. 1*. Tokyo: Tokyo Daigaku Shuppankai.

———. 1983b. *Sengo Seiji 1945–1955 Vol. 2*. Tokyo: Tokyo Daigaku Shuppankai.

———. 1988. *Nihon Seiji-shi vol. 4: Senryo Kaikaku, Jiminto Shihai*. Tokyo: Tokyo Daigaku Shuppankai.

Matsukawa, Shigeru. 1978. "Fukuri Kosei Shishutsu to Rodosha no teichakuritsu tono Kankei ni Tsuite." *Keizai Kenyu* 29 (2): 135–139.

Matzner, Egon, and Wolfgang Streeck, eds. 1991. *Beyond Keynesianism: The Socioeconomics of Production and Full Employment*. Brookfield, Vt.: Elgar.

Maurice, Marc, François Sellier, and Jean-Jacques Silvestre. 1986. *A Comparison of France and Germany*. Cambridge, Mass.: MIT Press.

McCubbins, Mathew D., and Gregory Noble. 1995a. "The Appearance of Power: Legislators, Bureaucrats and the Budget Process in the United States and Japan." In *Structure and Policy in Japan and the United States*, eds. Peter F. Cowhey and Matthew D. McCubbins, 56–80. New York: Cambridge University Press.

———. 1995b. "Perceptions and Realities of Japanese Budgeting." In *Structure and Policy in Japan and the United States*, eds. Peter F. Cowhey and Matthew D. McCubbins, 81–115. New York: Cambridge University Press.

McCubbins, Mathew D., Roger G. Noll, and Barry R. Weingast 1987. "Administrative Procedures as Instruments of Political Control." *Journal of Law, Economics, and Organization* 3: 243–277.

———. 1989. "Structure and Process, Politics, and Policy: Administrative Arrangements and the Political Control of Agencies." *Virginia Law Review* 75 (2): 431–482.

McCubbins, Mathew D., and Frances M. Rosenbluth. 1995. "Party Provision for Personal Politics: Dividing the Vote in Japan." In *Structure and Policy in Japan and the United States*, eds. Peter F. Cowhey and Matthew D. McCubbins, 35–55. New York: Cambridge University Press.

McGillivray, Fiona. 1997. "Party Discipline as a Determinant of the Endogenous Formation of Tariffs." *American Journal of Political Science* 41 (2): 564–607.

———. 2004. *Privileging Industry: The Comparative Politics of Trade and Industrial Policy*. Princeton: Princeton University Press.

McKean, Margaret A. 1981. *Environmental Protest and Citizen Politics in Japan*. Berkeley: University of California Press.

McKean, Margaret, and Ethan Scheiner. 2000. "Japan's New Electoral System." *Electoral Studies* 19: 447–477.

Milesi-Ferretti, Gian-Maria, Roberto Perotti, and Massimo Rostagno. 2002. "Electoral Systems and the Composition of Public Spending." *Quarterly Journal of Economics* 117: 609–657.

Milgrom, Paul, and John Roberts. 1994. "Complementarities and Systems." *Estudios Economicos* 9: 3–42.

———. 1995. "Complementarities and Fit: Strategy, Structure, and Organizational Change in Manufacturing." *Journal of Accounting and Economics* 19 (3): 179–208.

Milly, Deborah J. 1999. *Poverty, Equality, and Growth: The Politics of Economic Need in Postwar Japan*. Cambridge, Mass.: Harvard East Asian Monographs.

Mincer, J., and Y. Higuchi. 1988. "Wage Structure and Labor Turnover in the United States and Japan." *Journal of Japanese and International Economies* 2 (3): 97–133.

Ministry of Construction. 1960. *Kensetsu Hakusho 1960*. Tokyo: Okurasho Insatsukyoku.

———. 1970. *Kensetsu Hakusho 1970*. Tokyo: Okurasho Insatsukyoku.

———. 1975. *Kensetsu Hakusho 1975*. Tokyo: Okurasho Insatsukyoku.

———. 1984. *Kensetsu Hakusho 1984*. Tokyo: Okurasho Insatsukyoku.

Ministry of Finance, Zaiseishitsu, ed. 1974. *Showa Zaiseishi vol.14: Finance*. Tokyo: Toyo Keizai Shinposha.

———, ed. 1983. *Showa Zaiseishi 13: Shusenkara Kowa made*. Tokyo: Toyo Keizai Shinposha.

———, ed. 1991. *Showa Zaiseishi: 1952–1973 vol.10*. Tokyo: Toyo Keizai Shinposha.

———, ed. 1997. *Showa Zaiseishi vol.15*. Tokyo: Toyo Keizai Shinposha.

Ministry of Health and Welfare. 1956. *The Ministry of Health and Welfare 1956 White Papers*. Tokyo: Toyo Keizai Shinpo.

——— (Insurance Bureau), ed. 1958. *Kenko Hoken 30nenshi, vol. 2*. Tokyo: Zenkoku Shakai Hoken Kyokai Rengokai.

——— (Pension Bureau), ed. 1962. *Kokumin Nenkin no Ayumi*. Tokyo: Ministry of Health and Welfare, Pension Bureau.

——— (Ministerial Secretary's Planning Office), ed. 1963. *Kosei Hakusho 1963*. Tokyo: Toyo Keizai Shinposha.

———, ed. 1972. *Kosei Nekin Hoken/Kokumin Nenkin Yushi Shisetsu Yoran*. Tokyo: Chuo Hoki Shuppan.

———, ed. 1988a. *Koseisho 50 nenshi*. Tokyo: Chuo Hoki Shuppankai.

———, ed. 1988b. *Koseisho Nenkin Kikin 10 nenshi*. Tokyo: Kosei Nenkin Kikin Rengokai.

———. 1997. *Shakai Hosho Nyumon*. Tokyo: Chuo Hoki Shuppan.

——— (Minister's Secretariat, Statistics and Information Department), ed. 1996. *Kosei Tokei Yoran 1995*. Tokyo: Kosei Tokei Kyokai.

Ministry of Health and Welfare (Pension Bureau) and Kosei Nenkin Kikin Rengokai, eds. 1979. *Kosei Nenkin Kikin Junenshi*. Tokyo: Kosei Nenkin Kikin Rengokai.

Ministry of International Trade and Industry (Industrial Policy Bureau, Enterprise Behavior Department), ed. 1981. *Nihonteki Koyo Kanko no Yukue (A Survey of Labor Mobility)*. Tokyo: Sangyo Noritsu Daigaku Shuppanbu.

Ministry of Labor. 1953. *Shiryo Rodo Udoshi 1952*. Tokyo: Romu Gyosei Kenkyujo.

—— (Chingin Chosaka), ed. 1960. *Nihon no Chingin Kozo*. Tokyo: Romu Gyosei Kenkyujo.

—— (Unemployment Insurance Section, Employment Stabilization Bureau), ed. 1960. *Shitsugyo Hoken Junenshi*. Tokyo: Ministry of Labor.

——. 1965. *Rodo Tokei Yoran*. Tokyo: Okurasho Insatsukyoku.

——. 1969. *Rodo Gyoseishi vol. 2: Sengo no Rodo Gyoseishi*. Tokyo: Rodo Horei Kyokai.

——. 1975. *Rodo Tokei Yoran*. Tokyo: Okurasho Insatsukyoku.

——. 1977. *Shiryo Rodo Undoshi 1973*. Tokyo: Rodo Gyosei Kenkyujo.

——. 1978. *Shiryo Rodo Undoshi 1974*. Tokyo: Rodo Gyosei Kenkyujo.

——. 1979. *Shiryo Rodo Undoshi 1975*. Tokyo: Rodo Gyosei Kenkyujo.

—— (Ministerial Secretariat Statistics and Information Bureau). 1982. *Koyo Kanri Chosa*. Tokyo: Rodo Horei Kyokai.

——. 1988. *Chingin/Rodo Jikan Seido to Kigyo Fukushi no Jittai*. Osaka: Rodo Horei Kyokai.

Mishima, Ko. 1998. "The Changing Relationship between Japan's LDP and the Bureaucracy: Hashimoto's Administrative Reform Effort and Its Politics." *Asian Survey* 38 (10): 968–985.

Mitchell, Paul. 2000. "Voters and Their Representatives: Electoral Institutions and Delegation in Parliamentary Democracies." *European Journal of Political Research* 37: 335–351.

Miura, Mari. 2002. "Atarashii Rodo Seiji to Kyohiken." In *Ryudoki no Nihon Seiji: Ushinawareta 10-nen no Seijiteki Kensho*, eds. Nobuhiro Hiwatari and Mari Miura, 259–277. Tokyo: Tokyo University Press.

——. 2003. From Welfare through Work to Lean Work: The Politics of Labor Market Reform in Japan. Ph.D. dissertation, University of California at Berkeley.

Miwa, Yoshiro, and J. Mark Ramseyer. 2006. *The Fable of the Keiretsu: Urban Legends of the Japanese Economy*. Chicago: Chicago University Press.

Miyatake, Takeshi. 2001. "Seikimatsu no Nenkin Kaisei wo Kensho Suru: Sono Seisaku Keisei no Tokucho to Kadai." *Kikan: Shakai Hosho Kenkyu* 37 (1): 17–28.

Miyawaki, Atsushi. 1995. *Zaisei Toyushi no Kaikaku: Koteki Kinyu Hidaika no Jittai*. Tokyo: Toyo Keizai Shinposha.

Moe, Terry M., and Michael Caldwell. 1994. "The Institutional Foundation of Democratic Government: A Comparison of Presidential and Parliamentary Systems." *Journal of Institutional and Theoretical Economics* 150 (1): 171–195.

Moriguchi, Chiaki. 2003. "Implicit Contracts, the Great Depression, and Institutional Change: A Comparative Analysis of U.S. and Japanese Employment Relations, 1920–1940." *Journal of Economic History* 63 (3): 625–665.

Moriguchi, Chiaki, and Emmanuel Saez. 2006. "The Evolution of Top Wage Incomes in Japan, 1951–2005," unpublished paper.

Morishima, Michio. 1982. *Why Has Japan Succeeded?: Western technology and the Japanese Ethos*. New York: Cambridge University Press.

Mulgan, Aurelia George. 1988. *Rice Politics in Japan*. Canberra, Australia: Australia-Japan Research Centre.

——. 1990. "The Last Bastion: Prospects for Liberalizing Japan's Rice Market." In *Report of Study Group on International Issues SGII No. 7*, ed. Food and Agriculture Policy Research Center, 113–44. Tokyo: Food and Agriculture Policy Research Center.

——. 2000. *The Politics of Agriculture in Japan*. New York: Routledge.

——. 2002. *Japan's Failed Revolution: Koizumi and Politics of Economic Reform*. Canberra: Asia Pacific Press at the Australian National University.

———. 2003. "Japan's 'Un-Westminster' System: Impediments to Reform in a Crisis Economy." *Government and Opposition* 38 (1): 73–91.

Murakami, Kimiko. 1987. *Senryoki no Fukishi Seisaku. Welfare Policy during the Occupations Period.* Tokyo: Keiso Shobo.

Murakami, Kiyoshi. 1979. *Kigyo Nenkin no Chishiki.* Tokyo: Nihon Keizai Shinbunsha.

Murakawa, Ichiro. 1985. *Zei no Urabutai: Seifu Zeicho to Jiminto Zeicho.* Tokyo: Kyoikusha.

Muramatsu, Michio, Mitsutoshi Ito, and Yutaka Tsujinaka. 1986. *Sengo Nihon no Atsuryoku Dantai.* Tokyo: Toyo Keizai Shinposha.

Muramatsu, Michio, and Ellis Krauss. 1984. "Bureaucrats and Politicians in Policymaking: The Case of Japan." *American Political Science Review* 78 (1): 126–146.

———. 1987. "The Conservative Policy Line and the Development of Patterned Pluralism." In *The Political Economy of Japan, vol.1: The Domestic Transformation*, eds. Kozo Yamamura and Yasukichi Yasuba, 516–554. Stanford: Stanford University Press.

Muramatsu, Michio, and Ikuo Kume, eds. 2006. *Nihon Seiji Hendo no 30-nen: Seijika, Kanryo, Dantai Chosa ni Miru Kozo Henyo.* Tokyo: Toyo Keizai Shinposha.

Myerson, Roger B. 1993. "Incentives to Cultivate Favored Minorities under Alternative Electoral Systems." *American Political Science Review* 87 (4): 856–869.

Myles, John. 1984. *Old Age in the Welfare State: The Political Economy of Public Pensions.* Boston: Little Brown.

Naka, Mamoru. 1990. *Rodosho Kenkyu.* Tokyo: Gyoken Shuppankyoku.

Nakamura, Keisuke. 2006. "Kaikaku no Naka no Itsudatsu: Rodo Seisaku." In *Ushinawareta 10-nen wo Koete II: Koizumi Kaikaku no Jidai*, ed. Tokyo University Social Science Research Institute, 246–277. Tokyo: Tokyo University Press.

Nakamura, Yashuhiko. 2000. *Norinzoku: Tanbo no Kage ni Hyo ga Aru.* Tokyo: Bungei Shunju.

Nakano, Minoru, ed. 1986. *Nihongata Seisaku Kettei no Henyo.* Tokyo: Toyo Keizai Shinposha.

———. 1989. "Wagakuni Fukushi Seisaku Keisei no Seiji Katei: Omoni Showa 60nen Koteki Nenkin Seido Kaisei wo Jirei toshite." In *Tenkanki no Fukushi Kokka to Seijigaku*, ed. Nihon Seiji Gakkai. Tokyo: Iwanami Shoten.

Narita, Junji. 1997. "Kodo Seichoki ni okeru Shanai Yokin Seido no Yakuwari." *Fainansharu Rebyu* 42: 69–87.

Nenkin Fukushi Jigyodan ed. 1972. *Nenkin Fukushi Jigyodan Junenshi.* Tokyo: Kosei Shuppansha.

Nicoletti, Giuseppe, Stefano Scarpetta, and Olivier Boylaud. 1999. "Summary Indicators of Product Market Regulations with an Extension to Employment Protection Legislation." OECD Economics Department Working Papers, No. 226.

Nihon Hokengyoshi Hensan Iinkai, ed. 1968a. *Nihon Hokengyoshi: Soron.* Tokyo: Hoken kenkyujo.

———, 1968b. *Nihon Seimei Hokengyoshi: Kaisha hen Gekan.* Tokyo: Hoken Kenkyujo.

Nihon Kangyo Ginko. 1967. *Nihon Kangyo Ginko 70 Nenshi.* Tokyo: Nihon Kangyo Ginko.

Nihon Kogyo Ginko Nenshi Hensan Iinkai. 1982. *Nihon Kogyo Ginko 75 nenshi.* Tokyo: Nihon Kogyo Ginko.

Nihon Kokumin Kyokai, ed. 1980. *Kokumin Nenkin Nijunen Hishi.* Tokyo: Nihon Kokumin Nenkin Kyokai.

Nihon Romu Kenkyukai. 1963. *Romu Nenkan 1963.* Tokyo: Nihon Romu Kenkyukai.

———. 1990. *Romu Nenkan 1990.* Tokyo: Nihon Romu Kenkyukai.

Nihon Shakaito Nosei Giindan, ed. 1981. *Nihon Shakaito Nosei Giinda Nijusshunen Kinenshi.* Tokyo: Nihon Shakaito.

Nihon Tekko Renmei. 1969. *Tekko Junenshi: Showa 33–42*. Tokyo: Nihon Tekko Renmen.

Nikkeiren Souritsu Jusshunen Kinen Jigyo Iinkai, ed. 1958. *Nikkeiren Junnen no Ayumi*. Tokyo: Nihon Keieisha Dantai Renmei.

Nikkeiren (Nihon Keieisha Dantai Renmei). 1963. *Nikkeiren no Ayumi: Showa 33 nen 4 gatsu – Showa 38 nen 3 gatsu*. Tokyo: Nihon Keieisha Dantai Renmei.

———. 1968. *Nikkeiren no Nijunen no Ayumi*. Tokyo: Nihon Keieisha Dantai Renmei.

———. 1973. *Nikkeiren no Ayumi: Showa 43 nen 4 gatsu – Showa 48 nen 3 gatsu*. Tokyo: Nihon Keieisha Dantai Renmei.

Nishikawa, Katsunori. 1991. "Shitsugyo Hoken to Rosai Hoken no Kakuritsu." In *Nihon Shakai Hosho no Rekishi*, eds. Kazuhiko Yokoyama and Hidenori Tada, 105–122. Tokyo: Gakubunsha.

Nishikawa, Satoshi, ed. 1994. *Zusetsu Nihon no Seimei Hoken*. Tokyo: Zaikei Shohosha.

Nishikubo, Koji. 1996. "Tenkanki wo Mukaeru Nihongata Fukuri Kosei." In *Seimei Hoken Keiei* 64: 1, 63–81.

———. 1998. *Nihongata Fukuri Kosei no Saikochiku*. Tokyo: Shaka Keizai Seisansei Honbu.

Nishimura, Mariko. 1996. "Shinryo Hoshuu Kaitei no Mekanizumu ni Kansuru Rekishiteki Kosatsu." In *Iryo Hosho to Iryohi*, ed. Shakai Hosho Kenkyujo, 37–70. Tokyo: Tokyo University Press.

Nishimura, Yoshimasa, ed. 1994. *Fukko to Seicho no Zaisei Kinyuseisaku*. Tokyo: Okurasho Zaisei Kinyu Kenkyujo.

Nishinarita, Yutaka. 1988. *Kindai Nihon Roshi Kankeishi no Kenkyu*. Tokyo: Tokyo University Press.

———. 1992. "Senryoki Nihon no Roshikankei." In *Nihon no Kindai to Shihonshugi*, ed. Nakamura Masanori, 189–227. Tokyo: Tokyo Daigaku Shuppankai.

———. 1994. "Sengokiki to Shihonshugiteki Saiken no Roshi Kankei." In *Senryo Kaikaku no Kokusai Hikaku*, eds. Daizaburo Aburai, Masanori Nakamura, and Narahiko Toyoshita, 132–161. Tokyo: Sanseido.

Niskanen, William. 1971. *Bureaucracy and Representative Government*. Chicago: Aldine/Atherton.

Noble, Gregory. 2006a. "Seijiteki Ridashippu to Kozo Kaikaku." In *Ushinawareta 10-nen wo Koete II: Koizumi Kaikaku no Jidai*, ed. Tokyo University Social Science Research Institute, 73–105. Tokyo: Tokyo University Press.

———. 2006b. "Seijiteki Ridashippu to Zaisei Toyushi Kaikaku." In *Ushinawareta 10-nen wo Koete II: Koizumi Kaikaku no Jidai*, ed. Tokyo University Social Science Research Institute, 191–218. Tokyo: Tokyo University Press.

Noguchi, Yukio. 1995. *1940nen Taisei*. Tokyo: Toyo Keizai Shinposha.

Noll, Roger, and Frances Rosenbluth. 1995. "Telecommunications Policy Structure, Process, Outcomes." In *Structure and Policy in Japan and the United States*, eds. Peter Cowhey and Mathew McCubbins, 119–176. New York: Cambridge University Press.

Odaka, Konosuke. 1993a. "Nihonteki Roshi Kankei." In *Gendai Nihon Keizai Shisutemu no Genryu*, eds. Tetsuji Okazaki and Masahiro Okuno, 145–182. Tokyo: Nihon Keizai Shinbunsha.

———. 1993b. *Kigyonai Kyoiku no Jidai*. Tokyo: Iwanami Shoten.

OECD. 2005. *OECD Pension Market in Focus Newsletter*, no. 1 (June 2005).

Ohara Rodo Mondai Kenkyujo. 1953. *Nihon Rodo Nenkan vol. 26*. Tokyo: Jiji Tsushinsha.

———. 1959. *Nihon Rodo Nenkan vol. 32*. Tokyo: Toyo Keizai Shinposha.

———. 1960. *Nihon Rodo Nenkan vol. 33*. Tokyo: Toyo Keizai Shinposha.

———. 1961. *Nihon Rodo Nenkan vol. 34*. Tokyo: Toyo Keizai Shinposha.

———. 1978. *Nihon Rodo Nenkan vol. 49*. Tokyo: Rodo Junposha.

———. 1981. *Nihon Rodo Nenkan vol. 51*. Tokyo: Rodo Junposha.

———. 1983. *Nihon Rodo Nenkan vol. 54*. Tokyo: Rodo Junposha.

——. 1984. *Nihon Rodo Nenkan vol. 55*. Tokyo: Rodo Junposha.

——. 1985. *Nihon Rodo Nenkan vol. 56*. Tokyo: Rodo Junposha.

——. 1987. *Nihon Rodo Nenkan vol. 57*. Tokyo: Rodo Junposha.

——. 1990. *Nihon Rodo Nenkan vol. 60*. Tokyo: Toyo Keizai Shinposha.

——. 1991. *Nihon Rodo Nenkan vol. 61*. Tokyo: Toyo Keizai Shinposha.

——. 1992. *Nihon Rodo Nenkan vol. 62*. Tokyo: Rodo Junposha.

——. 2002. *Nihon Rodo Nenkan vol. 72*. Tokyo: Junposha.

Okazaki, Tetsuji, and Okuno Masahiro, eds. 1993. *Gendai Nihon Keizai Shisutemu no Genryu*. Tokyo: Nihon Keizai Shinbunsha.

Okimoto, Daniel I. 1989. *Between MITI and the Market: Japanese Industrial Policy for High Technology*. Stanford: Stanford University Press.

Okuma, Yukiko. 2005. "Gorudo Puran to Otoko wa Dokyo Sannin-gumi." In *Kaigo Hoken Joho* 5 (10): 26–29.

Okuno, Masahiro. 1984. "Company Loyalty and Bonus Payments: An Analysis of Work Incentives in Japan." In *The Economic Analysis of the Japanese Firm*, ed. Masahiko Aoki, 387–411. Amsterdam: North-Holland.

Omoto, Keino. 1985. "Fukushi Kokka to Wagakuni Jutaku Seisaku no Tenkai." *Fukushi Kokka: vol. 6*, ed. Tokyo Daigaku Shakai Kagaku Kenkyujo, 397–452. Tokyo: Tokyo Daigaku Shuppankai.

——. 1986a. "Taidan: Sengo Jutaku Seisakushi Part I." *Tochi Jutaku Kenkyu* 143: 30–40.

——. 1986b. "Taidan: Sengo Jutaku Seisakushi Part II." *Tochi Jutaku Kenkyu* 144: 58–64.

——. 1991. *Shogen: Nihon no Jutaku Seikatsu*. Tokyo: Nihon Hyoronsha.

Ono, Akira. 1989. *Nihonteki Koyo Kanko to Rodo Shijo*. Tokyo: Toyo Keizai Shinposha.

Orloff, Ann Shola. 1993. *The Politics of Pensions*. Madison, Wisc.: University of Wisconsin Press.

Orloff, Ann Shola, and Skocpol Theda. 1984. "Why Not Equal Protection? Explaining the Politics of Public Social Spending in Britain 1900–1911 and the United States 1880–1920." *American Sociological Review* 49 (4): 726– 750.

Osawa, Mari. 1992. "Gendai Nihon Shakai to Josei." In *Gendai Nihon Shakai vol.6*, ed. Tokyo University Shakai Kagakau Kenkyujo, 33–79. Tokyo: Tokyo Daigaku Shup-pankai.

——. 2006. "Kudokasuru Shakaiteki Sefuti Netto: Shakai Hosho no Ushinawareta 15 Nen." In *Ushinawareta 10-nen wo Koete II: Koizumi Kaikaku no Jidai*, ed. Tokyo University Social Science Research Institute, 279–309. Tokyo: Tokyo Daigaku Shuppankai.

——. 2007. *Gendai Nihon no Seikatsu Hosho Shisutemu: Zahyo to Yukue*. Tokyo: Iwanami Shoten.

Oshio, Mayumi. 1996. *Kazoku Teate no Kenkyu: Jido Teate kara Kazoku Seisaku wo Tenbo suru*. Tokyo: Horitsu Bunkasha.

Ota, Hiroko. 1994. "Jutaku wo meguru Seifu to Kigyo no Shien." In *Raifu Saikuru to Shotoku Hosho*, ed. Tachibanaki, 103–124. Tokyo: NTT Shuppan.

——. 2006. *Keizai Zaisei Shimon Kaigi no Tatakai*. Tokyo: Toyo Keizai Shinposha.

Otake, Fumio, and Keiko Fujikawa. 2001. "Nihon no Seiri Kaiko." In *Koyo Seisaku no Keizai Bunseki*," eds. Takenori Inoki and Fumio Otake, 3–28. Tokyo: Tokyo Daigaku Shuppankai.

Otake, Hideo. 1986. *Adenaua to Yoshida Shigeru*. Tokyo: Chuo Koronsha.

——. 1991. "Hatoyama/Kishi Jidai ni okeru Chiisai Seifu Ron." In Sengo Kokka no Keisei to Keizai Hatten, ed. Japanese Political Science Association, 165–185. Tokyo: Iwanami Shoten.

——. 1994. *Jiyushugiteki Kaikaku no Jidai: 1980 Nendai Zenki no Nihon Seiji*. Tokyo: Chuo Koronsha.

——. 1997. *Gyokaku no Hasso*. Tokyo: TBS Buritanica.

———. 2003. *Nihongata Popurizumu: Seiji eno Kitai to Genmetsu*. Tokyo: Chuo Koron.

Otake, Yasuo. 2000. *Mireniamu Nenkin Kaikaku: 2000nen Nenkin Kaiseiho no Zenyo to Kaisetsu*. Tokyo: Kokusei Joho Senta.

Otani, Yasuo. 2000. *Mieniamu Nenkin Kaikaku*. Tokyo: Kokusei Joho Senta.

Pagano, Marco, and Paolo Volpin. 2001. "The Political Economy of Corporate Governance." Center for Economic Policy Research Discussion Paper No. 2682.

Palme, Joakim. 1990. *Pension Rights in Welfare Capitalism: The Development of Old-Age Pensions in 18 OECD Countries 1930 to 1985*. Swedish Institute for Social Research 14.

Patashnik, Eric. 1995. "Growing Importance of Trust Funds in Federal Budgeting." Paper presented at the Annual Meeting of the American Political Science Association, Chicago, August 31–September 3.

Pekkanen, Robert, Benjamin Nyblade, and Ellis S. Krauss. 2006. "Electoral Incentives in Mixed-Member Systems: Party, Posts, and Zombie Politicians in Japan." *American Political Science Review* 100 (2): 183–193.

Pempel, T. J. 1982. *Policy and Politics in Japan: Creative Conservatism*. Philadelphia: Temple University Press.

———. 1991. "Nihon to Sweden." *Rebaiasan* 9 (Fall Issue): 104–128.

———. 1998. *Regime Shift: Comparative Dynamics of the Japanese Political Economy*. Ithaca, N.Y.: Cornell University Press.

Pempel, T. J., and Keiichi Tsunekawa. 1979. "Corporation without Labor? The Japanese Anomaly." In Schmitter and Lehmbruch, 231–270.

Peng, Ito. 2002. "Gender and Generation: Japanese Child Care and the Demographic Crisis." In *Child Care Policy at the Crossroads: Gender and Welfare State Restructuring*, eds. Sonya Michel and Rianne Mahon, 31–56. New York: Routledge.

———. 2005. "New Politics of the Welfare State in a Developmental Context: Explaining the 1990s Social Care Expansion in Japan." In *Transforming the Developmental Welfare State in East Asia*, ed. Huck-ju Kwon. London: Ashgate.

Perotti, Roberto. 1996. "Growth, Income Distribution and Democracy: What the Data Say." *Journal of Economic Growth* 1 (2): 149–187.

Persson, Torsten, and Guido Tabellini. 1999. "The Size and Scope of Government: Comparative Politics with Rational Politicians." *European Economic Review* 43: 699–735.

———. 2000. *Political Economies: Explaining Economic Policy*. Cambridge, Mass.: MIT Press.

Pichler, E. 1993. "Cost-Sharing of General and Specific Training with Depreciation of Human Capital." *Economics of Education Review* 12 (2): 117–124.

Pierson, Paul. 1994. *Dismantling the Welfare State: Reagan, Thatcher, and the Politics of Retrenchment*. Cambridge: Cambridge University Press.

———. 1995. "Fragmented Welfare States: Federal Institutions and the Development of Social Policy." *Governance* 8 (4): 447–478.

———. 2004. *Politics in Time: History, Institutions, and Social Analysis*. Princeton, N.J.: Princeton University Press.

Piore, Michael, and Charles Sable. 1984. *The Second Industrial Drive: Possibilities for Prosperity*. New York: Basic Books.

Pontusson, Jonas. 1984. *Public Pension Funds and the Politics of Capital Formation in Sweden*. Stockholm: Arbetslivscentrum.

———. 1991. "Labor, Corporatism, and Industrial Policy: The Swedish Case in Comparative Perspective." *Comparative Politics* 23 (2): 163–179.

———. 1992. *The Limits of Social Democracy: Investment Politics in Sweden*. Ithaca, N.Y.: Cornell University Press.

Powell, G. Bingham, Jr. 1982. *Contemporary Democracies*. Cambridge, Mass.: Harvard University Press.

Prowse, Stephen. 1995. "Corporate Governance in an International Perspective: A Survey of Corporate Control Mechanisms among Large Firms in the US, UK, Japan, and Germany." *Financial Markets, Institutions and Instruments* 4 (1): 1–63.

Quadagno, Jill. 1985. "Welfare Capitalism and the Social Security Act of 1935." *American Sociological Review* 49 (4): 632–647.

———. 1987. "Theories of the Welfare State." *Annual Review of Sociology* 13 (3): 109–128.

Quadagno, Jill, and Melissa Hardy. 1996. "Private Pensions, State Regulation and Income Security for Older Workers: The U.S. Auto Industry." In *The Privatization of Social Policy*, ed. Michael Shalev, 136–156. New York: St. Martin's Press.

Ramseyer, J. Mark, and Frances Rosenbluth. 1993. *Japan's Political Marketplace*. Cambridge, Mass.: Harvard University Press.

Raunio, Tapio. 2006. "Finland: One Hundred Years of Quietude." In *The Politics of Electoral Systems*, eds. Michael Gallagher and Paul Mitchell, 473–490. New York: Oxford University Press.

Reed, Steven R. 1990. "Structure and Behavior: Extending Duverger's Law to the Japanese Case." *British Journal of Political Science* 20 (3): 335–356.

———. 2002. "Evaluating Political Reform in Japan: A Midterm Report." *Japanese Journal of Political Science* 3 (2): 243–263.

———, ed. 2003. *Japanese Electoral Politics: Creating a New Party System*. New York: Routledge.

Reed, Steven R., and Michael Thies. 2001. "The Consequences of Electoral Reform in Japan." In *Mixed-Member Electoral Systems: The Best of Both Worlds?* eds. Matthew Shugart and Martin Wattenberg, 380–403. New York: Oxford University Press.

Rein, Martin, and Richard Freeman. 1988. *The Dutch Choice: A Plea for Social Policy Complementary to Work*. Gravenhage: HRWB.

Rein, Martin, and Lee Rainwater, eds. 1986. *Public-Private Interplay in Social Protection*. Armonk, N.Y.: M. E. Sharpe.

Richardson, Bradley. 1997. *Japanese Democracy: Power, Coordination, and Performance*. New Haven, Conn.: Yale University Press.

Rodden, Jonathan. 2005. "Red States, Blue States, and the Welfare State: Political Geography, Representation, and Government Policy Around the World," paper presented at Comparative Political Economy Workshop, October 7–8, Harvard University.

Roe, Mark. 1994a. "Corporate Governance in Germany, Japan and America." In *Institutional Investors and Corporate Governance*, eds. Theodor Baums, Richard M. Buxbaum, Klaus J. Hopt, 23–88. New York: Walter de Gruyter.

———. 1994b. *Strong Managers Weak Owners: The Political Roots of American Corporate Finance*. Princeton: Princeton University Press.

Rogowski, Ronald, and Mark A. Kayser. 2002. "Majoritarian Electoral Systems and Consumer Power: Price-Level Evidence from OECD Countries." *American Journal of Political Science* 46: 526–539.

Rohlen, Thomas. 1979. *For Harmony and Strength: Japanese White-Collar Organization in Anthropological Perspective*. Berkeley: University of California Press.

Romano, Roberta. 1994. "Public Pension Fund Activism in Corporate Governance." In *Institutional Investors and Corporate Governance*, eds. Theodor Baums, Richard M. Buxbaum, and Klaus J. Hopt, 105–159. New York: Walter de Gruyter.

Romu Kenkyujo. 1975. *Fukuri Kosei Bijon: bijon no Tatekata to Roshi no Jissairei*. Tokyo: Romu Kenkyujo.

———, ed. 1990. *Shin Fukuri Kosei Hando Bukku*. Tokyo: Romu Kenkyujo.

———, ed. 1994. *Fukuri Kosei Hando Bukku*. Tokyo: Romu Kenkyujo.

Rose, Richard, and Rei Shiratori, eds. 1986. *The Welfare State East and West*. New York: Oxford University Press.

Rosenbluth, Frances. 1989. *Financial Politics in Contemporary Japan*. Ithaca, N.Y.: Cornell University Press.

Rosenbluth, Frances, and Michael Thies. 2001. "The Electoral Politics of Japanese Banking: The Case of Jusen." *Policy Studies Journal* 29 (1): 23–37.

Rosenbluth, Frances, and Ross Schaap. 2003. "The Domestic Politics of Banking Regulation." *International Organization* 57 (2): 307–336.

Rothstein, Bo. 1985. "The Success of Swedish Labor Market Policy: The Organizational Connection to Politics." *European Journal of Political Research* 13 (3): 153–165.

———. 1992. "Labor Market Institutions and Working Class Strength." In *Structuring Politics: Historical Institutionalism in Comparative Analysis*, eds. S. Steinmo, K. Thelen, and F. Longstreth. 33–56. Cambridge: Cambridge University Press.

Rueschemeyer, Dietrich, and Theda Skocpol, eds. 1996. *States, Social Knowledge, and the Origin of Modern Social Policies*. Princeton: Princeton University Press.

Saguchi, Takashi. 1957. *Nihon Shakai Hokenshi*. Tokyo: Nihon Hyoronsha.

———. 1977. *Nihon Shakai Hoken Seidoshi*. Tokyo: Keiso Shobo.

———. 1995. *Kokumin Kenko Hoken*. Tokyo: Kookan.

Sainsbury, Diane, ed. 1994. *Gendering Welfare States*. London: Sage Publications.

———. 1999. *Gender and Welfare State Regimes*. Oxford: Oxford University Press.

Sakaguchi, Masayuki. 1985. *Nihon Kenkou Hokenho Seiritsushiron*. Tokyo: Koyoshobo.

Salamon, Lester, ed. 1989. *Beyond Privatization: The Tools of Government Action*. Washington, D.C.: Urban Institute Press.

Samuels, David, and Richard Snyder. 2001. "The Value of a Vote: Malapportionment in Comparative Perspective." *British Journal of Political Science* 31: 651–671.

Samuels, Richard J. 1983. *The Politics of Regional Policy in Japan: Localities Incorporated?* Princeton, N.J.: Princeton University Press.

———. 1987. *The Business of the Japanese State: Energy Markets in Comparative and Historical Perspective*. Ithaca, N.Y.: Cornell University Press.

———. 2003. *Machiavelli's Children: Leaders and Their Legacies in Italy and Japan*. Ithaca, N.Y.: Cornell University Press.

Sato, Seizaburo, and Tetsuhisa Matsuzaki. 1986. *Jiminto Choki Seiken*. Tokyo: Chuo Koronsha.

Sato, Susumu, and Hiroshi Miyajima. 1990. *Sengo Zeiseishi*. Tokyo: Zeimu Keiri Kyokai.

Schaede, Ulrike. 1995. The "Old Boy" Network and Government-Business Relationship in Japan." *Journal of Japanese Studies* 21 (2): 293–317.

———. 2000. *Cooperative Capitalism: Self-Regulation, Trade Association, and Anti-Monopoly Law in Japan*. New York: Oxford University Press.

———. 2004. "The 'Middle Risk Gap' and Financial System Reform: Small Firm Financing in Japan." The Institute of Monetary and Economic Studies, Bank of Japan, Discussion Paper 2004-E-11.

Scheiner, Ethan. 2006. *Democracy without Competition in Japan: Opposition Party Failure in a One-Party Dominance State*. New York: Cambridge University Press.

Schmitter, Philippe C., and Gerhard Lehmbruch, eds. 1979. *Trends toward Corporatist Intermediation*. Beverly Hills: Sage.

Schoppa, Leonard J. 2006. *Race for Exits: The Unraveling of Japan's System of Social Protection*. Ithaca, N.Y.. Cornell University Press.

Schwartz, Frank J. 1998. *Advice and Consent: The Politics of Consultation in Japan*. New York: Cambridge University Press.

Seimei Hoken Bunka Senta, ed. 1990. *Kigyo no Fukuri Kosei Seido ni Kansuru Chosa*. Tokyo: Seimei Hoken Bunka Senta.

Seimei Hoken Kyokai, ed. 1973. *Showa Seimei Hoken Shiryo vol.6: Kaifukuki*. Tokyo: Seimei Hoken Kyokai.

Senkyo Seido Kenkyu Iinkai, ed. 2001. *Zukai: Senkyo Seido no Shikumi*. Tokyo: Natsume-sha.

Shakai Hosho Kenkyujo, ed. 1975a. *Nihon Shakai Hosho Shiryo I*. Tokyo: Shakai Hosho Kenkyujo.

———, ed. 1975b. *Nihon Shakai Hosho Shiryo II*. Tokyo: Shakai Hosho Kenkyujo.

———, ed. 1988a. *Nihon Shakai Hosho Shiryo III, vol.1*. Tokyo: Shakai Hosho Kenkyujo.

———, ed. 1988b. *Nihon Shakai Hosho Shiryo III, vol.2*. Tokyo: Shakai Hosho Kenkyujo.

Shakai Hosho Kenkyujohen, ed. 1992. *Nenkin*. Tokyo: Yuhikaku.

Shalev, Michael. 1983. "The Social Democratic Model and Beyond: Two 'Generations' of Comparative Research on the Welfare State." *Comparative Social Research* 6 (3): 315–352.

———. 1990. "Class Conflict, Corporatism, and Comparison: A Japanese Enigma." In *Japanese Models of Conflict Resolution*, eds. S. N. Eisenstadt and E. Ben-Ari, 60–93. London: Kegan Paul.

———, ed. 1996. *The Privatization of Social Policy?* New York: St. Martin's Press.

Shashi Hensan Iinkai, ed. 1981. *Honoo to Tomoni: Yahata Seitetsu Kabushiki Kaishashi*, vol. 8. Tokyo: Shin Nihon Seitetsu.

Sheard, Paul. 1994. "Interlocking Shareholding and Corporate Governance in Japan." In Aoki and Dore, eds., 310–349.

———. 1995. "Long-termism and the Japanese Firm." In *Structure of the Japanese Economy*, ed. Mitsuaki Okabe, 25–52. New York: St. Martin's Press.

Sheingate, Adam D. 2001. *The Rise of the Agricultural Welfare State: Institutions and Interest Group Power in the United States, France, and Japan*. Princeton, N.J.: Princeton University Press.

Shibagaki, Kazuo. 1985. "Nihon no Fukushi Kinyu." In *Fukushi Kokka vol. 5: Nihon no Keizaik to Fukushi*, ed. Tokyo Daigaku Shakai Kagaku Kenkyujo, 109–169. Tokyo: Tokyo Daigaku Shuppankai.

Shimada, Yoichi. 2000. "Kaisei Rodosha Haken Ho ni okeru tekiyou Taisho Gyomu no Negatibu Risuto-ka no Igi to Mondaiten." *Waseda Hogaku* 75 (3):119–144.

Shimizu, Masahito. 2005. *Kantei Shudo*. Tokyo: Nihon Keizai Shinbunsha.

Shinkawa, Toshimitsu. 1984. "1975 nen Shunto to Keizai Kiki Kanri." In *Nihon Seiji no Shoten: Jirei Kenkyu niyoru Seiji Taisei no Bunseki*, ed. Hideo Otake, 189–232. Tokyo: Saichi Shobo.

———. 1993. *Nihongata Fukushi no Seiji Keizaigaku*. Tokyo: Saichi Shobo.

Shinkawa, Toshimitsu, and T. J. Pempel. 1996. "Occupational Welfare and the Japanese Experience." In *The Privatization of Social Policy?: Occupational Welfare and the Welfare State in America, Scandinavia and Japan*. ed. Michael Shalev, 280–326. New York: St. Martin's Press.

Shinoda. Tomohito. 2004. *Kantei Gaiko: Seiji Ridashippu no Yukue*. Tokyo: Asahi Shinbun-sha.

Shinoda, Toru. 1989. *Seikimatsu no Rodo Undo*. Tokyo: Iwanami Shoten.

———. 1996. "Futatabi Niwatori kara Ahiru e?" In *Gojugo-nen Taisei no Hokai*, ed. Nihon Seijigakkai, 129–149. Tokyo: Iwanami Shoten.

Shinposa, Toyo Keizai, ed. 2002. *Keizai Tokei Nenkan 2002* (published as a special issue of a weekly magazine, *Toyo Keizai*). Tokyo: Toyo Keizai Shinposa.

Shiota, Ushio. 1985. *Hyakuchoen no Haishin*. Tokyo: Kodansha.

Shirahase, Sawako. 2005. *Shoshi Korei Shakai no Mienai Kakusa: Jenda Sedai Kaiso no Yukue*. Tokyo: Tokyo Daigaku Shuppankai.

Shiritsu Gakko Kyoshokuin Kyosai Kumiai, ed. 1965. *Shigaku Kyosai Junenshi*. Tokyo: Shiritsu Gakko Kyoshokuin Kyosai Kumiai.

Shleifer, Andrei, and Lawrence Summers. 1988. "Breach of Trust in Hostile Takeovers." NBER #2342.

Shleifer, Andrei, and Robert Vishny. 1997. "A Survey of Corporate Governance." *Journal of Finance* 52 (2): 737–783.

Siaroff, Alan. 1999. "Corporatism in Twenty-Four Industrial Democracies: Meaning and Measurement." *European Journal of Political Research* 36: 175–205.

Skocpol, Theda. 1992. *Protecting Soldiers and Mothers: The Political Origins of Social Policy in the U.S.* Cambridge, Mass.: Belknap Press of Harvard University Press.

———. 1996. *Boomerang: Clinton's Health Security Effort and the Turn Against Government in U.S. Politics.* New York: W. W. Norton.

Skocpol, Theda, and Edwin Amenta. 1986. "States and Social Policies." *Annual Review of Sociology* 12 (2): 131–57.

Soma, Masao. 1986. *Nihon Senkyo Seidoshi: Fuhen Senkyoho kara Koshoku Senkyoho made (The Institutional History of Japanese Elections)*. Fukuoka: Kyushu Daigaku Shuppankai.

Sone Kenkyukai. 1985. *Shingikai no Kenyu*. Tokyo: Sone Kenkyukai.

Sorai, Mamoru. 2000. "Jiminto Shihai Taiseika no Nomin Seito Kessei Undo." In *Senso Fukko Hatten: Showa Seijishi ni Okeru Kenryoku to Koso*, eds. Shinichi Kitaoka and Takashi Mikuriya, 259–295. Tokyo: Tokyo Daigaku Shuppankai.

Soskice, David. 1990a. "Wage Determination: The Changing Role of Institutions in Advanced Industrialized Countries." *Oxford Review of Economic Policy* 6 (4): 235–278.

———. 1990b. "Reinterpreting Corporatism and Explaining Unemployment: Coordinated and Non-Coordinated Market Economies." In *Labour Relations and Economic Performance*, eds. R. Brunetta and C. Dell'Ariga, 170–211. New York: New York University Press.

———. 1994. "Advanced Economies in Open World Markets and Comparative Institutional Advantages: Patterns of Business Coordination, National Institutional Frameworks, and Company Product Market Innovation Strategies," unpublished paper.

———. 1998. "Divergent Production Regimes: Coordinated and Uncoordinated Market Economies in the 1980's and 1990's." In *Continuity and Change in Contemporary Capitalism*, eds. Herbert Kitschelt, et al., 101–134. New York: Cambridge University Press.

Steiner, Kurt, Ellis S. Krauss, and Scott C. Flanagan eds. 1980. *Political Opposition and Local Politics in Japan*. Princeton: Princeton University Press.

Steinmo, Sven. 1993. *Taxation and Democracy: Swedish, British, and American Approaches to Financing the Modern State*. New Haven: Yale University Press.

Steinmo, Sven, Kathleen Thelen, and Frank Longstreth, eds. 1992. *Structuring Politics: Historical Institutionalism in Comparative Analysis*. Cambridge: Cambridge University Press.

Steinmo, Sven, and Caroline Tolbert. 1998. "Do Institutions Really Matter?: Taxation in Industrialized Democracies." *Comparative Political Studies* 31 (2): 165–187.

Steinmo, Sven, and Jon Watts. 1995. "It's the Institutions, Stupid! Why Comprehensive National Health Insurance Always Fails in America." *Journal of Health Politics, Policy, and Law* 20 (2): 329–372.

Stephens, John D. 1979. *The Transition from Capitalism to Socialism*. London: Macmillan.

Stevens, Beth. 1990. "Labor Unions, Employee Benefits, and the Privatization of the American Welfare State." *Journal of Policy History* 2 (3): 233–260.

———. 1996. "Labor Unions at the Privatization of Welfare: The Turning Point in the 1940s." In *The Privatization of Social Policy?*, ed. Michael Shalev, 73–103. New York: St. Martin's Press.

Streeck, Wolfgang. 1991. "On the Institutional Conditions of Diversified Quality Production." In *Beyond Keynesianism*, eds. E. Matzner and W. Streeck, 21–61. Aldershot: Edward Elgar.

————. 1992. *Social Institutions and Economic Performance: Studies of Industrial Relations in Advanced Capitalist Economies*. London: Sage Publications.

Streeck, Wolfgang, and Kozo Yamamura, eds. 2001. *The Origin of Nonliberal Capitalism: Germany and Japan in Comparison*. Ithaca, N.Y.: Cornell University Press.

Strøm, Kaare. 2003. "Parliamentary Democracy and Delegation." In *Delegation and Accountability in Parliamentary Democracies*, eds. Kaare Strøm, Wolfgang C. Müller, and Torbjörn Bergman, 55–106. New York: Oxford University Press.

Suganuma, Takashi. 1991. "Shitsugyo Hoken to Rosai Hoken Seido Kakuritsu." In *Nihon Shakai Hosho no Rekishi*, eds. Kazuhiko Yokoyama and Hidenori Tada, 105–111. Tokyo: Gakubunsha.

Sugayama, Shinji. 1995. "Nihonteki Koyo Kankei no Keisai: Shugyo Kisoku, Chingin, Jyugyoin." In *Nihonteki Keiei no Renzoku to Danzetsu*, eds. Hiroaki Yamazaki and Takeo Kikkawa, 191–231. Tokyo: Iwanami Shoten.

Sugeno, Kazuo. 1988. *Rodoho*. Tokyo: Kobundo.

Suleiman, Ezra. 1974. *Politics, Power and Bureaucracy in France: The Administrative Elite*. Princeton, N.J.: Princeton University Press.

Sumiya, Mikio, and Hiroshi Koga, eds. 1978. *Nihon Shokugyo Kunren Hattatsushi (Sengo-hen)*. Tokyo: Nihon Rodo Kyokai.

Swank, Duane. 1998. "Funding the Welfare State: Globalization and the Taxation of Business in Advanced Market Economies." *Political Studies* 46 (4): 671– 692.

Swenson, Peter. 1991a. "Bringing Capital Back In, or Social Democracy Reconsidered: Employer Power, Cross-Class Alliances, and Centralization of Industrial Relations in Denmark and Sweden." *World Politics* 43 (4): 513–544.

————. 1991b. "Labor and the Limits of the Welfare State." *Comparative Politics* 23 (4): 379–399.

————. 1997. "Arranged Alliance: Business Interests in the New Deal." *Politics and Society* 25 (1): 66–116.

————. 2002. *Capitalists against Markets: The Making of Labor Markets and Welfare States in the United States and Sweden*. New York: Oxford University Press.

Taagepera, Rein, and Matthew S. Shugart. 1989. *Seats and Votes: The Effects and Determinants of Electoral Systems*. New Haven: Yale University Press.

Tachibanaki, Toshiaki. 2000. *Seifuti netto no Keizaigaku (The Economics of Safety Nets)*. Tokyo: Nihon Keizai Shinbunsha.

Tada, Hidenori. 1991. "Seikatsu Hogo Seido no Kakuritsu." In *Nihon Shakai Hosho no Rekishi*, eds. Kazuhiko Yokoyama and Hidenori Tada, 70–84. Tokyo: Gakubunsha.

Takahashi, Hideyuki. 1986. "Nihon Ishikai no seiji Kodo to Ishi Kettei." In *Nihongata Seisaku Kettei no Henyo*, ed. Minoru Nakano, 237–266. Tokyo: Toyo Keizai Shinposha.

Takayama, Noriyuki. 1992. *Nenkin Kaikaku no Koso; Daikaisei eno Saishu Teigen*. Tokyo: Nihon Keizai Shinbunsha.

Takehara, Norio. 1988. *Sengo Nihon no Zaisei Toyushi*. Tokyo: Bunshindo.

Takenaka, Harutaka. 2002. "Introducing Junior Ministers and Reforming the Diet in Japan." *Asian Survey* 42 (6): 928–939.

————. 2006. *Shusho Shihai*. Tokyo: Chuo Koronsha.

Tamakuni, Fumitoshi. 1995. "Furinji Benefitto Kazei no Genjo to Kadai." *Zeikei Tsushin* (November): 38–115.

Tanaka, Kakuei. 1967. "Jiminto no Hansei." *Chuo Koron* (June): 284–293.

Tanaka, Kazuaki, and Akira Okada. 2000. *Chuo Shocho Kaikaku: Hashimoto Gyokaku ga Mezashita "Kono Kuni no Katachi."* Tokyo: Nihon Hyoronsha.

Tanaka, Nobumasa, Hiroshi Tanaka, and Nagami Hata. 1995. *Ozoku to Sengo*. Tokyo: Iwanami Shoten.

Tatebayashi, Masahiko. 2004. *Giin Kodo no Seiji Keizaigaku: Jiminto Shihai no Seido Bunseki.* Tokyo: Yuhikaku.

——. 2006. "Seito Naibu Soshiki to Seitokan Kosho Kankei no Henyo." In *Nihon Seiji Hendo no 30-nen: Seijika, Kanryo, Dantai Chosa ni Miru Kozo Henyo*, eds. Michio Muramatsu and Ikuo Kume, 68–94. Tokyo: Toyo Keizai Shinposha.

Teranishi, Juro. 1995. "Savings Mobilization and Investment: Financing during Japan's Postwar Economic Recovery." In *Corporate Governance in Transitional Economies: Insider Control and the Role of Banks*, eds. Masahiko Aoki and Hyung-ki Kim, 405–434. Washington, D.C.: World Bank.

Thayer, Nathaniel B. 1969. *How the Conservatives Rule Japan.* Princeton, N.J.: Princeton University Press.

Thelen, Kathleen. 2004. *How Institutions Evolve: The Political Economy of Skills in Germany, Britain, the United States, and Japan.* New York: Cambridge University Press.

Thelen, Kathleen, and Ikuo Kume. 1999. "The Effects of Globalization on Labor Revisited: Lessons from Germany and Japan." *Politics and Society* 27 (4): 476–504.

Thelen, Kathleen, and Sven Steinmo. 1992. "Historical Institutionalism in Comparative Politics." In *Structuring Politics: Historical Institutionalism in Comparative Perspective*, S. Steinmo, K. Thelen, and F. Longstreth, 1–32. Cambridge: Cambridge University Press.

Tilton, Mark. 1996. *Restrained Trade: Cartels in Japan's Basic Materials Industries.* Ithaca, N.Y.: Cornell University Press.

Tojo, Yukio. 1995. "Rodo Doin." In *Nihon no Senji Keizai: Keikaku to Shijo*, ed. Akira Hara, 237–282. Tokyo: Tokyo Daigaku Shuppankai.

Tomiyasu, Nagateru. 1963. *Kigyo Taishoku Nenkin Seido no Kenkyu.* Tokyo: Nikkan Rodo Tsushinsha.

Toshi Kaihatsu Kyokai Somu Iinkai, ed. 1985. *Toshi Kaihatsu Kyokai Junenshi.* Tokyo: Toshi Kaihatsu Kyokai.

Tsebelis, George. 2002. *Veto Players: How Political Institutions Work.* New York: Princeton University Press and Russell Sage Foundation.

Tsuchida, Takeshi. 1991. "Iryo Hoken no Seido Kaikaku." In *Nihon Shakai Hosho no Rekishi*, eds. Kazuhiko Yokoyama and Hidenori Tada, 277–298. Tokyo: Gakubunsha.

Tsuchiya, Moriaki, and Yoshiaki Miwa, eds. 1989. *Nihon no Chusho Kigyo.* Tokyo: Tokyo University Press.

Tsujinaka, Yutaka. 1986. "Rodo Dantai – Kyuchi ni tatsu Rodo no Seisaku Kettei." In *Nihongata Seisaku Kettei no Henyo*, ed. Makano Minoru, 267–300. Tokyo: Toyo Keizai Shinposha.

——. 1987. "Rodokai no Saihen to 86nen Taisei no Imi." *Rebaiasan* 1 (August): 130–150.

Uchida, Kenzo, Masao Kanazashi, and Masayuki Fukuoka, eds. 1988. *Zeisei Kaikaku o Meguru Seiji Rikigaku.* Tokyo: Chuo Koronsha.

Ujihara, Shojiro. 1985. "Koreika Shakai ni okeru Kigyo no Taiou." In *Fukushi Kokka vol 5: Nihon no Keizaik to Fukushi*, ed., 353–421. Tokyo Daigaku Shakai Kagaku Kenkyujo. Tokyo: Tokyo Daigaku Shuppankai.

Upham, Frank K. 1987. *Law and Social Change in Postwar Japan.* Cambridge, Mass.: Harvard University Press.

——. 1993. "Privatizing Regulation: The Implementation of the Large-Scale Retail Stores Law." In *Political Dynamics in Contemporary Japan*, eds. Gary D. Allinson and Yasuhiro Sone, 264–294. Ithaca, N.Y.: Cornell University Press.

Urabe, Kunitoshi, and Kihei Omura. 1983. *Nihonteki Roshi Kankei no Tankyu.* Tokyo: Chuo Keizaisha.

Uriu, Robert. 1996. *Troubled Industries: Confronting Economic Change in Japan.* Ithaca, NY: Cornell University Press.

Usami, Noriharu. 1984. *Seimei Hoken Hyakunenshiron*. Tokyo: Yuhikaku.

Uzuhashi, Takafumi, et al. 2004. "Seikatsu Hogo Seido Minaoshi no Ronten to Shiten." *Kikan Shakai Hosho Kenkyu* 39 (4): 383–388.

Van Kersbergen, Kees. 1995. *Social Capitalism: A Study of Christian Democracy and the Welfare State*. London: Routledge.

Vogel, Steven K. 1996. *Freer Markets, More Rules: Regulatory Reform in Advanced Industrial Countries*. Ithaca, N.Y.: Cornell University Press.

———. 1999. "Can Japan Disengage? Winners and Losers in Japan's Political Economy, and the Ties that Bind Them." *Social Science Japan Journal* 2: 3–21.

———. 2006. *Japan Remodeled: How Government and Industry Are Reforming Japanese Capitalism*. Ithaca, N.Y.: Cornell University Press.

Wada, Yakka. 1979. *Nihon Zaiseiron*. Tokyo: Nihon Hyoronsha.

Wada, Yoshitaka. 1997. Kaibo Nihon no Soshiki: Zenkoku Tokutei Yubinkyokuchokai." *Foasaito* (February): 120–123.

Watanabe, Osamu. 1990. *"Yutakana Shakai" Nihon no Kozo*. Tokyo: Rodo Junposha.

———. 1991. *Kigyo Shihai to Kokka*. Tokyo: Aoki Shoten.

———. 1998. "'Sengogata Seiji' no Keisei to Noson." *Demokurashi no Hokai to Saisei: Gakusaiteki Sekkin*, eds. Ryoshin Minami et al., 219–260. Tokyo: Nihon Keizai Hyoronsha.

Weaver, R. Kent, and Bert A. Rockman. 1993. "Assessing the Effects of Institutions." In *Do Institutions Matter? Government Capabilities in the United States and Abroad*, eds. Kent Weaver and Bert Rockman, 1–41. Washington, D.C.: Brookings Institution.

Webber, Carolyn, and Aaron Wildavsky. 1986. *A History of Taxation and Expenditure in the Western World*. New York: Simon and Schuster.

Weingast, Barry, Kenneth Shepsle, and Christopher Johnsen. 1981. "The Political Economy of Benefits and Costs: A Neo-Classical Approach to Distributive Politics." *Journal of Political Economy* 89: 642–664.

Weinstein, David. 1994. "United We Stand: Firms and Enterprise Unions in Japan," *Journal of the Japanese and International Economies* 8 (1): 53–71.

Weir, Margaret. 1992. *Politics and Jobs*. Princeton, N.J.: Princeton University Press.

Weir, Margaret, and Theda Skocpol. 1985. "State Structures and the Possibilities for 'Keynesian' Responses to the Great Depression in Sweden, Britain, and the United States." In *Bringing the State Back In*, eds. Peter Evans et al., 107–163. New York: Cambridge University Press.

Weiss, Linda. 1993. "War, the State and the Origins of the Japanese Employment System." *Politics and Society* 21 (3): 325–354.

Westney, D. Eleanor. 1987. *Imitation and Innovation: The Transfer of Western Organizational Patterns to Meiji Japan*. Cambridge, Mass.: Harvard University Press.

Whitten, Guy, and G. Bingham Powell. 1993. "A Cross-National Analysis of Economic Voting: Taking Account of the Political Context." *American Journal of Political Science* 37 (2): 391–414.

Wilensky, Harold L. 1980. "Leftism, Catholicism, and Democratic Corporatism: The Role of Parties in Welfare State Development." In *The Development of Welfare States in Europe and America*, eds. Peter Flora and A. J. Heidenheimer, 345–382. New Brunswick, N.J.: Transaction Books.

———. 1990. "Common Problems, Divergent Policies: An Eighteen-Nation Study of Family Policy." *Public Affairs Report* 31: 1–3.

———. 2002. *Rich Democracies: Political Economy, Public Policy, and Performance*. Berkeley: University of California Press.

Woodall, Brian. 1996. *Japan under Construction: Corruption, Politics, and Public Works*. Berkeley: University of California Press.

Yamaguchi, Jiro. 1986. "Zaisei Kochokuka Kyanpen no Zasetsu to Yosan Katei no Henyo." In *Kanryosei no Keisei to Tenkai*, ed. Kindai Nihon Kenkyukai, 279–304. Tokyo: Yamakawa Shuppansha.

Yamamoto, Yoshito. 1996. "Kyuyo Jutaku to Roshikankei: Part II." *Chingin Jitsumu* (December 15, 1996).

Yamamura, Kozo, and Wolfgang Streeck, eds. 2003. *The End of Diversity? Progress for German and Japanese Capitalism*. Ithaca, N.Y.: Cornell University Press.

Yamanaka, Hiroshi. 1982. *Seiho Kinyu no Mado kara: Seiho Kinyu 50nen no Ayumi*. Tokyo: Sangyo Noritsu Daigaku.

Yamazaki, Hiroaki. 1985. "Nihon ni okeru Rorei Nenkin Seido no Tenkai Katei." In *Fukushi Kokka vol.5: Nihon no Keizai to Fukushiu.*, ed. Tokyo Daigaku Shakai Kagaku Kenkyujo, 171–237. Tokyo: Tokyo: Daigaku Shuppankai.

Yamazaki, Kiyoshi. 1988. *Nihon no Taishokukin Seido*. Tokyo: Nihon Rodo Kyokai.

Yashiro, Naohiro. 1996. *Nihongata Koyo Shisutemu*. Tokyo: Toyo Keizai Shinposha.

———. 1997. *Nihonteki Koyo Kanko no Keizaigaku*. Tokyo: Nihon Keizai Shinbunsha.

———, ed. 1997. *Koreika Shakai no Seikatsu Hosho Shisutemu*. Tokyo: Tokyo Daigaku Shuppankai.

Yokoyama, Kazuhiko. 1976a. "Gendai Nihon no Nenkin Hoken." In *Shakai Fukushi no Shakaigaku*, ed. Yoshiya Soeda, 61–90. Tokyo: Ichiryusha.

———. 1976b. "Saigo no Shakai Hosho: Kazoku Teate." In *Shakai Fukushi no Shakaigaku*, ed. Yoshiya Soeda, 91–160. Tokyo: Ichiryusha.

Yokoyama, Kazuhiko, and Hidenori Tada. 1991. *Nihon Shakai Hosho no Rekishi*. Tokyo: Gakubunsha.

Zaisei Chosakai, ed. 1957. *Kuni no Yosan 1957*. Tokyo: Doyu Shobo.

Zysman, John. 1983. *Governments, Markets, and Growth*. Ithaca, N.Y.: Cornell University Press.

Index

Abe, Shinzo, 263, 264, 284, 289, 292
Abegglen, James, 171n10
Aberbach, Joel D., 74n55
accountability, 60–61, 62–65, 69, 70, 80, 99, 220, 236, 280
Acemoglu, Daron, 171n8
active labor market policy (ALMP), 30, 32, 47
Adams, Carolyn Teich, 38n52
Ad-hoc Research Council on Administrative Reform (Rincho). *See* Rincho
adjustment cooperatives, 125
administrative intervention, 32–34. *See also* anti-competitive regulation, cartels, Convoy system, market-restricting policies
administrative orders (*tsutatsu*), 123
Administrative Reform, 272–74, 282
aging (demographic aging), 202, 207, 209, 225, 226, 231, 234, 239, 284, 290
   institutional vulnerabilities in Japan's welfare state, 203
agriculture, 29, 142, 146, 202, 207, 209, 220, 244
   Agricultural Basic Law, 146
   agricultural cooperatives (*Nokyo*), 124, 156, 237, 244, 267
   agricultural income, 142, 285
   agricultural subsidies, 3, 35, 37, 48, 68, 69, 71, 72, 199, 205, 206, 237
   Farmers' Pension, 25, 160, 274

Food Control Law, 146
   Law for Stabilization of Supply, Demand, and Prices of Staple Food, 244
   liberalization of rice imports, 237, 244
   Norin Chukin, 156
Aizawa, Koetsu, 44n66
Akarui Senkyo Suishin Iinkai, 286
Albert, Michel, 16n39
All National Insurance (*Kokumin Kaihoken*), 138, 141, 147–49
Allied Occupation of Japan, 17, 78, 79, 100, 102, 103–11, 112, 114, 117, 124, 127, 287
Allinson, Gary D., 139n5, 245n1
Allmendinger, Jutta, 201n8
amakudari, 94, 95, 130, 131, 230, 281, 282, 283
Amenta, Edwin, 8
Amyx, Jennifer, 295n5
Anderson, Stephen, 4n7, 7n12, 13, 19, 44, 139n5, 194n75
anti-competitive regulation, 30, 186, 190, 252
Aoki, Masahiko, 93n50, 168n1, 170n5, 199n1
Aoki, Yasuko, 200n4, 216n45, 217n53, 218n55
Ariizumi, Toru, 184
Australia, 20, 23, 66–68, 168, 208
Austria, 69, 168

Other Books in the Series (*continued from page iii*)